EDGAR
CAYCE

MODERN PROPHET

FOUR VOLUMES IN ONE

EDGAR CAYCE

MODERN PROPHET

FOUR VOLUMES IN ONE

Edgar Cayce on Prophesy
Edgar Cayce on Religion and Psychic Experience
Edgar Cayce on Mysteries of the Mind
Edgar Cayce on Reincarnation

BONANZA BOOKS
New York

This 1990 edition is published by Bonanza Books, distributed by Outlet Book Company, Inc., a Random House Company, 225 Park Avenue South, New York, New York 10003, by arrangement with Warner Books.

Printed and bound in the United States of America

LIBRARY OF CONGRESS CATALOGING-IN-PUBLICATION DATA

Edgar Cayce : modern prophet.
    p.   cm.
    Summaries of Cayce's dictated readings, written by Mary Ellen Carter . . . [et al.].
    Reprint of works originally published 1967–1989.
    Contents: Edgar Cayce on prophecy — Edgar Cayce on religion and psychic experience — Edgar Cayce on mysteries of the mind — Edgar Cayce on reincarnation.
    ISBN 0-517-69702-5
    1. Cayce, Edgar, 1877–1945. 2. Prophecies (Occultism) 3. Parapsychology—Religious aspects—Christianity. 4. Consciousness. 5. Intellect. 6. Reincarnation. I. Cayce, Edgar, 1877–1945. II. Carter, Mary Ellen. III. Title: Modern prophet.
BF1027.C3E34   1990
133.8′092—dc20   89-28702
                                            CIP

8 7 6 5 4 3 2 1

CONTENTS

EDGAR CAYCE

On Prophecy

By Mary Ellen Carter
Under the Editorship of
Hugh Lynn Cayce

*This book is dedicated to all who are helping make
the way clear and passable for the New Age.*

CONTENTS

Introduction

WHO WAS EDGAR CAYCE?

THE EIGHT BOOKS which have been written about him have totaled more than a million in sales, and more than ten other books have devoted sections to his life and talents. He has been featured in dozens of magazines and hundreds of newspaper articles dating from 1900 to the present. What was so unique about him?

It depends on whose eyes you look at him through. A goodly number of his contemporaries knew the "waking" Edgar Cayce as a gifted professional photographer. Another cross section (predominantly children) admired him as a warm and friendly Sunday School teacher. His own family knew him as a wonderful husband and father.

The "sleeping" Edgar Cayce was an entirely different figure; a psychic known to thousands of people, in all walks of life, who had cause to be grateful for his help; indeed, many of them believe that he alone had either saved or changed their lives when all seemed lost. The "sleeping" Edgar Cayce was a medical diagnostician, a prophet, and a devoted protagonist of Bible lore.

In June 1954, the University of Chicago held him in sufficient respect to accept a Ph.D. thesis based on a study of his life and work: in this thesis the graduate referred to him as a "religious seer." In June of that same year, the children's comic book *House of Mystery* bestowed on him the impressive title of "America's Most Mysterious Man!"

Even as a child on a farm near Hopkinsville, Kentucky, where he was born on March 18, 1877, Edgar Cayce displayed powers of perception which seemed to extend beyond the normal range of the five senses. At the age of six or seven he told his parents that he was able to see and talk to "visions," sometimes of relatives who had recently died. His parents attributed this to the overactive imagination of a lonely child who had been influenced by the dramatic language of the revival meetings which were popular in that section of the country. Later, by sleeping with his head on his schoolbooks, he developed some form of photographic memory which helped him advance rapidly in the country school. This faded, however, and Edgar was only able to complete his seventh grade before he had to seek his own place in the world.

By twenty-one he had become the salesman for a wholesale stationery company. At this time he developed a gradual paralysis of the throat muscles, which threatened the loss of his voice. When doctors were unable to find a physical cause for these conditions, hypnosis was tried, but failed to have any permanent effect.

As a last resort, Edgar asked a friend to help him reenter the same kind of hypnotic sleep that had enabled him to memorize his schoolbooks as a child. His friend gave him the necessary suggestion, and once he was in self-induced trance, Edgar came to grips with his own problem. He recommended medication and manipulative therapy which successfully restored his voice and repaired his system.

A group of physicians from Hopkinsville and Bowling Green, Kentucky, took advantage of his unique talent to diagnose their own patients. They soon discovered that Cayce only needed to be given the name and address of the patient, wherever he was, and was then able to "tune in" telepathically on that individual's mind and body as easily as if they were both in the same room. He needed, and was given, no other information regarding any patient.

One of the young M.D.'s, Dr. Wesley Ketchum, submitted a report on this unorthodox procedure to a clinical research society in Boston. On October 9, 1910, *The New York Times* carried two pages of headlines and pictures. From that day on, invalids from all over the country sought the "wonder man's" help.

When Edgar Cayce died on January 3, 1945, in Virginia Beach, Virginia, he left well over fourteen thousand documented stenographic records of the telepathic-clairvoyant statements he had given for more than eight thousand different people over a period of forty-three years. These typewritten documents are referred to as "readings."

These readings constitute one of the largest and most impressive records of psychic perception ever to emanate from a single individual. Together with their relevant records, correspondence and reports, they have been cross-indexed under thousands of subject-headings and placed at the disposal of psychologists, students, writers and investigators who come in increasing numbers to examine them.

A foundation known as the A.R.E. (The Association for Research and Enlightenment, Inc., P.O. Box 595, Virginia Beach, Virginia, 23451) was founded in 1932 to preserve these readings. As an open-membership research society, it continues to index and catalogue the information, initiate investigation and experiments, and promote conferences, seminars and lectures. Until now its published findings have been made available to its members through its own publishing facilities.

Now Paperback Library has made it possible to present a series of popular volumes dealing with those subjects from the Edgar Cayce readings most likely to appeal to public interest.

In this volume Mary Ellen Carter has traced many fascinating threads of prophecy through the complicated tapestry of the thousands of individual readings. Dramatic personal prophecies are in contrast with the world prophecies whose validity is attested daily by our newspaper headlines. Though Edgar Cayce has been dead for twenty-three years, his readings seem very much alive as we examine his statements which have come to pass as well as those describing incidents which lie just ahead.

Mrs. Carter's examination of the major theories on time in the light of the Edgar Cayce readings will stimulate your thinking. She is a good reporter whose book will raise many questions for you, but also answer many which have been suggested by Edgar Cayce's strange prophetic capacities.

—Hugh Lynn Cayce

CHAPTER 1

PROPHET OF THE NEW AGE

EDGAR CAYCE WAS a prophet of the New Age.

It has also been called the "Great Dispensation," the "Age of Understanding" as he called it; "The Day of the Lord."

It might also be called "the end of the world as we know it."

Thinking about man's history on earth as compared with what the prophets of the past have held up to us as the ideal; considering man's present weariness with wars, degradation, starvation, and the meaningless treadmill that is our lot, maybe this is pretty good thing.

Looking through our most optimistic shade of rose-colored glasses, we think of the many changes that have already taken place in recent years which have made life better for mankind. The changes of which Edgar Cayce spoke were to be on all levels, including international relationships, science, social conditions, spiritual growth, and man's knowledge of his mind and his inner being. In all this, we find, was a clear sound of the ringing bell of hope, and not of doom. We face a glorious age of expansion and growth because "dispensation" means "special exemption"—"release from obligation." Not that we're worth it, but that God is good.

During his lifetime, Edgar Cayce previsioned the vicissitudes of the Great Depression, pointing out its reasons and its end. He warned of America's entrance into World War II unless she prayed and acted as she prayed. He foretold the New Age Dispensation, which he said would come when "those who are His" have made the way passable and man's history is "folded up."

He was a world prophet, speaking for all the nations, for ancient nations long forgotten by man, and for future centuries hence. He spoke in terms of the long view, in which he himself had been a prophet in at least one past life, and foretold that he would return again in 2100 A.D., remembering his identity as Edgar Cayce!

In January, 1945, Edgar Cayce stepped through "God's other door," as he had often called death, and in five months, World War II was ended. It seemed the end of an epoch during which he had lived to bring what many have taken to be an unmistakable message of God's love to the world during its worst trials in modern times, and from then on, his message was enough to carry us into the millennium.

As we look back twenty-three years later, we see that man had then needed a prophet and that Cayce said what had to be said, just in time!

Like prophetic passages of the Bible, Cayce's forecasts could become a relic of the past which generations of the future might remember as a curiosity and a strange myth of the twentieth century. Or they could serve to be a source of hope to generations wiser than we.

Unlike most prophets, he spoke in a self-imposed hypnotic trance and did not know what he had said until he returned to consciousness. He depended all his life on others to record and evaluate what he brought forth. It was left to others to present his work to the world, or to forget it.

The readings state in one place that, like Cayce, Ezekiel had a secretary or scribe to take down his utterances.

Also, like Ezekiel, he spoke forcefully of our social ills. He predicted the present race riots and labor troubles as inevitable unless regard was given the underprivileged and disadvantaged. For too long, the social and economic sins of America have been covered up, as in the days of that ancient Hebrew seer, when God likened the hidden evils of Jerusalem to a wall that had been "daubed with whitewash."

If you had compared Edgar Cayce with Ezekiel to his face, he would probably have laughed. His self image was not such that he ranked himself with the major prophets, nor even called himself a minor one. He was a southern Presbyterian Sunday School teacher, a photographer by profession. He was a family man. And then, there was this matter of being psychic. He had a kind of wonder about it all, like everybody else. He was never able to hear himself say all these wonderful, frightening, joyous, terrible, crazy un-Presbyterianlike things recorded by his secretary, whose accuracy his wife confirmed.

By all other psychics of this age, however, he is acknowledged generally to be the greatest among them. In a public talk given in July, 1967, to a Virginia Beach audience, the beautiful prophetess Jeane Dixon said of him, "Edgar Cayce is the expert." She had been asked about predictions she had made regarding many earth changes in the future, which agree with those Cayce made.

He said that he would return in 1998 as a world liberator if he so desired, to help bring about the New Age. "Is it not fitting then that these [old souls] must return?" states this message for Edgar Cayce himself, "as this priest may develop himself to be in that position to be in the capacity of a *liberator* of the world in its relationships to individuals in these periods to come; for he must enter again at that period, or in 1998."

Furthermore, this will also be a time of liberation for Cayce: "When the day of the earth, as earthy, is fulfilled in Him," states Reading 254-83, "this body, Edgar Cayce, shall be rejuvenated, shall be purged, shall be made free."

In the parlance of reincarnation, this doubtless means that he will be freed from the need to reincarnate again. This is possible, say the readings, for any soul who is willing to live as close to spiritual law as did Edgar Cayce.

Following his next incarnation in 1998, however, he will return at least once more by his own volition, if his prophetic dream of being born again in 2100 A.D. is true!

In this dream, he had been born in the year 2100 in Nebraska, and as a child, told his elders that he had been Edgar Cayce in the early twentieth century. The scientists who investigated him were quite bald, and wore long beards and thick glasses.

He recalled his former home states of Alabama, New York, and Virginia. He journeyed with the scientists on their visit to these places, traveling in a long, cigar-shaped metal ship which moved at high speeds through the air.

On this venture he saw that New York had been destroyed and was being rebuilt. Alabama was partly under water, and Norfolk, Virginia was now an immense seaport. Industries were scattered over the country instead of being centralized in cities. Houses were of glass. Many records were discovered proving that Edgar Cayce had lived when he did. The group returned to Nebraska, now America's west coast!

The world was at a low ebb in its history in 1936 when he had this dream, and it was also a personally difficult time for Edgar Cayce. He, his wife Gertrude, and his secretary, Gladys Davis, had just gone through the humiliating experience of being arrested in Detroit for practicing medicine without a license. The court trial ended in their favor, but it had come after months of uncertainty, and as a result, Cayce had suffered in mind and in body.

He dreamed this account of the future the night following the trial. Later, he obtained an interpretation through a reading which assured him that the dream had been for his "understanding that though the moment may appear dark . . . though there may be periods of the misinterpreting of purposes, even these will be turned into that which will be the very proof itself in the experiences of the entity and those whom the entity might . . . help. . . .

"Though the very heavens fall, though the earth shall be changed, though the heavens shall pass, the premises in Him are sure and will stand—as in that day—as the proof of thy activity in the lives and hearts of thy fellow man. . . .

"For indeed and in truth ye know, 'as ye do it unto thy fellowman, ye do it unto thy God, to thyself.' For with self effaced, God may indeed glorify thee and make thee stand as one who is called for a purpose in thy dealings, in thy relationships with thy fellowman. Be not unmindful that He is nigh unto thee in every trial, in every temptation, and hath not willed that thou shouldst perish. Make thy will, then, one with His. Be not afraid. . . ."

As one might suspect, he also had some rather unusual experiences while in the waking state. He lived as a child in Hopkinsville, Kentucky, the life of a typical farm boy. At twelve, he became very religious and spent many hours reading the Bible and praying. One evening after he had gone to bed, he awoke to find his room full of light.

"I thought that my mother had entered the room with a lamp," he told friends years later. Then he realized that the figure which he saw was not that of his mother!

"I heard a voice speaking to me, and was told that a power was going to be given me to help others if I used it properly.

"The next day, I found that by losing consciousness, as if in sleep, after reading or hearing read a lesson, I could remember it all when I awoke."

After this, Cayce advanced rapidly in school. After the seventh grade, he had to quit his formal education and go to work however.

He gave his first reading for himself at twenty-one to find out how he might regain his voice, which he had lost a year before. The reading was his first psychic diagnosis, describing "a congestion in the area of the voice box." The suggestion was given that it could be cured by increasing the circulation in that area. He regained his voice at once.

When news spread of this, people came to him for readings. Newspaper publicity followed. When he was thirty-three, Dr. W. H. Ketchum became interested in him and cooperated with him in diagnosing and curing ailments, for many readings required the skills of a physician to carry out the suggested treatments.

In a speech to a Greek letter fraternity in Pasadena, California, Dr. Ketchum told of his investigation of Cayce. "My subject simply lies down and folds his arms, and by autosuggestion goes to sleep," he began. "While in this sleep, which to all intents and purposes is a natural sleep, his objective mind is completely inactive and only his subjective is working. . . ."

Typical headlines of the earliest newspaper accounts stated "Illiterate Man Becomes a Doctor When Hypnotized" *(New York Times,* October 9, 1910). According to a note in the files, the first record of Cayce's early work was actually made before 1910, but that year seems to be the beginning of his public service as a psychic.

He had learned photography and was anxious to succeed in that profession and to live a normal life. His marriage and the arrival of two boys certainly were reason enough for him to want a stable and secure life for himself and his family. His mysterious ability to help people, which had come to him just as the strange lady with the light had promised, was a wonderful gift. But he found it took much time from his career and family.

But as the lady had prophesied, he was to spend a lifetime using his gift for the good of others. As his work spread, the A.R.E. was told that "the day will arise in thine experience . . . of this group who seek, of those present, when they will see, will hear it sounded about the earth. . . ."

This has come to pass, for Cayce and his work have been the subject of books and articles which have indeed "sounded" about the earth. First there was *There Is a River,* the endearing—and enduring—biography of Cayce by his friend, the late Tom Sugrue, published in 1942. Others followed, and at present, Jess Stearn's, *Edgar Cayce: The Sleeping Prophet,* has been a best seller for the past year. Since its publication, interest in and knowledge of Cayce's life and legacy of fourteen thousand readings has mounted. Membership in the Association has tripled and inquiries are swamping the A.R.E. offices. People who never heard of Cayce before 1967 are reading of him, talking about him, and speculating over the many new ideas his life represents.

Foremost among these, of course, is reincarnation. "I don't know whether I believe in it or not," a housewife told me after reading about Cayce recently. "But it's an interesting idea."

There are many such "interesting ideas" in the files which are awaiting perusal of the kind of scholars and researchers—and just plain folk—who insist on leaving no stone unturned in the search for the answers to many questions.

Cayce wrote to a friend in July, 1926: "Of course, don't everybody agree with what the readings say—won't everybody try them all out, and under the circumstances and conditions, I wouldn't blame you one bit. . . ."

He had a very realistic outlook regarding his gift. He was as much in the dark as anybody when he opened his eyes after a reading! But he had also the gift of faith which anyone can have through prayer, reading the Bible, and doing the right thing, day by day. This was all he asked of himself and others. But he knew also how much patience this daily regime took.

He received letters from people for whom he had given readings, attesting to the rewards they had brought. A friend who had lost his job wrote, "When I look at these readings that have been given me for health, life, and work and see how they come jamb up to the line, I am made to know that they cannot be doubted. . . ."

Cayce wrote him, "Don't make plans too far ahead . . . That it [adversity] has taken you almost over the fire, with just seared threads holding you off, is not in condemnation—rather that you might be better acquainted [with God] for we must oft remember that 'though He were the Son, yet learned He obedience through the things which He suffered.' "

This man must have had a prophetic bent, himself, for he replied, "Where a man, country, nation or any organization works and keeps the Will of the Father, no power is greater than He. So I fully believe this work is just being born and will grow to be a worldwide thing, and much quicker than any expect. Why? Because truth and results is what counts, and no arguments can retard it."

The range of universal concepts to which prophecy of this high order was applied was as wide as the mind of man can stretch. It embraced man's deepest yearning to know what lies beyond himself, and beyond the farthest star. It accommodated itself to man's most trivial concerns—one woman asked where she might locate her lost emeralds. In a word, it reflected man himself, which is perhaps what made it all so wonderful.

Specifically, many events of world significance were foretold, including major earth changes in the near future. In the realm of archeology, fascinating forecasts were made concerning the Great Pyramid of Gizeh, and a number of other sites not so well known. Another meaningful body of material is contained in the "Palestine Readings," given for people who were told they had been together during the life and times of Jesus. This data includes a description of the Essenes and their part in the advent of the Messiah, and is prophetic of the light thrown upon these mysterious people by the discovery of the Dead Sea Scrolls in 1948, fully ten years later.

Many personal readings were given in guiding the vocations and health—spiritual, mental, and physical—of hundreds of persons. Some of this was guidance through his interpretation of other people's dreams. Cayce, himself, had many precognitive dreams.

He, of course, guided his own life and that of his family by his clairvoyance. Finally, he guided the work of the Association with the various committees and study groups organized to carry on its work. Much of this was prophetic. Hardly a move was taken in those days by the Association without the help of the psychic sources.

And yet, prophecy was not the main concern of Edgar Cayce. It was respected and heeded when given, but, just as we in our dreams don't look for predictive messages, so it was with Cayce. Helpfulness was the rule, and prophecy is helpful. Thus was it given. It was both volunteered and sought.

For, of course, he and many others did ask for answers to the riddle of the future. They asked about everything that is humanly possible to ask—about marriage, careers, ending of wars and financial problems. Sometimes they asked about very unusual things, such as oil wells, and buried treasure, about the future of air travel (back when the dirigible was really big!) and they received startling answers at times.

The year 1924 marked a turning point in Edgar's Cayce's life. He gave a reading on Psychic Sources on February 9, just a few weeks before his forty-seventh birthday. It predicted that he would bring through his psychic gifts "joy, peace, and quiet" to the masses and multitudes. This would be done through the efforts, however, of other individuals.

In 1924, the reading went on, after the twentieth of February, when influences astrologically would be those of Pisces (Edgar Cayce's sign) and the sun, he would go forward to develop his psychic and occult abilities for the benefit of great numbers of people that would turn to him.

This reading then foretold that all of his work in this lifetime would be judged by the public according to his own spiritual life, and his manner of living.

He was told to teach psychic and occult ability.

All this unfolded in the latter part of his life.

Mysterious Virginia Beach

On a clearing among the sand dunes at Fort Story, on Cape Henry, guarding the entrance to the Chesapeake Bay, stands a large, stone cross. Here, every Easter morning, sunrise services are held by devout citizens as the sun slides up out of the ocean and seagulls cry and wheel beyond the gentle surf.

This was the place where in April, 1607, a group of 104 Englishmen rowed ashore to seek their fortunes in the wilderness that then was Virginia. They planted a cross on the shore of Drayton's "Virginia, Earth's only Paradise." They were set on finding gold, the Northwest Passage, and some Indians to convert. They also planned to send home commodities.

They had lost sixteen of their number in the four-month crossing, and after they went to Jamestown, a malarial lowland, they suffered privation and sickness that whittled them down to fifty-three. The history of this nation was indeed begun with a cross.

For three centuries, Cape Henry remained a windswept wilderness of silent sands and forbidding swampland. Toward 1900 there grew up around the Coast Guard station a couple of miles south of the first landing site, a tiny community of perhaps a hundred people, one hotel, one grocery store, and an Episcopal church which was shared by the Methodists.

By 1925, Virginia Beach had grown a little, but it certainly was not a place where you'd invest your money anticipating a real estate boom, nor was it a likely place for even a first-rate clairvoyant to hang out his shingle. And yet, Edgar Cayce was told he should leave Dayton, Ohio, where he had lived for several years, and settle in this lonesome outpost.

The destinies of Edgar Cayce and Virginia Beach seemed to have a mysterious affinity. He was told both in his readings and his dreams that this was the place for him, and that a large institution for learning would be built there, as well as a hospital.

He was told that he should be near large bodies of water for the best use of his powers. In all his incarnations, water had been of great significance for him, and many events important in his development had taken place near water.

Water, so the readings say, is the symbol of life, or spirit, or of the relationship between God and man, or man and his fellowman. Its spiritual symbolism is expressed in our ritual of baptism. So for him, it was particularly significant that his work entered its most important phase after he came to Virginia Beach and settled in the "old headquarters" on Arctic Avenue. This was near a lake separated from the ocean by only a few hundred yards. Here he was to live and give readings for twenty years until his death at 67.

The Cayce Hospital, which came about as predicted within a few years after he settled there, was built on the highest sand dune at Virginia Beach, overlooking the Atlantic, commanding a view of beaches and ocean. Back of it broods the Cape Henry Desert, a symbol of contrast between primeval history and the twentieth century—a reminder of how impenetrable and vast is the mind of man—and how our explorations remain on the edge, only, of its mysteries!

While still in Dayton, Cayce had dreams for several weeks of "a ship off the coast of Virginia where a very hilarious party was going on." People were fishing and making good catches.

When he asked for an interpretation, he was told that it meant that many people would become interested in his new interpretation of life, as symbolized by the many people on the ship, and their "fishing" (for knowledge) and "catching fish." These symbols, he said, show the "special, specific work that is to be done by individuals . . . the truth of the fact more apparent to all, the work cut out, or set." The individual "fish" caught meant "a lesson to the chosen people that will give the closer understanding between the laws and lessons as were given to a world through the peoples whom the Master came to save."

Another dream earlier that year had told him that "from this place, Virginia Beach, will flow out a great force which will build greater forces or power that will be discovered by means of the phenomena. Not that there will not be hardships, yet let each know, now, when established in the correct place, we will build, knowing we are following the suggestions, the outline from the Force [God] in which we gain the knowledge of all. . . ."

Some others closely associated with Cayce also had dreams predicting the major events of the Cayce work. One person reported for interpretation: "Then I saw a hospital. It was a good one and seemed the result of Henry S's donation. . . ."

The university and the hospital became realities, but only for a few years. They were lost after the 1929 crash, but hopes of their revival have remained with many members of the group. As early as 1931, it was asked if the University could be rehabilitated, and Cayce answered that this was possible.

The hospital building was regained in 1954, when the A.R.E. was able to sell the old headquarters and buy it back. It had changed hands a number of times since 1931, having been a night club, a Navy Nurse's home, and, at the time of its restoration to the A.R.E., it was a Shriners' home. Painted on the walls in the living room were, appropriately, scenes of Egypt with pyramids, palm trees, and burnoosed desert people, reminding everyone of the place Egypt has in the prophecies of old, and its ancient influence on the story of mankind.

How much significance, too, for those to whom the fatherhood of God, the brotherhood of man—the Masonic ideals—mean much! For Cayce had predicted it would be these very ideals upon which would be built the peace of the world!

Those first Englishmen who came to Virginia looking for gold had no idea that it could heal more than economic problems. But, Cayce said, there was gold in the sands that could heal ailing bodies! He told many persons to lie in the warm sands of the resort city and to take "sand packs" for the beneficial effects of the gold there.

"Of all the resorts on the East Coast, Virginia Beach will be the first and the longest lasting of the increasing of the population, valuation, and activities. Hence, we would give, the future is good," said Cayce in 1932. A boom began just after World War II. Now the city ranks third largest in the state. An annual estimate published in the Virginia Beach *Beacon,* November 1, 1967, by the University of Virginia's Bureau of Population and Economic Research, gave the city's population as 145,843. The town has come a long way since the days of its first "gingerbread" hotel, the Princess Anne . . . and one hundred citizens.

Norfolk, also, was in for a good future. "With the years that are to come, conditions that are to arise, as we find, eventually—and this within the next thirty years—Norfolk, with its environs, is to be the chief port on the East Coast, this not excepting Philadelphia or New York; the second being rather in the New England area" (August 27, 1932).

According to "Earth Changes," a booklet written by a geologist who studied the readings, "In 1957 Norfolk Harbor and the Port of Newport News together shipped and imported a total of 59,920 short tons of cargo. Ports of the 'Delaware River and tributaries' were second with 47,569; New York Harbor was third with 42,003; Baltimore Harbor and Channels, Md., handled 32,044; and Portland Harbor, Me., was fifth with 12,935. (U.S. Bureau Census, 1959, table 776.)

"The opening of the Hampton Roads Bridge Tunnel took place in 1957, and in October of this same year approval was granted for construction of the 200-million dollar Chesapeake Bay Bridge Tunnel," the author of "Earth Changes" states further, in reference to a prediction that changes in Norfolk and vicinity would start around 1958. "As the longest fixed-crossing in the world, this structure would make the Norfolk area a "port" for auto and truck traffic along the east coast. In 1959, the engineering and cost analyses for two huge new general cargo facilities at Newport News and Norfolk were completed."

My own recollections of Edgar Cayce are vivid, however confined they are to brief encounters. I remember him with a great deal of understanding that I didn't have then. I had just celebrated my twenty-first birthday, was a newspaper reporter for the Norfolk *Ledger-Dispatch* (now the *Ledger-Star)* and was not about to believe in fortune-tellers!

Before 1944 I had never heard of Edgar Cayce and not until June and Harmon Bro came down from Chicago did I find out about him. They were here to learn more about this man of whom Dr. Bro's mother, Margueritte Harmon Bro, had written in the *Coronet* Magazine article, "Miracle Man of Virginia Beach." I met the Bros through my mother, to whom they had been introduced at a Methodist Church function.

Edgar Cayce's birthday was traditionally celebrated each year with a fund-raising party at the old headquarters on Arctic Avenue. On this March 18, my mother and I arrived at the green-shingled headquarters building which was set against a lovely backdrop, Lake Holly. On the way toward the office entrance we passed a doorway where, tall and brooding and alone, stood Edgar Cayce.

A lean, kindly man, he looked down at us from his vantage, a rather thoughtful smile on his face. He did not of course recognize us and so we merely nodded and went on by. But the memory of that strange personage whose reverie we had momentarily broken will never leave me. He stood in a relaxed pose, in his shirtsleeves, hands on hips, gazing out at the world and thinking—what? Perhaps he was tired and welcomed the moment he had taken from the demands of an ever-needful humanity. Perhaps he read our minds, or at least our auras, as I later learned he could do. Perhaps he saw the vast doubt we shared about him. We were not sure just why we had attended this particular party, but were drawn by the Bros' earnest persuasion that we know more about this man.

Later that summer I attended a reading session. Well, I didn't really attend it. I was such an unbeliever then that they were afraid my negative attitude would be a disturbing influence on the sleeping seer! So while Harmon was inside recording the proceedings in the little corner office (Cayce's son Hugh Lynn, normally in charge, was in the army over in Europe), June and I sat outside on the grass, leaning against a tree, trying to catch what was going on through the open windows.

We could understand very little . . . we heard only the rise and fall of Edgar Cayce's voice as he spoke in his self-imposed sleep. It was maddening. I really was getting curious, in spite of my prejudices, and wished very much that I was inside.

"Why don't you ask for a reading?" June urged me many times. Harmon was quite enthusiastic by now, after spending several months with the Cayces, and was increasingly respectful of Cayce's ability. He and June had readings, but I remained uncertain.

Edgar Cayce was to die within months. I never had my reading. Later, however, I did begin to study the readings and parallel material in the A.R.E. library. I became a member of the Virginia Beach Study Group, met and talked with many of his friends, and grew aware of the undercurrents of feelings about him on the part of local townspeople. To this day the feelings appear to be mixed. To those who knew him, he was a great soul. To many who had readings from him, and were associated with him through the physical readings and their effects on the health of local people, he was "Dr. Cayce." Interesting testimonies are recorded in the files from Virginia Beach people who saw the results of his readings on their lives. Yet many others have never known, or cared to know, about the work. Over the years, at times, I have heard doubting remarks about the beliefs among Association members, particularly their belief in reincarnation. But in knowing the people in the Association, and in studying the data myself, I have gained a better insight into life.

For a long time I could not accept the idea of reincarnation, which is part and parcel of the Cayce phenomenon. But as I attended lectures by Hugh Lynn Cayce, Harmon Bro, Eula Allen, Esther Wynne, Hannah and Noah Miller, Harold Reilly, Lydia J. Schraeder Gray, and many others, my sympathy for the work grew and so did my understanding.

I regret never having really talked to Edgar Cayce or obtaining a reading. But I have one memory I value—the memory of a man standing in a doorway, casting his glances at sky and budding trees of spring, and thinking his own thoughts about a world that is so ready to see the worst and so slow to accept the best.

The people who knew Cayce first hand, who worked and grew with his work, have lived to see many of his predictions come to pass. They have also seen new people come to help, people who never had a reading but who were attracted by the story told in books, newspaper accounts, magazine articles. Cayce had predicted that those who weren't ready for the "work" would not be with it long. Those who have stayed through the years have had a long time to observe the many ways in which human nature reacts to the unknown, and have been witnesses to a unique kind of experience in history involving God's ways with His children.

There seems to be a testing that takes place. But the human will being what it is, and the human capacity to change and drift, react, and blossom with almost no discernible pattern, many come back who first were repelled. A few drop away, finding other interests or simply becoming discouraged. The work has its requirements: one must seek to be a channel of service to others, put away prejudices and materialistic tendencies, and come with an open mind.

Without these basic qualities, those who have lived through the testing period agree, one could never make it.

Cayce said in his "Work Readings" that the A.R.E. should be first a research organization, then an enlightening one. The research should precede the enlightenment. It would be "in keeping with those things that are sacred, those that are true, those that are helpful, and yet being tolerant to all. . . ."

Furthermore, its members are to present to others only those experiences that have proven valid at first hand. Those who didn't find within themselves that an idea was good shouldn't advocate it.

He said that those who had found this work compatible should never find fault with others who disagree with them, but that they should "glory in the promises of thy Lord, thy Master, thy brother, in those things that He would do in the earth through thine feeble efforts."

There is throughout the readings a pervasive compassion for those who committed themselves to the task of first living, and then presenting the standpoints in the Cayce files. Whether it was experimenting with the effects of atomidine and prayer on one's dreams, or whether it was taking osteopathic treatments, or whether it was speaking kindly to one who was unkind, the *research* in life should come first, before one talked about it.

Study groups sprang up, following the Norfolk Study Group One, which Edgar Cayce led. Now there are over two hundred such groups all over the country, and more forming all the time. These attempt to guide the research and enlightenment at the "grass roots," so to speak. They are formed to study and to try Cayce's numerous suggestions to a better life. Some of these follow the "Search for God" Books One and Two, written by members of the first A.R.E. Study Group during months of efforts to apply the wisdom of the readings. This group had literally prayed, suffered, and wept its way through the readings, giving guidance and counsel in order to bring to others what they had found.

Never do the Cayce students proselyte, nor insist that anyone take part. The facts are there at 67th Street, Virginia Beach, Virginia. How important they are remains always for the individual to find out for himself. They can seem inconsequential, even ridiculous and to some they have. Or they can mean the difference between life and death, and they have, to uncounted numbers.

In the following pages we will present the major prophecies of Edgar Cayce, taking "first things first" as he emphasized. The readings on World Affairs, given in the twenties through the early forties in answer to questions about global problems, present the case of his veracity for themselves, as do the many on scientific developments of recent years, which Cayce predicted forty years ago. This book comes to be written with what seems to be excellent timing: the great upheavals that allegedly will affect millions of people were predicted to begin in 1968 and continue to 1998. An atmosphere of revelation now seems to be present as we see history unfold in the light of the Cayce predictions. To have lived with the readings as the predicted events were ticked off through the decades has been for the Cayce students a unique manifestation of clairvoyance. But one becomes used to it. As each important world event takes place, one is no longer surprised.

As for Edgar Cayce, he seemed to step aside and join the onlookers with their peculiar brand of savoir faire regarding their inside position to Time's secrets. In his simple wisdom, he regarded it all with a great deal of patience for those who scoffed. He of course did not live to see many of his world prophecies come true, because they were about events following his death. Others are happening now, and some are still to be proven.

In his readings he equated the Spirit of God with Time, Space, and the useful virtue Patience. He explained prophecy against that equation. However, it is one thing to repeat the formula, and another to get up before the class and explain it. Given a little of each—Time, Space, and Patience—I will attempt to present some of what Cayce said about prophecy.

CHAPTER 2

THE NEW AGE

Hell, her numbers full,
Thenceforth shall be for ever shut. Meanwhile,
The world shall burn, and from her ashes spring
New heaven and earth, wherein the just shall dwell,
And, after all their tribulations long,
See golden days, fruitful of golden deeds,
With joy and love triumphing, and fair truth.

Milton's *Paradise Lost*, Book Three,
300–335

This is the New Age?

Low morals, spreading anarchy, juvenile crime, drug addiction and a war which half the nation condemns; riots that bring death and injury to hundreds, dissent that divides us: This is the New Age?

"What do you think will happen in the twenty-first century?" a scientist was asked recently.

"I'm not convinced we'll have a twenty-first century," was the answer.

In trying to reconcile the Cayce predictions for an ever-better world during the last part of this century, we are hard put to figure out the inconsistencies of what we see and what the readings say is happening.

But, despite wars, riots, dire predictions of earth upheavals, we are reminded that this is a time of change, and like the bull in the china shop, it's upsetting a lot of dishes.

It is, in the words of St. Paul, "the day of the Lord," and a lot of housecleaning is being done, according to the Cayce data. In passages that are awe-inspiring in their majesty, we are told: "That as has been promised through the prophets and the sages of old—the time and half time—has been and is being fulfilled in this day and generation; and that seen there will again appear in the earth—that one through whom many will be called to meet those who are preparing the way for His day in the earth. The Lord then will come, even as ye have seen Him go . . . when those who are His have made the way clear and passable for Him to come."

"The way clear and passable" seems to refer to spiritual conditions in the earth. We are suddenly aware of the magnitude of the many basic reforms now being wrought within the Church, which are in keeping with our new understanding of righteousness in this day. We are sharply aware of the great struggle between two nations which is primarily of a spiritual nature, for America, founded upon religious principles, is at natural odds with a nation which denies the very existence of God.

Then, as such reforms and struggles take place in the ideological arenas of this age and the way is there being made "passable," we see again that it is by the will of man—of man making his will one with God's—that he makes for himself a better world in which the Christ can abide.

Man seems ready for a step up in his evolution, according to the Cayce readings. We are poised on the beginning of the Aquarian Age, following the one just ended—the Piscean—which has lasted for two thousand years under the symbol of the "fish" of the early Christian Church. These ages overlap and we will not begin to fully understand all that the present one brings until the turn of the century. By then, we will see the Day of the Lord at a more completed stage, not only in our imaginations, but in actuality. It will be the beginning of the Millennium. "As given," says the reading, "for a thousand years He will walk and talk with men of every clime. Then, in groups, in masses, and then they shall reign of the first resurrection for a thousand years, for this will be when the changes materially come."

It appears that first He, the Christ, will be in the hearts of mankind then and will begin to walk and talk with men in our physical world. Meanwhile, we will experience the effect of the Christ upon the hearts of individuals.

It will be in the hearts of leaders, as has been in the past, as the following example shows:

"In the manner as He sat at the peace conference in Geneva, in the heart and soul of a man not reckoned by many as an even unusually godly man [Woodrow Wilson] yet raised for a purpose, and he chose rather to be a channel of His thought for the world. So as there has been, so will it be, until the time as set. As was given of Him, not given to man to know the time or the period of the end, nor to man, save by their constituting themselves a channel through which He may speak."

The year 1998 is given in a number of readings for the time of this great event. By that time, the world will have seen much drastic change and upheaval of both a geologic and social nature. Thus far the change has been gradual, but will become more pronounced.

"In 1998 we may find a great deal of the activities as have been wrought by the gradual changes that are coming about," states another reading. "These are at the periods when the cycle of the solar activity, or the years are related to the sun's passage through the various spheres of activity, become paramount, or tantamount to the change between the Piscean and the Aquarian Age. This is a gradual, not a cataclysmic, activity in the experience of the earth in this period."

What specifically can we expect for 1998? The readings firmly state that there will be "less of wars" even before then, that peace will come to the world, and that man will learn more and more how to benefit from scientific discoveries still in the offing!

For centuries people have been predicting the end of the world and have been fooled every time. Even the Christians of the early church expected it in their day. People have been preparing for it in every generation since. Why should we believe it's really happening now?

The answer is: Look within. If you have ever experienced a moment of true brotherly concern for another person, or expressed a kindness to someone, or showed patience toward an erring child, you know something of the New Age and what it will bring. It has been gathering force throughout the ages in just this way. It will happen because the way has been made "clear and passable" not only by formal action taken in self-reform in the church, but by the good we ourselves are responsible for.

In this reading on "Spiritual Evolution" given September 22, 1939, a student asked, "What will the Aquarian Age mean to mankind as regards physical, and mental and spiritual development?"

Cayce replied tartly: "Think ye this might be answered in a word? These are as growths. What meant that awareness as just indicated? In the Piscean Age, in the center of same, we had the entrance of Emmanuel or God among men, see? What did that mean? The same will be meant by the full consciousness of the ability to communicate with or to be aware of the relationships to the Creative Forces, God, and the uses of same in material environs.

"Then, as to what will these be—only those who accept same will even become aware of what's going on about them!

"How few realize the vibratory forces as create influences from one individual to another, when they are even in the same vibratory force or influence! And yet, ye ask what will the Aquarian Age bring in mind, in body, in experience!"

As the entrance of Emmanuel or God among men meant the salvation of mankind in the Piscean Age, so will the next great step be given man: the full consciousness that he can communicate with God! How many of us even comprehend the advent of God two thousand years ago? The New Age we are entering will hold for us just as tremendous a concept in our evolution!

In 1942 a young man asked, "When this [peace] does come about, can you advise some of the world conditions and how to meet them?"

The answer was, "This will depend upon much of the activities of those who have the establishing of the relationships.

"Individually, know that right, justice, mercy, patience—as was represented and presented by Him—the Prince of Peace—is the basis upon which the new world order *must* eventually be established before there *is* peace.

"Then, innately, mentally, and manifestedly in self, prepare self for cooperative measures in all phases of human relations in this direction."

Another man, concerned about his personal responsibility in helping to bring about world peace, asked in March, 1944: "What can I do to help bring about the New Age?"

He was told, "As just indicated, you will have to practice it in your own life. These are the manners and channels through which this might be better expressed by this particular entity."

Does the New Age, then, depend upon God's will or man's? If this man was told that he could help bring it about by "practicing" it in his own life, what good was the age-old prophecy anyway? What if this man decided *not* to practice the new understanding of peace and brotherhood (which is ever new, it seems, in every age)? If he said, "I will not," would the New Age grind to a halt?

Well, it seems that the New Age is coming about both because of—and in spite of—mankind! God doesn't really need man. Man needs God. But man can, by his own free will, *delay* or *hasten* fulfillment of God's plan.

This is indicated plainly in the following message to a group seeking spiritual help: "And so may ye, as seekers for divine guidance, be uplifted and thus may ye hasten the day when war will be no more."

During the dark days of World War II, many such messages were given to persons bowed down by the sorrows of the time. A week before Pearl Harbor (November 29, 1941), this heartening word was given for Study Group One: "Though troubled and a blood-stained world, thy prayer, thy blessing may bring a new hope, and may blossom into joy on earth, peace among men."

Invariably, when people or groups asked for help in what to do about bringing lasting peace, the responsibility was thrown right back into their own laps. The search for world peace became just such another personal challenge to a woman of sixty-three who asked, "Will I live to see this war ended and peace and happiness in America?"

"The peace and happiness must first be within self," she was told. "You will be living when war is ended, but when peace is established—that's something else!"

Eight years later, she wrote "My life reading gave me a clearer idea of my responsibility and obligation to serve humanity. . . ." She reported that in spite of bad health, nervous exhaustion, and a crippling fall which left her in a wheelchair, at seventy-one she became a diagnostician and found a measure of the peace and happiness she had sought within herself. For her the New Age had already come!

The motto on the Great Seal of the United States, *"Novus Ordo Seclorum,"* means "A new order of ages." It is not by chance that America has that mystical motto, according to what the Cayce readings say about this nation's role in the world's destiny.

America's Role in the New Age

"The spirituality of the American people will be rather as the criterion of that as is to become the world's forces, for, as has been given in that of the peace table, there sat the Master in the American people; with the brotherhood of the world accepted, war was at an end. Without [the brotherhood of the world] there will again come the Armageddon, and in same there will be seen that the Christian forces will again move westward!"

So spoke Cayce on October 9, 1926, during a period of great scandal and immorality on the part of America, reveling in unmatched national prosperity and pursuing at the same time a policy of isolationism from the rest of the world. This was the "Roaring 20's."

It was this nation, Cayce reminds us, which was founded by devout and religious men, and which declares on its money, "In God We Trust." Specifically, as was mentioned earlier, Cayce pointed to President Wilson, who, although not known to be particularly godly, was yet "raised for a purpose" and who "chose to be a channel of His thought for the world" as he strove to create peaceful measures in Geneva. This is elaborated upon in another reading given January 15, 1932:

"Some years ago (this, we understand, is out of line with what many would have one believe) there was a Peace Table, and about same were gathered representatives of every nation under the sun! In the soul of the representative of the United States sat the Prince of Peace—yet many would have you believe, that in the economical world, the financial world, had that man never left his home, his own shores, the world would be better today. Not so; for 'Ye shall pay every whit'; for 'The heavens and earth may pass away, but My Word shall not' are the words of Him who made the world.

"As to whether it will be in three years or five years [that peace comes] depends upon those who would rally to 'I will make of my life a channel of blessing to *someone* today.' "

In a biography published in 1960, President Wilson was championed by his physician and naval aide, Rear Admiral Cary T. Grayson, who served during Wilson's two White House terms. Admiral Grayson asserted that Wilson would have given his very life if he could have saved the League of Nations. In a conversation on March 25, 1920, Wilson told Grayson that he would run for a third term "even if I thought it would cost me my life." He died February 3, 1924, only three years following his presidency, from the effects of a stroke brought about by his strenuous crusade for the League.

All during the years before World War II, individuals asked if America would be drawn into war and what could be done. "What is the outlook for war?" was asked in the thirties.

"If America acts as it prays" she would not be drawn into the war, Cayce repeated.

But three months before Pearl Harbor, this hope was withdrawn. On August 31, 1941, the picture changed. No longer did Cayce state that we might be spared involvement, but that war was imminent for us.

It was man's will which had made the difference. A study of one nation's going to war affords us an opportunity to learn how individuals, like nations, create their own destiny: prophecy is only flexible to a certain point of no return. God will not always wait for us to turn to Him, but permits His laws to operate. If a man or a country continues to act in a way that leads to disaster, the disaster will come.

The reading of August 31, 1941, that marked the turning point in America's destiny stated: "It is evident that there are strenuous conditions imminent in the affairs of the land, owing to thought as respecting the relationships in varied portions of the world.

"And, as has been and is indicated, unusual combinations are being made; and those individual groups or nations that have heretofore manifested friendly or brotherly relationships are now seen to be as enemies . . ."

Thus he predicted the reversal in Japan's attitude toward the United States from that of friendship to enmity.

Following the prophecy of war for America, this same reading predicted the date war would end and discussed the principles upon which world peace would be built: those inherent in American ideals, including the brotherhood of man, and of Masonry!

"For with those changes that will be wrought, Americanism—the ism—with the universal thought that is expressed and manifested in the brotherhood of man into group thought, as expressed by the Masonic Order—will be the eventual rule in the settlement of affairs in the world.

"Not that the world is to become a Masonic Order, but the principles that are embraced in same will be the basis upon which the new order of peace is to be established in '44 and '45."

This reading also advised Americans to guard against Communism and Fascism, and to take a stand for Christ and His principles rather than becoming involved with questionable groups. "A great number of individuals formulated into groups who have declared specific or definite policies will be questioned as to purpose and as to the ideal. Some of such will be drawn into coalition with questionable groups."

There was once a time when nations lived unto themselves. Even America practiced isolationism, and considering her role in the affairs of the world, it is surprising that she should have refused to join the League of Nations. According to Cayce, it was Americans who must carry the spirit of cooperation with them to other lands, in the postwar world of twenty years ago.

It was December 8, 1941, the day after Pearl Harbor, when this message was dropped in the lap of one person seeking information: "While there will not be the reversal of the capitalistic system, there is to be the establishment more and more of the cooperative basis—in local, state, county, national, and international activities. Cooperation must form the basis of activities, such as has been indicated here, and is to be applied not only in the home, but in corporations, in mines, in manufacturing, in the nations—more and more.

"There will be the greater abilities, the greater possibilities—not of America becoming again as the land to which others will flee, but *Americans* must go to the other lands and carry cooperation with them!"

We think of the Marshal Plan, the Peace Corps, and of the many cooperative measures we have taken in helping the less fortunate nations during those years. International cooperation has been created through many agencies, including the North Atlantic Treaty Organization, Organization of American States, and other regional groups.

It was a war-sick world by May, 1944. On May 10, someone asked Cayce, "What can be done specifically by the American people to bring about a speedy, lasting peace?"

Consistently, Cayce continued to put the responsibility with ourselves. "We haven't the American people," he said. "The thing is to start with yourself. Unless you can bring about within yourself that which you would have in the nation or in any particular land, don't offer it to others."

On May 14, another person asked for affirmations or little prayers that might be used in praying for peace. "As to affirmations: these should be towards that of peace through the next six to eight months. For then through this period will the earth and its peoples be passing through the most strenuous period of the world's history since the Master walked in the earth!"

The six to eight months following May, 1944, held the heaviest destruction by American and British bombing raids on Nazi-held Europe of the entire war. Two-thirds of the destruction was carried on *after* July, 1944! The year 1944 saw the great invasion of Europe by the Allies in June; the breakthrough at St. Lo; the Battle of the Bulge. The Japanese stepped up their attack on China late in 1944 and the war in the Pacific was being fought with the heaviest losses and fighting in which Saipan, Guam, the Philippines fell to the Allies by Christmas.

After January, 1945, the worst was over. The predicted eight months of trial, the worst in history since the time of the Master two thousand years ago, had come to pass.

Leaders in the New Age

In 1942, a young woman of twenty-five was told, "Be *glad* you have the opportunity to be alive at this time, and to be a part of that preparation for the coming influences of a spiritual nature that must rule the world. These are indicated and these are part of thy experience. Be happy of it, and give thanks daily for it."

The "Day of the Lord," that St. Paul foretold, is coming, according to Cayce. "The Lord will come . . . when those who are his have made the way clear" for His return.

Who are "those who are His?"

Evidently, they are among us now, seemingly quite ordinary people—because they are people we know. They are leaders who are quietly carrying out their task, we gather. Throughout the files are mentioned appearances of many who will prepare the way. They are coming to leadership at a time when they are sorely needed—a high-minded breed of individuals who have incarnated in large numbers in recent years.

Among these are several outstanding world spiritual leaders who were incarnated around 1935 and 1936. According to one reference, St. Martin, patron saint of France, is to serve in some manner in 1989 at the age of fifty-four.

As early as 1931, a woman was told that she would see the "greatest development in spiritual affairs that the world has known."

There seems to be an intensified incarnation of Atlanteans now, or those souls who had incarnations in the Atlantean civilization. (See chapter on Atlantis.) Especially was there an influx of these souls between the years 1909 and 1913 inclusive. Now fifty-five to fifty-seven years old, these are doubtless among those in authority in positions everywhere today throughout the world.

These people may "rule or ruin" the character of man's condition, bringing from Atlantis their extremes in character—the very worst, the very best. They have strong emotional and mental traits combined with a past record of "engorgement of carnal influences in the experience of others, of self-indulgence." They also were scientifically advanced, and so possess technical knowledge, or an inherent ability in technology.

On July 4, 1939, a thirty-one-year-old music teacher, Protestant, with unorthodox leanings, was told that she was "one of those of the new order of the Atlanteans that will either make for a great development" or help repeat the errors of the past. These errors are described as "of the natural tendencies of the material aspect of the world" at the time of Atlantis when that nation had become proud and self-destructive.

Others were similarly told that they were among "those individuals upon whom the real future of the state or nation will depend" and "may in this experience be the mother of those who may fill high places; . . . be well guarded in the law of the Lord, for it is perfect and will convert the souls of men."

A sixteen-year-old boy asked on June 24, 1940: "Will I or any of my immediate family reincarnate with Mr. Cayce in 1998?"

He was told: "This is not to be given, or things of such natures, but is to be determined by the desire, the need, the application of those who may desire to do so."

Another excerpt stated: "For as has been indicated now, in the next few years, there will be many entrances of those who are to prepare the way for the new race, the experiences of man, that may be a part of those activities in preparation for the Day of the Lord."

To another: "All that are in the earth today are thy brothers. Those that have gradually forgotten God entirely have been eliminated, and there has come—now—and will come at the close of this next year [1943] the period when there will be no part of the globe where man has not had the opportunity to hear 'The Lord He is God.'

"And, as has been indicated, when this period has been accomplished, then the New Era, the New Age is to begin. Will ye have a part of it, or will ye let it pass by and be merely a hanger-on, or one upon whom your brother—the Lord, thy Christ—may depend?"

CHAPTER 3

CHOOSE THOU!

"There is this day set before thee good and evil. Choose thou!"

JANE HARRINGTON LOOKED across the breakfast table at Claude, her young husband. "I dreamed," she said slowly, "of a weak-minded boy." She frowned. "What could it mean?"

Claude swallowed a sudden sense of foreboding with a gulp of coffee and replied, "It's probably a symbol of something the matter with your head." He returned her troubled glance with what he hoped was a grin.

"I am *not* weak-minded!" Jane pretended insult, tossing her lovely bobbed hair. It was 1925, she had been married one month, and she resented the dream's intrusion on her happiness.

"Was that all you remember?" Claude asked lightly.

"That's all. Could it be precognitive?"

"Oh, it doesn't have to be literally so. . . . It can be symbolic, you know, of some conditions you might be running into."

Jane was silent for a moment as she stared out of the window at the city skyline, as if the answer skipped along the tops of the buildings there in the blue summer sky. "Or could it actually be the prediction that . . . someone we know . . . is going to have a . . . retarded child?"

Now Claude fell silent. Finally he said, "It could be."

The Harringtons were no ordinary dreamers. For several years before his marriage, Claude had been a student of dreams. He had been recording his dreams and sending them to Edgar Cayce in Virginia Beach for interpretation. His bride, a bright psychology major planning to work for her master's degree, became fascinated with the project and began recording her own dreams for the southern psychic.

This particular dream was so disturbing to Claude that he decided to write Cayce that very day. "I am indeed anxious to get an interpretation of Jane's dream of a weak-minded boy or child," he wrote, "for we have had certain discussions and maybe it is a warning to her. Of course I am guessing."

They had already learned much of the nature of dreams, from past discourses given them by Cayce. They knew that dreams often are symbolic, rather than literal. Thus a dream of death usually means the "death" of one's past and the beginning of a new and better future; "putting on clothes" symbolizes for most people the putting on of various states of mind or attitudes.

However, Cayce's reading shortly after was not reassuring. He told them that any condition becoming reality is first dreamed. It was, he said, "a projection of thought, of conditions" that were indeed possible in the future.

When Jane became pregnant a year later, they set aside all doubts. This would be a very special child, for the Harringtons had faith that through preparation and dedication of themselves to high ideals founded in their religion they could produce a great spiritual leader.

Dreams, they argued, did not have to come true—not that kind. And their confidence was later bolstered by further information from Cayce that although there were laws in operation which governed the possibility of dreams being an accurate indicator of the future, the "maybe" factor was always very strong.

Unfortunately, their joy in anticipating their child was marred. Quarrels and misunderstandings arose, and the conflict was not to be resolved. Even as they looked forward to the birth of their child, they were torn by their growing estrangement.

On April 4, 1927, a son was born to them. He was normal. Now, there were to be many readings for this new little person in whom the unhappy parents still placed such high hopes.

After the excitement of the new arrival had worn off, the Harringtons turned away from each other with mounting bitterness. Then came the stock market crash . . . a time when fears for the future ran high and lives were drastically changed overnight. Within a few years, the Harringtons found themselves in the divorce courts. Jane was given full custody of young Edward, who was never to see his father afterward. Edward later wistfully wrote to Edgar Cayce that he had tried to get in touch with his father, to no avail.

Edward possessed a brilliant mind. He studied in a university for several years and valiantly followed his leanings to spiritual matters. He had a high temper, of which Cayce had warned. At twenty-five he had a mental breakdown and was admitted to an asylum. Thus, his mother's precognition two years before he was born had become a tragic reality.

Jane, and all those involved, may well have asked years later, as she did when she first "saw" the event: "What could it mean?"

In this sad account of the fulfillment of a twenty-seven-year-old prophetic dream, we have a study in precognition and the many questions it raises. It is more than just an emotional experience, a mysterious experience; it has lessons not only for the people it involved, but also for anyone who cares to seek them out.

Our first reaction to such a story is perhaps best expressed with a shudder. Who, we cry, needs such previews of tragedy? And yet, we want to *know*, transfixed as we are midway between dread and anticipation, whatever the future may hold!

The reason for this lies in what the Cayce readings tell us is our "birthright." For in our dreams, he stated, we are given our own personal prophecies. In addition, these visions from the subconscious and superconscious warn, prepare, advise, rebuke, goad, remind, inspire, cheer, reassure, chide, and guide the dreamer toward doing better. If we don't remember our dreams, or are poor interpreters of them, we miss out on our birthright. By recording them daily, we can increase our memory and ability to interpret the messages that are meant for our use.

As for Jane and Claude, what went wrong? We have, thanks to their intelligent and avid interest in dreams, a fund of information on the subject which has contributed greatly to our knowledge. At the same time, no amount of knowledge prevented them from ultimate grief and disaster. Claude had dreams to indicate that their child would become the spiritual light they had hoped for, and they were apparently encouraged to believe this by Cayce's analysis. But there were the *two* possibilities which awaited them: what could have tipped the scales against the happier ending?

According to the readings, the answer, painful as it is, lies in the failure of the parents to live up to their sacred marriage vows, to give the boy the stability he needed in order to carry out his life work. He was brilliant but highstrung—his very sanity depending upon the kind of home life created around him. Had he been more stable, he perhaps would not have been affected by these conditions.

We would not judge this beautiful and highly motivated couple of the "roaring 20's" and their hope of rearing together a spiritual leader. We only know that Edgar Cayce gave us, and them, in their earnest soul-searching during those early days of their marriage, the understanding that "we find there are no coincidences, or chance coincidences. Each and every individual follows out that line of development of the entity in the present earth plane as it has received from the preceding conditions, and each grain of thought or condition is consequence of other conditions created by self. And in this particular condition, we find this is a condition wherein the body [Claude] may choose that which will give development for self. For this body should remember this injunction, as was given:

"It is not that one should ascend into the heavens to bring the Force [God] to man, or that one should ascend into the elements, or go into the depths, to bring up the Forces, for there has been set before you, this day, good and evil.

Choose that which will bring the better development of self, and in lending to the Lord is the service that man renders to his Maker. . . ."

To another person at another time, Cayce said, "In the spiritual aspects [of life] everything is good. As the individual works out his destiny by application of mind, his experiences become bad or good, depending upon his choices."

See Deuteronomy 30:12-20!

In April, 1930, the Cayce Hospital was admitting patients for treatment according to the suggestions in the readings. Fred Pelham, then fifty and suffering from neurosis of five years' standing, entered on the twenty-second and had his first reading.

He asked the sleeping Cayce, "Is the case curable? If so, approximately how long?"

Cayce answered, "Curable, sure—it's curable! How long? How hard will the body not try, but just get well?"

Evidently, it was a matter of Fred's choice!

His readings called for changes in diet, for sandpacks and violet-ray applications. Later, Fred lay on the beach that stretched below the hospital, covered by the warm sand which he had been told contained gold which was healing to the body.

"Just what can this do for me," he grumbled, "a man who's gone through the crash, lost everything—for a man whose wife has turned against him!" He stared moodily at the blue sky above. The cool salt breezes on his face felt chilly to him. He sighed with the heaviness of Job.

A sense of failure had dogged him here. In his heart he told himself that it had all been too much for one man. His marriage was gone, and he might as well face up to it. Slowly he got up from the sand and brushed it off his body. He thought, "This is crazy. How can lying out here . . . taking those light treatments . . . eating that silly rabbit food change things back home? Crazy doctors, crazy me for thinking they know!"

But he found himself in the water, and the salt sting of it dashed his dark thoughts momentarily away. They washed off with the sand and when he plodded back to the hospital a little later, he discovered he was hungry. "Wonder what they'll have for supper?" he mused. "Rabbit food, no doubt!"

And so the summer went. Fred took his treatments among the other patients and gradually he seemed to be feeling better. He had another reading on August 29, four months after entering. It stated: "When the body physical, body mental, has so attuned itself as to be able to face self and self's obligations, self's relations one with another, in that period there will come changes in the business associations and business relations such as to enable the body to make that as is built in the interim in the mental and physical body. . . .

"Three to five weeks . . . and then the body will find that there will be those aids for seemingly unseen sources as will make for the better relations, the better associations, in the marital and domestic relations, and an understanding reached. Do not falter in self."

Fred asked in this reading, "How can the body go about to create the harmony that is desired in the home life?"

The answer was, "By taking a stand for that as is known in self as to be the proper, the correct relationships as must and will exist, and keep to that as is known, and felt, irrespective of anything else."

By now, Fred had been exposed to the attitude toward prayer and its healing power prevalent at the hospital and engendered by the devout Edgar Cayce himself. The atmosphere of cheerfulness and good will that was breathed in along with the salt air had worked wonders for Fred. His next question was tendered with great sincerity: "What prayer can be held by the body as a guide to that he wishes to attain?"

"May the meditations of my heart, my mind, my body be wholly acceptable in thy sight, My Lord and My Redeemer," was the reply.

His next question was one which he had been pondering for some weeks now, for he had begun to think it might be possible to make a new start at home. He was advised to take things easy in this direction, until he had become strong enough to maintain his equilibrium. "This should not be considered too fast, for the inclination will be to worry over same. Will that as has just been given be held, the place, the position, will be seeking the man as much as the man seeking the place . . ."

On September 20, Fred Pelham was dismissed to return home and to a new life. For him, Edgar Cayce had been the best sort of prophet—and doctor! For Fred was a changed man, and a changed man can do anything—including winning back a place in business, and the woman he loves!

"For remember, the Creative Force [God] has made man with a will of his own. As to what a man will do with same, only he himself *can* know! Only the tendencies and the inclinations may be given; and these, as indicated here, at times have seemed bad choices, and at times there have been helpful influences. These must depend upon the entity himself."

To others, Edgar Cayce expressed much the same thought. He explained to one this: "As He has given, God has fixed the doors. . . . He has fixed the purposes through which man's own activity may pass. Yet He leaves the choice to man."

The attitude of expectancy is very important in directing our future lives. "He that expects—and acts in an expectant manner—consistent with the mental and physical activities—will be rewarded."

And yet, when Cayce gave a prediction, it was often unqualified and seemingly irrevocable. He had predicted that Claude Harrington would marry Jane months before Claude proposed or was sure he would! A friend of the Harringtons wrote: "You are a wizard when it comes to marrying people. I don't know whether Claude sold the proposition to you or you sold it to him, but he certainly is going to marry the girl in —— and you said it would be in the Southwest and you also said within a year."

Evidently, then, understanding destiny is not as simple as we would hope. "The race is not to the swift, nor the battle to the strong, neither yet bread to the wise, nor yet riches to men of understanding, nor yet favour to men of skill; but time and chance happeneth to them all." (Ecclesiastes 9:11)

What is it that brings order out of chaos, then? To some who asked Edgar Cayce if it were possible to understand, he replied, "His ways are not past finding out, to those who attune themselves to that inner consciousness which is the birthright of each entity—that privilege, that opportunity *given* to each soul. . . ." Thus, man is right in pursuing his attempt to understand destiny a little better, to find his place amidst its mysterious workings.

CHAPTER 4

DESTINY AND THE LAW

"MY SON, in all thine getting, get understanding" is the biblical injunction. Cayce added, ". . . and the ability to apply it."

We are living under what he referred to as "Universal Laws" which were in effect for the Harringtons, and have not reportedly gone out of existence since their time.

He said that the purpose of life is "to gain the understanding of all universal laws." The knowledge attained by living these and making them a part of our second nature brings development: spiritual, mental, and even physical.

The application of the law leads to the understanding of the basis upon which destiny is founded. For it is man's use or abuse of the law which is destiny's prime mover.

Man has, furthermore, the gift of free will. If he chooses to break the laws, he must abide by the consequences, for "God is not mocked and whatsoever a man soweth, that must he reap."

It is this Law—the whole gamut of many laws—which undergirds the earth and the universe, unchanging and sure. It is what brings order out of chaos. In a time when there is a breakdown of respect for the laws of both God and man, a look at Edgar Cayce's explanation of the present dilemma of man in the earth seems to be helpful.

It was "lawless men," said Peter, who crucified Jesus of Nazareth. Edgar Cayce was no less concerned with upholding law and order. He inspired respect for one's country, one's leaders, and for the rights of his neighbors. He told us to do all things in "decency and order, doing first things first." He followed Christ's admonition to "render unto Caesar what is Caesar's." Man as he is today must still have laws based on those of God, and once established, the laws must be respected and obeyed.

The current rejection of law and order in favor of anarchy and "mob rule" which Cayce predicted for this age, expressed in race riots, pot parties, student demonstrations, and all the rest, is not in the spirit of the Cayce philosophy. Nor is childish rebellion against one's parents the mature way to change one's world, as the psychologists and Cayce agree. Change comes about by working to improve one's self, coordinating the emotions with the mind, and keeping what is good from the past. This is best expressed by observing the orderly function of the laws of the universe, which direct the movement of planets and temper for us the heat of the sun, as they govern the fate of the humblest child.

In comparing Paul's letter to the law-conscious Romans with what the Cayce readings say, we find a freer interpretation of what law is. It covers every avenue of life, and is to be found, it would seem, as much among the unwritten truths we live by, as those that are in the books. It is to these unwritten laws that Paul seems to be referring, and these are brothers to those in the Cayce files. Nearly all the first ten chapters of the book of Romans speak of these spiritual laws. "I find then a law, that, when I would do good, evil is present with me" (7:21). Paul further speaks of the "law of the Spirit of life in Christ Jesus," the "law of faith," the "law of righteousness" and the "law of works."

The Law of Karma

One of Cayce's most repeated references is to "that first rule, a law that is eternal: The seed sown must one day be reaped." This is a key to understanding reincarnation and karma, which demonstrate the law of cause and effect. It applies not only to the present life we are living, but to past and future lives. Our present life is the result of those we have lived; it is the cause of our future experiences, for they will be determined by our thoughts and actions now. Cayce emphasized the biblical statement: "The Law of the Lord is perfect; it converteth the soul."

We may avoid learning these statutes, much less put them into practice. But they are there and we daily come under the "law." "If you would have friends, be friendly. If you would be loved, be loving." Reminded the sleeping seer: "There are laws—law is love, love is law. . . ."

In the case of the Harringtons, we see that the destiny of their child born into tragic circumstances was ordered for him by his karma. For, if nothing is by chance, and if we create our future, then birth into this or that situation must have its cause. He had been born into this by his actions in a past life, as we interpret it, and was to learn a lesson which his soul would never forget. He was paying for some transgression of spiritual law he had committed long ago. A hard punishment? Yes, but no doubt it was one he had earned; it was therefore appropriate.

And yet his parents, with their free wills in this life, shared the responsibility. How do we decipher this facet of their joint destiny?

Parents attract the children that come to them by their prayers and hopes, as did the Harringtons, or their *lack* of these, as the case may be. They set the stage, so to speak, by the way they live, long before the child is born. This illustrates still another law, the law of attraction. The boy which Claude and Jane received was bright and sensitive, like themselves, but their disharmony was reflected in his very personality through the years in the form of insanity. He was very much their child, their spiritual and mental progeny!

We carry over character traits and influences from past lives. These, therefore, are to be considered in predicting what we will do in this life. This point is made clear in the case of a young man who was in the Civil War "in the name of Artemus Davies . . . strong-minded, very central [single-minded?] in thought and action. Hence the necessity as will be of the training of the direction of the mind and of the developing of same . . ."

This fellow, named in his present incarnation Robin Belote, was born in Selma, Alabama, and had a reading in 1925 at the age of five months. He would take up religious study "as pertaining to psychological and astronomical conditions," said his reading, because he had been influenced by a "heralder of new religious thought" in Arabia in some remote past. Furthermore, he had abilities as a trained mathematician or banker.

From a life in Atlantis when he taught psychology and "the transmission of thought through ether," he would carry over these interests.

At twenty-two, these influences were evident. Cayce's secretary, now married and known as Gladys Davis Turner, had followed this child's progress personally, and in 1947 she reported that he was "always an honor student; worked his way through school.

"Very centered in thought and action as a leader and teacher (heralder) in the Seventh Day Adventist religious movement.

"Always made his own way financially; family received help from him in this respect very early. Outstanding in his religious leadership in the Seventh Day Adventist Schools which he attended. Is now a teacher in the school himself. Always good in mathematics.

"Very devoutly interested in 'transmission' of messages from God to old prophets, etc.—a 'heralder' of a return to religion and especially to *his* chosen religion."

Robin eventually obtained his doctor's degree in chemistry and became head of the department at the Seventh Day Adventist College in Nebraska.

"Not of Thyself . . ."

The Law of Karma is not all, however.

This would be a hopeless world if it were, for we would be so bogged down by our accumulation of karmic debt that we would be paying from now on.

There is, to those who choose it, the Law of Grace. "For the Law of the Lord is perfect," explained Cayce, "and whatever an entity, an individual, sows, that must he reap. That as law cannot be changed. As to whether one meets it in the letter of the law or in mercy, in grace, becomes the choice of the entity. If one would have mercy, grace, love, friends, one must show self in such a manner to those with whom one becomes associated. For like begets like.

"There are barriers builded, yes. These may be taken away in Him, Who has paid the price for thee; not of thyself, but in faith, in love, in patience, in kindness, in gentleness may it be met.

"That these have been the experiences [this particular person's ill fortune] may appear to the entity as rather unfair. Is it? The Law of the Lord is perfect. His grace is sufficient, if thy patience will be sufficient also. . . ."

Karma, Cayce told another, is met either in self or in Him. If we commit a sin, or entertain fear, the soul must die. Not in that moment or even that era, but if the soul continues in sin, it is subject to its effects. "But God has not willed that any soul should perish; He has with every temptation prepared a way of escape.

"Hence, He, the Word, the Light, the Truth, came into the earth, paid the price of death, that we through Him might have life more abundantly; eternal life, the consciousness of eternal life, the consciousness of eternity, and that we are one with Him."

At two days, little Alice Luane had no way of protesting her karma. Her reading on April 20, 1933, stated, however, that she would go into the field of vocational training, thus "enabling others to choose their own activity." She would show "high mental abilities," and, her parents were told, "many shall be those influenced by the . . . entity's sojourn through this experience."

She was, strangely, warned of great anxiety which would surround her at about the age of fourteen. This was hardly to be interpreted that she would contract polio, but that's what happened when she reached that age.

"She will make many men step around!" had read her forecast. This was proven true and when she married at twenty-three, her bridegroom carried her down the aisle!

Her high-spirited determination and ability for leadership which her reading foretold served her well as she grew to womanhood and rose above her handicap, which had put her in a wheelchair. When she was eighteen, according to her grandmother's report, Alice was "intending to teach disabled people handicrafts after she leaves school where she is majoring in art. . . . Her reading said she might go in for vocational guidance and I think her work will be very similar to that idea."

After graduation with high honors from junior college at twenty-two, Alice Luane did teach handicapped children and her influence on their destinies was obviously a fact.

In studying the many readings for children and their accompanying reports in later years, one is struck by the number of tragedies which occurred among them. At least two were drowned; there were at least two emotional and mental problems, and Alice Luane was crippled by polio.

Of course, this is partly due to the fact that the children were in tragic straits before being brought to Cayce for help. But if ill-fortune was to strike later, this was never held over their heads. It is characteristic of the Cayce readings that always a sense of optimism, of the possibility of good, prevailed. When trouble loomed, the prediction was tempered by compassion. Thus, Alice's polio perhaps had been foreseen, but in her reading, the parents were merely warned of a bad time for her at fourteen.

Cayce seemed to be treating each case as if it were in the law of Grace that it could be met. Certainly, Alice Luane was a sparkling example of that Law.

Once, in 1952, I attended a lecture by Tom Sugrue only months before his death. He sat in the living room at the old headquarters in his wheelchair, his face lean from pain and great self-discipline, his eyes bright with the wisdom it had taught him. He spoke then of this very subject, the prophecies regarding "The New Age" and the time of the return of Christ. He had suffered for years with crippling arthritis, had triumphed over his infirmities, and was a living demonstration of the virtue by which destiny is carved: patience.

Now he reminded us that we, too, had pain waiting for us in the future, perhaps, and that we had best prepare ourselves for it. It was a jarring reminder that we all err and are under the Law. He explained that karma was sometimes delayed for several lives until we were strong enough to accept it.

"Patience, love, kindness, gentleness, long-suffering, brotherly love. There is no law against any of these," Cayce had said. "For they are the law of consistency in the search for peace . . . they themselves bring peace." In his way, Tom Sugrue had discovered this for himself. He lived to tell about it.

CHAPTER 5

ATLANTIS RISING?

"POSEIDIA (ATLANTIS) to rise again. Expect it in '68 and '69. Not so far away!" Such was the amazing prediction given on June 28, 1940. Can we count on it? Science has taken a look at Cayce's forecast and has stated the equivalent of "Maybe so!"

It is difficult to believe there ever was such a continent as Atlantis or its Pacific Ocean counterpart, Lemuria. And yet the idea intrigues us, and becomes more believable the more we study the Cayce data.

From the readings we find that a great civilization once existed in the North Atlantic, in the location known as the Sargasso Sea, on a large continent about the size of Europe and Russia combined. Cayce said that it was first populated about ten and one half million years ago, that many upheavals and changes took place during the 200,000 years of its culture, and that it was finally destroyed after three major cataclysms several thousand years apart, the final one being about 10,100 B.C.

In 1958, a highly qualified research geologist* compared Cayce's reading on Atlantis with geologic concepts of the present day, and then compiled a study of this in a pamphlet with a jawbreaker of a title: "A Psychic Interpretation of Some Late Cenozoic Events Compared with Selected Scientific Data." (In later reprintings by the A.R.E. Press, the title became, thank goodness, simply "Earth Changes.")

This revolutionary study represents a new approach—he has given a new dignity to seemingly farfetched ideas of man and his history.

Science agrees tentatively now that the earth is about five billion years old,

* As he prefers to remain anonymous, he will be identified throughout as "the author of 'Earth Changes' " or as "the Geologist."

and has been changed about many times in its long life. Where there was once ocean, there are now cities. Where there are cities and farms, great fishes once swam. Volcanoes, earthquakes, floods and just plain erosion have shaken up the crust, wrinkled it, smoothed it out, washed it down, and set it out to dry in the sun. In the long process, many species of life have flourished and then become extinct.

Geologists have long known of a vast undersea mountain range in the North Atlantic. When the ocean cable was laid in the late 1870's, a systematic mapping of the area revealed a great mountain chain running north-south through the Atlantic. Lava found in the ocean bed of Atlantic waters dates within the past fifteen thousand years and shows evidence of having cooled *above water*.

Ancient maps indicate continents occupying the Atlantic and Pacific, and archeologists today are discovering artifacts and other evidence of buried cities predating Egypt—for example, the pyramids near Mexico City, judged from the lava found there to be eight thousand years old. Central America and Egypt have similarities of pyramid structure, although separated by the Atlantic. These and other lands apparently survived the last great balancing up of ocean and land, and yield their secrets slowly as science learns how to seek them. Scholars and philosophers have brought to literature a wealth of legend, lore, and speculation on the fabled lands of Atlantis and Lemuria. Plato, Francis Bacon, and the Roman scholar Pliny wrote of them.

Egerton Sykes of England, foremost world authority on the lore of Atlantis, who in 1965 visited Virginia Beach and lectured during the A.R.E. Conference on Atlantis, pointed out that many cultures in the world have "deluge legends." The legend of a great flood that long ago destroyed many lives and inundated the land is common to many peoples, including the American Indians. Belief in the advent of a savior who comes from the East is universal. There are common legends of lands in the Pacific and of a highly advanced race of people, remembered in the lore of China, Greece, South Pacific islands, and South America. If these similarities in religions, architecture, and traditions have existed since ancient times, how did it happen unless there was a common origin of the world's far-flung cultures?

Socrates, as reported in Plato's *Republic,* revealed that in about 590 B.C. the Greek philosopher Solon visited in Egypt and asked the priests there about antiquity. An old priest replied, "There have been, and will be again, many destructions of mankind arising out of many causes; the greatest have been brought about by the agencies of fire and water . . . You remember a single deluge only, but there were many previous ones." He then adds that "there formerly dwelt in your land the fairest and noblest race of man which ever lived, and you and your whole city are descended from a small seed or remnant of them which survived."

The old Egyptian went on to say that at that time the Egyptian constitution was eight thousand years old, while Greece was a thousand years older.

He might have been speaking to us, for we of course "remember a single deluge only"—that which Noah survived and which is recorded in Genesis.

Several thousand books have been written on these last continents. Their authors include Lewis Spence and Colonel James Churchward, the latter claiming to base his several volumes on Mu and its culture on ancient tablets he found in a temple school monastery in India.

To the questions raised from spontaneous references Cayce made from time to time to Atlantean peoples, he gave detailed descriptions of the lost civilization. He said that it occupied the Atlantic, extending to include our eastern seaboard and further, to the Mississippi River. He said that the people were highly developed but degenerated after they misused God's gifts to them, and brought about their own destruction in their later period.

In the age of their enlightenment, they worshipped the One God, using the sun as their symbol of Him. But in her later days of chaos and dispersion, refugees who went into other lands to begin new colonies gradually came to worship the sun itself, as the English colonists found the American Indians doing. Among the Indians, the Iroquois were the direct descendents of the Atlanteans, as were the Mound Builders.

But perhaps America's most significant tie with Atlantis is her character as a nation, which Cayce says resembled theirs as a gifted, scientifically minded, and enterprising people. They were originally a peace-loving people but later were divided into two factions: the "children of the Law of One" and the "Sons of Belial." Atlantean ideals of the Fatherhood of God and the Brotherhood of Man, says Cayce, have been reflected in our own American ideals, perpetuated from the time of Atlantis.

As a nation, they were for long periods a righteous people who discovered the uses of gasses for balloons, and electricity for lighting and heating their homes, for elevators, and one-line cars. They discovered and developed radio and television, and later, air power and aerial photography. They even had amphibian planes which carried them through water and over land.

Finally, they solved the mystery of solar energy conversion, using what Cayce called the "Great Crystal" to harness the sun's energy. This was originally used as a kind of oracle or communication with God, but it could also be used to regenerate the human body, to heal it and otherwise perfect it. Thus, Atlanteans discovered the secret of youth and lived for hundreds of years thereby!

The crystal operated by reflecting the sun to a greater or lesser degree, depending upon how it was "tuned," and could be tuned up to a pitch so devastating that the rays could destroy rather than restore. When those in power forgot their responsibility to use the crystal for good and gained supremacy over the moral elements of the society, the crystal was used destructively. An accidental tuning of it to a high degree brought about volcanic activity in the earth, which led to the final deluge.

After the first destructions about fifteen thousand years before Christ, the nation was no longer one large continent. It had been broken up into five smaller islands, the main ones being Poseidia, Aryan, and Og.

The end of Atlantis was the beginning of Egypt, Greece, and the Incas. This would corroborate the statement of the Egyptian priest in *The Republic* dating his nation and that of Greece at around eight or nine thousand years B.C.

At the time of Atlantis, there existed also the older continent of Lemuria. This one sank beneath the Pacific before Atlantis' downfall, under similar conditions. It was another highly civilized land, the survivors of which established a new culture in America and Mexico, perpetuating their ancient religious concepts very much as the Atlanteans perpetuated theirs in the Mediterranean.

Harking back to the beginnings of man's history, even before Atlantis, Cayce gives us a picture of what the earth was like ten and one half *million* years ago, when the poles were changed around to make what is now frigid, tropical. He says that the Sahara and Gobi deserts were fertile, prosperous lands in the first days of human life on earth. He identified Iran as the Garden of Eden referred to in Genesis. In America the Mississippi basin was an ocean bed. In the west, only the "plateau" of Nevada, Utah, and Arizona was above water, the rest apparently having been ocean bed, also. The Atlantic seaboard was the Atlantean lowlands. The Ural Mountains were tropical, as was Siberia and Hudson Bay! The Nile River then emptied into the Atlantic.

In his study of the psychic data of Edgar Cayce, the Geologist wrote that he found the readings both logical and consistent. He studied fifty readings, twenty of which describe events of earth history that occurred ten million years B.C. or since then. He said that some of these agree, others disagree, with present scientific concepts.

He then pointed out that recent scientific research, such as deep-sea, paleomagnetic, and that on the absolute age of geologic materials (e.g. radiocarbon dating) have tended to render the readings *more probable*.

He further points out that recently maps thought to be "many thousands of years old" have been discovered in Greenland, Antarctica and other portions of the world. They are highly accurate, he says, showing mountain ranges which have since been found by the Army Map Service. What is the more remarkable, he says, is that they show both Greenland and Antarctica in an unglaciated state. (This seems to agree with Cayce's views of a tropical Arctic and Antarctic.)

He adds that expeditions to Greenland and Antarctica have since verified the mountainous topography beneath the ice, by means of seismic surveys. He points out that the authority who solved the map projections, A. H. Mallory, "thinks it possible that the ancient cartographers . . . might have accomplished their feats by mapping from the air."

The Geologist then cites many more favorable comparisons between Cayce's views and scientific discoveries of recent date. In addition to the maps cited above, there have been findings that support Cayce's assertion that the temperatures were different from what they are today.

The date of Stonehenge in England has been found to be about 1848 B.C. and was referred to by Cayce as having been built by refugees from the Holy Land when it was sacked by the Chaldeans and Persians.

The Geologist also suggests that a discovery made in 1958 of a unified field theory which relates mass, energy, and gravity, may bear out a 1932 Cayce prediction that in 1958 the secret of how the Great Pyramid of Gizeh was built would be discovered.

Such events, says the Geologist, lead us to think that "it is no longer necessary to accept some psychic statements on faith alone."

There are new techniques of determining the ages of organic substances rich in carbon by means of radiocarbon dating. Geologists can test the contents of the stomach of a mammoth pried from frigid Siberian wastelands; they can take "cores" of the ocean bed materials beneath several miles of water and can determine the ages of the various layers of the ocean floors and their geologic history. They can tell the temperature at which ancient shells grew 200 million years ago! With such tools, the story of Atlantis does seem to have some chance of being told with ever-increasing accuracy by science.

Other readings given in the 1930's and '40's tell of *future* geologic changes which Cayce says will take place in the earth. One of the most startling predictions is that Atlantis will rise once again, first to be seen in the Bahamas where is located that submerged continent's highest land areas. Here, southwest of the island of Bimini, specifically, is where we can expect it in 1968 or 1969!

There will be a shifting of the poles so that "where there have been [temperatures] of a frigid or semi-tropical will become the more tropical, and moss and fern will grow." Climate changes and final shifting of the poles will occur approximately forty years after geologic disturbances first in the South Pacific and in the Mediterranean. The volcanoes Vesuvius and Pelee are also mentioned in connection with trouble in California and Nevada, which will follow their eruptions.

Disturbances will be felt throughout the world, but particularly in the western part of America, in the eastern New York state area, in Japan, northern Europe, and the Arctic and Antarctic. Land will appear both in the Atlantic and in the Pacific, and there will be oceans and bays where there is now land.

The standard geologic concept of earth change is that it takes place slowly over long periods of time, the Geologist states. He adds that "the large number of 'catastrophic' events predicted for the period from 1958 to 2001 A.D. are out of harmony with this concept of gradual change."

He confirms tendencies toward the possible fulfillment of the Cayce predictions, in pointing out the worldwide earth events that have been taking place in recent years. The waters of the North Atlantic are warming up. It's getting warmer around the poles, and since 1900 the thickness of the polar icecap in the Arctic has decreased by three feet. A new pattern of hurricanes which strike inland as never before adds to the list. These changes, which include rising and sinking of land and more frequent volcanic eruptions, indicate something could be happening to our earth that will have a bearing on future conditions.

Upheavals!

By 1932, Cayce said, the changes in the earth would begin to be evident, at the same time that a change occurred in the consciousness of mankind as we entered the Aquarian Age.

In 1936 there would be catastrophe in the form of great political changes "that will make different *maps* of the world." The very earth would be disturbed, as there would be a shifting of the interior of the earth in relationship to the poles. There would be upheavals in the earth's interior and wars in the affairs of men.

This was given on February 8, 1932, in answer to a request that Cayce "forecast the principal events for the next fifty years affecting the welfare of the human race."

"This had best be cast after the great catastrophe that's coming to the world in '36," replied Cayce, "in the form of the breaking up of many *powers* that now exist as factors in the world affairs. . . . Then, with the breaking up in '36 will be the *changes* that will make different maps of the world." (See pp. 62–65.)

A later question in another reading was: "What will be the type and extent of the upheaval in '36?"

"The wars, the upheavals in the interior of the earth, and the shifting of same by the differentiation in the axis as respecting the positions from the Polaris center," was the answer.

In August of 1932 someone asked if there were to be physical changes in the earth's surface in Alabama, which seemed to be a kind of testing for more specific and localized predictions. The answer was affirmative.

"When will the changes begin?" was asked.

"Thirty-six to thirty-eight," was the answer.

"What part of the state will be affected?"

"The northwestern part and the extreme southwestern part."

In November, Alabama's future was again predicted, when Cayce was asked if that state's physical changes were to be sudden, or gradual. The answer was "Gradual." They would take the form of sinking and inundations.

There is no doubt that if there had been time enough, in the crowded schedule of readings Cayce was committed to give, that he could have gone over the entire globe with a fine-tooth comb and described the physical changes of every section. However, specific predictions were given for larger areas, and these are next described.

Major Earth Changes Prophecies

The major earth changes prophecies cover a period of sixty-two years, from 1936 to 1998. The changes were to begin in a gradual way and become more pronounced beginning in 1968 or 1969.

They were to come about by earthquakes and volcanic action, sinking and rising of land, flooding of some lands and rechanneling of existing waterways. Some lands would be devastated, others would be perfectly safe. Coasts were to fall away or be inundated, leaving new coastlines.

Major earthquakes and other natural disasters have been recorded over the centuries. They include the city of Lisbon, Portugal, which in 1755 was engulfed by ocean waves created by an earthquake which killed up to 60,000 people. In 1811-1812 a new lake, Reelfoot, was formed in Tennessee and Kentucky, when part of the Mississippi floodplain sank. In Japan, the cities of Tokyo and Yokohama, Mino and Owari have been destroyed or greatly damaged by quakes since 1897. Other countries have suffered similar disasters—in India four major quakes have occurred since 1897. In that year, they were so severe that thirty lakes appeared in Bengal and Assam.

Certain regions of the world have earthquake "faults" or breaks in rock strata, and contain the world's active volcanoes. Seismologists report around eight thousand earth disturbances annually throughout the world. Japan lies astride the great Pacific rim earthquake belt, and has a number of faults, making it highly susceptible to major disturbances.

This earthquake belt borders the Pacific along the western edge of the Great Basin, extending along the coasts of North and South America and the eastern coast of Japan. Here are located the East Indian and West Indian islands and the islands of the Pacific. Other earthquake regions are the Mediterranean coastal areas of Italy and Greece, and the Himalayas.

So earthquakes were certainly not new when Cayce forecast big changes for the second half of the century: They were occurring along with other lesser forces that alter the topography. The year 1936, in fact, was not the first time in earth's history to see the shifting of the poles, according to Cayce.

This is challenged by science, which in general maintains that the continents and poles have remained in position throughout the history of the globe.

There is, however, the "continental drift" theory which holds that the continents drifted apart and are still slowly moving farther and farther from each other. Some think that the poles have shifted in past geologic times, creating opposites in climate conditions. One group of scientists seeks to explain the glaciation that is known to have taken place in India, South America, South Africa, and Australia at one time by assuming that the North Pole had then been in the vicinity of Hawaii. Then, the arctic climate would have been centered around the North Pacific.

Cayce spoke in his readings of "the turning of the axis" and the "changing of the poles" around 50,772 years ago! In this connection he told also of a strange event which occurred at that time involving the problem of "enormous animals" in Atlantis. He stated that nature took a hand and in the changing of the poles, with the sudden change in temperatures, the animals were destroyed by ice.

According to the author of "Earth Changes," as science interprets this, the north pole shifted from a position outside the Arctic Ocean to its present position inside this ocean, thus initiating the ice age described. It is a hypothesis which in 1958 was presented by the scientists Ewing and Donn, he says. It was anticipated by Cayce fourteen years earlier.

The earth changes as forecast by Cayce are as follows:

SOUTH PACIFIC: The changes will begin to be apparent "when there is the first breaking up of some conditions in the South Sea (that's South Pacific, to be sure) and those as apparent in the sinking or rising of that which is almost opposite it, or in the Mediterranean, and the Aetna (Etna) area. Then we may know it has begun."

THE ATLANTIC: "Lands will appear in the Atlantic as well as in the Pacific." "And Poseidia will be among the first portions of Atlantis to rise again. Expect it in sixty-eight or sixty-nine. Not so far away!"

THE PACIFIC: "Lands will appear. . . ." "The greater portion of Japan must go into the sea."

EUROPE: "The upper portion of Europe will be changed as in the twinkling of an eye. . . ." "Even many of the battlefields of the present [1941] will be ocean, will be the seas, the bays, the lands over which the new order will carry on their trade as one with another."

AMERICA: "All over the country many physical changes of a minor or greater degree. The greater change will be in the North Atlantic Seaboard. Watch New York, Connecticut and the like.

"Many portions of the East Coast will be disturbed, as well as many portions of the West Coast, as well as the central portion of the United States.

"Los Angeles, San Francisco, most of all of these will be among those that will be destroyed before New York, even.

"Portions of the now east coast of New York, or New York City itself, will in the main disappear. This will be another generation, though, here; while the southern portions of Carolina, Georgia, these will disappear. This will be much sooner.

"The waters of the Great Lakes will empty into the Gulf of Mexico.

"If there are greater activities in Vesuvius or Pelee, then the southern coast of California—and the areas between Salt Lake and the southern portions of Nevada—may expect, within three months following same, an inundation caused by the earthquakes.

"Safety lands will be the area around Norfolk, Virginia Beach, parts of Ohio, Indiana, and Illinois and much of the southern portion of Canada and the eastern portion of Canada."

ARCTIC AND ANTARCTIC: "There will be upheavals in the Arctic and the Antarctic that will make for the eruptions of volcanoes in the Torrid areas, and there will be the shifting then of the poles—so that where there have been those of a frigid or semi-tropical will become the more tropical, and moss and fern will grow . . ."

SEALANES: "Strifes will arise throughout the period. Watch for them near the Davis Straits, where there will be attempts to keep open a life line to a land.

"Watch for them in Libya and in Egypt, and in Syria. Through the straits around those areas above Australia; in the Indian Ocean and the Persian Gulf.

"Ye say that these are of the sea. Yes, for there will be the breaking up, until the time where there are people in every land who will say that this or that shows the hand of divine interference—or that nature is taking a hand—or that this or that is the natural consequence of good judgments . . ."

GENERAL: "The earth will be broken up in many places. The early portion will see a change in the physical aspect of the west coast of America. There will be open waters appearing in the northern portions of Greenland. There will be new lands seen off the Caribbean Sea, and dry land will appear . . . South America shall be shaken up from the uppermost portion to the end, and in the Antarctic off Tierra del Fuego, land, and a strait with rushing waters . . ."

The shifting of the poles as a logical consequence of large scale crustal displacements, according to the Geologist, will be due much later. According to Cayce, this will occur around the year 2000 to 2001.

But it will begin with the signs in the South Pacific and the Mediterranean which Cayce describes, and the appearance of land near Bimini. The West Coast destruction will be early on this time clock of events, as will the inundations of parts of the Carolinas and Georgia.

To show how unlikely is the safety of relatively high ground when this begins is the example of Norfolk, which was told it would remain a good place to be even though it is low and close to the sea. "Norfolk is to be a mighty good place, and a safe place when turmoils are to arise," one person was told; "Though it may appear that it may be in the line of those areas to rise, while many a higher land will sink. This is a good area to stick to."

More Scientific Observations

"How soon will the changes in the earth's activity begin to be apparent?" one person wanted to know in 1932.

"The indications are that some of these have already begun," Cayce said, "yet others would say that these are only temporary. We would say they have begun."

The Earthquake Information Bulletin of the National Earthquake Information Center (NEIC) states: "The strongest earthquake ever located in this area [Mississippi] occurred December 16, 1931." This brings to mind that Mississippi and its general locale has never been an earthquake center but has had three quakes in recent history, the third occurring in June, 1967. Thus, for that state, something new is going on. It could be what Cayce was referring to. Other areas have increased in earthquake activity since 1932, according to the *Bulletin* of the Seismological Society of America (Vol. 57, No. 3) for June, 1967: "There appears to be an increase of larger intensity and magnitude earthquakes since 1936 in Washington State, and especially in the Puget Sound area since 1949."

Strangely, the year 1932 marked the beginning of a program by the Coast and Geodetic Survey to record accurately earth motions in the seismically active regions of the western United States. "Fortunately this was done in time to record the notable 1933 Long Beach, California and 1935 Helena, Montana earthquakes," states the NEIC *Bulletin*. "These provided the first data of destructive ground motions for engineering applications, and an impetus for strong motions studies."

In 1936 the Seismological Field survey was established to carry out earthquake investigations in the western United States.

The June, 1967, issue of the *Bulletin* reveals that nearly a million lives have been claimed by earthquakes in this century alone. Bahngrell Brown, in an article entitled "Geology of Disaster" *(The Professional Geologist,* November, 1966), estimated that since the time of Christ, five million lives have been lost by natural cataclysms. From this, it would seem that earth activities are increasing in severity.

Brown is interested in geology's potential ability to *predict* earthquakes and other disasters of natural forces, allowing evacuation of endangered masses of people to safe ground. His thinking in regard to the imminence of a major change is markedly in line with the Cayce predictions. "It may be noted that the spacing of these events over the last one hundred years would suggest that sacrifice in life is imminent.

"As we face the future, we might let our imaginations dwell on the likelihood of these long-overdue possibilities for that future:

"1. A Crater Lake type eruption in the belt of the "dormant" U.S. volcanoes.

"2. A recurrence of the terrible 1811-12 earthquake in the Mississippi Valley, where there are now great cities.

"3. An unlikely (but possible) tsunami in the Gulf of Mexico.

"4. Any mountain city in an avalanche path."*

A major seismic disturbance now seems about to occur in the area of the San Andreas fault, according to scientists. It is a trench six hundred miles long running along the coast of California, with many branches cutting into wider areas to the east of it. The earthquakes of 1906, 1957, and 1838 were the largest which have happened there in recent times.

Active earthquake regions have mainly been in the western part of the United States and Alaska and so we are not alarmed at statistics concerning that section.

What does alarm geologists is the fact that for the past several years the usually rumbling San Andreas Fault has grown quiet—too quiet, and they fear that it may be building up for real trouble.

The year 1966 was a "dry" year for earthquakes, according to Jerry L. Coffman, who in the March, 1967, NEIC *Bulletin* states: "We have not had a 'great' earthquake since the Good Friday shock of March 28, 1964, in Alaska, and only one other—on October 13, 1963, in the remote Kurile Islands north of Japan—since the May, 1960, earthquake in Chile. . . .

"Does this mean we are about to have several great earthquakes? Not necessarily. We may complete an unprecedented fourth year without a great

---

* Quoted by permission of the American Institute of Professional Geologists.

earthquake, or a single great event may occur at any time. Earthquakes are not yet predictable."

The August, 1967, *Bulletin* says, "Statistics developed over the first half of this century indicate that about one great earthquake will occur annually on the average." Even major shocks are absent, it adds, in recent years. "Most seismologists believe that strain is constantly increasing until released by an earthquake. If this is true, then it is only a question of time—and where—until the next 'great' shock strikes."

Japan is the most seismically active nation in the world. Again, we wrote the NEIC *Bulletin* for March, 1967: "An unusual earthquake swarm has been experienced by the people of Matsushiro, Japan, a town of 22,000 inhabitants about one hundred miles northwest of Tokyo. It all began August 3, 1965, and is still continuing.

"The inhabitants of Matsushiro are quite familiar with earthquakes, but the continuous shakings which have awakened them throughout the night for months and caused them to take to the open fields at times for refuge are something different. Some have said that the 'gods' are angry because instruments were set up near the shrine on Mount Minakami, the focal point of the shocks.

"From August, 1965, to December, 1966, over 565,000 earthquakes were recorded, with about 59,000 of these strong enough to be felt. On April 17, alone, 6,780 shocks were recorded and 661 were felt. Three hundred homes were damaged on this date as the repeated shaking continued to reduce buildings and walls to rubble. . . .

"There is no conclusive evidence of the cause of these earthquakes. One theory is that molten rock is pushing up toward the now dormant Minakami volcano. But would this explain the alteration of the surrounding landscape? Highly sensitive instruments have indicated a very slight rising and tilting of the mountains east of Matsushiro and a sinking of the valley floor. Still another theory relates these observations to tectonic (mountain-building) forces.

"This series of earthquakes has subsided somewhat, to 7,371 in December. Meanwhile, the residents of Matsushiro still live an uneasy life. Some think the shocks will eventually cease, but the less optimistic believe the earth is building up to an eventual major blow-up."

Disturbances that lead to earth changes include volcanic action, which scientists have observed have been on the increase since 1947. According to Cayce, the first breaking up was to happen in the Pacific area and a check by the author of "Earth Changes" shows increased activity in the Hawaiian Islands since 1958; a violent eruption on Bali in 1963; and a new volcano being built over the shattered remains of Krakatoa (blown apart in 1883). North of Auckland, Rumble III, a volcanic island, was violently active in November and December of 1964.

In the Pacific, the Alaskan earthquake in 1964 was preceded by the appearance in November, 1963, of a volcanic island off Iceland, called Sursey, near the Arctic Circle. According to "Earth Changes," "Recent measurements of crustal upwarping in the Canadian Arctic, Spitsbergen, and Greenland show relatively rapid rates of uplift—believed due to unloading by recently vanished or presently melting ice masses."

Volcanic activity has also been stepped up in the Atlantic, particularly in the Azores, site of the Atlantis mainland. A paper by F. Machado presented at the IAV Symposium on Volcanology (New Zealand) in November, 1965, entitled "Activity of the Atlantic Volcanoes, 1947-1965," points out that "since 1947 volcanic activity increased considerably in the oceanic volcanoes of the Atlantic." He adds that "eruptions were reported first in Iceland, and then successively in the Canaries, the Cape Verde Islands, the Azores, Tristan da Cunha, and again in Iceland, where an eruption is still going on (June, 1965)."

He goes on to state that Hekla in Iceland had been quiescent since 1913. On March 29, 1947, a new eruption started, causing a huge cloud to be carried to Finland by high atmospheric winds. Lava flooded the area, and the activity lasted for thirteen months. In 1961, a new Iceland eruption occurred, and an explosive submarine eruption off the coast began in 1963. In 1964 it "became effusive and continued thus until May, 1965."

Earthquakes preceded similar eruption on September 27, 1957, off Fayal Island, Azores, when a new sand isthmus was formed to the main island, states the report.

On May 30, 1967, the Associated Press reported that the four mouths of the volcano on Stromboli Island, Messina, Sicily, "have fused into a single lava-spouting crater lake three hundred yards across. This occurred over a fifty-day period of eruptions, with lava flowing down to the sea at safe distances from fishing villages."

The Etna area (mentioned by Cayce as an important area which will be active at the beginning of earth changes) is an active volcano of historic renown. It exploded in 1960, and in 1964 experienced its most violent eruption in ten years. It is not so much the volcanic activity which will signal other major earth disturbances, then, but the sinking or rising of the area around it.

The author of "Earth Changes" suggests that Cayce's "perplexing statement about the *sinking* or *rising* in the Mediterranean area may possibly be connected with the recent water-level drop in Greek harbors. The drop would indicate *rising* of the land in this eastern part of the Mediterranean."

He quotes a Reuters dispatch from Athens which describes the drop in 1959 as being more than three feet in many places, causing small boats to sit on the sea bottom. The condition remained; and scientists cannot explain what caused it.

Lest we underestimate the power of the 1964 Alaskan earthquake, we have the report in the *Virginian Pilot* (November 12, 1967) that it literally moved mountains! It also temporarily raised the level of the Mississippi River, and sent a seismic wave as far as the Antarctic!

"The [Commerce] Department's Coast and Geodetic Survey, more than three years after the Good Friday disaster, is still gathering data on the effects of the strongest earthquake ever recorded on the North American continent," states this Associated Press story.

"Some of its findings are incorporated in a technical report issued by the Environmental Science Services Administration.

"It said some Alaskan mountains subsided because of the quake, the sea floor in one area rose as much as fifty feet, and a seismic wave was recorded in the Antarctic 22½ hours after the quake.

"This giant wave, the report said, had traveled 8,445 miles at 430 miles an hour.

"The earthquake caused one hundred thirty-one deaths and more than $750 million in damage not only in Alaska but along the U.S. Pacific coast as well.

"Here are some findings from the report:

"Mountains on Kodiak Island and the Kenai Peninsula and the Chugach Mountains near Prince William Sound subsided seven feet or more. Earlier surveys revealed that some Kenai Peninsula Mountains shifted laterally about five feet.

"The ocean floor rose in an area 480 miles by 127 miles with the highest upheaval fifty feet—the biggest ever recorded—between Kodiak and Montague Islands.

"Shock waves oscillated the water as far away as Key West, 3,968 miles distant. Surges of water began along the Gulf Coast of Louisiana and Texas between thirty and forty minutes after the quake."

On Tuesday, December 5, 1967, South America was again in the news, this time because of a volcano erupting on the Antarctic island of Deception. This is in the area of Tierra del Fuego, just to the north of the Antarctic Peninsula. As Cayce predicted, "South America shall be shaken up from the uppermost portion to the end, and in the Antarctic off Tierra del Fuego, *land,* and a strait with rushing waters. . . .

"There will be upheavals in the Arctic and the Antarctic that will make for the eruptions of volcanoes in the Torrid areas. . . ."

This particular eruption came "from the depths of an ancient lake on the island, and wrecked the scientific bases of three nations, forcing researchers to flee," according to Chilean officials. Braving a rain of ashes and rocks, Chilean navy helicopters took thirty Chilean and eight British researchers and military personnel to the Chilean ship *Piloto Pardo* waiting off shore.

"An Argentine group of fourteen was to be taken off by the Argentine ship *Bahia Aguirre,*" the Chilean navy said.

"No volcanic eruption had been reported in more than 120 years on the island until geysers of boiling water from the lake began shooting up several days ago.

"Then the volcano erupted in full fury Monday, sending ash and rock into the air and sending lava down ravines from the lake. A dense cloud of smoke shrouded the island and ashes blanketed the white ice caps.

"The Interior Ministry said the British, Chilean, and Argentine bases, hewn from the bitterly cold wastes, were wrecked by the volcano's force. The bases are used for weather and oceanographic research.

"A Chilean navy spokesman said helicopters had to be used to bring off the

Chileans and Britons because rough waters and the eruption of ashes and stones made it impossible to use boats.

" 'We shall not be returning to the island until we know it is completely safe,' said a British spokesman."

CHAPTER 6

PEOPLE RISING!

God has taken his place in the divine council;
in the midst of the gods he holds judgment:
'How long will you judge unjustly and show partiality
   to the wicked?'
'Give justice to the weak and the fatherless;
maintain the right of the afflicted and the destitute.
Rescue the weak and the needy:
   deliver them from the hand of the wicked.'

They have neither knowledge nor understanding,
   they walk about in darkness;
   all the foundations of the earth are shaken.

I say, 'You are gods,
   sons of the Most High, all of you:
Nevertheless, you shall die like men,
   and fall like any prince.'

Arise, O God, judge the earth;
   for to thee belong all the nations!

—Psalms 82

ON JULY 2, 1967, as the Detroit riots were in progress for the third consecutive night, I was in the midst of researching the Cayce files on race relations. I found the readings chillingly immediate—they could have been uttered during the long, hot summer of '67 instead of that far-off summer nearly thirty years ago.

During the time this book was being written, in fact, much has happened that was directly related to the readings' picture of this era. Most dramatic and obvious were the racial conflicts which Edgar Cayce predicted, pointing out that this was the way men took "when there is the plenty in some areas and a lack . . . in the life of others."

Unless, in fact, we remembered that we are indeed our brother's keeper, there would be a revolution in this country and "a dividing of the sections one against another.

"Ye are to have a division in thine own land before there is the second of the Presidents that next will not live through his office—a mob rule!"

"Unless there is, then, a more universal oneness of purpose on the part of all, this will one day bring—here—in America—revolution!" (June, 1939)

He laid America's problems for these times to her "unbelief." In 1943 he delineated the errors and their results for us "today," meaning the period that included that time and this, old problems which have festered over the years, stemming from centuries past.

"The ideals, the purposes that called the nation into being are well," he said. "It might be answered by saying that there needs to be on the part of each man, each woman, the adhering to those principles that caused the formulating of the American thought.

"Yet in the present there are seen many complex problems, many conditions that are variance to the First Cause (God) or first principles, not only among groups and individuals in high places, both from the political and the economic situations, but the problems of labor-capital, as well. As all of these are problems in America today, as well as that of religious thought, religious principles, racial concern—which are mass as well as individual and group thought. . . .

"To meet same? Only that each soul turns not to self alone and cry for strength, but that each soul lives in such a manner that there may be the awakening to the needs, the purposes, the causes for the nation coming into existence!

"That such is, and is to be, a part of the experience of America is because of unbelief!"

The riots were met with horror and acknowledgment of wrongs long existent, mingled with the soul-searching which Cayce predicted when he advised that "each soul lives in such a manner that there may be the awakening to the . . . purposes for the nation coming into existence." This was countered by the die-hard expressions that will not quite let these people go. There was emotion and hard thinking and a genuine effort on both sides to do something, and do it now. There were the stirrings of the old cry "Am I my brother's keeper?" and the answer, from pulpits, streetcorners, homes, and many groups was "Yes!"

Edgar Cayce never condoned the riots, crime, revolution which he warned about. He merely predicted them, saying that these were the natural result of injustice. He said that conditions as they have been over the years just could not go on.

On November 22, 1963, I was on the staff of the A.R.E. and remember the anguish of that day and the awe we felt that another prophecy had been fulfilled. As in offices all over the nation, we gathered around a radio and listened to the strained and conflicting reports that President Kennedy had been shot. Then we heard the terrible news that he was dead.

We looked at one another in shocked amazement. "Edgar Cayce predicted this," we reminded ourselves. Franklin Roosevelt had been the *first* president to die in office since 1939, when the prophecy was given: "Ye are to have a division in thine own land before there is the second of the Presidents that next will not live through his office—a mob rule!"

John F. Kennedy was "the second of the Presidents."

The readings of Edgar Cayce are for all people. However, their message for the New Age is meant no more for the extreme rabble-rousers, the lawbreakers, than it is for the "status quo." It is for all those who are sincerely trying to use their talents, understanding, knowledge, position, and money—in harmony with the laws of God and man—for the constructive goals of mankind, which President Kennedy so well crystallized during his brief tenure in office.

In 1937, Cayce predicted that there was to be a "new awakening" in many portions of the earth.

The social revolution which has been going on since that time is a part of the new awakening, we think, and it refers to that in Africa, South America, and many other continents and nations which are shaking free from colonialism of the past.

Ahead of time, and the times, was this statement given as to our rightful attitude toward all people: "Whoever, wherever he is, that bears the imprint of the Maker in the earth, be he black, white, gray, or grizzled, be he young, be he Hottentot, or on the throne or in the President's chair—all that are in the earth today are thy brothers!"

During the 1920's, a group of idealists asked Cayce how to build a "great society" (although they did not use that term) such as is the goal under President Johnson today. They wanted to build "a world organization" which would ensure hospitals, churches, schools, farm loans, rural road construction, for the underprivileged people of the earth, for the "upbuilding of mankind."

This, said Cayce, has been the dream of many people in times past, who have had much more to work with than did the friends of Cayce. "Same was the idea of Alexander when he sought to conquer the world"—yet he forgot his high purpose which had been bred into him by Aristotle.

"In the tenets of the Christ" may such a plan be brought to realization most successfully. It would take the old-fashioned virtues of faith, hope, love, to bring about the conditions necessary to build a social structure in which people might then help themselves.

An outstanding example of modern progress toward this goal is the Alliance for Progress in South America.

This organization was inaugurated under President Kennedy in 1961, with twenty American nations signing the Charter of Punta del Este. United States aid to these countries was pledged and now, seven years later, a vast business boom and a program for road building, education, and hospitals has been established. Political despotism has been replaced with democratic elections. College students have gone to work in their own poverty-stricken areas to teach the people new skills. The success of the Alliance, which is yearly becoming more effective, has elbowed out Communism, which once threatened these neighbors.

The "awakening" goes on in many places, filling many needs. In not only the Americas, but in India, Africa, illiteracy is being tackled by the teaching programs of many agencies. And in the ghettos, boys and girls are given opportunities to develop many skills under trained supervision. There is a stirring among the impoverished and the low in every corner of the world, and a rising to a common level.

"The leveling must come," Cayce predicted.

Edgar Cayce attributed the division in this country to "fear on the part of those who control capital investment" and a lack of universal oneness of purpose.

Economic Changes Predicted

On the night of March 3, 1929, Gerald Bailey dreamed that he and his friends in the stockbroking business "ought to sell everything, including the box stock."

"A bull seemed to follow Doris Morrow's red dress. . . ."

Cayce was asked to interpret this dream. It was, he said, a key to the stock market situation and should certainly be heeded because he had dreamed correctly. On March 6, Gerald asked for a fuller interpretation. The bull, he learned, was the bull market, of course. "The red indicating the danger in the bull market, yet—as seen—there will still be the continued attempt to keep the market a bull market.

"Hence, we will have a mixture, but gradually sliding off, as seen in the present . . . though this . . . whole condition may change . . . This issue being between those of the reserves of nations and of *individuals* and will cause, unless another of the more stable banking conditions come to the relief —a great disturbance in financial circles. . . ."

On October 29, less than seven months later, the crash occurred. Another of Cayce's interpretations of a prophetic dream was confirmed.

More may come as disturbances to America from within than from without, Cayce said in 1941. This was true. After the war, labor and racial frictions mounted.

But before that, the Depression which followed the crash was the all-consuming world dilemma and for this, he had both immediate and far-reaching predictions. Just before Christmas, 1930, when a bleak Yule was in store for millions, came the question: "When will economic conditions throughout the United States be improved and the present depression be at an end?"

"Beginning with the spring [1931] there will be, in various portions of the country, a change in economic conditions. Another year [1932] will bring those of a greater disturbance in many centers. Then, unless there is the adoption of other conditions, a still greater disturbance in this present land. Then, '34 or '35, things will gradually adjust themselves to the uphill, as it were, for the general conditions."

The Depression deepened in 1931. As Cayce had forecast, the world-wide disturbance reached its lowest point in 1932.

In January of that year, Edgar Cayce was questioned about the Depression's cause and the time the nation could expect a return to normalcy.

"The United States may not expect to recover sooner than any other nation unless its basis for recovery is founded in that that brings peace, harmony, and understanding. As it, the U.S. (in the present) is the leading nation in attempting to give an understanding of the principles of 'Thou shalt love thy neighbor as thyself'; it stands above all others in its financial, in its social positions in the world; yet it has faltered, and—as of old—when troubles arise, when fearful conditions beset thee, the same answer was of old 'Know ye that *sin* lieth at *thy* door!'"

That same year, 1931, he said that depressions and good years come and go in cycles of about twenty-four to twenty-five years. The last one had occurred in 1907. Although he did not give the date, we have since lived through another low period, that of 1954, termed a "recession" and occurring right on time.

The causes of the Great Depression were different, he said, from those of other times, for they were the "combination of wrath, oppression, and sin."

In November, 1939, he told a labor-management mediator that general changes in financial structures in America were to come about. He said that a greater stabilization of currencies would be needed with the general international conditions, and that it would happen in early summer of the following year. These must be the basic conditions of capital as related to the individual or personal finance, and as to the Government, he added.

An economist asked in June, 1943, "What could our own country be doing toward equalizing opportunities for trade among the nations immediately following the war?"

He answered, "In some quarters, too much is being done already! These are the things over which many disputes will arise. But there must come some basis for an economic situation in all lands, in those that are a part of the united effort against . . . aggression . . . as well as those devastated by war."

This reading went on to say that we would move toward a lowered tariff in many directions, and that it was not only possible to raise the economic standards of the world, but it *must* be done if there was to be a lasting peace.

He likened social ills to cancer cells that rebel, causing destruction.

Although it would take a long time to establish, he predicted an international stabilization of exchange values and said that "there may indeed be another war over just such conditions."

In 1944 he said that there would be many economic changes after World War II and that there will be "more and more upsetting in the monetary units of the land."

The depression of the thirties turned in the forties to inflation and a rising cost of living, thus general instability. According to L.V. Chandler's *Economics of Money and Banking* (New York: Harper and Row, 1964) bank failures and closing of other types of financial institutions led to the adoption since the 1930's of better practices, including better regulations of financial institutions and procedures, insurance of mortgages, Federal Home Loan Banks, etc. There were "many economic changes," as Cayce had predicted, including these and the rise in employment and many shifts in the economy. The peak year of 1948 was followed by a mild recession year, and these were followed by quick recovery. Easy and tight money followed each other during those years of ever increasing prices.

Concerning the prediction that a change in our whole financial structure would come about, let us again turn to Chandler: "The whole structure of financial institutions in the United States has undergone tremendous changes since 1914. Perhaps most striking has been the rise of institutions sponsored in one way or another by the federal government: For example, the whole complex of farm-credit institutions, the many new institutions in the housing-credit field, and the Small Business Administration. . . .

"Private financial institutions other than commercial banks have also undergone great changes. Among these are the phenomenal growth in the number and resources of savings-and-loan associations, the rapid growth of credit unions in some areas, the greater aggressiveness of mutual savings banks, the rise and rapid growth of pension funds, and so on."

He cites the decline in banks and their absorption into mergers.

Cayce's prediction of an international stabilization of exchange values is still in the future. Says Chandler: "The international reserve system and international monetary policies have not yet approached a final stage of evolution. The International Monetary Fund has been highly useful, and it continues to grow in usefulness and prestige. But its policies are still undergoing change, especially those relating to the terms and conditions under which it will make its resources available. . . ."

Many questions need to be answered and many financial problems will arise, it is pointed out, before this will become fully workable.

Cayce told us, "These questions [of stabilization of currencies] must be the *basic* conditions of capital as related to the individual and as to the Governments . . ." But the fear of financial woes might be corrected by a return to the trust in God.

Authors William and Paul Paddock have recently predicted worldwide famine which only the United States will be able to alleviate effectively.* This emphasizes Edgar Cayce's warnings of "hardships" and "extreme periods" regarding future food supply. The time ascribed for this could be that generally predicted by Cayce in 1943 for land upheavals "in the next generation."

Back in 1943, Edgar Cayce was asked by a Norfolk resident if the purchase of a farm in the region between Washington and Norfolk was still advisable. Cayce replied that it was advisable "because of hardships which have not begun yet in this country, so far as the supply and demand for foods is concerned."

To another at that time, he said, "Anyone who can buy a farm is fortunate and buy it if you don't want to grow hungry in some days to come."

"Should I hold the twenty-five acres of land near Oceana (Va.); also, two

* *Famine-1975!* (New York: Little, Brown, 1967).

sites in Linkhorn Park and lots on 54th Street (Virginia Beach, Va.)?" Cayce was asked by still a third person.

"Hold them until at least the early spring; that is, the lots," Cayce advised. *"Hold* the acreage, for that may be the basis for the extreme periods through which all portions of the country must pass—for production for self as well as those closer associated with the body."

Still another reference to the "return to the soil" was made as early as 1938: "All that is for the sustenance of life *is* produced from the soil. Then there must be a return to the soil. Every man must be in that position that he at least creates, by his activities, that which will sustain the body—from the soil; or where he is supplying same to those activities that bring such experiences into the lives of all."

In June, 1938, the Works Progress Administration and the Civilian Conservation Corps had provided many people with jobs. A typical paycheck was $17.50 a week—yet it meant the difference between going hungry and having food to eat.

There were all kinds of projects involving many construction laborers, as well as projects employing destitute people in the arts. Symphony orchestras, writers' workshops and art classes enriched communities wherever they appeared.

But Cayce advocated the "return to the land" all over the country, and "not so much of the makeshift of labor in various fields . . . for unless this comes, there must and will come disruption, turmoil, and strife."

In addition to the population explosion of this age, and the many long-standing economic causes of poverty and hunger in the world, it is possible that the predicted food crisis of which the authors of *Famine-1975* and Cayce speak will be due to impending earth changes. As lands rise and sink around the globe, a lot of bread-baskets will be upset in the process! If the Great Lakes, for instance, are to empty into the Gulf of Mexico, this can only be by way of the Mississippi Valley. Thus will be lost an important food-producing region in this country. Other places for food raising will obviously have to be developed.

Casually, as was typical of the way such information came about, the possible answer for this future problem was volunteered. Bill Howard was told in 1944 that his birthplace—Livingston, Montana—was one day to be an important place. This city of the southern part of the state and its surroundings "will have much to do with many, many nations!" said his reading. He had been with Eric the Red in Minnesota, he was told, and had been one of those remaining there. He seems to have been drawn back to that area in this lifetime for a special purpose.

His reading went on to state, then, that "Saskatchewan, the Pampas area of the Argentine . . . portions of South Africa . . . these rich areas, with some portions of Montana and Nevada, must feed the world!"

There seems to be a tie-in between the two prophecies for Montana, particularly since they were given in the same reading. Livingston is not in the wheat-growing region of Montana but in the foothills of the Rockies. Could

Cayce have meant that Livingston would become a food distribution center for the nations? This appears likely.

Saskatchewan in Canada adjoins Montana, making that part of the state likely to be most important as a source of food, as it is now. From the mention of the Pampas in the Argentine and parts of South Africa and Nevada, we have a clue as to what other lands might be relatively undisturbed by earth changes, if this is what the reading is referring to.

The trend has been away from the farms, for the little farmer, leaving food producing to the big business it has become. But has this been the best for our people, altogether? A Negro leader in October, 1967, might have set a new trend when he appeared on television and told about a group of his people in the Brooklyn ghettos who were planning a mass exodus to a farming community where they could "live under the sun." They wanted to get away from the ghetto slums and crime, where their children had no place but the streets to play. They would establish farms for themselves and their families, he said, and "toil by day, plan by night."

Is a return to the soil the answer to much of our social and economic trouble? Cayce said in a reading that it didn't hurt anyone to get his fingers in the dirt now and then and work with the soil! Perhaps for many people this will be the answer.

Rural poverty, particularly in the South, is the opposite of what Cayce meant by a return to the soil, however, and of seventeen million such poor, only two million are served by Federal food programs, according to recent reports. Millions more, however, are benefiting from the "war on poverty," a program which has brought about pre-school training in the Head Start Project, job training under the Job Corps program, Vista and the Youth Corps.

In Norfolk, as its school systems' Office of Special Projects takes stock of twenty months of educating slum children better, a project spokesman states, "It will be ten or fifteen years before we see if we've been successful or not."*

In Los Angeles, "Operation Bootstrap" is a community project which approaches the problems of interracial understanding with practical classes in work skills and sessions in learning to communicate. In cities throughout the country "cultural enrichment" measures are being taken to give youngsters in slum areas an opportunity to learn dramatics, painting, dancing, writing.

These are the right steps, but they are late. Edgar Cayce warned in 1938 that unless America remembered to apply in its economic and political life the idea that we are our brother's keeper, there would be a revolution.

On November 1, 1967, Senator John McClellan, Chairman of the Senate Permanent Investigations subcommittee, told the opening hearing on slum violence that the riots over the past three years are becoming a "tangible threat to the preservation of law and order and our national security."

The subcommittee has found that since 1965, 130 persons were killed and 3,623 wounded in major racial disturbances in seventy-six cities across the nation. The survey included the first civil rights march in Selma, Alabama, where no sniping, looting, arson or vandalism occurred, and followed

---

* Quoted in the *Virginian Pilot,* November 8, 1967.

through to the violence of the nation's cities in the summer of 1957. The statistics included "7,985 cases of arson, 28,939 arrests, 5,434 convictions, and economic loss estimated at $504.2 million."

Chairman McClellan expressed fear that this will "sweep us swiftly down the road to chaos and anarchy." Immediate causes of ghetto rioting, and later causes of longstanding social problems such as unemployment, were to be sought. Senator Karl Mundt, the subcommittee's senior Republican, warned that there was no limit to conflagration which could sweep this country and said that the first order of business should be "to lay down more firmly the law of the land."

If Edgar Cayce were living today, he could say no more to us than what he said on June 24, 1938, regarding the course to be taken now. "Since the application of these truths or tenets [the ideals of brotherhood] as indicated becomes the basic needs for the peoples of every land in the present, to be sure it behooves those in America, then, to apply same in their dealings with the situations that exist respecting the political, the economic, and the general situations throughout the land.

"This at the first glance may appear to be an impractical thing; yet these are the conditions to be met:

"Every phase of human experience and human relationship must be taken into consideration, just as indicated from that given, that we are our brother's keeper.

"Then if those in position to give of their means, their wealth, their education, their position, do not take these things into consideration, there must be that leveling that will come.

"For unless these are considered, there must eventually become a revolution in this country—and there will be a dividing of the sections as one against another. For these are the leveling means and manners to which men resort when there is the plenty in some areas and a lack of sustenance in the life of others.

"These are the manners in which such things as crime, riots, and every nature of disturbance arise—in that those who are in authority are not considering every level, every phase of human activity and human experience.

"We find these conditions have been in other lands centralized, localized into individual activities—as in Russia, Italy, Germany. The conditions that exist in Spain, in China, in Japan are what? The oppression of the producers by those for whom and to whom such power has come to be used as their opportunity for becoming their brother's keeper: and not as represented in some lands, the disregarding of the other's rights.

"Then those who are in power must know that they are their brother's keeper and give expression to that which has been indicated in 'Thou shalt love the Lord with all thy heart and mind and body, and thy neighbor as thyself.'

"This rule must be applied. It is true that in some of these factions in Russia this is an attempt, yet there are those who have applied and do apply same in not only the economic life but attempt to in the mental and spiritual life. And this brings or works hardships where it should not be. . . .

"True, in other lands, whether the Communism, the Fascism or the Nazi regime, there are missions to be filled, and these are opportunities. But when there becomes class or mass distinction between this or that group, this or that party, this or that faction, then it becomes . . . a class rather than 'thy neighbor as thyself.'

"For all stand as one before Him. For the Lord is not a respecter of persons, and these things *cannot* long exist.

"From the conditions in these other lands, then, America—the United States—must take warning.

"For to whom does the wealth belong? To whom do the possibilities of the land belong?

"Does it belong to those who have inherited it? To those who have been given the position by power? Or to those who have, by their labor, by the sweat of their brow, produced same?

"Not that all would be had in common, as in the communistic idea, save as to keep that balance, to keep that oneness, to keep that association of ideas of activity, of the influences throughout the experiences of all. These are to be kept in those attunements which there may be the land, itself, defining what freedom is; in that each soul is by his own activity to be given the opportunity of expression, of labor, of producing.

"But all of these, also, are not to say where or what, but are to seek through their own ability, their own activity, to give that of themselves that is in keeping with those who labor in the vineyard of the Lord.

"Hence these may apply in the national and international relationships.

"For there must come, first, a stabilization of the monetary unit. There must come then the exchange of commodities of trade in a way and manner in which not merely sections, not merely distinctions made of one portion of the land against another, but all are taken into consideration.

"Unless this is done, turmoils and strifes will arise. And that which has made and does make the people of America afraid is the fear of servitude in any manner!

"All, though, must learn that those who are to be the greater, those who would make the greater contribution to activity in every sphere and phase of influence, are to be the servants of all; not those who would be lords over others. . . ."

On June 16, 1939, a questioner asked: "What should be our attitude toward the Negro and how may we best work out the karma created in relations with him?"

"He is thy brother!" Cayce reminded this person. "They that produced, they that brought servitude without thought or purpose, have created that which they must meet within their own principles, their own selves.

"These should be taken in the attitude of their own individual fitness, as in every other form of associations. For He hath made of one blood the nations of the earth."

"Is there a racial or social problem facing America?" asked one person.

"As indicated, these all depend upon the effort of individuals to all live as brothers one with another!" was the reply.

"How can it be met for the protection of our democracy?"

"Raise not democracy nor any other name above the brotherhood of man, the fatherhood of God!" Cayce reproved him.

"Since we are fighting for the freedom of all races," asked another person on June 20, 1943, "what suggestions could you give us toward effecting greater equality of opportunity for minority groups in our own country?"

"As indicated, in the first [reading on this subject], all groups must have their representation and their privileges, that they, too, may have the opportunity. Unless we begin within ourselves and our own household, we are false to ourselves and to the principles that we attempt to declare. By setting classes or masses against other groups, this is not brotherly love. . . ."

But the most final and ringing statement was given earlier than these, in 1938: "Though there may come those periods when there will be great stress, as brother rises against brother, as group or sect or race rises against race—yet the leveling must come.

"And only those who have set their ideal in Him and practiced it in their dealings with their fellowman may expect to survive the wrath of the Lord. . . .

"And then there should be, there will be, those rising to power that are able to meet the needs. For none are in power but that have been given the opportunity by the will of the Father—from which all power emanates.

"Hence, these will be leveled with the purpose 'My Word shall not fail!' "

CHAPTER 7

DESTINY OF NATIONS

THE PEACE OF the world will be shaped upon the American ideals and those found in the Masonic Order! "Not that the world is to become a Masonic Order," Cayce explained, but that the *ideals* will prevail.

The remarkable series of twenty-nine readings on world affairs—on peace, on world economics, race relations, and on America's place in the world—were given from 1921 to 1944. They became increasingly important as the world seemed to be getting into deeper waters. First the Depression, then World War II forced Cayce's friends to dig deeply for answers.

The destiny of nations is concerned with man's collective relationships with himself and with God. We can make of the world what we will—and we have! Future wars can be prevented by man's will, just as they are started that way. All evils begin in the hearts of men, and there they can be resolved. Cabot Lodge, on the televised program "Face the Nation" (September 17, 1967), stated that if the United Nations wanted to, it could mobilize member nations to thwart Communist aggression in Vietnam—*if* they had the will to do so!

In the readings on world problems are both prophecy for the latter part of this century, and counsel that is just as applicable now as when it was given.

It is counsel that pulls no punches, for "God is not a respecter of persons." America has her faults, just as do other nations, and criticism of her was not withheld. Russia's religious development is to be the "hope of the world" one day, and China will be the "cradle of Christianity," although the implication is that the latter will not happen for a long time yet.

The gloomy picture we have of an earth changed and broken by natural disturbances is offset then by a much brighter picture of a world that *is* getting better, that is moving toward peace and order, in spite of the chaotic conditions in some respects. Cayce told us to measure whether or not the world was getting better by the same criterion which Christ used when He affirmed His Christhood—"Tell them the blind see, the lame walk." It is this kind of proof which we will see in the future, in fact, even now—and unless mankind is benefited in a real and practical way, we are deluding ourselves. He who tells a person who is starving, or without adequate housing, or without a job or self-respect, "Go in peace," is a "thief and a liar," said Cayce.

It is significant that he lived out his most effective years of service in Virginia, within a few miles from the place where a few Englishmen first set foot on these shores to begin there a new nation! It was in March, 1938, when many nations were about to be plunged into war, that he pointed out: "Each nation, each people have builded—by the very spirit of the peoples themselves —a purposeful position in the skein, the affairs, not only of the earth, but of the universe!"

In February, 1932, he was asked: "Please forecast the principal events for the next fifty years affecting the welfare of the human race."

"This had best be cast after the great catastrophe that's coming to the world in '36, in the form of the breaking up of many powers that now exist as factors in the world affairs. The first *noticeable* change will be the acceptance or rejection of the world's interference of Court of Last Resort in the world, in the present meeting as presented by France, and as rejected by America. Then with the breaking up in '36 will be the changes that will make different maps of the world."

"Name the powers that will be broken up in '36."

"Rather by '36. Will be Russia, U.S., Japan, and England or United Kingdom."

"Who will be the controlling power?"

"That depends upon who is closer to those sources of power."

In going back to the time of this reading, history has recorded a decade of shaken world powers, during which 1936 was a particularly violent and fateful year. Leading up to those years was Hitler's rise to power in 1933, and Germany's withdrawal from the League of Nations.

But in 1936 we find these events:

In England, George V died in January and Edward abdicated in December, causing his brother, the Duke of York, to become King George VI.

Spain began civil war.

Russia's Stalin started conducting his Great Purge Trials (half a million people executed, imprisoned, or put into forced labor camps).

Italy and Germany formed the Rome-Berlin axis in October.

Hitler denounced the Locarno Treaty and marched into the Rhineland.

By the end of the year, almost all nations had abandoned the gold standard.

In 1938, Spain was presented as a trouble spot for the rest of the globe. "This is that whereunto the real troubles, here, are only beginning," stated a reading. "For unless there is to be the consideration given to each factor, then others will come in and devour the spoils.

"This is the outcome of seed sown in the ages past, and from same man can —as a whole—and should—take warning."

Spain's war was the preamble to World War II when German Nazis, Italian Fascists, and Russian Communists took sides by sending troops, supplies, and technicians.

On January 15, 1932, Cayce was asked: "Will Italy adopt a more liberal form of government in the near future?"

"Rather that of a more monarchical government than that of the liberal," Cayce replied. "Italy, too, will be broken by what now is an insignificant or small power that lies between those of the other larger, or those of the moment, of the larger. These will not come, as we find . . . before the catastrophes of outside forces to the earth in '36, which will come from the shifting of the equilibrium of the earth itself in space, with those of the consequential effects upon the various portions of the country—or world—affected by same."

Italy met defeat in Greece and in North Africa in 1940.

On June 13, 1939, Cayce stated, "Then ye ask, What is to be the outcome of England and France in their efforts to join hands with Russia as an encirclement of the totalitarian regime? These, so long as they are in keeping with God's purposes with man, will succeed. When they become active for self-preservation without thought or purpose of their fellowman, they must fail.

"So it is with the endeavors of Germany, Italy, Japan. As they attempt to preserve their own personalities, their own selves without thought of their fellowman, they may succeed for the moment, but 'God is not mocked!' And whatsoever a man, a country, a nation sows, that it must reap."

In 1932 when Great Britain was trying to cope with the "non-cooperation" of Gandhi in India's civil disobedience campaigns, the World Affairs series answered this question: "From the general trend of events, what is to be expected in the struggle between Great Britain and India?"

"Great Britain is *losing* an excellent fight. Non-resistance is hard to be broken! As to whether those peoples will remain or whether the prayers and supplications of others will be with those, depends upon individuals."

A year later, Cayce was asked: "Give the outstanding events which may be expected in the struggle between Great Britain and India."

"Those that have already come to pass, in the things that have just happened, in the recognition of the low caste and the outcasts, or the untouchables. And this *has* been accomplished and will go farther."

England was described in the readings as the "balancing power" in the world. When England begins to consider every phase of her relationships with other countries, "more and more will it be able to control the world for peace."

"The spirit of France will not be broken," Cayce predicted on January 21, 1944. That was a dark time, indeed. France had been occupied by Germany since 1942 and it was to be five months before her liberation by the Allies.

States another reading: "There is that which is the spirit of France. Don't ever get the idea that even under the stress through which the nation of France is passing, it will be eliminated from the earth. It is as one of the seven sins, as well as one of the twelve virtues in the human family."

He described the French situation then as "an old debt that must eventually be paid."

So nations, like people, have karma and must pay for past crimes against brother nations!

China

A book publisher in August, 1943, planned to visit China on a mission "for improving the future of cultural relations as they affect books between this country and China in the years after the war." He asked Edgar Cayce for advice for making his mission a success.

Cayce began: "As will be seen, the greater rule in the next twenty-five years in China is to grow towards the Christian faith (though it may appear to some at present that this is lacking). . . ."

Would China's leadership take a more democratic or more authoritarian turn in the next twenty-five years?

"More of the democratic" was the answer. "For, as has been indicated, more and more will those of the Christian faith come to be in political positions, and this in China will mean the greater rule in certain groups—according to how well they manifest. And these will progress, for civilization moves west.

"The various sects of China (Christian, Buddhist, Confucian?) will all be united more and more towards the democratic way—just as it has begun and as it has been in the last twenty years, and it will grow and spread faster in the next twenty-five, and more in the last five, than in the first ten."

For a prediction to be so explicit and emphatic, this one would appear twenty-five years after to be dead wrong. Those years—1923 to 1968—have seen a distressing turn, not toward Christian leadership, or a free democracy, but toward a ruthless dictatorship under Communism.

It is true that China had already taken a step towards democracy in 1911 when she revolted against the ineffectual Manchu dynasty. The Nationalist Party ruled beginning in 1928 and represented a people's government which made quite a contrast against the emperors of the past. But Chiang Kai-shek's forces were defeated in 1949 and a new government, the People's Republic of China, was set up. Millions of Christians and people of other faiths, and other intellectuals, were now killed off or "re-educated" in Mao's purges.

Could prayer have saved China from this? "If the same attitude (of prayer) is kept in China," Cayce told another person about that time, "the eventual conquering of self in China will be brought about and there will be lack of interference then from without."

There had already been "interference from without" for years in China. In 1938, Edgar Cayce was asked about the "Japanese and Chinese situation," referring to Japan's undeclared, all-out war on China beginning the year before. "These bespeak of themselves that which is happening and has happened," was the reply. "But might does not make right. Rather will the principles of the Christian faith be carried forward in and through the turmoils that are a part of both China and Japan. For without those cleansings and purifyings, tradition (of feudalism) alone may not be destroyed. For it is through the purging that the strength and the beauty of each will come forth."

The purging by war, by Mao, and by civil war—the last of which still goes on—is what Cayce meant, we think. That any religious life can still survive the watchful and ever present eye of the present government is almost too much to hope. Yet, that is what Cayce seems to say, and what is more, the principles of Christian faith will be carried forward "in and through" these turmoils.

But there are other predictions he made which tell the present picture quite accurately, if we interpret them aright. In 1932, he declared: "The international interference will make for a repeopling of portions of China, and the ultimate destruction of China or Japan as a nation!"

It appears that he meant the time of wars between China and powerful nations including Great Britain, Japan, and France at the turn of the century. The victors in each war, in which China was consistently defeated, took over much of her territory, "leased" her ports, maintained troops on her soil. It was this desperate and humiliating situation that led the Chinese to overthrow the Manchus and reform their government. Under Mao, many people have been transported from the east to the western lands to develop towns, industries, and agriculture. Is this what Edgar Cayce meant by "a repeopling of portions of China?"

The last part of this prediction sees "the ultimate destruction of China or Japan as a nation!" This was, as we interpret it, to be an outcome of the "international interference" spoken of in the first part of the prophecy. If a nation consists in its traditions, its religions, its arts, the philosophy which gives it the indefinable character distinguishing it from other nations, then the old China has been destroyed as a nation. In Mao's "cultural revolution," the young men of his Red Guard have recently led in an unbelievably savage rampage to tear down and to demolish every vestige of the symbols of China's past. Temples and their ancient treasures have been burned, along with books and religious statues. Poetry inscribed on mountain rock among the temples in Central China has been obliterated *(Life,* October 7, 1966).

The American book publisher in that far-off day in 1943—when the temples still stood, and one could talk about an interchange of ideas between the United States and China—was told by Cayce that he should cultivate the intelligentsia. The most helpful would be the Christians and those Chinese who had been educated in America. He was told also that an exchange of books between the two countries should be accompanied by stressing ideas upon which both could agree. He was advised to avoid getting side-tracked into one sect or group.

In our continuing attempt to understand China in the light of the Edgar Cayce prophecies, we might turn to *The Nature and Truth of the Great Religions* by Dr. A. K. Reischauer (Charles E. Tuttle, 1966) which states: "for more than a century now the Chinese have come more and more into contact with the Western world and a civilization enriched by what modern science can provide for a good and better life. As a result of this China is seen now by many Chinese themselves as a backward country and it is perhaps only natural that some of them should blame especially Confucianism just because of its traditional glorification of the past. . . .

"Sooner or later even those who are now so favorably impressed with the Communist program of doing something positive about their country's backwardness and improving its economic conditions, will realize that man, just because he is man, 'does not live by bread alone.' Whether that means that the Chinese people will then turn again to Confucianism and their other age-old spiritual heritage remains to be seen. That there is much in the best of this heritage that is of permanent value cannot be questioned by any fair-minded student. It is, however, quite likely that this heritage will be reinterpreted and modified by the influence of the Western world's spiritual heritage and so bring it more in line with what might be called our developing common World culture. . . ."

Russia

Echoing Dr. Reischauer's above statement, the title of a recent book by novelist Vladimir Dudintsev about the "dreariness and stagnation of Russian life"* is *Not By Bread Alone.*

In 1932, Cayce prophesied that "on Russia's religious development will come the greater hope of the world." He gave a cosmic picture of what had happened to Russia in the years of revolt against the Czar and he described that country as "being born again." He defined America's relationship to Europe with the words: "the hope of Europe depends upon *you,* in your homes *today!"*

That thought was brought into sharp focus recently when Svetlana Alliluyeva, Stalin's daughter, appealed to the free world to speak out for freedom everywhere.

Cayce was asked, "What can be expected in the trends of events in the political and economic conditions in Europe?"

"Europe is as a house broken up," was the answer. "Some years ago there was the experience of a mighty peoples being overridden for the gratification

* Robert Sherrod, "Russia at the Crossroads," *Post,* March 26, 1966.

and satisfaction of a few, irrespective of any other man's right. That peoples are going through the experience of being born again and is the thorn in the flesh to many a political and financial nation in Europe, in the world. But out of same, with the prayers and supplications of those that may pray—even as Abram or Abraham, 'If there be fifty, will it not be spared? O, if there be ten faithful, will it not be spared?' Then, the hope of Europe depends upon *you,* in your own home *today!* In not the same way, but the same manner as did the life of Lot, or of the other peoples in Sodom and Gomorrah."

"What is the name of that nation referred to?"

"Russia!"

This was, of course, pointing to the sufferings of the Russians under the Czarist regime, and the overthrow of that regime in 1917. We might remind ourselves that Stalin's purges had not yet taken place, nor had Hitler risen to power, at the time of this reading. Cayce seemed to be urging Americans to pray for Europe to spare it the fate similar to that of the biblical Sodom and Gomorrah.

Five years later, in 1938, Europe was suffering that fate, and now Cayce said of Russia that "a new understanding has and will come to a troubled people. Here, because of the yoke of oppression, because of the self-indulgences, has arisen another extreme. Only when there is freedom of speech, the right to worship according to the dictates of the conscience—until these come about, still turmoils will be within." This time, it was not the Czar's Russia of which he spoke, but that of Stalin.

Cayce foresaw the changes that have come about economically between the two countries. When he was asked in 1933 if the United States should recognize the Soviet government, he said: "Many conditions should be considered, were this to be answered correctly. You could say yes and no, and both be right, with the present attitude of both peoples as a nation, and both be wrong, for there *is* to come, there *will* come, an entire change in the attitude of both nations as powers in the financial and the economic world. As for those raw resources, Russia surpasses all other nations. As for abilities to development of same, those in the U.S. are the farthest ahead. Then these united or upon an equitable basis, would become or could become, powers (for good); but there are many interferences for those . . . investments (already made), those already under questions; (these) will take years to settle."

Recently, Russia has become increasingly capitalistic in her economics, according to reports. The U.S. has, we see, turned from isolationism since 1938 to a policy of worldwide involvement in the financial and economic welfare of other nations.

As for the prediction that her religious development will be the basis for the "hope of the world," we are reminded by experts on Russia who have lived and traveled in that country that her Russian Orthodox Church has never been entirely eliminated from the life of the people. To some extent, marriages, baptisms, Easter and Christmas celebrations continue to take place in the ancient churches. The experts further tell us that the ideal of brotherhood and the community working together for the common good is also a part of the Russian heritage, which perhaps explains the emphasis they have accepted, in the extreme, on the collective society, at the expense of the individual.

This is not to obscure the facts that children are taught atheism from the cradle onward, with "no other principles than what the Party teaches," that all religions are scorned; and that church leadership is kept subjugated and ineffectual for the general masses.*

But out of extremity often develops the opposite extreme, and within the past ten years, a stirring has been felt among the religious and intellectual elements in Russia, an evidence of desire to break the bonds that hold mind and spirit. In the 1950's, Boris Pasternak's *Dr. Zhivago* spoke for the "other Russia." In reporting the effect of this novel, Eugene Lyons stated that "there is more than a chance that the outlawed novel will do its destined work of spiritual mobilization."** More than five hundred copies of the book in its original Russian have circulated in that country, according to Lyons, and we assume they continue to do so.

Another hero, in Western eyes, is the late Oleg Penkovskiy, key member of the Soviet intelligence service, who was shot in Moscow in 1963 for passing top-secret documents to the west for a period of sixteen months. According to the editors of a book telling his views on Russia, *The Penkovskiy Papers* (Doubleday and Co., 1965): "Experts assess Penkovskiy's achievement as the greatest intelligence *coup* of modern times. Singlehandedly he sabotaged Kruschev's threatened Berlin showdown in 1961 and his information lay behind President Kennedy's successful defeat of the Soviet Cuban missile threat in October, 1962."

His friend Greville Wynne, a British spy who was his go-between, described Penkovskiy as being "interested in religion. He had indeed been baptized himself by his pious mother. . . ." And further: "He believed simply that a free society should emerge in the Soviet Union, and that it could only come by toppling the only government he knew. He was a heroic figure."

Incidents such as this one, and others which have been recounted in the press, seem to point to a growing movement in Russia toward freedom of religion and expression, and while they do not do more than provide a hopeful glimmer, they could be the beginnings of the "religious development" which Edgar Cayce said would one day prove to be the "hope of the world."

Further evidence for this trend is presented in the account of still another observer, James H. Billington, who spent seven months in Russia in 1966.

In the November 10, 1967, issue of *Life* Magazine, Billington wrote: "Svetlana Stalin is not alone in rejecting the faith of her parents for that of her grandparents. Repelled by both the manipulative morality and monotonous art of the Stalinist bureaucracy, young Russians now seek a deeper basis for human conduct and esthetic inspiration. 'Faith proved itself worthy of fresh respect in the camps,' one survivor of more than a decade of imprisonment told me. 'Those who believed in God often seemed the only ones able to go on acting like men.' But the intellectuals are not seeking mere return to the

* *The Penkovskiy Papers* (New York: Doubleday, 1965).
** The Book the Kremlin is Afraid to Let the Russians Read," *Reader's Digest,* February, 1959. Used with permission.

Orthodox Church of yore. 'Even if I were free to do so, I could never join a church which did not even pray publicly for those in the camps during the Stalin era,' one writer explained."

Mr. Billington goes on to say that "the Russian intelligentsia has a kind of undoctrinal ecumenical movement of its own; it brings together Christians and Jews (far closer in Russia, where they share a common persecution, than in the West, where they share an occasional brotherhood banquet table), neo-Kantian scientists, pro-Buddhist Orientalists, and many other forms of believers. All identify vaguely with Russia's religious past; and many feel attracted to new sects or religious-philosophical discussion groups, where they hope to find more satisfying human association than in the philistine society about them. Youthful members of such a religious-philosophical group were apparently victimized by the wave of quiet arrests conducted in Leningrad early in 1967. . . ."

Edgar Cayce's suggestion that Americans and Russians might learn to cooperate in solving the world's supply problems is brought to mind by Mr. Billington's proposal that "new bi-national Russo-American scientific and cultural projects might start us on the path toward new practical forms of collaboration that should help bypass old hostilities. Such projects (preferably under auspices of the U.N.) would never seek to exclude others, and should begin with projects of common concern to all humanity."

"What Then of Nations?"

In the last World Affairs reading, given June 22, 1944, Edgar Cayce said that spiritual laws govern the actions of nations as much as those of individuals. He had, as we pointed out earlier, said that nations had their characters, and that by their choices and actions they created their places not only in the world, but in the universe, as well.

Cayce explained how the nations became separated by languages or "tongues," when they "set about to seek their gratifications." "There are then in the hearts, the minds, of men, various concepts of these [spiritual] laws and as to where and to what they are applicable. . . ."

It was in misapplying God's laws that the nations have suffered, he said. "What is the spirit of America?" he challenged. "Most individuals proudly boast 'freedom.' Freedom of what? When ye bind men's hearts and minds through various ways and manners, does it give them freedom of speech? Freedom of worship? Freedom from want? Not unless these basic principles are applicable, for God meant man to be free. . . .

"What then of nations? In Russia there comes the hope of the world, not as that sometimes termed of the communistic, of the Bolshevik, no; but freedom, freedom! That each man will live for his fellow man! The principle has been born. It will take years for it to be crystallized, but out of Russia comes again the hope of the world. Guided by what? That friendship with the nation that hath even set on its present monetary unit 'In God We Trust.' (Do ye use that in thine own heart when you pay your just debts? Do ye use that in thy prayer when ye send thy missionaries to other lands? 'I give it, for in God we trust'? Not for the other fifty cents, either!)

"In the application of these principles, in those forms and manners in which the nations of the earth have and do measure to those in their activities, yea, to be sure, America may boast; but rather is that principle being forgotten when such is the case, and that is the sin of America.

"So in England, from whence have come the ideas—not the ideals—ideas of being just a little bit better than the other fellow. Ye must *grow* to that in which ye will deserve to be known, deserve to receive. That has been, that is, the sin of England.

"As in France, to which this principle first appealed, to which then came that which was the gratifying of the desires of the body—that is the sin of France.

"In that nation which was first Rome, when there was that unfolding of those [Christian] principles, its rise, its fall, what were they that caused the fall? The same as at Babel. The dissensions, the activities that would enforce upon these, in this or that sphere, servitude, that a few might just agree, that a few even might declare their oneness with the Higher forces. For theirs was the way that seemeth right to a man but the end is death. That is the sin of Italy.

"The sin of China? Yea, there is the quietude that will not be turned aside, saving itself by the slow growth. There has been a growth, a stream through the land in ages which asks to be left alone to be just satisfied with that within itself. It awoke one day and cut its hair off! This, here, will be one day the cradle of Christianity, as applied in the lives of men. Yea, it is far off as man counts time, but only a day in the heart of God—for tomorrow China will awake. Let each and every soul as they come to their understandings, do something, then, in his or her own heart.

"Just as in India, the cradle of knowledge not applied, except within self. What is the sin of India? Self, and left the 'ish' off—just self!"

Israel

Edgar Cayce said that human affairs move in cycles. Concerning Palestine, God apparently worked in cycles of millenniums. In studying the biblical prophecies and those of Cayce we arrive at a better understanding of prophecy in general, and that concerning Israel, in particular.

The Israelites first moved into Palestine about 2,000 B.C. according to history. Egyptian texts mention Jerusalem about 1,900 B.C. A thousand years later, King David set up there the Ark of the Covenant. After another thousand years, Jesus of Nazareth was born in Bethlehem and the Temple which had been destroyed by the Romans was rebuilt by Herod the Great. Approximately a thousand years after the Jews left Palestine in 70 A.D., the Turks captured Jerusalem. It remained under Moslem rule until freed during World War I, 1917, and under the British mandate the World Zionist Movement to bring the Jews back to their homeland began. But it will be 2,072 before the cycle is completed.

In 1933, fifteen years before the Jews proclaimed the state of Israel, Edgar Cayce foretold that, as it had been prophesied in the Bible, the Jews would return. This came about in questions on the part of some who were then concerned about Hitler's attitude toward the Jews.

When this reading was given (November 4, 1933) Hitler had just come into power and as Cayce has stated elsewhere, "even God does not know what man will do." Cayce could not at that point foretell what course Hitler would take.

He termed the events then happening and consequent events involving the Jews' return to Palestine "the beginning of the return that must come throughout the earth."

How timely are the biblical prophecies for the Jews of the 1960's! Palestine was, under the British, divided for fifty years into Arab and Jewish nations. By June, 1967, in the "Seventy-two-hour War," they fulfilled the final prophecies concerning their long struggle with the Arabs and their other traditional enemies:

"Thus says the Lord God: Behold, I will take the people of Israel from the nations among which they have gone, and will gather them from all sides, and bring them to their own land; and I will make them one nation in the land, upon the mountains of Israel; and one king shall be king over them all; and they shall be no longer two nations, and no longer divided into two kingdoms." (Ezekiel 37:21-23)

We think of the amazing development since 1948 of Palestine from an arid land and swamp to the garden place it is now becoming. The Jews have answered a call home from far places, a call that is two thousand years old.

A special insight into the restoration of Israel is given in the Cayce readings which see the Jews and their long history of wandering as the dramatization of all of man's spiritual condition, and not just that of one small nation. Israel, said Cayce, is all those on earth who are seeking a way back to God. Thus, we share vicariously with the Jews their heritage, their traditions of oneness with God, their falling away from him, their trials. "Israel" means the spiritual seekers of the world, no matter if Buddhist, Christian, American, French, German, or "Hottentot," as Cayce said it.

The Bible itself brings all of us into the picture in predicting that there would be no more wars, which Cayce emphasized was coming about for us in this century:

> For out of Zion shall go forth the law,
>   and the word of the Lord from Jerusalem.
> He shall judge between many peoples,
>   and shall decide for strong nations afar off;
> and they shall beat their swords into plowshares,
>   and their spears into pruning hooks;
> nation shall not lift up sword against nation,
>   neither shall they learn war anymore;

but they shall sit every man under his vine and under his
fig tree, and none shall make them afraid;
for the mouth of the Lord of hosts has spoken. (Micah 4:2-4)

A particularly inscrutable prediction was given in 1941 for a two-year-old boy that he would live to see a "religious war." So far, this is one problem the world hasn't had to face, unless it could be the Israeli-Arab conflict which still goes unresolved.

CHAPTER 8

"FOR THE SEEKER TO KNOW"

IN THE DESERT near Cairo the pyramid ruins extend for sixty miles west of the Nile River. The one nearest the Nile is the oldest, the Great Pyramid of Gizeh, called by Cayce the "Pyramid of Understanding." It is the largest of them all, standing 481 feet high. Between this and the Nile is the Sphinx, facing east.

The Great Pyramid is conjectured to have been built around 2,885 B.C. The Egyptian King Khufu built it as a tomb, say historians, after a mere century and a quarter of progress from the time stone masonry was first used. Suddenly, Egypt leaped in architectural prowess from constructing primitive pit graves to the most advanced building ever known. Clearly, there is something wrong with our understanding about the culture that produced it!

Much has been written about the mysterious Pyramid and its guardian Sphinx. Studies by mathematicians, historians, and architects reveal it to be a puzzle in stone, based on mathematical, geometric proportions.

According to Dr. Browne Landone, author of "The Prophecies in the Ancient Temples,"* the mathematics involved in the Pyramid of Gizeh is the Teleois, "a mysterious series of numbers and proportions found . . . in musical scales, distances of planets from the sun, designs in snowflakes, et cetera. It also determines the structures of all key temples of Palestine and Tibet, ancient Cathay, Mayaland and the eastern Andes. . . . In the structure of the Pyramid of Gizeh the Teleois is so dominant that we are forced to believe that it was intentionally used to symbolize and record knowledge of the past and prophecies of the future. . . ."

Out of the hundreds of references to what are called in the Edgar Cayce data the "Pyramid Prophecies," or "Egypt, Prehistory," comes a story that, if true, is of the greatest importance to our understanding of both the past and the future. In the story of Atlantis and the earth changes that continent

---

* In Gordon Collier's *Will You Be Alive in 1975?* (Tarrytown, N. Y.: The Book of Destiny. 1961).

suffered, we have the background for Cayce's prophecies dealing with the Great Pyramid Mystery.

The ending of Atlantis was roughly the beginning of Egypt, and other cultures. One of the major ideas to come out of the Cayce data is that the time of the construction of the Great Pyramid was not 2,885 B.C., as is suggested by James Henry Breasted in *Ancient Times* (Boston: Ginn and Co., 1935) but 10,490 to 10,390 B.C.!

Scholars are bemused by the unbelievably rapid technological and scientific progress which the Egyptians are supposed to have made in little more than a century, in building the Pyramid. That they must have developed such a sophisticated concept of architecture under the leadership of a more advanced people seems more plausible than that they achieved these highly complicated arts suddenly, by themselves.

According to Edgar Cayce, just such a culture emerged from the ingress of hordes of Atlantean refugees into Egypt 12,500 years ago. Egypt was one of the safety lands during the destruction of the Lemurian and Atlantean civilizations. These destructions occurred, Cayce said, over long periods of time: The break-up of Atlantis took place over a period of 7,500 years, between 15,650 and 8,150 B.C.

By dint of their superiority over the native Egyptians, the Atlanteans conquered the latter and imposed upon them their religion and civilization. A peaceful settlement was brought about by Atlanteans and Egyptians but there were many races and nations now existing here and therefore a conglomerate of ideas and influences.

Egypt was thought by the Atlanteans to be the ideal place in which to establish not only a high culture, but a new spiritual understanding. This was due to the persistent influence of the "children of the Law of One," or the religious element. There grew up an exchange of ideas with people of other lands such as the "Poseidian (or remnants of Atlantis) Og, Norway, China, India, Peru and America." At that time, there was also one common language. The Atlantean leaders made visits to these other lands to study and collect spiritual ideas from other centers.

Egypt became a "land of plenty" in "foods, in ornaments, in the recreation, in the needs of the inner man, in the many material things of life, and in the development of the sciences." The land was visited by the "wise men" of other countries now, which was in reciprocation to Atlantean visits. A wise government was established, evolving a "national spirit and centralization of interests."

The leaders of this new nation had the task of teaching spiritual laws that "there might be a closer relationship of man to the Creator and of man to man." This was the thesis of their mission, which they felt inspired by God to carry out.

In special temples they prepared the records of Atlantis from its beginnings and "those things that were to make known later in the minds of peoples as the changes came about in the earth." The Great Pyramid, however, was the final statement. Begun in 10,490 B.C., it was to take one hundred years to build. "The rise and fall of the nations were to be depicted in this same temple that was to act as an interpreter for that which had been, that which is, and that which is to be, in the material plane." It would record further "all changes in the religious thought of the world."

It was in the Hall of Records, however, that actual written documents were put which would explain in full the message of the Great Pyramid.

Concerning the magnificent achievement in establishing the records in stone and in written hieroglyphics, Cayce raised the question as to why this would be accomplished in Egypt, rather than some other place. "Why Egypt? This had been determined . . . as the center of the universal activities of nature, as well as the spiritual forces, and where there might be the least disturbance by the convulsive movements which came about in the earth through the destruction of Lemuria, Atlantis, and—in later periods—the flood . . .

"When the lines about the earth are considered from the mathematical precisions, it will be found that the center is nigh unto where the Great Pyramid, which was begun then, is still located.

"Then, there were the mathematical, the astrological, and the numerological indications, as well as the individual urge. . . ."

One person was told by Edgar Cayce that he had helped to build the Sphinx!

"In what capacity did this entity act regarding the building of the Sphinx?" he asked.

"As the monuments were being rebuilt in the plains of that now called the Pyramid of Gizeh, this entity builded, laid, the foundations; that is, superintended same, figured out the geometrical position of same as [in] relation to those buildings as were put up of that connecting the Sphinx, and the data concerning same may be found in the vaults in the base of the Sphinx. The entity was with that dynasty . . . when these buildings [were] begun. This laid out, base of Sphinx, in channels, and in the corner facing the Gizeh may be found that of the wording of how this was founded, giving the history . . ."

Information regarding the Sphinx "and many findings, as given, may be found in the base of the left forearm, or leg, of the prostrate beast, in the base of foundation. Not in the underground channel (as was opened by the ruler many years, many centuries, later) but in the real base, or that as would be termed in the present parlance as the cornerstone. . . ."

The Hall of Records

Scores of allusions are made to the future opening of the Hall of Records "when much may be brought to light." Located in a small tomb or pyramid of its own, according to Cayce, it lies between the right paw of the Sphinx and the Nile River and is a kind of "time capsule." Cayce calls it "the pyramid of unknown origin, as yet"—a "storehouse of records"—"that holy mount yet not uncovered."

These, first, include the "precious" records of Atlantis put there by one who was in charge of the records when the last of the Atlanteans scattered. A good number of others brought records with them, as well. These documents, described as "copies" of the Atlantean originals, included their scientific knowledge, their literature, history, laws, and treatises on "the abilities to use the unseen forces in the . . . material things of man."

Still other works were "for the interpreting of the earth as it was, as it is, and as it is to be" for the "seeker to know his relationships to the past, the present, and the future when counted from the material standpoint."

Such data is gleaned from readings like the following: "The entity was among those of the Atlanteans who came into Egypt and whose land was destroyed during that period. Hence, the entity was among the Children of the Law of One that entered the Egyptian land, being a priestess of Poseidia, and brought much of the record that was attempted to be preserved for future activity, future proofs of those who would seek out those influences that were the happenings in the Atlantean land. . . ."

Another reading, for one of the builders who laid out the plans for these tombs, speaks not of only one Record Chamber, but of "many."

According to Cayce, the people who had gathered and compiled the sacred records were buried there in those tombs, along with many artifacts which will provide further meaningful evidence of the existence of this people. Among them are innumerable articles which had been deposited in the tombs as having particular significance to the persons buried there. These include musical instruments, such as harps, lyres, lutes, and even violas. There will be found "the hangings, the accoutrements for the altar in the temple of the day." Gold and precious stones, used for both healing and for exchange, are there. There will be uncovered "the cymbals for the calling of the people to worship"; plaques and life seals; surgical instruments and medical compounds.

A woman named Ammelle of Atlantis "persuaded her countrymen to preserve drawings, recipes, placards" and led in "the first attempt to make for a written language" in order to preserve the records in Egypt.

Another's "harps and menus" will be "in the storehouse of records."

In the Hall of Records, the linens one woman prepared will be discovered. "Caskets of gold, or the golden bands about those [bodies were] put into the burial chambers."

In the "mount not yet uncovered" is buried the king, together with a number of his effects. At least one person for whom Cayce gave a reading was told that he, too, was buried there. Besides the many temples built around the Sphinx, mention is made of an area or city that is just beyond the Great Pyramid. "And many of the inner shrines will today, now, be found bearing the inscription of the entity in that period—Isssi—"

Of particular interest to scholars is that the records were put in forms that were "partially of the old characters of the ancient or early Egyptian and part in the newer form of the Atlanteans."

Here in this hidden chamber, then, is "a record of Atlantis from the beginnings of those periods when the Spirit took form or began the encasements in that land, and the developments of the peoples throughout their sojourn, with the record of the first destruction and the changes that took place in the land, with the record of the sojourning of the peoples to the varied activities in other lands, and a record of the meetings of all the nations or lands for the activities in the destructions that became necessary, with the final destruction of Atlantis and the buildings of the pyramid of initiation, with who, what, where, would come the opening of the records that are as copies from the sunken Atlantis; for with the change it must rise again."

"This in position lies, as the sun rises from the waters, the line of the shadow (or light) falls between the paws of the Sphinx, that was later set as the sentinel or guard, and which may not be entered from the connecting chambers from the Sphinx's paw (right paw) until the time has been fulfilled when the changes must be active in this sphere of man's experience. Between, then, the Sphinx and the river."

These records were made from the standpoint of world movements, and not merely from that of one nation, Cayce reminded one person. He said that it would be necessary to wait until the full time has come for the breaking up of much that has been in the nature of selfish motives in the world, before they could be obtained.

One woman was told that her tomb was a part of the Hall of Records and that there were thirty-two plates or tablets there which "may be discovered by 1958." That date is now a decade past and so the world still waits. As for herself, this person was told she was so gifted intuitively that she might obtain the records mentally!

In the reading on the prophecies of the Great Pyramid, the question was asked, "Are the deductions and conclusions arrived at by D. Davidson and H. Aldersmith in their book on the Great Pyramid correct?"

"Many of these that have been taken as deductions are correct. Many are overdrawn. Only an initiate may understand," was the answer.

The volume is entitled *The Great Pyramid, Its Divine Message.* This classic, now out of print, was first published in 1924. Its final and seventh printing was in 1948. Just what parts are correct and what are overdrawn would indeed take an initiate to know, so that the reader must decide for himself what to take for his authority. There are many charts and diagrams of the Great Pyramid showing its perfect placement in relation to the Sphinx, the earth, and the universe, of which Cayce made mention. There are, however, many statements and a good deal of lore that match other sources, and the book is founded upon the day's best scholars of the antiquities, including Breasted.

Like Cayce, Davidson and Aldersmith describe a highly developed civilization in pre-dynastic Egypt. There was a catastrophe of worldwide proportions after which nothing tangible remained. Modern civilization was founded upon oral traditions brought over from former civilizations. The authors point out that in all the ancient cultures of Egypt, Mexico, Peru, Babylonia, Assyria, and China there are various versions of the Noachian Deluge.

They further state that "the day generally celebrated throughout the world in ancient and modern times as the Anniversary of the Catastrophe, is November 1, with variations generally from October 31 to November 2. These represent in modern times All Hallows' Eve, All Saints' Day, and All Souls' Day."

One particular statement stands out in bold-face: "The object of the Pyramid's Message was to proclaim Jesus as Deliverer and Saviour of men, to announce the dated circumstances relating to His Coming, and to prepare men by means of its Message—whether they believe it or not in the first instance—to adapt themselves spiritually to the circumstances of His coming when the fact of the Message becomes to them a matter of certainty."

This agrees with the Cayce interpretation, and, as we see it, is the key to all the rest. We leave to students a comparison of the contents of this book with what we present here from the Cayce record.

At 3 p.m. on June 30, 1932, members of the Norfolk Study Group One and friends of A.R.E. met to hear Edgar Cayce give his usual reading for the Annual Congress. References had been made many times to the Pyramid prophecies and now, details were to be requested as to the origin, purpose, and the prophecies, themselves. The reading was as follows:

"Yes. In the information as respecting the pyramids, their purpose in the experience of the peoples, in the period when there was the rebuilding of the priest during the return in the land, some 10,500 years before the coming of the Christ into the land, there was first that attempt to restore and add to that which had been begun on what is called the Sphinx, and the treasure or storehouse facing same, between this and the Nile, in which those records were kept. . . .

"Then . . . there began the building of that now called Gizeh, with which those prophecies that had been in the Temple of Records and the Temple Beautiful were builded, in the building of this that was to be the Hall of the Initiates. . . .

"This, then, receives all the records from the beginnings of that given by the priest . . . to the return of the Great Initiate to that and other lands for the folding up of those prophecies that are depicted there. All changes that came in the religious thought in the world are shown there, in the variations in which the passage through same is reached, from the base to the top—or to the open tomb and the top. These are signified by both the layer and the color in what direction the turn is made.

"This, then, is the purpose for the record and the meaning to be interpreted by those that have come and do come as the teachers of the various periods, in the experience of this present position, of the activity of the spheres, of the earth.

"In the period that is to come, this ends—as to that point which is between what is termed in chronological time in present—between 1950 and 1958, but there have been portions that have been removed by those that desecrated many of those other records in the same land. This was rejected by that Pharaoh who hindered in the peoples' leaving the land.

"Q. 1. Are the deductions and conclusions arrived at by D. Davidson and H. Aldersmith in their book on the Great Pyramid correct?

"A. 1. Many of these that have been taken as deductions are correct. Many are overdrawn. Only an initiate may understand.

"Q. 2. What corrections for the period of the twentieth century?

"A. 2. Only those that there will be an upheaval in '36.

"Q. 3. Do you mean there will be an upheaval in '36 as recorded in the Pyramid?

"A. 3. As recorded in the Pyramid, though this is set for a correction which, as has been given, is between '32 *and* '38—the correction would be, for this—as seen—is '36—for it is in many—these run from specific days; for, as has been seen, there are periods when even the hour, day, year, place, country, nation, town, and individuals are pointed out. That's how correct are many of those prophecies as made.

"Oft may there be changes that bring periods, as seen in that period when there was an alteration in that initiate in the land of Zu and Ra that *brought* a change, but at a different point because of being driven by those that were set as the guides or guards of same.

"In this same pyramid did the Great Initiate, the Master, take those last of the Brotherhood degrees with John, the forerunner of Him, at that place. As is indicated in that period where the entrance is shown to be in that land that was set apart, as that promised to that peculiar peoples, as were rejected—as is shown in that portion when there is the turning back from the rising up of Xerxes as the deliverer from an unknown tongue or land, and again is there seen that this occurs in the entrance of the Messiah in this period—1998."

Here the reading stops. A continuation was given the following day, July 1.

"Much has been written respecting that represented in the Great Pyramid, and the record that may be read by those who would seek to know more concerning the relationships that have existed, that may exist, that do exist, between those of the Creative Forces that are manifest in the material world. As indicated, there were periods when a much closer relationship existed, or rather it should be said, there was a much better understanding *of* the relationship that *exists* between the creature and the Creator.

"In those conditions that are signified in the way through the Pyramid, as of periods through which the world has passed and is passing, as related to the religious or the spiritual experiences of man—the period of the present is represented by the low passage or depression showing a downward tendency, as indicated by the variations in the character of stone used. This might be termed in the present as the . . . age . . . in which preparations are being made for the beginning of a change, which—as indicated from the astronomical or numerical conditions—dates from the latter portion or middle portion of the present fall [1932]. In October there will be a period of in which the benevolent influences of Jupiter and Uranus will be stronger, which—from an astrological viewpoint—will bring a greater interest in occult or mystic influences.

"At the correct time accurate imaginary lines can be drawn from the opening of the Great Pyramid to the second star in the Great Dipper, called Polaris or the North Star. This indicates it is the system toward which the soul takes flight after having completed its sojourn through this solar system.

In October there will be seen the first variation in the position of the polar star in relation to the lines from the Great Pyramid. The dipper is gradually changing, and when this change becomes noticeable—as might be calculated from the Pyramid—there will be the beginning of the change in the races. There will come a greater influx of souls from the Atlantean, Lemurian, La, Ur, or Da civilizations. These conditions are indicated in this turn in the journey through the Pyramid.

"How was this begun? Who was given that this should be a record of man's experiences in this root race? For that is the period covered by the prophecies in the Pyramid. This was given . . . in that period . . . when there were many who sought to bring to man a better understanding of the close relationship between the Creative Forces and that created, between man and man, and man and his Maker.

"Only those who have been called may truly understand. Who then has been called? Whosoever will make himself a channel may be raised to that of a blessing that is all that entity-body is able to comprehend. Who, having his whole measure full, would desire more does so to his own undoing.

"Q. 4. What are the correct interpretations of the indications in the Great Pyramid regarding the time when the present depression will end?

"A. 4. The changes as indicated and outlined are for the latter part of the present year [1932]. As far as depression is concerned, this is not—as in the minds of many—because fear has arisen, but rather that, when fear has arisen in the hearts of the created, *sin* lieth at the door. Then, the change will occur —or that seeking will make the definite change—in the latter portion of the present year. Not that times financially will be better, but the minds of the people will be fitted to the conditions better.

"Q. 5. What was the date of the actual beginning and ending of the construction of the Great Pyramid?

"A. 5. Was one hundred years in construction. Begun and completed in the period of Araaraart's time, with Hermes and Ra.

"Q. 6. What was the date B.C. of that period?

"A. 6. 10,490 to 10,390 before the Prince entered into Egypt.

"Q. 7. What definite details are indicated as to what will happen after we enter the period of the King's Chamber?

"A. 7. When the bridegroom is at hand, all do rejoice. When we enter that understanding of being in the King's presence, with that of the mental seeking, the joy, the buoyancy, the new understanding, the new life, through the period.

"Q. 8. What is the significance of the empty sarcophagi?

"A. 8. That there will be no more death. Don't misunderstand or misinterpret! but the *interpretation* of death will be made plain.

"Q. 9. If the Armageddon is foretold in the Great Pyramid, please give a description of it and the date of its beginning and ending.

"A. 9. Not in what is left there. It will be as a thousand years, with the fighting in the air, and—as has been—between those returning to and those leaving the earth.

"Q. 10. What will be the type and extent of the upheaval in '36?

"A. 10. The wars, the upheavals in the interior of the earth, and the shifting of same by the differentiation in the axis as respecting the positions from the Polaris center.

"Q. 11. Is there not a verse of scripture in Isaiah mentioning the rock on which the Great Pyramid is builded?

"A. 11. Not as we find; rather the rock on which John *viewed* the New Jerusalem—that is, as of the entering in the King's Chamber in the Pyramid.

"Q. 12. What is the date, as recorded by the Pyramid, of entering in the King's Chamber?

"A. 12. '38 to '58.

"Q. 13. If the Passion of Jesus is recorded in the Great Pyramid, please give the date according to our present system of recording time?

"A. 13. This has already been presented in a fair and suitable manner through those students of same, and these descriptions have been presented as to their authenticity.

"Q. 14. How was this particular Great Pyramid of Gizeh built?

"A. 14. By the use of those forces in nature as make for iron to swim. Stone floats in the air in the same manner. This will be discovered in '58."

". . . With the storehouse, or record house (where the records are still to be uncovered) there is a chamber or passage from the right forepaw to this entrance of the record chamber, or record tomb. This may not be entered without an understanding, for those that were left as guards may *not* be passed until after a period of their regeneration in the Mount. . . ."

CHAPTER 9

"THE RECORDS ARE ONE"

ELEVATORS IN the Gobi Desert!

A Poseidian temple near Bimini!

A blue vase from Ur!

These are some more of the tangible evidences of Atlantis which Cayce said were still around after 12,500 years, waiting to be discovered.

The specific directions, the intriguing hints, scattered among the readings are enough to make an archeologist grab his pick-ax and head for the nearest jet.

An aviatrix did just that back in 1935—headed for the nearest prop job, that is—and discovered a well with spooky inscriptions carved on it at Bimini.

Most of this fabulous collection of leads to new, important archeological finds has been left untouched.

Some of it has been partly uncovered, such as the Dead Sea Scrolls in

Palestine: Cayce indicated that the scrolls' owners lived and taught at Mount Carmel. So far, little has been done there to prove or disprove this.

Matching and comparing lean and fat references, entire readings at times, we begin to see and to know the world as it was in 10,500 B.C., according to Cayce. This period was emphasized because it was the time of the breaking up of Atlantis, when migrations were going on and new nations were being born. Thus, this period is more sharply drawn for us than others Cayce described. Specific dates are offered marking events of that era. Prehistory was given not only for Egypt, but also for Yucatan and the Gobi Desert, for Persia, in many references given in individuals' life readings. In these cases, involving Yucatan, Gobi, and Persia, as well as Egypt, we have an amazingly consistent picture of their life and character in prehistoric times, which attest to high levels of culture.

An example of Cayce's plausibility in fixing the dates for this period is this list of historic events as culled from various readings:

The westward migration to Yucatan from Atlantis occurred around 10,600 B.C.

The city of Ur was flourishing from 10,500 B.C. to 10,420 B.C.—probably much earlier and much later as well, for these dates merely mark the time of one person's birth and death, in her individual reading.

The Great Pyramid of Gizeh was built from 10,490 B.C. to 10,390 B.C.

A library was established at Alexandria in 10,300 B.C.

The Gobi Desert's City of Gold, in the nation of Taoi, was a thriving metropolis in 10,000 B.C. and was contemporary with equally cultured nations of India, Norway, and Og (Peru).

The sprawling democracy of Taoi in the Gobi Desert of Mongolia and Northern China had its own independent and highly advanced civilization. There was an interchange of scientific, religious, and social ideas among these countries. Trade flourished among them, bringing "spices from India, cut stones from Egypt."

Cayce declared that the temple records that will be found in Egypt, Yucatan, and off Bimini will be found identical! In a reading on Mayan prehistory, he states: "Yet as time draws nigh when changes are to come about, there may be the opening of those three places where the records are one, to those that are the initiates in the knowledge of the One God.

"The Temple [built] by Iltar (Yucatan) will then rise again. Also, there will be the opening of the temple or hall of records in Egypt, and those records that were put into the heart of the Atlantean land may also be found there— that have been kept, for those that are of that group [Poseidia at Bimini].

"The *records* are *One.*"

We can expect to find the artifacts in these three places to be similar.

But we cannot expect them to be marked "Made in Atlantis"! No. In fact, archeologists will be dealing with a whole new level of study that will probably take quite a while to carry out. We may be years in comparing the records and relics of the many sites yet to be excavated, if the exciting finds the future holds take as long to evaluate as have the Dead Sea Scrolls. We can envision a whole new generation of "Atlantologists" who will specialize in knowledge of that period. Certainly, it will take all the skills archeology has developed in recent decades to verify and explain the meaning of Atlantis.

Archeology has "grown up" in modern times. Its techniques were once haphazard, and in the process of digging, many people destroyed as much as they found. Now there are many scientific aids to make this an increasingly efficient science in itself. There are the carbon dating tests that can measure the age of a skull. There are new code-breaking techniques to decipher texts; more careful digging methods and labeling of artifacts; and lately, the use of X-rays to look inside such otherwise enigmatic structures as the Great Pyramid!

The Atlanteans used these very techniques, we conclude from Cayce's records, and they're back, to put their scientific know-how to work in every field! Cayce said that archeology was practiced in Egypt. If the people of that period had solar power and the laser, they were also pretty good archeologists.

In the overall picture Cayce presents, a pattern in man's development emerges, involving his innate need to remember, to preserve his identity and his past. Man needs his traditions to give him a sense of continuity and permanence. In knowledge of his history, he can better control the future and understand the present.

We enter the 1970's on the threshold of what can become for us and future generations "the best that's yet to be." This will be made clearer when "the records that are one" are found, and, with the record temples, or chambers that are opened, the minds and hearts of mankind in the twentieth century.

We note, the timing is perfect.

Bimini!

It is not the jewelry and the vases which archeologists prize, however real they make the people of the past seem to us. It is rather the clay tablets, the parchments by which the past is communicated. We can expect that when the documents of Atlantis are found, they will represent a tremendous breakthrough for historians as well as scientists. However, Cayce's predictions come with the understanding that "yet as time draws nigh when changes are to come about, there may be the opening of these three places where the records are one, *to those that are the initiates in the knowledge of the One God.*" (Author's italics.)

What does this mean? Only that we will need to be spiritually mature, as well as scholarly, to appreciate the value of the discoveries in full. These will not be just another cache of exotic baubles. These will be the sacred relics of a God-fearing people who acknowledged Him above nationality and wealth. We do not begin to comprehend the powers they had in posting guards about the record chambers until they had been "regenerated in the mount." This is a mystery among many mysteries surrounding the Great Pyramid. But the Cayce readings have said that when the time is fulfilled, the right people will appear to undertake the opening of the records, and it will be by the hand of God.

Appropriately, the first inkling Cayce and his friends had of this trinity of sacred temples was in 1926 with the first mention of Bimini, which concerned nothing more important than oil wells. The Great Pyramid and the Hall of Records in Egypt was described in 1932. The idea of a "Temple of Iltar" at Yucatan was introduced in 1933.

Bimini! It consists of two very small islands among several thousand in the Bahamas, just forty-five miles east of the Miami coast and a haven for deep sea fishermen. But in 1926 when it first figured in the Cayce annals, it was virtually isolated and served chiefly as a station for rum-running.

Cayce described it as "the highest portion left above the waves of a once great continent, upon which the civilization as now exists in the world's history [could] find much of that as would be used as a means for attaining that civilization [Atlantis] . . ."

". . . for this is of the first highest civilization that will be uncovered in some of the adjacent lands to the west and south of the isles, see?

"Q. 1. Was this the continent known as Alta or Poseidia?

"A. 1. A temple of the Poseidians was in a portion of this land.

"Q. 2. What minerals will be found there?

"A. 2. Gold, spar, and icthyolite."

This seems to indicate a temple of Poseidia is located in the vicinity of Bimini.

Besides, there's a lot of gold in those (underwater) hills, according to Cayce!

As may be surmised from various statements in the readings, not only Bimini itself, but the area to the south and west of it—the Gulf Stream—is the location of the new land to rise. This is part of the island of Poseidia, and "under the slime of the ages of sea water" near Bimini, part of the Poseidia temples may yet be discovered. With them, said Cayce, would be records like those in Egypt.

When land rises in this area, many "Atlanteans" will be drawn back to rebuild it! "There are, as has been given, many peoples being born again into the earth's plane who were, through their experiences, in this land. With the building, then, again, we find the innate desire will come to an innumerable number to be in some manner or way associated—either as dwellers for a portion of the time or the whole time, or as the investors in the project—to make this not only a habitable place, but as a resort equaled by none."

Other big things were suggested for Bimini. It could be made into a shipping port, with its many natural harbors and its convenient position on the waterways. It could become a strategic point in the affairs of several continents "as it has been in the eons past."

It could become a center for archeological research.

Hydroelectric power could be obtained from the tidal currents which "would supply all of the power necessary for any project that might be even undertaken here."

Bimini could be one of the biggest health resorts in the world. Cayce said that wells could be drilled there from which would flow the healing waters used by the Atlanteans. Was this, then, the legendary Fountain of Youth which Ponce de Leon came so close to finding?

There are actually two main islands of Bimini: North and South. The underground waters on these islands are very different, and yet both are excellent, according to Cayce. He said, "The northern portion of South Island will lend itself to the water supply—a sweet water—adaptable not only for the drinking purposes but for all purposes of the body. This will be found by drilling to the depth which will be, true enough, below the sea level, yet the source is from far, far away. Better water will be found (here) than in those lands known as the continents."

There are sulphur waters on the North Island: "The sulphur waters may be obtained where there is seen an old channel on north end of the south portion of the North Island. These will be of the black sulphur, yet for certain conditions, and for the baths as may be instituted through same, will be quite beneficial to health, and especially to those of the neuritic conditions—nervousness and the general rheumatic conditions, see? This will be found only eighty-nine to ninety feet deep."

But after the land around Bimini rises, the possibility of Bimini's becoming a resort, a shipping port, and all the rest changes. As the geologist author of *Earth Changes* remarked recently, this prediction seemed to indicate that Bimini's future as a resort and shipping center was limited to the time when there were opportunities for this.

Cayce did predict that a temple, its records matching those in Egypt, would be found. In fact, that there would be the remains of "temples" found in this part of Poseidia, when it appeared.

Where are these temples, or their ruins? Someone asked Cayce, "How deep in the ground will the [minerals and archeological remains] be found?"

"These will be found in the twelve to fifteen-foot levels," he said. "The vein, as workable, would be found extending in the northeast-southwest direction. . . ." These are below sea level.

Since "archeological remains" referred to in the record seem to indicate the temples Cayce had mentioned earlier, did Cayce mean that these would be found at the same level with the vein of gold?

Concerning the accuracy of the dating of the final destruction of Atlantis, the Geologist says that this might be determined by radiocarbon dating. A sample of mangrove peat encountered at a depth of nine feet below mean low water in a core boring on Bimini in 1957 was reported by Columbia University scientists to be 4,370 years old. "The date suggests that any materials encountered in the twelve to fifteen foot levels would be only a few thousand years older than about 4,372 years, and might possibly be of the order of 10,100 years or slightly more, the date given for final destruction of Atlantis."

Cayce's interest in Bimini began with a man who showed up with an apparently sincere sympathy for the work. He enlisted the clairvoyant's cooperation in trying to locate oil in Florida, promising that a hospital could finally be built from the proceeds of such a venture.

Edgar Cayce thus seemed drawn to this part of Poseidia by chance circumstances, without funds, but with a dream for healing his fellowmen fixed firmly in his heart and mind.

A whole series of readings followed the initial request for information on oil, Cayce directing operations in Florida from his couch in Virginia Beach. Several of the readings of pirate treasure which he said was also located there giving the precise location were never returned by his opportunistic friend, who disappeared shortly afterward.

But as was given in a reading on the work of Cayce: "Oft will it be learned by the study of phenomena of people's actions, that seemingly all forces in the universe are used to bring about that which is good, for it has been said, 'I will harden the heart of Pharaoh, that he will not let my children go.' Through this same seed came the Son of Man, and through these same trials through which the forefathers passed, the burdens and sins of the world were laid upon that Son.

"Then through the trials, the temptations, the besetters of evil from within and without, may any work that is His be expected to grow, and in that manner become polished bright, and a shining light unto the world; yet though He were the Son, He learned obedience through the things which He suffered."

In 1935 Melaney Freeman, a licensed pilot, learned of the well of fresh water on Bimini and was curious.

"Edgar Cayce must have talked to her about this well in discussing Atlantis," noted Gladys Turner in this file, "because I can find nothing in her life reading mentioning it. Edgar Cayce had visited Bimini in February, 1927; possibly he heard a story from the natives about a supposed fresh water well which was visible at certain times with the flow of the tide."

Melaney decided to fly down to Bimini and look for herself. From Miami she wired Cayce: "Please send me directions to locate well in Bimini. Also sea tide incoming or outgoing best to get sample of water. Expect to go next week by plane for the day."

Cayce wired back, "Well in Bimini southeastern position of North Bimini. Tide only changes flow of well."

She found a fresh water well, she reported, marked or walled around the top with stones of peculiar composition and strange symbols. She asked in her next reading: "Could the well in Bimini be promoted and reconstructed?"

Cayce stated in reply that a center could be established for two purposes: regeneration from the well, and its surrounding waters for those who are ill, and a center for archeological research. "And as such actions [dredging for harbors] are begun, there will be found much more gold in the lands under the sea than there is in the world circulation today!"

"Aid may be found from the varied societies that have been founded for the geological and archeological activities . . . for much will be found. . . ."

There is that assurance again, despite Bimini's uncertain future, that "much will be found."

The Geologist who has done considerable work at Bimini, was unable to locate the well. Melaney Freeman said she found it below the water line on the southeastern part of North Bimini.

I asked Gladys Turner where Melaney Freeman is today, nearly thirty-three years later. Gladys stated that she had been out of touch with the aviatrix for a number of years, and has no way of locating her for help in rediscovering the well. Perhaps future excursions to Bimini by the Geologist and other researchers will yet yield knowledge about the well, the vein of gold, and those elusive Poseidian temples that lie beneath the sea!

Yucatan!

Among the Children of the Law of One, a certain Iltar led a group of ten people in one of many westward migrations to Yucatan in about 10,600 B.C. The Cayce readings indicate that these migrations were by air as well as by boat.

In Yucatan these Poseidians began a new civilization. They worked with those who had preceded them and others who had followed, keeping the spiritual tenets of their old homeland and building temples to their One God. They found here refugees from the Lemurian (Pacific) and Mu (lower California and Mexico) upheavals. Together they created a new culture—for the latter were equally anxious to preserve their religious principles. When the final upheavals in Atlantis occurred several hundred years later, much of the contour of the land in Central America and Mexico was changed to what it is now. Cayce stated that the first temples erected by Iltar and his followers were destroyed as this happened. But the temples which were built later by the combined peoples from "Mu, Oz, and Atlantis" were those which were being discovered at the time he gave the reading on this in 1933.

The most ancient and inscrutable pyramids in Mexico are at Teotihuacan, thirty-two miles from Mexico City. Here is located the Pyramid of the Sun, which is nearly as large as that called Gizeh in Egypt, but only 216 feet tall. Another was dedicated to the moon, and according to Ignatius Donnelly's *Atlantis: The Antediluvian World,** covers forty-five acres—or four times as much space as Gizeh. He cites the many similarities between the Mexican and the Egyptian monuments.

Donnelly states, "In Mexico pyramids were found everywhere. Cortez, in a letter to Charles V, states that he counted 400 of them at Cholula. Their temples were on those 'high places.' "

In reference to Cayce's statement that "the first temples that were erected by Iltar and his followers were destroyed" during the later upheavals, we would point out that Donnelly relays to us an observation of Bancroft that "In many of the ruined cities of Yucatan one or more pyramids have been found, upon the summit of which no traces of any building could be discovered, although upon surrounding pyramids such structures could be found . . ." He adds, however, that there is in Egypt another form of pyramid called the *Mastaba,* which, like the Mexican, was "flattened on the top"

* New York: Harper & Row, Publishers, Inc.

and is in fact found from Mesopotamia to the Pacific Ocean. These pyramids of Yucatan without temples could be of this order.

In her article, "Atlantis In Mexico," *(Searchlight,* June, 1963), Clare Templeton states that "there are some arresting comparisons with the Cayce readings" and the Toltecs, who some researchers think were the first high culture above the archaic level, and the originators of the calendar. The mass of legendary material about them is as heroic as it is confusing, but researchers agree that they did not practice human sacrifice. One legend which qualifies by sheer persistence is that they had airships and arrived in Mexico by this means. . . ." She states that the calendar stones, "on technical precision alone" are "more apt to be survivals from the earlier culture."

These pyramid ruins were also Incal in influence, though the Incals were themselves the successors of Oz or Og in the Peruvian land, and Mu. These same ruins were added to later, when there appeared on the scene members of the Lost Tribes of Israel! Thus these are remnants of Egyptian, Lemurian, Oz, and even Mosaic influences.

The Lost Tribes left Palestine three thousand years before Christ, and part of them came into Mu, or extreme southwestern United States, and then moved on to Mexico and Yucatan, centering in the area of Mexico City. Here arose a mixture of races again, and a different civilization.

Cayce referred to the civilization in Yucatan and Mexico as a "high" civilization, and that more than one such will be found as research progresses. But the Aztec people were a much later nation, which flowered around 1479 A.D. According to the Encyclopedia Britannica, "The word *Azteca* is derived from Aztlan (white land) where, according to the Aztec traditions, their tribe originated. . . . The Aztecs were people of the sun."

The Aztecs, however, were influenced by the Mosaic laws of human sacrifice, and combined the Atlantean worship of "God the Son" and the symbology of the *sun* with this later ideal of sacrifice, and sacrificed human beings—usually their enemies—to the sun! Cayce tells us that among the ruins in Yucatan are "the altars upon which there were the cleansings of the bodies of individuals (not human sacrifice; for this came much later with the injection of the Mosaic, and those activities of that area). These were later the altars upon which individual activities—that would today be termed hate, malice, selfishness, self-indulgence—were cleansed from the body through the ceremony. . . ."

We recall the ideals of the Temple of Sacrifice, in which the earlier Atlanteans sacrificed, said Cayce, not human beings, but their baser emotions. Thus the Aztecs applied these inherited concepts in degenerate form, offering their victims on the altars in great numbers to "keep the sun moving," as H. R. Hays tells us *(In the Beginnings,* G. P. Putnam's Sons, 1963).

In addition to the altars, Cayce said that further specific proof would be "the pyramids, the altars before the doors of the varied temple activities," an injection from the people of Oz and Mu.

The Aztec "Calendar Stone," which seems an interesting but primitive piece of gibberish, embodies, according to George C. Vaillant *(Aztecs of Mexico,* Doubleday and Co., 1941), a finite statement of the infinity of the universe." It was made in 1479 A.D., he states, and weighs over twenty tons. It is twelve feet in diameter.

Vaillant describes the relic thus: "In the center is the face of the Sun God, Tonatiuh, flanked by four cartouches which singly give the dates of the four previous ages of the world and together represent the date of our present era. The twenty names of the days circle this central element, and they, in turn, are ringed with a band of glyphs denoting jade or turquoise, which give the idea of being precious, and symbolize the heavens and their color. This strip is girdled by the signs for stars, through which penetrate designs emblematic of the rays of the sun. Two immense Fire Serpents, symbolic of the year and Time, circle the exterior to meet face to face at the base. Boring back through these forms to the significance behind them, we have a grandiose conception of the majesty of the universe.

"According to Aztec belief," Vaillant adds, "the world has passed through four or five stages or Suns. Details differ, but the record on the great calendar Stone may be taken as the official version in Tenochtitlan. . . . Our present age, Four Earthquake, is under the control of the Sun God, Tonatiuh, and it will be destroyed, in time, by earthquakes."

But these beliefs are Aztec, you say. Not originally, according to Cayce. For he states that further evidence of the time of Atlantis were "the stones that are circular, that were of the magnetized influence upon which the Spirit of the One spoke to those peoples as they gathered in their service, are the earliest Atlantean activities in religious service, as would be called today."

Cayce speaks of another kind of stone—the "Great Crystal," a "large cylindrical glass" cut with facets so that the capstone on top of it controlled the power concentrated in it from the sun—the "firestone" of which he spoke in the data on Egypt. He says that in Yucatan there is the "emblem of same." This is stated to be the circular stone of the Aztecs (or their Atlantean forebears)—a *symbol* of the firestone. "Let's clarify this," Cayce continues, "for it may the more easily be found. For they will be brought to this America, these United States. A portion is to be carried, as we find, to the Pennsylvania State Museum. A portion is to be carried to the Washington preservation of such findings (Smithsonian Institute), or to Chicago."

Records as to how to construct the firestone will be found in Yucatan, Bimini, and Egypt. "As indicated, the records of the manners of construction of same are in three places in the earth, as it stands today: in the sunken portions of Atlantis, or Poseidia, where a portion of the temples may yet be discovered under the slime of ages of sea water, near what is known as Bimini, off the coast of Florida. And in the temple records that were in Egypt, where the entity later acted in cooperation with others in preserving the records that came from the land where these had been kept. Also the records that were carried to what is now Yucatan in America, where these stones (that they know so little about) are now—during the last few months—being uncovered." This was given December 20, 1933.

By way of Oz and Mu (or Peru and Mexico) the Lost Tribes injected their influence in the religious culture of Yucatan. "The pyramid, the altars before the doors of the varied temple activities, was an injection from the people of

Oz and Mu; and will be found to be separate portions, and that referred to in the Scriptures as the high places of family affairs, family gods. . . ." Also, "The stones that are set in the front of the Temple, between the service temple and the outer court temple" were later adopted by the Hebrews in their worship.

There still remains a temple of Iltar in Yucatan, where the records are waiting to be discovered. As for what happened to Iltar's later people, we are told "Those in Yucatan, those in the adjoining lands as begun by Iltar, gradually lost in their activities (through generations); and came to be that people termed, in other portions of America, the Mound Builders."

But Yucatan, Bimini, and Egypt are not the only places where there may be found evidences of Atlantis. Cayce added other places in the following statement: "The position the continent Atlantis occupied is between the Gulf of Mexico on one side and the Mediterranean on the other. Evidences of Atlantean civilization may be found in the Pyrenees and Morocco and in British Honduras, Yucatan and parts of the Americas—especially near Bimini and in the Gulf Stream in this vicinity."

CHAPTER 10

TAOI!

THOUSANDS OF MILES east of Atlantis, on the vast plains of Mongolia, in 10,000 B.C. throve a nation covering 102,000 square miles.

What fabulous secrets now lie hidden under the sands of the barren wastelands of the Gobi Desert? In this part of the world which has seen little geologic change in centuries, gazelles graze and fierce winds howl. Beneath the sparse growth of sagebrush and thorn, says Cayce, one day will be found the fabulous City of Gold—Taoi!

A prophecy in 1935 linked Alexandria, Yucatan and Gobi, as archeological "interests that are arising in the . . . unearthing—as in Alexandria, as it will be in Yucatan, as is to be in the next two and one-half years in the Gobi. . . ."

Just what archeological research went on in the Gobi at that time (1937) is not clear. Certainly no City of Gold has yet been reported found there. At the time of the readings, archeologists had been working at Angyang, south of Peking, under Chinese and American auspices. Civil War stopped it in 1930, vandalism by grave robbers hampered later attempts, and by 1937 the Japanese were invading North China. However, says H. R. Hays in *In the Beginnings,* "Despite interruptions during the war with Japan, the fall of Chiang Kai-shek and the formation of the People's Republic, excavation of sites in North China has gone on since 1928 until we can form a picture of a great culture as significant and sophisticated as that of Mesopotamia or Egypt."

Judging from Edgar Cayce's dissertation on the prehistory of the Gobi Desert, the civilization of Taoi shared that status, and it still remains to be one of the major discoveries of the future.

Cayce said Taoi had been peopled by migrations from Lemuria, more as a latter-day contemporary of that civilization than as a refugee center. It was thus influenced by this early advanced race, about whom very little is given in the Cayce files. Taoi became "among the highest state of advancement in material accomplishments for the benefit or conveniences for man's indwelling. . . ." As a colony (?) of Lemuria and as a nation in its own right, it was led by the ruler Mu, the "prophet, the sage, the lawgiver."

Among the materials used for construction, we are told, were precious woods and metals: "And here, as may be discovered when these are excavated, the greater use of timbers or wood as a building material was exercised. . . ." He adds that there was constructed a "temple of gold—overlaid —its beams, its walls, its panelings—with many colored polished woods."

This was a very democratic nation with democracy extending into its religious practices. The people gathered in a temple "for speech-making. There were no priests as in many other lands." They *all* spoke and had what "would be called a forum, such as a group known in thine own land as the Quakers— who spoke when they were moved by, not anxiety, not wrath, but by the spirit of thoughtfulness—or the recognizing of Mind, the Builder. But the laborer was heard as well as those that were of every trade as would be termed in the present."

Cayce states: "There was equality between the sexes during that experience. There was only, as has been indicated, monogamy; not polygamy *ever* practiced among these peoples. The rights of each were the rights of the other. When by injury, wrath, accident, the mate was destroyed or killed, or by [natural] death, then the choice was made by the individual and seconded by those that were in the authority as to judgments. But those that judged were as the common people, as those in authority. For only the Prince, only those of the household of the Prince, were the 'last word'—but they never as lords, priests, presidents or dictators, but as interpreters of the law between man and man! And all interpreters were of the law between man and man! And all interpreters were moved to speech, or moved by the spirit in that ye call religion in the present, though these later—with the mixing of those from India and especially from Caucasia—made for disturbances in the second generation after Muzuen."

Muzuen was the name of the son of Mu, or the Prince who was the same as the person for whom this reading was given by Cayce. He took his place as heir to the throne at the age of sixteen and proved to be an enlightened ruler, a "prepared pacifist." He unified his country and later saw the development of explosives for defense.

During his time there occurred "the destruction of the mighty forests to the north, upon what are now the mountains of lime, salt, and sodas."

Muzuen was described as "five feet eleven. Blue of eye. Hair dark gold. Six fingered; five toed."

(Six fingered?)

"In dress: leather, linen, cotton, silk—in their varied seasons, their varied activities. Not given to ornaments as much as many, and this gradually turned the peoples from personal adornment to their home, their cities, their recreation places, their preparations for defense, their preparation for offense."

Adornments included "the finer works in laces, fabrics, spun gold, silver, carved ivory, and the like."

Elsewhere, the people are described as wearing clothing of "flax, cotton, ramie, silk" and using articles made of "gold, silver, lead, radium."

They had also a technology like ours, for they had electricity. They even had elevators! Cayce declared that there will be found here "lifts or elevators, the one-line electrical car, the very fast aerial locomotion—these were a portion of these experiences. . . ."

"The communications—not the telegraph as is known today; more of that of the voice transmission of quite a different type and nature."

"As to the manner of defense and offense, as has been indicated, much that is yet to be found again was a part of those preparations in those periods. For these then had to do with the setting of long-period drums for defense in which there might be any attempts by others to interfere, to cause their *own* undoing."*

Although Cayce does not say so, we can probably expect that gold coins which the people used as means of exchange will be found at Taoi. These he described as being "edged or etched; but no figures, no individual heads. These came later. But *holes* in same; almost square pieces, strung." The square coins were thus notched—"smooth but edged that it might be known from other groups that gradually used the same—and was changed to this when it was found that the Atlanteans' were almost the same." They were "strung to be worn about the waist or about the neck."

As each labored, said Cayce, as each saved, each received from a common storehouse, a common bank. There was no Government Bank and no taxation. Everyone worked, including the women and children, and all were paid the same: a piece of gold for a day's labor, for all did what they could. It was "all for the one, and one for all."

In trading with other countries the same coins were used.

Gold existed in fabulous quantities: "For with the City of Gold there will be found—well, there is not so much now even in the treasury or vaults of the U.S.A.!" There was much pomp, much use of gold trappings in the heraldry —"for gold was then as the sands to these peoples."

Unimpressed by gold except for ornament and as a means of exchange, these people had great regard for the religious life. One person was told he had been a missionary to Taoi, and had built a temple as the "representation of the understandings in the moral, the mental, the religious and spiritual life."

Another was told that he had helped with the "Temple Beautiful that was established in Taoi which may some day be brought to light . . . when there

* This is explained in Chapter 12.

have been those concentrated efforts in the direction to uncover the activities that will make for a greater correlating of the fact that Truth is that which grows in the hearts of men to make them aware of their relationships to their Maker. . . ."

A woman was told that she had ministered to the needs of the peoples in "the Temple", providing "ointments, lotions, odors," which were typical aids for worship at the altars of that time.

What will be found of the democracy of Taoi, one day? Elevators in the Gobi Desert? Gold coins that are square? A city of gold? And if these people preserved their dead as did the Egyptians, perhaps the mummy of Prince Muzuen will be found—with those twelve fingers!

Indo-China

Thailand and Cambodia were in the world news early in November, 1967, when Mrs. Jacqueline Kennedy visited there to fulfill a childhood dream— that of seeing ruins of the ancient Cambodian city of Angkor. Here is the largest religious building in the world, the Angkor Wat.

And there is another "City of Gold" to be discovered, said Cayce, in Thailand.

Evidence of a life in "Siam or Indo-China" was promised one person when "there will one day be opened the proof of those activities and experiences of that person there; the proofs of what this entity, with the companion, wrought in the experiences of the people of that land—that caused eventually those changes in the trend westward of what man has called civilization!

"A whole city—yes, a temple—will be uncovered, as will be the City of Gold in the Gobi land."

Such "proofs" suggest that here may be found, as in Egypt, tombs or buildings containing written documents which will bear an account of a re- mote history of that people. Whether the time was 10,000 B.C. or 100 B.C. is not even hinted at. The only clue is that the people referred to somehow caused changes to come about in the westward trend of civilization. This sounds as if we might place it only in prehistoric times.

"Thailand," whose name means "land of the free," has enjoyed centuries of independence. It is located in Indochina, between Burma and Cambodia, and bordered on the northeast by Laos. Its central region is a fertile river basin of farmland and among the mountain valleys to the north are more farmlands, growing rice, tropical fruits, and vegetables. The present people are originally from China; their religion, Buddhist.

Cayce made reference to another city "in Indo-China, where there are uncoverings even now of the city in which the entity resided." More combina- tions of iron will be found here, according to another reading.

But where is that City of Gold of old Siam?

Lemuria

Lemuria, which was destroyed before Atlantis, is not so clearly drawn for us among the Cayce records. He told one person that she was among those who established a temple of worship near what was her birthplace in this life, or Santa Barbara, California. This, he said, "must in the near future fade again into those joinings with the land of Mu"—that is, sink into the Pacific with the Lemurian inundations.

We find few evidences of the Lemurian civilization suggested for future excavation, except those which were left by peoples who came from that continent, mixing with other peoples, such as at Gobi or Yucatan.

One instance, however, stands out. A man was told he had come from Mu "when there were being those banishments and preparations for the preserving; for they had known that the land must soon be broken up."

This person was "among those that journeyed from Mu to what is now Oregon; and there still may be seen something of the worship as set up, in what was the development from that set up by the entity . . . as the totem or family tree."

In other words, the totem pole is a direct "descendant" of Mu. Another equally intriguing lead is indicated off lower California, where a "Princess Shu-Tu" of Lemuria journeyed "to see, to know." Here may be found a certain Canyon Island which "will be a part of the discoveries of . . . natural formations."

"For *this* was the entity's place of the temple."

CHAPTER 11

CARMEL: A SCHOOL OF PROPHETS

IN THE NORTHWESTERN corner of Palestine, in Haifa on Mount Carmel, stands a Carmelite monastery, a thriving center which includes a church, a school, and a shrine of the early Carmelite monks.

A quarter of a mile away at Wadi es Siah are the ruins of the *first* monastery of this order, the place where Elijah was supposed to have started the order known as the Sons of the Prophets who lived to prepare their community for the birth of the Messiah. Here are a garden spot and a cave which has a famous spring—Elijah's Spring. Still another spot is supposed to be where Elijah slew the four hundred priests of Baal.

Another cave and spring revered by the Jews is located at a distance from the first, on the northwest side of Carmel, and is also claimed to be that of the prophet.

Scattered over the entire mount, which is shaped like a loaf of bread, are the unexplained ruins of entire cities.

Although scholars have not yet linked this place with the community of Qumram, one hundred fifty miles away, where the Dead Sea Scrolls were found in 1947, the Edgar Cayce readings abundantly suggest that Mount Carmel was the original "School of the Prophets" of the people of Qumram, and furthermore, that an Essene Temple was located there at the time of Jesus.

This mass of evidence is to be found in what is known as the "Palestine Readings." We have here without doubt predictive material that can be compared with the Dead Sea Scrolls, and that was given the world ten years before the scrolls were found! Will the Temple of the Essenes at Mount Carmel perhaps be found some day? This will be for the archeologists to answer.

Twenty years ago seven of a vast library of parchments were discovered—scrolls written by an obscure Jewish sect, the Essenes, who lived at the time of Jesus. These were followed by lesser finds in later years. Among the first was a *Manual of Discipline,* which tells of the Essenes' communal life at Qumram. Others found with it included the Book of Isaiah, a commentary on the Book of Habakkuk, and an addition to Genesis written in Aramaic. The scrolls were in various states of disintegration and had to be reassembled before they could be edited and published.

Bibles in use today, based on manuscripts dating only to the ninth century, have thus come to be questioned by scholars who are comparing them with the original manuscripts.

The Essenes were destroyed by the Romans in the first century A.D., but before their dispersal they collected their precious library of important records and teachings of the prophets, which date from 100 B.C. or earlier, put them into large jars, and hid them in the caves of Qumram. Although the sect was destroyed, the scrolls were kept from utter decay by the fortunate climatic conditions prevalent there.

Information gleaned from the giant work of assembling the badly fragmented scrolls for editing and publishing is eagerly awaited by Christians and Jews for the new insight into their histories it will bring. The scrolls are termed by some scholars as "revolutionary," written on the eve of Christianity and therefore of more authority than those produced later.

Of major importance already is the contribution which the Essenes made to Christianity. According to certain of the scrolls, the Essenes were a people "set apart" from the Pharisees and Sadducees at the time of Jesus. Their communal and ascetic life, their persecution at the hands of the Romans, and their adherence to a form of Judaism which later paved the way for Christianity, are vividly set forth.

The Essenes are not mentioned either in the Old Testament or the New. But what the Dead Sea Scrolls reveal about them was indicated and anticipated in the Cayce records as early as 1936. Their daily lives, studies, customs, all centering around the Holy Family, were set forth in great detail in readings given for many people allegedly associated with the Master during His life on earth.

The Cayce readings state that the Essenes provided the social and religious setting into which Jesus was born, that their goal, years before Jesus' birth, was preparing a fit community into which the Messiah could be born. The meaning of *Essene,* the readings state, is "expectancy."

These were a dedicated people and evidently existed only to nurture this great Event into the world, as their existence is not recorded for us in the orthodox sources of the present day.

Exquisite insight is given into the hearts and minds of Mary, Joseph, and many others surrounding them. Of special interest are those who helped Joseph and Mary in the care and teaching of Jesus at Mount Carmel, in the Temple. It was in the Temple, also, that Mary was chosen, and it was there that she and Joseph were married.

Essenism has been known to scholars through the works of Pliny, Josephus, and Philo. Now the Dead Sea Scrolls will give us new understanding of the beginnings of Christianity. They will be confirmed by another approach: the Edgar Cayce readings.

A typical reading from the Palestine group was given June 27, 1937:

"In the days when more and more leaders of the people had been trained in the temple at Mount Carmel—the original place where the school of prophets was established during Elijah's time—there were those leaders called Essenes who were students of what ye would call astrology, numerology, phrenology, and the study of the return of individuals, or reincarnation.

"There were certain reasons why these proclaimed that certain periods formed a cycle—reasons which grew out of the study of Aristotle, Enos, Mathias, Judah and others who supervised the school, as you would term it.

"These men and women had been persecuted by leaders of the people, and this had caused the saying of which ye have an interpretation, as given by the Sadducees, 'There is no resurrection' or 'There is no reincarnation'—which is what the statement meant in those periods.

"In the lead of these reasons were those changes . . . from the position of the stars . . . that stand, as it were, at the dividing of the ways between the universal vision of the solar system and those from outside the spheres. The North Star in its variation made for those cycles, and this began the preparation for the three hundred years, as has been given. Then in these signs was the new cycle which was . . . the beginning of the Piscean Age—of the position of the Polar or North Star, as related to the southern clouds . . .

"These, then, were the beginnings. Then there was the prophecy of old which had been handed down from the experiences of the sages of old—that an angel was to speak. When this occurred at the choosing of the maiden who (as known only by those close to her) had been immaculately conceived, the preparation of the Mother was brought to a focal point."

"In the Faith of the Fathers"

"Much might be given as to the how, why, and when of the purposes that brought about the materialization of Jesus in the flesh.

"In giving then, the history: There were those in the faith of the fathers to whom the promises had been given that they would be fulfilled as from the beginning of man's record.

"Hence there was a continued preparation and dedication of those who might be the channels through which this chosen vessel might enter—through choice—into materiality.

"Thus in Carmel, where there were the priests of this faith, there were the maidens chosen who were dedicated to this purpose, this office, this service. Among them was Mary, the beloved, the chosen one; and she, as had been foretold, was chosen as the channel. Thus she was separated and kept in closer associations with and in the care of this office.

"That was the beginning, that was the foundation of what ye term the Church.

"Then, when the days were fulfilled that the prophecy might come that had been given by Isaiah, Malachi, Joel, and those of old, she, Mary, espoused to Joseph, a chosen vessel for the office among those of the priests, the sect or group who had separated and dedicated themselves in body, in mind, in spirit for this coming—became with child."

Jesus' Childhood and Training

"There was a period of purification according to the law, then the days in the temple and the blessing by Anna and by the high priest. And these constituted the early days of the beginning of the entity called Jesus, who becomes the Christ, the Master of Masters. During this period there was the return to Nazareth and then the edict that sent them into Egypt so that the prophecy might be fulfilled, 'My son shall be called from Egypt.'

"There five years were spent, as you term time, by the mother, Joseph and the child. Then there was the return to Judea and to Capernaum, where dwelt many of those who later were the closer companions of the Master.

"Here, after the period again of presentation at the temple, when there were certain questionings among the leaders, the Entity was sent first—again—into Egypt for only a short period, and then into India, and then into what is now Persia.

"Hence, the Entity was trained in all the ways of the various teachers.

"From Persia He was called to Judea at the death of Joseph, and then into Egypt for the completion of His preparation as a teacher. He was with John, the messenger, during a portion of His training there in Egypt.

"Then He returned to Capernaum, Cana, and there came the periods of first preparation, in the land of His nativity.

"The rest ye have according to Mark, John, Matthew and Luke; these in their order record most of the material experiences of the Master.

"Many details may be given as to the varied fields of preparation, but these were the main experiences."

Jesus' first teacher, Josie, was Mary's handmaid. Mary and Josie knew the Mosaic law and the Prophets, as well as the mysteries of astrology. They were by no means ignorant of the culture of their world and they taught the Boy entrusted to their care until He was twelve, when He was sent to the prophetess, Judy. This woman taught Him "the prophecies" and at sixteen He was sent to Persia and then to India. After that, He went to Egypt to be taught by the temple priests.

The myriad of data given for the people who had experiences in Palestine would be too much to present here, but the quotations given here afford some glimpses into the wealth of material that one day should be compared with the Dead Sea Scrolls.

The prophetess Judy figures large in the Cayce panorama of events surrounding the life of the Master, because her influence did not end with her guiding Jesus' education, but continued throughout long years following His death, among the Essenes and the early Christians. Perhaps her records are among the Scrolls, for she not only helped to shape events, but she recorded them, as well. These records were studied first at Carmel, then by the other Christian communities, including Antioch, Jerusalem, Smyrna, and Philadelphia (Amman).

Bible Land Prophecies

Tombs of Theresa and Herod the Great

One woman was told she had been Theresa, the Roman Queen of Palestine, wife of Herod the Great. She lived from 28 B.C. to 6 A.D.

In 1940 she asked, "Can I find my name Theresa written in any history?"

Said Edgar Cayce: "Best to find it written in the tablets in the burial places about Jerusalem. There it will be found, as with The Great."

She was writing then a book as yet unpublished on the Palestine Period, drawn to this because as Theresa she had been sympathetic to the Essenes and secretly had helped their cause. In that life she was murdered after the death of her husband, upon his previous orders.

She now asked Cayce, "What should be the title, purpose, and general outline of this book on the Palestinian Period?"

"The Dawn of a New Day (or Era): the needs of the world for the new message, which is in keeping with the needs in the present—as then. There was the looking forward to the coming of the Prince of Peace, the new era. These are before you, even as then. These presentations would make same timely."

Nor have the tombs of Herod and Theresa yet been found. Now that the Israelis again control Jerusalem, perhaps they will attempt the archeological excavation that will lead to this important find.

An Essene bishop evidently traveled as far as Chaldea to establish a church. According to a reading about him, documents bearing his sermons will be found near Ur of the Chaldees.

A young girl of twenty-one was told that she should wear a replica of King David's seal, and she asked where she could find such an article.

She had psychic powers, Cayce told her, so that it would be easy for her to make a seal that would be correct in design. The original "will one day be uncovered in Jerusalem" and "could be duplicated in either ivory, coral, or gold."

This is another discovery which will create great excitement and will be of great meaning to both Christians and Jews.

More records will be found in Iran, or Persia, following excavations which will uncover stores and records which were put there by one Artial. This prediction was given in 1927. Another prediction states that in the Arabian desert, near Shuster, lie the ruins of a city that will soon be discovered. Among the temple ruins will be "the dressings for the altar—or as would be called the accoutrements of the altar service that was carried on there."

When this city existed and when it will be discovered were not given. One reference to this was given August 7, 1926.

And then there was the lady who was told that her vase had just turned up in Ur after 12,500 years! Cayce said that in recent excavations in old Ur, where she had lived from 10,500 to 10,420 B.C., there was a vase "where there is the piper, with the drawing of the chariot" that had been among her own possessions. "It's blue in color," he added.

Africa

Far to the south of Egypt, where the Nile has its beginnings, is Ethiopia, a mountainous plateau with peaks ranging to fifteen thousand feet in height. The emperor of this ancient land boasts that he descends from Solomon and the Queen of Sheba. These people have been isolated from the world by their mountains until the 1930's and archeology reportedly has not yet come upon the hieroglyphics which Edgar Cayce says are there: ". . . There still may be seen in some of the mountain fastnesses of that land, particularly in the Upper Nile where there were those activities in the mountains, the images of the entity that are often worshipped . . . [and] the entrance to the tombs there.

"Then the name was Ai-Ellain and the hieroglyphics will be found to be marked as these: The Ibex (the bird of same), the hornheaded man, the Ibex turned in the opposite direction, the sacred bull of Ipis [?], the hooded man as of the Ethiopian people, the cross, the serpent (upright), the staff with the symbol (that should be the symbol of the entity through its experience) as the B's turned towards each other . . . or one upright with two loops on either side of same, with the serpent head two ways from the top of same . . ."

Such a discovery, were it to take place, would link Egypt with Ethiopia by inscriptions, images, and tombs, as well as by the ever-constant Nile.

Opposite Ethiopia on the African map is the little country of Liberia on the west coast. It was founded for Negro slaves—escaped refugees from the United States in 1822—and is covered by tropical rain forests which repel travel. In the southernmost part, says Cayce, is "a city upon top of the city" and much may be found of a school established there by another refugee, of another time: one in exile from Egypt at the time of Atlantis!

This school taught the "ideal relationships between individuals," and its leader disseminated "the tenets and laws in many lands."

In this city may be found the name *Cubri,* the man's name in that life, according to Cayce.

CHAPTER 12

THE PRISM

"ALL POWER IS from one Source: God." Edgar Cayce thus put on an equal basis the laws that govern material science with those that govern spiritual realities. In this orderly universe, everything has its place and its function. The same God which says "Love is law . . . law is love" on the spiritual level, tells us "Matter doesn't change in chemical transformation" on the scientific level.

Cayce used the example of a prism separating the rays of light. The various colors thrown out are like the various aspects of the universal laws, but all from the same source. These laws become manifest in our material world as we develop our sciences and gain knowledge of their existence.

"All such laws," he predicted, "as man develops, will come to the use and benefit of man, there being many illustrations in the present age."

That was January, 1925.

Cayce described the use of these laws by the Atlanteans and said that they were being rediscovered. From this same fundamental Source are derived the laws described in the chapter "Destiny and the Law." It was because the Atlanteans abused these that they were doomed. This age is subject to the same rules because they are eternal.

Some of the important scientific discoveries based on these eternal principles, said Cayce, would be those which have since been recognized by students of the readings as the laser, solar power, hydroelectric power, electromagnetic power, infrasound (see p. 106).

Cayce also described techniques of healing which sometimes had nothing to do with medicine or surgery and are so simple and mild as to make us doubt their effectiveness. His many physical readings reflected, not one limited approach to healing, but all agencies within the powers of man to employ. Healing by electrotherapy, healing by light, infrared-rays, shortwave, physiotherapy, diet, vitamins, packs, oil rubs, poultices, osteopathy, were what worked for his patients, and in this they were predictive of what modern medicine will hopefully acknowledge in the future.

Surgery was often bypassed in his suggested treatments, in favor of these other techniques. They were prescribed, too, as preventive measures, for the saying that "Prevention is better than cure" was an underlying philosophy. Cayce was, however, quick to suggest surgery when it was really needed.

The Physiotherapy Research Division

The clear-eyed, ruddy-faced man stood on a slope of the hill outside the A.R.E. headquarters building and vigorously led a breathless group of young people through a stretching exercise.

"Hands above heads—good!" Silently, the motley collection of "athletes" followed through.

"Circular motion with your body . . . now bend forward. Breathe in and through the nostrils, as you rise on your toes. That's right! Now breathe deeply!"

He paused; they breathed.

"Exhale quickly through your mouth, not through your nose . . ."

Sounds of exhalation nobly accomplished.

It was a recent summer day and a lot had happened since Dr. Harold J. Reilly first heard of a Cayce reading. That had been forty years ago, when physiotherapy was young. Reilly is founder and head of the Reilly Health Service, Rockefeller Center, New York. He has worked in the field of physiotherapy and drugless therapy since 1916.

He first heard of Cayce when a patient of the latter was referred to him. He has been working with the Cayce suggestions ever since, and has lectured on them many times to audiences in many cities.

In the summer of 1967 the Edgar Cayce Foundation announced the formation of a Physiotherapy Research Division with Dr. Reilly as director. He has donated to the Foundation specialized equipment used by the Health Service. With the equipment, students are being trained in the Cayce-Reilly methods at the clinic set up in the basement of the headquarters at Virginia Beach.

The Cayce-Reilly methods include exercise, manipulation, hydrotherapy, and application of light, heat, electricity. Later, these kinds of therapy will be researched with members of the Association.

Dr. Reilly is a trustee of the Edgar Cayce Foundation and the author of two books, *The Secret of Better Health* and *Easy Does It.* In a *Searchlight* article once, he described the progress physiotherapy has made since it was discovered fifty years ago.

This healing art was developed by the Army during World War II, Reilly explains, when many boys back from the battlefields needed whatever help they could get.

Amazingly predictive in respect to this field is the fact that the therapies now in use were described by Cayce in detail forty years ago! "There was no chance at that time (1924-1929) of Edgar Cayce's having been familiar with these types of physiotherapy, yet he gave readings containing electrotherapy, short wave, and ultra short wave," he states.

"Even now I can take the latest findings in the field of physiotherapy and

compare them with readings given forty years ago and I assure you the
readings do not come out second best! For instance, a famous Russian scientist and several of the other experts on longevity and geriatrics have said that
the average age of man should be about 140 years. In one of the Cayce
readings, a question was asked about old age. The answer was that if the
person lived properly, ate properly, didn't worry too much and kept an optimistic outlook on life, he could live to be 120 years of age.

"So the facts that we continually get from scientific sources, and facts given
in the readings, can more and more often be reconciled."

The Medical Research Division

Another man who is working with the Edgar Cayce Foundation to further
its research in healing is William A. McGarey, M.D., who, as head of the
Foundation's Medical Research Division, Phoenix, Arizona, spent six weeks
during the summer of 1967 in this endeavor. He conducted a study of the
research program and, on the basis of his work over the past ten years with
the readings, sent a letter to interested physicians throughout the country to
enlist their cooperation in the use of the concepts in the readings.

"The medical concepts and treatments contained in many thousands of the
Edgar Cayce readings have frequently proved to be remarkably effective,"
writes Dr. McGarey in this letter. "This has led to a demand reflected in
scores of the letters received at the Headquarters of the Association for Research and Enlightenment, Inc., for advice and help in receiving aid of a
medical nature embodying the knowledge imparted through the Edgar Cayce
readings."

He requests physicians to accept as patients those A.R.E. members seeking
help from the readings. The Foundation will furnish data from the readings
as it is requested by member patients.

In conversation with Dr. McGarey this summer, I asked him why the
medical profession has been so slow to research such healing agencies as
suggested in the Cayce data.

"A scientist, it seems to me, either accepts the reality of God or rejects it,"
he said. "The scientist who rejects the reality of a creative God cannot come
to a satisfactory understanding of the energies as they are existent. He may
measure the energies, but this is like taking measurement of a house and
never taking consideration of the materials, the people who built it, the architect who makes the plans."

I asked him about appliances for healing by electric current.

He pointed out that there has been in the past a sporadic, insignificant
interest in the healing properties of electric currents. He feels that the use of
this principle—low-voltage electrical impulses which are sent through the
body—is a legitimate means of healing.

"It's described in a book by L.E. Eeman—the only other authority I have
seen about it," he told me.

I looked up the book—*Cooperative Healing* by Eeman, published in 1947 in

England. It tells of "experiments which can be repeated at will and of facts which can be controlled and measured by instruments." Basically, it seems to describe experiments using electrical current for healing.

In France, Russia, and Japan, electrical current is sweeping the population! According to a report in the November, 1967 issue of the *Ladies' Home Journal,* no one in those countries is waiting for science to research this method of healing. The people there are going ahead and using it, not for the entire body, just the head.

Bob Gaines states in his feature "You and Your Sleep"*(Ladies' Home Journal,* Nov. 1967), "In France and Japan, insomniacs drop into local drugstores to pick up tiny, transistorized gadgets with electrodes that send a mild electric current through their heads. In the Soviet Union, there are 300 'sleep stations,' where patients in beds are plugged into a communal electrical outlet. It's not electrocution, it's electrosleep—and it's becoming the rage of Europe. Partisans claim it can produce the equivalent of a night's sleep in two hours and can cure everything from schizophrenia to ulcers. Somehow, the small current is supposed to cause a beneficial electrical discharge from the brain. The Russians claim seventy-five percent of all patients at the sleep stations rest better after treatment.

"American sleep researchers are uncertain. Our foremost electrosleep authority is Dr. Sigmund Forster of Maimonides Hospital in New York City. Forster's objection is that no one knows what happens when current goes through the brain. 'It could easily be the power of suggestion that makes people sleep when the machine's on.'

"At the moment, no one in the U.S. is using electrosleep equipment for anything other than experiments. You'll probably have to fly to Moscow if you want to get *really* charged up for the night."

As a key to understanding this form of healing, the following reading is important, though not among the material relegated to physical healing techniques. It is, in fact, from a reading on "psychic healing," an entirely separate field covered at length in the readings, yet containing basic ideas related to electric current healing.

"Each atomic force of a physical body is made up of its units of positive and negative forces, that brings it into a *material* plane. These are of the ether, or atomic forces, being electrical in nature. . . ."

Is this a clue as to how electric current could heal the body?

Like so many other suggestions of a unique nature in these files, this has a predictive quality. The report that "electrosleep" is the rage in Europe, claiming cures for "everything from schizophrenia to ulcers" surely seems to be a fulfillment of this particular suggestion.

What is Healing?

No healing, said Cayce, is perfected without some psychic force exerted.

In the reading in which he said the body was made up of electrical, atomic units, Cayce said further that Jesus while on earth only used the "universal law," which implies that he made this manifest "in the last overcoming even the disintegration of the spirit and soul from the physical or corporal body. . . ."

So Jesus was "able to force all law to become subjugated (by His will) to the body, or, as shown in the electrical forces as used by man." He demonstrated for us that "the body is only atoms in motion and was able to heal others (to raise the dead) to raise Himself after death, and to become proof thereby that physical and spiritual laws emanate from the one Source."

This is applicable to more than psychic healing. The entire man is involved in his well-being—his emotions, his attitudes, even his purpose in life. Doctors in recent years have become aware not only of the physical nature of healing, but of the many other aspects, including marital, vocational and social problems, which create the total health picture. Cayce predicted this, for he said that one's emotions could make him sick or well. Moreover, he advised that the person caring for an ill person should be one who "exerted psychic force" by prayer, and a loving and sympathetic rapport with his patient, for the best healing results.

Immunity to the Law?

Sometimes, in working with the laws of which Cayce spoke, people close to the readings became puzzled because they still didn't understand that the laws work on various levels. As was pointed out, the laws are of the same Source, but they operate true to their function, and within the realm they govern.

But when it comes to the matter of praying for others, isn't one immune to physical ailments, protected and guarded by one's love for others?

"Why should one develop organic trouble while praying for his fellow man?" asked one person, herself suffering perhaps from a disability, and dismayed that this should happen in spite of her sincere prayer life.

"A natural consequence of being in organic matter," answered Cayce. "There are laws in organic influences that are seen through the natural chemical reaction, and those that pertain to the natural forces or environs; for under whatever environ an individual is, it is subject to the laws of that!"

This is a very important key, we believe, in separating the laws as to their various levels, for a better understanding of them. We are in a physical environment and a physical body which needs physical care, and we are subject to the laws of that body. That we work in the spiritual realm, also, using the laws of prayer and meditation, does not necessarily mean we are freed from the physical laws, themselves divine, after all! The approach to physical laws in the Cayce readings is a step up in our human concept of spirituality, for it holds that all laws are divine.

The only law that does intervene for us, in our karmic pattern, is the Law of Grace, and in this, all may be forgiven, even as we forgive, and we may be absolved from our debts because Christ died for us.

But otherwise, the laws are strict and operate without change—or they would not be divine laws!

How good it is to know that they do work, as demonstrated for us in the physical world plainly enough! From this, we can learn to respect the spiritual laws and to realize that they are not to be broken, but are to be understood and lived by, for the good of all.

Research

Research to a limited degree has been done on the Edgar Cayce readings, on such diverse subjects as epilepsy, the use of castor oil packs, multiple sclerosis, the use of Glycothymoline, pyorrhea and leukemia, says Dr. McGarey. Many doctors have reported favorably on cases brought to Cayce. In recent years, a medical doctor studied all the readings on four different diseases—multiple sclerosis, pyorrhea, leukemia, and epilepsy—and evaluated them for future researchers. The readings had given unorthodox and unheard-of suggestions for treatment, and so, also, these treatments might be considered prophetic.

There are many uses for the laser, as all are aware. Scientists—including Edgar Evans Cayce, Edgar Cayce's second son—understand this to be the same instrument described in the readings as "The Great Crystal," which the Atlanteans used for many purposes. While this could be used for destructive purposes such as "death rays," it could also be used for healing and regenerating the body. In the A.R.E. *Journal,* July, 1967, is the following: "An article entitled 'Laser—the Light Fantastic' by Thomas Meloy in the April, 1967 *Reader's Digest* tells of the recent development of this device, which emits beams of light so intensely concentrated that they can pierce steel. Many uses and possible uses are discussed, including adaptation for surgery. Already eye surgeons are using the laser photocoagulator to repair torn retinas and so ward off detached retinas and resulting blindness. In the laser laboratories of the University of Cincinnati and Children's Hospital in Cincinnati, Dr. Leon Goldman is experimenting with burning off from the skin, blemishes and tumors of a certain kind. Melanomas or cancerous black splotches have turned to healthy white skin tissue in areas touched by the laser beams."

The Cayce readings state: "About the first one (the Great Crystal) . . . It would be well that there be given something of a description of this, that it may be understood . . . how both constructive and destructive forces were generated by the activity of this stone. . . .

"The concentration through the prisms or glass . . . was in such manner that it acted upon the instruments that were connected with the various modes of travel . . . Through the same form of fire the bodies of individuals were regenerated, by the burning—through the application of the rays from the stone, the influence that brought destructive forces to an animal organism. Hence the body rejuvenated itself often. . . ."

The glands, which had been greatly ignored in medical research, have in the past several years become recognized as important in our immunization against bacteria and viruses. This is *not* new, in the Cayce story, for he had much to say about the glands and their function. He said that every organ in the body, in fact, might be termed a gland, but that there are seven centers, or glands, which work together in a healthy body in an intricate way.

In answer to the question, "What relations do the vitamins bear to the glands? Give specific vitamins affecting specific glands," Cayce replied:

"You want a book written on these! They, the vitamins, are food for same. Vitamins are that from which the glands take those necessary influences to supply the energies to enable the varied organs of the body to reproduce themselves. Would it ever be considered that your toenails would be reproduced by the same gland as would supply the breast, the head, or the face? Or that the cuticle would be supplied from the same source as would supply the organ of the heart itself? These [building substances] are taken from glands that control the assimilated foods, and hence require the necessary elements or vitamins in same to supply the various forces for enabling each organ, each functioning of the body, to carry on its creative or generative forces, see?"

Researchers at Wayne State University in Detroit found in 1966 that globulin from a rabbit linked by an organic chemical to cancer cells from a patient, when injected back into the same patient caused antibodies to be developed in his body to fight the cancer!

But back in 1926, a man suffering from cancer was prescribed a highly predictive treatment, for it was that he be injected with the same kind of rabbit serum! "There may be prepared a serum from the infusion from the pus of this body injected into the rabbit," said Cayce, "between the shoulders, and when this brings the infection, this injected or placed on the sore will heal, see? or the culture of same may be made and injected in the blood of this body."

Technological Predictions Infrasound

The chic secretary in the French National Center for Scientific Research in Marseilles rested her head on her desk. She felt sick, and her pale face looked it.

Soon others on the staff complained. They were nauseated and held their heads in pain. The aspirin bottle was passed around.

What had started as a fine spring day had become a nightmare in which everyone in the building was seized by a mysterious malady.

Investigations revealed that it was not electromagnetic waves, nor was it ultrasound waves, which the laboratory had been researching for eighteen years.

"At this point" states a report special to the *Virginian Pilot,* April 28, 1967, "one of the technicians got out an antique apparatus for detecting infrasound; that is, air vibrations which oscillate at less than ten vibrations a second, or 10 hertz. (The human ear registers, as sound, vibrations from 16 per second, or 16 hertz, to 20,000 hertz.)

"It quickly identified the source of the unease: the giant ventilator of the factory next door. After changing the ventilator's frequency, the five-man team, headed by Prof. Vladimir Gavreau, decided to find out more about the properties of infrasound."

The article goes on to say that "fast sound vibrations go through or bounce off solid objects, usually doing relatively little harm even when very powerful. But slow air vibrations, below the hearing level, can create a sort of pendulum action, a reverberation in solid objects that quickly builds up to intolerable intensity."

To study this phenomenon, the team built a giant whistle and hooked it to a compressed air hose. Then they turned on the air.

"That first test nearly cost us all our lives," Professor Gavreau says. "Luckily, we were able to turn it off fast. All of us were sick for hours. Everything in us was vibrating—stomach, heart, lungs. All the people in the other laboratories were sick. They were very angry with us."

This vibration caused "an irritation so intense that for hours afterwards any low-pitched sound seems to echo through one's body."

"In developing a military weapon, the scientists intend to revert to the policeman's whistle form, perhaps as big as eighteen feet across, mount it on a truck, and blow it with a fan turned by a small airplane engine. It could kill a man five miles away.

"There is one snag. At present, the machine is as dangerous to its operators as it is to the enemy."

This use of "infrasound" to destroy or sicken the enemy seems to have been what was meant by a reading Edgar Cayce gave on September 10, 1936, for Muzuen of Taoi, in the Gobi Desert, 10,000 B.C.:

"As to the manner of defense and offense, as has been indicated, much that is yet to be found again was a part of those preparations in those periods. For these . . . had to do with the setting of long period [slow frequency?] drums for defense in which there might be any attempts by others to interfere, to cause their own undoing."

Whether produced by a whistle or a drum, infrasound seems to be extremely effective!

Electromagnetic Power

The "submarine" looked like a child's toy—only ten feet long, approximately eighteen inches in diameter, it weighed only nine hundred pounds. It was pretty, sleek, white, and of course, unmanned. It had no propellers or jets!

The group of engineers, including senior mechanical engineering students from the University of California at Santa Barbara, who had helped to construct the craft, slowly set it down in the ocean at Guleta by means of hoists. The model was launched and after final balance adjustment, the switch was closed and acceleration began immediately. It moved through the water "at better than design speed" or at 1.5 knots, according to a report by S. Way, consultant for Westinghouse Electric Corporation Research and Development Center.

Now the submarine ploughed along parallel to the shore, turned, came back, and then circled for about twelve minutes. Then it was hauled in and given an inspection and battery check.

And that's how it was launched on July 21, 1966, the world's first submarine—since Atlantis, anyway—powered by "those forces in nature as make for iron to swim."

Or, as science has discovered, by electromagnetic forces.

This type of sub could operate just as well in large sizes, says Mr. Way. Such a craft might be considered as an effective cargo carrier.

But the story of the electromagnetic submarine actually started some years ago, when "there was an awakening of interest in the idea of electromagnetic propulsion *in about the year 1958.*" (Author's italics.)

So?

"How was this particular Great Pyramid of Gizeh built?" was asked, we will recall, in 1932.

"By the use of those forces in nature as make for iron to swim," said Cayce. "Stone floats in the air in the same manner. This will be discovered in 1958."

A preliminary memorandum on the subject describing Mr. Way's own examination of electromagnetic propulsion was sent to our geologist friend, who relayed his whole story to us. It was dated October 15, 1958! And this was, he stated, its beginning—when memoranda and seminars were presented at the Westinghouse Laboratories dealing with this kind of submarine propulsion.

Hydroelectric Power

The suggestion in 1926 to set up at Bimini a hydroelectric power plant "in the waves . . . by the tides, such as built in the Bay of Fundy" has gone untried. But in 1967 has come the report that a lighthouse in Tokyo Bay has been successfully operated by electricity generated by wave action.

This is Hikajima Lighthouse, and the operation was for a trial thirty day period. The lighthouse, unmanned, is perched on a ledge of rock in the rough surf. The waves flow in, creating air pressure in the tube which is carried through the pipe to an air turbine generator that charges the batteries which operate the light.

The Japanese intend to build a number of these if this one continues operable.

Laser-Operated Space Ship?

On July 2, 1966, *Nature* Magazine carried an article by Professor G. Marx on the possibility some day of space travel powered by laser beams! The author says it would solve the problem of speed, but slowing down the vehicle

neutralizing Gravity

upon landing on another planet would be difficult—unless we could radio the planet to let them know we were on the way! Then, after traveling at 0-99c among the stars, the ship could be slowed down by the planet toward which it was headed. The home journey could be made in the same way.

Professor Marx suggests that the difficulty in landing without Earth's technological cooperation probably explains why we haven't been invaded by extraterrestrials so far.

Cayce definitely reported Atlantean travel in craft that "soared through the ether." One such reference was for a man who in 1927 said that at various times during the past six years he had dreamed of an airship heavier than air, which collected its lifting and driving force from the atmosphere by means of *points* on top of it.

"Underneath this machine there are apparently two heavy copper bars running the length of it, having small points underneath which, when charged with the force, lifts the machine from the air, apparently neutralizing the force of gravity.

"The machine was driven by the power streaming from points attached to the rear.

"You will give the interpretation of this dream or vision, tell us if such a machine is practical, and if such a power is available, and how such may be made . . ."

Cayce told him that this was "emblematical" of the "higher forces" for spiritual, mental, and physical development. He would have the same dream three more times.

Then Cayce interpreted the dream on a material level, and said that "from the purely mechanical forces, these, as they are presented from time to time, will bring to the knowledge of this man that necessary to bring about the changes in mechanical appliance of that force known as the 'earth side' force as has been applied in eons ago to those crafts that soared through the ether."

Sound like a flying saucer? We think it does! This was twenty years before the first publicized reports of such things, and air travel was in its infancy.

Air Travel

In 1936, you traveled around "upstairs" in dirigibles. You could go to Europe and back that way, although planes were available. But for a number of years, air travel was very unsafe. "Barnstormers" accounted for the high statistics in fatalities, and accidents in general were numerous.

But Edgar Cayce predicted a brighter picture for air travel, and told one traveler: "Regular air travel will become more and more safe. More and more are . . . the airways to become the use of man. . . ."

"Air transportation will become more and more the basis of *all* relationships with other nations, countries, as well as the internal or national activity," he told another.

"No town or city or community off an airline will be in the thick of things," was another prediction in 1944. "It might as well be out of the world, almost!"

Thus Cayce recognized today's jet age. Today, it's safer to go by air than to drive an automobile. All kinds of safety equipment and safety practices have been provided to cut the hazards.

And although airlines have replaced train travel to a great degree, the railroads are still with us. Cayce had a word to say about that, too: "Railroads will never be entirely eliminated."

Importance of Radio

Although the air was to be the greater means of communication between nations, Cayce said then that radio and telegraph would both be developed as important fields, and that they "must eventually be one." In 1943 he said, "this radio field has only begun to occupy its place in the affairs of men . . ."

He was right. Radio in the form of television, which uses the radio sound system, is with us in a big way. Radio is used now in radio astronomy, in air travel, police communications, and still retains its usefulness as a medium of entertainment.

Electrolysis of Metals

To a man who had in an Egyptian incarnation worked with metals, he said, "Do not give up those ideas of some day experimenting—or this will bear fruition, and you will see it come to pass!"

"What specific experimental work should be done now?" the man asked.

"The combining of the metals in their crude state by the passing of current in the various forms through same, during the period of smelting same, see?" He added, "Copper and brass, gold and iron, through the combinations in their crude state, may be made to be much stronger in usage, lighter in the needs for present development, and not as expensive in the combinations."

The man to see about these possibilities would be Henry Ford, Cayce advised, "if he was approached right."

Electrochemistry has enabled modern industry to make use of this idea but whether or not Henry Ford was approached, in a right or a wrong way, was not given in the record!

Glass That Bends

And then, there was the prediction that it would be possible to make glass that would bend!

The A.R.E. *Journal,* July, 1967 [in *Science News,* Oct. 22, 1966], reports: "A three-page article on the subject of glass reminds us that it was first created when intensely hot volcanic materials flowed over sandy soil and fused this into a smooth, uncrystallized solid. Later, primitive man constructed glass beads as his first manufactured product. Today the making of glass is approached from many angles so that different kinds may answer the varied needs arising in a technological world. The Corning Glass Works has developed a product which is five times stronger than ordinary glass due to a special chemical treatment known as Chemcor. This glass can be bent and twisted without breaking and is especially useful for back windows of sports cars. The Pittsburgh Plate Glass Co. has evolved a method by which chemical tempering replaces heating and quenching. An ion exchange takes place in the glass, bringing greater strength. It can be made very thin and even bent around corners to give streamlined effects without impairment of its toughness."

From the Edgar Cayce readings, the *"World News Spotlight"* report continues: "April 13, 1926. As to what as may be applied in malleable, or in glass that will bend, as is seen and known, the same manner, the same way, of making glass . . . from the elements of the earth's storehouse, is in all practical applications the same as was used twenty-five hundred—yes, forty-five hundred years ago . . . yet there may be still applied those physical elements, now known to man's consciousness, to produce such an element that will act in the place of . . . glass. This, too, however, necessitates the more perfect consciousness of those elements that go to make up flexibility of that called hardened or crystallized substances; for . . . there is no element in the physical plane with the present elasticity of that called glass—that is, a piece, strip of glass, bent in a manner, after becoming crystallized, bended to that point of not breaking, but of its own flexibility, no matter how long same may be kept in that position, the moment it is released, it retains the first or former place or condition. No other element will do such. Hence, as there is seen then, necessary that a greater consciousness of that called crystallization of substances as are known in the make of glass, be gained; though, with study, with a higher concept, a more perfect concept of same, this may become possible."

Remember the glass houses in Edgar Cayce's dream of the twenty-first century? Do you suppose this will be the natural development from this new discovery? Very likely!

It is not possible here to review all the scientific developments in the Cayce files without a thorough knowledge of science. The many uses now being found for the laser, for instance, were foreshadowed in the Atlantean device, the "firestone" or Great Crystal, which we described in "Atlantis Rising?"

Healing Sound

That infrasound has the power to kill has been demonstrated. But sound has its happier use, as well.

Just as the laser may be used for destruction or for healing, so, too, can

Deafness

sound. It is the low-frequency vibrations which are destructive, and which, when produced by an instrument, can kill a man five miles away.

But Cayce had much to say in other readings concerning the use of healing vibrations for people who are both physically and mentally ill, and even for deafness!

Certain kinds of music are more desirable for healing than others. Cayce told several deaf persons, including a child, to listen to music, even though they might not hear it. How would it help? By the vibrations, Such persons should even be encouraged to play an instrument, so as to be healed by the music's resonance.

The most helpful kind of music he said, would be Mendelssohn's "Spring Song," "The Blue Danube," and similar classical and light airs.

"Have you considered the great artist as a pianist who accomplished his greater works when little or no hearing was available of a physical nature?" Cayce reminded one suffering from deafness. "As to how the inner sense was attuned to the infinite?" This, of course, was Beethoven.

Today, many doctors' offices have music piped in to soothe their patients, and music is, in fact, heard in more and more commercial places, including supermarkets, to soothe the customers' pocketbooks!

CHAPTER 13

THE PRISM TURNS

EDGAR CAYCE DID not try to convince anyone about God, or to set up a cult. Members of the Association have realized this and tried to show that the A.R.E. was a "research organization" rather than a religion. And yet, many people think of it as a form of religion.

This is because many religious ideas have come out of the readings, and are couched in the context of Christian principles. What has emerged has been a much broader understanding of what Christianity is: that although *not* at variance with other religions, it is, after all, the ideal, the most complete faith and the one which is the future religion for the world.

It seems a paradox that the readings present Christianity in this way, until we see what they have to say regarding our relationship to God, and what evolution is all about. Thinking in these terms, considering evolution's span over ages of time, and trying to imagine what we will be like eons from now, the differences between religions seem to dwindle.

"So we see that the coming into earth is—and has ever been—for the soul's evolution," said Cayce, "unto its awareness that there are effects of all influences, in all its experiences, in all its varied spheres of activity. Yet only in Him, the creator and maker who experienced mortality, spirit, and soul, could all this be overcome. For has it not been said and shown . . . that He has not willed any should be lost?"

SETH

He went on to say that His Spirit has been in the leaders of all religions and "in every race and color." In another reading he states that the Christ "as an entity influenced either directly or indirectly all those forms of philosophy or religious thought that taught God was One" such as "Buddhism, Muhammedanism, Confucianism, Shintoism, Brahmanism, Platonism, Judaism."

Religion in the Cayce records cannot be confined to limited boundaries. It runs throughout every reading, whether physical, mental, or spiritual, whether on science or sociology, for all ages, for people of all faiths. There is an underlying truth which is consistent, and which cuts across all manmade lines.

In 1931, Cayce predicted that one woman would live to see "the greatest development in spiritual affairs that the world has known." In the thirty-seven years since that time, has the world developed spiritually? Memories of personal experience and of what has happened to the world during that time would probably make most people answer *No!* After all these years, on the eve of upheavals in the earth we don't quite believe will be possible, and amid the very real upheavals going on in our cities and among the best and the worst of us, the answer seems to be the slogan "God is dead!"

But even science is not quite convinced of this idea, as Dr. A. K. Reischauer points out in *The Nature and Truth of the Great Religions*. He states: "The older materialistic and mechanistic cosmologies are no longer intellectually respectable. To be sure, the concept of mechanism will continue to function for certain aspects of the physical cosmos, but to accept it as adequate for reality on all its levels or for reality as a whole is regarded as naively childish."

"Mind is the Builder," said Cayce many times, explaining how a life, a concept, a nation, a world is created. Never did he say that the universe is a mechanical toy operating mindlessly and without the concern of a Creator out there!

Dr. Reischauer quotes a passage from *The Mysterious Universe* by Sir James H. Jeans, one of the greatest astronomers and physicists of modern times, that confirms what Cayce has said all along about the Mind of the Universe: "Today there is a wide measure of agreement, which on the physical side of science approaches almost to unanimity, that the stream of knowledge is leading towards a non-mechanical reality; the universe begins to look *SETH* more like a great thought than like a great machine. Mind no longer appears as an accidental intruder into the realm of matter; we are beginning to suspect that we ought rather to hail it as the creator and governor of the realm of matter. . . .

"The new knowledge compels us to revive our hasty first impressions that we had stumbled into a universe which either did not concern itself with life or was entirely hostile to life. The old dualism of mind and matter, which was mainly responsible for the supposed hostility, seems likely to disappear; not through matter becoming in any way more shadowy or insubstantial than heretofore, or through mind becoming resolved into a function of the working of matter, but through substantial matter resolving itself into a creation and manifestation of mind. We discover that the universe shows evidence of a designing or controlling power that has something in common with our own individual minds—not, so far as we have discovered, emotion, morality, or aesthetic appreciation, but the tendency to think in the way which, for want of a better word, we describe as Mathematical. . . .

"It is, in fact, most striking," Dr. Reischauer continues, "how many modern scientists and philosophers give recognition to the mental and spiritual aspect of the physical cosmos. It is as Eddington puts it when he says rather whimsically, 'There *is* an external world . . . But I think there can be no doubt that the scientist has a much more mystical conception of the external world than he had in the last century where every scientific "explanation" of phenomena proceeded on the assumption that nothing could be true unless an engineer could make a model of it.' "

This kind of thinking is bound to filter down from the Olympian heights to the common man! Thus, the old materialism seems to be giving way to a fulfillment of Cayce's prophecy of "the greatest development in spiritual affairs the world has ever known."

The reforms that have been going on, both in the Roman Catholic Church and in the Protestant churches, as the result of self-criticism and a general reassessment of their role in today's changing world, are another part of the prophecy come true. Who can say fully what is going on in the spiritual world, or who is the final authority? We observe these movements from a limited vantage point, and do not attempt to evaluate their meaning. We can only point out what seems to have been meant by Cayce's prediction.

At a time in which every churchgoer, every college and high school student, is dismayed and intimidated by the conflict between science and religion that still is felt, crippling the layman's ability to accept the Bible's great truth, and yet undermining our understanding of what science's ultimate gift to mankind is, we are refreshed by such statements made by scientists for the general masses as acknowledge the existence of God.

Such a statement is the following by Dr. Wernher von Braun, director of NASA's Marshall Space Flight Center in Huntsville, Ala., from an article in the *Tampa Tribune,* July 30, 1966 (quoted by permission of the North American Newspaper Alliance): "The two most powerful forces shaping our civilization today are science and religion. Through science, man strives to learn more of the mysteries of creation. Through religion, he seeks to know the Creator.

"Neither operates independently. It is as difficult for me to understand a scientist who does not acknowledge the presence of a superior rationality behind the existence of the universe as it is to comprehend a theologian who would deny the advances of science. . . .

"Today, thousands of scientists all over the world are engaged in the greatest intellectual adventure ever undertaken by man: Attempting to understand the origin and functioning of a physical universe that is vast in space and time, complicated in detail, and awesome in its orderliness.

"Thus, to say that science's only purpose is trying to discover physical laws to increase man's control over the forces of nature is no longer an adequate explanation of science's goal; for the concept of science itself has grown. The raw material of science is a set of experiences, observations, and measurements with which the scientist attempts to build a model of time, space, and matter. When new knowledge is discovered, the old model is not discarded; it is simply changed according to the pattern of relationships which the scientist finds in this set of experiences.

"By his willingness to change his model or his concepts, the scientist is admitting that he makes no claim to possessing ultimate truth.

"You cannot build a wall between science and religion. As science explains more of the intriguing mysteries of life and the universe, its realms expand into those areas which previously were either unknown or accepted solely by faith. Every experience we have—physical or spiritual—must fit together into a pattern that is credible and meaningful. Man is the observer of the universe, the experimenter, the searcher for truth, but he is not a spectator alone. He is a participant in the continuing process of creation. . . .

"In our modern world many people seem to feel that our rapid advances in the field of science render such things as religious beliefs untimely or old-fashioned. They wonder why we should be satisfied in 'believing' something when science tells us that we 'know' so many things. The simple answer to this contention is that we know many more mysteries of nature today than when the Age of Scientific Enlightenment began. There is certainly no scientific reason why God cannot retain the same position in our modern world that He held before we began probing His creation with telescope and cyclotron. . . .

"Our decisions undeniably influence the course of future events. Nature around us still harbors more unsolved than solved mysteries. But science has mastered enough of these forces to usher in a golden age for all mankind if this power is used for good—or to destroy us if evil triumphs. The ethical guidelines of religion are the bonds that can hold our civilization together. Without them man can never attain that cherished goal of lasting peace with himself, his God, and his fellow man."

As has been observed, religion is not confined to a special category in the Cayce readings and is hard to separate from the general picture of his prophecies. We have already pointed out that the spirituality of the American people would be the criterion for the peace of the world. We have had the shocking prediction that "out of Russia's religious development would come the hope of the world." We have the amazing forecast that China will one day be the "cradle of Christianity."

These, given in the chapter "Destiny of Nations," emphasize that the spirituality of a people shapes their destiny. It was the loss of religious ideals, we recall, which brought about the Atlantean catastrophe. Then to what religious thought will the world turn in the days ahead, to shape its future?

"That as is comprised in that as has been given, whether it be the Greek or the barbarian, whether it be from the bond or from the free, 'Thou shalt love the Lord thy God with all thine heart, and thy neighbor as thyself!' " said Cayce.

He stressed that religion was not a matter of belonging to a church but that "the church is within self." He advised that one should join a church, not for convenience, but "where ye may serve the better."

This understanding as to what true worship is was given us in John 4: 19-26: "The woman said to him, 'Sir, I perceive that you are a prophet. Our fathers worshiped on this mountain; and you say that in Jerusalem is the place where men ought to worship.' Jesus said to her, 'Woman, believe me, the hour is coming when neither on this mountain nor in Jerusalem will you worship the Father. You worship what you do not know; we worship what we know, for salvation is from the Jews. But the hour is coming, and now is, when the true worshipers will worship the Father in spirit and truth, for such the Father seeks to worship Him. God is spirit, and those who worship him must worship in spirit and truth.' The woman said to him, 'I know that Messiah is coming (he who is called Christ); when he comes, he will show us all things.' Jesus said to her, 'I who speak to you am he.' "

Someone asked Cayce, "Is there any indication of what church I should join and associate with?"

"Remember, rather, the church is within self," he answered. "As to the organization, choose that, not as a convenience for thee but where ye may serve the better . . . whatever its name, let it be thy life proclaiming Jesus the Christ."

"For the Master built no churches, but He laid the foundations." He told another person that the church was within, as he had learned in a former incarnation: "Before that, the entity was in the English land during those periods when questioning arose between church and state. And there the entity for itself settled that question for good: the church is within yourself and not in any pope or preacher, or in any building, but in self. For thy body is indeed the temple of the living God and the Christ becomes a personal companion in mind and in body . . ."

Individual preferences and temperaments should be considered, Cayce said, in choosing one's church. "Then let each test themselves with that chosen. That it will make for life in thine own experience will aid another. Not that each has the same vision, or the same experience, but the Lord addeth to the church daily such as should be saved, when all of one mind!"

Cayce interpreted Jesus' prophecy: "Upon this I will build my church." "What church? The Holy Church! Who is the head? That One upon whom the conditions had been set by that question asked. For here ye may find the answer again to many of those questions sought concerning the Spirit, the Church, the Holy Force that manifests by the attuning of the individual; though it may be for a moment.

"He asked, 'Whom say men that I am?' Then Peter answered, 'Thou art the Christ, the son of the living God!' Then, 'Upon this I will build my church and the gates of hell shall not prevail against it!' "

"The New Jerusalem"

"In Revelation 21, what is the meaning of the new heaven and the new earth; for the first heaven and the first earth were passed away and there were no more seas?"

This question was answered by Cayce as follows: "When the foundations of the earth are broken up by those very disturbances. Can the mind of man comprehend no desire of sin, no purpose but that the glory of the Son may be manifested in his life? Is this not a new heaven, a new earth? For the former things would have passed away. For as the desires, the purposes, the aims are to bring about the whole change physically, so does it create in the experience of each soul a new vision, a new comprehension.

"For, as has been given, it hath not entered the heart of man to know the glories that have been prepared, that are a part of the experiences of those that love only the Lord and His ways."

We recall that Jerusalem was the place of the Temple rebuilt for the Jews by Herod, where for two thousand years before Christ's Advent, the Jews had worshipped. Jerusalem has long been an important city to the nations, and to the Christians, Jews, Moslems, it has held a special significance.

An explanation of the following verse was then asked of Cayce: "And I saw the holy city, new Jerusalem, coming down out of heaven from God, prepared as a bride adorned for her husband, and I heard a great voice from the throne saying, 'Behold, the dwelling of God is with men. He will dwell with them, and they shall be his people, and God Himself will be with them: He will wipe away every tear from their eyes, and death shall be no more, neither shall there be mourning nor crying nor pain any more, for the former things are passed away." (Rev. 21:4)

Cayce explained, "[To] those then, that are come into the new life, the new understanding—the new regeneration, there *is* then the new Jerusalem—not as a place, alone, but as a condition, as an experience of the soul.

"Jerusalem has figuratively, symbolically, meant the holy place, the Holy City, for there the Ark of the Covenant—in the minds, the hearts, the understandings, the comprehensions of those who have put away the earthly desires and become as the *new* purposes in their experience, become the New Jerusalem, the new undertakings, the new desires."

Here we find echoed what Cayce described for the conditions of the New Age, and that it is both of the future, and, for those who are truly one with God's purpose, *now*. Jesus told the Samaritan woman that "the hour is coming, and now is, when the true worshippers will worship the Father in spirit and truth." Even then, the New Age had begun, and the New Jerusalem was present!

We remember that Cayce said that during this age many high-minded individuals are being incarnated on earth to assist in its culmination. Cayce was asked to explain this admonition: "Do not seal up the words of the prophecy of this book, for the time is near. Let the evildoer still do evil, and the filthy still be filthy, and the righteous still do right, and the holy still be holy. (Rev. 22: 10-11)

Cayce's interpretation: "As that period approaches when there shall be the influences of the power of those incarnated in the activities of the earth, then the purposes become set as in that indicated by the activities of each being in that to which they have then given themselves."

That we can use power either for good or for destruction is by now a familiar statement of the nature of man's full abilities. So great is man's power of free will, said Cayce, that he literally doesn't know his own strength!

This idea appears in a reading given in 1935. Cayce was asked, "Regarding general world conditions, is it likely that changes in the earth's surface in the Mediterranean area will stop Italy's campaign against Ethiopia?"

"Not at this particular period," was the answer. "Such changes may eventually be part of the earth's experience, but not just yet."

"When is this likely to occur?"

"As to times and places and seasons—as indeed has been indicated in the greater relationships established by prophets and sages of old—especially as given by Him: 'As to the day and hour, who knoweth? No one, save the Creative Forces.'

"Tendencies in the hearts and souls of men are such that these upheavals may be brought about. For as often indicated through these channels: Man is not ruled by the world, the earth, the environs about it, nor the planetary influences with their associations and activities. Rather it is true that man brings order out of chaos by his compliance with Divine Law. Or by his disregard of the laws of Divine influence, man brings chaos and destructive forces into his experience.

"For He hath given: 'Though the heavens and the earth pass away, my word shall not pass away.' This is often considered just a beautiful saying, or a thought to awe those who have been stirred by some experience. But let us apply these words to conditions existent in the affairs of the world and the universe at present. What holds them together—what are the foundations of the earth? The word of the Lord!"

In *The Dawn of Conscience* (New York: Scribners, 1933) James H. Breasted gives us an insight strangely parallel to the Cayce view of history and how man shapes it. At the time his book appeared, the world was still thinking in the old ways, so that his thoughts are all the more remarkable for their timeliness now. In his final chapter, "Power and Character," he says: "In Palestine this is indeed the supreme transformation, from Elijah to Jesus, from Carmel and Armageddon to Nazareth.

"But this culmination in Palestine was a later process, a fruition made possible by that far earlier transformation—what we have called the great transformation—which lifted man from the exclusive struggle with nature alone and shifted him into a new arena, the struggle with *himself* for the conquest of his own soul and those new values which transcend the material world and make up the substance of a new reality which we call character. We have seen that the forces which wrought this earlier transformation were born in Egypt and passed thence to Palestine and the later world. It was no merely accidental coincidence that Hebrew history should have traced Hebrew national origins back to Egypt, a tradition of which there is an echo in the Christian belief, 'Out of Egypt have I called my son.'

"Today in the lands of the ancient East we too look out upon the works of nature and the works of man, and in a New Crusade of scientific endeavor, we are striving to recover the story of both. But already we have discerned enough to realize that they are *one:* that the processes of nature and the unfolding life of man are but chapters of the same great story; that looking down into that appalling chasm of the Dead Sea which so terribly confronts us with Professor Haeckel's question (Is the universe friendly?), we may find an answer which natural science cannot give us—an answer which comes to us only as we contemplate human experience in the Ancient East and realize that the culmination of a developing universe is *character.*

"It has been the purpose of this book to furnish an historical demonstration that the process of human advance which brought forth character is still unfinished—is still going on. The possibilities of its future are *unlimited,* and it is our responsibility to bring the vast significance of this new fact to bear as a practical influence upon our own conduct. In doing so we gain the full realization that we are no longer carrying forward merely traditional truths and inherited teachings with which we may have little sympathy, but just as the light of character once dawned in a darkness which had never known such light before, so there is no reason to doubt the growth of that light to illumine realms of being that still lie all unrealized in the unfathomed ages toward which our limited vision of today looks out but does not see."

In November, 1932, the physical changes predicted in Alabama for 1936-38 were on the mind of one person, and Cayce's answer to the question "What form will they take?" was also the answer to a much larger question, for it pointed to the idea that man's character and the processes of nature are, in Breasted's words, "but chapters of the same great story."

"To be sure," said Cayce, "that may depend upon much that deals with metaphysical as well as what people call actual, or in truth! For as understood —or should be understood by the entity—there are those conditions that in the activity of individuals, in line of thought and endeavor, oft keep many a city and many a land intact through their application of the spiritual laws in their associations with individuals. This will take more of the form here in the change, as we find, through the sinking of portions, with the following up of the inundations by this overflow.

"In all these times, let each declare whom ye will serve: A nation, a man, a state, or thy God?"

CHAPTER 14

EVOLUTION: IT'S WHAT'S HAPPENING!

THREE-YEAR-OLD Belinda Le Blanc crept softly behind her mother's chair and said in an awesome treble: "Ooooh! I'm a ghooost!"

Silence. Mother looked back of her chair. "Ooooh! I'm a bigger ghost than youoooo!"

Belinda shrieked with delight.

It was December, 1932, and her mother sought a reading for Belinda from Edgar Cayce.

Belinda was, said her reading, talented in music, and one who loved mysteries. "Coming under the influence of Neptune makes for mystic forces . . . in making a mystery, in soft whispers, in creeping about. . . .

"This may be enhanced or entirely eliminated by the trend of the development."

But Belinda poses a lesson for all those interested in training and teaching unusual children, in developing a better society, in helping to work out man's destiny. For she was first described as a very "old soul" who would be "unusual."

Her reading volunteered the prediction that man would come to understand an important fact—that the development of the human mind will represent the development of the human race not through biological, but through sociological conditions in man's progress or evolution.

An old soul, such as Belinda, then, was "the more highly evolved" or "greater developed soul" because, Cayce said, she had lived a great period of time in history.

There are old souls and there are young souls. Some of us have grown spiritually, others have regressed. Some have many experiences on earth to their credit; others, few. But it has been according to the will of the individual, not God's. We call to mind Cayce's statement that "all those who have forgotten God have gradually been eliminated," and that only souls that have reached a certain level of development (for to remember God must be the requirement) have been permitted to incarnate.

There is a place for all of us in the great Heart of the Universe. It is, however, given us to know that it is a special privilege to incarnate, and that many souls crowd about the earth, seeking an opportunity for rebirth.

But from the above, we infer that for this age, the standards are higher and the restrictions more stringent. As we have come along, throughout many lives, we have matured in soul attributes and gradually the human race has gotten better.

A New Step in Man's Understanding

Evolution, we said in the chapter on the religion of the future, was for the soul's growth: "Coming into earth has been for the soul's evolution."

There is a double prediction given in the Cayce record that we almost overlooked, it was so mildly put. And yet, to me it seems quite a special kind of prediction. It was given for little Belinda and it related to her because she was an old soul. Cayce seemed to be prompted by some soul records to call up the most amazing observations! This was one.

It dealt with the workings of reincarnation as being for the soul's evolution: "As may be well understood (and will become gradually more and more understood by the mental-mind of man), the developing of the mental attributes of the human family will grow more and more to represent the whole period of transition, in the way of developing the human race of family through that known as the form, not of biological, but of sociological, conditions in the evolution of man in each experience (or incarnation)."

To paraphrase, he is saying that (1) the developing of human mental attributes will in the future represent, not biological evolution, but sociological; and (2) the mind of man will gradually understand this new concept.

A *third* prediction is implied: that man will accept reincarnation as a fact, because this is necessary in order to accept the first!

What would sociological evolution be? That Breasted referred to in his *Dawn of Conscience,* in which man is pictured developing a social consciousness and character based on his humanitarian insights. Not that man *inherited* his character and his nobler instincts, so much as learned them from the examples of a few good, upstanding citizens, and taught them to his children.

At least, that is what is meant generally to distinguish from biological evolution, in which survival of the fittest has been the teacher.

But Cayce added, "in each experience (or incarnation)," thus including the factor of reincarnation. So the sociological evolution he predicted must be understood to be accomplished by man learning to do better through his own personal soul growth, rather than the hand-me-down methods we have thought were sufficient.

For the rebirth experience is, according to reincarnationists, much more effective for teaching the lessons of soul growth than any teacher or text!

Or, to put it another way: The science teacher can talk all he wants about a theory, but it's in the laboratory where the student experiences the realities of that theory.

When Cayce gave this prediction, science was closer to the Darwinian theory of evolution, and the widespread misconceptions concerning his *Origin of Species.* The public thought he had said that man came from monkeys, whereas he had avoided man's evolution in the book.

But Cayce reflected the *future* thinking in his readings on evolution, and anticipated science's modern and enlightened stand on theory that man came from monkeys: by disagreeing.

"Archeology has made great strides in the century since Darwin set the world agog," writes Dr. Webb B. Garrison, author of *Strange Bonds Between Animals and Men.* "Mounting numbers of finds in Africa and Asia, as well as in Europe, have clarified the evolutionary paths of both men and apes. Today, no serious scientist supports the notion that humans are descendants of living anthropoid species—to say nothing of the long-popular view that Negroes sprang from gorillas, Mongolians from orangs, and whites from chimpanzees!

"New fossil finds plus more accurate dating by means of radiocarbon and other recent techniques have given conclusive proof that man is far older than any Victorian dared guess. Peking man, one of several human species long extinct, seems to have been using bone tools and fire some 400,000 to 600,000 years ago. Even Neanderthal man, whose skullcap was ammunition for Huxley's assault upon the taken-for-granted, is no longer considered to have been a direct ancestor of *Homo sapiens.*

"Most specialists now think that modern man, several extinct groups, and today's great apes are descendants from an unknown type of primate that thrived at least 30,000,000 years ago. Vague and scattered clues suggest that the family tree branched some 25,000,000 years ago. One line is thought to have produced the gibbon, while the other is believed to have continued toward human and ape types.

"At least half a million years ago—and probably much earlier—still obscure genetic changes led to the appearance of *Homo erectus.* . . .

"Long extinct, this early human was followed by big-brained *Homo sapiens,* to which species belong all the varied races of men. . . ."

Cayce's interpretation of evolution holds that man evolved biologically but that this has always been that his "flesh . . . was always to meet the needs of man for which there was made all that was made." He added that our evolving had been "the gradual growth upward to the mind of the Maker."

Instead, however, of evolving from lower forms of life, we originated from "the First Cause, or God, in creation, and the preparation for our future needs has gone down many, many thousands and millions of years." This is in preparation "for the needs of man in the hundreds of thousands of years to come."

According to Cayce, this is the only inhabited planet in this solar system and all the universe was indeed created for man's evolvement back to God! Our other planets, he said, don't even have animal life of any kind.

The predictions here given are in need of fuller explanation and analysis by a more competent mind; I will not attempt to do more than state them. I conclude that Cayce is saying that man is a social being more than a biological being, and that this will be very important to us as we learn more about the mind. He is basically from the "First Cause" which commands him to be a cooperative, peaceful, loving part of a larger Being. He develops *to* this and learns by experience over long periods of time, his character and his mental attributes being shaped by his own trial and error in many lifetimes. He learns, not in a vacuum, but in a universe that is a *social* universe which includes many mysteries—not the least of which is man himself. But he finds within himself all that is in the universe, and all that is finally necessary, and he translates this to his attitudes and his actions toward God and his fellow man.

Foreshadowing this predicted change in scientific attitudes toward man's high status in the scheme of things is this statement by Dr. Garrison: "Maturing knowledge has led to a new understanding of the grandeur of the creature who is unique as asker of questions and finder of answers about animals and men."

"It's What's Happening"

Where are we headed? If we have gradually changed and developed for the better, as Cayce says, where do we go from here? Is it possible we could be improved as a race? Yes, said Cayce, that's what's happening! Man is growing up.

Suddenly the world is aware of the powers of the mind, the ability of some people to predict the future, to see colors with their fingers, to practice thought transference. This awakening is everywhere and in many areas of activity. The religious awakening among people both in and out of the church is a part of it, as are the rise of many new scientific ideas and revival in the arts, we believe.

The riots, the violence, the immorality, the minority of our youth who rebel against the traditional good life, are happening, too. The awakening is a two-edged sword and brings with it a negative side to which some are drawn.

But the meaning is there. It is the pervasive, unspoken and yet very real feeling which runs through all of it that man is coming into his own, and that we are being thrust forward toward something better than before.

We have been told, in fact, in the Old and the New Testaments (Psalms 82; John 10:34), that we are gods! But we're self-made gods, and have to earn the right, on every level, for what we claim.

Cayce predicted that we will develop psychic powers just as we have developed our senses; through long generations of the *need* for such abilities. Just as we acquired eyesight, rather than the sharp hearing of the dolphin, so will we acquire extrasensory perception. Our sight was sharpened because we have an environment of light which makes vision possible. The dolphin, however, has developed in the sea where sound carries, but vision is hampered in the murky depths.

Dare we assume, then, that it will be because we are entering a new environment of the universe in which Earth has never before found itself, as Cayce suggests, where the vibrations are such that we will need psychic ability? If man has developed, as he says, according to biological needs that have been fulfilled to help him grow "upward to the mind of his Maker," then there is no reason to doubt that he will do so according to new needs taking him even closer to that goal.

Cayce stated we would develop intuition and telepathy, and that in fact this has been going on among various cultures over centuries of time. The Bible is perhaps our best guide to this side of man, for both the Old and the New

Testaments are actually an account of man's psychic experience, although primarily of the Jewish heritage. Joseph's predictive dreams, the story of the witch of Endor, the visions of the prophets, the early Christians' speaking in tongues, the appearances of angels and cherubim, all this is of the past. But these stories are still told as unusual happenings, as extraordinary then as they would be for us today. So we know that psychic powers have manifested only here and there, and have always been a source of much doubt and speculation.

Cayce defined psychic phenomena with the explanation that "psychic" means "of the Spirit or soul." He added that psychic forces are "of the imagination when attuned to the spirit or the soul of the individual" or they may be from other entities or souls that have passed on. They are real. They are not understood from the physical standpoint, but may be understood by an intuitive, receptive mind.

Without the psychic world, the physical world would be in a state of "hit or miss" or as "a ship without a rudder." It is the *building force* in each and every condition. No healing, for instance, is perfected without some psychic force on the part of a doctor, nurse, or loved one.

Psychic readings such as Cayce gave were given among the Chaldeans four thousand years before Christ. They seemed to be accompanied, said Cayce, by magnetic healing, of "that life-giving flow" of psychic force.

Such readings *should* be given, if not used for selfish reasons, and the use of this force is only "using the spiritual law that makes one free." This does not mean the freedom to take advantage of one's fellowman or to hurt him.

Where did the information given through Edgar Cayce originate? It was, said he, gathered from the sources from which the suggestion (given at the beginning of a reading) may derive its information. His mind communicated with those like minds having to do with the person involved. There is a vast fund of information in the collective unconscious whereupon Cayce drew, mysteriously and unerringly.

Not only will we develop the ability in this Aquarian Age to communicate telepathically, Cayce predicted, but we will have the full consciousness of being able to communicate with the Creative Forces and to make use of them as scientific laws for our material benefit!

This means we will have a kind of "mental radio" which will put us in touch with the universe! But only those who can accept it will even know what's going on.

It is difficult for our practical, scientifically-geared minds to believe what was said here about the future nature of man's mental abilities, and yet the stirrings are evident everywhere around us. Psychics like Peter Hurkos and Gerard Croiset are being employed by police departments to help solve crimes. Scientists are conducting experiments in ESP, life after death, psychic photography, color vision. Universities around the world are granting doctorate degrees for this kind of research, including Yale, Cambridge, and Oxford. Leningrad University has a special department for this.

The novelist Taylor Caldwell has recently revealed in *This Week* magazine (Oct. 15, 1967) that she has the gift of ESP and the ability to predict events.

She describes her attempts to be understood for her insights, and the negative reactions which she received. Only now has she broken her long silence regarding her gift, for she feels she has important predictions to make.

It was Jeane Dixon's unique influence in the world today which broke the spell—Jess Stearn and Ruth Montgomery, her biographers, making it possible for such people as Miss Caldwell to speak up to a world turned more sympathetic to people of her unusual abilities. And even for this, Edgar Cayce had a prediction: He foretold that a man by the name of Stearn or "Sterne" would make Cayce's work known in a big way. And he did!

Developing Psychic Abilities

One of Cayce's predictions was phrased in this way: "The individuals of this plane [Earth] will and are developing this [thought transference] as the senses were and are developed."

Some people who came to Cayce for readings were already aware of their advanced mental abilities, and asked questions to explain the phenomena they had encountered. One person asked: "In the physical plane, do the thoughts of another person affect a person either mentally or physically?"

Cayce replied: "Depending upon the development of the individual to whom the thought may be directed."

Apparently, then, we are on various levels of this evolutionary progress. It was in this reading that he volunteered the prediction that this would develop among all of us as a general trend.

Another person who perhaps did not have psychic ability but who was interested in cultivating it asked, "How does one develop psychic powers?"

"The preparation for tomorrow is builded on today," Cayce told her. Those experiences we have now are used for the growth of mental and spiritual attributes of the future. Of course, we can choose not to develop them, just as we can choose to shut off sounds audible to our normal hearing. It is our will which, after all, is paramount in our progress. "That the will must be the ever-guiding factor to lead man on, ever upward" was the understanding to be gained from our study of the planets.

"To him that hath, and uses aright, to him shall be given. To him that hath and abuses that privilege, to him shall be taken away even that he seemed to have," was a statement Cayce made elsewhere, but which seems to apply here. As we use our psychic powers, however slight, we will be given more. But we must really want to do so, to acquire them.

In a sense, Ella Johansen was asking for all of us who might want to be more psychic, when she posed the question: "While in this body will I ever be able to see and hear on a higher plane? How can I develop this power?"

This attunement, Cayce said, is accomplished only in concentration and in attuning oneself to those forces on higher planes. A person is made up of various consciousnesses. As he opens himself to these "various spheres of understanding," he gains "an access, a vision, an insight, a hearing, a feeling, into these various planes." He attains the next plane by using the gifts at hand.

Belief in the psychic sources available to us, as they were to Cayce, can only come with personal experience. There are laws that govern the use of these powers, just as laws that govern the use of electricity—and they can be just as dangerous if used wrong! Even Cayce was not able at all times to read the record or the collective mind for a person if the person was unwilling to submit to the suggestion. Sometimes his own ill health hindered. Or perhaps the mental attitude of those about him was not in accord with the kind of information sought.

In one instance, no information at all came through, because of the "feelings of those present that made for a deflecting of that being sought."

"The development must be self-development, soul development."

Thus Cayce advised a young electrical engineering student on "correctly developing psychic faculties." He said that this person was well balanced mentally, physically and spiritually, but that he could use his psychic forces for either very high development or for the turning of it into destructive forces, though not intentionally at all times.

So he was warned, "Find self. Find what is self's ideal. And as to how high that ideal is. Does it consist of or pertain to self development (or selfless development) for the glory of the ideal? And be sure that the ideal is rather of the spiritual. . . .

"And do not be satisfied with a guide other than from the Throne of Grace itself! . . . And who better may be such a guide (to teach him) than the Creator *of* the universe? For, He has given that 'If ye will seek me ye may find me' and 'I will not leave thee comfortless' but if ye are righteous in purpose, in intent, in desire, 'I will bring *all things* to thine remembrance' that are needs be for thy soul, thine mind, thine body, development. . . .

"This is a promise from Him, who is able to fulfill that which has been promised to every soul that seeks His face, His ways.

"Then, speak oft with thy Maker. And let thine meditation be:

"Lord, use thou me in that way, in that manner, that I—as thy son—thy servant—may be of the greater service to my fellow man. And may I know His biddings, Father, as Thou hast promised that if we would hear Him, that we ask in His Name may be ours. I *claim* that relationship, Father, and I seek thy guidance day by day!"

This young man was told that he would receive guidance within, knowing the answers "in the spirit." When some associate, or friend, or brother came along "as a guidepost along the way of life," he would know that he had been guided to that person and "must walk that road," learning what that person could teach him.

The Key to Telepathy

Telepathy seems to be the most common form of ESP and the most easily developed. "Give the principles and techniques of conscious telepathy," one person asked.

"The consciousness of His abiding presence" was the answer. "For He is all power, all thought, the answer to every question. For, as these attune more and more to the awareness of His presence, the desire to know of those influences that may be revealed caused the awareness to be materially practical."

"First, begin between selves. Set a definite time and each at that moment put down what the other is doing. Do this twenty days. And ye shall find ye have the key to telepathy."

Possession To Be Understood

To accept that there is such a thing as demonic possession is to accept the existence of an invisible spirit world. For this reason, despite Jung's assertion that possession exists, psychology still does not recognize that premise.

However, in giving help for a case which he named possession, Cayce made the prediction that although this interpretation would not be admitted by some as an explanation, "there will come those days when many will understand and interpret properly." Several cases of insanity brought to Cayce for readings turned out to be cases of possession, he said. Such was a young man who would not respond to the usual treatment for schizophrenia, and whose condition was only worsened by sedatives given him.

As man applies the laws of the universe, he develops and brings up the whole generation of man, said Cayce. Individuals carry out certain elements and laws, and gradually man becomes capable of applying and using these in his everyday life. This, whether applied in medical science, anatomical science, mechanical science, or whatever, is merely discovery of universal laws that have ever been existent in the universe.

"Many times has the evolution of the earth reached the stage of development as it has today and then sank again, to rise again the next development —some along one line, some along others: for often we find that the higher branches of so-called learning destroy themselves in the seed they produce in man's development, as we have in medical force, as we have in astrological, spiritual, destructive forces. . . ."

Our example here is, of course, that of Atlantis. The people of that highly developed continent were, said Cayce, a "thought people," with greatly evolved mental and intuitive abilities. They had a better understanding of spiritual laws than we do today; yet they were weakened by the "Sons of Belial"—those who served the dark forces—and were destroyed from within. As we learned from their history in the readings, they had developed on all levels: they were gifted in science and the arts, and possessed the psychic abilities we are just becoming aware of in this age. They had many conveniences—necessities to them, although we would think of them as luxuries. They were able to use ESP to their own advantage, and many of them used it for good. Some men and women were told in the readings that they had been prophets in their own right, and thus would take in stride the many supernatural events that are a part of their experience. For instance, they knew from the prophecies of their leaders that Atlantis was doomed, and were able to prepare well in advance for the breaking up of their civilization. They collected their documents and put them into the Tomb of Records, knowing that centuries might follow without so much as a hint of their having existed, and yet, knowing, too, of the prophecies of this age, when all would be revealed.

The experience of Atlantis, then, is a lesson to this generation in the evolution of the earth, and man's capacity for making a total shambles of his sojourn here. For, says Cayce, not only has this happened to the Atlantean civilization, it has happened to many before it!

"You remember a single deluge only," states the Egyptian priest, in Plato's *Republic*. "There have been, and will be again, many destructions of mankind arising out of many causes. . . . You remember a single deluge, only, but there were many previous ones."

This time, we believe, things will be different.

We must believe it.

CHAPTER 15

TIME AND PROPHECY

How is prophecy possible?

Destiny, said Edgar Cayce, is created in Time and Space.

"Those activities (of men) make for such an impression upon the realm of data, or between Time and Space, as to make for what men have called Destiny . . . in the material affairs of individuals."

Then, we might ask along with J. B. Priestly, author of *Man and Time,*[*] "What is Time?" Or, as he states it, "What is the future?" For of course the future is a part of time. "The future can be seen, and because it can be seen, it can be changed. But if it can be seen and yet be changed, it is neither solidly there, laid out for us to experience, moment after moment, nor is it nonexistent, something we are helping to create, moment after moment. If it does not exist, it cannot be seen; if it is solidly set and fixed, then it cannot be changed. What is this future that is sufficiently established to be observed and perhaps experienced, and yet can allow itself to be altered?"

* New York: Doubleday, 1964.

SETH

God, said Cayce, is Time, Space and Patience. And all Time is one: the past, present, and future.

"For to the entity—as to the world—patience is the lesson that each soul must learn in its journey through materiality. And this is a thought for the entity: Time, Space, Patience are in the mental realm the same as implied by the expression "Father-God, Son, and Holy Spirit"; or as Spirit, Body, Soul. They are expressions of the three-dimensional thought. And in Patience then does man become more and more aware of the continuity of life, of his soul being a portion of the Whole. . . ."

Time and Space are difficult concepts to grasp. We can take them in limited portions, only. And yet, they do not appear quite so awesome when we realize that they are a part of our everyday lives. The daily, three-dimensional events which we can understand are, after all, events which are a part of Eternity.

For instance, at the time of the Deluge, according to Genesis, people were going about their daily lives pretty much as usual. They were "eating and drinking and marrying" at the very moment disaster overtook them. They obviously didn't know what Time it was!

All that we know in our lives materially is measurable, evaluated in terms of the abstract realities we call time and space. We move around in space without much thought. Sometimes we are forced to be aware of it when we stand on a crowded bus, and sometimes, looking at the stars, we are bowled over by its magnitude. We buy and sell footage in county fairs; we rent it in parking lots. It takes half an acre or more to build a house and plant a tree.

We are conscious as never before, in the history we know, of the galaxies and universes. We find ourselves in a "space race" to control the square mileage out there.

By means of the sun, or a watch, or a Stonehenge, we measure time. We are aware of time in relation to our lives and the events they encompass—or in relation to history and the happenings recounted in their sequence.

Time is precious to us all, but we use it each in his own way, and out of it are shaped individual lifetimes, are they not? Time is not the same to us all, however, nor is it the same to us at all times.

So time and space remain mysteries that bring forth all kinds of speculation. We have lately been jostled out of our comfortable delusion that time and space are the same over there as over here; they have been simply past, present, and future marching along at an even rate; and height, width, and breadth have been the unalterable containers of the universe.

Now, we are told by scientists familiar with Einstein's theories of time and space that both are flexible.

"We might compare our traditional idea of Time to a rope that seems whole and unaltered as it passes through our world but is now frayed and insecure at each end far away from us," writes Mr. Priestly. "But if it will no longer do for stars and atoms, it is still good enough for man. In other words, I believe that many scientists (perhaps most of them) cling all the more tenaciously to the classical concept of Time, so far as our life in this world is concerned, because it has been so successfully challenged in the application elsewhere, on the largest and smallest scales. They feel strongly that nobody must start picking at the middle of the rope, where it seems still to hold. This explains—though in my opinion it does not justify—the shouts of 'Bosh!' 'Not tested!' 'Not proved!' 'Mere coincidence!' that greet any appearance of parapsychology and ESP, precognition, and new theories of Time. I can imagine them crying to each other, with Yeats: *Things fall apart; the center cannot hold.*"

This is running a little ahead of us, but it demonstrates the occasional similarity of thinking between Priestly and Cayce. The former is concerned in his book with time as it relates to man's entire experience: his world of thought and dreams, his unexplained and unaccountable adventures beyond the five senses. He seems to arrive at the same conclusions suggested by Cayce, and even the imagery they use to describe time and space (because we must attach them to some material concept in order to work with them at all) is identical. He compares the idea of time here to a "rope"; Edgar Cayce speaks of the "skein of time and space."

Just as is this modern writer, Edgar Cayce was quite explicit on the two different kinds of time in our experience. Cayce indicated this in many references to these abstract ideas and said that actually there was *no* time and space, and that these terms are merely conveniences for us here in a three-dimensional plane. "Time and Space are the elements of man's own concept of the Infinite and are not realities as would be any bodily element in the earth . . ." he explained.

Time and space are moreover manifested in the vastness of the heavens, said Cayce. "This becomes hard to conceive in the finite mind; as does the finite mind fail to grasp the lack of, or *no,* time." He speaks of a certain date in history as being "as Time is counted now, or light years—day and night years." This is *our* way of counting time. Then he adds: "Not light years as . . . counted by astrology or astronomy, in the speed or the reflection of a ray of light . . ." This is seemingly a reference to the new concept of Time which is "frayed and insecure at each end," as Priestly describes it.

Just as Priestly has surmised, the mysteries of ESP, including precognition, can be better studied by way of grappling with the nature of time and space, as we find in Cayce's statements. Priestly tells of a "torrent of correspondence" which he received in response to an appeal once on television to the public for letters of personal experience with ESP. He states, "Comparatively few of them were concerned with any theory of Time, even though they might have read—or tried to read—Dunne. They believed in their experience—and in some instances this might go back half a century, my correspondents being of all ages between eighteen and the eightys—and so they were glad to pass it on. . . .

"The prevailing notion of Time was not then challenged. Our contemporary idea of ourselves was not questioned. Something odd had happened, that was all; it could not be fitted into the accepted pattern, so it was ignored. Nobody, man or woman, in this great middle range pointed out that if one, just one, precognitive dream could be accepted as something more than a coincidence—bang goes our conventional idea of Time!"

This is a familiar reaction to these concepts. We are too close to our own experience of life to be able to be objective and to see the larger issues.

But if most people do not relate their subjective perception to the problems of time, Priestly brings to us the thoughts of several great minds who have. One chapter is devoted to the scientist's contribution to our understanding; another, to time as presented in fiction and drama, reflecting, of course, our many kinds of approaches to time in real life. He presents the theories of J. W. Dunne, who described in *An Experiment with Time* the dreams he had which set him to puzzling about time. Led into this brilliant scientist's maze of reasoning, we see in it, here and there, some thoughts comparable to Cayce's. But Edgar Cayce said in a few words what most scientists must take hundreds of words to say, and he said it with authority.

Priestly also discussed the Esoteric school, where we feel more at ease. Here is reviewed the influence of Ouspensky in *Tertium Organum* and his other works. He describes the "Work" of Gurdjieff and Ouspensky as "far removed from the usual soft and sentimental doctrine of Higher Thought, Theosophy, and the rest: it is hard, demanding, grimly unsentimental."

In his chapter on "Time and Ancient Man," Priestly points out that primitive man had ideas of time different from ours today. Modern man feels his life being "ticked away" by an inescapable beat; primitive man, such as the Australian aborigine, has a more meaningful rapport with time. "Their myths relate the deeds of great ancestors or heroes," says Priestly. Quoting A. P. Elkins' *The Australian Aborigines,* he says that to these people, the "past" belongs "to that same sacred time of the spirit homes—it is also present. The usual term that they use for the past creative period also means 'dreaming'; their myths are about the eternal dream time. . . . The time to which they [the myths] refer partakes of the nature of dreaming; as in the case of the latter, past, present, and future are, in a sense, coexistent—they are aspects of the one reality."

Priestly then cites other ancient cultures in which time was undifferentiated, and decries by contrast our own culture with its absorption in technology, materiality, and the mechanical living which becomes meaningless for us. Picturing the "eternal dream time" of the primitive man, with his ritual and myths, heroes, and gods, he says that Elkins considers this the life in which any human being really finds his place in society and in nature, whether primitive or civilized, and in which he is brought in touch with the invisible things of the past, present, and future." From it, "men obtain courage and strength, but not if they desecrate or neglect the sites, break the succession of initiates, forget the myths, and omit the rites, all of which results in the loss of an anchor in the past, a source of strength, and a sense of direction for the future."

Modern man yearns for this kind of relationship to time, says Priestly. We are "haunted" by the various kinds of similar relationships enjoyed by the ancient Egyptians, Mesopotamians, East Indians. Even the Greeks, he states, had a different and more inclusive viewpoint. They imagined time to be moving in a circle in which things repeat themselves.

It is in the arts rather than in formal scientific reasoning, Priestly finds, that modern man has more easily managed to keep, or perhaps only lately to discover, his new understanding of time. "Erich Kahler, who was enthusiastically praised by Thomas Mann and Einstein, is not primarily concerned with Time in his wide-ranging study of modern man, *The Tower and the Abyss*. But he observes, in his notes on various great modern poets, 'a profound feeling of contraction not only of space but of time—a gathering of all times and their contents, of our entire existence in one sublime moment, a concentration which is almost equivalent to an abolition of time.' And in his later examination of the 'stream of consciousness' techniques so characteristic of modern fiction, he turns to Time once more. These new techniques, he tells us, having broken through the bottom of our consciousness, have likewise 'cracked the supposedly solid foundation of chronological time. A new time begins to germinate within time, the time of inner experience within the time of outer happenings. This new time has no definite limits—the depths into which it expands are practically infinite. It cannot be measured by means of chronological time.' "

Among the many ways to observe time is through the phenomenon of dreams, as Priestly points out.

In dreams, time seems to have no existence. It is not its passage which occupies us, but the reality of the message. Nor is space given a rational treatment. It is as if the mind no longer needed to be bound by time and space, but could see in this state what is important.

If we deal then with time as an artist does, we are freed from the bonds of definite, conventional limitations, just as we are in dreams. If we are thus freed, we say, "This old man with the sad eyes lived in Time and Space for a while. But let me show you the eternal truth about him! He exists yesterday, today, and tomorrow, though his body decay and this canvas will not always be intact!"

If a writer wishes to bring home to his reader the impact of an incident upon one of his characters, he uses the "flashback" technique which carries the reader to another scene in the story, to juxtapose events not as they occurred in historic time, but for the truth as it exists eternally.

And so, Priestly was concerned with the way time has changed for us since the theories of Einstein were introduced. He sees this new view (as opposed to the old, Newtonian concept), as related to the problems of understanding precognition, ESP, dreams. He finds that Einstein's theory, however, "gives no allowance for any mechanism for reaching into the future. Past and future are very clearly separated in the relativistic models—in a sense more clearly than in previous views."

In a discussion with a high-ranking professor of physics, Priestly learned that "the theory of relativity, and particularly Minkowski's contribution to it, led people to adopt a certain attitude to time. (Minkowski said something like 'From now on space and time will lose their independence, and only their union will be real.') This tended to encourage people to think of space-time as ultimate reality which we experience section by section. This has some resemblance to Dunne's theory, but the latter assumes that all events, both past and future, are *there. . . .*"

More and more like Cayce!

In general, Edgar Cayce's readings tend to confirm all that the scientists, the modern writers, artists, and scholars are thinking these days about time and space being one and the same, and yet different "at both ends of the rope." But Cayce carries this further, and helps us to understand the riddle which Priestly poses for us, "What is the future?" The answers lie in the confirmation of quite another idea that has long been with us in our Judaic-Christian heritage and is found in the Old Testament. It is, we think, the "book of remembrance" referred to in Malachi 3:16, and is the "data . . . between Time and Space" which we quoted from the readings at the beginning of this chapter.

It is, said Cayce, this "book of remembrance," the record of all that happens in time and space, which he "read." It may be read, he added, by anyone sufficiently gifted to do so.

The Akashic Records

Would you believe that everything in history, everything that is happening on earth today, is being recorded on an etheric television screen, sound and all?

Remember, television and radio waves have always existed in the ether, and that man has merely *discovered* them, not created them! All man has done is to find mechanical ways to use them for his benefit, and this is, of course, remarkable in itself. But they have been there all along, down the centuries and eons of time: the *recorders* of the universe!

A popular television program illustrates this—in it, people are televised and recorded all unaware and unrehearsed.

We are, to be candid, on record—what Cayce calls the "Akashic Records." The records of what a person does and thinks are thus forever preserved. It was this record which Cayce said he was able to "read" clairvoyantly. It is, he added, a scientific fact, the laws of which are possible to discover and which will be discovered one day.

This record is called in the readings at various times, "The Akashic Records," "The Book of Life," and "God's Book of Remembrance." It is, he said, "the record that the individual entity itself writes upon the skein of Time and Space, through Patience, and is opened when self has attuned to the Infinite, and may be read by those attuning to that consciousness."

"For the light moves on in Time, in Space" is given further, "and upon that skein between them are the records written by each soul in its activity through eternity—through its awareness—not only in matter, but in thought in whatever realm the entity builds for itself in its experience, in its journey, in its activity."

These records are made in relation to our environment, our heredity, and according to our ideals. Thus not only the factual record, but an evaluation of the record is there. When the Akashic records are "read," these factors of environment, heredity and ideals are taken into consideration.

It is from the Akashic Records that knowledge of the future is possible. This is because, said Cayce, all time is one: past, present, future. "Do not confuse present and past—they are one, if the entity, the soul, will make itself attuned to the whole purpose of Creative Energies and forces that manifest themselves in the activities of the individual.

The fourth dimension in Einstein's treatment of the "space-time continuum" was spoken of by Cayce, who described the fourth dimension as "an idea"—or an idea is the best we can comprehend of the fourth dimension! Therefore, of course, it cannot be envisioned, but we have a clue to what it is like in other words of Cayce's which describe the records as being "upon the esoteric, or etheric, or Akashic forces, as they go along upon the wheels of Time, the wings of Time, or in whatever dimension we may signify as a matter of its momentum or movement."

The Akashic Records began, said Cayce, with Creation. "For, in that creation in which souls of men were given the opportunity to become aware of those forces without themselves, when Time and Space began, there was given that incentive for each entity, each soul, in whatever environment it might be, to make a manifestation of its (the entity's) awareness of its relationships to the Creative Forces, or God . . .

"Thus, irrespective of what the entity has done or may do, there is *within itself* the records of what it has done, upon the skein of Time and Space." (Author's italics.)

Describing creation in another reading, Cayce tells of the appearance of matter, space, time. He gave a special place to patience, for he said that it was "in Patience" that all the rest of creation has evolved!

"Even being God ain't no bed of roses!" God says in the play *Green Pastures.* The line serves to tell us something of the patience that is required even of the Almighty in dealing with creation!

Cayce said, in analyzing self, the entity finds itself body, mind, and soul that answers in the three-dimensional plane to the Godhead—Father, Son, Holy Spirit. God moved, the Spirit came into activity. In the moving it brought Light, and then chaos. In this Light came Creation of that which in the earth came to be matter; in the spheres about the earth, Space and Time; and in Patience it has evolved through those activities until there are the heavens and all the constellations, the stars, the universe as it is known—or sought to be known by individual soul-entities in the material plane.

"Then came into the earth materiality through the Spirit pushing itself into matter. Spirit was individualized and then became what we recognize in one another as individual entities. Spirit that uses matter, that uses every influence in the earth's environment, for the glory of the Creative Forces, partakes of, and is a part of, the universal consciousness.

"As the entity, an individual, then applies, it becomes aware—through Patience, through Time, through Space—of its relationship to the Godhead —Father, Son, Holy Spirit. In self it finds body, mind, soul. As the Son is the builder, so is the mind the builder in the individual."

One day, perhaps the mechanical means will be discovered which will enable us to "tune in" to these records. This is possible, Cayce said, so that we will be able perhaps to tune in to the conversations of Socrates, or of Jesus, or the First Continental Congress! For these records are like radio waves which can be picked up from the ether, if we but know how to locate them.

But as we learn to apply ourselves to finding our relationship to the God-head, as the above reading instructs us, and to understand and use our minds to the fullest extent, even such a mechanical device for communication with God will become unnecessary. However, as not all of us will be able to "tune in" psychically, the invention of a "universal radio" will be perhaps as impor-tant to us as television is now. We don't all develop at the same pace, as Cayce reminded us, and some will even prefer the "cosmic sets" as being more "scientific," more accurate receivers than mental ones.

Probably, we will develop our mental capacities—that is, our reasoning and thinking abilities—right along with the psychic ones. This is what Cayce said was true of the Atlanteans. Therefore, we will be still highly individual in the use of mental powers. Prophecy, psychic healing, creative and artistic ability, will all likely be commonplace everywhere, and will be as "normal" as intellectual attributes. The ideal will conceivably be a combination of all of these in each person!

Time and the Psyche

Not only can precognition be explained against the formula of Time, Space and Patience, but so, too, can intuition, perception beyond mere factual knowledge, telepathy, teleportation. Priestly tells of his own experience in still another realm of the mind: creativity. He wrote, he says, several plays within a very short time, hardly laboring over them at all, and yet they were well-written and pleasing to him and others. He felt that he was not really doing the writing, but that there was a selflessness involved.

This is a joyous experience for a creative person, and when he finds he has "dashed off" some excellent work, he is as amazed as anyone else that this happened to him!

Thus, artists, composers, writers, poets—all, in fact, who lend themselves to creative endeavor—partake of this freedom from conventional time, as do those gifted in psychic ability.

"In spite of this astounding speed of composition," writes Priestly, "it did not occur to me then that any Time element was involved. With Jung's theories in mind, I felt that the hard work in this apparently effortless playwriting had somehow been done in and by the unconscious, which had then broken through and taken charge and used my conscious mind simply as a transcribing instrument. So it did not occur to me that there was any Time element in this almost magical creation—for however modest its results may have been in terms of world drama, it was almost magical to me.

"But now I see that we cannot rule out Time, which has its own relation to the unconscious. We know that on one level the unconscious is capable of keeping an eye on chronological time for us, waking us if necessary at any hour we choose. But this is not its own time. It refuses to accept, when it is about its own business and not acting as an alarm clock, our whole idea of temporal succession. Its time is not ours, as Jung himself pointed out to me, some years later. . . ."

As we indicated in the chapter on the Pyramid Prophecies, a woman was told in a reading that her tomb was a part of the Hall of Records in Egypt, where there are thirty-two tablets with inscribed information. She asked how she might find the records and was told that she would be able to obtain them "mentally," even as far as interpreting them. "Seek through those (psychic) channels for guidance—as it is felt that it is needed," she was advised. This applied to her work in the Association, as well.

Once, Tom Sugrue asked Cayce how to go about describing an event he knew only at second hand, with but a few facts to guide him, in building a general picture of conditions in a story he was writing. "Use the imagination!" said Cayce.

Thus, we have two kinds of psychic perception suggested for these people, and they both demand a certain independence from time and space. The woman would have to defy the centuries of time that existed between the twentieth century A.D. and the eleventh century B.C., not to speak of the physical distance between herself here in the United States and the pyramid ruins of Egypt! Yet how else would she be able to obtain those records?

Tom Sugrue's problem, we would think, was similar. And yet, Cayce implied that the information they both received would be as accurate as though they had obtained it in materiality.

In using the imagination, in using our psychic intuition, we move around in infinity! Others were told to do the same, and a few more "Atlanteans," at least, were told that their activities in Egypt (or in other areas, but particularly in Egypt), were still a part of them and could be a meaningful influence in their present lives. They were stirred by these influences. If they were to go back to Egypt, they would be overtaken with old emotions—a kind of nostalgia?—that were engendered there.

One such person was an Egyptian who had built temples. "And if the entity but gazes upon those builded—by self, even, or under self's supervision —there comes the feeling of awe in the present; not only from that those meant to the entity during the experience, but from the constant harking— mentally, spiritually, to those tenets through the experience. . . ."

Another person was termed to be "the eighth from Adam," who, according to the Bible, was Methuselah. We are given that he lived "in the days of the exodus, and the periods of understanding through those activities." He had traveled from Chaldea, but spent time studying the records that were being compiled at that time "for the seeker to know his relationships to the past, the present, and the future, when counted from the material standpoint. And as the entity sought in those experiences to make Time and Space, as well as Patience, the realms that express the universality of the Force called God, so may this become in the present experience that in which the entity may excel

—in giving that assurance to those who seek their closer understanding of the relationships one to another."

Now, this person (who was, by the way, the grandfather of Noah) was told that often "he may lose self in those things that are found there."

No Time, No Space

It is difficult to realize the magnitude of space, and furthermore, to understand that there actually is no time and no space. These are merely concepts, Cayce said, for our use in our limited condition. An interesting idea then is that if this is so, this would explain how we can go "back" in time or "cross" space, or look "ahead" into the future, for if these are but illusions, there are no barriers to our consciousness!

One person was told by Cayce that this was an explanation of how the effects of an event which happened in his childhood were being *re-enacted* years later. This man asked: "Did the fall I had, out of a swing when a child, hurting my head, cause an injury, causing a nervous condition all these years?"

Cayce replied: "This, of course, is—Remember that Life as a whole is one. If no Time or No Space—and these are elemental facts—then the *effect* of same is being *re-enacted* as it were into the body at present, but it is the general debilitation that is setting in. This may be a few weeks, it may be a few months; but these are beginning."

Cayce is saying here that the effect is *"re*-enacted," which means it must have been *enacted* at the time of the injury. And yet it is being re-enacted in time (or our illusion of time) because that's the way results are brought about in our three-dimensional world.

But in the realm of no-time, the result had already happened simultaneously with the accident. For "that as lived today is as tomorrow today, for today is tomorrow, tomorrow is today."

Cycles and Deadlines

There is a discipline in our dealing with time, however. For there are both cycles and deadlines, which work like our own concept of time: according to clocks and calendars. The ancients were aware of these cycles, as Priestly indicates. Cayce stated that time moves in cycles, and that much repeats itself. And so we find that although man has free will, he is also under the influence of these great circles. They are frightening, because one feels caught between the pincers of two points in time—one in the past, the other in the future. Having seen, for instance, that a certain type of event take place every twenty-five years, or every hundred years, or whatever, we find the next recurrence inevitable.

And the inevitable is what our free wills try to avoid!

In fact, nothing else in the study of time seems inevitable except the kind of prediction based on cycles; and even this, Cayce implies, can be modified by our wills.

But if we make the record in time, time, nevertheless, has power over us. There are, as we pointed out in "Destiny of Nations," cycles of millenniums, as was shown in the history of the Jews. We indicated the workings of the economic cycles for the world, which Cayce said occurred every twenty-four or twenty-five years, as given in "People Rising." He also spoke of the seven-year cycle of the body, which, he said, renews itself completely during each.

A spectacular example of the manner in which the stars repeat their influence over long periods of time was given in the reading for a woman in 1941: "Unusual astrological aspects affecting every soul in the earth to 'think differently,' to 'have varied urges' in the next two weeks—April 29 through May 12. It has been over eight hundred years since such has been the urge. . . . Think of the darkness of the spiritual life as was enacted then, and see what is the experience through which so many souls are passing and we pass during this period in the relationships of man to man.

"Will ye as a Soldier of the Cross do thy part?"

Spring, 1941, found the world at war although America of course was not yet in it.

But what dark time comparable to the early days of World War II had existed eight hundred years before?

This was the time the Second Crusade failed, and Jerusalem fell to the Moslems! The date? 1147-49—or 794 years before 1941.

In a World Affairs reading given the same day, Cayce explained again that beginning April 29, 1941, the Sun, Moon, Jupiter, Uranus, and Venus would all be in one sign. "When last this occurred," he said, "the earth throughout was in turmoil, in strife."

He went on to say that sixteen hundred years before this present conflict, when the earth was under these signs, that the powers of light and darkness were clashing, just as at the time of the Crusades, and World War II. "As in those periods, so today—we find nation against nation, the powers of death, destruction, the wrecking of that which has been and is held near and dear to the hearts of those who have through one form or another set ideals."

To what third world event was this related? By 340 A.D. the Democracy of Rome had been replaced by oriental despotism, first under Diocletian and later under Constantine—sixteen hundred (and one) years before 1941!

It would seem that the combination of these five heavenly bodies does this earth no good.

Further study of these two readings given on the same day brings up the question of why Cayce treated these events as he did. The woman was given the time of the Moslem capture of Jerusalem; the group inquiring on World Affairs, the Fall of Rome.

Cayce was being appropriate, as usual. The woman had evidently been a part of the unsuccessful Second Crusade and stood to gain from that experience in this present life. The Fall of Rome was of special significance to World Affairs students.

It would seem that prophecy has a definite advantage in taking into consideration the cycles of time. Astrologers, of course, know the zodiac and predict from a purely calculated basis, knowing the stars' influences and how they bear on individuals and nations.

Analyzing every hidden thought or intuitional insight, as Priestly does throughout his book, he gives us some valuable thoughts on the cycles of time as the East Indians believe they are. He is dismayed by their overwhelming view of time, which dwarfs our everyday attempts to live in the here and now. He describes the "Indian Time Trick: . . . an old emaciated Indian magically appears in your office. He begins by pointing out that a single daytime of Brahma lasts 4,320,000,000 of your years . . . and how the mahayuga consists of four ages each of them longer than your historical records, and that one thousand mahayugas constitute a kalpa, and that fourteen kalpas make up one manvantara. . . ."

Certain periods in time are good, others not so good, whether a cycle can be discerned or not. Such a time was the year 1936, when the Spanish War flared, Stalin began his mass purges, and Hitler marched into the Rhineland.

But the most interesting year, we think, was 1932, when Edgar Cayce made many important predictions for this century—perhaps his most important, from a world standpoint. At the same time, the events of that year had great bearing on those predictions.

Some of the events of 1932 were:

As given in the Cayce readings, the New Age was officially "begun."

The Pyramid Prophecies were given and interpreted by Edgar Cayce.

The Depression was in its worst year.

Cayce made an interesting prediction on the future understanding of evolution.

Cayce predicted earth changes, wars, and political upheavals, to begin 1936.

Wilson's role as peace-maker was made clear.

Cayce declared Russia's future religious development to be the hope of the world.

Related to these were several events which by themselves do not seem significant, but when taken in this context, point to a general stirring in the world to the unseen influences arising. Probably much more could be told, but those that pertain to world conditions are very relevant here.

In 1932 many areas of human endeavor revealed a concern for earthquakes, volcanoes, and their effects—and man's dominion in the earth! The Coast and Geodetic Survey began to record earth motions in the western United States. That same year, geologist Ugo Mondello stated that new lands would probably rise "one day" in the South Atlantic. James Henry Breasted gave the world his scholarly insight into the unity of "the works of nature and the works of man"—at the same time that Cayce was saying that man's relationships to his fellowman, or his spiritual life "oft keep many a city and many a land intact."

What a time to begin the New Age! At the bottom of the barrel, we *had* to start improving. Another decade and we had landed ourselves in another world war. But in 1950 we began a new period symbolized in the Pyramid

Prophecies as "the King's Chamber." The meaning of this, said Cayce, was "the joy, the buoyance" promised for this new age.

If there are cycles and deadlines, their existence is for our benefit, we think. Time, Cayce said, was relative, often, but for some matters he was quite specific. When he predicted that China would one day be the "cradle of Christianity" he added that it was "far off as man counts time, but only a day in the heart of God." In the reading on Jesus' childhood and training, he said that the Master was in Egypt for five years "as you count time." These brief phrases encountered here and there emphasize the dual nature of time and affirm that there is another way of viewing it.

This was quite distinct, however, from the definite deadlines he gave, the towering beacon of them all being the year 1998 A.D. All along, there have been predictions that certain years would bring certain events. Such a year was 1958 when the principles of electromagnetism were to be discovered, and they were! Yet, in the same year the records of the Great Pyramid were to have been uncovered, but because of man's unreadiness for this, it did not come about. Destiny is influenced by man's will, but there is a time when it is rendered irreversible, by his will. It is even left to man his "time to be born, to die." Certain times were allotted for the influx of Atlanteans, and the year 1943 was the year after which no one would be born who had not heard "The Lord He is God."

The Great Pyramid as a Monument of Time

The Great Pyramid utilizes space mathematically to interpret time.

If the Hall of Records contained the written past, present, future of man in the earth, why was it necessary to record this in stone? The Pyramid of Gizeh is this record expressed in terms of space, as well as in terms of time. There is need to identify time with space. Without the Pyramid, the full significance of the Prophecies would be lost to us. The Pyramid would appear to teach, even by an imaginary walk down its corridor and into the different chambers, a lesson in the unity of time-space,

So, too, the Sphinx was built to make space articulate, its location being in deliberate relationship to the rays of the sun falling in a certain way. "As the sun rises from the waters," said Cayce, "the line of the shadow (or light) falls between the paws of the Sphinx."

Then, the Pyramid and the Sphinx are studies in infinity. It is the Pyramid, however, which represents, embodies the ideal of time as no other structure on earth. Its secret is to be revealed "when the time has been fulfilled." Its very position in the center of the earth, as Cayce said, further clarifies for us the importance of space in presenting its message of, in, for all time. It occupies space in a special way, and from the center of the earth, its relationship to the universe is made plain by a mystical affinity to the stars. "At the correct time, accurate imaginary lines can be drawn from the opening of the Great Pyramid to the second star in the Little Dipper, called Polaris or the North Star. . . ."

"Time, Space, and Patience"

The sad part is that the world could not make better use of the Cayce data and has had to wait for the future to take it by the scruff of the neck and drag it into the light. Things would have been easier, it seems, if the world had had Cayce's ideas to work with.

Prophecy about what man would do, though, was qualified often and took into consideration the human will, many times. Gathering from what the readings said about future events he predicted, it would seem that *all* of these events were originated in the *wills* of individuals in times past, and were only now becoming predictable without further room for change. He spoke of "tendencies in the hearts and souls of men" as being such that upheavals may be brought about.

"Our decisions undeniably influence the course of future events," said Dr. von Braun. This is attested to by Cayce, who had much to say about decisions and their effects on our future destiny.

One such study in decisions involves a time span of nine hundred years, between decisions made and the time of reckoning with them. And, although it bridges a perfectly measurable length of time as we understand it in the old way, the time measured by calendars and clocks, it tends to give a picture, too, of the way time is condensed for us in living out many lives. For, in reincarnating, we pick up where we left off in the last life, or perhaps we take up a karmic debt after many lives—but the continuity of cause and effect is there like a river flowing along.

Marcia Delgado wrote Edgar Cayce that she "sought advice dealing with the problems and conditions which have come about as the result of the decision made January 1, 1944."

Cayce began her reading with: "These are decisions which were made first in December, 1020!"

Marcia was reminded of her decisions made in December, 1020, in connection with her present husband. Her relationship with him had not been a happy one, we assume, nor the decision altogether wise, or there would be no painful repercussions from it now.

"In, then, the undertakings of the problems of today, each of these will be found to be part of that to which ye attempt to attain. Not merely the experiences of the moment, for that which happened in time, years ago, is today bearing fruit. Are ye gathering it ripe, or are you letting it destroy itself on the tree of life? Or are ye ignoring it altogether?"

The report reads that Marcia remained with her husband and children, due to the counsel she received in this reading, and thus rectified a wrong decision of the past with a right one in the present. The decision was obviously not easy, for she soon had a nervous breakdown. After a brief period of hospitalization, however, she returned home to fulfill those eleventh-century decisions.

How can we know when we are making the right decisions? "By the listening within. . . . For the answer to every problem, the answer to know His way, is ever within," Cayce answered.

The inner self is a part of the Infinite, while the self-will or personality (which may lead us astray) is ever at war with the infinite "for the lack of what may be called stamina, faith, patience. . . ."

Actually, however, we are living the past, present, and future all at one time, said Cayce. Our lives are divided into "lives" for our own convenience, only: all time is one and all life is one.

Earlier in this chapter, we had a hint as to how this works in the example of the man who fell in childhood and was suffering from after-effects years later. This was a natural consequence of the fall, of course, but there is another quality of time at work which is apparently the secret of cause and effect zeroing in so accurately on our lives, in every circumstance. How is it that we meet an old enemy of the past, or a dear friend, or some other important person in our lives, in a chance meeting? How is it that we find ourselves involved in accidents, or financial straits, or an emotional problem that seemingly has no justification in this life?

According to Cayce, the debilitation going on in the man's body was being *re-enacted* because it had occurred already! In this is the key to the law of karma. "Do unto others as you would have them do unto you" is a wise maxim, because it takes cognizance of this hidden characteristic of time. For as you treat others, you are setting up in that very moment the way you will be treated later: You are *enacting* your own fate.

Thus, the answer as to how we "happen" to meet our fate is explained in this example. Since there is no time or space, the cause of the fateful event and the event are simultaneous. This is perfection, we would think, in fitting the punishment to the crime, or the reward to the good deed.

"For the Law of the Lord is perfect: it converteth the soul . . ."

In explaining how groups, nations meet their joint destiny, it would seem that their individual thoughts and actions are just as effective in bringing about their joint destiny as their individual destiny. France, we recall, was paying a karmic debt during her occupation by Nazi Germany. America's joint prayers could have kept her out of war. Cayce spoke of the "sins" of each nation as though he were speaking of individual persons. Thus, on a smaller scale, karma is then possibly brought about in the event of small groups of people brought together in some common endeavor—or plight. An airplane crash, for instance, involving a group of people is not, by these rules, by chance. We might turn this to a happier example as found in the family, brought together by karmic debts to spend a lifetime making amends or just learning to get along.

Just as the universe could not have evolved without patience, neither can we. "Time, Space, Patience—through these you possess your souls" said Cayce. We begin to see the relationship which patience has to time and space. It takes patience to do unto others as we would have them do unto us. We don't in that moment experience the reward. Cause and effect are years apart.

In patience we "become aware of our souls, of our identity, of our being each a corpuscle, as it were, in the great body, in the heart, of our God. And He has not willed otherwise." In fact, it is out of our awareness of these concepts that it is possible for us to *know* the Infinite.

The records of what we have done in the past are found within ourselves and they are there for us to remember if we wish, for we have been promised "all things to our remembrance."

Thus, if we are haunted, as Priestly suggests, by our primitive experience with time and space, we might be prompted to study these ideas for their value in the inner life. Not that we would go backward into a primitive expression of these values, denouncing all of civilization's achievements, but that we might re-examine our identity as a small part of a great Being and what this means to us as "children of God."

The ESP of which we hear so much these days can be seen to belong both to the primitive culture and to the most advanced, as shown in the Atlantean "myth" we have presented here. Or in a Peter Hurkos, or a Jeane Dixon. In another realm, there is the mysticism of Christianity and of Judaism, and in religious circles, ESP is being investigated, we are told, with great interest. Mystics of every kind have access to the world of the paranormal, and have reportedly practiced out-of-the-body travel, thought transference, soul memory.

For all, Edgar Cayce advocated that character development should precede ESP, and as one grows in virtue—in patience—one will receive these gifts as a natural result.

He advised that in all of our seeking in these strange paths, that we take on the Christ Consciousness for protection and guidance. For above all else, the highest use of ESP is to "know ourselves to be His."

"Time never was when there was not a Christ and not a Christ Consciousness," Cayce declared.

Contrary to theological thinking, the Christ has existed in all Eternity because it is of Spirit. Jesus, the man, took on the Christ Spirit. He lived in a temporal body, subject to physical laws, but was able to transform its atomic structure when He ascended into Heaven.

"And, as has been given, again the time draws near when there shall be seen and known among men, in many places, the manifestations of such forces in the material world. For 'As ye have seen Him go, so will He return again.'"

One seeker, puzzled about many things concerning the Christ, was told: "Oft, to be sure, it has come to thine own consciousness, how could, how *could* He be in Heaven, in earth, in this place or that place, and be aware of an individual and at the same moment or same time be aware of that same presence in places miles, yea, leagues and leagues apart?

"Then, in all, through all, is the permeating influence of the Christ Consciousness."

In another reading Cayce said: "Who of the whole peoples of that city that His Temple of Jehovah had been sat in, looked upon the King on the Cross and thought or felt that there would come the day when His words, even, 'My peace I give unto you' would change the whole world, and that Time, even, would be counted from that death, that birth?''

And in still another, "What is the water of life? What is this that the Spirit and the Bride, or the Spirit and the Lamb, say to come and take of freely? Patience, Time, Space! That we may know ourselves to be His; that our spirits, our souls, bear witness in the things that we do in which we bear witness of Him."

Just as Jesus dealt with the physical man, so, we are beginning to suspect, God is dealing with the physical heavens and earth. He is renewing them just as Jesus was able to regenerate the flesh. The body and the earth are, after all, made of the same stuff. If a new body, why not a new earth? Literally!

Then, the earth changes predicted for us were to be a very physical disturbance, according to Cayce, but the physical change will be due to the "desires, the purposes, the aims" of people everywhere. This will bring about a "new vision," a "new comprehension." "Can the mind of man comprehend no desire of sin, no purpose but that the glory of the Son may be manifested in his life? Is this not a new heaven, a new earth? For the former things would have passed away. . . ."

Why hasn't God done this long ago? Because, said Edgar Cayce, this is a joint project—the heavens and the earth are under the management of God and man. We are the ones who have held off new heaven and new earth and peace. "When there has been in the earth those groups that have sufficiently desired and sought peace, peace will begin. It must be within self."

Desire is the key. To attain peace, a new heaven, a new earth, we must desire them sufficiently, even as God desires them.

When we pray, "Thy kingdom come, thy will be done," we are saying the words that might carry this desire or that might remain empty words. Each Christian knows within when he says these words how much he really desires the kingdom and God's will be done.

This is the deepest prayer we know. It is the deepest and holiest of all Destiny. It sums up all other prophecy for all time, for it will be in earth as it is in Heaven. This is both prophecy and promise, as well as prayer.

"And yet, remember as He gave: Time is not yet complete, Time is not yet at hand. Why? The laws are set, love can only remove same. . . ."

EDGAR CAYCE

On Religion and Psychic Experience

By Harmon Hartzell Bro, Ph.D.
Under the Editorship of
Hugh Lynn Cayce

To my Duluth sponsors—who saw the need for this book and made possible the research behind it.

CONTENTS

PART III

Enhanced and Elevated Psychic Experience

PREFACE

HARMON H. BRO first came to Virginia Beach in 1943 as a young minister, just graduated from Divinity School at the University of Chicago. He was troubled that his mother, Margueritte Harmon Bro, had become involved with some pseudo-psychic or miracle worker called Edgar Cayce. He found something quite different—a psychic who became a friend. During those troubled war years, Edgar Cayce welcomed Harmon and his wife June. Accelerated activity in requests for Edgar Cayce readings had resulted from the publication of *There is a River* by Thomas Sugrue, which was followed by Margueritte Harmon Bro's article in *Coronet Magazine* entitled "Miracle Man of Virginia Beach." Harmon and June Bro had opportunities to work closely with Edgar Cayce and those around him. They listened to hundreds of readings. They had access to all correspondence and talked with those who came for readings.

From this point, Harmon became interested in psychology and decided to continue graduate work. He went on to Harvard and then to the University of Chicago where he did a doctoral dissertation based on a study of the Edgar Cayce readings. For this dissertation, he coined, in my opinion, an excellent title for Edgar Cayce—"a seer in a seerless culture."

As will be evidenced by this book, Dr. Bro has had a wide experience in investigating psychics and psychic phenomena. His work in psychotherapy, coupled with his background as a minister, provides excellent additional ma-

151

terial and insights for this volume, *Edgar Cayce on Religion and Psychic Experience.*

Rather than dealing with the Edgar Cayce readings on Bible passages, history or characters, Harmon has turned to the mental and spiritual readings which Edgar Cayce gave, and to a series of some several hundred readings on spiritual laws which are used as the basis of the A.R.E. study group program.

In each section of the book, Dr. Bro discusses Edgar Cayce on a specific spiritual law and then relates this to the field of psychical research concerned with parallel types of psychic phenomena.

This book should be challenging to any person interested in psychic phenomena and religion. Highlighted against basic religious principles, the varieties of psychic phenomena which are discussed come into much clearer perspective. I know of no published material which has made this focus so clearly as Dr. Bro's treatment here. This book also should be of great help to anyone involved in personal psychic experiences at any level. Ministers of all faiths should find these data of special value.

Edgar Cayce saw the psychic as related to the spiritual nature, the soul nature, of man. Here is a fine clarification of this point of view.

For some of you, this may be the first introduction to Edgar Cayce. "Who was he?"

It depends on through whose eyes you look at him. A goodly number of his contemporaries knew the "waking" Edgar Cayce as a gifted professional photographer. Another group (predominantly children) admired him as a warm and friendly Sunday School teacher. His own family knew him as a wonderful husband and father.

The "sleeping" Edgar Cayce was an entirely different figure—a psychic known to thousands of people in all walks of life, who had cause to be grateful for his help. Indeed, many of them believed that he alone had either saved or changed their lives when all seemed lost. The "sleeping" Edgar Cayce was a medical diagnostician, a prophet, and a devoted proponent of Bible lore.

Even as a child, on a farm near Hopkinsville, Kentucky, where he was born on March 18, 1877, Edgar Cayce displayed powers of perception which seemed to extend beyond the normal range of the five senses. At the age of six or seven he told his parents that he was able to see and talk to "visions," sometimes of relatives who had recently died. His parents attributed this to the overactive imagination of a lonely child who had been influenced by the dramatic language of the revival meetings which were popular in that section of the country. Later, by sleeping with his head on his schoolbooks, he developed some form of photographic memory which helped him advance rapidly in the country school. This gift faded, however, and Edgar was only able to complete his seventh grade before he had to seek his own place in the world.

By the age of twenty-one he had become the salesman for a wholesale stationery company. At this time he developed a gradual paralysis of the throat muscles which threatened the loss of his voice. When doctors were unable to find a physical cause for this condition, hypnosis was tried, but failed to have any permanent effect. As a last resort, Edgar asked a friend to help him reenter the same kind of hypnotic sleep that had enabled him to memorize his schoolbooks as a child. His friend gave him the necessary suggestion, and once he was in a self-induced trance, Edgar came to grips with his own problem. He recommended medication and manipulative therapy which successfully restored his voice and repaired his system.

A group of physicians from Hopkinsville and Bowling Green, Kentucky, took advantage of his unique talent to diagnose their own patients. They soon discovered that Cayce only needed to be given the name and address of a patient, wherever he was, to be able to tune in telepathically on that individual's mind and body as easily as if they were both in the same room. He needed, and was given, no other information regarding any patient.

One of the young M.D.'s, Dr. Wesley Ketchum, submitted a report on this unorthodox procedure to a clinical research society in Boston. On October 9, 1910, *The New York Times* carried two pages of headlines and pictures. From that day on, troubled people from all over the country sought help from the "wonder man."

When Edgar Cayce died on January 3, 1945, in Virginia Beach, Virginia, he left well over 14,000 documented stenographic records of the telepathic-clairvoyant statements he had given for more than six thousand different people over a period of forty-three years. These documents are referred to as "readings."

The readings constitute one of the largest and most impressive records of psychic perception ever to emanate from a single individual. Together with their relevant records, correspondence and reports, they have been cross-indexed under thousands of subject headings and placed at the disposal of psychologists, students, writers and investigators who still come, in increasing numbers, to examine them.

A foundation known as the A.R.E. (Association for Research and Enlightenment, Inc., P.O. Box 595, Virginia Beach, Virginia, 23451) was founded in 1932 to preserve these readings. As an open-membership research society, it continues to index and catalog the information, initiate investigation and experiments, and promote conferences, seminars and lectures. Until now, its published findings have been made available only to its members through its own publishing facilities.

—Hugh Lynn Cayce

PART 1
Introduction

CHAPTER 1

THE PUZZLE OF PSYCHIC EXPERIENCE

EDGAR CAYCE LOOKED at the waitress and grinned.

He had been through a hard day, handling part of the thousands of recent letters from all over the world that asked his clairvoyant aid on problems as varied as terminal cancer, early baldness, mental illness, a lost ring, unjust imprisonment, a missing soldier, whom to marry, and whether to begin a career in law. As usual, he had managed to answer personally only a small number of letters, explaining what he tried to do for people in his twice-daily unconscious trances, and why he gave priority to serious medical or psychological needs. To the rest of the letter writers he had been able to send only a form letter and a descriptive leaflet about his puzzling abilities, now the subject of investigation by a small research society which inquirers were welcome to join, if they wished to try his assistance. His secretary had made certain that all money other than membership fees enclosed in the letters opened that day had been sent back. Now it was time for him to relax.

His wife had just ordered clam chowder. They sat at a window table in one of the few restaurants operating in the winter along the oceanfront at Virginia Beach, Virginia, not far from his home. He was about to order the chowder, too, as were the present writer and his wife. Then Edgar Cayce caught an impression about the neatly uniformed young waitress, standing there with pencil and pad in hand. Perhaps because he was in high spirits after the day's work and enjoying the evening out (he always enjoyed good food, restaurants,

155

and new places), he did something rare for him in his later years. In mischievous solemnity he said to the waitress, "You shouldn't marry him."

The startled waitress turned to stare at Cayce. "Do I know you?"

"Nope," he replied. "But you know I'm right. You shouldn't marry him. You've had two husbands already, young as you are, and you're about to make the same mistake on a third as you did on the last two."

Flustered, she murmured something polite and hurried to get the clam chowder. Returning with the soup, she looked hard at Edgar Cayce, who again smiled broadly at her, and she decided to trust him. "Look here," she offered, "I don't know who you are or why you said that, but I think you might be right. Do you know something I don't know?"

"Maybe," he answered. "Why don't you sit down for a bit?"

She sat, while her other customers continued their leisurely winter dinners. "The part about the two husbands already was right," she began, "but I haven't made up my mind completely about the man I'm going with."

Everyone at the table laughed. Cayce had no business knowing about her two past husbands. The whole situation was ridiculous. But being around Cayce meant bumping into the impossible.

He told the waitress he had just felt an impression about her, and thought she might want to hear it. After a bit of bantering that she enjoyed, he began to speak seriously to her, pointing out that all three men were too old for her. She was being drawn to them, he explained, to get them to take the place of her father, who she felt had deserted her by divorcing her mother.

Her face grave, she nodded. "Right on the ages, though I never connected that with my father—especially because at times I have really hated him. Suppose you're right; how do I get over my father, anyway?"

Cayce was not flip. He spoke briefly about how hard it was to forgive and "turn loose of those who hurt us"—"hurt any of us," he added with a gesture that took in himself and the whole table. "But we all have to do it sooner or later, don't we?" His manner was gentle, playful, yet direct.

Customers were signaling her, and she rose slowly. "Can I talk with you sometime?"

"Sure," he responded. "You might want to visit our Tuesday night Bible class." It was unlike him to invite a stranger to the group that way. But he acted as he felt.

Visit she did, after getting the details when the check was paid.

She came only a couple of times, joining the dozen who had gathered weekly for several years in the library of Cayce's office, which adjoined his home, and who had now gotten to Matthew after starting in Genesis. But one of those Tuesdays she stayed to talk with Cayce in his little study crowded with souvenirs. When she left, her face was glowing.

"She's made it," he commented quietly as she left. He relaxed with a cigarette, and soon he was into the story of an earlier experience when he had also volunteered something to a stranger. The place had been the main street of a city in the Southwest, back in the days when he was using his abilities there to locate oil and raise money for the hospital he wanted to build, for those who sought his medical counsel. Standing on the street in front of a store, he had greeted by name a complete stranger who passed him. The man had nodded absently and then turned back to question Cayce, who admitted he had guessed the name through a psychic hunch. The stranger, a local bank official, took Cayce to lunch, and in the midst of the meal dared Cayce to write out the combination of the bank vault. Cayce scribbled it on a napkin and passed it over to him, electrifying his host and incidentally beginning a warm friendship that lasted for decades.

Can anyone read the life of a stranger as he would scan the contents of a book? Had Cayce made lucky guesses?

Was it also a lucky guess the writer observed nearly twenty years later when he sat in a crowded New York airport restaurant with a European psychic who asked the airport waitress, "How are your two children in England?" "Fine," was her answer as she started towards the kitchen. Then she did a doubletake as broad as classic farce. "Why did you ask about my grandchildren? Do you know them?" The psychic didn't. But when she produced from her purse in a nearby locker a photograph of the youngsters, he fell to chatting with her about the personal characteristics of each child, delighted with each new hit he made. He did so well, as the writer observed on other occasions, that the waitress actually forgot for a moment he was only a psychic. She was caught up in celebrating the youngsters with someone who so well appreciated and understood them—until she stopped in real bewilderment. "This is impossible," she objected. "Are you some sort of a relative?"

He wasn't.

Had it been a lucky, or unlucky, guess which led the third-grade schoolteacher in a Wisconsin town to phone the chief of police shortly after a county-wide hunt for a murder suspect had been announced, and to report his name? She was a quiet, loving spinster, the soul of propriety in the town where only a few close friends knew she could "see" things. She counted the chief of police among these friends, as she did the present writer, and did not hesitate to tell the lawman that the wanted man was the father of one of her schoolchildren. She "saw" the story when she looked at the child that morning, even though the boy did not yet know of his father's crime. And she felt she had to call, for the safety of the child, because she was sure the father was dangerously ill of mind, though a respected citizen in the community and an absurd choice as a murderer.

She proved quite right. "Of course," she commented when the writer reviewed the case with her; her mind was obviously on the boy and not on a psychic feat.

Does this sort of thing go on in the human family? How long has it gone on?

Did Nathan act on a prompting of this sort when he challenged David for taking Bathsheba and having her husband killed? Were Paul's friends guessing when "filled with the Spirit" they warned him not to proceed to Jerusalem and certain arrest, despite his Roman citizenship? What had Jesus seen about one woman's husband when he asked her for water at a Samaritan well?

Did Swedenborg "watch" a fire hundreds of miles away as it threatened his home, in the events recounted by that cautious philosopher, Kant, after he personally investigated them? Did that nineteenth-century one-man ecumenical movement, the Hindu Ramakrishna, really keep track of his disciples "psychically" while they were on their travels? In modern times, did that buoyant and devout Catholic socialite and crystal-gazer, Jeanne Dixon, actually foresee the assassination of President Kennedy and try to warn him through friends, as she had personally warned Roosevelt of imminent death before him?

Edgar Cayce Sharpens the Puzzle

The frustrating puzzle of such events, the subject matter of parapsychology, would be easier to ignore, were it not for the modern figure of Edgar Cayce.

What Cayce did not was not done in a corner.

He did not publicize his abilities, nor make extravagant claims for them. But during his lifetime he was several times the subject of extensive newspaper investigation, as well as of a sensitive biography. His work led to the building of a small but accredited hospital, and a modest liberal arts university, though both expired with the Depression. He became the center of a pioneering but knowledgeable national research society of hundreds of laymen and a few professional people.

He kept records of everything he did, after the halfway point of his career, so that at his death he had a fireproof vault almost as large as his study, jammed with filing cabinets for fourteen thousand transcripts of his trance discourses, together with many more thousands of relevant letters, medical reports, engineering and geological reports, records of historical digs, and results of psychological studies of his abilities.

He made his records, his person, his work, his finances, his family, and his friends and relatives open to investigators who came from Harvard, Duke and elsewhere—just as the present writer came for eight months of study, midway in a graduate program at Harvard and the University of Chicago.

Cayce did not claim to explain his abilities, though he had theories by the end of his life. He did his work, and he tried to increase its helpfulness by following it up with letters, personal friendships, a few study groups, and an informal "congress" of people he had helped, held every June.

He broke every stereotype used to discredit psychics.

Not other-worldly, he based none of his work on communication with the dead, though he was sure from his personal experience that the dead were not dead. Not worldly, he never got beyond making a good living as a photographer who built up several studios, and never managed more than a modest and irregular income from the research society that sponsored his work for the last twenty years of his life.

Not a showman, he turned down all offers from theaters, circuses, lecture bureaus, moviemakers, and radio (the writer watched him refuse a lucrative radio spot for a cereal company, not long after rejecting a trip to Hollywood pressed upon him by a star he admired). Not a recluse, he took his ability straight to the countryside of gushers and derricks, when he tried to raise money for his hospital by locating oil in Texas; he also went twice to the White House, and traveled to nearly every major city in the U.S. in a long lifetime of trying to discover how best to use his abilities. Not a saint, he had a temper and moods that sometimes strained, though they did not break, the mutual bonds of his family and many relatives. Not a religious fanatic, he taught Sunday School all of his life because he enjoyed it and was good at getting people to think fresh thoughts about the Bible. Not a simple man, he was an inventor, a prize-winning photographer, a raconteur, a green-thumb gardener, a memorable though rambling lecturer, an organizer of regional church activities, and an articulate letter-writer.

And through most of his life he was a walking museum of psychic abilities.

When he once needed a label for the door to the room where he gave free trances in early manhood, he called himself a "psychic diagnostician." Yet it was clear to the observer at the end of his life that he did not think of himself primarily as a chapter in the history of psychical research.

He knew psychics great and small, and once exchanged trance "readings" with the gifted medium, Eileen Garrett, in which each described from an unconscious state what he saw the other doing. He knew the jargon of psychic circles well, from "apport" to "yellow aura," and had a personal experience to tell about each classic phenomenon from ouija boards to levitation. He met or was studied by investigators of many kinds. And he encouraged his son to put on a New York radio program on telepathy, as well as to submit materials from his records for study projects at two universities.

But in his own mind and memoirs Edgar Cayce was no more a psychic wonder than he was a hypnotic freak—and he probably spent as much time in hypnotic trance as a busy corporation executive spends on the telephone. He thought himself, as his dreams and diaries showed, a man with a job to do —like other men with other talents.

He knew he had a talent and that it was at its best a remarkably good one. But he also knew it had missed a few times when he was under heavy strain, and that he was using it on medical matters where a mistake could cost a life, however much he warned that his trances were only "experiments" completely subject to medical interpretation and counsel.

He learned that his talent functioned best when he stuck close to his own religious norms. After reading the Bible or praying or teaching a class that discussed forgiveness, he was more fun to be with, more sure in his judgments about using his outrageous abilities, and more accurate and detailed in his next trance session. He saw his talent as operating lawfully, but knew that he understood only a little of the laws, and that while learning the laws he had better try to help others more than himself, and to stick as close as he could to "the Giver of all good and perfect gifts."

What were the psychic dimensions of Cayce's talent?

The question sounds redundant. If Edgar Cayce was a "psychic," how does one speak of the "psychic dimensions" of his talent?

He was a psychic. But it must remain an open question whether his chief talent, even in his trances, was extrasensory. For anyone who heard a number of his unconscious sessions, Cayce's work was as much poetry as prediction, as much renewing as reporting. He dealt in lives. Facts were instruments, precise and important for him to retrieve. But his "readings" were not readings of dials, nor even of omens and trends, and the name of "readings" only betrays how barren is American speech on this kind of phenomenon. Cayce's twice-daily trances had the character of encounters. They were speech between man and man which made all parties liable to think hard about life or even God, at any point in the exchange, though the readings be on colonies or colonialism or colleges.

There was a danger in his work that the visitor did not always see. His family and staff well knew that there had been times when it had been impossible to waken Cayce from his trance state, when none of the hypnotic suggestions worked and when the passing hours were marked by his flagging respiration and pulse, until they ended up quite simply on their knees, asking for his life. Little was said of these occasions, and good spirits prevailed at the entry of Cayce's "reading room" twice each day. But something more than a performance, a feat, was undertaken, as they saw it; the man's life was on the line, each time. This meant that his trances were to them not only "phenomena," however practical and concrete, but events which involved them all at their core. Not surprisingly, they distinguished carefully between what was said by the waking Cayce and what was said by "the information," as they called the unknown source or sources of his trances, which they viewed as inclusive of Cayce, yet independent, intelligent, impersonal, and in keeping with Biblical faith.

Still, Cayce was a psychic. Whatever else he might be remained a worse puzzle than his psychic ability. Perhaps his trances were wisest in the term they habitually used for him—"a channel," or "this channel"; it was precisely the term used in the same trances to describe every man, as each fulfilled his vocation.

What were the dimensions of Cayce's psychic ability, the amplitudes and modes of his being a psychic "channel"?

He appeared to the careful observer to be psychic in three different states of consciousness: while he was awake, while he was asleep and sometimes dreaming, and while he was in a self-imposed trance—also sometimes dreaming.

In each of these states his ability could be observed to operate in three levels that shaded into each other: (a) a "natural" or relaxed level, (b) an "enhanced" or focussed level, and (c) an "elevated" or visionary level. Observation gave little cause to expect flawless performance at any of these levels, but the impression grew on the observer that the chances of accuracy and helpfulness were better as Cayce entered the "elevated" level. Paradoxically, it was this level where evidential material was lowest, though breathtaking when it occurred, for Cayce seemed in this level to be primarily concerned with the life-situation of a man or a group as they stood before God and their own souls.

Cayce Awake

Awake, Edgar Cayce had a flow of psychic experiences sufficient for an exceptional lifetime without trances. He had to work to keep down the waking flow of impressions, he said, so he could enjoy normal relationships without seeing too much. He invented card games, including a noisy one called "Pit, or Corner the Market" which became an American staple for a generation, so that he could play cards, which he thoroughly enjoyed, without reading the minds of opponents who concentrated as they did in bridge. He told stories to strangers, more often than he engaged in real exchanges with them, partly because story-telling kept him from getting too close to them psychically. He kept his family and secretary and good friends and relatives close at hand, to be ready buffers between him and the problems of others, and to allow him to relax without stumbling onto unwanted material.

At the "natural" or spontaneous waking level of psi, or psychic ability, he seemed daily to pick up moods and thoughts of those around him, both in direct impressions and in casual glimpses of auras. Because of this, Cayce was not easy to live with, as the writer can testify; one could never be sure of privacy of thoughts, or whether Cayce might react to someone's ugly mood which nobody else had noticed. He seemed to have swift effects on the moods of others, even of those who were quite used to him, as though he were broadcasting depression or love or joy to those about him. Working with him was like working in a tank of fluid where everyone's movement carried promptly to Cayce and might come bouncing back with doubled force or a special twist. Just policing one's thoughts and emotions became a daily task for those who, like the writer, attended the twice-daily trance sessions, because experience showed that the quality and helpfulness of his productions would vary, though in narrow compass, with Cayce's sense of the buoyancy and peace of mind of those around him.

It was not unlike the man awake to mention someone he thought would telephone soon or to observe that a certain letter or visitor was coming—and be correct. When several times he told his wife and the writer that he would never again see his two sons in the service, he refused to be consoled by encouragement—and his own death bore out his prediction.

Surprisingly, he showed relatively little "natural" ability to affect objects or induce healing, although these abilities of "mind over matter" (which researchers call psychokinesis, or PK) were thought to run in his family.

A few moments of earnest concentration could lift his waking ability to an "enhanced" level. Holding a letter in his hand as he dictated, he would pause to tell a secretary what the sender looked like, of whether there was hope for the case. Dictating to the writer's secretary when his own was overloaded, he stopped to tell the girl she was pregnant, and to mention the sex of the coming child; he startled her, for while she had just been to the doctor and confirmed the pregnancy, she had not yet told her husband. Cayce had found years ago that he could send for others to come to him by concentrating on them, but had also decided not to play around with his ability. Probably some part of his "enhanced" waking ability further showed in deft probing and equally deft listening when friends and relatives came to him for informal waking counsel, approaching him not as a psychic but as a good man whom they admired and loved. Not infrequently they reported, "He helped me make my own decision and it worked out right." A similarly unspectacular ability might be suspected as he sorted out and responded to serious seekers among those in his Bible classes, where he would illustrate a point in imagery familiar to the questioner, or amplify a thought in an observer's own phraseology. In another kind of psychic event where only friendly interest appeared at work, he reported to the writer seeing a dead husband present in the room where he conversed with a widow.

What might be called "elevated" psi came to Cayce more rarely while awake. But there were visions, such as that of a chariot in the sky and a man beside him in full armor, when he looked up from gardening; these sights he associated with the devastations of World War II, and they shook him severely. Like other earnest Christians before him, he cherished a few times when he thought he saw and spoke with his Master, recording these experiences in his diary notes. Less dramatic instances of possible psi at an "elevated" level may have appeared when he prayed with great simplicity and sincerity until there was such deep peace in the room that nobody wished to leave, and one could see tears glistening in eyes across the room. Something like a current or field of goodness and promise seemed built up around him at such times, and not by eloquence.

Cayce Asleep

Even when Cayce went to sleep at night, he had his share of psychic happenings. Early in life, as the writer verified with townspeople from his boyhood home, he had discovered that he could pray over a schoolbook, touch down to an inward "promise" he had once received in a vision, and go to sleep with the book under his pillow. When he awakened, he would find a photographic image of the desired pages in his mind. It was not studying, but it was a help on tests. His classmates resented his unusual ability, enough to recall the feeling for the writer many decades later. Once in early manhood Cayce had done his sleep-learning so well, with the catalog of a book firm from whom he wanted a job, that at the end of his life he could still recite from it. Perhaps a similar process worked for him in his daily Bible reading, combined with lifelong teaching of the Bible, to help him to "know by heart" practically all of the New Testament and much of the Old Testament, as the writer repeatedly verified.

By concentrating and praying, Edgar Cayce seemed to have been able to affect his recovery from illness during his sleep, speeding up the recuperative process. However, during an illness of some six weeks which the writer witnessed, he did not succeed in doing it, and his own trance given on the subject told him that taking a sulfa pill had slowed down recovery more than usual for him.

Dreaming at night, Cayce seemed to be as naturally psychic as awake. He dreamed of stock market quotations, of people he should see to increase his income, of greed among associates, of trips he would take—right alongside dreams which a psychologist would recognize as normal accompaniments to daily living. But there were also "enhanced" levels of dreaming, in which he previewed step by step the development and loss of his hospital, or building up of study groups. Far more than most people, although still only a few times a year, he dreamed of detailed scenes and events from ancient times: Egypt, Greece, Israel. It had become his conviction that such dreams were accurate recollections from his own past lives, but of course such supposed retrocognition was impossible to verify. He had dreams of meeting on another plane some cherished relatives and friends who had died; to him, these experiences were real encounters, and the kind of psychic dream experience which many could have if they chose. Once he dreamed of his own death, with a physiology not unlike that of his final illness, and followed by his wife's early death—which proved accurate; in the same dream he saw sweeping geological changes in the U.S. as scheduled for late in the present century, when he saw himself again on earth.

"Eleveated" psychic experiences may have been present in a few dreams of his being summoned to another plane and charged with a work to do; but this too eludes verification. Real to him were a few dreams of meeting Christ—the more real because not pompous but built around themes of eating, talking, walking with "the Master."

Cayce in Trance

His trance activity also seemed to an observer to operate at different levels of psychic acuity. He had dreams during some of his trances, while busy exploring faraway scenes and talking in an unconscious state with some other part of his psyche; these were likely to be "enhanced" dreams, better focused than were many nighttime dreams—teaching him a lesson about laws of growth, or helping him understand the person for whom he was giving a reading, or taking him back to a vivid scene from another time in history, or showing him his own stages of consciousness while he was active in a trance state. But there were other dreams from the trance periods that had a visionary and "elevated" character, introducing him to the figure of Death, or reminding him of Christ.

In Cayce's trance speech itself, the level which appeared most like that of "natural" psychic pickup in daily life showed primarily in little asides, made before the start of the formal discourse of the trance. On medical or business or other practical readings Cayce was directed by his wife to locate the person in question, and after locating the state, the city, the street and address, he often astonished his listeners in Virginia Beach by commenting on the weather where "he" was, in Florida or Alaska, or by describing a sweeping view down an avenue in Denver, or by mentioning whether his subject were asleep or reading or talking, or feeding a pet. These observations proved so incredibly accurate and detailed, as they were investigated over the years, that they became one of the least controversial aspects of Cayce's clairvoyance. They were matched by equally brief asides as he gave "life readings," or vocational and character counsel, when he might mention items from the place and date of the person's birth—such as a dangerous storm that morning, or for whom the new baby was named, or how many boys were born in the U.S. that day, or whether there had ever been suicides in that county. In the same undertone he also went back through the years of his subject's life, starting from the present and running back to birth, mentioning times of severe stress, or noting, for example, that as a girl the subject had been "a very good little flirt," or pointing out just when the decision to become a teacher had been made. To the listeners these comments suggested eerily that everyone leaves somewhere in creation an impression of all he has been and done, which may be recaptured and reviewed by another intelligence, sometime, somehow.

Besides these comments, however, his readings contained occasional answers that seemed to originate from a "natural" level of ability—especially when he seemed impatient with a questioner's manipulative attitude. At such times the listener had the feeling that much of the waking Cayce was near the surface—as when he told one man asking about organizational activities to do some thinking for himself, lest he begin asking whether to blow his nose with his right hand or left.

In stately and rhythmic language, the content of most of Cayce's readings and trance experiences seemed congruent with "enhanced" psychic perception while awake or dreaming. In this formal vein the trance speech never failed to identify an individual for whom counsel had been given before, though the person might have sought aid decades earlier and have been forgotten by the waking Cayce and his secretary. In the same measured prose the unconscious source continued by describing where in the U. S. to find the best physician for surgery of nasal passages, or how to combine certain drugs that pharmacists averred would not combine, or which colleges a given teenager ought to consider, or the face of a woman to be met some years hence and best chosen as a counselee's wife, or how a given subject remarked that one should "Work hard, play hard," or the tide and winds that would make the best day of the month to dive for a sunken treasure, or how to study the camber of airplane wings, or the form of government of ancient Inca civilization, or when World War II would end. The rhythmic-breathing Edgar Cayce touched upon these matters instantaneously, as though some cosmic file or computer were open to him on any subject where he was directed by an individual's need.

The trance source seemed simultaneously aware of how much could be effectively communicated to the listener. Repeatedly the trances began with the warning that only as much would be given as could be helpful to the person listening; not surprisingly, specialists got more technical subjects than laymen, and conscientious listeners more encouragement and information than dabblers. While some kind of swift intelligence seemed to be moving through space and history and realms of present knowledge, not to mention commenting on happenings on planes beyond death, another part of whatever consciousness was at work in the sleeping Cayce was watching and correcting his secretary's spelling across the room, or answering typed questions before they could be read, or responding to unvoiced inquiries of a listener, or insisting on giving a reading for a seeker whose letter of application had not yet arrived.

The enhanced abilities of Edgar Cayce would have been striking if they had been separate bits, strung out as long lists of targets for him to shoot at. When, however, he produced an intricate medical diagnosis of every organ system of a body, or a picture of the layers in the character structure of a busy human being, or a comprehensive sketch of ancient Judaic schools of the prophets, or a discourse on the warring financial interests that precipitated the Depression, or a report on the fault lines that underlay a series of earthquakes, or the history of tensions in a marriage, or a review of real estate prospects in a resort town—the probability of each little hit was compounded by its linkage with the others in meaningful wholes, and the reflective observer could only gasp.

There were a few times when personalities identified themselves as speaking through Cayce as though he were a medium, usually at the end of a trance session; here, too, enhanced abilities seemed to be at work, but not of a "direct voice" type so much as mediated through the personality and vocabulary of Cayce—similar to the process which the writer has observed at work in the medium Arthur Ford. Generally, however, Cayce and his associates were convinced that discarnate personalities were not giving his readings.

There were also times when the language of the trances changed to a more stately and more urgent style, woven swiftly around Biblical quotes and paraphrases. When this "elevated" level appeared in trance material, it was likely to be the freest of all in time and space. There might be comments on the details of a Biblical incident, such as the walk to Emmaus, or predictions of the fate of nations, such as racial bloodshed in the U.S., or observations on cosmic events, such as the coming of Christ to His own. But these factual items seemed incidental, noted as one might pick jewels from the wall of a cave one was hewing for safety, when jewels mattered little. For the elevated material had the strong note of urgency which the scholar Rudolph Otto had noted years before about moments when man feels himself close to "the Holy." Typically this elevated material came in the midst or at the end of readings, and once Cayce had moved into the heightened state, he was not likely to return to the more detached discourse in which most readings took place. What raised Cayce to the elevated level was not predictable; usually it was something very beautiful or very serious in the person for whom the trance was being given, but sometimes it could be a need in someone else in the room, or a note that had great meaning to Cayce the man. On very rare occasions the elevated material came in a style of severe warning and call to righteousness, as stern as from some archangel of old. Even more rarely, the voice of the sleeping Cayce fell to a hush, and he said, "the Master passes by," or spoke his encouragement "as from the Master"; yet this material was handled with great care to claim no special authorization, but only that which every Christian may have as he "prepares" and "attunes" himself with his Lord.

In one trance session which the writer heard, a group of Cayce's associates and board members of his little psychical research organization were asked, "What will ye do with this man?" It was a question they found hard to answer, and in less than a year Cayce was dead, largely through self-imposed overwork of trying to give six or even eight readings at a session where he formerly gave but one—hoping to catch up on the backlog of misery which thousands of letters brought him each week. The same reading warned that what Cayce did and said was nothing new, and should never be made the subject of a "cult, schism, or ism." His listeners were not being asked to glorify Cayce, which his trances had uniformly refused to do (reserving for Cayce the most curt readings given, though also patient and helpful encouragement). And his listeners were not being asked to promote an organization or movement, the historic response to an unusual phenomenon with religious dimensions. They were being asked instead what they would do with their own lives, with their own abilities; they were being asked to understand and use the laws they were seeing at work in Cayce, seeming to produce goodness and health and joy in people's lives.

What were those laws? Neither parapsychology nor any other psychology is in a position to explain what Cayce did for so many years. But parapsychology is at a point in its history when it is ready anew to consider theories, ready to consider even unusual programs for developing psychic ability, so long as they work. Perhaps it is time to see how the Cayce source explained the workings of psychic ability at various levels, and how it coached a group of determined laymen for fourteen years in developing productive forms of such ability, in a series of tasks later written up as *A Search for God*.

CHAPTER 2

THE CAYCE VIEW OF PSYCHIC EXPERIENCE

IN THE VIEW of the Cayce trance source, both psychic perception and psychokinesis were advanced forms of creativity.

Psychic activity was not a phylogenetic remnant from an earlier state in animal evolution. To be sure, man had once found psychic ability more readily available to him than now. But man in that dim prehistory was not at first an early anthropoid. He was, according to this view, at first that part of creation called a "soul," given freedom to roam the universe and create playfully with the rest of the cosmos.

Some souls went their way, glorifying God by fashioning, through psychic energies, realms of beauty and form which had only to be intensely thought to be objectified. Other souls came upon the earth, tumbling its way through the heavens in its own plan of evolution through "kingdoms" of inanimate and animate matter; these particular souls used their native psychic force to interrupt and toy with earth's evolution, fashioning such beings as they wished out of animal forms, and entering into those forms to enjoy the play of earth's energies. Earth's energies and beings were good, as Genesis says, and fashioned by God for earth's own becomings. But the exploring souls, like wayward children, used their great psychic energies to divert genetic streams, forming their own mutants and monsters, as well as sexual playthings. Eventually these particular souls—millions on millions of them—trapped themselves in the kingdoms of earth, until they forgot their full destiny to become co-creators with God, and sought rather to identify altogether with animal "instinct" and life cycles.

To enable the self-snared souls to discover the goodness of earth as God's creation without hopelessly distorting themselves and earthly evolution, they were given their own "evolutionary" process. They were programmed to reincarnate in successive human forms, interspersing human lifetimes with periods in other planes of specialized consciousness that built intelligence or beauty or kindness or courage or purity. In living as human forms, souls would find their great psychic energies more difficult to tap, available only under stiff requirements, so that they could do less damage than before. But their original energies were still there, awaiting human development to a level of shared goodwill where souls might again be trusted with so much power.

In this picture, the state of the soul in between-life planes of "death" was nearer to its true nature, and accompanied by more free psychic ability, than the state of the soul in a human body, except when that human body was—as in devout men of God—bent wholly in service of its fellows. From this perspective the usual question of psychical research, "Does man survive death in some form which uses psychic powers for communication and manifestation?" was inverted, to become "Does man survive birth—with what measure of his true psychic powers?"

This cosmic mural from the Cayce source had elements to offend the common sense of modern man. The hard-won scientific truths of animal evolution would seem threatened by affirmation of a separate order of "souls." The Church's long battle to affirm the goodness of life here and now would seem lost in a view that might lead to escapism from earthly reality. And the claim of great psychic powers as the birthright of souls would seem an infantile wish to think man as a god, despite the evidence of finitude that crowds upon human life.

Yet the Cayce source picture was not that souls had ever possessed all knowledge or all creative power in some psychic superstate. They had available to them as lasting knowledge and power that which came from use; whatever they tried to build in the universe became permanently theirs. They could draw upon an infinite set of patterns and energies which the Cayce source called "the Creative Forces" (and which others may have at times called archetypes); what they used responsibly became a permanent resource to them. He who truly and unselfishly "loved" became increasingly capable of psychic awareness of the needs and states of those he loved, as well as increasingly capable of giving healing energies and refreshment to those whom he sought to love. What a man did, he had. He who built unselfish beauty had ESP to find the materials of beauty, and PK to bring people and things into actual relationships of beauty.

The source of all human becoming, whether psychic or any other, was "the Creative Forces"—those pattern-giving and energy-releasing designs or fields that danced forth from the One, affecting two other orders that also proceeded from the One: mind and matter. Creation on earth was a blend of matter with mind (however primitive, mind was there in the tropisms and reactions of microorganisms, and in the polarities and valences of chemicals); but the driving, evolving Force was superordinate to either matter or mind alone, and expressed itself through these.

The soul of man was a microcosm of the One, containing as potential in itself all the "Creative Forces" which God Himself had so far seen fit to call into being in creation. Each individual soul was made in the beginning with all other souls, and bore the character and drive of the Creator so faithfully as to be "in His image." Each soul was destined to be a full companion with God, creating and sustaining untold galaxies and planes of reality with Him, using its resources by free choice in harmony with the purposes of God, and relinquishing its wayward self-indulgence while remembering all it had been and done. As the Cayce "information" so often described the destiny of the soul, it was "to have that estate with Him which was in the beginning, and be conscious of same." In such a view the long journey of discovery and becoming of the soul was eternal gain not only to the soul but to God Himself, Who delighted in free and conscious companionship of souls. Yet God did not allow souls to turn from His ways forever, for after untold opportunities some who continued to reject His ways would be returned to their original estate with Him—*without consciousness* of what they had been and done, won and lost.

In this cosmic history-beyond-history, psychic ability was the birthright of every soul, part of its native creativity, ready to find and affect whatever the soul needed for its unselfish work in the universe. Psychic capacity was as native to the soul as were love, inventiveness, patience, integrity, wisdom; it came into play to serve these.

Psychic ability was not, from this perspective, a special prerogative for souls in planes which man calls "after death," though disembodied "entities" might use telepathy to communicate, and psi to precipitate invisible or visible forms by concentrated thought. A soul who had lived a miserable life or series of lives would find at death little to draw upon in his treasure house of activated psychic ability; he might be a psychic cripple on other planes as he had been but partly alive on earth. Quoting Jesus about the degree of creative force available to a soul after death, the Cayce source often reminded, "As the tree falls, so shall it lie." The popular view of jumping out of bodies into a "heaven" of freedom of awareness and productivity had little support in this picture of psychic abilities of the living and the dead.

Nor was psychic ability a strange, occult force to be mastered by alignment with stars, by the aid of spacemen, or by the invoking of principalities or demons or powers. Seeking along these lines might so concentrate the consciousness of a living person as to awaken for better or worse some realm of the soul's developed treasure of psychic capacities. But enduring growth in psychic ability was completely synonymous with growth in spirituality, growth in grace, growth in that Godly love which preferred others. Growth in psychic ability on whatever plane of life or death was growth in high creativity with God.

A given level of psychic ability in a human being could not, then, be used as a measure of his present spirituality; for he might be presently misusing this resource as he might misuse any of his talents. To be sure, a high level of ability was an indication that somewhere, somehow, the soul had chosen and used the psychic resource for good—exactly as high levels of musical or mathematical ability indicated. But the proper spiritual question for any man to ask of himself was not "What have I got, in which I may take my pleasure?" but "What am I doing with what I have?" The latter question alone was the question of spirituality.

There was no point in seeking psychic development as a shortcut to revelations, a shortcut to potency with one's fellows, a shortcut to supposed higher realms. It was fruitful to seek "the higher gifts" of psychic abilities insofar as they emerged for each as potentials from the One Spirit who "divideth to every man as he wills," but such gifts should be sought and used in "faith, hope, and love" or they would either disappear or actively harm the soul who sought them—even through mental or physical illness. The effort to force psychic manifestations by dissociation or trance would bring some results for almost anyone who tried these methods assiduously, for every soul had some psychic inheritance both built up and native. But the last state of those who forced psychic ability by these or any other methods might be worse than the first, if complexes from the unconscious were to rush into the void made by abdicating consciousness, or if unwanted discarnates took over the vacated personality.

Viewed against this life-and-death backdrop, what were the sources of psychic ability in everyday life?

Three Levels of Psychic Experience

According to the Cayce "information," every soul in a human body had some measure of psychic ability as its birthright from creation, helping the person to protect his existence and enhance his daily function. This was a level of "natural" psychic experiences, awake and in dreams, which operated to warn an individual of threats to himself and his loved ones, as well as to alert him for opportunities he was constructively seeking, and to guide him into better relations with other souls. Hunches, apparitions, premonitions, glimpses of auras, moments of healing energy and radiance, delicate outreach to affect other persons and things—all of these would stream into consciousness, through the unconscious; or stream out from the person, in greater or less degree depending on his awareness and use of them. These were the "natural" psychic happenings available to every soul whose life was not so cluttered with defenses and guilts as to block off the flow of such energies in the same way that he blocked off impulses to love, to play, to learn, to build.

In addition, each soul had ever available to it an avenue of psychic awareness and action which far transcended its own native inheritance. The soul might, when fears were laid aside and purpose and practice quickened it, reach beyond its natural endowment to the unspeakable riches of God, which flowed into consciousness to match the soul's resources. There were no necessary limits to psychic experience here, when need and opportunity joined with intent; as Jesus promised, "Greater things than I do, shall ye do," and "I will send you the Holy Spirit, to make known to you all things from all times." Yet this overall process of joining the native resources of the soul to the resources of the "Universal Forces" was not capricious or magical, but lawful and developmental in its general outlines, however freely the laws might be transcended on occasion by divine mercy.

A soul might expect its natural psychic ability to be enhanced by Universal Forces, along lines of its past endeavors and application of talents. One who had served at healing of any kind, not just healing by prayer, might expect readier hunches on medications for a sick child. One who had been an explorer of new lands might expect clearer impressions of buried mineral deposits to appear in his psyche—more readily than one whose preoccupation had been with sculpture. One who had sought to awaken and coach talents in others might expect to find rising in him the energy to psychically affect others by direct action, more quickly than one whose gaze had been upon interpreting languages. In such a process the natural psychic endowment of the soul was enriched by the overlay of specially developed psychic talents; enhanced abilities followed naturally upon concentration, or preceded shock, either to widen the aperture of the soul's native abilities or to join the soul to the larger resources of the divine, or both.

These were the usual lawful forms of psychic ability. Yet under pressure of great need and great love souls might at any time slip into harmony with the One so that treasures not yet fully earned might be poured into consciousness, either as knowledge and insight or as force and outreach. In these "elevated" states not only useful facts but the very bones of the universe, the pulse of creation might come into reach—as they did for Job of old when the vision from Yahweh broke upon him. Psychic ability then became not simply a useful tool for man's day-to-day operations, but an unforced awareness of "the way things are," and an invitation to work with the grain of life. Rightly seen, psychic ability was ultimately not a phenomenon of unusual perception, but part of the everlasting quickening and guidance called "faith"; it was not as a mysterious esoteric power, but part of the overflowing goodness which humans called "love." It was part of the eyesight of the soul into creation, part of the muscle of the soul to build and to give.

When and how was the soul given access to the largest psychic awareness? This was not for the soul to dictate, though it might build its readiness by use of chosen gifts and interests. What the soul could attempt, however, was to respond to a force like itself, loose in the universe, which "ever seeks his own." That force the Cayce source called "the Christ Spirit," answering to the "Christ consciousness" originally given to every man. Souls who had tangled themselves in the web of instincts and energies, in the panics of animal creation, might have great difficulty in finding their way out, great difficulty "in even beginning to think and love aright." But they would find as part of their natural psychic inheritance that they had an ability which they need never lose; it was an ability to turn toward the Christ Spirit, which would awaken answering chords within themselves. This Christ Spirit was not a vague ideal or idea, but a vital, living reality—a shaft of Light ever shining in a particular way, "the Light that lighteth every man" if he chooses it. The key to the highest psychic ability, then, was the effort to attune the deep springs of personhood to the Christ Spirit, whose life and being served to "reflect" God to man, focusing the One to become believable and bearable for the confused consciousness of man. Over and over the Cayce source spoke of the "other Force," the "Christ Force," ready to "bear witness with the soul," to meet and strengthen and guide the natural divine energies welling up in an individual. This Christ Spirit did not take a man over, nor make him an automaton, for that would frustrate the plan of creation for each soul to reach its own powers, its own full consciousness. And no soul's becoming was a matter of indifference to the Christ nor to the Father, for, according to the Cayce source, each soul was created at the beginning with its own unique inherent design, as original and delightful as each snowflake, and capable of glorifying God as could no other design. The primal energy and dream of each soul held the qualities of goodness and inventiveness and purity that men ascribed to the Godhead; but buried within this glowing field of forces was the soul's own seed of unique becoming—a seed which might predispose a soul to one kind of psychic gift or another, at various times in its journey.

The Process in Psychic Experience

But how did actual psychic experience come about in the consciousness of a human being? How did the events occur?

The imagery of the Cayce source was one of fields—fields exemplified by the dance of atoms in a bar of steel, or the play of energies in a thought, or the radiant presence of an angel. In this view, everything had its fields, and all fields had complex patterns of "vibration" of the One Force. When fields of the human psyche were set into phase with a given field "out there," then psychic perception or psychokinesis could take place, in greater or less degree —sometimes even by accident, or without conscious intent, as the phenomena of poltergeists suggested, or the phenomena of medieval saints having to be restrained from levitation, or the accurate perception of a future event in which the percipient was only marginally involved. As a rule, however, active desire and focus were needed along with attunement of fields to bring about psychic events. Accordingly, the Cayce source added to the word "attunement" a companion term, "service," as the other necessary pole for effective psychic happenings. What man sought to use in service to enhance human life, and had trained his psyche to employ creatively, would meet the possibilities given him by attunement and yield what are called psychic phenomena.

A wide range of variables might affect one's "attunement" with other event-fields. Important among these variables was the capacity to conceive what might be going on "out there"—whether in another person's mind, or in an event of geological importance. Psychic ability could operate most readily to validate or shape the natural flow of impressions from memory and the unconscious, or the natural flow of energies through habits and the unconscious into events, by way of psychokinesis. If the flow were barren, through disuse or inexpertness, then the heightening push of psychic force had trouble proffering itself. Accordingly, experience, application, cultivation of talents. were essential to enlarge the range of options upon which creative psychic impulses might assert themselves. Service created the tunes for attunement; there was no magical way to attunement.

Yet psychic attunement to desired persons and events, or to object fields, had its methods and procedures, yielding greater or lesser effect in a given situation.

Essentially, these procedures were what the Cayce source described as "turning within," or "seeking the still small voice," or "asking God's help." But in specific physiological terms, the Cayce source spelled out a chain of states in the fields that made up a human being, activated for effective ESP or PK. There was first of all an invisible force-field that surrounded and interpenetrated each cell of the organism; it was called "the real physical body," and guided the maturation of the body, as well as its healing. Psychic activity first of all took place in the real physical body, through seven vortices in this invisible but important field—vortices which Hindu tradition called "wheels" or "centers." Each was associated with an underlying endocrine gland in the physiological body, which it affected in delicate ways, stirring the discharges which in turn stimulated the flow of sensory imagery into the central nervous system—yielding ESP impressions—or stirring a flow of vital energy which poured out through the vortices as PK. These responses in the physiological body to the invisible "field body" were not random, but occurred in chains of interaction affecting the endocrine glands and both the autonomic and central nervous systems. The optimum interaction patterns within the body were those which the Cayce information called by the Hindu term of "kundalini" —a welling up of creative energy and focus in the person, a raptness which was also productive. Active in study, in work, in play, in loving, in suffering, in worship, this kundalini circuit was called into play in the best and safest psychic experience, and kept in alignment by the deep purposes or ideals of the person, as expressed in the choices made, insights reached, productive service rendered, and prayer and meditation undertaken. The channel for the best psychic activity was therefore kept clear and effective by all forms of creativity, not by isolated acts of incantation and concentration. Yet each individual had his own memories, symbols, hopes, intentions, places that aided his best flow of kundalini.

The physiological side of psychic experiences, according to this view, was affected by whatever affected the endocrine gland function, or the function of the body's two great nervous systems. Injuries might cause sudden activation of unwanted and uncontrolled psychic abilities (as the history of psychic research well illustrated), while changes in endocrine secretion or medication might quickly affect or shut off an ability (as the history of the field again showed). Variations of rest, of balance, of anxiety and tension, even of diet, might be traced in their effects upon psychic ability. And in the actual moment of a psychic flash, or psychic impulse sent outward, particular processes of breathing, posture, and even the invisible action of the force-fields of gems upon the body, might be traced.

Over and over the Cayce material stressed the lawfulness of psychic happenings. Yet the total picture developed was not a mechanical one. The body, including its delicate chemistry and nervous impulses, was in the last analysis a servant of the mind. What the mind chose and held before itself either quickened the body as one tunes a musical instrument or let it go slack to psychic impulses. If the mind and will were turned toward shared creativity, whether of loving or of fashioned forms, then resources would be drawn from the soul to yield helpful psychic impulses for these tasks. If, in addition, that creativity were carrying on creativity built in some earlier lifetime in the soul's journey, then the psychic capacities could be expected to flow yet more freely. And if the person achieved purity of heart and enduring love toward his fellows, he could expect to find as well those times when the psychic stream overflowed its usual channels, and he found himself supplied with whatever was needful for the situation, from the Giver of all good and perfect gifts. These were the basic variations in psychic performance, psychic gifts, psychic phenomena, according to this source.

Psychic Experience as Creativity

Ultimately, there was only one category which affected the development and safe use of psychic ability: creativity. Not creativity in the narrow sense of novelty, nor self-expression, nor cleverness, but creativity in the sense where God Himself was described as Creator. In this sense creativity was the soul's entering into events in such ways that the consequences were other events, each working to fulfill the promise of shared human existence. Some creativity built persons, as when a parent held the hand of a fearful child, yet released it when the youngster was ready to venture on his own. Other creativity built forms—as when an artist painted a portrait, and yet did not substitute a portrait for fully perceiving a human face, but gained sensitivity from the portrait for the next encounter with a real person. Creativity might be as little as not forgetting to water a garden, or as great as laying the foundations for a country in its constitution or its music. But in the real, shared work of giving and building, man could find his destiny, so like that of the One whose unseen image he bore. And reaching ever fuller stature in the long journey of the soul, each individual might increasingly expect to see, by what could be called psychic ability, "face to Face" instead of "darkly," and each might expect to bless and refresh and heal and renew another, through adding to the other's natural energy an energy which might be called psychic ability, but was more often called "love."

The question of the conditions for effective psychic ability then became the question of the conditions of any creativity. What were, indeed, the essential conditions of man's creativity with his fellow man and with his unseen co-Creator, the Father of both? In the view of the Cayce source, these conditions were what men have sought to understand and practice through the intricate forms and traditions they call religion. Myths, symbols, dogmas were employed, however clumsily at times, to increase the attunement which men sought with the Source, and to increase the service of the fellow man for whom that Source ever waited and whispered and reached. Likewise, rituals, initiations, processions, sacraments, codes and commandments all were developed to focus and train man's energies into alignment with the One, in a flow of new and abundant creations. This was the ultimate function of faiths, of traditions, of religious communities and covenants, according to the Cayce source.

Yet man had freedom of will, and godlike powers in his creativity. He might choose, and often did choose, to dally, to become bemused, to squeeze for himself instead of sharing with others the fruits of creation—whether in the primal Garden or in the ghetto. And he could use his religious forms and modes to justify his turning aside, to still his doubts, to cover over his sins. So the quest for creativity, for the effective conditions of creativity, must be made over and over again, in each generation, by each people, and at one time or another by each soul. For the altar which was supposed to reflect the glint of the One Light might easily be turned to reflect the face of the self-seeker.

He who would develop safe and useful psychic ability, then, had no choice but to work upon his religious understanding and practices, whether these were overt in theological propositions and duties, or covert in personal codes of honor and generosity. He must sooner or later ask about his relation to the ultimate Source of good in his life and in the lives of others, if he were not to coast on the achievements of a past life, or to slide into narcissism, or to develop that cruelty which seeks to force from others the secrets of life buried by his own concerns for power or possession or position or passion.

A group of Edgar Cayce's friends from Norfolk and Virginia Beach, who had together been attending various religious lectures and study groups, asked him one day in 1932 whether he could give them lessons in spiritual development through his readings. They were especially interested in developing some measure of the astonishingly helpful psychic ability which each of them had experienced through Edgar Cayce's trances—whether that aid had been medical or vocational or financial or marital, or something as elusive as peace of mind and soul. Cayce agreed to try, and together they sought lessons from his source. Promptly they learned that the lessons would be given them only slowly, under the requirement that they live out and talk through and practice each lesson in turn. There was no pressing ahead for secret wisdom; it would not be given them. They learned that the life of each one would come under examination of his own conscience, and under the loving concern of others in the group, stimulated by terse but firm encouragement and coaching from the trance source. And they learned that they had to undertake daily disciplines of prayer and meditation at times they agreed upon, as well as less scheduled but equally important disciplines of guarding their tongues and thoughts, or sorting out their ideals, or training themselves to see the best in one another, in spouses, in strangers.

They did not secure lessons in breathing exercises, or in concentration, or in astrological charts, or in crystal balls, or in dream prognostication, or in visualizing, or in laying on of hands—although all of these were mentioned and some treated at length, while a few processes such as healing became the subject of yet another group and project. What they received were lessons in the major conditions of creativity, one by one. There were twenty-four such lessons, later published in two little volumes which they wrote together under the title of *A Search for God,* and a twenty-fifth which was to have been the start of another series interrupted by Cayce's death. They were required to develop their own insights on the themes suggested in the trances, and to write these up in their own words, not parroting Cayce. Likewise, they were to work out their own illustrations from daily experiences of growth, not simply quoting from the Bible or from biographies.

Their task was long, and some of the personnel of the group changed. But over the years the members each grew. And they developed a startling variety of psychic experiences, of each major type, and at each level of intensity—some awake, some in dream, and some in vision or in rapt state of prayer or meditation. They developed helpful energies for healing and blessing those who needed their aid.

They did not become great psychics. None became an Edgar Cayce. Yet the development of their own limited talents to full flower was for them a greater source of satisfaction than the showcasing of genius.

For they were seeing and working out for themselves the conditions of creativity, step by step, together. And they were finding rewards of joyful, productive lives that far exceeded the novelty of psychic manifestations alone.

In struggling to grasp the mystery of psychic experience posed for them by the work of Edgar Cayce, they opened in their studies the way to a yet greater mystery—the mystery of man's full partnership with God. This, rather than blinding revelations or marvelous signs, became for them the religious significance of psychic experience. The unknown opened into the known, the hidden into the near at hand, and the mysteries of phenomena into the mysteries of the gracious love of God meeting each man on his way.

What was the path they took towards a creativity which was psychic and more than psychic? Exactly how did they find phenomena linked with fulfillment, happenings linked with habits, impressions linked with intentions, psi linked with the soul, service linked with the Servant?

PART 2

Psychic Experiences in Everyday Life

CHAPTER 3

COMMUNICATION WITH THE DEAD

IT WAS SUNDAY morning. Edgar Cayce stood before his adult Bible class in the white-steepled colonial brick Presbyterian Church at Virginia Beach. Some thirty men and women had gathered from neighborhood homes and from homes an hour's drive away. They were in good spirits, ready to think, to chuckle, to pray, to discuss, until time for the stately Presbyterian worship at eleven o'clock.

Cayce had read aloud the Old Testament passage describing Elijah's contest with the priests of Baal, where each sought to prove whose divinity was real by bringing down fire upon piled wood. Though the events were extravagant, Cayce had read the account thoughtfully, without flourish, as one might reread a well-worn letter from a battlefield, touching upon familiar but prized details. When he put the Bible down and began to speak, it was to characterize Elijah's stubbornness and fierceness; he began with the man, not the phenomena of fire from the sky.

Picking up one detail after another from Elijah's life, Cayce sketched a portrait of a devout man, an extremist, a reformer. He made the brooding intensity of Elijah seem almost a presence in the room, until his listeners were responding, nodding. Those who knew Cayce well may have recalled the portrait of a bearded old prophet which hung over the filing cabinet in Cayce's study—a photograph which had won him a prize, though his subject was a weary derelict whom he had pulled off of the street to pose for him at his studio in Selma, Alabama.

Elijah's faith was the subject; Elijah's extraordinary gifts and experiences were only workings of that faith. It was a perspective that Cayce always developed when treating the miraculous in the Bible, and one which appealed to his listeners; it suggested that God could still do mighty works in their lives, though the mighty works might be as unheralded as continuing to live with a drunken husband, or handling the shuffling walk of multiple sclerosis, or building an enviable reputation for integrity as a sales executive. Though Cayce did not refer to his own abilities as he taught the Bible, his own presence before his class was a quiet reminder that wonders were not yet over; he did not need to labor to evoke a Biblical world where man and God were not strangers.

Midway in the period Cayce paused to look intently at one side of the room; he pursed his lips and waited briefly. Then, as he continued, he spoke with a bit more emphasis, and a flash of a smile. His imagery sharpened, and none in the room had difficulty imagining the smoke from Elijah's fire, while the priests of Baal stared sullenly at their flameless logs.

The period drew to a close, the members greeted one another heartily, singling out the few visitors (such as the present writer) for welcoming hand-clasps, as well. The room held no sense of hidden secrets, no psychic mysteries; here Edgar Cayce had simply shared again a talent he had used every Sunday since boyhood: teaching church school. The class members had become part of a throng of hundreds in his home churches of Kentucky, Alabama, Ohio, and Virginia, and at stations of missionaries around the world; they were never gathered except in Cayce's imagination, yet were his own "people" and flock for half a century of service.

What had interrupted Cayce that morning? At Sunday dinner in his home, after his wife had served a tasty Southern meal, he told the writer and others present that he had seen a number of discarnates, "dead" people gathering from another plane to share in the class. They had seemed to him to file in and take the empty chairs at one side of the room, although a few had stayed in the back. The sight had not been new for him, because he felt he often saw these unseen visitors at his classes and at public lectures such as those he had given on alternate Sunday afternoons back in the days of the Cayce Hospital. They were similar to the unseen visitors he occasionally glimpsed in prayer moments just before giving his daily readings, as others sometimes reported seeing them in the room—"entities" which his trance source confirmed were often there, listening, and sometimes hoping to speak or be noticed in some other way by the living.

What had caught Cayce's attention that morning was a feature of his visitors which he had seen a few times before: they were primarily Jewish, some wearing skull caps and shawls. He did not see their presence as a special tribute to him, for he felt that the dead often gathered where devout people studied and prayed together, to learn and grow as did the living. Rather he spoke of the visitors' sincerity and seeking, and noted the love of the Bible, of the Law, which often marked Jewish faith more deeply than the life of Christians. To Cayce, awake or in trance, Old Testament faith was not a story outdated by the New Testament; he made no gratuitous comparison between supposed Christian "love" and Jewish "legalism." Instead he viewed the entire flow of Biblical history as a stream of men and women living on a high plane with their God—on a plane where the closeness of God made the differences of traditions, however genuine and important, seem less important than in the usual Sunday School homilies. Not church or synagogue, but the "promises" of God to the people who covenanted with Him were the heart of the drama—perhaps a note more real to Cayce because he felt his own life and work intelligible only in terms of a promise given him when he was thirteen, and often renewed in his quiet times since.

Some at the dinner table asked why the dead should wish to learn of the living. Did not they have their own places of study and worship? Were they not freer to seek and instantly attune to centers of spiritual teaching than when on earth? Responding along the same lines as his trance readings, Cayce commented that sometimes the dead needed the prayer-energy of the living, to find their way; they often needed, he said, to be prayed for by the living who remembered them, as well as welcomed in the inward thoughts of worshippers in churches and temples. But also, it seemed to him, there were lessons which the living faced and grasped, because of their freedom of will and choice, in a different way than could the dead; the "discarnates" or "entities" could catch the force of these lessons by being present at times of spiritual searching, as a music-lover might learn of the structure and phrasing of a symphony by seating himself in the rear of an auditorium where an orchestra rehearsed.

Cayce's view of the dead learning from the living was the same as that independently developed by the Swiss psychiatrist, Carl Jung, who did not, however, allow his observations to be published until after his own death.

How did Cayce feel about seeming to see the dead? He made no great fuss about it, for such glimpses had been a part of his life since boyhood. Yet he was interested in each experience and often prompted to tell a story. On this occasion it was his wife and secretary who told the writer their own story. They had heard Cayce go to the door one night and seem to greet somebody; the conversation which they heard from their rooms upstairs had lasted well into an hour. Mrs. Cayce had even called downstairs when the visitor left, to inquire who had been there—receiving the incredible reply that it was a woman they had known in another city who had since died, calling on Cayce to discover what had happened to her and what she should do next. The story was strange enough to bring forth humor at the dinner table, and yet nobody was prepared to say it was impossible. The writer in particular recalled it when one day later he and Mrs. Cayce both heard footsteps on the walk and the door opening to the library where Cayce sat. Yet inspection showed nobody there, only Cayce laconically remarking as he smoked a cigarette, that he had received a "visitor" whom others ought to be able to see if they looked a little harder on such occasions.

He had his store of experiences of the dead, both awake and asleep. There had been that night back in Selma when he and his wife had once tried a ouija board—and decided never to do it again. Messages had poured through, including one which helped to locate the body of a drowned child. There were those visionary experiences which came shortly after he went unconscious for his trance, when he seemed to see himself following a thread of light through plane after plane of beings, whom he took to be souls who had died and were in various states of development or growth, from earthbound states to states of light and song. He had even noticed waxy shells, which his trance readings told him were lifeless remnants left behind to disintegrate, as souls on other planes went on their way.

More than once his dreams had seemed to put him in touch with his dead mother, who had greeted him warmly, and had even assured him that she would soon be reborn as the child of a loved relative. In a similar mood were those times when his mother or a treasured family doctor had seemed to break through at the end of his trances with a stream of happy exchanges and encouragement, as well as messages to other members of the living family; on at least one occasion those in the reading room heard such an exchange as one might overhear one side of a phone conversation, while Cayce himself recalled it all as a dream, on awakening.

One man who secured hundreds of readings from Cayce over a period of eight years was especially interested in life beyond death, which he called, after Ouspensky, "fourth dimensional" existence. In his readings, more than in any other collection in the thousands of Cayce trance sessions, there were perhaps a dozen times when particular "entities" whom he sought to reach— and felt he did reach in his own dreams and prayers—seemed to speak through the entranced Cayce. These "entities" were mostly his father and his mother-in-law, but also two businessmen with whom he sought to work closely in earning money to found a hospital and university, as well as supposed philosophers and on two occasions characters from New Testament history. How much of all this was real, the waking Cayce, who remembered nothing of the content of his trances, could not specify. But the general sense of the closeness of the dead, in his trances as when he was awake, was a living part of Cayce's daily experience—even in that peculiar phenomenon, which he could not explain, of sometimes knowing instantly as he passed a cemetery the names and dates of those buried there, as he had often verified in detail. Asked about "apports," or objects materialized for the living by the dead, he showed the writer a silver dollar which he kept in his dresser as a memento of a time at a campfire in the Southwest, when it had been given him as from his mother.

How typical of the world of psychic phenomena were Edgar Cayce's experiences of the dead?

They were similar to claims which stretched back to antiquity, enshrined in stories like that of Saul and the Witch of Endor calling up the ghost of Samuel and perhaps having a variant in accounts of the post-death appearances of Jesus. They had features in common with anthropological accounts of the *shaman* of Eskimo and Tibetan tribes consulting the spirits of the dead. They had parallels in China, in Africa, in Sweden; for whether self-delusion or reality, reports of communication with the dead have been as old and wide as humanity. But which of these reports bears up under modern scientific scrutiny?

Today's empirical study of the possibility of survival of death and of communication with the dead began with the earliest investigations of the Society for Psychical Research in England of the last century, and continues into present-day inquiry in American research centers on what is today called IPA, "incorporeal personal agency." An early investigation was a census of hallucinations, conducted among thousands of people in England, and later repeated in both England and America, attempting to discover how people think they see the dead. Dr. Louisa Rhine's monumental file of spontaneous psychic cases, compiled at Duke University, also contains similar material, carefully organized as to whether the perception of the dead occurred awake or asleep, at the moment of death or later, with details of demise or not, and whether visually or in some other sense of presence and identity. The British inventor of research equipment, Tyrrell, completed a study of apparitions in the 1950's, at the same time the American sociologist Hornell Hart was reviewing the experiences of the living in seeming to leave their bodies in full consciousness—presumably as the dead might do. An American researcher, J. G. Pratt, devised a method for evaluating verbal material that might be presented from a supposed discarnate, by breaking it into items which could be scrambled and offered to various subjects for claiming, to determine the percentages of hits and probabilities. Karlis Osis of the Parapsychology Foundation in New York set about investigating what may lie beyond death by studying the deathbed reports of the dying, while Carl Jung, and more recently others working with LSD and terminal cancer, have studied the dreams of the dying, to learn how the unconscious represents the state and event of death. Hugh Lynn Cayce has reported on his studies of cases of mental illness developing out of the attempt to contact the dead.

But by far the largest body of research on communication with the dead has been on the work of professional or amateur "mediums," individuals who feel they have developed the capacity to contact the dead at will, whether in mental mediumship (receiving messages through impressions) or direct-voice mediumship (seeming to have their vocal apparatus taken over by other personalities) or writing mediumship (having their hands produce scripts while the medium is in trance) or physical mediumship (seeming to materialize parts of bodies, produce unexplained objects, or manipulate instruments or temperature or levitate the medium's body). The names of researchers on such phenomena vary from the literate amateurs such as Hamlin Garland (who found mysterious buried crosses) to careful modern psychologists such as Gardner Murphy (who discussed the obscure poems of classical literature produced independently by a number of mediums whose combined messages added up to "cross correspondences," an intelligent literary whole seemingly devised by one entity on the next plane). It was William James at Harvard who was so impressed by the mediumship of Mrs. Piper that he arranged for her to be sent to England for further study; it was the American investigator, Dr. Prince, who did the first thorough study of the St. Louis author, Pearl Curran, who claimed to be producing scripts in out-dated English by a discarnate named Patience Worth. Then that careful British worker, Carington, studied the controls of a number of able mediums in experiments which suggested that these "controls" may have been complexes of the medium, showing the obverse of the waking or conscious personality. More recently, the controversial Bishop Pike has reported his seeming contact with his dead son through the American medium, Arthur Ford—whom the present writer has also studied in repeated tape-recorded sessions.

Out of this immense total of man hours no agreed-upon conclusions have been reached. It would be safe to assert that all the investigators agree that some mediums, especially the famed Palladino, have at times produced obvious frauds, whether by conscious design or by the too-willing action of an entranced unconscious, and that such deception will remain a hazard so long as the research rests upon talented individuals, rather than upon processes demonstrable with a wide variety of subjects. There would also be considerable agreement that definitive experiments about survival of consciousness beyond death will have to wait until more is known about the modes and range of ESP; at present, every fact needed to document the reality of a discarnate can also be treated as a target for the medium's telepathy and clairvoyance, so that ESP and PK today account for too much, as raw effects, to allow the discrimination of perceptions and actions of discarnates from all other psychic happenings. Finally, there would be considerable agreement among investigators that ordinary people have experiences enough like those of mediums to suggest that communication with the dead, if it is ever convincingly established, will prove to be a widespread human phenomenon, and not one of professionals or religious spokesmen alone.

While in a state of trance or altered consciousness, Edgar Cayce had much to say to many seekers on the subject of communication with the dead. His "information" insisted that anyone could learn to recognize signals or impressions from departed loved ones, although it also developed a theory of post-death planes of growth where discarnates would be less and less easy to reach, in a full theory of reincarnation consistently maintained by this source as by such other modern psychics in trance as Arthur Ford and Eileen Garrett. Like many another source, Cayce's insisted that some entities slept for long periods on dying, while others hung about the earth in bewildered attempts to carry on as always. Part of this view was spelled out in case after case, where the Cayce source described how discarnates sought to aid the living in problems of health, vocation, business affairs, developing a philosophy of life, learning how to love in families, childbirth, and childcare; much of such guidance from discarnates came, it was suggested, in dreams and prayer periods.

However, the Cayce readings were slower than most psychic sources to encourage systematic mediumship with the dead. Partly this hesitance arose from the insistence that the dead did not know a great deal more than they did while living, for the subconscious of the living, it was claimed, became the functioning mind or consciousness when one died. But also there were warnings that dependence on the dead was as unwholesome as dependence on a living person, detrimental to both parties. One who clung to a discarnate loved one could hold back that soul from its proper development. Besides, the effort to compile experiences of the dead which could convince skeptics was hopeless; the state of death was so unlike that of earth consciousness that it would only be understood briefly by humans when they entered a "raised" state of consciousness and saw and understood things that words and analogies could not adequately convey. It was emphasized that one should not expect general revelations from discarnates, for the path of communication between the living and dead lay along the line of love, not wisdom. Finally, the Cayce readings never wearied of urging those who sought psychic development to make their attunement with Christ, not with the dead; in such attunement they would be brought spontaneously and safely to such experiences of the dead as they could handle in their own growth, without becoming inflated or distracted from the business of living. Moreover, in the spirit of Christ, the living would find themselves prompted to pray for the dead.

Both during Cayce's lifetime and afterwards, many individuals interested in the Cayce-source views of death and the possibility of communication past death have kept records of their experiences, and shared these in study groups and special seminars. Their preliminary findings have been varied, but with points of agreement. When unwanted "interference" occurred, as though from invasion or obsession by "entities," there were typically several elements found together: hormone imbalance created by illness or injury affecting the circulation to endocrine areas, conscious or unconscious desire to solve life problems by shortcuts instead of sustained growth and service, conscious efforts at dissociation or intense concentration, and underlying currents of sexuality and hostility such as are commonly found in neuroses. On the other hand, seeming contact with the dead which did no harm to the living appeared most often in dream material, or in times of prayer and meditation, or in flashes of subjective light associated with meditative states, or in experiences where the healing of guilt and regret seemed as appropriate as in forgiveness among the living. Over and over the Cayce counsel seemed borne out, that the *purpose* in entering relationships governed their helpfulness in meeting the dead, as in meeting living; whether one sought a belonging of childish dependency or of mutual maturity before God was a critical element.

Belonging in Creativity

In the view of the Cayce information, the first religious question for those who sought to grow in any form of talent or creative activity together, including psychic activity, was the question of belonging. The kind of relationships one sought with others, and the outcome sought from such relationships, would influence every aspect of one's growth and daily life—from child rearing to business acumen, from constriction of blood vessels to romantic love, from the making of music to the character and scope of contact with the dead. The first chapter of the little training manual, *A Search for God,* was entitled "Cooperation." Its emphasis on creative ways of belonging to one another would not surprise a psychologist investigating the conditions of effective psychic experience, including possible communication with the dead.

Those who seek to find and share with the dead as a means of enhancing their own importance, by identification with supposed super-beings, might well make the same mistake as those who seek self-fulfillment among the living by identification with the famed, the glamorous, the powerful. Not fulfillment but emptying of personality results from such projection, as Erich Fromm has so bitingly shown in his description of "symbiosis" where two needy individuals use each other but never really meet as human beings. If the psyche works to balance itself in encounters with the dead as with the living, then surely it would limit such uncreative encounters, or distort them in such a way as to bring the perceiver into mischief with himself so that he would have to grow up. Interestingly enough, this appears to be the path of many a journey through exercises to break the barrier of death: the seeker comes upon just enough evidential material to keep him going, but just enough sick material to put him into a jam with his associates and force him to insight. In his love affair with the dead he finds much the same outcome as the teen-ager in a crush on an older teacher: growth through pain of self-discovery.

Research might well bear out the contention of the Cayce source that the nature of belonging affects all psychic activity and all other creative activity. How far might the flow of helpful psychic impressions on business affairs be impeded by the desire to take advantage of others, even those in the same firm? How freely could the flow of healing energies occur if the concern were to impress or captivate the sick person rather than to set him free? And would not the issue of true and false, rich and shallow belonging, affect the originality of the artist, the faithfulness of the priest, the independence of the adolescent among his peers, the security of the scholar, the judgment of the over-promoted consumer? How far was the Cayce source, stressing belonging as the beginning of creativity, anticipating the emphasis on group therapy in modern psychiatry, so sharply espoused by theorists such as Mowrer, writing on the effectiveness of Alcoholics Anonymous?

What the Cayce readings set forth in their insistence on "cooperation" appeared to be one of the oldest religious questions: the theological issue of covenanting. What does it mean to be a church, a Chosen People, a Buddhist Sangha, a Jewish kibbutz? How does religious covenanting differ, if at all, from joining a gang, identifying with the firm in one's gray flannel suit, merely absorbing the values of "the establishment" in politics and art and sex?

In the Cayce view, mere joining and membership, even enthusiastic identification with religious institutions and leaders and causes, availed man nothing in itself except to get man moving, and might be dangerous. Cooperation was only rescued from conformity or escape to group identity when it was covenanting with God. Over and over, the Cayce readings referred people to Exodus 19:5, where there appeared a saying used in many variations in the Old Testament: "If you will be my people, I will be your God, and will make you a peculiar treasure unto myself." The cooperation in a family, a store, a football team, a nation or a union of nations, had to be essentially of this order, however unverbalized the pledge.

Knowledge quickened in such covenanting could be trusted; seasoned in the community of the faithful, it might even be called revelation. But private visions pursued for their own sake, not bent to the service of others, would destroy a man's sanity and usefulness. "Knowledge not lived is sin" was a frequent refrain of the Cayce readings. The right order, then, was living relationships which produced workable truth, whether by psychic means or by reason or science, rather than truths which called for promotion by religious bands and societies. "Christ ye serve, and not a church," people were warned, while at the same time they were as strongly encouraged to join a church as to seek to glorify God in families—those institutions which were, in their living fulfillment of cooperation, "the nearest shadow of the heavenly home."

Might one count on psychic quickening to arise from group fields where there was genuine cooperation before God? The answer offered was the Biblical reminder "Where two or three are gathered in my name, I am in the midst of them"—to encourage, to disclose, to heal, to bless. By the real force of an extrapersonal energy and intelligence which men called Christ, and which they approached when they put on the loving "mind of Christ," natural psychic ability was quickened into enhanced and even elevated psychic ability. Paraphrasing Paul, the readings insisted in literally hundreds of passages that "His Spirit is ever ready to bear witness with our spirits"; something quite literal was meant, including psychic quickenings and confirmations as well as heightenings of psychokinetic energy, rather than a vague goodwill which made men feel glad they were well behaved.

But what was the nature of cooperation which might be called covenanting with God, whether in the home or marketplace or playground or lovers' hideaway? According to the Cayce readings, such belonging would involve man's keeping the two great commandments, which these readings never wearied of rehearsing: service and attunement.

Cooperation embodied service when it was infused with the right answer to the question so often repeated in these readings, "Am I my brother's keeper?" That right answer lay in the boldest possible assertion that though God was not exhausted by the human soul, He was Himself in and of the nature of the human soul. As one served his brother and blessed him, then, he did so to God Himself, not symbolically but literally. The Cayce readings often made this point by quoting Jesus, "Inasmuch as ye did it to one of the least of these my brethren, ye did it unto me." And they went on to add a stringent injunction, "Until you can see in each soul that you meet, though in error he may be, that which you would worship in your Master, you have not begun to live aright." The firmness of these assertions by the Cayce source was often a shock to the listener who had accepted such teachings as poetic injunctions, not as statements about the real divinity in his brother; listeners realized that if Cayce were here speaking the truth, then a radical form of loving others, even the enemy and, as these readings put it, "those who reject His way," would be demanded.

Yet the commandment of service was no call to sentimentality or indulgence, in cooperative belonging. One's responsibility was to meet each person where he was and then build him, lift him, strengthen him—whether by prosaically bandaging his foot or by beseeching the help of angels from heaven for his stubborn temper. And cooperation could involve struggle, indeed would involve struggle if one took seriously the Christ way; each person who sought to learn cooperation would have to learn to "so live that you can look any man in the eye and tell him where to go." And each would have to develop that sturdy identity before God which the readings meant when they said, "Every tub must sit on its own bottom." The ultimate goal in cooperation was the little phrase so central to the Cayce readings that it appeared in scores of prayers suggested for people to put in their own words and use many times a day: "to be a channel of blessings for others." The blessings were of course God's blessings. They would be what each could best give out of his resources, without depleting the giver to his damage; yet they would be fully creative events or "happenings" of a given moment, not stereotyped blessings of giving away tracts or Bibles or holy sayings. Being a channel was not a matter of setting prim and self-righteous examples for others. "Don't just be good, be good *for* something," was the refrain of the readings in their continuous insistence on real creativity in every dimension of man's life—in man's money, his dance, his governing, his carpentry, his lovemaking, his ballgames, his temple rituals. And who was the brother to be served? As might be expected, the Cayce readings defined this brother as the next one needing aid, needing respect, needing an opportunity, needing an opponent to fight him for his best self; the "brother" could not be defined by ties of kinship or nationality or religious bonds, although all of these ties involved promises and duties that must in their place be kept.

Yet service without attunement might be vastly ineffective, a mere do-goodism or even an unconscious using of others. For cooperation really to succeed, the persons involved needed to work together with the wisdom known by the parts and cells of the body producing a whole out of millions of cells; they would need to work together as do the heavens in "unity, order, harmony." That kind of cooperation could require knowing that transcended the mind of man, though man must use his every wit to understand his brother. So there must be the effort to bring human consciousness into alignment with an over-arching Consciousness greater than its own, that of the Father. As the Cayce readings used the phrase beginning "Inasmuch" with which to tag the basis for service, so they used a quotation from Jesus to establish what was meant by attunement: "I go to prepare a place for you"— in consciousness, said the Cayce source—"that where I am ye may be also." As man turned his deepest desire in the direction of Christ, and paused for definite acts of attunement, he could hope to best guide his efforts at service, and to enrich his energies with energies beyond his own, from a source as high as God and as immediate as his own soul. Without such attunement, any soul could expect to slip into "selfish aggrandizement," the precise Cayce definition of sin. His supposed service could become seeking power for his own ends, rather than building for the greater good, and this was the root of evil in man, the perversion of his incredible capacities. However, attunement in cooperation did not mean shutting oneself away, any more than it meant pursuing a spiritual athleticism of self-development; one could seek guidance in the midst of a busy life of building and loving and serving. Indeed, without these active expressions, the channels for attunement in belonging would become clogged.

There was in the Cayce readings a remarkable absence of assurance that one could make it to a full human stature simply by belonging, by identifying, with the right groupings or traditions. To be sure, neither insight and truth nor love and productivity could be reached without full covenanting in groups—whether in the family or work groups or play groups or political parties. Yet there was no group or combination of groups that would allow the seeker to sit down and take his pleasure, not needing a living, provoking God. These readings offered no salvation by identification, and certainly not by inviting Cayce-ites. Nothing short of living, daily process of "self-bewilderment in Him" could be trusted.

How might the right kind of belonging be cultivated, so that it might bear fruit in psychic experience and other creativity as well? The answer of the "information" was painfully prosaic, beginning with "look to the little things." Helpful speech and deeds, kind thoughts, overlooking failures as far as possible; these were the basic disciplines of that belonging which was covenanting with God. One had to learn to be mindful of attitudes in each situation, often by specific exercises, such as trying to go one day without a harsh word. Yet not negative controls but positive, outgoing attitudes were the prize; over and over this source insisted: "magnify the agreements," or "see that which is good in the other fellow," or "know that each is trying to build with his life what he sees of God," or "be interested in the other fellow if you expect him to be interested in you."

Training for full cooperation required more than hygiene of attitudes; it also required active commitments. This source urged individuals to join in groups of like-minded seekers, for Bible study, for sharing personal experiences and insights, for tasks of service to others, for intercession, for meditation. And such groups should not rely overmuch on the stimulus of meetings, for cooperation must be built daily. They should keep a regime, which each group worked out together, including daily prayer and meditation, as well as exercises of growing in cooperation, and should keep records of their growth as shown in dream and vision. Prayer, including prayer at the same times of day by the whole group, wherever they might be, and prayer by each group member for other members as well as for strangers, was constantly stressed, with the admonition that one dare not ask God to do for himself what he would not himself be willing to do for his brother. Out of such shared disciplines a group might slowly come to be "of one mind," and that mind the mind of Christ in some measure, so that cooperation could produce a group field for protection of the members, as well as for drawing in the "answering Spirit of Christ" to meet the needs of others.

Could cooperation be worked out in small groups alone? The Cayce source was insistent that cooperation, the right kind of belonging before God, must first be learned and practiced in small groupings. But it was equally insistent that the same spirit had to come in time to pervade the affairs of nations. Cayce's readings honored the idealism of communism, though not its expression in either Russia or materialism, and prophesied that in the long, long run new leadership for mankind would come out of Russia and China. At the same time, the readings set a high value on the American dream of freedom and just opportunity, promising that if more and more cooperation in economic and business and racial affairs took the place of selfish exploitation or defensiveness, America could continue to offer genuine world leadership. God was seen as a God of nations and peoples as well as of individuals. Yet the key to changes in the life of nations might often be found in the disciplined, determined growth of individuals in small covenanting groupings. The final outcome of the work of a few was potentially more than most people imagine, for the prayers of but a few who were in accord and lived as they prayed might—as with Abraham of old—save a city, or even a people.

Communication with Dead and Belonging

The Cayce readings offered cooperation as the fully creative mode of belonging which was the starting point for development of all gifts, even for building of people and cultures. Might cooperation actually produce enhanced communication with the dead?

A long-time associate of Edgar Cayce's married after his death, and shared with her husband, an attorney, a rich pilgrimage of inward growth and outward service to fellow seekers. When her husband died, in his sixties, she was inconsolable, despite her studies of the Cayce ideas of life beyond death and her lifelong churchwork. Yet she continued in her occupation of librarian, guiding others to the volumes they needed; her manner remained cooperative, though the light was gone from her face.

On her first birthday after her husband's death, she awakened early and keyed up, her mind once more on death because of the demise of a friend. She had dreaded her birthday, because her husband had always celebrated it in some imaginative way, with a gift and a trip together. Yet on this day she felt her apprehension lifting, and a sense of quickening that helped her morning chores and prayers. Later in the morning she found that a much-needed book was not in its proper place, and was dismayed, for she needed it for a reader. Then a quiet and happy kind of closure occurred within her, as she was prompted to look in another section of the library, under a different though similar number. She found the book at once. A short time later another needed book was missing; promptly again came the sense of what number to look under. There she found it—and found something else, as well. She found an inward assurance, filling her with joy, that her husband, dead but a few months, had reached her through the barrier of death on her birthday, and joined her in this helpful prompting—an act of service for others. His formless yet real presence seemed to make it known to her, in the recesses of her thought, that he was following through on the intent he had often voiced when living, especially during the helpless days of his last illness, when he repeated that he would like to aid her in her work.

From that moment in the library her spirits lifted, and she never again tasted the deep loneliness and depression that grief had brought her. She did not seek to make her husband her errand-boy in the library, as she had not while he was alive. This was not the way in which they belonged to one another, not the nature of their covenant. Yet she knew, in a certainty that she found difficult to describe to the writer, that the cord of love joined them through death as it had in life, and that each could give assurance and aid and loving energy to the other as it was needed. She prayed for him afterwards as naturally as she used to do before she got up to fix his breakfast. And she understood, she felt, some portion of why the act of sharing and giving, in breaking bread together, had opened the eyes of two disciples after they had walked the Emmaus road with their unseen Master.

CHAPTER 4

HUNCHES AND IMPRESSIONS

EDGAR CAYCE SHOOK his head. "I don't sleep on books any more," he told the writer. "I don't have to." He was enjoying the puzzled looks of those standing about him in his library, as he spoke of his boyhood knack for securing almost photographic impressions by sleeping on books—an ability featured in his recently published biography.

"Here," Cayce said, reaching for a book in the writer's hand. The volume was still in its mailing jacket, unopened, having just been received for review in the little *Bulletin* sent out regularly to members of the Association for Research and Enlightenment. The writer was to read the book, and perhaps review it.

Holding the book in his hand, Cayce stood there thoughtfully. He did not attempt to read the mailing jacket, or stare at the book. Then he said, "It's about a death, of a young woman and her husband, together. The father saw them, had a psychic experience of them at their funeral, and this book is about what he saw and what it meant to him." Then he handed the book back to the writer and walked off into the other room, completely sure of himself and as pleased with his brief, spontaneous performance as if he had hit a beautiful golf stroke.

The plot of the book, entitled *Lighted Passage,* turned out to be exactly what he had described. A young woman and her husband had been in an auto accident on their honeymoon. Her father, a Presbyterian minister and the author of the book, had seen what seemed to be her spirit leaving her body in the last moments of her life in the hospital, and her mother had seen the same, independently. Later, at the funeral, the father had seen both bride and groom in the back of the church, glowing in the responses of relatives and friends who had come to share the memory of the two young lives. Still later he had received impressions—some of which he described to the writer when he later came to Virginia Beach to visit Edgar Cayce—of the work of helping souls on planes after death, in which he believed his daughter and son-in-law were now engaged.

The flow of hunches and impressions seemed as normal to Edgar Cayce as the flow of incidental memories in the minds of others going about their daily work and play. He seemed to sense which cases most needed his help as he glanced over letters, and he quietly added certain appointments to his crowded schedule of readings, while he put off other applicants for months. Strange, however, were his experiences of scheduling readings in such a way that unusual diseases turned up in "runs" of a day or two. Was it Cayce's impressions about the seekers? Or had his unconscious somehow drawn to him four cases of polio at once, or six of leukemia all in a couple of days, without another case of polio or leukemia for several months? While the cause of such baffling synchronizing might presumably have been that Cayce was giving the same medical information to each indiscriminately, medical follow-up reports made this explanation unbelievable, and the puzzle had to be left like so many puzzles about Edgar Cayce's abilities—unanswered.

His family and associates became accustomed to little events that betrayed Cayce's access to hunches and impressions: his hurrying home from a drive to meet a stranger whose visit had not been announced, his predicting a furnace breakdown, his "seeing" an opponent's hand of cards in a game, his encouraging a teen-ager to believe that his parents would forgive him, his detecting the marital troubles of someone in his office. The items were small, and none of them in themselves completely beyond the reach of coincidence. Yet, like his impression of the minister's book, they were often so accurate and prompt that the observer wondered whether there were a psychic flow in Edgar Cayce's mind as present as background music in a restaurant. The flow seemed to be there in his dreams as well, when he glimpsed the coming of relatives, the availability of a house to rent, a forthcoming quarrel with a friend, the commotion of moving his belongings from one city to another, and the source of new interest in his readings at a time when he needed the income.

An unusual aspect of his waking impressions was his claiming to see "little people" or "elementals" around plants. He even teased his staff for not being able to see them in a colored photograph on the shelf in his library.

How typical of the world of psychic phenomena were the hunches and impressions of Edgar Cayce?

They made a piece with claims as old as the daimon of Socrates, which had told him of danger to himself and others. They were of the order of Samuel's abilities to locate lost animals, which led Saul to him in Biblical times, and not too different from Paul's precognitive dream of shipwreck. To be sure, Cayce operated without the cards, thrown sticks, horoscopes or crystal balls used to enhance impressions by diviners, in the Orient, in Rome, in Asia Minor. But his quick impressions were not substantially different from those of others in modern times, as the writer has noted in observing Eileen Garrett sensing a publisher's response to a submitted manuscript, or Arthur Ford answering in Philadelphia a long-distance call from Tucson, and correctly describing while wide awake the illness of a stranger's wife. Cayce's ESP in handling a book was not unlike the clairvoyant associating to token objects which the writer has seen scores of times in the daily life of a European psychic, and not unlike the impressions of a housewife who touched a book and promptly gave an accurate description of the Russian ancestors of the Harvard author of the volume.

What is the scientific status of such claims of daily-life ESP?

One of the striking accounts in early research was that of the English scholar of Greek culture, Gilbert Murray, who showed that he could pick up complete book plots, or even imaginary scenes, from the thoughts of his family and friends who devised tests for him. The novelist Upton Sinclair tried similar experiments with his wife, producing results impossible to quantify but striking in their content, while the French scientist Warcollier sent impressions across the ocean to telepathic receivers waiting to draw the objects intended for them. Drawings taken from the dictionary made targets for the landmark experiment by Carington, in which he discovered that when elephant was the target on Tuesday night it also turned up with disturbing frequency on Monday and Wednesday nights in the calls of his unselected subjects. He drew from this experiment the idea of "displacement" of ESP onto adjoining targets which led him to prompt Dr. Soal to monumental research with two subjects. Hettinger and others reported on "psychometry," or the use of ESP under the stimulus of token objects, and more recently experimenters with LSD have recorded periods of ESP accuracy on a variety of targets over a period of an hour or more, occurring in subjects who have taken the drug. But of course it has been the patient work of J. B. Rhine and his many associates which has brought the order of mathematical probability into research on hunches and impressions.

Today most researchers on ESP would expect, as Schmeidler has shown, that a given subject who shows regular ESP ability will disclose a pattern of psychic perception not unlike that of his sensory perception, corresponding to the style of his personality and the character of his bonds with a "sender" or "receiver." They would not be surprised at occasions when the subject "knows he knows," or starts strong in his calling a given set of targets and grows stronger and stronger in his accuracy and conviction, finishing flushed but exhausted. They would expect the accuracy of a subject's hunches and impressions to vary from day to day, and in response to health and general spirits of the subject; they would be surprised to have high scoring continue for more than ninety minutes at a time in a given day. They would expect an individual who scored well on one type of psychic ability to show some ability along other lines as well, though one or two main types of ESP might be prominent and the others sporadic; a total psi endowment rather than a narrow skill would be their expectation in a given subject. They would look for one who could do well on cards to have helpful hunches in traffic, and for one who could identify a telephone caller by holding the telephone wire to know his unseen dentist bill, as well.

But these rudimentary pictures of a total psychic process are far from constituting a theory. To be sure, theories have been attempted, such as the provocative attempt by Toksvig to account for Swedenborg's abilities, or the field theory proposed in the Ciba Foundation symposium on ESP, or the theory which Carl Jung called "synchronicity," linking mental perception with external events by way of intermediary "archetypes" rather than by direct causation—in a type of theorizing also followed by the knowledgeable Australian investigator, Raynor Johnson. But a generally convincing theory of hunches and impressions has not yet been formulated.

When Edgar Cayce turned to his state of altered consciousness for a commentary on hunches and impressions, he found a great deal of material. Part of the picture from his "information" was an insistence that "thoughts are things," as constant investment of psychological energy in a train of thought produced fields of force which acted autonomously upon the thinker, and even upon others. The Cayce source appeared to describe something similar to what a psychiatrist calls a "complex" within an individual's psyche, but to give it external reality as well. Part of psychic experience, then, was bringing one's own thoughts into phase with the thought forms of others, from which events and mental states might be inferred. Though such a cosmos might be difficult to imagine, thought had force and weight beyond that which modern man usually gave it.

The Cayce source paid much attention to the work of the psyche in dreams, as a source of psychic impressions and hunches, both those which were enacted in the dream and those to which the dreamer was alerted for later reception by his dream. In a bold assertion, the Cayce information went so far as to insist that nothing important ever occurred to a person without being previewed in a dream; however, the body of Cayce's dream material made clear that such previewing could be of tendencies rather than of explicit objective details. While the Cayce readings interpreted much dream material along lines similar to psychiatric interpretation, stressing the efforts of the psyche to right itself, or to interpret the meaning of each day's experiences, they also went on a tack not common in psychiatric dream study, insisting that a significant proportion of the dream material of healthy people consisted of psychic material—warnings and promptings and alertings which occurred every night to keep the personality functioning in its biological and social spheres.

The flow of hunches and impressions might be impeded, according to the Cayce readings, by fear—and this became one reason for not overloading the psyche by making it guess on problems where reason and common sense, or hard study and practice, would suffice. Further, the flow would be more flexible and accurate in mirroring external events, or the thoughts of others, where there was a wide range of experience available to the percipient. One who wanted hunches on stocks ought to study and work with stocks; one who wanted impressions for medical diagnosis should work in healing. The quick mind could be quickened to do its job even better, while the stumbling mind had difficulty in securing impressions.

As might be expected, the Cayce information insisted that the purpose of seeking hunches and impressions had a marked effect on the flow of accurate material. Cooperating created a different mind set than exploiting, which would set the seeker at odds with his own best self—the natural source of his psychic impressions and expressions. However, it was also important to actively study the various types of psychic phenomena, and the laws of each. Understanding through practice and understanding through study were the watchwords. Seekers were encouraged to read such volumes as William James' *Varieties of Religious Experience,* where James first outlined his concept of the "subliminal" before Freud popularized the term "subconscious," and Ouspensky's philosophical *Tertium Organum,* or a practical little book on the role of suggestion in focusing awareness, entitled *The Law of Psychic Phenomena,* by Hudson. Ignorance was no aid to psychic development, in the view of the Cayce source.

Because of the living example of Edgar Cayce's gifts, scores of people during his lifetime, and hundreds since his death, have tried to follow his prescriptions for developing a helpful flow of hunches and impressions, in waking and sleeping states. In a series of experiments called "Project X," reported in his volume *Venture Inward,* Hugh Lynn Cayce tried on college students for several weeks a set of intensive disciplines—all drawn from suggestions in his father's readings. The students went on special diets, fasted, kept journals of dreams, used specific gems, undertook daily projects of serving the handicapped or disadvantaged, set about intensive study of their own psychological makeup, helped one another to grow, and especially undertook regular periods of prayer and meditation, some at two o'clock in the morning. The progress of these studies on ESP tests was impressive, as the writer reported at a briefing session at Duke University. Since that time in the 1950's, the methods used have been generalized to fit intensive "project" groups, not unlike "sensitivity training" groups, which have been held as part of annual summer school programs by the Cayce-oriented Association for Research and Enlightenment.

What have these many laymen discovered about cultivating hunches and impressions? They have learned to move slowly. The cases reported in *Venture Inward* of mental breakdowns among those who sought to rush into psychic experience taught many eager seekers that opening the door to the unconscious was easier than closing it. They have learned to wait upon the flow that comes normally, in dream, in waking impression, in prayer quickening, in the heightened sense of certainty that a job is done effectively. And they have learned to analyze themselves, their motives, their states of consciousness, their drives, their energies. For they have seen that many sources in the unconscious offer imagery and imaginative material, and that some of the most compelling material is not psychic but neurotic or even psychotic. They have learned that they needed to know themselves, if they were to deal effectively with the psychic flow in everyday life.

Self-Analysis in Creativity

In its characteristic approach to religion as the cultivation of the conditions of creativity in human existence, the Cayce source took as its second theme for study and practice the task of self-analysis. The second chapter of *A Search for God* was inscribed with the words from the ancient Delphic Oracle, "Know Thyself," and the Cayce source placed the topic ahead of such topics as faith, virtue, the cross.

No psychologist suggesting the elements in cultivation of creativity would hesitate to give priority to self-knowledge. Studies of creative individuals, both by observation methods and by giving them tests for fresh approaches to problems, have consistently shown that the more creative person is typically one who has access to his inward life, to his emotions and fantasies; he is one who can produce a fairly accurate appraisal of his own abilities and weaknesses. It was self-knowledge and self-acceptance at a deep level which the sociologist David Riesman suggested might be the essential distinguishing feature of the "autonomous" man, able to both conform and not conform to his culture—by contrast with the overadjusted or ill-adjusted person in his culture. And of course self-knowledge has been the hallmark of psychoanalysis, whether in its forms stressing free association and dream study, or its forms stressing study of daily life behavior.

It would not be difficult to picture how the cultivation of safe and reliable hunches and impressions might require self-knowledge, though popular thought might guess otherwise. The overcontrolled or repressed person, afraid of his unconscious energies and promptings which manifest sexuality or hostility or power strivings, would be likely to shut off psychic materials along with other material, in the same process which makes him forget his nightly dreams, as well as claim to be a purely rational man, master in his own psychological house. On the other hand, the person who indulges in flights of fantasy, solves problems by wishing about them or making up omens and signs, or lives reactively rather than in disciplined responses, would be likely to drown psychic promptings in the flow of other material from the darker realms just outside of consciousness.

Further research may continue to show that self-knowledge affects all creativity, and not merely psychic power; self-analysis may prove relevant to marital success, to selecting the motifs for a painting, to holding a managerial post, and to controlling the diet. But as the psychologist Erich Fromm has pointed out, most moderns know how to spot and get attention for new noises or knocks in their cars, but have little skill at recognizing and attending to noises or knocks within their own psyches, preferring instead to invest evil in the Reds or the Blacks, or to lurch along in half-distracted existence.

By placing cooperation at the start of religious disciplines, Cayce's source had planted itself firmly in the Biblical tradition of covenanting. But in turning next to self-analysis, it picked up a strand more central to the Indo-Aryan traditions of Greece and India. Where cooperation stressed the bending of the will to serve God in the other person, self-knowledge stressed the overcoming of ignorance. Yet while the two concerns have often seemed antithetical in the history of religions, they may also be complementary. Without a spirit of covenanting, knowledge and self-knowledge may become cruel or stultifying; yet without knowledge, without truth about human life and existence, the effort to help others may become trivial sentimentalizing or vicious totalitarianism in the name of a misconceived divinity.

While the novel concept of the soul might startle the Westerner approaching Cayce's materials on self-knowledge, the actual emphasis in these materials was upon the Biblical "heart" of man—his intentions, desires, purposes. Evil, in the view of the Cayce source, was that which put a man out of relation with his brother, with his God; evil was that which made man separate—sin was selfishness. By contrast, man in his proper stature was seen in this view as having what Paul called "fruits of the Spirit": patience, longsuffering, kindness. To undertake self-knowledge, then, was to learn to distinguish among the impulses in the heart of man.

In the Cayce readings there was no dualism of impulses. The evil in man was essentially misplaced good, to be treated as such and "raised" to higher levels of effectiveness. Man's animal passions were not in themselves evil, for animal creation was "good"; they were only dangerous to man if he limited himself to this kind of expression, forsaking his larger inheritance of becoming, for then his very soul would rise up against him. Two inner processes, instead, in the Cayce readings, first contributed to putting man out of relation with his God, and did so today: fear and doubt. Human wickedness was real, as seen in cravings for lust, power, position, and possessions: but such drives could be harnessed for effective expression, if man would turn to the Source too often obscured by fear.

Why man's fear? In the Cayce perspective, fear could be either destructive or helpful. As "the fear of God," it could be "the beginning of wisdom," a limiting, focussing element, the instrument of education of the soul, the bearer of what Eastern thought calls karma. What a man did to himself or others which was wrong, selfish, contrary to the loving force in his own soul, became his problem, his panic, his puzzle. He was held to his wrong activity by his very fear and defensiveness about it—whether his problem be with knowledge, power, love, or things—until he finally learned to work properly with it. He might overcome such karmic fear by a slow path of suffering, or by a swifter path of "grace"—involving insight, forgiveness, and giving to others at the very point of that fear. Learning about oneself, then, meant learning about one's evil and its cure, and discriminating among one's fears.

Yet the emphasis of the Cayce materials was typically on what was right with man, on those resources for good which could be studied under three ancient headings: body, mind, spirit.

Because for forty years the Cayce source was chiefly occupied with giving medical aid, it produced an immense amount of material about the human body, its systems and organs, its diseases and their cures. But on the subject of self-analysis, this source turned to the question of how the body could respond to the promptings of the soul and of Christ. It urged a distinction between the "flesh body" of cells and molecules and the "real physical body" which existed as a field in and around the physiological body and which mediated impulses from the mind and from the soul. Because of the delicate interactions possible in the "real physical body," one might see as a literal truth the claim that "the body is the temple of the Living God"—and it was a truth often repeated, together with the assertion that "there He has promised to meet thee." Man need not, and should not, try to leave his body aside nor rise above it, but rather should seek to quicken and use it for others, until it could respond to unseen impulses as though it were a finely tuned electronic instrument. By seeking "the mind of Christ," man could find "the Christ consciousness" present "in, with and under" his flesh—the last phrase being one which the Cayce source borrowed from Lutheran teachings of the presence of Christ in bread and wine, to suggest that holiness was possible in human bodies, not reserved for other planes.

As self-study meant investigating the body, it also meant investigating the mind. In the 1920's, when psychoanalysis was limited to sophisticated intellectual circles in the U.S., Cayce was insisting in his readings that exploring the mind through dreams, as they led on into awareness of the spirit, would be a central avenue for modern man's growth in spirituality. In dreams would be found the drives and impulses which made up "desire" in man. For the Cayce source, the mental realm in man was a bridge between his body and the soul, but not as a simple conveyor belt. The mind had formative power greater than most men realized, although that power was sometimes apparent in hypnosis (as in Cayce's own instance) or in crisis, or in the puzzling endowments of a genius. What man had first to discover about his mind was its dynamism, its tendency to construct whatever the person set before himself. What one thought about and sought, he became. Indeed, the heaven and the hell of the afterlife literally existed in one's own subconscious, no more, but no less. The key to the life of the mind then, was the choice of one's ideal. Whether an ideal were animal cunning or selfless spirituality, the mind would try to build what was constantly set before it, though the building would be harder when the ideal was out of phase with the soul. In the view of the Cayce source, the living mind had two spheres always before it: the complex signals of the physical body and its interlocking cells mediating the outside world, and the rich signals of the ancient and godlike soul, infused with the particular qualities gained on the long journey of reincarnation. Each night, the mind of a man would struggle in dreams to reconcile and interpret the current events of his outward life with the deeper ideals and directions of his soul.

Yet the mind was not purely private. Because of its ability to be tuned like an instrument, it could be put in rapport with other minds and events, yielding an endless supply of helpful psychic experiences, where the mind was in harmony with the individual's own developed talents and soul. Because of its psychic powers, the mind was an active system, affecting the universe with its every reflection; over and over the Cayce source insisted, "Thoughts are deeds, and may become miracles or crimes," depending on how mental energies were used. To find religious parallels with the emphasis of the Cayce source on constructive powers of the mind, one would have to turn to Jesus' morality of intention, where thinking adultery was ultimately the same as doing it. Or one would have to turn to the "right mindfulness" of the Buddha —if the mind were set aright and properly fed, it would lead man out of his suffering.

Finally, according to the Cayce readings on self-discovery, there was need for study of the soul—a structure which had little stature in modern religious reflection in the West. The approach to the soul should not be made, in the view of this source, from what man might produce in one lifetime that could endure. The Cayce picture, which seekers were invited to verify through dream and vision and quickenings in daily life, was of a soul which dated with other souls from the beginnings of creation. Every man on the street was millions of years old, in his essential being, however far from the surface that essential self might have been driven by his actions. Every man on the street was inwardly a veritable universe, staggering if one could visualize it.

According to the Cayce source, when God made man, He gave to man as his soul's treasure every pattern of creativity found as yet in creation; the Cayce term for them was "Creative Forces" or "Universal Forces," and the readings used these terms as synonymous with God Himself. God was not just another Person doing things; He was in some sense Doing Itself, the unspeakable creativity working itself out in all things and planes and realms, whose extravagance and brilliance were graciously shielded from man except in visions such as the one which overpowered Job. But God was no blind principle of evolution, either, as men had found in the swift intelligence and loving, personal responses of the Christ, or of their own souls. Man could make what he willed of his body, through lifetime after lifetime, for its destiny was given into his hands. And he might turn his mind in directions beyond counting, for it was a great storehouse of abilities, and could bring him what he set his heart upon, if not at the expense of his brother or his own integrity. But the destiny of the soul, said the Cayce readings, was with God. The proper end of the soul was not past finding out, but only God could establish whether an individual soul were reaching its opportunity or betraying it.

Where would a man turn to learn about the soul? Would he seek some special tradition, books, teachers? The Cayce source did not belittle these resources, but it placed an astonishingly heavy emphasis on what could be known in self-study, when conducted in prayer and disciplined meditation: "All that ye may know of God is within thyself." Very often, too, the Cayce source quoted from the last speech of Moses to his people, in Deuteronomy, where Moses told his hearers not to send over the sea or into the heavens for the word of truth, since the Law could be found within, "in thy mouth, in thy heart." Openings, disclosures of God, were every man's right, not limited to prophets, priests, founders or reformers. If a man sought to find his own soul, he would sooner or later find it, and its Author as well. For both were of the realm which Cayce called "force," using the term synonymously with "spirit." So conceived, "force" was not a higher realm detached and floating above matter and mind, but the infusing, activating, directing and striving quality found everywhere in matter and mind. To be spiritual was not to discard matter and mind; this was impossible, though one might indeed discard a body by dying. To be spiritual meant to become more perfectly aligned with the essential quality of this force, with the One Force, which poured forth from itself all Creative Forces. This formative "word" or pattern-giving element in the Godhead was to be given flesh in each man's real daily life, not alone by his moral propriety within certain established limits, but by his being alive, productive, a full son, a light within the Light.

Tracing out the body, the mind, the soul were the essential tasks, then, of man's self-knowing. The method was to be not merely introspection, but experiment. A man was best known, in the view of the Cayce source, not by what he had, but by what he could give. No course of study alone could reveal this potential; a man had to act, to serve, to love, to dare, if he were to know himself. While in action, as this source so often urged, he could "step aside and watch self go by." One could examine his effect on others, to see whether in truth they were "glad to see thee come and sorry to see thee go"— a devastatingly simple criterion of spirituality. The evil that one saw and bemoaned in others could also become a useful tool for self-understanding, insisted the Cayce readings, since such annoying traits were irritating because they were in the beholder—precisely the psychoanalytic concept of projection of rejected unconscious material. One's mistakes, errors, and failures could be food for study, as well, because they could disclose laws at work, and show the mercy of God in his tempering of the soul: "Whom the Lord loveth he chasteneth." Yet the ultimate resource for self-understanding was not an achievement, but a gift—the quiet prompting of the soul. As one slept or awoke, worked or paused, the soul could be trusted to bear its witness with the "still small voice that convicts, convinces," and to bring its everlasting promise of goodness, in oneself as in one's brother.

Hunches or Impressions and Self-Analysis

Could self-analysis actually affect the flow of psychic hunches and impressions in daily life?

A young English teacher, much taken with Cayce's readings on psychic ability, set out to awaken his own abilities. He concentrated his thoughts, tried special methods of breathing, fasted, studied his dreams for evidence of psychic awareness, meditated, prayed, used candles, took ESP tests, read books about psychic phenomena, joined groups interested in the psychic realm, and went among psychics. Still, his impressions were sporadic, his hunches hardly reliable. He worked harder at his teaching, spent much time with his students, tried to improve his school and his church and community. His psychic awareness improved a little. But he knew that if there were anything to the Cayce picture, he was far short of his potential for reliable promptings.

He attended seances, he tried automatic writing, he sought to bring out the psychic abilities of others, and he talked with researchers such as the present writer. But his experiences were still few. Finally his family problems drove him to psychoanalysis, a step that humiliated his pride. With his analyst he began to face crippling patterns within himself that he had only dimly glimpsed before. He worked on hundreds of dreams, and he kept his religious sensitivities alive through his religious painting, an avenue which always awakened deep and good currents within him. He became so absorbed in his growth toward balance and wholeness through analysis that he forgot about psychic abilities.

But then the hunches and impressions began to come, in dreams, in visions of the dead, in nudges about the affairs of daily life, in seeing auras, in experiences of healing within his Episcopal church life. Without any dramatic turning point, he reached the time when he could sit down and take inventory, discovering that not a day passed without helpful psychic impressions to meet his increasingly effective work as a teacher, and his efforts as a husband and father.

What had changed? Like Peter of old, had he been required to study himself until he could distinguish within himself Satan and rock, the voice from "flesh and blood" and the voice from the Father?

CHAPTER 5

AURAS

THIRTY PEOPLE WERE crowded onto couches and folding chairs in the library adjoining Edgar Cayce's home, part of the frame building housing his offices and files. Although some had come to Virginia Beach from as far as California, nearly half were from points in Virginia. All were in a mood of expectancy, and in good spirits, though most were also self-conscious. It was a Saturday morning in early June, part of the long weekend which was called the annual "Congress" of the Association which sponsored Edgar Cayce's work. Cayce was going to read their auras as he did each year at this time.

Most of those in the room had received trance readings from Cayce. Some had even received scores of readings, on medical problems, vocational problems, spiritual ideals, business problems, and influences from past lives. Some had shared in the readings for a study group. But even those most familiar with Cayce's work felt a touch of apprehension. What would Cayce see, wide awake and looking at them? It was one thing for them to come under the inspection of his altered consciousness while he was in trance and speaking impersonally. But it was something else to have him inspect them, wide awake, and describe the fields of force which he, like so many psychics before him, reported he saw in patterns of shapes and thrusts and colors. From these auras, as he had shown in Congresses for some years, as well as in informal moments with those close to him, he seemed to discern the quality of a person's life, at various levels. Would he warn of illness? Would he hint at marital infidelity, which a couple had so far concealed from others and almost from themselves? Would he find an outer shell of spiritual talk covering self-righteousness? Or would he mention a hidden talent, so far overlooked? Or growth of soul which was permanent gain? Everyone knew that Cayce did not expose people in front of others in these sessions. But they also trusted him to indicate something of the truth he saw as prominent for each. So they spoke nervously with one another, chatting of little things, and then lapsing into introspective pauses. Had Cayce asked around the room, just then, he might have received fair "readings" from each one about himself, as the responses to his comments would shortly show, when individuals spoke here and there with evident depth of feeling.

Cayce explained briefly that he could only see what he could see, and report it. Like so many other aspects of his abilities, there was much about his seeing auras which he did not understand. But he knew that others had found this experience helpful, so he would try it for them. He kept the mood gentle, often playful as he went around the room for nearly forty-five minutes, making certain that laughter protected people from feeling too exposed.

To a woman who had been in and out of hospitals for several years, he described colors and shafts he saw in the region of her lower body, and assured her that the surgery recently undergone had done its work, with no relapses coming (and the months that followed proved him correct). For a doctor he described the colors and patterns that conveyed to Cayce a sense of intense energy; then he added with a laugh, "But you should never run for political office, for you will surely lose." (Though the doctor came from a family of social philosophers, he had no intention at that point of giving up his practice for politics; yet within a few years he ran for a state office—and lost.) On around the room Cayce went. He saw a field of golden yellow around one person whom he described as outgoing, helpful to others. He saw an intense blue over the head of another, and reported that she always meant what she said, that she was a person without guile. To another he mentioned the little crown of white, almost like the headpiece of a bride, which to him meant that her prayers and meditations were reaching "unto the throne" and beginning to change her whole life and feeling about herself. To a young housewife he reported a divided field, almost like an egg with two yolks, which suggested to him that she had not yet resolved the tug between home and career, but that she was making it. For a young student there were flecks of gray for disappointment, and some patches of angry red for frustration that needed to be worked out. For a middle-aged man there was a swirl that warned of a potential ulcer if he did not revise his attitudes and diet. For a gray-haired woman there was an indication in green that she would find peace and self-expression in gardening. On he went, speaking of health, travel, friendships, money, faith. As he spoke, people responded with comments which indicated that in most cases they had some idea of what he was describing—at times a very clear idea, or facts to report which delighted the room and wreathed Cayce's face in smiles. Some shook their heads in bewilderment, but promised to think about what he had said. Those whom the writer interviewed later produced considerable corroborative detail. It seemed that in at least some instances Cayce's psychic abilities awake had been as accurate and helpful as when he was in trance.

How like the experience of others were Edgar Cayce's glimpses of auras? They appear to have been of the same order as those which prompted medieval artists to paint halos around saints, or led observers of Loyola in prayer to insist that there was a light around his head. Whether a similar phenomenon may have occurred to the disciples of Jesus on the Mount of Transfiguration is problematic, as is the question of the energy field around the quaking shepherds which made them see light on the night of Jesus' birth. But there are abundant anecdotal reports in contemporary Western biographies of psychics to suggest that some phenomenon actually occurs under the name of "auras."

Although the subject was studied in the early days of psychic research by a German investigator, and by an Englishman named Kilner who worked on a filter to enable ordinary percipients see the aura, the phenomenon has been less studied than most other forms of psychic experience. This is unfortunate, for it may hold the clue to a number of processes to which it has not yet been connected by experiment. Were the strokings or "passes" of Mesmer in early days of hypnotism a process of affecting the aura of the subject, as Hugh Lynn Cayce has suggested from his research on hypnosis? Is the meeting of aura fields an important part of healing by laying on of hands? Are there fields of force similar to auras which inhere in objects, and account for "object reading" or psychometry, and perhaps even for some forms of hauntings, as well as for part of the healing effects of shrines and holy places? The area of auras should not be too difficult to investigate, for it is one of the most familiar experiences of gifted subjects, as the writer has observed in studying a number of noted psychics from the U.S. and Europe, as well as a number of gifted but unknown subjects.

An excellent beginning on such research has been reported by Shafica Karagulla, a physician with credentials in neuropsychiatry. With the aid of a foundation grant, she spent several years seeking out individuals on both sides of the Atlantic who could see auras, and then developed a clinical procedure with several gifted subjects. Her reports in *Breakthrough to Creativity* make an intelligent whole that appears to confirm and extend what the writer and others have observed in individuals such as Cayce. Her best subjects saw the shapes and colors of several different interpenetrating fields around the individuals on whom they concentrated; from these fields they were able to make remarkably accurate medical diagnoses of individuals with glandular ailments, as well as of other illnesses. Particularly interesting, in the light of Cayce's claims about "the real physical body," were the reports of her subjects that they saw distinct vortices in the auric fields of subjects, located in areas roughly corresponding to what Cayce called "centers." Dr. Karagulla's reports of how individuals could be seen to draw energy from other fields, or to give energy, or to change the quality of others' energy, corroborate the tentative reports of those who have worked with the Cayce ideas on auras, as have her studies of force fields associated with certain gems.

The Cayce source produced considerable material on auras and related fields of force, over the years. Individuals were sometimes encouraged to look for auras, or were told that they had always seen them without recognizing what the colors and patterns meant. The workings of auras were closely linked to the operation of the kundalini "centers" in seven areas of the body, and some were advised to wear specific gems in the area of one of these centers, to heighten and focus psychic ability—provided that their bodies and lives were in good balance, and their purposes for psychic experience creative rather than exploitative. An instrument using crystals to enhance the seeing of auras was described for manufacture. The impression left by this material was that all such procedures could heighten abilities developed in "past lives" more readily than initiate new psychic ability in one who had previously tried to use it.

Along with psychic perception in dreams, those who have worked in small groups with the Cayce materials since the early 1930's have placed the seeing of auras and their interpretation as one of the most helpful and safe forms of psychic perception, for most people to try. Starting with impressions about the aptness of an individual's clothing and colors, one might seek in a relaxed yet attentive way to imagine and respond to various fields of color about another, especially while the other was concentrating and trying to express himself. For many people areas and hues of color would eventually begin to appear in the mind—and very often be similar for several independent observers of a speaker or performing musician or one conducting healing services. Over the years few have shown the ability to see fields at will as did Edgar Cayce, although some who have grown up accepting auras as natural seem to be able to do so. So far, none have been reported who saw auras as Cayce appeared to do in trance state, when he described level on level of color from an individual, together with associated symbolism which constituted an "aura chart," and which have in a number of cases been painted according to the instructions of the readings, for study and for use as an aid to attunement and the strengthening of "ideals" by those who secured the special readings. These charts might carry such symbols as the all-seeing eye, the sunrise, the cross, the lotus, which might also appear in the individual's life-seal as described in Cayce's "life-readings"—incorporating themes from the best choices and experiences of an individual's past lives. But the aura charts were less representational, more purely esthetic in their dependence on tongues of color shading into one another.

Is it possible for ordinary people to learn to see auras? Could such impressions guide a mother on the degree of illness of her child, or a foreman on the disturbed state of an accident-prone employee, or a physician on the location of an infection (as the talented healer, Ambrose Worrall, has reported to the writer and recounted in his biography, *A Gift of Healing*)? Are processes involving the aura incorporated in such sacraments as baptism, confirmation, ordination, and extreme unction—not to mention the force fields in the communion elements? Has the ancient practice of crossing oneself, or the threefold gesture of Moslem piety, some basis in affecting the outreach of one's aura to another, as in all gestures of prayerful blessing? Fortunately, the literature of LSD research affords cases of apparent inspection of such fields for brief periods, mixed in with accounts of imagery which seem more like sensory overloads; new approaches to the study of auras may soon be found, including correlating the color material in dreams with other impressions of color about individuals dreamed.

Out of the reports of many persons in prayer groups, AA groups, therapy groups, sensitivity-training groups, it has begun to appear that at least one factor in seeing auras is important: the percipient must look to see what is really there in the person whom he is observing. To do this, he must look with an open mind and receptive attitude, relatively free of the constricting force of his own conscience, standards, ambitions, and evaluations, except insofar as these may sensitize him to matching concerns in the other person. He needs to have a conscience structure, a value system, which enlivens his perception but does not cramp or dictate it. What would such a conscience be like?

Conscience in Creativity

The third area of religious concern which the Edgar Cayce source identified as essential to consider in creativity was the general area of conscience. The Cayce source headed the third lesson in *A Search for God* with a question, "What Is My Ideal?"

To link the psychic perception of auras, or any other targets, with conscience structures would seem arbitrary only to someone not familiar with the abundant literature linking sensory perception to the selective attention and image-making processes of the unconscious. The famed Rorschach tests with inkblots, or the less well-publicized but equally dramatic projective cards and drawings, each show how individuals perceive ambiguous situations according to patterns below the surface of consciousness, though often within reach of consciousness and fed by it. Repressed people may see others as controlled or uninhibited. Perfectionists may see others as ambitious, driven, or despairing. Self-indulgent people may see others as selfish, lazy, or missing life's fun. What we perceive in others is located somewhere on an axis of our own concerns, interests, defenses, fears, wishes, conscience. A large part of psychotherapy is the reevaluation of these conscience controls systems, bringing them into line with realistic goals and limits in a given culture. Whether approached in terms of Freudian superego concepts, or the "parents" within so neatly described by Eric Berne in *Games People Play*, or in terms of compensatory strivings and "guiding fictions" postulated by Adler, or in terms of dominant archetypes in Jungian language, or in terms of masculine and feminine values described by Erich Fromm as fatherly and motherly conscience, the drama of conscience development and operation within the person holds a critical place in theories of therapy and education alike.

The problem of all creativity is to stimulate and tolerate the flow of relevant material from the unconscious, delaying selection until likely options are identified, and then following through with the creation of necessary products or events to embody the desired values. For this process a certain playfulness and tentativeness is needed, with an ability to endure the strain of no solution, crowned with drive to finish up and follow through. There are a number of reasons to suspect that psychic ability may operate in this way, involving the creation of special states of altered consciousness and the matching of inner material with outer events, rather than operating on an inspectional basis as do the usual senses. For this reason, parapsychologists have long wondered whether the term ESP may have misled researchers by suggesting too strong an analogy with sensory operation, rather than an analogy with problem solving.

In taking up the question of ideals as a religious contribution to creativity, the Cayce source addressed the thorny problem of bringing together God's controls and man's. It was a question as old as religious commandments in any culture, as pressing as burning at the stake, as modern as stands against war or contraception, as personal as love and child rearing. It was a question addressed by Jesus as well as his Jewish ancestors and contemporaries, some of whom took positions like his on both moral and ritual law—and all religious laws tends to be both. It was a problem which has split Buddhism into two great camps or "rafts," over the adequacy of a religious ideal of personal fulfillment and perfection versus an ideal of serving others and even the very blades of grass.

As the Cayce information approached the question of ideals, it was insisted that "idea" be contrasted with "ideal." An idea was the product of purely mental activity, whether stimulated by the needs and activity of the body, or by the soul; an idea was a creation of the imagination and the heart of man, which might or might not be in line with his "ideal." It was just a unit of mental activity. On the other hand, the "ideal" was a pattern-giving structure of great importance, the character of the soul's energies available to the person. The ideal was not the same as a goal, which a person might invent and set for himself, but was in the last analysis a gift from the soul, which a person might welcome and use well, or answer indifferently or perversely. In the language of Hebraic thought, an ideal had to be thought of in terms of being called and answering. Yet a man might take a "call" from his own soul, in its godliness, to be just, and turn this very justness into condemnation of others—eventually of himself, as well. Or he might take an ideal of beauty and answer it with manipulative entertainment. Or he might take an ideal of wisdom welling up within him, and answer it with craftiness in crime. The value and the energy and the interest were given in the mystery of becoming, which followed laws not always clear to man's sight. But each person had the free will to recognize or ignore the beckoning of each ideal within him, or to perfect or distort its promise. Each man's soul had its own crest, its coat of arms, made of the ideals he had truly chosen to answer when his soul spoke to him, though some crests were smirched by misuse.

Approaching the high value given to conscience in Catholic tradition, the Cayce source insisted that each man was judged by God only in terms of his own ideals—not in terms of the ideals of his brother or the norms of a church or culture, however valuable these might be for orienting the growth of a person, or for sensitizing him to what was unfolding within him. But the ideals or standards that each man chose, deep within his own being, when in some lifetime he sought one or another human quality, talent, virtue, were ever after used upon him; they were his private bar of justice, though in a given lifetime he might seek to ignore or repress them. To be sure, these ideals were not simple verbal labels, but dynamic wholes, containing within them the seeds of opposites and of ever richer ideals. One who chose justice as an ideal inevitably chose its twin, mercy, as well, though it might take him long to discover this and respond to it.

A man who at some point in his soul's journey set for himself an ideal, and then later ignored or defiled it, might find himself destroyed or crippled in body or mind by the negative action of a force so great in him that it overrode his thoughts and psychosomatic controls. For these ideals were described as dynamic structures, unleashing the creative energies of the universe itself through the soul, and as capable of producing insanity as sanity, sickness as health, if not properly handled. This was the working of karma: sooner or later a man had to face what he chose, what he held up for himself or for his brother. Over and over the Cayce readings insisted, "Be not deceived, God is not mocked. Whatsoever a man soweth, that shall he also reap." Far from being mere trappings of the mind, then, ideals were dangerous and important business, central business for every life. In the view of the Cayce source, each soul came into each lifetime with one overarching ideal or cluster of ideals before it, always both personal and social. "For no soul enters by chance," it was insisted, but always on a trajectory of encounter and discovery to enlarge its treasurehouse of becoming, on the long journey to conscious co-creatorhood with God.

Ought one then to leave ideals alone, just living his life from day to day, and speaking when he is spoken to? He might take this path, to some degree, for God is merciful, and, in words from the New Testament repeated often by this source, "God hath not willed that any soul should perish, but hath with every temptation provided a means of escape." It was an affirmation which came as fresh air to many an anxious person who sought aid from Cayce—this categorical affirmation that God was no impatient perfectionist, no tester of men. Yet the warning was there, too, that every soul would sooner or later find its temptation, its choices to make, its moments of truth, when it would either answer or betray its chosen ideals, or those aborning in its deeps. For creation itself, the Creative Forces, the One Force, was pouring itself through the human soul, bent on making companions for Itself; and though the process might take uncounted eons, it never ceased. Each man would face his own next self, sooner or later.

When such choices came, each man had two options. He could "come under the law," which meant that relentlessly he would be drawn into exactly the situations he forced upon others, in his secret or avowed ideals, until he finally knew with acute participation just what true and merciful justice meant, for instance, as distinguished from condemnation of self or others. But there was an alternative. A man could choose the "way of Grace," could enter into the full mystery of a chosen ideal by sharing it with others. Even when he betrayed an ideal, he could be freed of its destructive consequences, though not of all its consequences, if he turned again and sought to give of that very ideal to others in a spirit of humility and generosity. A man who set for himself an ideal of loyalty, and then broke it by taking his chief's wife, might go two routes. He could become so transfixed by his own ideal, within, that he would become defensive about his own wife, and eventually alienate and lose her, learning about loss the hard way—in one life or another. Or he might recover his true ideal, and begin to help others live out the severe task of loyalty, not narrow bondage but covenanted loyalty to the best in each before God—whether he did this in aiding others with marriages, or in political bonds, or in theological loyalties.

Yet in the view of the Cayce source, no man was expected to wrestle alone with his ideals, nor with the consequences of ignoring or violating them. There were social structures and traditions, such as the church and the principled idealisms of national heritages, to help him to reorient himself. But his greatest aid was always the Christ, who had gone before him as the "Ensample," the "Elder Brother," and who represented a kind of ever-present Field below or beside his own that might tug his own being into shape, if he would allow it. So the Cayce readings repeatedly urged people to "know in Whom you have believed, and that He is able to keep unto the last day that which ye have committed to Him." Of himself, a man could not choose his best ideals, nor live up to them. But in the most literal sense he had Help, if he chose it. Every ideal needed to be thought out to its ultimate grounding in God; every ideal needed to be given living footing in one's best understanding of the Christ way, the Christ life. Every ideal should be set "in Him."

Far from producing a religious legalism, or perfectionism, then, the Cayce approach to conscience was meant to set before man the hope of controls as flexible as the next moment, as living as the Man. It was an approach similar to that of Augustine in his famous dictum, "Love God, and do as you like." The Cayce way of putting it was to say that Christ so fulfilled the Law that he *became* the Law—so that even the elements of storms and sickness obeyed Him. Not that He achieved some totalitarian authority over natural and moral law, but that He was able to so live that all things worked together with Him. This goal, the Cayce readings firmly asserted, was the destiny of every soul—not alone to obey the Law and laws as a child obeys a parent, but to choose becoming, and to understand by doing and creating, until one became the Law.

Working with ideals was made complicated, in this view, by the fabulous creative powers of the mind, which would tend to build for a man whatever he set his desire upon. If he chose to become a crook, his creative unconscious, "ever the Builder in man," would take him a long ways in that direction, until he was finally faced in some way with a question—such as integrity in workmanship even for a criminal—which might force him to face himself and grow a new ideal. For the soul never quit trying. If, however, he finally answered the call to strategy within him by becoming a legal strategist, he might go through experiences in one or many lives which would enable him to draft the very constitution of a people, and to frame the temper of their laws so as to minimize crime. Constructive ideals would be found to come more quickly to realization than destructive ones—though the universe was big enough to hold plenty of the latter and made room for a man to hobble himself with his own lasso. The Cayce source insisted that no ideal was beyond the reach of a soul, in the fullness of time: "As ye abide in me, ye shall ask what ye will, and it shall be done upon you" was a typical Cayce variant on a saying of Jesus. Power, love, possessions, wisdom, patience—the possibilities were endless, if one began by being true to the ideals he already had, and used their energies and resultant imagery and interests in service to others. However, one need not expect to do all of this in one lifetime; the Cayce source was no exponent of riches by positive thinking (though ready to explain in terms of reincarnation and past ideals why some men had so little difficulty in achieving riches in a given lifetime).

Where ought a man to begin, who sought to grow with respect to those treasures of his soul, his true ideals? The rule of thumb in the Cayce materials was always "Be true to the best you know, and the next will be given to you." Being true to what rang clear in one's own depths was critically important, and must be followed, even at the price of social rejection; it was the point at which the person would be judged, or judge himself from the standpoint of the soul. Yet one had to sort decisions with care, for there was often a way that seemed good and compelling to a man whose end was destruction. The Cayce information was as clear as psychoanalysis that man's unconscious is a wily thing, a natural force not wholly subdued to the soul in any but Christ, and in those who achieved at times perfect attunement with Him. One must judge his own promptings, even the strong ones, by the legacy of his people— as the Cayce materials so fully used the Bible—and ever keep in mind the commandment to serve the other, to be one's brother's keeper. But against this background, the seeming imperative had further to be checked by attunement, by waiting upon the still, small voice, by prayer and reflection and the weighing of dreams and impressions. When an individual sought such counsel as to whether he was hearing from his own depths an "idea" or an "ideal," he could—if his purposes were sincere—unfailingly count on guidance, for "God hath not left himself without a witness." The guidance might take time, and be crowded out by other impulses at first, but it would be there, and man could count on it—even as Edgar Cayce could count on aid to give his readings, so long as he gave them to be helpful rather than to advance himself alone.

The Cayce source was ready with practical steps in working with conscience and its ideals. One should take a piece of paper and draw upon it two lines, making three columns, to be marked "spiritual, mental, physical." In each of these columns one should set down as honestly as he could his real ideals, from keeping his body at a fitting weight to loving his enemies—the whole gamut of what made sense for sure, right then, to the person. Then the entries in these columns should be worked with, checked against the life, made more clear. "Often you will find yourself rubbing out," the Cayce source warned, for some ideals would drop away, or be incorporated in better ones. In time, each column would begin to show the real uniqueness of that soul, on its special pilgrimage, with its strengths and weaknesses appearing side by side in specific ideals. At the same time, each column would be cast more and more in ways that to the person meant the mind of Christ: the ideals would be "grounded in Him"—not by imitation but by intent, quality, direction. In time one would come to see, said the Cayce readings, that there was no way forward except the Way that Christ showed and was—a living way, not a book of rules or behaviors or taboos or formulas. It was so not by special decree, or any excellence of Christians who often missed the point by identifying with Christ as a hero rather than as a personal challenge, but it was so because of the way the universe was built—a way of wise love and radical creativity which Christ walked and opened out for others. Setting the ideals in Christ was not a merely rational matter, in this view. As one chose to organize and think his ideals in this way, he automatically set his unconscious building in His direction, and he also called into being native psychic ability to seek and find that Reality in the present universe, not merely in history, which was the Christ Spirit. The soul would seek its own, by the most valuable kind of psychic capacity, and find it.

To be sure, some souls might require much time to build their ESP awareness of the living Christ, so that they could daily orient themselves by this lodestar. In the meantime, there was a practical method by which they could check their actual, functioning ideals. They could look to see to what they responded in others. Each would find that what he weighed and measured in others, or was drawn by, was the standard actually at work in his own soul. If he saw beauty, then beauty called him; if purity, if play, if patience—each was nudging him for decision or action within. If he saw mostly evil, or selfishness, or betrayal, then he should know that his own soul was holding him tightly to his own ideal, pressing him to it until he changed his ways or broadened his idea. If in time he found a new thing, a new hunger, a new longing arising from his own soul, he could make it real not alone by praying for it nor by studying about it nor by associating with the like-minded— although all of these things profited the birth of ideals. But above all, he could bring his new treasure to life by giving it away. Money might not be buried, but must be invested in life, said the old parable; it was so with ideals. Said the Cayce readings many times, "If ye would have love, give love; if ye would have friends, be friendly; if ye would have mercy, be merciful; if ye would have beauty, make your world beautiful for others." For this was a law, not just a good thing, but a law.

It was important, too, to think of ideals in positive terms, rather than negative: Better to seek to love than to omit hating. Even in matters of physical health, just avoiding illness was not enough. Not a few times the Cayce source put a direct question to a sick person, "What would ye do if ye were well?" It was made clear that the very body would not respond sufficiently to the life-giving patterns destined for it, unless the life were under the guidance of a fitting ideal, one that belonged to that special soul. He that had no notion of what to do with health might not receive it until he did. For those responsive to the Christian ideal (and the Cayce source said that by the 1940's there were no souls anywhere in the earth who had not been faced with the Christ way in some lifetime; the rest had been separated out for other paths), one might find the way to think his ideals by asking in a given situation a simple, blunt question, "What would the Master do?" No pat answer should be expected, but the question, truly put, would start the seeker in the right direction.

Auras and Conscience

Are there cases which seem to link the seeing of auras with maturity of conscience development?

A busy young Congregational minister set about building the membership of his Southwestern church. He drove himself to make calls on homes; he raised money for a new organ; he attended community functions; he worked on his sermons. The membership increased a bit, and then leveled off. He pushed himself harder. There were denominational conferences to attend, inspirational books to read, causes to espouse, including the reality of psychic experience. He became known as a promising young minister, and denominational executives looked on him with favor, assigning him to city and state committees.

But his wife was lonely, his children difficult. His prayers of thanksgiving sounded forced, even to him. Then he went to a pastor's conference at his seminary where an older pastor preached, and simply talked with the young ministers. The older pastor reached him, not by claims about his ministry—though his church was immense, with a full staff of ministers—but by using the language of psychotherapy. He spoke of self-acceptance, of insight, of the treasures hidden in the sick complexes of a man. And he put the ministers at the conference into small groups, where many dared to speak freely with one another. At the same time, he spoke of prayer, and showed in his own unforced praying an emblem of one man's relationship with God. The young preacher went home and took stock of himself. He did not like what he saw—a driving perfectionism that was killing whatever he sought to create. He began to read, to confront his own conscience with the materials from psychiatry. Cautiously, he introduced a few small study groups in his church, and began with his wife to set a pattern of speaking honestly in them.

The first development was that his parishioners seemed to go to pieces. Or at least more went through breakdowns and near breakdowns than he would ever have expected. It was as though they had been waiting, holding on by force of will, until someone was ready to hear and to help. With each new set of problems he thought he saw more of his own weaknesses, new symptoms of his own failings. He was near distraction, many times, and even contemplated suicide. But he stayed close to his people, and listened to them, and prayed in his own way. Some of his sermons were poor, and he missed enough meetings to make a few church stalwarts angry with him. But a new spirit began to show in worship. People sang from their hearts, every now and then. An alcoholic family changed, and the husband became an active building force in the community and the church. People came from nearby housing developments to see what made members talk about the life of the church, and often found the answer in the small groups.

The young minister forgot psychic abilities for weeks at a time. But then he noticed that faces were looking softer to him, people were looking to him like individual adventures, like paintings of themselves. And one day he was noting colors about them, rather absent-mindedly. He joked about the colors with a few of his laymen, and was surprised to find they were seeing the same things—especially two who had worked for years in Alcoholics Anonymous, and one young bookkeeper. They compared notes, and found themselves seeing similar colors and intensities, over and over again, with similar meanings. As time went on, seeing auras became as natural for the minister and for other leaders of the church as making phone calls to see how friends were doing. They made no special claims about it, yet enjoyed it among themselves, as was clear when the writer came to attend a conference in the same city, and became acquainted with the minister and leaders of the church.

What had been involved in one man's coming to see auras? He had come to see faces. Out of his own searching, his own sorting out of himself, he had begun to look at others, to care about them rather than to process them for church functions. And their faces and forms had lit up for him. He had meant more than auras when he spoke in a small group one day of "the true Light that lighteth every man in the world", as the inner radiance men had to seek in one another, rather than constrictive consciences. But he suspected that the true Light showed itself in colors, as well—helpful colors, psychically perceived.

CHAPTER 6

AUTOMATISMS AND QUICKENINGS

"HOLY FATHER," Edgar Cayce began to pray, using the phrase with which he often started his prayers. "We ask Thy presence here with us today, now." His voice was low, contained; his hands were folded on the library table before him, beside the large Bible from which he had read aloud.

"We have no secrets from Thee, for Thou knowest us altogether. Thou knowest how each of us has sinned and fallen short, even as thy servant David, of whom we have read." The words were earnest, steady. It grew very still in the room, for the mention of sin struck home to those gathered with him at the regular two o'clock prayer period of his family and office staff. There was silence around the library table, and heads were bowed.

Only a few days before, Cayce had recovered his voice after a month's illness, and taken a reading on his own health. He had been rebuked for not keeping better balance in diet, for not keeping more quiet times, for not preparing himself for each trance session—even to showering and changing clothes before entering the reading room. Then his voice, still hoarse, had suddenly changed to ringing tones of unbelievable loudness, and the source of the information had come right to the point. It was not Cayce alone who had broken the law, lost touch with his spiritual center, and contracted illness under the strain of giving so many extra readings each day. The weight of the trouble fell upon the entire staff, who were—with Cayce—called "ungracious, unrepentant" people who made a "garbage pit" of their negative emotions. With a severity the writer—who was present for the reading and included in the rebuke—cannot exaggerate, the stentorian voice had said, "Walk in the way of the Lord, or else there will come that sudden reckoning, as ye have seen. But don't be pigs!"

Nobody in the room doubted what was meant. Under pressure to handle the stream of mail, phone calls, and visitors, Cayce had hired extra typists and pressed volunteers into service until the small office quarters were jammed with people at makeshift tables and desks. People got in one another's way, bypassed one another's authority, strove to feel important. Tempers rose, bodies were weary from long hours of work, quiet times were lost. Bickering and jostling for position became so common that it was unpleasant to come to work. Edgar Cayce became entangled in the turmoil, growing morose in those few times when he stopped for a cigarette. Then he had become ill, and there had been no readings at all for a month, followed by the searing reading heard that day.

Now, a few days later, things were more controlled, and Cayce was praying aloud.

Then something strange occurred. Usually his prayers aloud were simple, Biblical, and somewhat halting; he once told the writer that "the man who prayed without stumbling very possibly doesn't mean it." But at this point Cayce's speech became steady, sure; each phrase was a finished thought, each word fitted securely into place, each image seized and focussed the attention. Without raising his voice, Cayce was listing the sins of those in the room, including himself. He named no names, he made no charges. He simply spoke the truth about one person after another and all in the room knew it. There had indeed been pettiness, boastfulness, backbiting, impatience, unforgiveness, indulgence—and more. Yet there was no condemnation in his voice, no reveling in trouble. For his prayer continued, "Thou has made it known to us that the effort to serve one's brother covereth a multitude of sins." He gave thanks that each in the room could aid in relieving pain, could light a path for the troubled, would "make the heart of many a man to sing." And in the same quiet, sure voice, he closed, asking "that we might be given the grace to follow Him, the Master whose Name we have named in our hearts, and for Whose sake we pray."

Something better than a lecture had taken place. Talking and thinking about David, who as the Lord's anointed had still so often sinned, and had repented, the staff had gathered into a common mind. The tight controls of the past few days since the painful reading had eased, and bodies leaned back a bit. Then had come this cleansing prayer, catching up each person in the room, enacting a shared confession, with the assurance of an absolution as real as the wrongdoing. Later that afternoon people were humming and whistling, as they had not done for weeks. And in the days that followed, something like teamwork began to emerge from a crew whose understanding of Cayce's work varied from almost nothing to years of experience, whose education varied from grammar school to graduate school, and whose devotional life varied from fishing to choir singing.

Had Cayce been taken over by another "entity" for this prayer? His vocabulary had not changed, although his sentence structure had tightened. He had said little that he could not have compiled in a conscious checklist of problems around the room, and yet he had said it with striking speed and fitness. His voice had not changed, except to reach the timber and depth that those who loved him associated with his best self. No revelation had been given, and yet his speech had revealed each one in the room.

Was this automatic speech? Was it of the same order as the Biblical "speaking in tongues"? Was it like automatic writing, so commonly reported in psychic circles, where words streamed forth from a pencil moving without the subject's intent, yet using his hand?

Those in the room would rather have described Cayce's incisive prayer and catalog of penance as a "quickening," a meeting of Cayce's psyche with a field or force or spirit wiser and richer than his own. He had, they would say, been "lifted up," in accordance with the promise so often quoted in the readings, "My Spirit beareth witness with thy spirit, as to whether ye be the sons of God."

It would be no surprise to those familiar with Edgar Cayce's work for his consciousness to change, allowing some new center of his being, or some other center of being, to guide his thoughts and speech. This was the substance of what he did twice a day, when hypnotized and speaking in trance.

Moreover he came from a family where he had seen his grandfather, in his childhood, make a broom move around the kitchen, and where his father had proven his ability to dowse for water with a forked stick. Those who had worked with Cayce in trance claimed that once he had even levitated, risen up from the couch in response to an urgent instruction meant to lift the level of his voice: "Up, up!" Not having seen this, Cayce did not have to believe it. But he had seen the little planchette fly, the night he and his wife had tried a ouija board.

Cayce's experience of being fully conscious, and yet having his vocal cords seem to leap to form phrases in prayer, placed him in the midst of a wide variety of psychic practices which had for centuries employed spontaneous muscular action. He was experiencing a variant of what the writer and many others have seen and studied in table tipping, the divinatory use of swinging penduls, ecstatic speech of "glossolalia," address in unknown foreign tongues, speech in what was claimed to be the language of angels, opening of the Bible to let the eye fall on guiding passages, staring at imagery in crystal balls, arranging Chinese sticks in symbolic patterns, turning up cards in fortune telling—and still other practices where men have sought to let unguided activity mediate the messages of the gods or fate or spirits.

The literature of parapsychology includes many investigations of automatisms and quickenings, where the response of muscles appears to precede or accompany conscious thought, rather than to follow it as is usual. Researchers on both sides of the Atlantic have spent hundreds of hours observing and interpreting automatic writing, reporting it to be often trivial, sometimes sensible, and occasionally erudite (as in the famous cross-correspondences), or artistic (as in the poetry and prose of Patience Worth), or inspirational (as in the Betty books of Stewart Edward White). They have also shown that more material proceeds from unconscious complexes of the writing subjects than most laymen would believe, to the degree that some psychiatrists today employ automatic writing to disclose a patient's real responses to touchy material which his conscious mind denies.

The novelist Kenneth Roberts has reported on the water dowsing of Henry Gross, and investigators such as the present writer have watched psychics accurately locate underground water and minerals by touching a map or drawing on it. A considerable literature and interest in automatic speaking in tongues, long practiced in Holiness churches, has emerged in such staid church circles as Episcopalian and Lutheran.

If there is any agreement at all among seasoned investigators, it might lie in warning against wholesale abdication of consciousness for automatisms, because of risks as dangerous as playing with hypnosis. Many have personally observed cases of mental illness, such as those described by Hugh Lynn Cayce in *Venture Inward,* which began as harmless dissociation with a ouija board and turned to engrossing automatic writing, then finally to uncontrollable hearing of voices or experiencing sexual sensations. Few investigators would suggest that the dissociation or automatisms caused the illness, for underlying neuroses seem always present in such cases. But the method appears to be a problematic approach to dealing with unconscious contents.

Yet other investigators, including such psychics as Arthur Ford who have reported on their own experiences, have argued that automatism can be safely attempted by anyone who first does a responsible inventory of his own problems and attitudes.

Over the years of Cayce's trance activity, many sought from his information some guidance on automatic writing or other automatisms and quickenings. The answer often given was that anybody could develop such abilities, if he set about practicing properly. But with the answer always went a question: Why? In part this was a question of motive, for impulses to self-glory or power over others were potentially dangerous impulses, according to this source; such attitudes might release unwelcome contents of the unconscious that would be difficult to control, and might draw to the person "disturbing forces" in the form of discarnate entities enjoying full or partial takeover of willing subjects. But the question of *why* was also the posing of a choice. For the Cayce source insisted that the same energy used to achieve "automatic writing," for example, could achieve "inspirational writing." The former would be limited to discarnate entities, at best, while the latter might give the individual access to the best of his own soul, and whatever additional resource he might need, according to his abilities, from the treasure house of the "Universal Forces." Not Uncle John, but the Christ, was the better focus in this view. And not abdication of consciousness but alignment, attunement, elevation of consciousness, until it was infused from beyond itself, rather than displaced or destroyed. Yet various twilight stages of consciousness had their usefulness, as the trances of Edgar Cayce showed. One woman was urged to cultivate along with her prayer life the ability to talk in her sleep, for some of the counsel she would give would be found similar to Cayce's readings. In the view of the Cayce source, many variables had their effect on what "came through" a person who sought to "open himself" to other energies and insights than those afforded by normal consciousness. Any injury or illness affecting the endocrine gland operation (and associated "centers" in "the real physical body") might turn quiet times into nightmares of unwanted promptings. So might habitual dwelling on sexual or hostile material, creating "thought forms" which would trouble the percipient as though they were separate beings. So might participation in a group whose intentions were thrills or distractions, bringing forth responses in the dissociated person which were not his own intention.

But one whose physical and mental life was in some balance, and whose intention was to secure aid to increase, rather than supplant, his waking gifts, might find that through quiet times, prayer, Bible study, and the cleansing-arousing flow of meditation, he could be lifted beyond his usual conscious abilities. According to their gifts, some might recall scenes of past lives and be able to write them as stories; others might hear music as though from the spheres, to incorporate in their music-making or poetry; others might have flashes of light, where the face and form of a loved one, acutely real, came momentarily before their minds, together with a helpful impression or prompting for daily life.

Over the years since Cayce's death, individuals interested in his approaches have tried various forms of dissociation and focusing, attempting to stretch their consciousness to levels beyond its usual function. A few have interpreted dreams and performed well on psychic tasks under hypnosis, though most who have tried it have not. Some who have tried automatic writing have found bits of helpful or evidential material, though most have not, and a few have found to their horror that they entered unconscious depths which they could not control. Others have tried writing out Bible passages in their own words by "inspiration" and have achieved results varying from good poetry to gobbledegook. Still others have tried to let "messages" come from them while laying on hands in healing, and a few have experienced apt leading, while others have produced wordy generalities. In all of this experimenting, there has been highlighted the problem of initiative: What is man supposed to do, and what is man supposed to let God do?

Initiative in Creativity

The Cayce source took up the difficult problem of initiative in its fourth lesson for trainees seeking psychic and other creativity. It titled the chapter "Faith" in *A Search for God.*

Emphasizing initiative would seem appropriate to a careful observer of the phenomena of automatisms. In any major city, and certainly at a Spiritualist summer camp, one can find individuals practicing automatic writing to secure messages from discarnates, and sometimes to seek counsel for problems of daily life. Some of these practitioners report themselves authorized by heavenly beings, and present their materials with boldness and fervor. Some present their materials with a touch of whimsy, as surprised as any at what seems to "come through them." Others wait until "caught up in the Spirit" to do their work, in accustomed piety. What seems to be evidential material at times results through any of these methods. But in all of them the psyche appears to take its stand on some flow, whether personal or transpersonal, which the individual has learned to trust. What is such trust, such "faith," and how does it act to free the psyche for useful parapsychological material, or to flood it with irrelevancies?

Erich Fromm has argued that "faith" in the orderliness and helpfulness of the universe and other people must underly any creative loving and working; he has distinguished what he calls rational faith from blind faith. Gerald Heard, writing of the Buddhist call to "right belief," has insisted that man's "deep mind" must be convinced of what he sets out to do, or it will not build for him in the direction he seeks his growth. Both have touched on the relation between understanding and trust, in probing the issue of faith. It is an issue as old as man's religion. In Christianity, the issue has been approached by those who like Tertullian rejoiced in believing the absurd, and those of scientific temper who reserved belief and trust for things demonstrable through the senses. While these viewpoints may seem at times "merely theological," it is clear that important issues in any kind of creativity—whether psychic or political or laboratory or philosophical—can be involved in the controversy. To be creative often involves some suspension of judgment, in the trust that a solution will present itself—but from where? It involves also the commitment to take action on a solution, rather than daydream more and more solutions, in the trust that such action will be worthwhile—for whom? It involves the ability to overhaul one's functioning after repeated failures, in the trust that one can arrive at better patterns of problem solving—from where? Repeatedly the issue emerges of what man can trust when habit and experience, counsel and expedience fail, whether in child rearing or moneymaking or facing death—where no man has conscious experience.

The approach of the Cayce source on the initiatives in faith was remarkably literal. Faith was described as a flow of promptings with definite content, coming into consciousness from beyond itself, ultimately from the soul as it "answered" the force of the life. One might learn to recognize the flow, to respond to it with assent, to improve it with a godly life of service. But the flow of faith might neither be taught nor learned, could not be forced, and could not be destroyed—though it might be ignored. For it was a gift, a fundamental attribute of the soul, welling up from the soul's intimate knowledge of the Creative Forces. In every realm of a man's life, from the most practical problem of starting a stalled car to the blinding problem of handling the sudden death of a loved one, he could count upon a quiet flow from within, trying to show him patterns, meanings, connections, directions, until he could say to himself in a click of recognition, "So that's how it is!" Faith in this view was not a specifically religious or churchly phenomenon, but the evidence of many things unseen, as wide in range as God's love for man or a parent's love for his child. It was the everlasting prompting of the next step, the next insight, the next commitment—not a series of tests nor a series of propositions. It was a steady flow of inward knowing, a living business, to be tried out daily. When Jesus described Peter's insight about His Messiahship by saying, "Flesh and blood hath not revealed this to thee, but the Father," he meant, in the view of this source, the kind of helpful certitude which did not overwhelm the person nor displace him, but quietly fed and strengthened his understanding, in little moments or in crises of judgment. Such moments as Peter's declaration might be elevated, when man's spirit was fused with a Spirit from on high, but there would be other moments of prompting, equally the flow of faith, when the certitude would seem more ordinary—as when a parent was prompted to trust that his child told the truth, or a woman was prompted to trust life until she could better afford a new dress. Whenever something within seemed to say, "Yes, you can trust that," man might be brushing against the gift of faith.

Yet in the view of the Cayce source, faith was not an all-or-none business. Man's proper prayer was, "I believe; help thou mine unbelief," for one had to grow in faith. One had to learn to empty the heart of selfishness, which could block the flow; he had to learn through meditation and often-repeated prayer to become a channel—and then act as he prayed. One had to learn to distinguish faith from unconscious compulsions, for faith would not come as a noisy absolute, taking a man over, but as a steady beat, an assurance, an awakening, a "shadow" cast by real events over the mind of the seeker. One had to learn to use constructively what had for him the quiet, steady assurance of faith—and even to be willing to make mistakes; it was "better to do wrong with good intent than to do nothing at all."

Over and over the Cayce source insisted that man could count on the divine initiative within, to stir him, to guide him, to strengthen him. Faith was a "gift from the Throne, implanted in the soul." Yet no more could rightly be sought than the next step, and the next—although sometimes far vistas might briefly show, in dream or vision or reasoned understanding. For the gifts of faith were always contingent upon man's using what he had now: "Use what you have in hand, and the next will be given to you." This contingency was not a matter of God's being despotic or arbitrary in his self-giving through the soul, but of lawful processes that kept the person from destroying himself with the knowledge and power he could attain through faith. In general, a person would recognize only those opportunities he could use, if he did not delude himself with his imagination, while others would also be prompted by their faith to recognize and honor his opportunities—though not always, if they ignored their inner promptings. Likewise, one would not be led by his faith into more than he could handle, for "God hath not willed that any soul should perish"—though man could trap himself by his will and imagination.

How might one distinguish between faith and imagination? The rational mind could help, by providing clues to a Christlike life, and by orienting one's native psychic ability towards attunement with the Spirit of Christ. The Cayce source offered no encouragement to discard thinking, but urged people to "get understanding," both by study in all its forms and by experiment or "application" in real life situations. Faith was not a flow to be damped or disturbed by responsible reasoning; it would give life to reason by supplying connections, inferences, even factual data in psychic perceptions. But the ultimate task of responding to faith was not formulating facts or dogmas; it was seeking and hearing the Father, not announcing that God was a fact.

How might one help the flow of faith in others? First of all, by trusting that God was working to fulfill His purposes "in the other fellow." Second, by fulfilling the duty of having faith in oneself, in the action of God in one's own life—for one who doubted himself soon doubted others. The life lived in this vein would soon begin to shine with good energies—as in the aura—and with effective deeds or good works, and such a light should be trusted "to so shine before men that they may glorify your Father in heaven." There was no need to set out to work miracles, though remarkable things could come about under the quiet stimulus of promptings called faith. For the Cayce source insisted that no material emergency was beyond solution by spiritual inspiration; God would be found fantastically creative, if man would learn to listen to Him. For example, the Cayce information insisted that there was no disease which did not have its cure available somewhere on earth, a cure that could be found and used through the psychic capacities that were an integral part of faith. There were no incurable diseases, although there were specific cases of deterioration that had progressed too far to be reversed, when the soul would soon leave the body.

How might one cultivate the lively flow of faith—of practical, helpful promptings as well as ultimate assurances about the meaning and place of suffering and freedom? "Let us humble ourselves," began one reading. Man must use his initiative, his will, his consciousness, to set himself before God, and to bow his will to the One. "Let us open our hearts in meditation," the reading continued, stressing that extraordinary state of altered consciousness which could come from daily quiet focus on a Biblical prayer or affirmation. Further, one could set his mind to remember, in times of stress, the faith of others in distress, their trust and steadfastness; for this purpose the study of the Bible was man's best resource, though every great life or biography might carry assurances—as the Cayce readings often referred to Woodrow Wilson, and at other times to such figures as the Buddha, Lao Tse, Swedenborg, or the founder of Zoroastrianism. As part of cultivating the flow of faith, one would have to analyze himself, not forgetting the loving help of others, and seeking to find the typical weaknesses which would block the flow—then asking for faith to show him the next step in dealing with these very weaknesses. One would need to determine where he actually put his trust, lest he proclaim faith in God, but enact faith in power, or wealth, or charm, or some other ultimate. And in moments that seemed to contain assurance, one could learn to distinguish, said the Cayce source, between "confidence" which might be based on sensory data or emotional vigor alone, and "faith" which came in quieter, deeper tones, but allowed acting in no fear at all. For as a man grew in awareness and response to this flow, he could become as a rock, and upon such a rocklike trust Christ Himself could build a Kingdom.

Automatisms or Quickening and Initiative

Can building a living awareness of the gift of faith affect psychic performance with the muscles and nerves, in automatisms and quickenings?

A young choral conductor, trained in Navy musical groups after his college experience in singing and conducting, tried repeatedly to find the way to a larger guidance than his own in his work. He tried closing his eyes and losing himself at important passages; he tried concentrating intensely on the score, on the singers, on his conducting technique. He tried sitting in silence before performances, and tried fasting and special breathing techniques on days of concerts. Learning of Cayce and other psychics, he sought and achieved the ability of automatic writing, securing a variety of messages that purported to come from entities wiser than himself. Still, his conducting was erratic; trying to lose himself, he sometimes lost the choir.

He joined a weekly study group, some of whose members were church people and some not, but all of whom were serious. He tried meditation, and at first made of it another attempt to abandon himself to the unconscious. But he worked hard in the Bible study of the group and in the shared discussions during the next four years. Slowly it began to come clear to him that creativity was not leaving himself out in favor of something better, but using his every skill and understanding to answer the quickenings to beauty that might come within him. He worked harder at his music and began to listen ever more carefully to chords and balances, to the contributions of each section of his choir. One day he caught himself knowing, really knowing, exactly how the sopranos would sing the next phrase, though they had never sung it before in such marked accents. Spontaneously his arms joined his consciousness in conducting the sopranos through the phrase, adding his force to theirs, and then carrying the force onward with the tenors. The effect was electric. It had come after long practicing, but it was new. Neither conductor nor singers had created the result alone; it had flashed to life in all of them together, using all their training and skill.

For a while the conductor could not find the way to the same state. But in time he did, learning that he could sense not only the strengths of his singers, but their weaknesses, and respond accordingly. He thought at times he was using his rational inference alone. But how would that account for his knowing when a given singer would be absent, or when a choir bus would miss its route and be late, or when a recording date would be called off? These items came into his consciousness in the same stream as the signals to create beauty. And how was he to account for something the choir itself noticed and commented upon, that at times—and he knew the times—he could add a vital force to the singers, feeling a flow go forth from him that helped the basses reach notes usually out of range, or prompting deftness beyond the usual reach of the second sopranos? It was not that he did something to the singers, but that something good in him seemed released to trigger something good in them, and to guide and shape it with them. An important part of the process was listening to the singers, training them to sing, to be artists, to answer the call of each performance from their own creativity. "We hear each other all the way down; we really do," he once told the writer. "If men could act out with one another the way God hears and responds to us, this would have to be something like it."

Had he found his way to a process to which Jesus pointed when His touch brought movement of a withered limb, or sight to a sightless eye? Jesus' typical response had been not to take credit nor reject it, but only to strengthen the flow in the person before Him: "Your faith has made you whole." Perhaps this was the psychic quickening, the ecstatic speech, the spontaneous movement that could be trusted.

CHAPTER 7

ACTION ON PEOPLE AND THINGS

THE IDEA SEEMED RIDICULOUS, but Edgar Cayce was confident. "I'll waken you," he said. He was offering to waken the writer and a few others at the same time every night by thinking about them. "It will work," he added; "I've done it before."

The group was studying *A Search for God,* attempting to keep daily meditation times with the specific procedures outlined in the Cayce readings for stilling the mind and body. But the distractions of daily life in wartime seemed too much. Nobody in the group was meditating every day, and few were doing it at the agreed-upon times when all would be invisibly together. As a consequence, nobody's meditation was going through the complete arc or cycle, but instead each was finding himself sidetracked into introspection or unconscious imagery or psychic promptings. At last the group had decided to follow a method suggested in many a Cayce reading. That method was to arise at two a.m. for thirty days and keep first a half hour of prayer—drawing close to God in adoration, petition, dedication—followed by a half hour of nonreflective meditation, in which the effort would be made to empty oneself of whatever hindered the divine force from "rising" within the individual. Several, however, confessed that they could not waken from a sound sleep, even with an alarm clock. And two or three were hesitant to use an alarm clock, lest they disturb a spouse not so interested in the devotional life. They were discussing the problem as they stood in Cayce's hallway after a Bible class. It was then that he offered to waken them for a time, until they became used to the nightly hour.

But the idea was certainly strange. The sleepers would be scattered over a twenty-five mile radius, in Virginia Beach and Norfolk and Oceana. The thought that Edgar Cayce or anyone else could exert a force to awaken all these people at the same time was farfetched, even to those who had become accustomed to fetching far with Edgar Cayce.

The experiment was begun the next night. As did the others, according to the shared reports at the next meeting, the writer found himself wide awake at two a.m., roused from a sound sleep, and feeling no inclination to return to sleep. Was it the power of suggestion? Experimenters with hypnosis have shown that every adult has a sense of the hour of the day, accurate within a few minutes, and that posthypnotic suggestion can awaken a person at a desired time—or put someone to sleep in the same way. But posthypnotic suggestion usually does not work night after night without reinforcement, and frequently disturbs the depth of sleep. Yet here were the group members popping awake night after night to keep their appointed devotional hour, free from telephone calls or children or business demands. And nobody was hypnotizing them, although each was telling himself he wanted to cooperate. During the experimental period when Cayce added his aid, two reported thinking that on given nights they would skip the time, because of illness— yet were unable to keep from waking up. Later, when Cayce discontinued his efforts, some members of the group found they had to try harder to wake up, or could sleep through the time if they chose.

Nothing was clearly proven by this little experiment. But those who took part had an eerie sense that the mind might have more powers of outreach, of action on people and things, than was usually assumed in daily life.

For Cayce the experience was less strange. Years ago in his photographic studio in Kentucky he had taken a dare to summon a man to his studio by concentrating on him, and had seen the bewildered man enter, within a relatively few minutes, apologizing for coming up without a definite reason, yet feeling that Cayce wanted him. It was one of a number of experiences which had taught Cayce the power of thought to affect events—as had the events which he told the writer, involving two men at Virginia Beach. They had wanted $1500 for a business deal by a certain date, and had begun concentrating on bringing the money forth, "manifesting it." Not praying, they were simply willing the money to appear. Day and night they "held the thought." The appointed day came and there was no sign of the money—but that day a severe automobile wreck hospitalized them both. An insurance agent came to the hospital to offer them a settlement at once, protecting his client who was also in the accident. The amount? $1500.

Cayce trusted the flow of energy going out from his being, so long as he kept his attunement in prayer, and his purposes those of service. He was immensely successful in vegetable gardening, as his friends were reminded by an abundant crop of asparagus that spread over an adjoining lot after Cayce's death. It was not strange to him that plants should respond to loving care. Nor did he consider that healing by touch was impossible, although he felt it was not his gift for this lifetime. The only form of direct action on the body that the writer saw him attempt was a bit of folklore practice: stroking someone's warts to make them go away—which they did (as research has shown they will also do under suggestion). But the outreach of psychic ability was as real to Cayce as the inreach. There had been those times in his life when it seemed that people were acted on in ways that completely passed understanding. For example, there had been the time—one of many—when he had been anxious for money to meet household needs, and had prayed earnestly for aid. Taking a reading on the subject, he was told that he should have no fear as long as he kept close to God; it was the same counsel he was always given by the information, except with a slight addition this time. He should watch what happened now for thirty days, to learn the truth in the Biblical phrase often repeated by his trance source: "The silver and the gold are mine, saith the Lord: the cattle on a thousand hills." He watched, and his whole household watched with him, as something developed that none of them have yet explained. For exactly thirty days there was some form of money in every letter he received. People long forgotten remembered to pay for their readings (about twenty-five percent, in the author's experience, never paid, and Cayce never dunned them). Friends sent a dollar bill, or a five-dollar bill—"just to help out." Creditors sent adjustments on accounts. One way or another, everyone who wrote, from points all over the country, tucked in some money—even coins for return postage. Then at the end of thirty days the phenomenon stopped, and money came irregularly as always—somehow enough, never too much. Had a signal gone forth from Cayce by some form of psychic ability? Or had he reached unto "the Throne" which his readings described as in touch with every man, according to his desire and intent?

Cayce's seeming ability to affect people and things at a distance from him was a reminder of claims as old as antiquity: of Joshua making an ax to float, of Jesus stilling the waves, of Peter triggering the death of Annanias when the latter held back money he had agreed to share. It had in it elements of the claims in firewalking, of mediums claiming to produce fresh roses from out of the air in seance rooms, of Haitian needles stuck in Voodoo dolls. It raised questions long raised in the human family about the powers of "mind over matter."

Parapsychologists have tackled these questions in different ways. Dr. Karagulla set her psychics to observing auric fields of force sweeping out from a compelling speaker to embrace a room of people and pull their fields into a shared unity. The present writer studied a European psychic as he held his hand near sections of the backs of volunteer subjects, making the subjects' flesh jump and muscles activate at his will—but only by dint of exhausting concentration on his part. He said it was the same ability which he also used to produce images on unexposed film held in his hand or—when he failed—to produce peculiar flecks of light that ruined packs of film. J. G. Pratt and others investigated the action of so-called poltergeists, seemingly disembodied centers of activity which threw furniture and objects around a home by undetermined force. Gerald Heard analyzed in his technical studies of prayer how asceticism may have produced in certain subjects, such as the Cure d'Ars, a piled-up charge of psychic energy which spilled over in the movement of objects around them.

But by far the most careful and valuable work on psychokinesis—PK—has been that done by J. B. Rhine and associates at Duke and elsewhere in the

U.S. and Europe, exploring the effects of concentration of the fall of dice down chutes onto marked tables. Thousands of runs have been conducted by a score of investigators, including engineers and professors of biology and physics. In general, their findings have been less spectacular than those on telepathy or clairvoyance, yet still statistically notable and showing lawful patterns which have convinced at least the dedicated workers that they are dealing with a measurable force. Yet the difficulty of conceiving of such a force along lines of presently known forces has challenged philosophers such as Professor Margenau of Yale and physicists such as Professor McConnell of Pittsburgh, as well as engaging that wide-ranging intellect, C. G. Jung, who undertook his doctoral dissertation on the seeming direct action of the mind upon a table, a knife, and a bookcase.

From time to time the question of the direct impact of the mind upon external events, objects, and persons came up in the Cayce readings. Here such phenomena were treated as further exemplification of the claim that "thoughts are things," and at least one researcher was encouraged to believe that he could train himself to move such objects as a spoon (he was told to start with objects made of silver) which he saw himself affecting in a dream. However, he was warned that such activity was much more taxing for the body than ESP, and that he would have to cleanse his body and emotions alike to accomplish it—as well as hold to a purpose which did *not* include impressing other people, whether for the sake of his own ego or to advance a supposed religious cause. In the Cayce view, the actual energy involved in psychokinesis came from the action of the delicate "centers" of the body, the same ones involved in psychic perceptions; the training of these centers was a matter of training the whole person, not simply a training of psychic musculature. Once the way had been found and the gift used in service, probably over many lifetimes, it would be reliable and could even be used spontaneously as Jesus had used it to change water into wine (in a process, the Cayce source noted, where the actual change had not taken place until the water was poured).

During Cayce's lifetime and since, his associates and those who have together worked with his materials have concentrated chiefly on absent healing through prayer as their means of using psychokinetic force. In developing this ability, as in developing other forms of psychic phenomena, they have been mindful of the Cayce source's injunction to seek "the mind of Christ." Repeatedly it has become clear that no form of ritual, no method of concentration or breathing, no circle in the dark or in daylight, no chant or incantation, would bring about an apparent operation of energy flowing out to people and things, except as the individuals brought their whole lives into harmony with the spirit of their prayer. It did no good to ask for God's help unless one were willing to offer his own—through a telephone call, a visit, the securing of a good doctor, the giving of a massage. Those who sought the capacity for sharing with others an energy broader than the body and consciousness had to "live as they pray," as the Cayce source so often put it. Integrity was crucial.

Integrity and Creativity

The Cayce source took the issue of integrity as the fifth area of religious concerns in training for creativity. The chapter of *A Search for God* on integrity was named, after two components of integrity, "Virtue and Understanding." In this view "virtue" was consistent behavior from pure motives, which freed the flow of insights that made "understanding," leading in turn to more effective behavior.

That personal integrity affects the flow of psychokinesis in everyday life would seem reasonable if in fact psychic activity is a total creative act of a person, rather than a trick of an obscure nerve or gland. One living without integrity by a double standard might be subject to the same censorship which disguises the contents of dreams; psychic energy used to justify oneself with others could hardly be expected to work effectively. A man with hidden and unresolved anger or sexuality could hesitate to broadcast his force by PK, just as he might be guarded in other areas of life. And an individual whose behavior led him to fear punishment would be as likely to have the "will to fail" in psychic matters as any other. At the same time, a self-righteously virtuous person, whose proper behavior lacked human understanding, could not expect to mobilize PK for others more readily than he would his handshake or his money.

A number of individuals with what appears to be healing gifts—for example, Ambrose Worrall—have told the writer that the use of such energies for show or personal advantage tends to limit their availability the next time they are needed. For Worrall, this has meant making his living as an executive for the Martin Aircraft Company, and accepting no fees for his healing work. For a psychic from China whose psychokinetic abilities with coins, dice, living tissue, and chemical solutions has seemed to the writer to be extraordinary, the question of stability of his talent appears directly linked to his motives. What he does for research or as a contribution to healing seems to leave him peaceful and ready for the next assignment; what he does for entertainment, or for publicity, seems to render his next efforts less reliable.

Insofar as many psychics can describe the difference between "natural" everyday psychic experience and "elevated" psychic experience, where the sense of a cooperating divine reality is unshakeable, the role of integrity seems to them prominent in making the difference. Edgar Cayce once lost his ability for a year, after it was used to predict the results of horse races. At another period when it was used for mixed motives in locating oil wells, it seemed to describe oil accurately as it had been present thousands of years ago. Something beyond Cayce's consciously feeling "worthy" or "unworthy" may have been at work in such experiences, for those who have elevated psychic experiences do not typically claim to be "worthy" of these at all. Instead unconscious processes may be chiefly involved, where the entire psyche takes account of its controls, ideals, and defenses—its integrity.

Investigation of creativity in problem-solving and the arts has not always shown a high correlation between public norms of virtue and the productivity of the creative man. However, when his productivity is measured against his own consistency with inner stances disclosed in dreams and introspection, another picture emerges. The man who prostitutes his art, or solves strategy problems for industrial spies, may produce results, but there are often suggestions that he operates below his best capacities. An experience such as Samson's, where an individual recovers his full potential in a burst, after breaking vows he has made, also raises the question of integrity in the generation of creative energy. On the other hand, those who practice proper but stale virtue, as the story of Job may suggest, may find that only crisis and accompanying vision may free their best energies. Understanding, or wisdom, may indeed be the twin of upright behavior in all creativity. Carl Jung and his associates have traced the spontaneous emergence of "archetypes" from the deep unconscious as occurring in an orderly sequence of "understanding," which is the accompaniment of productive activity in the "individuated" person. In a provocative essay, Jung has suggested that Paul's phrase might read, "For now abideth faith, hope, love—and insight." Virtue seems to require understanding.

In taking up the question of integrity Edgar Cayce turned to the ancient religious question of how a man may do that which he knows he should. In the Cayce view, no man alone had sufficient resources to keep true to his present ideals and open to new ones at the same time; he must have the continuous aid of his own transcendent soul, and seek the help of the ever-aiding Christ Spirit. "None can choose aright without the Holy Spirit" was one statement on the problem. Yet he who patiently hoped and tried to do the best he knew would find help, until one day it might be said of him as the Cayce information occasionally observed of an individual who asked guidance: "Who can tell a rose to be beautiful? Who can tell the wind to blow? Who can tell a baby how to smile?" Purity of heart was not beyond man's reach, with God's help.

Part of God's help would be understanding. Not necessarily learning, or knowledge of facts, but the sense of meaning, of design, of the connections in behavior. He who tried to control his anger might learn how the energies of anger can work effectively, so that one can "be angry but sin not." He could learn how to convert hostility to courage, violence to vigor, aggression to boldness, explosive episodes to steady fierceness over poverty and bigotry and epidemics. For there were laws for the operation of the adrendalin glands, just as there were laws for everything else in the universe. Man could learn how he uses anger for cheap catharsis, or to cover up threatening sexuality, or to impute his own guilts to others, for these things were not past understanding —just as he could learn that "a person without a temper isn't worth much." Virtue could be grounded in intelligent understanding. By self-study, even by the study of the glandular function, as well as by the study of literature and the Bible, one might grasp little by little the essential truths of any area of his behavior. But introspection alone would not take him far, and knowledge not tested could be a pit, a snare. For the primary activity of human consciousness was comparison, correlation—and these processes could only be brought fully into play in activity, in experiment, in trying out the laws of being. No virtue worth having would be mere artificial control. As already noted, the Cayce materials insisted, "Don't be just goody-goody, be good *for* something" —for in productive creativity, in shared making and loving and giving, man could find the precious wisdom he needed to conquer himself.

Part of every man's task of integrity would be making sure that his "personality" was in alignment with, and grounded upon, his "individuality." By *personality,* Cayce's source meant a man's public self—his offices, roles, trappings, standards, station, titles, vestments, and the rest of the image that he asked the world to accept of him. By *individuality,* Cayce's source meant something not so easy to inspect, but which was evidently the unique thrust of a soul in a given lifetime—with certain ideals to the fore, certain vows to be kept, certain talents to be used, certain life-riddles to be solved. Individuality was what the Cayce information probed in life readings, as well as in "mental and spiritual readings." Dreams, prayer, meditation, the tiny daily promptings of the stream of faith, all might bring to consciousness the true individuality, upon which the personality might be properly grounded in virtue. Other aids to discovering individuality could also be found in the loving responses of group members, in the ring of biographies within the self, in the construction of "life seals" based upon the best elements in past lives, and even in travel to sites where one had grown most beautifully in former existences, or in cleaving to associates who seemed to elicit one's best self. For the individuality upon which virtue must be grounded was not hopelessly hidden; what covered it over would be so acting toward one's brother as to blind oneself from the light of one's own soul, in the very act of blinding one's brother. To grapple with virtue and understanding, then, one had to work to see behind the vice of others, had constantly to discover what good thing sought to work itself out in another, however clumsily. Always, one had to go beyond vengeance to compassion for the offender, for it was a law that the psyche would exact upon itself the same standards used upon others. "Judge not, that ye be not judged" was more than good advice; it was reality as sure as gravity.

Yet not every trial that came upon a person meant that he was being judged, that his virtue and understanding had failed him. There were, in the view of the Cayce source, those times when—as Job discovered—tribulations were the mercy of God. Weakness might yield to strength, timidity to certitude, hope to performance, under a duress that had its origin in what was to come as much as in what had been. "Whom the Lord loveth He chasteneth" was used by this source to forestall the endless computing of karma by those who sought, like the friends of Job, to rationalize all stations and developments in life. A man's journey was ultimately known only to God, and to be measured only by God and the individual's own soul, born of the same Godhead; it was possible (as Jesus said, according to the Cayce readings) for a boy to be born blind "that God may be glorified" in his life and in his fellows, by the choice of that soul. Hardship was not always the sharp justice of karma for deserting virtue and understanding (which was in the minds of those questioners who asked whether it could be the boy's fault that he had been *born* blind).

How might one begin to cultivate integrity? There was that remarkable creative power of the subconscious, which would build whatever it was consistently offered. Therefore, "whatsoever things are true, beautiful, just, of good report, think of these things." And one could make choices of his thoughts, beginning again and again. The power to choose, to throw the switch of meaning, to pick, to determine, to take a stand, was in the view of the Cayce source a final attribute of the soul, never fully lost. This did not mean one could invent or imagine his life to be what he pleased; the universe was not that chaotic. But in the real choices that faced man, not his hypothetical one, he would find he had the power of choice—and a tiny bit more each time he used it constructively, in the way or "mind" of Christ. Such power of choice, to recognize and answer calls from the soul and one's brother, was of more value than attainment of skill or position that men prize. On that account, each would find that what God asked of him in any lifetime was not that he succeed in some notable way, that his virtue and understanding bring him public results; God's ultimate question of him was only whether he tried. "Try, try again," the Cayce readings urged upon alcoholics, quarreling lovers, struggling scientists, repentant parents, regretful politicians, fumbling artists. This was the commandment: not to succeed, not to be perfect, but to try—with all the heart, mind, soul, strength—until the whole being burned with single light in the effort to glorify God. That alone would be gain, eternal gain, if the effort were made in order to be a channel of blessings—that blessed channel—to others. For man would not get "into heaven," into new and free consciousness of creating daily with God, except "leaning on the arm of someone ye have helped." This was the refrain of hundreds of the Cayce readings.

Integrity and Action on People and Things

Can growth of integrity actually be accompanied by growth in psychokinesis, in capacity to direct an unseen flow of energy towards people and things? Do virtue and understanding play so large a part in the development of psychic gifts?

The writer interviewed a psychiatrist who has practiced in New England for years, working long hours with troubled people. A student of parapsychological research and of dream research, he described a process which he had found emerging in recent years of his practice.

Early in his practice he had conceived his role as explaining people's problems to them, helping them name the goblins of the mind, equipping them with the courage born of knowing that others had faced and met such problems, and sharing his professional treasure of procedures which they could use to meet and tame their demons. In this process, he often found himself touched to the quick by the situation laid bare in a life before him, which so closely paralleled his own weaknesses that had led to divorce in early marriage. As many another therapist has done, he found himself as much healed as his patients, through what he came to face and to understand, as well as in the impact of those telling moments when his patients chose fidelity or trust or risk, and showed the human spirit shining, even out of sickness.

His perception of unconscious contents in his patients grew keener, his empathy warmer, as he brought his own life under the same standards, the same disciplines, the same covenants he fostered in his patients. But more, he had found recently in his practice that something beneath the level of words was occurring at critical moments in therapy. He was slipping into a total stance of prayer, like his own best private devotional life, while before him a father chose whether to forgive a son, or a painter whether to live in reality, or a child-molester whether to face his own childish aggression. And in those moments he could feel a flow of energy go out from him that seemed to have an almost physical impact on the patients. Tears came more freely when they were needed by a patient, a patient's anger reached catharsis rather than staying sullen poison, fear sharpened a patient's desire to dig out his deceptions, truth recognized by a patient could resonate into a huge laugh. Patients repeatedly commented on the vital boost of help they felt at turning points, and relatives even mentioned hearing of the incidents. Not every sick person recovered. Not everyone was significantly helped. Yet there had appeared what seemed to be a force that could be relied upon in the consulting room (though not for too many hours in a given day), a force that at least triggered or restricted responses in others, if it did not act directly upon their minds and bodies.

The psychiatrist did not abandon his psychiatry. Instead he pressed his studies ever harder, reaching into further research on dreams, and into the biochemistry of traumas and their release. But his chief hope to be helpful to patients at turning points, critical incidents when they needed an extra vital boost to code the struggling energies within them—this resource, he told the writer, came from the effort to keep his own life straight, to walk in the way of the best he knew. As he managed to do this, or to try again, under all the temptations of professional prestige, wealth, women patients proclaiming love for him, and potential competition with colleagues, he found that he was "not against myself," that he could reach for aid as far down as the center of his selfhood, and find there forces not wholly of his own making. Asked if he believed in spiritual healing, he always answered "yes" with a smile. While his questioner might refer to a superior occult power from some other plane, he meant, as he would explain when pressed, that "spirituality" was not violating one's own foundations, and was the basis of the healing he trusted most in his consulting room. "If ye continue in my word," he once reminded a group that Jesus had said of purity in behavior and understanding, "then shall ye be my disciples; and ye shall know the truth, and the truth shall make you free."

CHAPTER 8

OUT-OF-THE-BODY EXPERIENCES

EDGAR CAYCE SAT up and rubbed his eyes. He had finished a long trance session, and awakened with a slight start, asking his wife who sat beside him to give him instructions during the trance, "Did you get it?" Having been unconscious, he had no idea what he had said, or whether he had said anything at all—for there had been times when he was very tired that he could not enter the trance state nor give a reading. After his wife nodded, he buttoned his collar and smiled. "I had a dream," he said to the writer and others in the room.

The idea of Cayce dreaming, while he was busy talking in deep trance about people scattered around the country, seemed absurd. Yet from time to time it happened. This time the dream was a little unusual.

"I went fishing with John, James, Andrew and the Master," he explained. "I asked where Peter was. 'Oh, you know Peter isn't here!' said James. Thomas said, 'Oh, yes, I was a fisherman—don't let them fool you, telling you to quit fishing. We are all eating fish.'" "All of us," Cayce added, "were in the nicest little boat on a lake."

Cayce had obviously enjoyed the dream. The center of his entire devotional life was "the Master," and any sense of closeness to Him, even in dream or waking reverie, gave Cayce a lift as could nothing else.

In earlier days, when the pressure to give readings for those in pain and illness was not so great as this year—the year that proved the last of Cayce's life—he might well have taken a reading on the dream, to get an interpretation to match his waking judgment. But now he had to be content with what he could consciously make of the dream.

He knew it was important, for a dream of the Master was one which touched his very soul. He also knew it was not a warning, from the happy mood of the fishing. He also knew it was not literal, some sort of gathering of those particular souls in another plane, or at least he thought this unlikely. For his readings had told him that at least one of the disciples in the boat had already incarnated, and Cayce had met him—a man in England. Further, he had been assured that two others, including Peter, would incarnate during Cayce's lifetime, or soon after, to help in preparing the way for a new growth of spirituality across the earth. He took this to be the meaning of the comment in the dream that Peter would not be found with the other disciples, and it gave him a sense of promise. For Cayce was weary, and he welcomed every prompting that told him others would provide new kinds of leadership in a world at war.

More practically, he took the comments about fishing as encouragement from his own best self to get out on the dock behind his house, where there was a little fresh water lake, and to renew the fishing times he so loved. In the quiet at the water's edge, practicing a ritual as old as man on the earth, he had always found refreshment, balance, steadiness, assurance that "underneath are the everlasting Arms." But in the press of hundreds of pleading letters each day, since the publication of his biography, and in the demands of long-distance phone calls so numerous that the phone company limited the number of his incoming calls each day, in order to let others use the lines out of Virginia Beach, he had put his fishing aside. After this dream he returned to it, at least for a while. He even ate more fish and seafood, in the light of his feelings about the dream, for he had long been convinced by his readings that dreams deserved to be examined for content at several different levels at once —physical, mental, spiritual.

But there was a puzzling element about the dream, as about many dreams. Was there, in addition to the various symbolic contents meant to give him aid and encouragement from his own best self, also a residue to suggest that he had "moved" somewhere in consciousness while having this dream? For it had the qualities of sunlight and beauty that he had learned to associate with dreams which his information said signaled a dreamer's entrance into another plane of consciousness. Had he for a flash been "caught up," as Paul said he had been so lifted into the "third heaven," and had Cayce retained only the sense which had been elaborated in the little dream? Did people actually leave the body in some way to be "present with God," as Paul had suggested?

The idea of leaving his body, or at least having part of his consciousness leave his body, was not strange to Cayce. He had learned from painful experience that nobody should pass his hand or an object over his solar plexus while he was in trance, for it would instantaneously stop his speaking. His source had warned him that carelessness in this matter could cost him his life, by separating an invisible connection between his sleeping-speaking body and that other part of him that was abroad seeking aid for someone through a reading.

He knew that he could be directed in trance to go anywhere and give such explicit detail about what he was watching that those who had listened, over the years, had become convinced that an important part of him was really on the distant scene. For example, early in his career, according to Mrs. Cayce, Cayce had been asked to "follow" several of his Kentucky townspeople each day, while they went about touring spots at the Paris Exposition. He had supplied such abundant detail that when his friends returned and examined the records, they made the case celebrated for years in that section of Kentucky. (Mrs. Cayce, however, had been unhappy with this use of Edgar's abilities, fearing that such a relatively pointless exhibition would not afford him the same vital energy and protection as when he sought to help the sick).

Over the years he had experienced a few dreams which in their form and content left him convinced that he had "been somewhere," out of his body, during the dream. For example, there had been the dream when he found himself with Dwight L. Moody, a gifted preacher and evangelist who had given Cayce much encouragement at a chance meeting early in Cayce's manhood. Other ministers he had known were present in the dream, too, all of them by that time dead, as were the others in a great meeting hall which they entered from a dark hallway, where the light was dark blue and made people's faces look purple. In the meeting hall itself he noticed that all wore robes and were standing. They were waiting to hear the Master speak, as Cayce had been told He would, when invited to go to the meeting at the start of the dream. In the hall was somehow a light, which Cayce couldn't see, but realized it came from a Voice, which he knew to be "the Lord" speaking, though He could not be seen. The Voice asked, "Who will go to bring peace again on the earth?"—a fitting question in the midst of World War II. Then, Cayce reported of the dream, Jesus had stepped forward and said, "I will go. It is time for me to go again into the earth to strengthen my brethren, though I will not be born on the earth . . ." And the dream ended, leaving Cayce with a sense of joy and promise he could not put into words, but which had often returned in his thoughts since the dream. The dream had left him with a sense that his work was worthwhile if in even the smallest way it helped to set men wondering and thinking, so that they might better recognize the closer Presence of the Master, when He came among them.

In reflecting on the possibility of being fully conscious, yet out of his body, Cayce joined a long parade of those who made such claims in various cultures. It was the heart of the trance experience sought by the shaman among the Indians of the Pacific Northwest, and the essence of old Hindu claims that holy men could be seen in two places at once, miles apart. European folklore celebrated the claim in stories of the "Doppelganger" or double who walks abroad, while men in battlefield experiences of World War II were currently reporting leaving their bodies after severe wounds, to travel over the terrain about them, seeing every detail with indelible clarity, while seeming to seek aid for their battered bodies.

Possible out-of-the-body experiences had been reported by investigators of hypnosis from its earliest days, where it was quaintly called "traveling clairvoyance." Hugh Lynn Cayce and other investigators such as Charles Tart and Andrija Puharich have reproduced the early hypnosis experiments with their own subjects, in cases, for example, where subjects supplied such abundant detail of adjoining rooms unknown to them (rooms deliberately set to fall into disarray after the door was closed and all observers outside) that the hypothesis of some sort of "leaving the body" seemed worth considering. Under the influence of LSD, or of sensory deprivation tanks, others who were not hypnotized sometimes also seemed to inspect their immediate surroundings as though from outside their bodies, while still other subjects reported similar experiences after surgery or in critical illness—where they seemed to look down on their bodies with detachment. Cases where people were seen by others in an apparition miles from their bodies were studied and reported in considerable numbers by Muldoon and Tyrrell in England, as well as by Hart and Louisa Rhine in the U.S.

Can some portion of a man's consciousness leave his body, split off and have its own perceptions? Could this be trained, as some of the earliest investigators had reported? Edgar Cayce in trance was asked a number of times, over the years, about such a possibility.

The "information" responded that such experiences did occur, most often in dreams, where few were aware that they were abroad, although the careful study of anyone's dreams might reveal such incidents after a time. It was also reported that accident or injury, especially to endocrine gland areas and associated "centers" of the "real physical body" could bring about out-of-body experiences where they were not sought, usually with some peril to the subject. The attempt to induce such experiences while awake, rather than in dream or trance states, held considerable danger, and most people were advised by this trance source to "place self wholly in Christ, and let Him determine" when such experiences might be fruitful for the person. To be sure, the regular practice of meditation might keep free the channels within the personality and the body, along which such unusual experiences could occur, if there were the need to know another soul with the extraordinary vividness which such experiences made possible (as compared with the mental attunements of hunches and impressions), or if there were the need to make one's presence so felt by another living person that only an out-of-body experience would accomplish the goal.

Those who have kept records of their dream and fantasy experiences, in the effort to verify some of the claims of the Cayce source, have noted the relative rarity of material which would suggest that the individual was detached from his body and looking back at it, while also inspecting in veridical detail some adjacent or distant area. Yet the experiences do seem to occur, sometimes with a suggestion of slipping out of the top of the head. A few have reported hesitation about whether to return to their bodies, and one psychic whom the writer has studied has for this reason vowed he would never again try to induce such an experience. Several have reported wondering whether the Cayce material might be correct in suggesting that leaving the body for such experiences was not unlike the parting at death, and have wondered whether a lifetime of meditation would make it easier to undergo the transition of death, when that time finally occurred.

Asking why extra-body trips have taken the dreaming or conscious person in one direction rather than another, investigators have raised the question of bonds with others. In psychic experience as in waking experience, do people take "trips" to see those upon whom their hearts are set? Does this account for the high proportion of out-of-body visits to loved ones by those who are ill or apparently have just died? Does like attract like, in the psychic world as in the world of vacations, letters, phone calls, and dinner parties? If so, then it becomes important whom one chooses in his heart as his associates, and perhaps even more important what one seeks from the meeting. When the spirit or force of a man goes forth from him, whether in a waking handshake or in an eerie dream, what kind of relationships does he seek with others? Does he exploit others for his own justification, convenience, power, position, advancement, or theories? Or can he meet people as subjects in themselves, as independent centers of reality, as points of becoming as cosmically significant to God and to his own soul as himself? The thrust of the Cayce materials about meeting others out of the body was that attitudes toward others were critical in determining whether such experiences would be helpful, or—more basic—take place at all.

Acceptance in Creativity

To the Edgar Cayce trance source, the question of radical acceptance of others was important enough to take sixth place in a graded set of foci for training in creativity. The chapter on this topic in *A Search For God* was entitled "Fellowship."

There are indications that while awake we all avoid those whom we have hurt or condemned; guilt is a barrier in the affairs of daily life. And those whom we have not rejected but treated by an opposite extreme, identifying and fusing with them, rather than accepting them as separate beings, find themselves rebelling against such assimilation to ourselves, and often turning upon us with surprising force, as we may do with them when we do not feel appreciated. Further, while we may find the flow of fantasy heightened over an idol, such fantasy is rarely creative until it is tempered by full human relationships; "love is blind" especially in early stages. May it be as blind for ESP as for other perception? In a similar fashion we are bound to our enemies if we hate them, finding that "hate is blind" as well; while we may be fully aware of the faults of an individual whom we feel has outraged us, we are usually singularly ineffective in generating changes in the other, while obsessed by him. It appears that people cannot function at maximum creativity in psychic ability or other relating, so long as they cannot approach others with an acceptance transcending both uncritical identification and unqualified rejection. As Martin Buber has so eloquently written, the "I" of an "I-thou" relation with another is a different "I" than the "I" of an "I-it" relation, where another becomes our thing, our abstraction, our convenience. We are whole and have access to our fullest selves, in Buber's terms, as we are able to stand, however fleetingly, in fully accepting relations with others. By contrast, when we stand in partial relations, necessary for the ordered affairs of daily life, we are but partly ourselves, for any kind of creative task.

Further evidence regarding possible "laws" by which we associate with others in psychic experiences, including those where we may leave our bodies behind and see them there, may lie in dream material. The interpreter of dreams so often finds that the characters in them represent parts of the dreamer that he usually begins on this assumption in clinical practice. However, he also finds those dreams where individuals appear not so much as flags or signals of something as they appear in the knobby uniqueness felt in their living presence. Such dreams leave upon the dreamer a sense of the peculiar combination of promise and problem, presence and potential, biography and becoming, which lights the face-to-face meeting with someone well known to him. Such dreams produce more fitting, more authentic encounters with the dreamed-about one, if he be living, or more apt memories and prayers for the dreamed one, if he be dead. Full encounters shatter stereotypes. Is it possible that dreamers leave their bodies to become present with others for just such full encounters?

Studies of the psychology of creativity have accented the factor of attitudes towards others, even though few others may be involved in the actual creative act. Self-justification before imagined others is a burden upon the flow of imagery and form, for a painter or a businessman alike. And self-justification is the typical concern where scorn has reduced the cast of respected associates on the stage of one's life. Likewise, belittling of others makes it more difficult to accept and use their contributions as valid for one's own creative work, while destructive efforts toward competitors or relatives alike tend to leave the actor afraid of himself being destroyed.

Taking up the issue of acceptance as a religious concern in creativity, the Cayce trance source turned to a religious question as widely distributed as men's faiths: Who is to be considered "justified," worthy, before God? Ought the answer to be "the people of the Book," as it was for Moslems who did not slaughter those who had a written scripture, in the days of their early conquests? Ought the answer to be those of doctrinal conformity, as it was for the Inquisition? Ought the answer to be those untainted by visions, as it was for early American witch-hunters? Are the justified the upright saints or arhats of Southern Buddhism, or the penitent seekers for heavenly compassion in Northern Buddhism? Ought man to emulate the ardent asceticism of John the Baptist, or the more relaxed city-trafficking ways of Jesus?

The Cayce source claimed that no man could properly be approached as a self-made product, either good or bad. Every man had to be understood as sprung from a seed planted by God, his living soul. Since souls were of the nature of God himself, in their love and purity and vital creativity, they need not be justified, and could not be; their very existence commanded respect, even when individual entities had to be avoided at times, or struggled with unto physical death. Nobody could rely upon a political or religious grouping to tell him whom to take seriously in his encounters, as Jesus had made clear in the parable of the Samaritan, where both distinctions were present. On the contrary, every man had to learn, sooner or later, that he must answer life with a consummate affirmation: "I am my brother's keeper." Who, then, was this brother? Potentially every man. Actually, the one whom he found before him needing his aid, his talents, his encouragement. Not some distant benighted savage for whom he might give missionary dollars, although such work had its place, but above all the one across the office desk, across the tracks, across the room in the hospital, across the prison wall, across the line of political right and political left—wherever someone stood or stumbled in need of aid that could be given.

The Cayce information was explicit that the economically disadvantaged, and the members of racial minorities, were direct challenges to every man; it asserted that these people must be given their rights, not only as individuals but as groups of people, for brotherhood did not stop with personal kindliness. Brotherhood also involved social responsibility, the taking of stands and the carrying of duties, even to the penalty that Jesus paid, if the individual had set his ideal "in Christ." Yet not martyrdom but creative service with the best of one's talents was the goal. To be one's brother's keeper was something more than cheering for him from a safe distance; the musician had better make music for him, the doctor heal him, the organizer bargain for him, the manufacturer employ him, the waitress serve him, the psychic "read" him— or health was not in any of them, and they might one day hear from their own souls "Depart from me," instead of the words from the Throne so often cited by the Cayce readings for the end of the soul's journey, "Well done, thou good and faithful servant; enter into the joy of the Lord."

For the brotherhood of man was not a deduction from something else, not a moral precept. It was a "shadow" of man's fellowship with the Father. Responding to a man was not identical with responding to God as Father; one had still to pray in secret to the Father, and to engage in meditation where all other beings but the One disappeared from view. But responding to man was of the same order as responding to God, requiring no less than the elements of worship: thanksgiving, adoration, repentance, celebration, forgiveness of sins, dedication, and more. The nearest house of God to where one stood was the next human flesh. For this trance source the theme was never reduced to poetry or religious scruples; as one treated another man, one was actually—not figuratively—treating God. In the other person burned always that "spark of the divine," that "celestial fire deep down," which the forces of another man's soul could "fan into flame." Even in dealing with the enemy, the reviler, the outcast, one could not settle for thinking positive thoughts, but must come to a "yearning" for the other to fulfill the promise of his being. Such acceptance would not by sympathy, which was simply a sometimes-helpful emotion, but would be a total response of love to the enemy which could only properly be called "adoration," in the sense of a turning toward him much more complete than affection or liking or attraction. One had to pray actively for the "One Force" in another, not merely overlooking shortcomings, but having a vision of something better emerging directly from the shortcomings, as the good in the other which his failings were blindly seeking to express. For such a purpose one might call upon his native psychic ability with his whole heart, and ask the aid of Christ as well, that he might be shown how to pray and how to act with an erring brother.

If every man were one's brother, did one then merely wander about doing indiscriminate good deeds? Sometimes. But the first stage of creativity to be practiced was cooperating, covenanting. One had to enter into specific bonds, specific groups, specific traditions, or he could not reach his own depths for the resources he needed to fully love and accept others. Such associating would at times take precedence in activity, though not in attitude, over even the bonds of family life. As the Cayce source reminded, even Jesus had asked, "Who are my mother and brothers? They that do the will of the Father in heaven." One had to gather with the "sheep," mature individuals who consciously chose the Ideal, in order to be able to feed the "lambs" who would become sheep if they knew how. Every devout man, as Peter in the Gospel of John, was called to feed both.

Could a man by will alone choose fully to accept his brother in fellowship? Not in the view of the Cayce source. Such fellowship was ultimately found by alignment with God, Who alone could open one's eyes and soul to the other. In the vein, the Cayce source chose an appellation for Christ which differed from the terms most common in the surrounding culture, though it did not contradict them. More often perhaps than any other phrase, the designation given to Christ by the Cayce readings was "the Elder Brother." The phrase had about it the insistence that one dare not give honor to Christ which was not matched in principle in the way one looked at his other brothers. The face of every man would look different immediately after looking at the face of Christ, for in such a glance the destiny of souls could be known: to have again with the Father that "perfect fellowship which was in the beginning." Yet no trivializing of Christ, nor reduction of Him to religious leader rather than Messiah, was allowed by the phrase. For often the terms used were Lord, Master, Son and Light—to remind men of the gulf between their easy earth-trimmed ways and that transcendent creativity which someday, somehow they had also to make theirs. The ultimate destiny of every man was to become as Christ, no less. A soul might require eons to do it, and move through regions and planes unknown to man on earth, but the journey had to be made, and God had time that matched the size of His purpose.

How might one begin to practice the radical acceptance that marked true fellowship? As always, self-evaluation was one essential. One had to look at his day, his week, to find out whether in fact he brought peace or contentiousness to those near him. He had to ask, with the aid of dreams and prayer, whether he would be willing to be represented in the very presence of the Almighty Father, solely by the way he treated his fellows at that time. One had to pry open the apertures of his mind and heart to others, and it was as fitting to pray "help thou mine unbelief in my brother" as to pray "help thou mine unbelief in my God." At the same time, acceptance and rejoicing in oneself, one's own secret identity and soulship, would be linked with one's capacity to accept others. For the Cayce source, self-condemnation was a dangerous sin. One could repent, be sorry, set about changing. But one could not punish nor condemn and exile himself, any more than he could his brother, for his own soul had equally regal status in the Kingdom with all others who sought to "inherit the Kingdom." Needless self-doubt, self-castigation would be found to be a defense against responsibility for one's own life, and an unworthy attempt at placating God with a sacrifice not approved by Him. The man who did not rejoice in the gift of his own life and his opportunities rejected God as truly as the one who ignored his neighbor; indeed, the two attitudes were secretly linked within, for the loss of the sun of the soul, with its gift of love and vision, was the natural consequence of any eclipse of human dignity and worth. Every man, oneself included, needed to be properly seen as striving to give form to his final understanding of God, though he might never use the word, for this was the force that set all souls and lives in motion and kept them on their journeys.

Specific disciplines might help to build the full acceptance which marked fitting fellowship of man with man. One could practice much at home, where it would be seen that no answer at all was better than an unkind one. There, where defenses were properly dropped, one could learn that a long face never glorified the God who spun the worlds and found them "good, good." In the daily walk of life, the beginning could ever be made, and the right direction made into a highway for the life, by being kind, considerate; more would be accomplished by little deeds wholeheartedly done than by great resolves honored more in speech than act. And again and again one would find the opportunity to risk a response to another soul, as he would want God to risk on him. "For if ye were judged by God as ye judge others, where would ye be?"

There was a bit of homey verse which the Cayce trance source often used, apparently taken from Edgar Cayce's own personal store of maxims, to sum up the challenge of fellowship, the dangerous and beautiful business of risking with one's brother and partner in creation itself: "It is better to trust one soul, and that deceiving, than to doubt the one in whom believing would have blessed thy life with truer meaning." Yet the point of fellowship was greater than self-serving. It was no less than "glorifying God in the earth," in the brother whose soul was as unspeakably precious to God as any soul created, "be he black, white, gray, or grizzled."

Acceptance and Out-Of-The-Body Experiences

Might the individual seeking helpful psychic experiences find that his growth in ability truly to accept others would at times free him to leave his body, in dream or in prayer, and stand close to another for sharing?

An able, elderly "sensitive" described to the writer an experience which followed shortly after painful chest surgery nearly cost him his life. Prior to the surgery, he had been involved in lecturing and demonstrations which took him across the country once or twice a year, as well as in counseling friends old and new who had come to rely on his aid. Often he was in trance, and he knew there were conditions of rest and diet and relaxation he would have to meet, to keep his physical resources intact under the strain of the trance work. Still, he pushed himself, responding to requests which in a year's time might include those of researchers, college professors, ministers, even government officials. Since he traveled so much, it was difficult for him to meet with the little study and growth group which had been the instrument of his healing once before, and the vehicle for his helping people of many walks of life, over the years. He struggled to keep his balance with his own devotions, but his health failed, a lung collapsed, and he required major surgery to remove part of his lung. During the painful convalescence he had time to think, time to talk with people on the phone, time to greet visitors, some of whom came from long distances to see him. He began to be able to look deeply into faces, unhurried, to cherish those about him, rather than to feel he must lead them. To some of these visitors, as to the writer, he told the story of an experience which followed shortly after his surgery.

He had fallen asleep thinking of the one man in America whose healing prayer he most respected, a man he had not talked with or written to for years. The friend was hundreds of miles away in another city. He wanted his aid, for the pain was great, and often his spirits flagged, while doctors were not encouraging about his recovery, as a man in his seventies. But he hesitated to call his friend the healer, for he had long failed to write, and the barrier created by ignoring loved ones intruded itself. Then during the night he had a vivid dream. He found himself standing in the bedroom of his friend, hundreds of miles away. He saw his friend stir, noticed a score of little details in the room, felt the lift of love for his friend, and then was gone from the place. Even in his dream he found himself noting that he had been out of his body.

He slept soundly, unaware of pain for the first night since the surgery, and in the morning woke refreshed. His recovery grew more swift, from that time on.

Two days later came a special delivery letter from his healing friend. "What were you doing in my room the other night?" it began. The letter told how clearly the friend had seen him, even to the extent of noting bandages on his chest, for just a moment. The friend had then stayed awake to pray, and poured out earnest intercession for the psychic whom he had not seen for so long. "I know you were here," the letter continued, "and I only hope I understood the reason for your coming and was able to help a bit." He had helped. Or at least that was how the psychic saw it. He saw his out-of-body experience not as a psychic feat, put on like so many of his demonstrations, but as a cry for help from his own soul, leading him forth along lines of companionship strung anew in the quiet times of his illness.

Had he moved out from his body in a process foreshadowed long ago, when an empty tomb led to an out-of-body meeting with bewildered disciples, and the flesh refashioned itself for Love?

CHAPTER 9

PRECOGNITION

EDGAR CAYCE WALKED through the little workroom where the writer sat typing, preparing questions for the next day's readings.

Somebody had to read the correspondence with each application for a reading, in order to formulate questions for the end of the reading. Cayce was swamped with just sorting each day's mail to schedule appointments. Besides, he was not too interested in the fine details of a given person's need. His source had told him that one reason he did his work in trance was to keep some measure of distance between himself and all those problems and personalities with which he sought to work psychically. So he was content to glance at the first letter of inquiry or application, and to let others study the correspondence to make up each day's readings and questions. Sometimes when the membership form in the little research association was in good order, he did not even see a note from an applicant. And sometimes people sent no information nor questions whatsoever, content to see what Cayce would get about them, or testing his ability. He did not seem to mind being tested, for he understood the doubts which people must have about his strange abilities. But Cayce's secretary had her hands full transcribing the many readings given each day, as well as supervising a busy office which at one point employed ten additional typists and file clerks. So the present writer had volunteered to prepare the correspondence, instructions, and questions for each day's readings, and was busy on this task when Edgar Cayce walked past to his lunch, saying nothing.

A moment later, Mrs. Cayce came from her kitchen, through the dining room and into the work area where the writer sat. "Edgar says you are leaving on the 11:40 a.m. Norfolk and Western train next Tuesday. Can we drive you to the train?" Her offer was spontaneous and genuine, quite like her. Indeed, there was nothing unusual about the incident, except that she named a precise train time and day for the writer's forthcoming trip—a time and day that had not yet been settled.

To be sure, her husband may have been guessing when he gave her the information he "picked up" as he simply walked past the writer. There were only a few trains each day from Norfolk to Chicago, anyway, and only two railroads to consider, leaving from different terminals. Yet it was wartime and Norfolk was a busy seaport, so that it was difficult to secure Pullman berths on short notice, as the writer had sought without success to do in his own lunchtime that day. He had been trying for one of three times, including the Tuesday departure which Cayce had quietly announced.

Not surprisingly, though not without humor, the writer and his wife began their packing and arrangements for their apartment, effective on the coming Tuesday. Cayce proved right. This was the day, the railroad, the time, when the departure occurred.

What had happened? The writer verified that he had left his home phone number with the railroad office, not his office number, and that no call had been made which Cayce might have overheard. There seemed little reason to doubt that there had occurred yet another in the little forays into the future which had become second nature to Edgar Cayce. Whether Cayce had secured the correct train details by simultaneously piecing together the mind of the writer and the appropriate railroad officials, or whether some part of his psyche had simply constructed a whole event and felt it "fit" with the future, would be impossible to say. Cayce himself could not describe the elements of such events in his mind, except that he "knew," and knew he knew.

How far is it possible to know the future? Is such psychic experience the direct inspection of a future event which has not yet occurred—which seems impossible? Is it a computerlike assessment of a score of variables all swept into a glance, and totaled up to reveal the future? Is it the inspection of a "pattern" element within the psyche, which may be similar to the "pattern" working itself out in the world beyond the psyche—so that a "fresh start in late morning" feeling in Cayce coincided with the elements working toward a "fresh start on a train trip on Tuesday morning"?

However it occurred, Edgar Cayce found the experience of certainty about the future familiar. Most of his detailed precognitive promptings had come in dreams. He had dreamed repeatedly of the founding and progress of his hospital, even while living in Dayton, before moving to Virginia Beach. He had dreamed of its medical staff, of its board, of its front steps, of the strains that would lead to its closing. He had dreamed of Atlantic University, founded on his work, and its personnel and backers. And his wife dreamed of the future even more often: she dreamed of a trip, of visitors, of a quarrel, of investment opportunities. Together they had learned to follow a piece of counsel from the readings about such dreaming: Man and wife, as well as close relatives and business associates, should learn to check their dreams together, for often one could dream more clearly of a coming event than another, or could supplement the dream of another with further pieces. (It was a kind of "cross-correspondence" between dream contents, similar to that which engaged parapsychologists in the study of messages from discarnates through mediums.)

But Cayce did not have to be asleep to be prompted about the future. If he were rested and in good spirits, he would know when he was about to receive a letter from one of his sons in the Service overseas, or when a check from a donor to research was on its way in the mail, or when a relative of one of his employees was ill enough to die—though doctors had not yet diagnosed the case. He seemed to "see" at times the outcome of pregnancies, the likelihood that a marriage would hold together, the prospects for a piece of real estate, the tendency to an auto breakdown.

His daily life experiences of precognition were not unlike those which had engaged soothsayers and diviners and prognosticators from time immemorial —except that he used no special divining equipment and most of the time did not seek information about the future. His dreams had in them a larger proportion of psychic material than the dreams of others his age studied by parapsychologists, but the range of subject matter and imagery was not essentially different from that in dreams of ancient times, where the story might say, "And they, being warned in a dream, departed by another way." As the writer has compared Cayce's dream experiences with those of other psychics, the content and symbolism has not seemed exceptional in Cayce's instance.

The question of how far an individual may accurately "know" the future has puzzled researchers from the beginning of modern work on psychic experience. What occurred in the case of seeming apparitions who appeared to warn against a train, which later wrecked? What led a dreamer like the Englishman, Dunne, to foresee catastrophes and the results of horse races? How could Soal's subjects, the photographer Shackleton and the housewife Mrs. Stewart, correctly call cards which had not yet been determined by the selection of a counter from a bowl of mixed counters? In the U.S., how were some of Dr. Rhine's best subjects on ESP tests able to score on a target sheet to be prepared in a few days or weeks, based on tables of random numbers selected in turn from newspaper figures on the weather?

No researcher today has the answer to these questions. What has become apparent is that individuals tend to have their own profiles in ESP touching the future; they seem to be interested in different kinds of events and people, and in different spans of distance ahead. Further, their test scores on targets in the future tend to vary in much the same ways as their scores on targets in the present, under the influence of drugs, hypnosis, competition, encouragement, injury, or helpful partners; what seems to be one process of "psi" confronts researchers, rather than a separate process for the perception of the present and the future.

People from many walks of life asked Edgar Cayce in trance how to become more effectively aware of the future. Mothers asked how to keep alerted for the danger of epidemics to their children. Businessmen asked how they might determine market trends. Inventors asked how they could safely get their devices to the patent office. Homeowners asked how they could be warned in advance of threatening earthquakes. A few eager students of mysteries asked how to foresee where they would be born in their next life on earth. Most of the seekers for the future were encouraged to study their dreams. But there was no magical divining screen offered in dreams; one could not usually expect to dream of the future of others, except his loved ones or close associates. Further, one could not usually expect to glimpse the future in areas outside his round of interests: A businessman would not be likely to dream of developments in Tin Pan Alley, nor an athlete of developments in theoretical physics. The subconscious, which accounted for most of the spontaneous psychic experiences in waking and dreaming life, was coded on what to expect of the future by exactly what the individual held and worked on in consciousness. The subconscious was not a ball of mirrors flashing aimlessly at the dreamer, correctly reflecting to him a bit of the vast future every now and then; it was a highly directional capacity, responsive to the conscious studies and work of daily life. To improve one's glimpses of the money market, one had to become a responsible banker, not attempt concentration on a dollar bill. If one worked creatively at his life, and with motives of integrity and service, he could expect glimpses of the future in the areas of his own responsibility as truly as he could expect to breathe, for natural psychic ability was constantly at work in a process which the Cayce source described as "similar to self-preservation."

Of course there were things to learn about subconscious renderings of the future, both in dreams and waking hunches. One had to learn to distinguish between a signal to pay attention to something—an opportunity or a warning to be studied—and a signal to act now on something coming about. One had to learn to use his reason, the "deductive mind," in harmony with the raw data of psychic perception supplied by the subconscious, the "inductive mind"; better rational judgment supported and freed the psychic processes to function, rather than supplanting them. Further, one had to learn not to take too seriously all images of the future, even those that seemed notably psychic, for it was the way of the subconscious to depict things as present trends would bring them out if unchecked, in that strange inner landscape where time and space were ignored, and all things of the past and future tended to be set forth as now. A dream of the death of a loved one could mean many things, including the death of an unhealthy relationship with that person; if the dream were the warning of a future development, it might more likely be an indication of a serious concern which unattended would be grave, rather than impending extinction for the loved one. Yet the subconscious was not erratic in what it fed an individual of his future, for it would tend to give him only what he could handle—if his nervous system and glandular system were not in some way damaged. One needed have no fear of being swamped in dire warnings, if his desires to know the future were only to see that which he could constructively use without exploitation of others.

The quiet flow of assurances which the Cayce source called faith, the evidence of things unseen, was the source of constant psychic impressions, even when not stimulated by great devotion or great need to reach an "enhanced" or "elevated" stage. Recognizing that such a flow would be there, one ought to pause briefly before making decisions involving the future, according to the Cayce information, and seek a "witness" from the "still, small voice." Before stepping into a stressful situation such as a quarrel or an accident or a delicate performance, one ought to pause and make conscious attunement with the good and godly spirit which could prompt him to an awareness of what was ahead, and prepare him for it. In an emergency, where one had to act but had no idea what to do despite his best efforts at quiet and reflection, then one could pray for the answering "Spirit of Christ" to respond to the trembling of his soul, bringing him into touch with what he needed to know of the future. Cayce's source offered no magical trick, nor claim that the effort to grapple with the future would be instantly effective. But on the other hand, this source gave the impression to those who sought counsel through many readings that man had more resources for knowing the future than he usually used, in an age when Biblical accounts of guidance seemed more quaint than real.

In the years since Cayce's death, hundreds of people have used his suggestions for working with dreams of the future, and have shared their dream content in small study groups and in intensive "project groups" held during the summers by the Association for Research and Enlightenment at Virginia Beach. Others have kept journal records for months, even years, of promptings of the future which occurred to them in waking life. There are many leads for research on precognition in all of this raw data. Varieties of temperament and interests are readily apparent in this material, as well as degrees of accuracy based on the use made of precognitive material. But one of the interesting variables which stands out appears to be the question of how much of the future one can handle. Fear, as the Cayce source suggested, may be a swift crippler of most kinds of psychic experiences. One who is afraid of a certain future, or afraid of his own adequacy and the trustworthiness of life itself, will not be a good candidate for the full range of psychic awareness of the future. It does not seem to work to seek awareness only of the pleasant that lies ahead; unless one can face the trying and frustrating as well, his unconscious appears to shut off most of the flow—as many people suffer spontaneous amnesia of dreams, while they are hiding from an unwelcome problem. Insofar as freedom from fear may be important for precognition, then the ability to handle stress may be critical in glimpsing the future.

Handling Stress in Creativity

As the Cayce source took up the next religious theme in its examination of the elements of creativity which man must work out in his pilgrimage with his Creator, it labeled the lesson "Patience." This was the word which summarized the essential capacity to handle stress, in working towards worthwhile goals.

Some of the earliest studies of creativity by psychologists have identified "endurance of unresolved tension" as the hallmark of the creative problem-solver. After he has defined a set of opposed values which he wants to reconcile in a productive solution, the creative person is notably the one who can wait, without losing track of the problem. He may go on to something else, or sleep, or go to a movie, or pray. But always he holds onto his problem. He may try out possible solutions from time to time, but he resists the temptation that seizes less able individuals, to simply take a solution and make it work as well as possible. At the same time, the person who scores well on tests of creativity is not a perfectionist, afraid to try a solution unless success is guaranteed. Characteristically, he will make his effort, but in due season, when he feels his problem has ripened into solution stage.

Does such endurance affect not only the composing of music, the solving of equations in physics, the joining of wood in carpentry, the timing of an auto race, but also the accurate glimpsing of the future by psychic means? Does the ability to handle stress, including the stress of coming frustration and disappointment, color the capacity to stand in a larger "present" than is usually scanned to consciousness? It would not be surprising to researchers to find this the case. Most human beings handle stress by some combination of skill, defenses, and what is loosely called "ego strength"—capacity to endure tension and uncertainty, or insecurity. Where the defenses of rationalization, projection, repression, or other largely unconscious mechanisms predominate, the helpful flow of the unconscious seems impeded or distorted, in the ordinary problem-solving of daily-life. It would seem reasonable to suspect that defensiveness might cripple the flow of helpful psychic promptings as readily as it cripples the flow of love, play, or study. Defensive postures of abandoning oneself to the unconscious in orgiastic bouts of emotion, or in hypochondria, or in paranoid fantasies, might also impede precognition. Insofar as the psyche is a self-regulating system, it would seem likely that frantic efforts to solve problems would endanger the channels of precognition as readily as tendencies to avoid or deny problems. A steady posture of readiness to tackle what comes might prove to be most valuable, not only for marital success or business adroitness, but for opening the aperture of perception of the future.

In approaching patience as a religious question, the Cayce source appeared to be taking up the old religious question of how to correlate "man's time" and "God's time," how to recognize the *kairos,* or moment of readiness in one's affairs, when the personal and the transpersonal meet. It was the question of the Kingdom of God, always here and always coming—how to stand in its shadow and face the future. It was the question of "storming the King-dom" about which the prophets of Israel warned, as has the modern philoso-pher, Martin Buber: Each person must find the line which defines the differ-ence between his readiness to act and his willful seizure of affairs. It was a question similar to those in Chinese discussions of the silent way of the Tao, similar to the encouragement of the Hindu *Bhagavad-Gita* that man could find a way to act without "attachment to the fruits" of the action, and like the question of living faith in Muslim references to the "will of Allah."

In the picture of patience developed by the Cayce source, what emerged was not passivity, but active alignment of the person with the timing which comes from God. Such alignment was not skill, though it might be perfected by experience and practice; in the last analysis it was a gift, the gift of the soul of man. Hearing the call of patience, which was more than dilatory waiting or restless pacing, and responding to the call in decisions of daily life, one might in time come to stand in steady relation with the soul which was a man's mediator of God's wise time. "In patience possess ye your souls" was the Biblical quote so often used by the Cayce trance source on this subject.

However, the Cayce information had one typical way of speaking of pa-tience that was less Biblical than metaphysical or philosophical. Over and over again this source spoke of growth to full personhood before God as occurring "in time, in space, in patience." Unmistakably, the Cayce readings were picturing patience as a third correlate of all events, beside time and space, when those events were seen—as Spinoza had long before suggested—under the aspect of eternity. But God's realm was not static and absolute, above all change, but the heart of all change, meaningful change; was not He the "Creative Forces"? Therefore, events could be described as occurring not only in time and space, but also in a dimension which both the soul and God knew: patience. It was the biographical, historical dimension. It was the di-mension where grace met law, for—said the Cayce source repeatedly—"ye grow in grace." Man would like to leap into the Kingdom, to establish him-self as "saved" in a single decision or act. But the Cayce source kept asking people whether anything valued in Nature behaved that way. Did plants leap into bloom, mountains leap into the air, babies leap to manhood? God's way was slow, steady growth, in which the laws of becoming were both exempli-fied and—in the case of man—learned. Hundreds of times the Cayce readings insisted that whatever was valuable for human beings developed "little by little, line upon line, precept upon precept." It was a perspective fully in keeping with a view of reincarnation, where the opportunity to grow through many lives, and grow in a fruitful direction, was hinted as Jesus' intention when he said, "I am come that ye might have life, and life more abundant." Each life could be lived out to the full, in its own character, as one might value a jewel, a beautifully fashioned antique, an exquisitely bred blossom—for each life would prepare yet another part of the body of awareness and choices that grew upon and completed the very soul.

In the view of the Cayce source, creation was for keeps, and need not be rushed nor anxious. Even movements and institutions and causes, revolutions and new world views, should be approached in the patience which was God's own timing—a timing neither fatalistic nor frantic. Repeatedly the Cayce source insisted on one formula for effective and lasting social change: Each new idea or new way of living must come "first to the individual, then to the group, then to the classes, then to the masses." Man would like to jump at once to influencing the masses, as though to prove the rightness of his ideas by sheer numbers of converts. But such change was not durable. Minds and hearts had to be won, not just votes or shouts, and this required each individual's experiencing the change that was sought, as well as nurturing and celebrating it in small groups, out of which in time public leaders and larger institutional changes might emerge. The Cayce source was often tested on this formula by those who sought to publicize or promote Cayce's own work. "First sell self" was always the answer. One had to have a living experience not simply of Cayce but of a living process, of the "Creative Forces" helping him in his life, before he had any business serving on the Board of the Cayce Association, or helping in any such endeavors. In God's time, in the patience which only the soul rightly understood, there was time to discover about Cayce's work or any other, "Does it make you a better husband, a better businessman, a better neighbor, a better artist, a better churchman? If so, cleave to it; if not, forget it!"

The opposite of patience was to be found where the person confused his birthright from God with being God, where one tried to force his will upon affairs. The essence of sin, said the Cayce source, was "self-aggrandizement," the clutching to oneself of one form of power or another which should instead be held in partnership with God and one's fellows. Behind the violation of the call of patience would be found an attitude which sought to force the hand of God. As a soul, one could use his free will to so force events; but the consequences were always fear, fear that one might be so forced by others and by the universe. And of such fear the destiny was made, the anxious drawing to certain events and associations, which men called karma—the reaping of what is sown. In living by grabbing one might even find "hell," which was described in one reading as becoming impatient with oneself.

The man who lived in patience, seeking and trusting "God's time" would one day see that in the long journey of the soul all his trials were of his own making. Though he might not consciously recall what he had done to bring upon him illness or failure or loneliness, these matters were not past finding out. Through prayer, introspection, analysis, and the cleansing of the channels of aid in meditation, he might come to understand what in his own heart needed the lesson he was undergoing, and how the trial would have come elsewhere if not in the events then upon him. Though man was bound with others in families and teams and churches and other groupings, and shared in the struggles and guilts of all through "group karma," it would be found that in the important matters each man met only himself. Christ had taken on the sins of all, in His unswerving journey to fulfill the will of God in His life; since Him, said the Cayce source repeatedly, "no man pays for the sins of others." Therefore patience was enjoined, not railing at life.

Patience, said the Cayce source, would be found to be the watch at the gateway between body and soul. The soul had unspeakable force at its command, when used for good. Yet that same force could destroy a man who was unprepared to handle it. Patience was the timing that screened one's promptings for him, and shaped the calls of opportunity that he would properly hear or ignore. In this vein, every life reading—Cayce's best effort to characterize the fundamental character, weakness and promise of a man—began with a phrase such as "Not all may be given at this time, but this we would give with the desire that this may be a helpful experience for the entity." It was made clear that not all of the urges, talents, past lives would be mentioned, but only those which the person might then safely handle; months or years later additions might be made—as was the case when Cayce was late in life given the supposed details of a lifetime never before mentioned in his readings—but only when his source felt he could handle it. There were many things in this view of which it might be said as by the author of the Gospel of John, "Ye cannot bear them now." Patience would be found the key to the steady, safe unfolding of talents in the round of one's life—including psychic talents. These would begin to show themselves in dream, in vision, in times of prayer, in crisis, in quiet reflection, in helping others—but a little at a time so that the person would not "think more highly of himself than he ought," nor abandon good sense in favor of psychic flashes.

Was there a way to learn patience so that nothing ever went wrong in one's affairs? Emphatically not, according to this source. "When one is without crosses, one is no longer among the Sons"—among the children who knew their Father and chose Him. With patience was linked "longsuffering" and the other fruits of the Spirit. No man could expect to grow in patience without growing also in love, and love meant bearing the burdens of others. Not being trapped by others, for they had not that power, but being ready to ease the pain of others, lighten their way, make their spirits glad. Man's goal was to serve others, but this was in fully creative ways that brought others to their feet and running; like Christ, each man was to be a "servant of servants," not a doormat. Patience was not synonymous with indifference or detachment; it was apt response, in God's own timing.

How might one cultivate patience? Nothing less than steady prayer, seeking an Aid greater than one's own to guard his impulses and defenses, could be trusted to nurture patience. And such prayer would be found no burden; for most people the time given to useless worry, spinning anxiety, could be better turned to quiet prayer—and then followed by creative action upon timely prompting. "Why worry, when ye may pray?" was a phrase frequently used in the readings, not as a churchly aphorism so much as an invitation to an experiment in problem-solving. "Try Me," "Call upon Me," "Ask," "Seek" were bits of Biblical admonition that sparkled through hundreds of readings, even the most prosaic medical diagnoses.

Yet prayer alone might seem moody and cloistered to some. Cultivating patience involved choosing a total way of being alive that embodied the trust which patience mirrored. So the Cayce source often repeated, "Keep the heart singing," or "He that would know the way must be oft in prayer, joyous prayer." Vital, delighted enjoyment of the journey of life would free the soul for its work, or allow it to run up its kite for energies and wisdom beyond its own. A sunny way was not simply a social asset, but an existential asset. The life lived in proper balance was marked by humming, whistling, teasing, playing, joking, seeing "the ridiculous, oft." "For if God be for us," the Cayce source often asked, "whom need we fear?" And as though to emphasize the point, the readings themselves sometimes parried questions with jaunty responses; a man who asked how much his childhood traumas were affecting his present responses might be told that the figure was "thirty-six and twenty-two hundredths percent."

While one might think that cultivating patience meant ever looking to the future, when things would be different, the Cayce source did not see patience that way. Instead, when asked to outline a prayer for someone to use as a model for his devotional life, this source usually focused at least part of the prayer upon the "this day" theme of the Lord's Prayer, by inserting the words "today, now," or "just now." The effect could be electric, in its contrast with the traditional religious focus upon an unchanging vast "heaven" beyond the present vale. In the perspective of this source, the keener the focus on being alive and giving and aware now, the more fully one exemplified patience. Indeed, said one reading, "Let us live each day as though the whole race depended on it"—in a variation on a Biblical passage often quoted in readings: "Let us run with patience the race that is set before us." A steady jog, whose pace was set by a Source within "not to be effaced," would bring the soul quietly closer each day to a conscious awareness of Whose companion, Whose partner in creation it truly was. How be patient? How handle stress? How face the fear of the unknown future? The phrase that sometimes appeared in the Cayce readings, as in Cayce's own letters to friends, was "Just keep on keeping on."

Precognition and Handling Stress

Can the growing ability to handle stress affect the emergence of psychic experiences of the future?

A committee on which the writer served, invested more than a thousand hours in redesigning a college curriculum, and eventually in reevaluating the fundamental goals and character of the campus. Also on the committee was an eager and enthusiastic college teacher, anxious to get results in whatever he touched, whether it be his drama class or his friendships or his faculty duties. Young, he was determined to make his mark on campus.

He was also interested in developing psychic ability, which he was tempted to view as the hallmark of spirituality, although he also knew psychics of no little ability who were petty, vain, and even dishonest. He joined an occult group which held training sessions in the dark, as well as practicing incantations and fasting, with the promise of developing psychic visions for each of its members. He saw much color and imagery, but little of it resembled outward affairs, and he worried about his spiritual health because he seemed so little psychic.

At the same time he entered more and more deeply into the struggles for self-definition of his college, participating in systematic studies fostered by a regional accrediting association, and investigating with his committee the development patterns of other campuses. In time he came to see that little would change in his school until the leaders were replaced, and he realized that such changes might be long in coming—though in fact they were not. Weighing the nature of institutional life, he came to see why so many checks and balances existed among faculty, administration, students, alumni, board, and philanthropic constituency, as well as with other colleges and learned societies. He matured a bit in his perspective, and was given more and more responsibilities on his campus. His friends noticed some new notes of humility, and finally even of patience.

Then one day he was watching a play where the hero was shot, the killing brought about in a circumstance in which many participated. It rang true to the sense of fateful but necessary slowness which he had discovered in his work at the school; it spoke of things ending out of their season, but in patterns which of themselves were ultimately good. And at that moment he had a sinking sensation in the pit of his stomach, one which made him weak and ill. He went home and lay down, where it came to him with a certainty that gripped his whole consciousness that somebody he loved was about to die. He had never had such an experience before, but it was for him beyond mistaking. He could not place the person, though he prayed and thought about it long, except that it was not a member of his family.

The feeling stayed with him as a memory, a nagging reminder, until a few weeks later at a faculty retreat he was informed one morning that his best friend, the dean of the college, a man in his thirties, had died of a heart attack in the night. At that point the feeling left, but in its place came quiet assurance that the dean, who had worked so hard in college reforms, would not have held back his life energy from the task he had shared in so abundantly. The young drama teacher led in the memorial service for his friend, helping to keep it from needless sentiment, as the writer well remembers. Speaking of the death later, he was sure that his warning had been of this death, this loss. And he was almost equally sure that the factor which was responsible for opening the eyes of his perception to the event coming upon him was his newly won ability to be patient, to accept and begin to understand the cycles of the life and death of a college—or a friend.

When Jesus learned of the untimely death of John the Baptist, and the collapse of John's movement, did his retiring to the mountains with his disciples allow him to find the perspective, the patience, the time beyond his own, which shortly would enable him to tell his disciples, without fear, of his own forthcoming death?

CHAPTER 10

RETROCOGNITION

EDGAR CAYCE WAS having a haircut. He looked over at the writer, waiting his turn, and said, "I'll tell you a story that happened right here." Nodding at his barber, he added, "He will confirm it."

The barbershop was modest, located on a business street a few blocks from Cayce's home. It was a place where Cayce knew he was among friends. Diagonally across the street was the railroad station, whose executive manager was on the board of the Association. Around the corner was the office of a long-time real estate agent at Virginia Beach, a member of his Tuesday night Bible class. Down the street a block was the drugstore whose pharmacist had for years mixed the compounds called for in his readings, and kept on hand the commercial products so often stipulated in those same readings: Atomidine, Glyco-Thymoline, Castoria, Black and White Cream, Patapar paper. Not much farther away was a photographic studio where he sometimes stopped to chat about photographic equipment, or to order pictures of his grandson, in terms reminiscent of his own days as a photographer. Across Atlantic Avenue and down a ways was a gaunt frame hotel on the ocean, owned by another member of his Bible class. All of these solid citizens were frequent visitors at his home and office, or attended his Presbyterian Sunday School class, as did the printer who prepared forms for him, operating from his home not far away. Here Cayce was among friends who had come to like and trust him as a neighbor, as a figure of spiritual depth, accepting the contrast of his strange reputation as a psychic with his relaxed, open manner.

Cayce began his story.

He had been sitting in the same place, getting a haircut, while among those waiting was a man he did not know, who had brought along his small son. The boy was tired, yawning, and took out a peanut butter sandwich from a paper bag, apparently packed for a picnic later in the day. As he munched, he almost dozed. Then he walked over to Cayce's chair and without a word offered him part of the sandwich. The two had never seen each other before, yet the boy moved as surely and unaffectedly as to a relative. "Here," the father called, "he doesn't want your sandwich!" "Yes, he does," the boy replied without moving. "He was very hungry on that raft. Weren't you?" he asked, looking up at Cayce in the barber chair.

Cayce stared the boy hard for a moment, and then grinned and nodded. Like the boy, he had remembered something that linked them. He thanked the youngster and declined the sandwich, but with appreciation. The boy went back to the arms of his father, and fell asleep, while his puzzled parent explained that he had never seen his son do anything of the sort.

Where was the raft on which the boy knew Cayce had been hungry? Cayce waited until he left the barbershop to finish the story. The raft which his own mind connected with an image of the youngster had been, he felt, part of another life. It had been on the Ohio River, in the early 1800s. There Cayce had finished what his own life readings described as a largely wasted and irresponsible life as a wanderer, a show-off, and even a bit of a rake, by fleeing from the Indians with others on a big raft floated down the Ohio River. The Indians were so hostile that the passengers on the raft could not land for food, and became painfully hungry on their journey towards freedom. Here Cayce had lost his life, according to his own trance source. Sitting in the barber chair, he had seen the boy's face become that of a young man, on the raft so long ago. Had the boy, drowsy and with the unconscious near the surface, also recognized Cayce? He thought perhaps so.

Over the nearly twenty years since his "information" had begun to discuss reincarnation, Cayce had slowly become accustomed to such seeming memory flashes in daily life, as to other forms of psychic experience. Receiving a letter from someone asking for medical aid but wondering about seeking a "past life" reading as well, he would sometimes offer unusual encouragement, saying, "I think you will find there a Palestine experience" or "You may be surprised at the talents which the information will show." He was not promoting his own readings, for he never did that, but responding out of his own waking sense that seemed to place the person in a given epoch of history, with perhaps a special talent. As might be expected, his readings bore him out.

Occasionally someone who had secured a life reading would want what had come to be called a "check-life reading," following up in detail on a particular incarnation. When Cayce was asked which lifetime of several might be most fruitful to explore, he would sometimes pause and smile, adding, "The one in Early America, not the one in France," because of sensing what the person had been like in each place—or even momentarily seeing the face and form of the person before him change, as other psychics have reported.

Talking with his family about a distinguished person whose reading was scheduled for the day, he sometimes mused, "I wonder if he was one of the twelve judges." Over the years his "information" had tagged a number of individuals as having been involved with him as judges in a lifetime in ancient Egypt when he had been a priest. It was the lifetime when he had reached, partly through exile and suffering, what he felt was perhaps his highest spiritual development, and the one his trance source told him bore most significantly upon the present life. As a consequence, he was always more than a little interested when something inside himself seemed to place a person in his "memory" or retrocognition as an associate from ancient Egypt. He enjoyed more the associations that linked with Palestine in the time of Jesus and shortly afterwards, where he had lived in Asia Minor, he felt. But the Egyptian "memories" were the ones which bore upon the critical struggles for growth in this lifetime, affecting the growth and dissolution of his hospital and university, and he always approached them with alert interest. Visitors who saw a head of the ancient Egyptian Queen Nefertiti on his filing cabinet may have thought it a quaint decoration, but friends knew it was an informal

symbol of a stream of retrocognitive reflections which were always meaningful to Cayce.

In dealing so naturally with reincarnation, Edgar Cayce was handling the
one phenomenon of his work which more than any other alienated him from
responsible people in his times. Doctors were often keenly interested in his
medical diagnoses and detailed prescriptions, as well as the theories of physiology which streamed through Cayce in thousands of readings—until they
learned of the reincarnation material. Ministers and priests were fascinated by
his detailed descriptions of Biblical times, which included accurate accounts
of clothing, coins, food, languages, customs, and even the correct distribution
of names of the time in various languages familiar to scholars and archaeolo-
gists—until they learned of the reincarnation material from the same source.
Scientists responded to the chemical analyses, psychologists to sophisticated
descriptions of hypnosis, government officials to theories of social change in
various nations—until they came across the reincarnation material.

It did not help that details had been so often verified, by old court records
or archaeological finds or history books—for this might only demonstrate
that some part of Cayce's mind had access to factual sources about the past.
Perhaps, as the writer surmised at times, the Cayce source was using all of
this "retrocognitive" material in a reincarnation framework only to shock or
interest people. Yet there was no interest in sensationalizing such material on
the part of the Cayce source, and often warnings were given against stressing
novelty to foster a "cult, schism, or ism." Those who were sure that the
trance information must have unaccountably failed in accuracy whenever it
took up reincarnation sought without success for evidence of such a failure,
or explanation of it. The writer was fairly well convinced at one point that he
had located a massive error in the Cayce materials, when he came across
frequent references to the Essene group of Jews at the time of Jesus, or to
similar groups of Covenanters, described in the Cayce life readings as significant precursors of Christianity. During the 1920s to 1940s when Cayce was
supplying abundant materials about this sectarian movement in Judaism,
alongside of convincing material on Jewish temple leadership, and other pur-
ist or Hassidic groups, there was not a responsible Biblical scholar in the
world who would have endorsed Cayce's picture. Yet not long after his death
the Dead Sea Scrolls were found, and confirmation poured in of many of
Cayce's reports on sites, practices, and even the presence of women in the
retreat centers—so long denied by scholars.

How representative of the psychic experiences of others were Cayce's seeming experiences of retrocognition of the past, which occurred to him in daily
life? He dreamed at times of ancient Egypt or Greece, or some other area
where he had been told by his source that he had lived; the dreams were vivid
and always presented an issue that needed facing in his present life—they
were not simply colorful excursions in the night. But while such material
seems to appear in the dreams of others his age, and with his interests, it is
rare in the experiences of dream researchers to find as much of it as Cayce's
dream records showed. To be sure, Cayce also dreamed often about photogra-

phy, more often than most people—perhaps because he was much involved in photography, as he was much involved in reincarnation.

In the writer's experience, most of the best-known psychics in the U.S. and Europe today take reincarnation as a matter of course, and report their waking experience of retrocognitive glimpses as naturally as they report imagery from out of the past coming into consciousness when they hold a token object —a wrist watch or medallion—for psychometrizing. But such agreement proves nothing, for it may be a tradition, a stereotype among psychics; one seeking a census of psychic experiences in India finds an even larger proportion of "sensitives" reporting such past-life material. Retrocognition has long been a part of the thought world of much of the Orient, where a Buddhist monk may expect as a natural part of his growth and training to recover in detail material from his past lives, and will ascribe a ready meaning to the promise of Jesus that the Holy Spirit "will make known to you all things from all times."

Parapsychologists have tackled the question of whether such direct inspection of the past is possible. Much examined has been the case of the two English ladies who reported a waking journey through French palace gardens, in which everyone they met seemed dressed as though from a past time. And two other British women reported hearing the full noise of a long-ago battle, one night when they stayed at an inn located where such a battle had in fact occurred. But such instances might be chains of coincidence. Hypnotists have sought to tackle the problem of retrocognition by the bold method of age regression, which psychiatrists had used effectively to take patients back to detailed memories of childhood. Why not, the hypnotists asked, take people back beyond childhood, to previous lifetimes? The results in the case of a supposed Bridey Murphy made newspaper headlines not many years ago, and were carefully examined by Professor Ducasse of Brown University; even better cases were reported by Ruth Montgomery in *Here and Hereafter*. Others, notably Professor Ian Stevenson of the University of Virginia Medical School, set out to interview people around the world who thought they could remember and prove details from past lives. With the aid of a research grant, Stevenson explored subjects young and old in India, in the U.S., in the Pacific Northwest, and elsewhere, producing the first careful research report on this topic in the modern West. Still other investigators have probed the ancient phenomena of seemingly haunted buildings, trying to develop theories of how a living person might perceive appropriate details from the past in such buildings, while Hettinger, Karagulla, Puharich and others such as the present writer tested seemingly able psychics on the stretch of the past, including even ancient cultures and languages, which they seemed to bring to consciousness by touching objects from those times.

No consensus has emerged from these investigations, except perhaps an interest in keeping open the possibility of retrocognition—direct inspection of past events by psychic means, whether in personal "soul memory" or some other process free in time. Too little is firmly established about the nature of any kind of psychic ability to allow specification of when it is used in viewing the unknown past—for such an unknown past must always be represented by present records or facts to be verified, and nobody knows whether a psychic is viewing the past or the present verifying records.

Edgar Cayce's trance source was of course questioned repeatedly on how one might have psychic experience of the past. Such knowledge was not particularly stressed by the Cayce information, for this source gave detailed medical, vocational and spiritual aid to thousands of people without ever mentioning the subject. Yet those who sought to understand their own makeup, and the forces which drive men, were encouraged to explore the realm of reincarnation as matter-of-factly as they were encouraged to explore childhood memories, or ideals, or hidden defenses. Most commonly, the Cayce source encouraged the exploration of retrocognition through dreams, where one might find he was already recalling bits of an unknown language, or scenes of an ancient place, or artifacts that bore directly on present problems and opportunities; one could expect retrocognition as well as precognition. It did not help the individual enough to see in advance a crisis which he would meet the next day; he also could profit from discovering why he so disliked certain kinds of people, or feared authority, or made sure decisions about textile marketing, based on past-life experiences which might come back in dreams.

Not all retrocognitive dreams would be pleasant, according to this source. The writer heard two Cayce readings which interpreted the battle nightmares of young children as memories of having been killed as children in early days of World War II; here the solution, according to the Cayce trance source, was quietly calming the child as he fell asleep, when he would be most open to helpful suggestion from a parent. But in general, when the body was not injured, the unconscious would supply only retrocognitive dream material which the dreamer could safely use and handle.

Might the doorway to psychic perception of the past be opened by sustained effort? Many who have been interested in the Cayce theories have recorded their dream and waking perceptions which might be of the past, and studied the possible accuracy of these perceptions. Abundant evidence has emerged that the mind can fool itself, for an individual seeking to establish his importance can produce fantasy-chains which any psychiatrist can recognize. The writer heard one person interested in the Cayce materials sententiously pronounce that he was Peter, reincarnated, only to be told by an alarmed associate, "You can't be! I'm Peter!" But others in less need of ego-supportive imagery have recorded suggestive experiences—including those of perceiving awake the face and character of an associate or loved one in exactly the same details which the entranced Cayce saw. But none have yet duplicated Cayce's ability to take a newborn baby and sketch from past-life influences, as he saw them, an entire personality structure of talents and urges and weaknesses and interests—often borne out in astonishing detail in later years (though possibly by conscious or unconscious imitation of the reading).

Some have found unusual quickenings occurring to them in reading historical novels, or visiting museum wings of ancient cultures, or wearing costumes of a certain period. All of this material is difficult to verify as retrocognitive, and for the present can usually only be studied for the depth of response in the percipient (as indicated, for example, in his dream responses to the stimulating exposures), and for the general usefulness of the experience in the life of the percipient (producing better self-insight that enables him to operate, for example, less defensively). If any one factor stands out in the tentative explorations of those who have sought to open their minds' eyes to the unknown past by retrocognition, it may be the importance of approaching such material for its usefulness in the present, rather than for verification of philosophical theories of human destiny. For the key to psychic experience of the past may be one often noted as important in psychic experience in the present: how far the individual is prepared to make productive use of what he receives.

Productiveness in Creativity

The Cayce trance source rated productiveness as such a basic religious issue in the development of creativity that it focused upon the question in the seventh lesson suggested for the little book, *A Search For God*. The chapter on this concern was entitled "The Open Door"; in the chapter was emphasized the helpful resource of the Christ Spirit, standing at the door of every man's life and ready to enter, if only the individual sought to employ such aid in practical, productive service of others.

The American psychologist, William Sheldon, developer of somatotyping theory and methods, has suggested that adults can be usefully divided into the wasters and the productive—with the distinction revealing much about all kinds of creativity in the person. Writing from Mexico City, the psychologist and analyst Erich Fromm has defined productivity as one of the two ways in which a mature person can make meaningful closure with life and other persons, alongside of loving. Distilling what he believes an important contribution from among the irrelevances of Marxist thought, he also emphasizes how cooperation in productivity affords a more promising framework for the development of all kinds of human creativity than can ruthless competition.

Is it possible that the degree and kind of services rendered, forms created, work turned in, may contribute not only to artistic quality and business progress, but to ESP workings as well? Can the use to which one seeks to put his psychic cognition affect its flow, whether in revealing the present, the future, or the past?

It seems likely that the person who has not found a productive way to live, whether in employment or in the duties of household and family life, would be particularly vulnerable to the cheap satisfaction of fantasy, especially fantasies of contacts with the dead or fantasies of having been someone important in a past life. On the other hand, lacking useful circuits in which to channel psychic material might have the effect of closing off some of the flow of material from the unconscious, as well as distorting it. Both developments would seem to be potentially harmful to the function of ESP. To be sure, laboratory experiments on ESP have shown many subjects able to score briefly when they are doing no meaningful work except guessing—and yet guessing in the context of research may prove to be exhilarating work indeed.

A barrier to creativity sometimes discussed by artists, scientists, and inventors, lies in talking too much and too soon about one's work. The effect of such verbalizing at times appears to be the dispersal of creative energies and imagery; some scholars have even speculated that this was the process seen by Jesus when he warned many whom he healed to tell no man about it. Those who can, do; those who can't, teach—so runs an aphorism warning against overtalk in creativity. It would seem possible that the effort to secure retrocognition into one's personal "past" or into some period of history or chain of events might be frustrated by doing so for the sake of talk, rather than for the sake of making a difference in some creative, productive act.

Psychiatrically, adult living is marked by willingness to take the responsibility for one's own life, to develop a way to be *for* something, rather than merely against grievances; to come alive in shared effort, rather than wait for a parental figure or lover to "turn me on." Is the same requirement of responsible productivity to be found guarding the way to retrocognition? Is one more likely to have useful glimpses of the unknown past to heighten his labors, rather than to charm him into beginning long-postponed labor and loving?

In taking up productivity as a religious issue, the Cayce source touched upon an old theological riddle. Much of man's religiousness, as seen for example in early Buddhism, has been focused on getting out of a predicament, on God's work in what theologians call "the order of redemption." Man is often seen first of all as a sinner, as a sufferer, as a prisoner, in which the agency of the divine is needed to redeem, heal, or free. On the other hand, there have been strands in religious history and thought where the focus has been upon man's reaching for his full stature as a builder, as a lover, as an artist, through the aid of the divine. Taoism, Confucianism, and some of the devotional Hinduism have at times stressed this approach, as have robust forms of Judaism. Here man is seen first of all as a creator, a gardener, a fashioner of cultures charged to "multiply, and subdue the earth"; he is viewed in "the order of creation."

The Cayce source in its essays on religious themes was never far from touching upon man's sinfulness, his selfishness, his pride or lust or self-will. No prayer suggested by this source omitted such reference, and no encouragement to positive thought suggested that human evil might be ignored. Yet there could be little doubt that the Cayce source placed radical emphasis on man's role in "the order of creation," ahead of the "order of redemption." Creation was man's very name, for he was made in the image of his Creator and destined to become a conscious co-creator with God. Redemption occurred to get man back on to this track, rather than creativity being a far-off reward for faithful participation in redemption now. As the Cayce source asked many a sick person, "Why do you want to get well? What do you seek to do when you are well?" so it seemed to take a similar approach to man's broader predicaments of sickness of soul. Man had to keep his eye on his potential for good, for beauty, for love, for truth, or he would not achieve sufficient motivation to change. In this context, psychic ability was simply one more area for seeing that God's ways toward men were ways of promise, of astonishing creativity and goodness. If someone could find by psychic ability the cure for a disease, then this was only part of the work of the Creative Forces, which ever sought man's health and joy. And if someone by psychic ability learned to make a good living, or grow prosperous, this was no affront to the Creative Forces, which sought man's material welfare just as truly as any other end of man. To be sure, the human journey would be found in the long run to be a "crucifying of the carnal," where man would learn to live in an animal body without identifying with it, or "seeking the flesh." But creation was not first of all punishment, nor testing, nor temptation, nor torment. When these things occurred, they were of man's doing, and always remediable by his return to his Source for guidance.

The emphasis on God's incredible helpfulness was a major part of the religious thrust of the Cayce information. The emphasis was not merely verbal, but seemed acted out by Cayce's own helpful work, as well as by the rich guidance appearing in dreams and prayer life of those who were coached by readings. A God who has chosen to "give the Kingdom" to his sons was the God the Cayce trance source unfailingly communicated. Such a God could not successfully be identified with religious scruples or taboos, although men could quickly learn the value of restraints. But in this perspective it was clear that religion was made for man, not man for religion; the Sabbath was to be kept that man might prosper in his journey Godward, not as a duty but as an opportunity.

In the perspective of the Cayce readings it did not make sense to speak of miracles. The Creative Forces did not now and then break through the lowering skies to give men a helping hand, even in the startling phenomena associated with figures such as Edgar Cayce. The Creative Forces were always at work, showering their blessings on man, seeking his full becoming as co-creator, but in lawful ways. The very law was itself God's mercy. The regularity of grace, its dependability, was the assurance that it was grace, not a passing marvel.

In the approach of the Cayce readings, God was to be found ever at hand, helping, through "the open door." That door was the readiness of the flesh to respond to the divine, if man sought aid for the right purpose, for service rather than for selfishness. As one reading put it, "spirituality must be expressed in materiality." There was no room in this picture for a Gnostic devaluation of flesh. Although flesh was neither man's ultimate home nor his best creativity, it was his present opportunity, and he dare not ignore it. The flesh was a cloud, a barrier to full psychic perception, and probably to full awareness of beauty and truth as well, for man had donned earth-consciousness as a diversion, in the long journey of the soul. But once he had entered into this realm of creation, into the ways and laws of the earth, he would never find his pathway out by pretending he wasn't there. He could not "rise above" the human condition. Rather, he must "lift up" the very flesh itself, in its concrete life of glands and nerves, by using his material existence as a channel for helping others. When the body was spent in sweat that another might find life sweeter, then God Himself stood at the open door, and a body was a treasure to wear, to use—it was even the temple of the Most High.

There was, in the view of the Cayce source, a law that man could have only by giving. What he sought to share with others, this was what grew in his ideals and his talents, until it became his lasting resource throughout his lifetimes. No scheme of self-development, self-perfection alone would work for long, for it was out of harmony with the soul of man, with the Creative Forces. No man should seek simply to be saved in some private journey of justification, for this was not the pattern of the Christ, Who freely gave Himself to others.

The precise mechanisms of worship would be found to be the same as those of all other truly creative effort—in this the Cayce theory of kundalini energies rising within man found a parallel to the old Latin saying that to work is to pray: *Laborare est orare*. Man could not separate his religiousness from daily loving and manufacturing, for these acts occurred along the selfsame channels of creativity. There were only whole acts of giving, where the thanksgiving was intertwined with willingness to carry, to push, to heal, to teach. One might step aside for times of quiet alone with his Maker, but never aside from the intent to make the way brighter for someone else, or the prayer itself would falter, betraying the character of the soul which sought to present the petitioner before the Throne. Although the Cayce source enjoined daily meditation upon everyone who truly sought to walk with God, and regular intercession for others, it matched this almost athletic program of piety with insistence upon creative action. "Do, do, do," or "Try, try again," or "Ye only learn the laws in action," or "True understanding comes in application" were notes at which the Cayce information hammered away over the years. The Christ Spirit could be found knocking at every man's door, but it would not enter until asked, and the asking must be for more than self. It might be easy to say, "The Son of Man came not to be ministered unto, but to minister," but the fact was that all souls came into being for the same destiny—a destiny which they could not fulfill by ritually celebrating the self-giving of Jesus.

Yet the open door which man might find within him, ready to welcome a Christ who would give him aid for his brother, was not to be swung by blind activism in productiveness. The very revelation of God to man occurred through the same door. Insight into the workings of the Creative Forces, vivid imagery of the structures of the soul and its Lord, might be found in dream and vision as one sought to serve. Truth and judgment would be given as readily as energy and love, if one sought to be fully productive in his life. It was not wrong for a man to seek to know God Himself, if the desire were motivated, as Paul had said, by love. Each time one earnestly chose to do the will of the Father, and consciously sought the aid of the Christ, he would discover that he had attained a new "concept" of the Father, however difficult this might be to verbalize. Knowledge would come as well as good will, through the open door which God Himself had fixed in man.

How might one begin to cultivate, to train in himself, the productivity which could find an open door for aid beyond his own? He might begin with expectancy. It could make all the difference in the affairs of one's life whether one really expected healing, solutions to problems, a better world, or whether one only sought to endure, grieving his lot. The Essenes were characterized by the Cayce source as a model of an expectant community, as were the early Christians who literally expected the coming of the Holy Spirit to their aid. Yet expectancy was not a dwelling on some unknown religious future, or upon a past Biblical age to be restored. Expectancy was a matter of how one might approach each present task, each present relationship, ready for the most valuable outcome to emerge from the play of all the factors involved. Expectancy was exemplified in the growing trust that "All things work together for good to them that love the Lord," for having all things work together for good was the true business of the Creative Forces, the very character of God at work in each situation, however unseen. The formula was an exact picture of true creativity. He who knocked at the open door would find a way to reconcile quarreling lovers, to match prices with costs, to combine chemicals into new compounds, to embed worship in the day's work, to fight leukemia with special transfusions—for the Lord of the Universe was the Lord of all this becoming, and not the God of shrines and structures alone. So one might show forth his expectancy by a process as concrete as choosing a truth each day and living it out, inviting the partnership of that endlessly creative mind below the surface which was the builder in man.

As one worked at productivity, at partnership with God through the open door where extra energy and wisdom flowed, it would be found that increasing one's own usefulness went hand in hand with increasing that of others. One had to stop before each man whom he truly engaged, and find for himself the way in which that person was trying to build his image of God, however haltingly or perversely. This was not kindness, good manners, but a law as fixed as any in electricity or chemistry. There was no way to be more loving without helping others to love, no way to work longer hours without enabling others to enjoy their work, no way to build a better world except upon the talents of others. For one's own soul, the source of a man's every talent and prompting, the mirror for the Everlasting Creator, shone like the even sun upon the face of the other man as upon oneself; it was of the same Force as God.

Finding productivity meant studying the conditions under which one found he could become rapt, caught up in a task, swiftly and surely responsive in a situation. One of these conditions would be balance, in every level of one's life. To keep his mind and body alert for productivity, one had to eat what he knew was best for him, in his own experience. He had to discover his own right balance of quiet and activity, of solitude and companionship, of work and play, of study and application. Each who sought to find more and more easily that open door would need to work out his own guidelines, his own regimes, not as burdens but as good sense for greater aliveness. Part of such a regime would be found to be the choosing of a household of faith, a church or a synagogue or whatever it might be called, where one might truly serve—not just attend services. This kind of association was not a mere accident of history, but an expression of elements of man's journey that could not be fulfilled without covenanting. Each different faith, each sect, would be found to have its special secrets, its special celebrations, its special tasks, its special functions—for none would survive without meeting some human need. Yet each would also have its own temptations, weaknesses, and perils, so that the servant who joined with others to find the open door to true productivity would need always to remind himself Whose were the kingdom, power, glory.

Productivity and Retrocognition

Might one find that working to give away his talents released in him a capacity for seeing things helpful out of the past? Does productivity, along with other elements, genuinely affect retrocognition?

A young mother found herself swamped in the duties of childrearing and homemaking, shortly after leaving college. She had never been an especially good student, although she also knew she had never tried very hard, preferring instead to concentrate on her drama roles in her extra-curricular theater work. She was interested in psychic things, and once had a reading from Edgar Cayce. With her husband, she attended lectures on parapsychology and sought out demonstrations by a medium.

But she could find little time for study, and precious little time for prayer and quiet, with four young children. Still, she kept a sunny spirit, doing what she could to enrich the life of her church, especially by guiding a play-reading and discussion group. Years went by in which she occasionally had dreams that seemed to her linked with what Cayce had described as her past lives, and she had a few experiences of warnings that helped her protect her children. But she could hardly think of herself as psychic.

Then—it seemed almost overnight—her children were grown. What was she to do now? With much hesitation she agreed to share in the leadership of a discussion group on a retreat weekend. She did better than she had ever thought she might. Those in the group felt the steady flow of love which had become second nature to her as a mother and a wife, and they began to relax, to speak deeply of their lives, their failures, their hopes. She took the responsibility for guiding a weekly study group and again did well. To her surprise, she now began to be keenly interested in reading, especially in history, and sought every chance she could find, at the beauty parlor or on a bus or waiting in line at a shopping center, to snatch some reading time about the development of myth and ritual in ancient cultures. She found her sense of the drama helping her to feel her way into long-ago materials, and her sense of family life helping her to understand social structures of other times. Now she began to teach a more formal class, and to lead people in workshops, where the writer saw her at work, comparing dreams with historic myths and symbols.

She was becoming a productive person in her second life, in the career she had once put aside to rear her children and serve her husband. She was using her mind thoughtfully, carefully, systematically, and beginning a new program of graduate studies. At the same time, she began to notice a striking development as she worked with people in small groups. She would see, when someone leaned forward to disclose himself to others, from his own real center, that for her the features of the person's face changed somehow before her eyes. At first she saw the images of that person's childhood, the point at which he had been hurt, or lost trust in himself and life. But then there began to be other images, quietly superimposing themselves. Here was something Chinese—and it led her to perceive better the other person's sense of courtliness. There was something Hungarian, in this case military and aggressive, to be tamed and redirected. Another might present a Greek countenance, with a love of rationality and dialectic exchanges which made others impatient, yet always clarified discussions. Was this imagery entirely from her own mind, a fantasy projected onto others to facilitate her better response to them? Perhaps so. She could not prove what she saw. She could and did share her impressions, which she rarely mentioned to anyone, with two different psychics who felt they could see "past lives" as they saw other things about individuals; to her surprise, they corroborated her judgment. When she learned that one of her group members had received life readings from Cayce, she was again surprised to learn that she was hitting the same themes he had struck, though not as fully nor as many. Slowly she began to wonder whether her psyche had, in her efforts to become fully productive and helpful as a teacher and group worker, opened the door to retrocognition. But the question had to remain a question, for there was no way to prove the accuracy of what she saw. It did leave her wondering about certain Biblical materials.

What had Jesus seen, when he looked over Jerusalem and wept, speaking of how that city had stoned the prophets? Had he known only a poetic reminder of its long history as a center of faith and a center of idolatry? Or had his vision opened for a moment into a living impression of the city's whole history, rolled out before him, so that he could only weep for its betrayed promise? Perhaps it did not matter whether his vision that day was poetic or retrocognitive. What mattered was that he went on into the city to do his job, sharing every ounce of his being with his fellows, on a journey sometimes lonely but finally resolved in the events of the resurrection which still stagger men's imagination, and point to a productivity that does not fail.

PART 3

Enhanced and Elevated Psychic Experience

CHAPTER 11

PROPHESYING

EDGAR CAYCE LAY in quiet trance on the couch in his library. It was a sunny June afternoon, and his wife had just given him the hypnotic suggestion to speak on world affairs to the forty or so persons packed into the library. This was Congress weekend, when his friends and well-wishers came from all over the country for several days of lectures led by Cayce and other speakers. Now was the time for the "information" to give counsel on a subject of general interest, as had become the custom each year. Past subjects had included the times of Jesus, the nature of psychic ability, the nature of sleep, and prehistoric peoples. In this war year of 1944, it was to be the affairs of the major powers, and their destinies.

Among those present were the writer and others who had heard readings tersely predicting the end of the war in 1945, with the end coming suddenly once it began. The room was hushed, for all longed to hear some assurance that the war would soon be over. But when Cayce began to speak in his state of altered consciousness, he did not speak as a political or military commentator, though he had shown many times that he could provide accurate analyses of economic, political and military affairs of specific nations. Indeed, he had done so well recently in briefing a diplomat on China that interest in Cayce's work had grown in Washington, and the writer had answered the phone one

259

day to hear "This is the office of the Vice President of the United States"—requesting three days of readings from Cayce (though Cayce's death intervened before they could be given). But here at the Congress, the entranced man spoke not of strategies but of morality. He spoke little of the Axis nations and much of the Allies, and he addressed himself not to their righteousness but to their national sins.

Cayce's emphasis might have been predicted. Whenever earnest seekers came together with serious and highminded intent, his trance discourse tended to become "elevated," tended to turn to questions of man's relations with God. What so often was practical counsel, factual information, would take on a note of urgency, as listeners were offered choices. The man who functioned most of the time as a seer, concerned with the problems of individuals, now functioned as a prophet, and addressed himself to the concerns of groups of men. His speech as a prophet was not merely prediction, for there were bits of prediction all through his readings, as through his dreams and waking hunches. It was speech that was not so much "foretelling" as "forthtelling"—speaking the truth of the human situation as he saw it. Prediction was incidental; a direct encounter with his listeners was the intent.

He began by speaking of spiritual laws, and indicating that each nation over the centuries had developed its understanding of these laws and their application. "There are, then, in the hearts, the minds of men, various concepts of these laws, and as to where and to what they are applicable. . . ." The weakness of each nation would be found to be its own form of gratification, as it attempted to use these laws.

The trance voice took up America. Although it was wartime, and most Americans were inclined to make comparisons with others nations to the disadvantage of foreigners, the Cayce source reminded listeners of themes developed in many other readings, where it was warned that the American people had to face racial problems, problems of poverty, problems of indifference to minorities. "What is the spirit of America? Most individuals proudly boast 'freedom.' Freedom of what? When ye bind men's hearts and minds through various ways and manners, does it give them freedom of speech? freedom of worship? freedom from want? Not unless these basic principles [of man's relationship to God] are applied. For God meant man to be free. . . ."

"What, then of the nations?" The voice of the unconscious man was measured, firm. It began the roll call.

"In Russia there comes the hope of the world. Not as that sometimes termed of the communistic, of the Bolshevik, no. But freedom, freedom! That each man will live for his fellow man! The principle has been born. It will take years for it to be crystallized, but out of Russia comes again the hope of the world." Listeners stopped breathing for a moment. This was a hard teaching. As middle-class Americans, they had been trained by a generation of newspaper articles and political speeches to despise Russia. While they might celebrate Russian idealism in novels, it was alien to them to consider that Russia's Marxist dream might have a good core, an ideal that could one day break off the husk of bureaucratic Communism and become the seed of a new type of cooperative society around the world. Yet here was the Cayce source insisting that they pay attention. Russia might be atheist, but it was, as other readings had insisted, touching a pattern well pleasing to the "Creative Forces" insofar as it strove to build a society where man would be his brother's keeper.

Yet the Russian momentum would need guidance, and that guidance should have religious depth, of the sort that could come from America, if America lived up to her dream rather than selling out to a materialism which only masqueraded as holiness. The voice continued, asking how Russia's future should be guided: "Guided by what? The friendship with the nation that hath even set on its present monetary unit, 'In God we trust.' "

Here the Cayce source stopped to place a challenge squarely before the listeners, as was often the case in readings of a prophetic character, which insisted that all lasting social change must begin with the individual. Taking the image of the slogan on the coin as an emblem of American ambivalence, the voice asked of the motto "In God we trust": "Do ye use that in thine own heart when you pay your just debts? Do ye use that in thy prayer when ye send thy missionaries to other lands—'I give it, for in God we trust'? Not for the other fifty cents, either!" The sarcasm was pointed. People laughed, but nervously. Caught up in the soul-searching of the occasion, they were flicking back in memory to ask what indeed they trusted in their lives, how much in God, justice and kindness, and how much in financial canniness.

Then the voice went on to charge America with the sin of self-righteousness. "In the application of these [spiritual] principles, in those forms and manners in which the nations of the earth have and do measure to those [American dreams of freedom, brotherhood, trust in God], in their activities, yea, to be sure, America may boast." The American dream of self-determination of peoples, of a society of shared plenty, of not treading on the rights of minorities, of religious concern framed in religious freedom—this was a valid dream for all peoples, as Americans were quick to insist. Yet American boasting in itself violated the spirit of true brotherhood; chauvinism was no substitute for respect for the unique contribution of others. "But rather is the principle [of freedom based on a spiritual ideal] being forgotten when this is the case, and that is the sin of America."

The quiet voice continued, turning to the land from which America had drawn language and law; it spoke of the temptation to snobbery, to imperialism, in both politics and culture. "So in England, from whence have come the ideas—not the ideals—ideas of being just a little bit better than the other fellow. [What does England forget?] Ye must *grow* to that in which ye will deserve to be known, deserve to receive. That has been, that is, the sin of England."

Moving to the Continent, the voice of the entranced man contrasted the birth of modern France in ideals of freedom, equality and fraternity with France's more recent focus on sensate values. "As in France, to which this principle [of freedom in shared responsibility] first appealed—and to which then came that which was the gratifying of the desires of the body. That is the sin of France." Was the entranced Cayce merely expressing American middle-class disapproval of Parisian mores? Or was he striking at real decadence in

France, which would one day have to be met in the struggles of colonials, students, strikers?

"In that nation which was first Rome," the voice continued, bringing into focus the heritage of Roman law and Roman right which was the foundation of all Western social structure, "when there was that unfolding of those principles [of freedom in shared responsibility], and its rise, its fall [as a people], what were they that caused the fall? The same as at Babel. The dissensions. The activities that would enforce upon these, in this or that sphere, servitude —so that a few might just agree [politically], or that a few might even declare their oneness with the Higher Forces [religiously]." Here the sleeping man spoke sternly of the human temptation to bring about social and religious conformity by force, by empire, by ecclesiastical power. "For theirs was the way that seemeth right to a man but the end is death. That is the sin of Italy." Nobody listening could have foreseen the changes toward permissiveness and internal freedom which were to come in the Italian church within two decades.

The trance source moved to the other side of the world. It spoke of Chinese isolationism as its sin, yet warned that all had best be alert for what would come from China. "The sin of China? Yea, there is that quietude that will not be turned aside, saving itself by slow growth." But then the Cayce source went on to speak of the strength of China. "There has been a growth, a stream through the land in ages, which asks to be left alone, to be just satisfied with that within itself. It awoke one day and cut its hair off! This, here [in China], will be one day the cradle of Christianity, as applied in the lives of men. Yea, it is far off as man counts time, but only a day in the heart of God —for tomorrow China will awake." It was a promise which the Cayce source had made before, and not especially flattering to American listeners, who prided themselves on providing political and religious leadership for the future. The insistence here was on something different than the political and economic justice which one day would be distilled from Russian experiment; the Chinese contribution would specifically be to the rebirth of Christianity— not to the Christendom of missionaries and church empires, but to the real faith which might draw men together "in Christ."

Typically, the Cayce source paused in its flow to challenge listeners to examine their own lives, to determine whether they were individually ready to share in such a rebirth of faith from out of China. "Let each and every soul, as they come to their understandings, do something, then, in his or her own heart."

Finally the voice took up India. Here the Cayce source showed clearly how its fundamental outlook differed from much of historic Hinduism, by its insistence on service of fellow man ahead even of self-development—although the Cayce framework contained strong teachings on individual disciplines and self-understanding. "Just as in India—the cradle of knowledge not applied except within self. What is the sin of India? Self. And leave the 'ish' off, just self." Not greed, not imperialism, not taking from others by being selfish. Yet stopping short of full giving to others, in a path of development too often limited to the self.

The reading was soon over, and people spoke quietly around the room as Cayce sat up and rubbed his eyes. What had they listened to? Had it been a collection of meaningless generalities, of platitudes and prejudices? Or had they heard an incisive judgment of the trends of nations and peoples, warning them of their own temptations to narrow vision? And how were they to take the little exchange which had occurred in the question period, when a question was asked as to how Germany might be taught "democracy" after the Allies had conquered her. The answer had come back sternly, "Raise not democracy nor any other name above the Fatherhood of God and the brotherhood of man." This had been a shock. Were not American-style democracy and the laws of God practically synonymous, as any American could testify? Or would it be necessary to try to fully understand separate peoples when the war was over, helping each to develop its own government, ideals, dreams—whether or not these copied American ways?

Nobody in the room felt he had taken part in something sensational. If this was "prophecy," it was certainly not very entertaining. Instead, there was over the group an air of soberness, a sense of having been judged and warned.

Readings on such broad subjects had been slow in developing in the history of the Cayce information. Most of his readings had been strictly medical, and most for individuals, until one day in Selma, Alabama, when Cayce's Sunday School class gathered on a Sunday evening to see whether they could secure a different kind of material, just at the end of World War I. To everyone's astonishment, they did. One of those who heard about it was a Selma relative of Woodrow Wilson, who arranged then, in great secrecy, for Cayce to go twice to the White House, giving readings on the famous Fourteen Points, and insisting that the League of Nations was the right direction for America at that time. The Cayce family was sworn to secrecy and to this day will not discuss this material, though old records have brought it to light for investigators.

Over the years there had been many occasions when the Cayce information slipped into an "enhanced" or "elevated" state, and offered its firm challenges on human affairs. To be sure, these occasions numbered only in dozens, out of thousands of readings; but they were memorable. It was insisted that there had been an ancient civilization called Atlantis, as Plato had said, and that this civilization had destroyed itself, by the misuse of inventions. Today, said the Cayce source, the same souls who had once before obliterated a civilization were back on earth again, either to learn a lesson or to repeat their mistake. Great numbers of children were being born who understood electronics and atomic power, as well as other forms of energy; they would grow into the scientists and engineers of a new age which had the power to destroy civilization, unless this time they learned spiritual law as well.

Looking at the American racial turmoil, the Cayce source quietly observed that many who were today born black had been white slave owners and importers before; now they were having an opportunity to build the very people and heritage they had destroyed—or again misuse their power.

Describing changes in the crust of the earth, oftentimes with startling geological accuracy as to fault lines and minor quakes, the Cayce information warned that human activities (nuclear bombs? draining oil fields?) were affecting the crust of the earth. In terms reminiscent of Noah's time, the Cayce source insisted that the activities of Nature were not impersonal forces, but responsive to the same order that governed moral affairs; men could so live as to bring on their own destruction—this time by fire, not water, as the New Testament warning had correctly envisioned. In particular, the coastal cities of California could be destroyed, the farmlands of Alabama and neighboring states inundated, and a crippling breakdown of the American economy follow, so that each man who wanted to eat would need a plot of ground on which to raise his own food. Yet these predictions were not offered for the newspapers, but quietly given to individuals who sought aid in planning their lives and their service to their fellows. And always the Cayce source insisted that some of these changes were reversible. At the very least, men who lived good lives would be warned of catastrophes. And there was still, as to Abraham of old, the assurance that even a few godly men working together could save a city, or a region, if they prayed—and worked as they prayed.

How typical of the psychic experiences of others were the Cayce prophetic materials, where his information spoke to groups of people?

Each year prognosticators with varying degrees of psychic ability announce lists of coming events. However, it is not always typical of them to couch these warnings in terms of national ideals, nor to set existential choices before their fellows. For parallels, one would need to turn more to philosophers, theologians, poets, playwrights—men of impassioned vision. For this was the quality of the Cayce material which could rightly be called "prophetic"; it was "elevated," shot full of an earnest sense of man's opportunities with God. In this material the factual element which drew Cayce admirers fell into the background, and the heart of the exchange was one man speaking with all the force of his being to his fellows. The subjects were not all "religious," such as the work of Christ or the nature of the church; neither were they all "political," such as the systems of government and the economics of nations. Some were psychological, calling men to better self-understanding through dreams. Some were sociological, urging a better understanding and keeping of marital bonds. Some were esthetic, reminding of the opportunities that men had for creating beauty and loveliness for their fellows, through the arts. But whatever the topic, the language was strongly Biblical, and the thrust was man's opportunity to become a co-creator with God—now, today, in this present walk of life. Though the language was Biblical, the sense was not one of returning to hometown religiousness; there was no magic about answering the prophetic challenge, nothing to be gained by empty chanting, "In God we trust."

Parapsychologists have tended to ignore the prophetic type of psychic material, because it is relatively unusual, and because it carries an aura of dogmatism from which science has only recently rescued itself. However, anthropologists studying primitive leaders with psychic endowments have noted among them unusual states of ecstasy and impassioned address, while researchers on LSD have wondered at the gripping sense of certitude which appears to accompany certain types of personal and social insights of those who take the drug and remain permanently changed afterwards. On the other hand, Biblical scholars, classicists and Orientalists have often tended to study the endowments of religious leaders of ancient times as though nothing of the sort could ever occur in the present; exceptions have been the French scholar Guillaume and the German scholar Wach.

Unfortunate confusions in the study of psychic experience might begin to disappear if the phenomena were looked at as a whole. Those who have only experienced little promptings or auras, even from the dead, often tend to trivialize all psychic experience, while those who have had some experience of astonishing "opening," where they saw and heard more than they could ever put into words, tend to ignore the physiological and psychological mechanisms studied by parapsychologists.

The Cayce source was asked about the operation of psychic ability in those experiences here called "prophetic"; it always ascribed the action to the "superconscious"—that portion of man's unconscious which could place him in direct relation to the Creative Forces of "the Holy Spirit." This kind of attunement was to be distinguished from the normal promptings of the soul, for it far transcended them in scope of awareness and capacity to formulate issues. To be sure such enlarged awareness did not come at the expense of the soul, or in violation of its ideals, but in amplification of its daily work and commitments. A small-minded person could not expect to have large visions —unless he had sought and won and shared these in some former life, so that they might flash back to him again as a challenge to awaken him. But even where the capacity for attunement through the "superconscious" was available, the actual occasions of operation were affected by many things: the needs of listeners, their readiness to act on what they heard, the longing in the heart of the psychic, the helping presence of those on other planes, impending crises or trials. For the gifts of higher attunement were man's to seek, but God's to dispose, according to a Wisdom which saw all the needs and intentions in a given situation.

Those who have been interested in the Cayce materials for several decades have sought to cultivate with some care the conditions of what is here called "elevated" psychic experience, such as prophesying. Most often they have noted it as coming in a vision associated with prayer or meditation, sometimes in a dream. Occasionally they have found that words came to their minds and lips in a steady, helpful flow while making a speech, and a quiet and peace settling over them and their audience, which have led them to think of attunement with the "superconscious." Individuals have sometimes found they could "speak the truth in love" to spouses, or children, or business associates, and do so caring as deeply as they spoke helpfully. Like many who have worked at their sharing in groups of Alcoholics Anonymous, some in their study groups and project groups have been surprised at how penetrating could be the address of one to another, when supported by a loving, praying group field. But the one discipline critical in opening the way for psychic ability of a higher order has seemed to many to be meditation.

Meditation in Creativity

The Cayce source considered the place of meditation in training for creativity to be so significant that it instructed the compilers of *A Search for God* to place a chapter on meditation as a preface to each volume of that work. Then it returned to the subject, in a broader context of living in conscious awareness of communion with God, in a chapter entitled "In His Presence."

The term "meditation" has come to stand for a variety of practices, from introspection to concentration, from visualization to emptying the mind. The Cayce source used the term in a strict technical sense, to refer to a specific discipline and process which when properly practiced would move through a series of stages, completing itself in the gaining of deep subjective quiet and a sense of holiness, often accompanied by having the field of consciousness filled with light.

To associate a specific discipline of emptying consciousness with creative activity might seem far-fetched. Creativity by itself sounds like action, the bringing about of something new or appropriate in a given form. What could silence have to do with action? How would one fill the mind with a needed solution by emptying it?

In the view of the Cayce information, meditation was the twin sister of prayer. By specific acts of prayer, one might bring his consciousness to focus on the divine, might enter into attunement with the "super-conscious" realm of his own being, and into relation with the Creative Forces. Through thanksgiving, praise, adoration, penitence, contrition, dedication, and the others acts of prayer, one might humble himself before the Throne, might bring his wayward psyche into a plastic state where a Source greater than itself might affect it. But getting ready for change and accomplishing it were two different things. Meditation ought to follow prayer, as the time for a movement in consciousness, a shift in values, a quickening of some needed center within. The initiative for such change would need to lie wholly with the divine, for in meditation man sought only to get out of the way of the gifts of being which were prepared for him, however wordlessly and dimly perceived. After meditation one might find a problem spontaneously resolving itself, or a helpful image presenting itself to the mind. But meditation was not to be entered into for the sake of some special goal; this was the business of prayer. Yet it was the nature of meditation to free the channels of the person to receive guidance, and if he did not receive it shortly after meditation, he could count on the action of such guidance when next he faced a decision or need for invention. Through the channels cleared and kept fresh by meditation could come more swiftly the flow of imagery and assurances that made up faith, "the evidence of things unseen," including helpful psychic promptings of all sorts.

Researchers into creativity have studied the process of "incubation," where an individual codes his mind with a problem and then waits for a solution to present itself, often after sleep. But they have rarely studied the specific religious processes of prayer and meditation, in part because these make assumptions about the nature of man and God which remind scientists of an unwanted medieval world view, and smack of magic. Nevertheless, there are hints that prayer and meditation might be highly effective in freeing creativity. These processes may serve to confirm an individual in his own identity and ego-strength, so necessary to face a difficult problem and endure the strain of waiting for an answer. Further, they may serve to lower defenses which impede the flow of helpful unconscious material into consciousness, and they may bring to bear powerful motivation on the solution of a problem, by turning the individual toward his highest values.

If ESP is a reality, then the seemingly pointless process of focusing the mind to empty consciousness may foster a flow of ESP signals into the psyche and out of the psyche in a state of rapt attention that has often appeared in effective psychic functioning in the laboratory. Moreover, prayer and meditation may have some place in fostering that elusive changeover from normal to "elevated" psychic activity which can be observed in any highly gifted sensitive from time to time. Prayer and meditation might make the difference between an individual's helpful promptings, largely for himself and his loved ones, and those larger openings which seem to take up his group, his people, his times, in ways so abundant and effective as to merit the terms of "prophecy," "wonderworking," "guidance," and "healing."

Might prayer and meditation be critical not only for development of higher forms of psychic ability, but for other types of creativity as well? Could the handling of political conflict, the marketing of products, the fashioning of symphonies, the solving of medical problems, the teaching of children, all be made more sensitive by such processes? A hallmark of the highest creativity appears to be that the solutions presented take account of the needs of all who are involved, not just of the primary creator. The best leader often leads people to arrive at needed decisions by themselves, out of their own resources. The best artist requires that the viewer invest himself in the painting, and invites him to do so. Do prayer and meditation add to creativity the extra dimension of how the other person can respond, what he can see, how he would put it? If so, they do in fact offer a larger dimension to every creative act, which can become an event with several centers, instead of a purely personal expression.

In taking up meditation as a key process in creativity, the Cayce source raised the question as old as any form of religion—the meaning of devotional acts. It turned its attention to the common base of the whirling of Muslim dervishes, the human sacrifice of ancient cultures, the totem meals of primitives, the handclapping of Shinto, the flower offerings of Hinduism, the swinging of the resonating bull roarer by Australian bushmen, the Hebraic practice of circumcision, the Catholic mass, the Quaker devout silence. Insofar as some aspect of prayer and meditation could be found at work in all worship, what was happening? And in particular was there a process of wordless meditation such as that long practiced under the Hindu term dhyana, the Chinese term Ch'an, and the Japanese term Zen, which ought to interest Westerners as well?

The Cayce trance source began its treatment of the theme "In His Presence" by insisting that there was no way to glorify God in worship or devotion which set Him apart from His creation. His presence would be found "in, with, under" all of His creation; any effort to limit God's presence to sacred things, times, places would quench the spirit. Unless He were the One Force sought in play, in study, in belonging, in work, He would not be found in worship; for exactly the same channels of energy were called upon in the physical body, in the action of the autonomic nervous system upon endocrine glands, under the stimulus of conscious thought in the cerebrospinal system, and with an impact from unseen sources, for all of man's creative activity of any type. Indeed, meditation was itself a very high order of creative act, in which something real and new was brought about, "released" in physical consciousness, however little perceived at first; it was its own form of conception and birth, in consciousness. What happened in meditation was some form of "raising" of the ideal into consciousness, some movement of emphasis and quality in the very center of the human being. An ideal would be activated in the imagination and begin to do its work throughout the life, if the ideal were of a high enough order to draw from the soul a full burst of energy and meaning in meditation.

Prayer, according to this source, was "a concerted effort of physical consciousness to become attuned to the Creator," while meditation was "an emptying of self of anything that might hinder the Creative Forces from rising along natural channels to sensitive spiritual centers in the body and psyche." As William James had said of prayer real work was done by it. But because real energies, real patterns were handled in prayer and meditation, these also held dangers. So strong were the currents once they were trained that as Paul had said of taking communion, he who did these things without the proper preparation of body and mind did them "to his own destruction." So the Cayce source warned that there should be cleansing in connection with regular devotional times—cleansing of the body, cleansing of the thoughts from all distractions and worries (even if one had to stop and dispose of these before continuing, as Jesus had warned about placing a gift at the altar while hostile towards one's neighbor). There needed to be balance in diet, rest, recreation, work, in order for the natural processes in prayer and meditation to move smoothly.

Exactly what needed to be done in meditation, as it was presented by the Cayce source as a way to stand "in His Presence"? The process was one of first freeing the body to enter into a delicate act of concentration and focus of energies. One needed to sit up straight (or lie straight) in a poised and unforced state. There needed to be a time of prayer, sharing with the divine both one's sins to be forgiven and one's honest gratitude, as well as the longings of the heart; the essence of the prayer would be found to be communion, however, more than anxious instruction of God. One could stand before the divine as he might stand with the sun at his back and the wind blowing over him, sure of eternal support and action from realms he had not created. Then the body would need to be quieted for meditation—and each person could find what worked best for him. Cayce took seriously ancient traditions of breathing procedures, even to tracing their physiology and the delicate pressures these placed upon endocrine gland areas. This source also treated chanting, incense, gongs and bells, instrumental music, candles, lights—each of which might work for some according to what they may have effectively used in some past life.

But there were no mechanics of meditation that would force it, only that which in its own way spoke of the divine as a real Presence to the individual. Meditation was not a focusing upon aids, for meditation had but one purpose, "the coming of the Lord" into an individual life. To make certain that this was the focus, the Cayce source offered a series of "affirmations" which might be held in the mind as microcosms of God's coming to man, and man's responding. Biblical in their phrasing, they evoked the whole sense of the pilgrimage of the people of God, seeking to understand and glorify Him. Each affirmation contained some note of service, each contained some note of man's shortcomings. The tone was warm, strong, earnest. The person seeking to meditate was invited to reflect on the force of the affirmation at some other time, perhaps in a study group, or when working on his ideals. But at the time of the meditation, reflection, reasoning and analysis were to be laid aside. One was to hold the action, the movement, the total thrust of the affirmation gently before his mind, until all other thought and sensation dropped away. Where prayer was a deliberate filling of consciousness with high resolve and awareness, meditation was a stilling of consciousness. Practicing meditation daily, one ought to find he could keep only the Presence before his mind, drawing attention back from the rippling play of thoughts, until one day he could not locate his body, nor be affected by outward sounds and sights. In this deep abstraction, a number of events would occur to signal that real inward action was taking place. Currents would seem to move along the spine, or dizziness to take over consciousness, or swaying from side to side or back and forth become evident. None of these were in themselves important, nor were sensations in particular parts of the body, from the gonads to the head, where the sensitive "centers" of the real body were located. In patience, and in steady waiting, one should be at peace with his Lord. In time there would come those moments when the whole arc of meditation was completed, and consciousness was filled by an indescribable stillness and peace, as well as often by a flowing, melting stream of light that filled the entire field of awareness.

These were merely accompaniments. What was really happening in meditation? The aftermath might tell. Often one would find such abounding good stirring within him that he might call this the most blessed of human experiences, consummated in the next generous handshake or helpful word or work on a committee. For one fruit of meditation could be release of ancient guilts and defenses, stilling of fears and compulsive drives. Problems could slip into perspective as challenges and opportunities; one might look upon his whole life as God looked upon creation, and call it good. For hours, or even days, after meditation had done its proper work, one would find that the answers he needed would occur to him—not in some strange occult way, but in a heightening of the flow of ideas and impulses that had always been there. He could go to bed at night aware that he had been more truly alive than ever before, and more truly himself.

Sometimes meditation would bring tears, tears of parting from old ways that no longer seemed worthy, or tears of rejoicing at the incredible goodness of God to so give himself to man. Sometimes it would bring a heightening of sexual energies, or a quickening of other emotions and drives, which then needed to be faced and given constructive expression. For this process was calling forth the total life force in an individual. Worship of this kind could be dangerous to the person if it were not anchored in loving service of others, in energetic self-giving. There was no way to seek to be "in His Presence" in meditation, if one did not strive to find himself "in His Presence" as one stood before another person, or before the realm of Nature—buying groceries, pruning plants, making a speech, reading a book, repairing a vacuum cleaner, struggling with an enemy, supporting a drunk. God was either a Presence with all of His Creation or he would be found in none of it.

The Cayce trance source never wearied of encouraging people to meditate. It was not, in this view, a luxury for those with time on their hands. It was a necessity for the human being to be human, as essential for the total growth of a man, and for his health and balance, as breathing was for his body. One could survive for long periods without it, perhaps for lifetimes, but only by developing halfway substitutes—various rituals of the arts or crowd gatherings or sexuality or Nature worship. Better to do that which was the way appointed in the human frame and heart, as a way to meet God. Then what was good in private and corporate rituals would thrive from the ground supplied by this primary devotional process, while that which was unworthy would fall away.

In the view of the Cayce information, meditation, accompanied by prayer, was no less than man's meeting God in his body and consciousness here on earth, not waiting for some other plane. It was "Good News" that "He walks and talks with thee"; it was a promise not reserved for holy men, prophets, and saints, but for all men who would accept it and act on it.

What was necessary to cultivate meditation? One had to set before his consciousness some concept of God, the best he could conceive, and let it be prepared to grow. In the view of this source there was no way to dare God to present Himself, to reach Him at the conclusion of an argument. One had to make the initial gamble of setting such a possibility before the mind, and allowing experience to stretch and enrich it.

Further, one had to set his house in order. If there were practices contrary to one's true ideals, however little these might be voiced, then these practices —whether of cheating, of boasting, of belittling, of cruelty, of using others— would make the individual afraid, in his heart. And fear could block meditation, as it blocked the flow of so much else that might be helpful to man from his unconscious. "When there is fear, know that sin lieth at the door" was frequently said by this source. Not the reasonable fear from a momentary danger, but the anxious fear that nagged at the back of the mind, that daunted the spirit of a person. One had to set his paths straight, in order for meditation to work for him.

It was needful to be regular, for at least fifteen to thirty minutes a day. Most would find that an early morning time was best, although some could begin by a period in the middle of the night, when distractions would be at a minimum. But as in prizefighting or singing or any other complex skill, regularity was essential, for the mind and especially the body to find its way into meditation. Moreover, once the flow had begun, one ought to seek to touch it in moments of quiet during the day, by memory and focus. The much discussed "still, small voice" would be found to work, to answer, to supply helpful nudges all day long, if one opened the channel and kept it open through meditation. Yet even as meditation began to yield its treasure, its indescribable honey, one had to choose to rejoice in it only before God, not to make it the basis for special claims before one's fellows; Jesus' parable of the Pharisee and the Publican at prayer was to the point, for boasting could stop the delicate process by distorting it.

What would be found the greatest reward of meditation? Special skills and gifts? Remarkable powers? Fortuitous events? All of these might occur, for God was a Creator God and sought His children to be creative. But the greatest gift in meditation was the self-giving of God, the bringing to human consciousness of greater and greater awareness of One who was not a person yet intimately personal, and the bringing of a way of life meant by "abiding in Him." There could come a sense of partnership with the Nameless One which made every day an adventure, and the long journey of the soul a pilgrimage into active joy that defied description.

Meditation and Prophesying

Probably many factors affect the emergence of that rare experience which might be called "prophesying"—speaking the truth to a group of people in terms that they can hear and receive, with a wisdom and love and helpfulness beyond one's own. The entire force of a life may be involved, as well as the need of others, and one's readiness to be strange, to be a fool for God, while yet to be ordinary and keep all the commandments. Yet it may be that meditation has a special way of quickening a realization that all one's days are lived "in His Presence," so that when a Presence beyond one's own is needed, it can be found.

An able psychic once visited the same New England campus the writer often visited. He had shown in many settings that he could at times give "readings" of striking accuracy, by having individuals write their names on a piece of paper which he then held in his hand. Details of their health, their marital status, their religious life, their vocation, their homes and clothing— all came easily to him. His accuracy varied with his good spirits and the general good mood of those he sought to help. Standing before the entire faculty at a special meeting, he dazzled them with his undeniable virtuosity. Then he visited some classes, and spoke of his experiences. At first his presence was merely an adventure and a campus challenge. Professors who had been sure there was nothing to ESP were shaken by his performances as they observed him at work, not only in groups but in the quiet and privacy of their homes. Then the atmosphere on the campus grew serious.

Students and faculty alike began to look at their own lives. What might an able psychic see, if he really looked at them? They sought him out for conversation where they did most of the talking, conversations which became confessionals. The psychic in turn felt the force of the stirring about him, and took himself off for long walks in the woods. He stayed on campus longer than he had planned, and night after night he met with small groups, speaking ever more deeply to one person after another. He recalled days in his early manhood when he had studied the Bible more than of recent years, and he reexamined his own life, to see where it was going and what kinds of associates he had drawn. He spent time in quiet, he touched a flow within him that he had learned to trust in times of meditation which he had too often allowed to be squeezed out of his life.

Then he turned back to trying to aid one person after another, offering new directions in vocation, new hope for worn-out marriages, new promise to homosexuals and alcoholics and compulsive gamblers—each represented in some small way on the campus. He worked so hard that more than once his face grew pale and his nose began to bleed; often he went back to his room utterly exhausted. Something more than phenomena was astir on that campus, and he knew it. A few times he spoke fiercely to a whole room of people. Difficult days were coming to America, he said, and this campus had to be making its contribution to understanding, to good will, to research, to community built on love of truth. He found himself speaking, as he rarely did, of God's impatience with men who forever turned their backs on Him. Students and faculty heard him without affront, and without indifference.

When he left the campus, students and faculty continued to talk, but not of his striking psychic accuracy, so abundantly shown to so many of them. They talked of their lives, of their times, of their world view. So many made plans to begin a new life that by the next fall over a third of the faculty had sought new positions and found them, while the school itself began an entirely new chapter in its self-definition and service to its constituency.

Had his psychic tidbits slipped into prophecy? Had "the Word of the Lord" been spoken, not so much by the psychic, who spoke much and earnestly, but by those who answered him in their hearts and with their lives? Was this possible both because of the openness of the campus and the readiness of the psychic to find his way back to a quiet spot within, to that flow of meditation he knew how to trust? Had he, in his groping and well-meaning way, found his way to the kind of consciousness that had enabled Nathan to speak the truth in love to wayward, wife-stealing David, saying "Thou art the man"? And in his efforts to help people find and trust their best selves, had he touched some part of what came upon Samuel when he took Saul, seeking lost farm animals, and anointed him as the future king of Israel? He made no claims, and in later years he often wished he might get back to the sharing he had found at that college, when things came to him straight and deep, and he knew it was right that he should be given to "shake up" a whole campus.

CHAPTER 12

WONDERWORKING

THE READING FOR the afternoon was to be a strange one. Instead of being given the exact location of his subject, Cayce would be given only his name and the designation, "missing in action in the South Pacific," together with the base post designation used by the Post Office. The effort would be to locate the man from his birthdate and place in a life reading.

In the reading room, Cayce's small office filled with mementos and photographs, sitting beside his desk piled high with letters to be attacked by his portable typewriter, sat the parents of the missing Navy airman. Frantic with worry since their son had been reported missing in action, they had decided to risk all their resources on a trip to seek Edgar Cayce's aid in locating their son.

Cayce had given them little encouragement, explaining in letters and phone calls that his gift required having the location of a person, in order to give a reading about his present circumstances. He knew that in the past he had been able to locate criminals by being first directed to the scene of the crime, but he also knew that becoming immersed in a crime, even while unconscious, tended to upset him. He had found that he might be caught up in the emotion of watching a murder, with his voice rising to an unaccustomed shout of warning, in the midst of a reading, and with a disturbed feeling for days afterwards. More than once he had located embezzlers, thieves, murderers in the past; but his information had warned him that while he could do it, the process was dangerous to his own balance, and like using a razor blade to chop down a tree. He knew that on occasion his information had been able to locate one person out of millions in a given city, when an address supplied proved faulty and the need was critical to get a medical reading; only recently he had done this in locating an individual in Los Angeles, after a period of silence and seemingly intense effort, accompanied by a quiet aside, "Pretty big place to have to look." He knew, too, that his trance source had once located the lost aviatrix, Amelia Earhart, in a location which sounded reasonable to her relatives and associates, but that the exact instructions given had not been followed out by search planes. What good would it do to locate someone if nothing were to be done about it? Why locate the Navy officer if the Navy were unable or unlikely to act on the information? If the man were dead, why give his parents—and his wife back home—the end of hope earlier than necessary?

But the parents had pleaded, and perhaps Cayce had touched within himself some sense of the probable outcome, for he finally agreed to try to locate the officer, and the writer and Cayce's secretary sat down with the parents to work out the instructions and questions which might bring results in the reading.

The room was quiet and everyone in keen expectancy when the reading began. Perhaps the expectancy, as well as the presence of the relatives, added to the attunement involved, for the voice of the sleeping man had hardly begun by locating the officer from his birth date and record (those strange "Akashic records" in "time and space" which the Cayce source seemed to turn to for life readings), when it went right to the question in hand. The airman was alive, but wounded, it said, and was being cared for by natives. He was ill, yet should recover within a few weeks, if all went well, and be rescued by American forces. Meantime, all that might be done by the parents and others who loved him was to pray for him. And in a quiet way the assurance was given that the prayers would have effect, being met by the same forces which made possible Cayce's giving of readings—these forces would also aid. The location itself would not be given, except that it was on an island in the area where his plane had been reported downed. Then, with one more admonition to pray, the reading was over.

The parents left, carrying hope even though disappointed at not being given the location of their son. Something of the quiet authority of the voice giving the reading had reassured them that their son was really alive and might make it back to them. Several months later they sent word that their son had indeed been found as promised, after having been wounded and cared for just as the reading had described.

Why had not the entranced man given the rest of the details? Was it a part of the usual restriction that people would only be given information they might act upon, in their own round of life? Did he foresee the awkward struggle that might occur in persuading the Navy to institute a search on the word of an ex-photographer speaking while unconscious in Virginia Beach, Virginia? Did he fail to locate the boy and only imagine the details which later happened to coincide with events? Or had the source been protecting Edgar Cayce from the flood of inquiries which would swamp him if he located even one flier by his unusual ability—or from Cayce's own inflation over such a feat? It had been made clear over the years that final details on locating buried treasure, or collecting rewards in the Lindbergh kidnapping, for example, had to come from some other person—usually in dream—which the Cayce source could then verify. But Cayce himself could not be asked to perform feats which would turn him into a sideshow marvel, stopping the quiet flow of helpful medical, vocational, and religious counsel.

And what had been the substance of the process hinted at, that the aid normally given through Cayce would this time be given in the form of a helpful force reaching out to affect the wounded man and his helpers—both native and American rescuers? Was Cayce's gift, whatever it was, capable of being used not simply as ESP, but as some form of psychokinesis as well, impressing itself upon people and perhaps even upon the tangle of signals that made up the work of a search party? Once before there had been such indications in the readings, when relatives sought to locate a businessman who had left home under mental and emotional strain caused by financial collapses of the Depression. They were given the answer that he was alive and well, but not given his location, for this would violate his freedom. They were urged to pray for him, and encouraged also to secure some of the strangest readings on record, when for about two weeks the sleeping Cayce was simply silent during the reading time, lending the presence of a helpful, loving force to the runaway man. In time the man returned, and his account of the lifts he experienced during his agony of decision whether to return home or even whether to go on living made striking parallels with the times of the readings taken.

In general, Edgar Cayce was not inclined to use his ability as a direct force to affect objects or people. As he told the writer, he believed he had previously developed such a psychokinetic ability, when he had healing force and the capacity for moving objects, or "materializing" objects psychically. But in a recent lifetime he felt he had misused the ability by showing off in a carnival setting, as well as to attract attention to himself rather than to help others with their needs. So he had come into this life without the ability to work wonders, or to influence flesh by direct flow of healing energy, except as he would be able to link the desires of his heart with the Spirit of Christ, Who could indeed do any such thing that was needful. Accordingly, he was inclined not to experiment with "physical manifestation," although he gave the impression that if he were ever in desperate need for aid for some member of his family, he would probably try to serve as an instrument through heartfelt prayer.

Often those close to him sought his aid in those little crises when psychic guidance or psychic outreach might seem to help. But his answer, typically, was prayer. For example, the writer and his wife once lost a beloved dog, when a car drove up at the end of the block and strangers scooped the dog into the car, driving off. Three men were in the car, and the indications were that they might want the dog to train as a hunting animal. Asking Cayce about the event, the writer was told that he and his wife should "release" the dog completely, "blessing it to the use" of the men, if the abductors needed it more than the present owners. It was a hard teaching, and Cayce was not dogmatic about it, yet obviously sincere. With considerable effort, the writer and his wife made the attempt, and nothing less than prayer would have made it possible. Cayce grinned, when he saw that the effort had been made, and said only, "Watch." He refused to make any comment when a few days later the same car with the three men drove up and let the dog out where they had picked him up. It was clear that he took no credit, but also that he felt that the prayers of each who offered them could help to make the best outcome for everyone, in such a situation.

Cayce's limited experiences with the possibility of "wonderworking," performing the movement of objects, the changing of storms and climate, the affecting of events, placed him in distant touch with the most controversial aspect of the history of psychic phenomena. In every culture of the Orient and the Near East, as well as in primitive tribes from opposite ends of the earth, there have been tales of men or women who could "make things happen." Biblical accounts would be representative of those from India and elsewhere: a jar that would not empty, a plague of locusts, bringing water from a rock, bringing victory in battle by an upheld arm and staff, quieting the sea, evoking an eclipse, walking on water, feeding a multitude out of little food, changing water to wine, and even raising the dead.

In modern times there were parallels to investigate in the astonishing mediumship of D. D. Home, who performed without fees for some of the best minds of the nineteenth century in Europe—and seemed to have levitated out a window and back, as well as moving chairs and tables so forcefully that strong men could not hold them, or changing the temperature of a room in a few minutes. Indian rainmakers challenged the observation of anthropologists, while Carl Jung and others studied the ways in which alchemists had sought to invest psychic energy in the action of metals upon one another. What set these processes apart as "wonderworking" from the more commonly studied psychokinesis with dice was their performance in a setting where they were a "sign," where they were used to convey to a group, rather than only to an individual, a force that would "show forth" the Grace of God. Drawing this line was not easy, but the distinction so often mentioned in these chapters between ordinary psychic experience of daily life and "elevated" psychic experience seemed to be a valid one in the manipulation of objects, as with perception of the unknown. Jung's suggestions that the symbolisms of alchemy were meant more to influence the deep reaches of the unconscious than to influence metals alone would be representative of the psychology under investigation in "wonderworking" as a phenomenon. What was it which, in classic Biblical cases, allowed a prophet to say, "The Lord will do a thing at which every ear shall tingle," and even as he spoke to have it happen? Was he merely predicting, or was the prophet given power to bring it about, in the very act of speaking—as Guillaume has suggested in his study of "the acted sign"? Something of this process seems to have been at work in the activity of an able psychic whom the writer observed trying to heal a little girl from seizures. The psychic said one day, "Something has been shown to me, which I will show you to study. She will never again have a seizure when I am in the same town with her—although when I am away I will have to pray to prevent or stop one. This will be true whether she knows I am in town or not—and I do not know why. But I know it is important to study, to understand, to see how we all need and help each other." Over a five-year period, his prediction has proven correct, as far as her family can determine. The events were small, compared to Biblical wonderworking—small, that is, to everyone but the suffering girl and her family. But they may have operated along the lines of "wonderworking" which needs further study, for the psychic seemed clearly in an "elevated" state when he grasped the promise for the girl, and for those who were trying to learn and grow with him.

From time to time the Cayce source spoke of Biblical incidents of wonderworking as though they had actually occurred. Sometimes the source corrected details, as in telling that Jesus had touched a man presumed dead on the forehead, to raise him from the dead—not taking his arm, which was bound according to the custom of the time for corpses. At other times the information gave supportive details on how Moses used his staff, or how sheep were bred to bear different markings, or how the multitudes were fed by

Jesus, or how Mary had conceived without being given to a man. This material was given spontaneously, and in a vein of helping listeners to understand laws which they might study—in patience—to employ helpfully in some measure in their own lives; it led those familiar with the Cayce materials to view the Bible much less as the "religious fairy tale" it seemed to many of their contemporaries.

In the view of the Cayce source, specific energies were involved in wonderworking, operating through the delicate seven "spiritual" centers of "the real physical body." Because of the notoriety involved in such phenomena, inquirers were repeatedly told that these were the most dangerous of psychic phenomena to attempt. Yet they were also assured in a few cases when dream material specifically showed a person he could develop such ability for others, that the force to "move" objects or "materialize and dematerialize" objects could be brought to work under the terms that Jesus had stipulated for difficult healing: "prayer and fasting." However, only those should make the attempt who had the prompting which Jesus had also mentioned, namely "faith"—not simply blind confidence, but the quiet springing up from within which promised them such ability as part of their lives and work. He who had the necessary faith to move mountains would then be the one who sincerely listened to the stream of assurances and promptings from his own soul, and answered with all the force of his being; if such a stream included a call to move mountains, then he might move mountains, in time—and patience.

Some have been drawn to an interest in the Cayce materials on wonderworking in the hope of developing a psychokinetic force which might be used either for personal gain or public service—perhaps in the field of electronics or photochemicals. But as they have experimented with the laws suggested in the Cayce materials, they have repeatedly found that beyond little bursts of happenings—such as seeming to dislodge a picture, or to break a glass, or to open a book repeatedly at a desired passage, or to affect the preservation of food—they have been unable to sustain such a force as an independent gift. Their observation has usually been that much more development of prayer, especially group prayer, would probably need to be developed. And that something in their own purposes probably needed to be cleansed and strengthened, before they could handle such a force if they succeeded in developing it in a stable, public way. Studying dream material accompanying such efforts, they have reported that central to the achievement of "physical phenomena" which might be used openly with others would appear to be complete purification of the will—sacrifice of all striving for attention and power over others. Seeking to cultivate this end, they have often been led into quite different avenues of creativity than they intended—including child guidance, the making of music, and the developing of medical appliances.

Sacrifice in Creativity

Martin Buber has written that two forces stride as twins down the centuries wherever men have practiced their religions: prayer and sacrifice. Having turned to the focus on prayer and meditation in the previous lesson in religious dimensions of creativity, the Cayce source turned to sacrifice in its lesson entitled "The Cross and the Crown," as part of *A Search for God.*

Linking sacrifice with the psychic phenomena of "wonderworking" would be strange only to those who have not studied the correlation between asceticism and "wonders" in the lives of the saints of West and East—whether those wonders were the moving of objects or the more practical manifestations of driving men to build churches and hospitals. Gerald Heard has suggested, following Hindu traditions about the building up of vital force and energy, that the intense religious focus of holy men, matched by strenuous athleticism and the narrowing of bodily expression, under the impulse to sacrifice one's will to God's, could indeed produce the phenomena described, though little accredited by modern men. While such sacrifice might at times have about it elements of masochism, it need not, but might be of the order of idealism which motivates a monk to lay aside sexuality for generalized tenderness—even if the goal is not always reached. Whether such asceticism reached all the way to abandonment of identity, as the Buddha had tried and rejected, or included only the sacrifice of self-will and idolatrous urges symbolized in the Hebrew tradition of an empty "Holy of Holies" at the center of the temple to Jerusalem, would have to be explored. But the content of many ancient accounts, including that of Samson's vows and accompanying strength as a Nazirite, would suggest a linkage between sacrifice and wonderworking.

If, as the Jewish analyst Neumann has suggested, there is at work in every man a tendency which can be called "centroversion" in comparison with introversion and extroversion, as a tendency to orient the ego to a superordinate Self below the surface of consciousness, then sacrifice of self-will, of complete ego autonomy, might affect the flow of all kinds of creativity. Not only psychic phenomena, but all artistic creating, invention of machines, building the United Nations, development of new forms of culture—all might be affected by whether the necessary inward promptings were organized to support a faltering ego or to link together a strong and capable ego with another Center of the person, his specific point of contact with the divine. Such a person might indeed act, as the Hindu Bhagavad-Gita pleaded, without concern for the personal benefits of his actions; he might act without self-justification or self-defense. But to arrive at such a new structuring of his psyche he might have to undertake a veritable "journey to the underworld," meeting the tests and developing the abilities suggested in ancient myths, or dramatized for Christians in the life and work of Christ, where the cross was followed by the crown of free companionship with the Father.

In taking up the theme of "the cross and the crown" the Cayce source was not only touching on the problem of voluntary sacrifice, as in all forms of asceticism, but also on the problem of involuntary sacrifice—that theme which in Catholic tradition has allowed baptism to the unbaptized, and therefore salvation, through the blood of martyrdom. What indeed is man to make of suffering? How is he to understand God's action with him in pain and death, and how is he to respond to trials? Why is the sacrifice of human life upon an altar wrong, or what is the error in impassioned suicide with the hope of reaching a better world? How is man to distinguish between the sacrifice of giving something up, and that sacrifice which Erich Fromm has called "giving out" as the truer form of sacrifice?

In the Cayce view the historic symbol of the cross represented man's having to make right his relation with matter. The action encountered in each man's having to bend his will through what seemed like the ultimate test to flesh—pain and death—had begun when souls first entered the earth, and "reversed law" by seeking to find gratification in "lower vibrations" than their proper realm of being. As a consequence they had to find not simply an exit—which of course death provided in itself—but a transformation, a way of working and living with matter that would give to them an understanding of its laws, and a way of sharing with one another through the right use of matter. Bodies had to be tamed, to be tuned, to be "lifted" until they were developed channels of grace from God, and from man to man. In this process, by many lifetimes of learning and giving, man could revise the original "fall of souls," and in fact make the whole journey worthwhile, a glorification of God.

But man would have to undo certain attachments in the process, and insofar as he identified with animal creation, he would experience the loosening of these attachments as pain and humiliation, or even as punishment. Yet the crosses in a man's life were not punishment, but focused opportunity. They allowed him to learn the laws of whatever ideals he chose, however falteringly. If he chose earthly possessions as an ideal, he would have to learn the place of things. If he chose and used power, he would have to learn how power was affected by the purpose for which it was used. If he chose love, then he would have to learn all the laws of love, perhaps even of incest and loneliness if necessary, until his soul stood free in the capacity for Godlike love. In the long journey, each would find that his crosses were also his crowns. He would also find that none but himself determined his crosses, that he brought upon himself each trial that came his way. He would, however, find that he could draw aid unfailingly from the One who had walked the way of the Cross before him, in all things tempted like other men, the One who "though He were the Son, yet learned He obedience through suffering." In the Cayce view the soul who was the Christ was fashioned at creation as were all souls, but given special charge over His fellows who sought their way into the earth, and given the opportunity to show His fellows the way to new life in the flesh, until it might truly be said that "the Word was made flesh and dwelt among us, full of grace and truth," and "from Him have we each received, grace upon grace," to become with Him true sons of the Father.

The concept of the necessary cross was a hard teaching, not congruent with the usual cheery optimism in psychic circles which asserted that man could have whatever he wanted by mastering occult powers, or by securing the marvelous aid of the departed. In the Cayce view man could have all of creation, all of the "Creative Forces" of God Himself; but man had to earn these through growth and proper use—and growth could often mean release of lower forms of creativity in order to achieve higher forms. One might have to give up the beating of sticks and logs, one day, if he were to play the piano. One might have to give up military drill with its pomp and killing, if he were to teach others the full art of dance that celebrated a national heritage. Each giving up would at times seem a cross, and require a genuine sacrifice. But the sacrifice would in fact be no greater than that made by a fetus upon leaving its lovely womb—a shock, not destruction. The cross was always also the crown, if chosen not "for narrow mindedness" but "for freedom."

The beginning of right understanding of cross and crown, then, would be to know oneself and every other soul on earth, even newborn babies, as sinners. No other view would be realistic, or even helpful. Here the Cayce source presented a view that closely paralleled ancient doctrines of original sin, even to linkage with sexual gratification in the "fall of man"; yet the sin had been not of one man such as Adam, but of every soul, and not a taint imparted by birth, but a problem brought upon each soul in its own past choices. Such sin would be known and found in every soul's efforts to play God over its fellows —in a fashion that made the Cayce view not dissimilar to Freudian views of the universality of the child's Oedipal strivings to use the parents. But understanding oneself and others as sinners did not define man's destiny; it only enhanced the understanding of present choices. For the promise seen in Christ was everyman's promise, "to be able to live a perfect, blameless life on earth," truly overcoming the flesh without deserting it nor belittling it. To find this promise, each soul had sooner or later to choose "to know only Christ and Him crucified" as his ideal. By any other choice, one made himself "a thief and a robber" to his best self. Such a choice was not a "religious" choice, not merely a matter of church membership and assent to creeds or rites. It was acceptance of a pattern which would be presented spontaneously in the soul of each man, in its own way and time.

Furthermore, that pattern would have its representation, for those who answered to the best within them and around them, in other religions than Christianity. The Cayce readings were adamant that wherever men had sought the One God in true faith and love, there the Christ Spirit had led, "in every age and clime." It was no handicap to be a Buddhist, a Moslem, a Jew, even a primitive sun worshipper, provided one followed out the highest ideal he knew; in time each soul would find his path led to the same Father as Christ had proclaimed. And that journey would be found not simply waiting, not punishment, not exile, but fulfillment, becoming, true creativity. For "He will withhold no good thing from those who seek His Presence"; the tales of the mighty works of God among men were not deceptions. He chose to give them no less than the Kingdom, no less than Himself as their birthright, if only they would use their energies to bless one another, in every concrete way their talents afforded. The Cayce picture of crosses, then, was not of hard gemlike souls being polished by abrasion, but of living branches and vines, finding always new shoots put forth precisely where the hurts were—and bearing fruits on every branch in a kingdom of becoming which was not dying to life but awakening to it.

If one's crosses were ultimately his own, then was life to be lived to meet one's own trials, and not those of others? By no means. There was in fact no way to meet a cross but to turn it into a crown. Each curse had to be made a course of blessing for others. Blindness allowed one to help others to see, poverty to give treasures not for sale, tyranny to open the door to freedom; for each man, "stumbling blocks must be turned into stepping stones." The Cayce source was definite about this, in pointing to the process which—for example—has made Alcoholics Anonymous such a success. Each person would learn that where he could most effectively aid his fellows was likely to be where he himself had to struggle the most; a man's weaknesses were not simply to be overcome, but made slowly into his wonders, his points of greatest strength and love and understanding. In this process the swiftest growth would be found to be "joyfully taking on the cares of others," wherever these might be found and rightly approached "in our own little world." For truly helping others should be seen as an opportunity, a privilege of helping none other than Christ Himself to bear the burdens of the world. Each man could make the force of his life-field available to that larger, purer and infinitely creative Field which men called "the Christ," and in so doing he could come under the law of "mercy" rather than of "karma." For the destiny of souls was to become "heirs and joint heirs" with Christ, and leaving out the "joint heirs" would block the entire inheritance, however dutiful the life—as Jesus had shown in the image of the elder brother of the Prodigal Son.

Were there not accidents, blind happenings which punished and destroyed a man? Asked about this, the Cayce source replied that indeed there had been accidents, "even in creation," but that no man should use this as a justification for blaming others for what came upon him. Far more than men realized, they drew upon them, in infinitely subtle ways which included psychic manifestations, exactly the predicaments in which they found themselves. This process extended even to lifetimes as mentally retarded or defective—which Cayce's source added then indicated that such people should be worked with in definite ways, not abandoned to strangers. The process extended to sudden death, or to the soul withdrawing quickly from life at any age, when the task which it entered to accomplish was fulfilled or blocked. The picture drawn by the Cayce source was one of staggering wisdom in the spinning universe, operating under laws of justice and soul-development which both transcended and harmonized with what men called "natural law." If the picture of this source were taken literally, the universe was not only "friendly," as philosophers often asked, but unspeakably loving, fired with love from God Himself.

How might one begin to meet his crosses, his trials, so that he could find them crowns? How might one undertake sacrifice of his own willfulness without abandoning his own creative will as an instrument for glorifying God? A beginning would need to be made in attitudes. Resentment at strains would unfailingly block the transformative process, as would blaming others. When pain and frustration came, and the temptation to flee to safety, or to thrills, or to try to corner life within some human power, a man should stop and say in his heart, "Lord, to whom shall we go?" Slowly, the fear in each crisis would begin to diminish, as one found that he had been protecting things, images of himself, which did not need to be protected. "Turmoils" would lessen, and "consternation" depart, as one sought to be conscious of the force of the divine in and with every important action and decision. One did not always have to solve problems correctly, nor should he expect to do so as much as he should expect increasing capacity to try, and try again.

And if one wanted to know whether he was making progress in the realm of sacrifice, the answer was not to be found in psychic feats alone. For signs and wonders and miracles were not God's way, as Jesus had showed in handling his own temptations. Remarkable things could come about lawfully as a man grew and worked with others who together sought the will of God. Indeed, the Cayce source insisted, nothing in the Biblical record, even the raising of the dead, was impossible for those who sought to train for such things for the right purpose—especially because they could count on an aid which the man Jesus had not known, the aid of the Risen Christ, to guide and resonate and focus their creative energies. But the right measuring sticks for men of good will and humble spirits would be found much simpler than miracles. Were they entering each new trial with a little more joy, a little more good nature, a little more spirit of adventure? Then all was well with them, whether they were moving objects by hidden powers or simply moving dirt with shovels as ditchdiggers. And yet better as an indicator of growth, were they taking up the burdens of others where they rightly could, and in good spirits that forbade martydom or boasting? This was the final way in which they or anyone else might know for sure whether they were becoming disciples of "the Master": "that ye love one another"—and not only the ones who loved them back, or even thought like them, or responded to kindness. What was the sign that could be trusted? Not that sacrifice which was a slaughter of oneself and others in the name of a fixed righteousness. Not that sacrifice which turned good energies aside for feats, and made stones into bread instead of bread into vehicles of feasting and communion. But the sacrifice which was service, imaginative and people-building service, wherever a trouble could be turned into a talent, and a crippling into a clap of insight, a cross into a crown.

Sacrifice and Wonderworking

Might sacrifice have anything to do with capacity to work wonders upon people and things? Cases are difficult to find, but hints are there to raise the question.

A European psychic who had made a reputation at solving crimes came to the U.S. for a series of demonstrations, and to participate in some modest research projects. During his visit he drew good-sized crowds at his demonstrations of seeming mind-reading and clairvoyance, and not surprisingly he was called upon by the police force of several cities to help solve crimes—

sometimes in their good faith and sometimes in suspicious tests. In one case in a large Eastern metropolis he correctly found a young man who had committed several murders, and had himself placed in a cell with the psychotic lad. After talking many hours with the suspect he had suddenly broken into a painful memory of the young man's past, when his parents had tortured him, and he was able to get the boy talking of this and start him toward rehabilitation. He was given an honorary police badge by the city for his work, and it was a source of much pride to him. He carried it in his wallet, and often showed it.

Then one day he was in a city on the West Coast when he was called by a frantic doctor, seeking help in reaching the mind and spirit of his troubled son, who had repeatedly tried to commit suicide. He went and talked with the boy, establishing a rapport by reference to the lad's inner thoughts and hopes and fears, which several psychiatrists had failed to achieve. He saw the lad several times, and helped him, but he knew he would soon have to leave to return to his native country. In one touching visit, he heard the boy plead with him for some means of remembering him, some way of recalling what their relationship had meant. And the psychic knew instinctively he should give the boy something of his own, some object that was stamped with his own identity. He had done this with others before. It was not enough to assure the lad that he might telephone him at any time, nor to promise him that he could slowly gain his balance through psychotherapy. What should he give him? His pen? His watch? He knew in an instant it would have to be the police badge, the object that had caught the boy's imagination when first they talked. It was part of him, part of his very self-image, his sense of worth in a strange land, and therefore the right thing to give.

The psychic was not surprised when the months that followed turned into years, without the doctor's son again trying suicide. Nor was he surprised that he did not really miss the badge, nor surprised that his work from that time more and more turned to work with doctors and less with police and the stage. He was beginning to find that he could muster a force that read x-rays without seeing them, that located strange roots to be used in medications, and could even guide a surgeon's hand and timing in a delicate brain operation. Some sort of "wonderworking" was coming into his reach, and though it frightened him with its responsibilities and often made him to want to turn back, it also opened up for him the meaning of the Old Testament as he had never felt or understood it before. He began to understand that one could make many mistakes, have many failures, yet if he were willing to share his real being with others, something promising would keep occurring. He saw at times that he might one day be more than a psychic—a man. Like Daniel of old he might cease one day to bow before wealth and power, trusting his abilities even to the point of discarding the love of others' lionizing, which was his own lions' den.

CHAPTER 13

GUIDING

THE LITTLE BOY was screaming. It was time for Edgar Cayce to start the afternoon reading, but it seemed impossible to get the necessary quiet. How was Cayce to pray and go into trance in his study, when right outside his door, in the library, a three-year-old was crying at the top of his lungs in pain and fear?

The child's parents had brought him all the way from a Midwestern suburb, to make a personal contact with Cayce and to beg for a "physical" or medical reading. The young Army officer and his wife knew their youngster's case was virtually hopeless; the boy had cancer of the eyes and had already been operated on eight times. He was now blind, and in constant pain. With the aid of sedation and loving care, they could keep his crying to a whimper, much of the time, but now they were not certain they could get him quiet enough to leave him for the hour and a half they would be in the reading room.

One of the secretaries in the office took the lad in her arms and began to talk to him, to rock him. Then she carried him into the next room where there was a parrot in a cage, an old sea salt of a parrot retrieved from a German submarine, who swore and who whistled at girls. As the boy quieted down to little gasps and coughs of crying, she described the parrot to him and explained that the parrot always knew exactly when readings were to begin, though nobody told him. As soon as the door to Cayce's study closed, the parrot would fall silent and stay that way until the reading was over, when he would begin once more with "Whatcha want?" or "Who's there?" or something a bit less refined. The boy caught the spirit of the comparison with the parrot he could not see, and snuggled into the girl's arms. He, too, it turned out, would stay quiet while the readings were given, including one on him.

The writer sat across the room from the unconscious Cayce, watching the boy's parents as the reading began. "Yes we have the body, present in this building." The parents were tense, earnest, obviously never far from prayer. The entranced voice traced the history of the ailment, examining contributing factors in the circulation, in the nervous system, in endocrine function. The history of the surgery was reviewed, and a sketch given of exactly how the boy felt, and how his cycles of pain developed through each day. At this last, the parents turned to each other open-mouthed in astonishment. How did Cayce know about the timing of the pain peaks? For that matter, how did he know what medication they were using, and the name of their doctor? Their faces were flushed as they leaned forward to listen to the steady voice explain what should be done, and explain whether there was hope.

Indeed there was hope, said the firm voice. Recovery would take a long time, but if the beginning were made at once, relief would be found before long, and in time healing. The boy would even regain his sight.

The mother wept, and the father bit his lip. It was evident that the assurance had struck home to them, touching their own inner spring of faith. In that moment they, too, were sure that their boy could be helped, in spite of all the negative medical judgments that had been given. How could Cayce be so right about the boy's history, his behavior, his care, and be wrong about his prospects? As the secretary took down the full medical regime of electrotherapy, chemotherapy, physiotherapy, and even diet, they listened as though to burn the instructions into their minds. They were surprised to hear the name of a doctor in Philadelphia recommended—someone far from their home and of whom they had never heard.

After the readings were over for that period—four of them—they went into the other room to get their son, who clutched at them. They thanked Cayce with evident feeling, and the young wife hugged him. Making arrangements for a copy of the reading to be dropped off at their hotel that night, they left.

It was nearly a year later when the writer had the opportunity to interview at length the Philadelphia doctor, a woman who taught medicine as well as conducted her private practice. She reviewed her doubts about the hope that Cayce had offered when the parents had come to her, and her hesitation to use the Cayce treatments. However, the essence of the Cayce approach was similar to her own, placing heavy reliance on stimulating better circulation to the cancerous area, and she decided to take the case. She described how frantically the boy had cried each time he was brought to her waiting room, his little mind filled with memories of visits to doctors, and of painful surgery and shots. It tugged at her heart when he fought to get away from her, groping in his blindness. But she made a friend of him in time, and even began to look forward to his visits for treatment, as she knew the boy did. Then came the day when she looked into the waiting room and noted with astonishment that the boy seemed to be reaching for a hat on a chair next to him. Quickly she took the mother aside to ask whether the youngster was seeing, however dimly. The mother responded that she had been wondering, too, though it seemed too much to hope.

But sight had begun again for the boy. And the time came, months later, when the doctor had one of the happiest moments in her long and busy practice. She stepped into the waiting room and saw the lad across the room catch sight of her. Without a word he slipped from his mother's arms and ran to the arms of the doctor. Though she was a professional person, she was also a woman. She wept, and scooped him up in her arms.

Was she able, the writer asked, to definitely establish that the Cayce treatments had stopped the course of the cancer and aided in the restoration of the vision? She could not. There were too many unknowns involved. And in fact, cancer—like other diseases—sometimes showed spontaneous remission of symptoms, when the growth would stop of its own accord, or by some process not initiated by physicians. All she could say was that if she had it to do over again, she would follow exactly the same regime of treatments, until research—on which she and her colleagues were making a beginning—could establish which part of the Cayce treatments if any had been effective, and how. Further, she responded, she was going to make a trip to Virginia Beach that year to study the Cayce medical materials, and hoped to be able to return for the same purpose regularly, though without publicity.

What had Edgar Cayce done, what had changed and moved in his consciousness, when he began to speak, saying "Yes we have the body, present in this building"? Had he really inspected the very tissues of the boy's body, and examined associated events of surgery and medical care carried in the boy's own unconscious and aura (the process described by his own information as the source for such readings)? Or had he developed fantasy material which happened by sheer coincidence to fit exactly with the facts of the case—as he had by similar coincidence in thousands and thousands of readings before this one? And where did he get the name of the doctor, whom he had not known previously? Not to mention the details of a therapy for a particular kind of cancer, which was by general medical knowledge not yet susceptible to therapy. It had all gone by so swiftly in the reading room; he had done it so many times before, for so many sick people and for so many doctors, even doing it twice a day for years in a hospital devoted entirely to treating people on the basis of his readings. His capacity could be accepted as some sort of a natural wonder, a sort of Grand Canyon of the mind, when one was right there looking at it. But when one stepped back and asked what might possibly have gone on, the mind boggled. Tales of "traveling clairvoyance" under hypnosis only made the phenomenon of such guidance more tantalizing, for such hypnotic phenomena had proven impossible to duplicate at will, and far less accurate medically than the usual Cayce performance, as well as lacking Cayce's precise medical terminology. Instances of medical counsel from supposedly discarnate doctors speaking through mediums offered certain parallels, sometimes even exceeding Cayce's medical fluency; yet the best of such mediumistic work had not yet proven under research investigation to be as stable as the Cayce phenomenon. Even hard-boiled university investigators, interviewed by the writer on their personal experiences with the Cayce readings, tended to lean to interpretations not far from Cayce's own, positing some sort of "universal intelligence" that Cayce might be in touch with, through his own procedure of prayer and trance.

The kind of guidance given to the parents of the cancer-ridden boy could hardly be called prophecy, for there had been no attempt to link the factual counseling with any group trend or commitment, nor with any immediate character concerns. There was no mention of the affairs of nations, of churches, of movements and causes and leaders. Just definite, detailed medical aid, for a family that desperately needed it. Yet the aid given was clearly of a different order from the little helpless flashes and promptings that had become a natural part of Cayce's waking life—far more detailed than he would be likely to see in an aura. And even though Cayce's dreams showed him capable of grasping the needs of a situation or individual in considerable psychic detail, they were never as rich in detail of aid for others as was such a reading. Compared to these other phenomena, the guidance that came in readings would seem to require description as "enhanced" or "elevated" psychic experience.

Cayce's speech in giving readings would become measured, rhythmic, stately. In spite of its grammatical omissions, based on an oral rather than written style, the discourse of the readings could often be scanned as free verse. At their best, these readings had little of the turgid personal style so familiar in the records of automatic writing, and little of the snips and snatches that sometimes characterized mediumistic or psychometric material. A complete creative form seemed to be instantly fashioned—at times re-minding a listener of Japanese haiku poetry. Yet the form varied in complete-ness and polish from day to day, and from period to period in Cayce's life, just as did the amount and precision of detail in the content of the readings. Enhanced or not, some readings offered only the bare minimum of factual material and recommendations, while others flowed and sparkled with both facts and value judgments. Some were awkward in grammar, while others were smooth.

Was Cayce in his readings conforming to the type of the "seer" in the history of religious, as that encyclopedic scholar, Joachim Wach, suggested on the basis of his comparisons with Greek, Hebraic, Peruvian, Hindu, and Chinese figures? Unlike the more striking figure of the "prophet" in various traditions, Cayce was limited in healing and wonderworking gifts, limited in administrative and organizing gifts as a reformer. But when it came to gifts of vision, his limits were difficult to determine.

Indeed, it sometimes appeared that the only limits on the scope of the Cayce counsel were (a) those of proper instructions given to Cayce, at a time when he was sufficiently rested, peaceful of mind, and healthy (not too soon after a meal), and (b) those of the seeker's capacity to use information in his own life, in constructive service of others, without unfair advantage of any man, nor damage to the seeker or Cayce in personal and social functionings. Within these broad limits, many factors appeared to affect the quality and scope of each day's readings—factors in Cayce, in those around him, in the seeker, and perhaps in the times as history or part of God's "plan of redemp-tion." But the range of targets demonstrated over the years had been stagger-ing.

There were readings in the files on buried treasure and buried talents, on investment opportunities and on opportunities with the Infinite, on leukemia and on loving, on child rearing and on crime control, on Egyptian architec-ture and on endocrinology, on fluoridation and on the fields of stars, on ancient gods and on airplane design, on chemical compounds and on Christ, on stock markets and stock-taking of ideals, on angels and on anger, on movie scripts and on motions below the crust of the earth, on marital covenanting and on merriment, on death and on dentures, on visions and on viscera, on the Bible and on bile. The list of material in this guidance process was evi-dently of about the same size as the material in human affairs, past, present, and—less sweepingly—future. The writer once undertook a study of what subjects were *not* dealt with at any length in the readings then indexed, and came up with agriculture as somewhat under-represented—probably in part because Cayce's work seemed to draw relatively few farmers over the years. The list could be lengthened, but because of the range of the life readings, which claimed to offer snapshots of people in all sorts of occupations and stations in life from many periods of history, the list of fields of human interest not at least suggestively touched on in the Cayce readings would be surprisingly short.

But as might be expected of a phenomenon which might truly be called guidance, rather than mere supplying of information in a kind of psychic computer service, the range of human value questions dealt with was as great as that of the factual material, and equally a hallmark of the Cayce phenomenon, though not as widely celebrated in his lifetime nor since his death. In the field of ethics and morality were issues of war and peace, family living and the character of corporations, race relations and sexual relations, taboos and trade practices, penology and panaceas, Biblical norms and basic cosmology of the soul and God. In the field of aesthetics were more limited treatments of norms and masters in each of the major art media, as well as studies of symbols and signs, of periods and pressures in art history, of the relation of beauty to love and truth and godliness ("For music alone may span the distance from the sublime to the ridiculous"). In the field of logic and the search for truth were treatments of perception and cognition, of hunches and hypotheses, of conscious logic and unconscious logic, of syllogisms and of statistics, of archetypes and analysis, of thought processes in half a dozen different states of consciousness besides waking attention, and of revelation and reason, theology and theorizing, myth and mindfulness. In the realm of values called the holy, there were materials on rite and on resurrection, on sin and on God's secularity, on penitence and on praise, on creation and on caring, on faith and on Fatherness, on Jesus and on judgment, on healing and on happiness, on brotherhood and on borrowing Grace. While there were essaylike passages on each of these topics, the general treatment was situational, personal, existential. People were not given maxims alone, but choices. They were not fed teachings so much as met where they were, and taken seriously in their own value thrusts. In the handling of what mattered in the quality of people's lives, both ultimately and proximately, the method of the Cayce source was to work with what was given in the seeker, either in his consciousness or just below the surface in the working of an ideal. For it was the perspective of this source that the relation of evil to good was not poles apart, in a given individual, but evil was "just under good." Evil was good energy and values, misapplied, misunderstood, misused, misfocused in the blind willfulness of souls; but evil was not so much to be exterminated as "raised" to the good which it could be. Psychosis was not far from prophecy, cruelty not far from carrying another, withdrawal not far from wisdom in silence—if only people could see the gap and make the effort. The gap between right and wrong was a cosmic gulf in the eyes of God, and yet right and wrong were as close as seed and shell in God's view of each man's growth.

These were perspectives which questioning drew, when the Cayce source was asked how a high form of psychic or seerlike guidance was possible among human beings. Characteristically, the Cayce source insisted that individuals could use the same processes Cayce used, to secure the guidance they needed for their own lives—in dreams and prayer and meditation, with waking hunches and judgment. The difference between most people and Cayce was only that most people could secure guidance for themselves and their loved ones, while Cayce was able to make his psyche available—through long training and dedication in past lives—for anyone to seek the guidance he needed. But others would be found to have natural endowments similar to and greater than Cayce's, his source insisted right up to the end of his life. Such souls could be "drawn into the earth" by parents who lived upright lives and prayed to be given the treasure—and to bear the trial—of a soul with such special talents for service and guidance of others.

During Cayce's lifetime, especially from 1932 until his death in 1945, his close associates and his family sought to cultivate their own gifts of guidance along lines suggested by "the information." Usually they were most successful in giving aid to family members, on a wide variety of topics which included medical information, vocational guidance, business judgment, child rearing, and psychotherapy. But at times they could give similar guidance, and even secure insights and visions of genuine theological depth, for members of their prayer and study groups. They found that many factors affected their ability, which seemed to have a different profile for each person; some were able to offer health hints to others, some able to counsel on marital relationships, some able to touch hidden value springs of a life, some able to interpret Biblical or other material to make a meaningful world view. But among these factors one that stood out was care not to divide the universe too far into realms of sacred and secular, of holy and unholy, of God and Nature, of religion and business. Unless they could find themselves working with the same springs of creativity, the same Source, in the same Spirit, in whatever they undertook, they would not be likely to secure effective guidance in any realm for long. God was either to be God of their whole lives or hidden from their view. It made a difference how they polarized their universe.

Polarizing in Creativity

After dealing with prayer and with sacrifice, the Cayce source turned to the question of religious understanding, religious belief, for its next area of focus among the religious conditions of creativity. Characteristically, it took up a perspective in which both idea and act were united, by using a phrase from Biblical history which was both a proposition and the heart of the Jewish prayer of faith, the Shema. The chapter on polarizing, on conceiving the fundamental structure of religious thought and action, was entitled "The Lord Thy God Is One" in *A Search For God.*

Psychic ability of every sort seems so irrational, so unpredictable, so much at the mercy of controls outside of consciousness, that linking guidance with any particular convictions may seem arbitrary. Yet every approach to the depths of the unconscious, where psychic ability seems clearly to take its origin, as viewed by modern research, shows how responsive the unconscious is to conscious thought and plan and stance. Dream material is full of commentary not only upon the activities of the previous day's consciousness, as Freud so well showed, but upon the conscious formulas and trends of the life style—as contemporary research in dream laboratories suggests. Psychotherapy in all its forms is based on the conviction that the unconscious material in certain neuroses and psychoses can be changed by changing the work of consciousness—its names, plans, claims, poses, formulas, convictions, abdications. Inventors correlate their flow of new material with conscious coding done by studying a problem, while most artists come to expect their inspiration to need matching and stimulus by conscious technique. It would not be surprising if the flow of helpful unconscious material called "psychic" were also responsive to the basic structures of thought and conviction, held in consciousness.

However, the choice of the ancient formula "The Lord Thy God Is One" as a focus for the polarizing of the mind by understanding and conceptualizing would seem a difficult one. Is the "Oneness" the transcendent holiness of Hebraic tradition, or the immanent One behind all things in Hindu tradition, or a One Mind of philosophical idealists, or a One Energy of philosophical vitalists? Is the God under discussion a personal or an impersonal being or reality? What kind of thought is implied in the use of the phrase "The Lord"—how far devotional and within a covenant, and how far philosophical and objective?

Behind all of these questions, it was at least clear that the Cayce source was struggling against all kinds of dualism, all efforts to make the split between matter and spirit, between God and creation, between reason and revelation, into cosmic splits rather than conveniences of thought. How might dualism affect creativity, whether psychic creativity or any other? The Swiss psychiatrist, Carl Jung, has suggested that most dualisms are rooted in an unhealthy separation of spheres of the psyche, of consciousness from the unconscious, of ego from a deeper Self. Insofar as Jung may be correct, then any ardent dualism tends to break up the effective harmony of surface and deeper layers of the psyche, which appear in creativity to stimulate and fructify one another. Insofar as such dualism is a defense against something felt unworthy and dangerous within oneself, then that part of the mind will be isolated, exiled, restricted, in its production of both negative and positive material. Freud's mission—as Fromm has called it—may be seen as a heroic struggle against one form of dualism which splits the mind by repression of primitive urges, rather than by large-minded acceptance of human motivation and controls.

In the area of high-level or "enhanced" psychic ability such as offering effective guidance and helpful information for others, the peril of dualism of attitudes towards the psyche—however projected outwards onto the cosmos—would seem to be the peril of invasion of spirituality by material from unrecognized personal conflicts. Something of this process may be seen at work in those lonely female automatic-writers whose discarnate "controls" appear to be dominantly masculine, bent upon serving the every wish of the medium—including unconscious erotic desires and power drives. The danger is no different from that encountered where people interpret dreams of normal psychological function and balancing as oracles from a "higher self" or from a "divine spirit." That many dream symbols, including sexual symbols, may be interpreted on both personal and transpersonal levels is hardly to be denied; what may be incest for one may be rebirth for another, and both for a third. But the peril in banishing part of human experience as unworthy in a scheme of grand dualism need hardly be labored. Amputation will never replace transformation, in the things of the human mind and spirit.

In taking up the question of dualism and monism, the Cayce source turned —surprisingly late in its progression of topics—to the question of religious belief and conviction which is as old as faith. When the Buddhist takes refuge in the Dharma, when the Hindu seeks direct knowledge showing "That art thou," when the Jew seeks to become bar mitzvah, "son of the commandments," when the Christian struggles for a creed, when the Muslim chooses to set Allah above logical necessity, when the Australian aborigine sets apart the circumcised male youth for instruction in men's truths—the question of religious belief and conviction is to the fore.

Characteristically, the Cayce source refused to separate knowledge from action. The right approach to God would be found in a combination of reflection and hard study with action which was at once attunement and service. Out of such an approach understanding would come. While the Cayce source often spoke philosophically of "the Oneness of All Force," and spoke psychologically of "turning within to the Christ consciousness which is One with the Christ," its characteristic formula was the devotional formula of ancient Judaism, "Hear O Israel, the Lord Thy God is One"—for here was a way of approaching non-dualism which was set in the living experience of a people, rather than in the armchair of the philosopher or the laboratory of the psychologist. The caution of the Cayce source regarding purely rational formulations of the nature of God and creation, of God and man, was in part grounded on a view of man where truth could only be found through transformation; the consciousness of a man could only fully grasp and use what he had lived out and activated in his soul. He could "understand" with wisdom, more than with learning, only as much of "the Creative Forces" as he had made his own through choosing and enacting an ideal. Concept and life-trajectory went hand in hand; concept not girded by experience could be a plaything or a snare. Even the most delicate interplay of senses and reason was not an adequate guide unless formed, quickened, prompted by unseen patterns coming into the background of consciousness from the soul and its "superconscious" awareness of the way things really were.

In the approach of the Cayce information it was necessary that the human mind be correctly polarized toward the divine at work, in order for the mind to achieve its maximum creative function. Such polarizing was of the order of tropism, as a plant turns toward the sun, rather than of the order of electricity, with positive and negative poles. The opposite of God was not some structured anti-God nor devil, though evil had its structures and some human patterns were assuredly devilish even to the extent of becoming autonomous thought forms. The opposite of God was that which was not yet fully in harmony with Him, and conscious of its nature and destiny. If one could talk about another direction from the One Force, it would have to be disorganized force, misused force, compulsive force—exactly what distracted souls showed in their spinnings, turnings, hidings, and masqueradings. But even the force to be selfish, to do wrong, was God's force—there was no other force in creation. And because it was God's force it would ever be transforming, turning into other modes, suggesting other meanings, calling forth new predicaments and results, turning man—and all creation—Godward. For even the creatures and things of the earth, said the Cayce information in one passage reminiscent of Mahayana Buddhism, must reach the consciousness of their Creator some day, and man could, in his journey in the earth, render this service to brother animal and sister stream. It was not a small canvas on which the Cayce source painted its sketches of creation and destiny.

To get at the conception of the universe which would free the soul to be itself, man had to learn that "dualism confuses and mystifies," that "all material things are spiritual," that "the Father doeth the works," and stands behind and with all His creation. From time to time one might even glimpse, as did Job, that "all things work together for good," that "God gets himself glory even out of men's evil." But this sense of the ultimate unity of the cosmos and Creator would be found to be the most difficult truth for human consciousness to fully attain, and in some sense would never fully be grasped except by metamorphosis, by the person's becoming more than he was. Likewise, man had to learn that God was not to be found in special "times and places" called religious or holy. He who could not find God in the face and heart of his brother could not find him in a temple or grove; he who could not find Him and share His presence in cooking and serving a meal would not find Him in serving communion. It was One Force at work in every aspect of man's life, and the point of elevating some segments to the status of holy things was only to emphasize that God was always there, in even the most ordinary things and events—like one day of the week, or bread and wine, or auras glistening out of sweat.

Yet to call God "One" and turn one's face towards Him might well require thinking meaningfully in Trinitarian terms, or some other symbolism which made the One luminous in its spectrum of Creative Forces. The Cayce source never wearied of saying that the formula of "Father, Son, and Holy Spirit" had come to the human mind and stayed there because it so well corresponded to three-dimensional existence—while on other planes perhaps six or seven dimensional existence would require different types of symbolism. On earth the primal symbolism of the Trinity was parallel with human three-ness: The Father was like the body of man; the Son—ever the Builder and Helper—was like the mind of man, while the Spirit was like the spiritual or soul realm of man's experience, ever tugging at him. So long as man had to contend with these three overlapping realms of reality, all drawn from the One, he would find Trinitarian thought helpful to him.

But there were limits in thinking of God in terms of substances, even metaphysical ones, for the primary category of the Cayce source was "force," in speaking of the divine. Not substance but process ran all through the readings. Even organs of the body were described as "those forces of the liver" more often than as "the liver." Mental tendencies and unconscious complexes were "forces of the mental." In the perspective of the Cayce information, the cosmos was seemingly an indescribably rich flow of interpenetrating fields and fluxes, of vortices and events, of vibrations and waves and harmonics, rather than of fixed things and structures which the conscious mind so liked to postulate. At times the Cayce source would be impatient with the neat structuralism which would incline a seeker to ask whether or not he had "arthritis" or "asthma" or some other patly labeled condition; the voice would indicate that the total condition of his body had been described, organ system by organ system, and the individual might call it whatever he wished, just so he set about treating those conditions. The Oneness, then, might better be grasped in a schema of forces and processes, of events and relationships, than in a schema of substances and structures, places and hierarchies.

The Cayce source moved freely back and forth between philosophical language and devotional language, in dealing with questions of polarizing man's thought and action about the divine. At times the concepts used were of laws, while at other times the same laws were described as "the promises" of God. Both ways of thinking were used as though they had value, even in intricate questions of "karma," where matters of justice and law were discussed as freely in terms of souls and "universal forces" as in terms of "meeting self, with the help of Christ." There was no clear priority given either to rational reflection, quickened by a life of commitment to ideals and the One Lord, or to "inspiration" welling up from the unconscious but requiring conscious interpretation and decision. There was, however, an insistence that no great vision or experience was needed to begin to live within the polarizing awareness "The Lord thy God is One." Even though the Cayce source insisted that Jesus had demonstrated the reality of direct, personal relations between man and God, so that every man could set as his destiny being able to say in the now, "I and the Father are one," there was no insistence that each person go through a conversion experience or turning-point revelation to find the Oneness. Like everything else of value in creation, this discovery of Oneness would come a little at a time. But entering into meditation on the assumption that the divine would really be there, touching the human field in some authentic way, would guide and speed the growth.

If not by seeking or waiting for some blinding invasion of God into consciousness, how might one begin to cultivate the polarizing of his life to the affirmation that "The Lord thy God is One"? The beginning might come in self-analysis, to discover just what sort of God one showed forth in his life. Was it a God of Sundays and public pronouncements, of religiousness? Or was it a God of love and work and play, as well as of worship, a God of dailyness? Was one's God the God of good behavior or of the whole man? Was it a God able to handle human evil as well as goodness, to turn crosses into crowns, for him who was hid with Christ—who had found a fully human Lord over "the imagination of the heart"? Each man was representing his own concept of God by his daily life as surely as if he were a sculptor carving it, or a singer intoning it, or a theologian explaining it.

But activity alone would not provide the index of one's polarizing towards that final One. There would have to be turning to the still, small voice, and toward the crowning Light and nectar of stillness that could be found in meditation. Only by entering into the "holy of holies" in one's own inmost being, through prayerful intent, could one find guidance as to whether his life was properly glorifying the One in the most creative way. For man could become easily confused and attempt without such guidance to live out spiritual laws on the physical plane, or mental laws on the spiritual plane. One might confuse sacrifice of the will to God with sacrifice of one's identity to parents or country. One might confuse trusting the constructive powers of the mind with an outlook where God Himself could be made to do the bidding of the mind through concentration. One might confuse the real physical laws of death with spiritual death and separation from God. There were laws for each realm, within the whole creation straining and dancing its way Godward, and only attunement could sort out the laws into their proper spheres, polarized around the One.

Polarizing and Guiding

The phenomenon of effective guidance, including psychic information for another person, may be more rare than the prominence of fortune tellers and soothsayers in human history might suggest. Yet some measure of it may go on all the time for those whom we find bound in the bundle of life with us, whether by love or fear. Of the many factors which may quicken and enrich such guidance, how far does the achievement of understanding about the non-dual relation of God and His creation make a contribution?

A nun in her thirties sat in her place in a sensitivity training group which the writer observed. Like many another of her sisters in these times, she was feeling the need to reunite the worlds of the secular and sacred, so divided in popular piety, however they may have been unified in the best of theology. She was wondering aloud again, before the group members whom she had grown to love and trust in a relatively short time, whether she ought to leave her habit and her community and take up a place in wholly secular life, bringing to those around her a sense that the gifts of God are for everyone, and not alone or especially for "the religious."

The group members, all lay men and women, were finding it difficult to respond to her question, and were surprised at how strongly they projected on her. Some wanted to see in her the purity they felt they had lost in their own lives; some wanted to see her choose the way of love and sex to justify their own life courses. Some saw in her the opportunity to be helpful to others without the burdens of family and children—burdens which they had always said kept them from real service to others (or had they?). Some saw in her work as a nun the possibility of a contemplative life where long hours might be put in searching out a direct relation with God. One after another, the group members contributed their subjective awareness that they could not see the nun for herself, in her own pilgrimage, because they were allowing her garments and office and vows to make her into a thing rather than a person— a religious thing, either great or small as the case might be, but a thing.

Further meetings came back to the nun's question, which she did not force upon the group during the week of close sharing, but which she addressed as honestly as the others were expected to address their own life questions. Finally, after the group had gone for a long walk together and settled down before the fire for a quiet time of prayer and talking with one another, one man spoke to her. "I think," he said, "you can have whatever you want, so long as it is within your capacity to handle, and you want it to share with others, and you are willing to pay the price of growth that is involved. You seem to want to love more deeply and personally than you have ever done as a very effective teacher and nun. My guess is that you may have this loving in or out of your Order, as you wish. For as I have looked at you this week I have seen less and less a representative of the church, and less and less a woman. I have started to think more in terms of life's possibilities and less in terms of its restrictions. If you want to love deeply and closely within the bonds of your vows, you can pray for this and I think you'll get it, though you may have to spend more and more time with children, and with trainees who really need you. But if you ask to love a man and have his children, that God may be glorified in this fashion, I think you'll get that. For the God we have been talking about this week is One Whom we have said withholds no good thing from those who love His coming. If it is true that He offers Himself unceasingly to us, then He is not first asking, what are you doing for My church and My traditions? He is first asking, how alive are you, how whole and how happy? For nobody can peddle joy who hasn't got it, can he?"

He spoke slowly, looking straight into the face of the nun seated on the floor before the fire near him. She began to weep as he spoke, although she was smiling as the tears ran down her face. Something in the way he had caught hold of her struggle, the way he had put it, had answered to her deepest self. As he finished, she reached over and seized his arm, and for a moment they locked arms, as wrestlers might, or companions on a long journey showing that each would hold the other from fainting or falling. The group was quiet, before the fire. Then a guitarist in the group strummed a little and began to sing, "Puff, the magic dragon, lived by the sea. . . ." The song made no sense for the moment at hand, but people laughed and sang it, while somebody passed cokes and potato chips, and the group settled down for the rest of the sharing at hand.

The nun went home and talked her heart out with a fellow Sister, one who was also considering leaving her role as a nun, though also remaining devout and active in the Church. Central for each of them was the man's perspective that God was a God who wanted to give Himself and His fullness of being to His children, in whatever way they sought it, in order to share it with others. The thought became guidance to them in the fullest sense, and they worked out their answers in terms of it. As events unfolded, one stayed in the life of a nun and the other left; when last the writer talked to each, they were both more fully alive and happy than ever before, growing into new ways in their respective spheres.

Had the man by the fire merely given advice? Was he simply projecting his own problems onto the nun? Or was he really looking at her as a person for the first time, free of the hidden spectacles which had divided his world into the things of God and the things not of God? Had his polarizing toward a God who streams into all creation, and seeks man's fulfillment over institutional offices, though not apart from them, given him the "opening" to speak the truth in love to the nun? He was not sure, when he described the tape-recorded event later to the writer, but he noted that he had trembled as he spoke. "Funny," he said, "but although I am a Presbyterian, I think I know where people got the name Quaker, from the quaking and trembling that I felt; it was good, it was great, and I don't know where it came from, but I felt clean and right and sure of myself, for once."

Had he found an attunement which led him to the surety with which Paul had spoken, when he said so many centuries ago, "Circumcision or uncircumcision, it availeth nothing" unless a man be in Christ? Had he found the direction in which to turn, the polarizing Jerusalem for his soul, so that he could stand secure and offer to a fellow pilgrim guidance as rich as it was simple?

CHAPTER 14

HEALING

EDGAR CAYCE WAS not following instructions. He had finished the readings sought from him that morning, and now it was time for him to awaken from trance. The phrase he should have used after the last reading was "We are through, for the present." Instead, he had said, "We are through with this reading," which was the usual signal for his wife to give him instructions for the next one. She leaned over her quietly-breathing husband to say, "That is all." He did not respond.

She was eager to give the suggestions for his body to reestablish normal waking patterns of circulation and "nerve forces," and to give the final instruction, "Now, perfectly balanced and perfectly rested, you will wake up." She knew that he had been giving more readings per session than before, spending between three and four hours each day unconscious, instead of the familiar total of an hour to an hour and a half. She feared for his health. He had recently been ill, and he showed the strain of the hundreds of requests for aid arriving daily—requests which had filled his appointment calendar two years ahead. She worried about him, aware that he had predicted he would never see his sons again.

The unconscious man cleared his throat and began to speak. "Now we have the body of M——— D———." Mrs. Cayce was startled, and looked hastily at the secretary, who was beginning to transcribe the words. They both knew the girl in question, as the daughter of a long-time friend and member of the study group working on *A Search For God*. But neither knew of a request for a reading for the girl, nor did the writer, who also sat there listening.

In the past a reading had been volunteered, on rare occasions, for someone not scheduled for the day; the reason always a crisis. A few times a reading had even been given before the application arrived, but after it had been sent, when medical aid for someone meant life or death. Now here was a reading beginning for a college girl, who they were sure was in good health.

The voice of the unconscious man spoke swiftly, locating the girl in the dormitory room of her college, not far away in Virginia. She had just fallen from the upper bunk in her room and injured her spine. She needed expert medical care of a specific type. Outlining which vertebrae had been injured, and how, the information went on to recommend exact treatments. Offering assurance that with the proper care the girl could recover without lasting effects, the reading closed, and the voice now came to its accustomed phrase, "We are through for the present."

The secretary hurried out to telephone the girl's mother, who lived nearby in Norfolk. To her surprise, she learned that the mother knew nothing of an accident. Concerned, the mother took down the essential details of the reading, and in turn telephoned the college. She found exactly what Cayce had described; her daughter had fallen from a bunk in her room and was in great pain. College health authorities had not yet decided where to take her for hospitalization, and the mother was thankful to be able to give them instructions. Then she packed and drove to the hospital herself, armed with a reading on her daughter's care. Meantime, the Cayces alerted the prayer group of friends and associates which kept regular times each day for a list of people in need, and the members of the group began at once to intercede for the girl in their prayers.

In time, the girl recovered completely, avoiding the paralysis which was feared.

As happens among good friends, all thoughts were on the girl's recovery. Little attention was given to the role of Edgar Cayce's information in bringing her aid. Given the nature of Cayce's work, as they saw it, why should she not have received a spontaneous reading?

But how had it happened? In what kind of a psychic field did Cayce operate, where he could be examining the bodies of others in points as diverse as Alaska and Florida, prescribing medications and physicians from anywhere in the country, and yet simultaneously keeping track of the emergency needs of those close to him? The only explanation offered by his family, who took the unusual reading in stride, was that at some level of his being Cayce was joined to the girl through her mother, who was close to him through her sharing in their search-and-study group. The family had seen before that the bonds of love formed invisible connections, over which aid flowed spontaneously when it was critical. If Cayce did not produce a spontaneous reading needed for someone close to him, he might instead dream of the person's need, and the answer to it. His own readings had said that everyone keeps track of his loved ones, below the surface, and receives helpful warnings or alertings in dreams or hunches.

Through his medical and psychological readings, Cayce had always been involved in some aspect of healing. This had been the central force of his work since it began years ago, in the office of a physician named Al Layne who had used him for diagnosis of cases under hypnosis. While the final purpose of his work might be felt by Cayce to be something like arousing people to a memory of their true identity as souls before God, as his dreams showed, his means had most often been the relieving of pain. Over the years he had been asked for readings on all sorts of physical suffering; each day was marked for him by the hope of helping someone's hurt. It was the focus which Cayce felt kept his feet on the ground, kept his purposes good, and enabled him to handle temptations to notoriety or wealth. Far back in his boyhood, when his unusual experiences first began at age thirteen and he found he could know the content of books by sleeping on them, he had first prayed to be of use like those he had been studying in the Bible—and "especially to children." He had then received an assurance that became the touchstone of his life, a promise that he could help people with their pain.

Yet his abilities in healing were sharply limited. He could diagnose, he could inspect like an x-ray to secure needed medical facts. He could present an entire medical history, including injuries long forgotten by a patient, and he could describe symptoms exactly as they felt to the sick person. He could explain an ailment and its development, step by step, in exact medical terms for an attending physician, if need be. And he could, through his readings, prescribe a complete regimen of treatment, seeming to draw on every major type of resource for healing: drugs, surgery, electrotherapy, diet, exercise, hydrotherapy, manipulative therapy, hypnotherapy, psycho therapy, serums and vaccines, and more. When asked by the proper person, he found that his source was able to describe microorganisms as they appeared under magnification by a microscope, could point to where researchers should seek a new cure for a dreaded disease, could report on cures as swiftly as they were developed anywhere in the medical world, and could lay out a complete theory of physiology. Yet the point at which Edgar Cayce's participation in healing stopped was the actual exchange of energy in what is often called "spiritual healing" or "prayer healing."

Others had to carry out the medical instructions of the readings. And if someone was called upon to aid another's healing by "the laying on of hands," or by round-the-clock prayer, it might have to be someone other than Edgar Cayce. He felt that he was not completely without such ability, and joined his prayers with others in his little group for healing prayer. But beyond that his psychic ability to engage in direct healing was limited.

To be sure, he often noted that some energy of his appeared to reach out helpfully to others. He could feel it when he counseled friends and strangers in his study, and could even see the changes in their auras. He could feel it when he spoke with all his heart to a lecture audience, and sensed their warm response coming back to him. And he could see for himself that his love and care made a difference, when a spontaneous reading like the one for the college girl initiated the healing which someone else would finish.

By his sharing in the events of healing, through his voluntary and involuntary psychic abilities, Cayce was touching a stream of claims of healings as old as the family of man. From every ancient culture, from every primitive culture, have come reports that certain individuals could contribute a special force to aid the recovery of others from disability of body and mind. Some did it by virtue of their office, as was the case with the supposed healing powers of "the emperor's touch" in the days of Rome, or the healing aid of anointed priests in Greece, Egypt, and elsewhere. Others made their contribution as a personal gift, perhaps from a vision such as that made famous at Lourdes, or from biographical developments of figures such as Ambrose Worall, who found their endowment thrust upon them as Cayce had his. The Biblical record offered evidence of both types, from the admonition for elders to pray for the sick person and lay their hands on his head, to the startling stories of healing that followed every step of the ministry of Jesus and appeared in the work of his apostles and followers.

What have modern investigators discovered about the question of paranormal ability to affect healing? The subject turns out to be immensely difficult for research. Because nobody yet clearly understands more than broad outlines of how the mind affects the body, all the processes of psychotherapy must be weighed in the search. Dramatic results obtained by hypnosis require that every form of suggestion be considered. Work with LSD and other chemicals affecting consciousness suggests that even small amounts of trigger chemicals or hormones may have large effects, if the individual is properly prepared in his attitudes, and is helped in a constructive and appealing setting. More promising than working with sick individuals, for careful research purposes, have been attempts to influence the behavior of bacteria, or to affect the growth of plants, because the range of variables to study is more limited than in a walking, talking, groaning patient. Yet this research effort to catch specific psychokinetic forces of the mind appears to have its own limitations; for the energies of love—whatever these may be—are likely to be mobilized and released differently toward plants than they are towards humans.

Interest in healing through some form of prayer activity appears to be growing, both in those churches which allow intense emotion in worship and suspend a certain amount of learned doubt, and in the traditional churches of the religious establishment in both the U.S. and Europe. In groups such as the Order of St. Luke and Spiritual Frontiers Fellowship, the interest of clergymen in healing has served as an ecumenical overpass across historic sectarian barriers. Around the world, comparable interests in religious dimensions of healing, especially through prayer, periodically come to the surface in Hassidic Judaism, in Sufi piety, in Bhakti Hinduism. But interest and stable knowledge are not the same, and the day of quality research on such healing seems yet far off.

Especially during the later years of Cayce's work, individuals sought readings on the processes of indirect healing, or healing with nonmedical energies. A group to study and conduct healing was formed as the result of a dream vision, and this group sought and received a long series of technical readings of the processes in healing. Consistently, the Cayce source affirmed that aid could be brought to the normal processes of healing by the resources in prayer and meditation, especially of a group. This aid was not designated as more "spiritual" in God's eyes than the work of a physician, and no encouragement was given to ignore sound medical practice and counsel—the very business in which most of Cayce's readings were engaged. Yet those who sought to understand nonmedical healing through prayer were told that definite energies and laws were involved, and that there would be times when such aid would be critical in the recovery of a suffering person.

Not every ill person would get well through paranormal healing. Some would die, and that would be their healing, as they came into a state of mind and body where they could enter death without fear. Others would only be helped to face some point within themselves where the distresses of mind and body originated—such as resentment which affected the respiratory system, or anger which affected the liver or stomach, or fear which constricted circulation to the limbs. At that point the individual would have to make his own choices, take hold of his own healing, and even God would not take this privilege from him. But always it would be found helpful to surround those in pain with the force which flowed out in honest prayer. The insights and decisions of the sick might be better reached against a prayer background, and at times the very life in the cells would respond where conscious thought could not.

An interest in healing which involved psychic and prayer energies has persisted over the decades among those informed of the Cayce ideas. Seekers after gifts of healing have fasted, meditated, joined hands, tried different times of day and night for intercession, followed the guidance of dreams on how to pray, created a healing field of force through group meditation, kept prayer lists, and tried to correlate beneficial medical procedures with nonmedical procedures. Results have been promising enough to keep the interest alive and growing, especially an interest in the Cayce theory of kundalini and "spiritual centers." Yet it has also become clear that many who seek to affect healing do so as a substitute for productive living in some other areas of their lives. Divorced persons and business failures may sometimes nominate themselves for special talents in healing, without first undertaking the discipline of bringing their own lives of loving and work into order. But the experience of suffering has proven no disqualification to healing, for it may sensitize an individual to the point of his choosing the relief of others' pain as an ideal, and out of this ideal talents in healing may grow. Whatever else appears to be critical to the development of effective healing gifts, and meditation would surely be high on the list of relevant factors, the simple matter of caring would seem to some of these seekers to be basic. There has been no sign of a technique which could by-pass real concern for the ill. Healing may rest on loving, as it appeared to do in Cayce's aid to the college girl, and appears to do in effective groups of Alcoholics Anonymous, not to mention groups studying *A Search For God*.

Loving in Creativity

If asked to name the elements of fully human creativity, many would begin by naming loving. Yet the Cayce trance source placed this subject twelfth and last in the first volume of *A Search For God,* in a chapter simply entitled, "Love." Only after prosaic beginnings in cooperation, self-study, and other disciplines, accompanied by prayer and meditation and growth in patience and sacrifice, would the full topic of love be taken up. By that time no mere attraction, nor vague good will, nor habitual association, nor mutual exploitation, would pass unexamined as love.

Approaching love as a precondition for effective psychic function, and especially for healing, would seem strange only if psychic ability is viewed on a mechanical model. If ESP and PK are merely the response of certain stimulated organs, rather than the matching of complex body-mental states with complex outer events through intermediary "forces," then asking about love would be as irrelevant for psychic ability as for asking how a finger perceives or radiates heat. If psychokinesis in particular is merely the focusing of a beam of invisible energy, as one might concentrate sun rays with a magnifying glass, instead of a complex triggering and releasing of healing energies by a strengthening of existent fields of force, then asking about love in healing would be as irrelevant as for asking how an arm pushes. But healing may prove in fact to involve the synchronizing of fields, not only the fields of the healer and the healed, but fields of a divine force and at times of cooperating agents both living and dead. If all these centers of being are involved in healing, then asking about the loving quality of their relationship may be highly pertinent.

Some of the most striking ESP research has shown that people in mutual bonds of affection and respect may make the ideal participants in experiments, even though they are not acting as sender and receiver. Experiments suggest that the presence of a loved schoolteacher acts as some sort of catalyst for the results of certain children on tests, and it is possible that the widely noted differences in results achieved by different ESP experimenters may also be traced to their capacity for genuine mutuality with subjects.

In many fields of creativity the question of the quality of bonds among participants holds the central attention of investigators. Why does the painter fail to transcend mere technical competence so long as his love for his teacher is idolatrous love, rather than the regard which frees him to use his own talents as his master used his? Certainly the love needed for a symphony conductor to wring the most from the performers before him is more than sentimental identification; conductors often have to be fierce, and to struggle with musicians to bring forth a creation worthy of their talents. Leadership studies circle around the question of the kind of regard and support which constitute effective, activated love, breeding confidence among participants and trust in their own talents, whether the leader be a football coach, master of a ship, a political reformer, or a salesman. Each leader must find some way to exert upon others the full force of his energy and talents and imagination, so that the others respond from their own creativity rather than with simple conformity or rebellion.

When the place of love is examined in the creative problem-solving of marriage and child rearing, the problem grows more difficult to study. Here talent and position count little and people must find the way to bring out the best in each other without benefit of spotlights and cheering. Battles must often be fought over breakfast tables or in the dead of night, if the divorce court and the juvenile court are to be avoided. Beyond the emotion in loving, beyond the cherished pairings and groupings, beyond the loyalties and identifications, there may lie a fundamental stance which unlocks all sorts of creativity. Martin Buber has suggested such an approach in his postulation of "I-thou" relations as over against "I-it" relations, in man's dealings with nature and with created forms, just as in man's dealing with his fellow man.

Taking up the question of loving, then, the Cayce source addressed a question central to viewing man as co-creator with God and his fellows. In so doing, the trance source grappled with religious questions centuries old, as men have tried to find what is the "apt force" (Gerald Heard's phrase) which they might bring to bear on one another and even on nonhuman creation. It is the question behind the Confucian ideal of uprightness and gentlemanliness, the question in the ecstasies of devotional mystics of India and medieval Catholicism, the question of whole-souled answering to the divine call in Judaism, the question of respect for orderly becoming in Apollonian Greek faith, the question of compassion for all sentient beings in Northern Buddhism, and the question of life-defining totem bonds of African primitives. How can man stand with his brother, so that life will flow between them, spilling over into their works and even into the Nature which supports them?

The Cayce information described love as "the healing, cleansing, blessing force." It was not a social invention, a convenience of relationships, but first of all an attribute of the soul. Indeed it was a force so truly of God that the Cayce source could say of Genesis, "the earth looked good to Love" at creation. As a soul attribute, love was that which enabled humans to "give without asking in return," just as God gives, "pressed down and overflowing" in the vessels of His love.

Such love was not merely emotion, nor interest, nor attachment, but a vital force, capable of changing the energy fields in oneself and other people by "raising the vibrations." It acted as directly as a musical instrument might set another instrument to resounding. This was why group fields of love, whether families or work groups or study groups or even cities and nations, had such potential for good; they could build up a group field of the force of love which was as great as the musical force of a symphony orchestra in perfect tune and rhythm. Those who sought to make love an active, helpful force in the lives of others, for their healing, strengthening, or transformation, would not reach their ends by solitary efforts alone, although solitude had its place.

Yet love was not mass enthusiasm, either, for one had to overcome in himself whatever he sought to help another overcome, or he would simply broadcast his troubles to another by native ESP, under the name of love. The Cayce source was firm that healing of every sort, physical and mental, social and financial, spiritual and aesthetic, had to come about in the one who sought to be helpful, before it could reach its maximum force for another. One had to choose his own Creative Forces before he would find the key to unlocking these in others. One who sought in love to free others from inward terrors had to work through his own panics; one who sought in love to help another fight disease had to overcome his own indulgences that lowered disease resistance. Love would be found a powerful force, bringing psychic energies and other energies to bear where they were needed. But love was no magical substitute for growth.

Truly loving others would be linked with one's love and regard for his own soul, as a gift from God. While "no man should love himself more highly than he ought," it was also true that false self-effacement or self-belittling or self-condemnation was crippling to the healing and blessing force of love. One had to learn to give thanks for his own growth and accomplishments as readily as for the fruits of the spirit in the life of another: "Thou shalt love thy neighbor as *thyself.*"

But the key to loving of both the neighbor and the self was not to be found in praise or favors. It was right where Jesus had put it, in the loving of God with all one's mind, heart, strength, and soul. Because love sprang as a force and pattern-giving element from the very Godhead, it was there that man must turn to learn how to love. In the view of the Cayce source, this meant "putting on the mind of Christ," turning the whole psyche by sustained choice to attune itself to the ideal found in Christ. Along the channel formed by such attunement, as surely as radio signals on a given frequency, there would come assurances, quickenings, promptings, and even strength and energy, to make love real in one situation after another.

The mind was not to be left out, and there were laws of love, such as forgiveness, just as there were laws of everything else in creation; these laws were to be studied, and learned by experimentation and practice. But love was that which could make law effective, make it helpful, make it relevant. Even karma, that seemingly impersonal process of visiting upon an individual exactly what he needed to round out his understanding of what he had chosen by actions, would be found to reach its maximum effectiveness in love. For "love is law," said the Cayce source, as "law is love." The orderliness of the universe was God's loving gift to man. Part of that very orderliness was that all law moved and swayed under the force of love, becoming man's living helper as the impersonal and threatening sea could bear up a craft, properly sailed.

Some souls mistakenly turned away from love toward an artificial righteousness, in the fear that the Creator did not mean for men to be happy. But, said the Cayce source, happiness was the very intention of God towards men, as seen in the use of the word "blessed" by Jesus. Even "blissful" would not be too strong, as one would find if he set about a life of love focused on others. The joy and peace that would follow would not arrive overnight, but as they came, they would be known by the person as transcending his other pleasures. There would be failures; there would be times when love did not reach the one intended; there would be crosses. But even as men knew in their hearts that love given in families was never lost, neither was love lost which was given anywhere in the family of God, to one's brother. As the Cayce readings often reminded, "A cup of cold water given in His name will in no wise be forgotten"; this was meant literally enough to indicate that one could risk loving when the cup might be rejected. The love intended was not an ethic of fairness, but of God-sized risks that the other man's soul would respond; such effort was never wasted, though it might take eons to bear full fruit, for fields invisible to senses were built up by true loving, and the very shape of "thought forms" was permanently changed. The concept of "nation" would mean one thing as a thought form in one age, and something else in the next generation, if love were brought to bear as the light of the nation's art.

There was a treasure to be found and shared in love, according to the Cayce source, which would not easily be found elsewhere. In the love of man for man, one might discover no less than a clue of the love of God for man. To be sure, God's love was there in Nature, as one would find if he sought it. But in becoming a "channel of blessings" each day, one was opening the way for others to find the pearl of great price: the One not far off, and ever ready to respond, even to be known. So the ways of love could afford to be simple, "just being kind," just turning aside to laugh and weep and work with others in the daily walk. Love was like light, ready to slip through the tiniest crack in the day's affairs, and the little things were its home. Celebrated and chosen in the washing of dishes, in the "preferring of another" in auto traffic, in playing with a neighbor's children, in the extra time given to a customer, in a chantey lifted among flagging spirits, love would one day be found strong enough for the test of difficult forgiveness. For "offenses must need come" in the human situation, but "woe unto him who brings them." The man who sought to love, to let his light shine in the sunlight of a larger purpose where his light might hardly be noticed, would find he could forgive, and forgive— seventy times seven. Not because he was wise, although wisdom might make forgiving easier. Not because he was without flaw, "for all have sinned and fallen short of the glory of God." But because forgiveness, the healing of doubt and fear and condemnation, was God's way, and the way in which his own soul sang.

Honestly sought, as one might dig a well in a dry land, the flow of love would be found within any man, for it was there as a fact from his own soul. Nothing could separate him from it, as the Cayce source often reminded in repeating a telling passage of Paul's in Romans: nothing of principalities or powers, of heights and depths, of life or death—nothing except one's self. Only the choice to turn away, to gamble on lesser creativity rather than the greater, would eclipse the inner sun of love. Man could choose to build barns and heap up a harvest, he could choose to build kingdoms of vassals, he could choose harems for his appetites, he could choose to withdraw from responsibility and to drift. Yet death would quietly end each such solution, and set the soul free for a further journey, even as the merciful karmic deaths of ambitions or property or prowess would allow fresh beginnings in this life. The love of God was never far away, ready to help a man who sought to make it his own; it could be found in dreams, it could be found in prayer and meditation, it could be found in dancing and play. It was the birthright of the soul.

What was involved in learning to love, training to carry the golden flow? "Let us consecrate ourselves," began one reading. Not tricks of remembering the names of others, no flattery, no gimmicks of manners. He who set out to love was setting out to adore and glorify God, for that was exactly Who dwelt in his brother, however hidden or covered over. The hearty confessions, the purifying of body and mind, the shared dedications which men reserved for their altars were no less proper for the approach to one's fellows, in the little things of daily life. Not in pomp, but in sincerity; not in rite, but in responsiveness; not in dogma, but in delight at the very being of another—these were how every man was a priest to his brother.

Prayer and meditation could keep love's channel open through attunement, while encouraging others and "magnifying the virtues, minimizing the faults" would increase the stream in service, as a spring feeds a river. It was, said the Cayce source, time to begin. For there was a sense in which the present age, despite the promises of God and the way shown by the Elder Brother, was still "a darkened and unregenerate world," in which "the laborers are few." The need and opportunity were great, for the tribulations foretold by Christ of old were coming upon man, and the end of an epoch upon earth was being shaped. As love was a reality, a living force, so great was the harm from its absence, the darkness from its eclipse. There was in very fact, in the hearts and experience of men, an "outer darkness" from which even God would not save them forever. So human loneliness and bigotry, sickness and ignorance, hunger and torture were the business of every man who saw them—"today, now."

Loving and Healing

In the uncertain state of knowledge about healing through prayer, can it be claimed that love may be decisive in freeing the flow of healing?

A psychic who had known much suffering stood looking down at the swollen legs of an old woman. The woman was merry and vital, despite her stumplike legs; she had just served a bountiful meal to the writer and others visiting her home in the country, where the psychic had gone for a rest.

He was weary inside. His efforts to find a niche in modern American society had never quite borne fruit. Two marriages had failed. Men of prominence in business, education, government, entertainment, and the military had come and gone in his life, each promising him aid in developing a foundation for research on abilities such as his, and each in time disappearing. Perhaps the fault was his. Why try any longer? Perhaps he should limit himself to stage and television appearances, and give readings now and then for the rich. He stared at the legs of the old woman seated in front of him, and thought his own dark thoughts of how unlovely life can be.

But the old woman teased him. She bantered with him, surprised him, badgered him, pleased him. She was as sly as a child, as supportive as a nurse.

The fullness of woman was in her, and she knew it. Cripple or not, she had known how to love and fight with husband, sons, employees; many a man had found he could not hide from her, when she set out to break his dark moods.

The psychic laughed, laughed full and free. Then he looked again at his hostess, and something moved within him. "I just said to myself," he told the writer later, "I like that old woman, I really do." His heart went out to her, and he felt a prompting he had not felt for years. "I can fix your legs for you," he said. She joked, "What is wrong with my legs? Don't you appreciate my legs?" But she could see he was as serious as he was suddenly free and happy.

He stripped off his coat and bent over her. Others in the room gathered, and speech stopped. All had been stimulated by his messages, his readings, his counsel, at one time or another. But nobody there had seen him attempt a healing; he had always said it was too hard, took too much out of him. Now he was evidently praying. Then he began to move his hands. He never touched the legs, which were propped on a footstool; he only ran his hands a few inches above them, in the air, as though stroking away the swollen tissue.

Those who watched expected that the woman might feel a bit better, for she had mentioned how her legs, swollen to unsightly shape for years, often pained her. But nobody was prepared for what happened. For stroke by stroke, the swelling was decreased. It was unbelievable, and the writer remembers saying to himself that it couldn't be done, that it was some sort of animated cartoon he was watching rather than real life.

The psychic was perspiring heavily; the back of his shirt was wet. His face was firm and concentrated, but not contorted; he seemed just deeply at work at a job he knew he could do. In a few moments he had finished, and the woman looked at her legs unbelievingly. They were completely normal and shapely. She tried to joke, but she was weak with amazement. The psychic told her exactly how she would have to sleep at night, to keep the legs from swelling again, and what treatments she would have to follow for about two months, to permanently improve the limbs. Then he paced the floor to "cool off," as he often had to do after intense concentration.

Was it hypnosis, the woman's body obeying her own mind under the power of suggestion from the psychic? Was it a force actually going out from the fingers and hands of the psychic, to touch and change the very cells of those legs? Or had the real force been there in the laughter and love in the old woman, which unlocked the heart and soul of the psychic, and let his own love come through in a burst of helpful energy? At least one who was there thought of the love and trust once in the heart of a sick woman, who only wanted to "touch the hem of the garment" of Jesus in a crowd. But he had felt a force go from him, and he had sought her out, even in the crowd. Was he, too, refreshed by the love she gave him, that day long ago?

EDGAR CAYCE

On Mysteries of the Mind

By Henry Reed
Under the Editorship of
Charles Thomas Cayce

CONTENTS

PART III

Hidden Powers of the Mind

Introduction

LOOKING INTO THE MIRROR OF THE MIND

IT DOESN'T SEEM possible, but it happened. It made electron microscopes, radio telescopes, radioactive carbon dating, and CAT scans, not to mention television and the telephone, seem trivial and unimportant or unnecessary. What kind of sophisticated electronic equipment do you think you would need to read a book that is sitting unopened in a distant library, to tell your friend what is happening to the atoms of his or her body, or to remember what happened thousands and thousands of years ago? Simply by lying down, relaxing, closing his eyes, and transporting himself from the limits of consciousness, Edgar Cayce was able to enter a superconscious trance state that made all these marvels of modern technology seem clumsy.

As a child, Cayce could sleep on a textbook and awaken with a photographic memory of its contents, without once having opened the book. As he grew and developed his gifts, he could diagnose the illnesses of people he had never met and otherwise knew nothing about. Moreover, his diagnoses included minute facts about the workings of the body that would take scientific medicine years to verify. With his farseeing eye he could locate an obscure medicine on the dusty stockroom shelf of a faraway pharmacy so that it could be located and used to help someone. His memory traveled far back into time and revealed the personal experiences of those who walked the planet before our recorded history. He went even further back and described the formation of the earth.

From this state of infinite knowing, Cayce claimed that he was doing nothing special, but something we could do ourselves. Although astonishing beyond belief, he indicated that all knowledge, that's right, *all,* is within. You and I already have within ourselves every bit of knowledge that has ever been known, as well as the seeds of all that will ever be known. It is all within, inside our own mind.

The mind is as infinite as the universe. No matter how far into outer space you can send your imagination, you still have not reached the boundaries of the mind. Nothing except creation itself is as unbounded and infinite as the mind—your mind, my mind. Explore it and you will see.

Before we can even catch our breath at the thought of an infinite mind, Cayce delivers another surprise. The mind not only is receptive, but active. It is creative. It creates the world that we live in. It gives form to the plants and animals, the rocks and the ocean, our bodies and our lives. Our minds create our experiences, our reality. The mind has an infinite capacity to know the world, because the mind created it.

How can this invisible, untouchable, seemingly unknowable thing we call the mind have such powers? How can it be? And if it is so, what does that mean for the way we live our lives? What are we to do with this knowledge? If it is so, it is so profound and fundamental a reality that it must completely upset all the ways we normally think of living or approach having a life. If there is something inside of you and I that is as immense as the universe and more powerful than any atomic bomb yet invented, how in the world could it possibly fit within our bodies? How does it get scrunched up inside our small skulls and how does it get out to do its magic?

Claiming these mysterious powers of the mind must be some form of poetic statement, not a literal truth. It couldn't be literally true.

But it is. And it has practical implications. As practical as staying healthy or finding a job. As practical as quitting smoking or getting along with people. It also has its spiritual side. Nothing is as essentially spiritual as learning to love. Nothing is as important to the development of our spiritual awareness as investing the gift of life with our own constructive efforts to nurture it. Thus the range of the implications runs the spectrum from the mundane to the spiritual. All this is contained within the mysteries of the mind.

Cayce's ideas about the mind, as farfetched as they may seem at first glance, have been receiving increased attention in recent years, as he predicted. As the twentieth century comes to a close, the many pressures and threats to our survival on this planet have been counterbalanced by much research and new thinking about the nature of mind and its role in our future. Research in many laboratories has verified many of Cayce's ideas. Theorists have developed perspectives on the mind that are similar to Cayce's view.

This book is the result of this scientific progress, for it is now possible to share the secrets revealed by Cayce in a way that is supported by scientific research.

Not only does scientific research now support the creative powers of the mind, but also hundreds of books, videotapes, audiocassettes, workshops, and seminars teach these principles. Many of the ideas first proposed by Cayce are now almost mainstream. Who hasn't heard of the power of positive thinking? Creative visualization and subliminal suggestion are now common items on the marketplace. The healing power of optimism and humor is routinely discussed on TV talk shows. Is there anything newsworthy left among the legacy of the Cayce readings?

Cayce continues to provide us with a new look at the mysteries of the mind. His body of work remains the only single source that provides a complete model, ranging from the spiritual to the atom, based on a few encompassing principles. Cayce was a pioneer in explaining matters of the spirit in psychological terms. The Eastern traditions have had their Yoga psychology for thousands of years, but Westerners have lacked an approach to the mystical side of life that was simultaneously compatible with their scientific worldview. Cayce's readings provided that approach. His was an integrated view, from the consciousness of the individual cell in the body to the holographic reality of the human soul. His was a practical view, providing the steps to take, suggesting techniques to use. His was what scientists call an "empirical" approach, meaning an emphasis on the facts of experience. He didn't ask that anyone believe what he said; in fact, he discouraged it. He didn't want your belief; he wanted you to experiment, to test his ideas in practice. Only what you have made your own through personal application is of any value. As I prepared for this book, looking through my files of research reports for experimental evidence corresponding to his ideas, browsing through libraries and bookstores stocked with books on the powers of the mind, and reflected on my own experiences developing my personal skills in this area, I was surprised to discover just how many important ideas and perspectives the Cayce material adds to the current culture of ideas on the powers of the mind.

A popular item on the market today, for example, is "subliminal suggestion" self-help tapes. Cayce was an advocate of the use of suggestion. He would applaud the technology of the cassette player that allows us to listen to suggestions that we ourselves design. He also recognized the power of subliminal suggestion. He saw it as a more active influence in our lives than we might suspect. As you learn more about our vulnerability to psychic influence, you will appreciate his surprising warning about the use of such methods as subliminal suggestion.

It is popular today to speak of "creating your own reality." That philosophy, as old as the first mystical experience, has taken on heroic proportions with the advent of our modern psychological technology of human growth. Yet it brings to the contemporary person its own set of new problems. Does it have any limits? Can I have anything I want? Does that mean I am to blame for my troubles? Those of us susceptible to the pitfalls of the "me generation" find creating our own reality leading us into a hall of mirrors. Everywhere we look, all we see is ourselves. Cayce's view adds a critical ingredient to the creation of reality formula that leads us out of the moral predicament of egocentricity without diminishing the incredible magic of our creative power. His perspective on this philosophy helps us get beyond ourselves, but without our leaving ourselves behind.

Self-help psychology has been with us for several decades. With the advent of the New Age perspective, however, the promises that are offered have become more optimistic and all-encompassing than ever before. For someone who doubts, or doesn't feel quite up to such heroic changes and self-improvement, these upbeat philosophies can be somewhat threatening. It's easy to feel that you'll never be enthusiastic enough, good enough, skillful enough to pull off such miracles of self-transformation yourself. Edgar Cayce's perspective, however, is intended to help even the most determined of self-doubters.

Although his psychic perspective reaches far into the heavens and deep within the soul, it is also grounded in the day-to-day rhythm of our emotional lives and the limitations we find there. While he suggests we can fly to the moon, he also points out the value of taking a simple step forward in our earthly life. Although he wants us to become aware of all the mysteries that the mind has to offer, he also assures us that there is nothing more important than loving those around us. While he explains how the powers of the mind can be used to extricate us from even the most impossible of situations, he realizes that all we might be able to manage for the moment is to slightly loosen the grip of such circumstances. Peace of mind, no matter how momentary, is of great value.

Above all, Cayce encourages us to make a start. Over and over he repeats this promise: If you will just do one thing that you know to do, if you will take but one step forward, something will happen to make the second step easier. There is a power within you greater than you realize. It awaits you, now.

CHAPTER 1

IT'S ALL IN THE MIND

For the time has arisen in the earth when men—everywhere—seek to know more of the mysteries of the mind, the soul, the soul's mind.

Edgar Cayce 254-52

WHAT DOES THE expression "It's all in your mind" mean to you? Ask many people and the answer is something like "Imaginary . . . not real." Do they think the mind is imaginary or not real? Not exactly. Many people *do* think that reality is one thing and the mind is another. As, for example, when the mind sometimes misses the mark and imagines something as real when it is not. Isn't that a fair description of the usual meaning of "It's all in the mind"?

Yet there is a totally different meaning to this maxim. This other meaning begins to appear when the mind is explored for its mysteries. The phrase becomes a teaser, almost a riddle. It becomes an invitation for you to discover a way to take command of your life and "have it your way." Let's see how that happens.

Common Mysteries

The mind usually seems more invisible than mysterious. Most of the time we hardly notice it's there. But there are those moments when we become aware of the mind. Sometimes strange events bring it to our attention. I'm sure you've experienced some of these very common little mysteries.

For example, you have been driving along the highway, returning home. As you approach your neighborhood, you realize that for the past several minutes your mind has been elsewhere. Daydreaming, thinking about things, your mind has been on anything but paying attention to the road. You wonder how you managed to watch out for cars, follow traffic signals, and make the right turns when you weren't even "there." There are a number of things we do without paying attention.

Suppose you are working on a problem and it has you stumped. Maybe it's about how to rearrange the furniture in your house, or it could be about designing a new procedure at the office. Nothing that you can come up with seems quite right. One day, in the middle of a conversation, or while out shopping or taking a walk, an idea suddenly comes to you like a bolt out of the blue. A perfect solution to the problem is simply handed to you, without apparent effort. You weren't even thinking about it. Perhaps there is another part of the mind outside of your awareness.

For no apparent reason, for example, you find yourself thinking of an old friend. Later that day, you receive a letter from that person, or the person calls you up on the phone. It was almost as if you were in mental contact or somehow knew the person was going to call. Perhaps the mind can reach out and touch someone without telephoning long-distance.

Another time you are sitting with someone having a cup of coffee when a remark is made that triggers a strange sensation. You have this odd feeling that you are reliving some experience from the past. You seem to know what the person will say next. It's as if you are repeating a scene you have lived before, even though you cannot remember when it was. Does the mind also reach beyond time?

You had a dream. Dreams seem real at the time. As a child, you may have wondered how it was possible to be fooled that way. As an adult you may be used to ignoring dreams, and would have forgotten about this dream. Maybe it was of a seemingly ordinary, everyday event, or it may have been an upsetting dream about something bad happening. A few days later, perhaps a few weeks later, the dream comes true. Many of the details of the event are just like what was in the dream. Was the dream real? Can the mind determine what is real?

We've all been in lousy moods. You know what it's like to be kind of depressed, a bit lonely. You've felt sorry for yourself sometimes because of your problems. At times they seem overpowering and unbeatable. You've probably also had those occasions where somehow you find yourself feeling better about things even though your problems haven't changed. Maybe you encountered someone who was in a really bad way and you reached out to the person and provided some cheer. Maybe you went to a comedy movie and laughed until your sides hurt. Maybe it was something else. But later you realize that your own mood has lifted. Your problems are still there, but somehow you feel better anyway. You look at the same facts with a different slant and you see things differently. It's almost as if you've changed your mind about what's real.

All these experiences are actually quite common. Some may seem easy to explain; others are perhaps more puzzling. Yet they all suggest that the mind is not as simple as it seems.

We take the mind for granted. We assume it is like a mirror that reflects the reality in front of us. It seems it is fed information by our five senses. We use the mind to think. Our thoughts feel as if we are talking to ourself silently. But where is the mind? Can you point to it or touch it? Is it in the brain? If so, then how do minds that are contained within skulls "meet" during those moments of intimate conversation? Just what kind of "stuff" is the mind? These kinds of questions show that the mind is actually the most puzzling mystery human beings have ever encountered.

Forgetting: Accidental or On Purpose?

Memory is one of those things that sometimes make us realize what a puzzle the mind can be.

How often do we make a promise to ourselves but fail to keep it? How many good intentions are "forgotten"? There are many things that we know would be good for us, that would increase the quality of our lives—relaxing, spending time with the family, perhaps taking up a new sport, developing different dietary habits. Yet we have trouble remembering to do them. There just isn't enough time in the day, and we "forget" those good things.

How often we find ourselves in a spot when we want to remember something but can't. Ever misplaced something and tried to remember where you put it? How is it that we have memories that we cannot recall when we want to, like a person's name, but which sometimes pop up all on their own? Apparently, the memories are there. Sometimes they just appear out of nowhere, clear as a bell. Often, however, they are unavailable to us. Yet they can still have their effect.

A colleague of mine once remarked that there is a strange irony to memory. On the one hand, our childhood experiences exert a powerful effect upon our adult personality and how we view the world. Yet the memories of these experiences are almost impossible to bring to the surface. How can something that we cannot remember have such a strong influence?

Forgetting can be such a problem that it is tempting to wish for a perfect memory. Yet our memory is already more perfect than you might suspect. And forgetting can play a useful role for us. What would memory be without forgetting? Who would want a pencil without an eraser? There are some things we want to forget. If you could not forget for the moment all the things that you *should* be doing right now, how could you concentrate on reading this book? Forgetting can be as important as remembering. It would be ideal to have both of these under our control, rather than our being at their mercy.

Learning how to forget can perhaps be as useful as learning to remember. Take a clue from a familiar, eccentric hero: the world's original detective, Sherlock Holmes.

He had just learned what he considered to be a piece of trivia. Although he was a gold mine of information, there were many surprising gaps in his knowledge. Dr. Watson had just informed him, in *A Study in Scarlet,* that the earth and several other planets with it revolved around the sun. Holmes replied that having heard this little tidbit, he would now promptly forget it— on purpose. He explained to the startled Watson that useless facts take up as much room in one's memory as does important information. By deliberately forgetting the trivial, he could more easily concentrate on the important.

Sherlock Holmes knew that the controlled use of his mind was the key to his success. He had learned that just as the mind can be trained to remember desired facts, so also can it be trained to forget.

Do you know Holmes's secret? Do you know how to forget on purpose? Can you do it at will? Can you control the process of forgetting and use it to your advantage? Suppose I tell you that the capital of Bolivia is La Paz. Now, can you forget it, the way Sherlock could? How would you go about it? Try it. Have you forgotten it yet? What is the capital of Bolivia? It's much like the old challenge to not think of the eye of an elephant. Once it's mentioned, you immediately see it in your mind. How can you get something out of your mind when you want to?

I studied this problem, as a graduate student of psychology at UCLA, and it proved to be my introduction to the mysteries of the mind. My mentor, Bernard Weiner, had discovered that people can forget on purpose. He was trying to figure out how they did it. He would give a person a word to read on a screen and then tell them to forget it. Here's a word for you to read:

Table

Now I want you to forget it. While you try, I'll continue describing our research as you read on.

If we gave people a word to forget and asked them to simply sit there and try to forget it, they just couldn't do it. However, after they saw the word to forget, if we then gave them additional material to read, they were more successful at forgetting the original word.

What about the word you just read a moment ago—do you still remember it, or have you been able to forget it while reading this paragraph? In our experiments, the chances were about fifty-fifty that a person would have successfully forgotten the word.

How do people forget on purpose? How did you go about trying to forget? It seems that the most natural approach is to try to think of something else. Did you, for example, try to concentrate on the reading, hoping that meanwhile the word would disappear from your mind? Trying to think of one thing in order to press something else out of the mind seems to be the way we try to forget.

Without doubting Sherlock's genius, we should rephrase his method by stating that in order to forget the trivial, *concentrate on the essential!* Focus on what you want your mind to retain, and what you want to forget will pass away. We will encounter many variations on this principle throughout this book.

Sherlock Holmes wanted to forget in order to keep his mind uncluttered. We often have other reasons to forget something. We might wish to forget a bad habit. Wouldn't it be nice to learn how to "forget to smoke" rather than having to struggle with willpower to fight the urge to smoke? What bad habit do you wish you could simply forget?

Sometimes we are bothered by something we can't do anything about. It would be pleasant to simply be able to forget about it.

In the book *The Little Prince,* the young hero visits several different planets. On one he encounters a drunkard sitting at a table with his bottle and cup. He asks the fellow why he drinks so much. The red-nosed fellow says he drinks to forget! How many times have we all used alcohol, drugs, or other forms of escape, such as shopping or watching TV, to forget our worries? By focusing on something else, we hope that our troubles will disappear from our mind. We all use a rough approximation of Sherlock's secret. We can learn to perfect this method to our better advantage.

Come On, Get Happy!

Peace of mind is perhaps one of life's most elusive treasures. Those who have found it value it highly. Most of us wish for it, but the pressures and uncertainties of modern life make it difficult. It is hard to ignore our problems. Many things that we would like to forget haunt us. Yet some people find that they can forget their worries by concentrating on something else, something positive or cheerful. That's how they get happy and stay that way.

You've heard about the value of keeping a positive attitude—it's called "looking on the bright side." You've probably experimented with this strategy yourself at various times. It may seem like a pleasant suggestion—it can't hurt—but of little use in actually dealing with problem situations. Attitude, however—that certain slant of mind that determines how we view things— has proven to have tremendous power.

Consider the case of people who have been confronted with a major trauma or disaster in life. I'm talking about being held as a prisoner of war, being taken hostage by terrorists or kidnappers, getting lost on a frozen mountain-top or down inside a mine shaft, having one's home destroyed by a tornado, or having one's life ransacked by a terrible disease. The victims of such catastrophes are often never the same afterward. It's as if they also lose something on the inside as a result of the ordeal. Social scientists have studied people who have gone through such traumas and catastrophes. While some people are destroyed by the experience, others survive and rebuild their lives. What seems to make the difference between succumbing or surviving is the attitude that was adopted during the ordeal.

Those who did not survive fell victim to an attitude of helplessness. It's an understandable reaction. Control over their lives had been stolen from them. There was little that they could do about the situation. The dark side of their predicament became imprinted on their mind.

Those who survived, however, managed to adopt a different attitude. They fought the temptation to give up and looked for some way to regain some small bit of personal control. Even being able to make decisions about a trivial aspect of their situation made a difference in their mental outlook. They searched hard for some way to look upon the bright side.

The psychology of survivors proves that a mental attitude can have a definite effect on how we deal with problems. It can make the difference between being victimized by problems or learning from them how to survive, and much more.

Surviving Daily Life

Ordinary life has its own ups and downs. On good days, when things are going our way, we're on top of the world. On bad days, it's not so good. Nothing is as we would have it, and life becomes a real struggle. We certainly don't feel on top of things; they feel on top of us.

On good days, we might say, "Life couldn't be better if I designed it myself!" On bad days, life can seem like a cruel joke. The joke is on us, and we become the tragic victim of circumstances.

The difference between the good times and the bad seems to be whether or not things are going our way.

On good days, you're on a roll and everything you do turns out well. You have hunches that pan out. Coincidences occur that make the day seem designed for you. Your every wish comes true. On days like that, you get the sensation that you can actually create the kind of life you would like to live. Life is like a fun movie and you get to write the script.

On the bad days, you feel helpless and out of control. You have no choices, you are under pressure, between a rock and a hard place, more is being expected of you than you can deliver, forced to do something you would rather not, and about to lose something you value—these are the sorts of things that make life seem like a mindless machine wearing you down.

It's almost as if there are two realities, two types of life.

In one reality, we are victims, we have to take what comes and cope the best we can. Sometimes the odds are against us. The best we can do is to minimize our losses. Life is bigger than us and has us caught in its grip. Life acts and we react.

In the other reality, it seems the reverse. We act and life reacts. We get to design the day our way. We become the scriptwriter, director, and actor upon the stage of life.

Which is the true reality? It may be clear which one we prefer, but which reality is the way life really is? Is there an answer to that question? Is it just what you want to believe?

Believing in the Possible

Suppose I were to ask you to assume that believing is everything. Suppose that it does make a difference what you believe. What if you were to believe that your mind creates the world you live in, the kind of day you have and the life you live. If you believe you can, you can create a good day or a bad day and take charge of your life. You can design your life the way you want it, because the mind creates the kind of life you have. If that were true, wouldn't it be an important thing to know?

Just think, if it were really not true that life comes to us on its own terms and we have to take what comes, wouldn't it be important to know that? If it were true that we can design life to our own patterns, wouldn't you like to know that? Couldn't you use that fact to your advantage?

I know it may not seem true. It's too hard to believe. For now I would like simply to suggest that the idea is important. It certainly is worth considering. It has important implications for your life. You may not be able to believe in the possibility yet, but do not insist that it is impossible. What we believe has important consequences. I'm sure you've heard of self-fulfilling prophecies.

We know a lot about self-fulfilling prophecies. Repeated classroom research has proven, for example, that students from whom their teachers expect good work do good work, while students whom the teacher believe cannot do well usually don't. Have you ever experienced the power of having someone really believe in you? It can be a wonderful source of support. On the other hand, we can feel uncomfortable around someone who believes only in our weaknesses. It makes us feel insecure, and sometimes we find ourselves stumbling. The expectation is confirmed.

What are the limits of this power of belief? Science is just beginning to explore the outer limits of this mystery. The power of belief is actually quite stronger than you might realize.

In medical history, for example, there is the well-known story of a Mr. Wright who had terminal cancer. He believed that there was going to be a drug that would cure him. He heard that his hospital was testing the experimental drug, Krebiozen, and he became convinced that this was the drug that was going to save his life.

Mr. Wright repeatedly requested that his doctor use the drug on his case. Finally, the doctor relented and gave it to him. Unlike the experimental patients, who were showing little response to treatment by Krebiozen, Mr. Wright made a rapid recovery and his cancer went away. He left the hospital and returned to a normal life.

Then Mr. Wright read in the newspaper that Krebiozen was proving ineffective against cancer. Within days, Mr. Wright's cancer returned to its former condition.

Mr. Wright's doctor decided on an experiment and told him that they had found that the problem with the Krebiozen was that it had a short shelf life. The medicine that had been used on him was old, the doctor said, but there was a fresh batch that could now be administered. This time he was given only plain water, but it provided him an even more miraculously quick and complete cure. He left the hospital once more to resume his life.

Unfortunately, Mr. Wright later read in the newspaper that scientists had proven without a doubt that the Krebiozen was worthless. His cancer returned and he died a few days later. In his case, and in many others like his, belief held the power of life and death.

From the Imagination to Reality

Belief and expectation have a powerful effect. If the power of belief, as evidenced in the case of Mr. Wright, could be bottled and sold, it would be a wonder drug. Actually, the power has already been bottled. It is in your mind. It is contained in the imagination.

Look around you. How many things can you see that first existed in someone's imagination before they existed in physical reality? Houses, cars, and clothing, to name but a few. All these human inventions were first ideas. They came from the mind.

Have you ever been to Disneyland or Disney World? Did you ever think how the world of Disney was first an idea in the imagination of Walt Disney? He began drawing cartoons and wondered how he could bring them to life. At the time, animated cartoons were just being invented. Disney worked hard to develop the technology of that art form. He finally brought Mickey Mouse to life out of his mind. When we watch Mickey Mouse in a cartoon, the character seems real. The child in you believes him to be real. And the holographic, 3-D cartoons that can now be produced make Mickey even more real. It all originated in the imagination of Walt Disney.

Imagination, together with a positive attitude and belief or expectancy, is a powerful combination. Just think of how many inventions that make our world as wonderful as it is came from this special combination we sometimes call "visionary determination"—the light bulb, the airplane, spacecraft, and surely you can think of many more.

The imagination, in fact, is the way to direct the positive energy of belief and attitude. With the imagination, we can do things that even today, before reading this book, you would have believed impossible.

Consider the case of Garrett Porter. When he was ten years old, he was told that he had an inoperable brain tumor. Radiation therapy did little good. He was going to die.

Garrett was fortunate enough to be in Topeka, Kansas, where the Menninger Clinic is located. Pat Norris, a psychologist at the clinic, was conducting research on the role of the imagination in healing. She taught Garrett how to use his imagination, in a specially concentrated form, to direct his body to destroy the cancer cells in his brain. They worked against time, day after day.

Once or twice a day, Garrett imagined the white cells in his bloodstream eating up the cancer cells. One day Garrett announced that he could no longer find his brain tumor in his imagination. A CAT scan of his brain confirmed the information provided by his imagination—the tumor was gone. He and Dr. Norris wrote their story, *I Choose Life,* so that other people can learn how there is hope.

Garrett's story is an example of the mind's directly changing the reality of the body. The mind took control and erased the tumor. Sometimes we think that a positive attitude, looking on the bright side or imagining the possible, is only a sweetener, that it adds a spoonful of sugar to help the medicine go down but otherwise has no effects. Garrett's story shows that a positive attitude can be more than simply adding a spoonful of sugar to the medicine. It was not simply making a bad situation more tolerable. Garrett changed the reality. The tumor was gone. The mind has the ability to control the events in the body.

The stories of Mr. Wright and Garrett Porter may seem like something out of *The Twilight Zone.* They are just too impossible to be true. But they are true. And they are not the only stories. The secret powers of the mind have been verified in laboratories and clinics all over the world, and more is being discovered every day.

The Consciousness Revolution

Things haven't been the same since the sixties. Something happened back then that has changed the way we have viewed the world ever since. It was the beginning of the "consciousness revolution."

It was the era of the Vietnam war, whose horrors, frustrations, contradictions, and confusions gave birth to the term "burnout." As the end result of a chronic gridlock of stress, fatigue, and discouragement created in the face of conflicting ideals and contradictory expectations, burnout has become a familiar word in many areas of today's life. It has led to an intense reevaluation of many of our assumptions. As old solutions no longer work there has now developed a realization that "trying harder" needs to be replaced by "trying smarter." Different approaches are needed that require a new way of looking at things.

As part of the shake-up of the times, the sixties also witnessed the explosion of the psychedelic scene. The use of drugs was not what was so uniquely influential about psychedelics. People have always gotten drugged, and we've always known that it isn't healthy. What was significant was that it was psychedelic drugs that were being used. The word means "mind-manifesting." These were drugs that "turned on" the otherwise invisible mind so that it could be seen. Psychedelic drugs revealed to many people in a dramatic fashion that the mind is an important and creative reality in itself. The fortunate ones got the message quickly and then turned to other methods of exploring the mysteries of the mind. Many people graduated from marijuana, not to heroin, but to meditation.

Among them were the Beatles. As they opened a new frontier in music and a new role for it in society, we watched them go from turning on with drugs to visits with the Maharishi. In their movie *Yellow Submarine* they announce the secret that becomes a time bomb for our lives: "It's all in the mind."

Beatle fans knew what was being said. There was the suggestion of "make-believe," as the animation effects of their movie made so startlingly clear. Yet there was also the understanding that a deeper secret was being revealed—the mind is both the origin and purpose of reality. All that we seek for can be found within ourselves. The love that we long to receive from others originates from the love we grow from within our own hearts. Ancient truths, actually, but now delivered by our culture's pop heroes on the large cinema screen and across the airwaves.

Twenty some years later, Shirley MacLaine announced on her television miniseries *Out On a Limb,* "You create your own reality." It is the Beatles' statement recast in a new vocabulary. Yet of the millions of viewers who watched this program, many seemed confounded if not outraged by her remarks. For a week afterward, I heard men in the steam room, who usually discuss only sports, sweating Shirley's story out of their system. For months, Shirley became comedy material for Johnny Carson and others. Clearly she touched a nerve, even if some misunderstood her message.

Yet there were many who found her show to be but a rerun of experiences they had had themselves and of ideas they believed in. In the two decades between the Beatles and Shirley MacLaine, in laboratories around the world, reported in books by the thousands and workshops and classes galore, the consciousness revolution had sprouted, planted roots, and borne many fruits. The neuroscience of the brain, the psychology of meditation, these and many other disciplines of study were accumulating facts and proving theories that point to new ideas about the mind. The provocative statements made earlier by the Beatles and now by Shirley MacLaine were being supported.

Edgar Cayce: The "Sleeping Prophet"

It was during the sixties, when I was in one of those laboratories working on the mystery of memory, that I was introduced to the work of Edgar Cayce. I was interested in the problem of amnesia, wondering how a person could forget their own identify and life history. I had decided to explore an everyday amnesia, the forgetting of dreams, where one's nighttime experiences are forgotten by morning. Did sleep have something to do with the forgetting? Could hypnosis bring the memories back? These were the questions I was contemplating when a friend brought me a book about Edgar Cayce and what he had to say about dreams. What I read changed the course of my life and work.

I discovered first that Edgar Cayce learned how to enter a self-induced hypnotic sleep. He would be amnesic later for what transpired during this sleep. On the other hand, while in this altered state of consciousness, his memory was immense. It went beyond his own personal experiences, to encompass events in history and other people's experiences dating back thousands of years. He entered a state of superconsciousness, showing an understanding of things that surpassed his humble waking state. In his waking life, he was a photographer and a Sunday-school teacher. But while in this special trance, he became "the sleeping prophet."

He was best known for diagnosing illnesses. Given simply the name of someone at a distant location, he could describe the person's illness and prescribe treatments. At the time of his work, between the years 1901 and 1944, his treatments sounded strange. Today he is recognized as the father of holistic medicine, that approach to healing that treats the whole person—body, mind, and spirit.

I found particularly important Cayce's psychology. In his superconscious state he presented a different view of the mind than I had learned in school. Yet his ideas seemed very important, because they helped to make sense out of many of the common mysteries of the mind that I wanted to understand. He also said that we are all amnesic for the powers of the mind, but that we could awaken to them and use them for our benefit.

I was amazed at what Edgar Cayce had to say. I began a search in the library to find out more about what he did. Was he a freak? I discovered that history contains the stories of other people like him. Many people had discovered that behind the normal waking mind there lies another, more knowledgeable, consciousness. I found that this superconscious mind, regardless of who it is speaking through, has surprisingly similar things to say about the psychology of the mind. I learned that what made Cayce unique was that he took these lessons from the superconscious mind to heart in his own life. By applying them in his daily affairs, he developed himself to be even better able to receive inspirations from the superconscious source. His primary motivation was to be able to obtain information that people could use to better their lives.

A New Look at The Mysteries of Mind

Although it seemed that Cayce's sleeping state was a very magical state of mind, it had a simple message for you and me. It was that the mind Cayce was using in his special sleep is the same mind that exists within each of us. It's there, waiting to be called upon, already active within us. It's active every night during our dreams. It is also available to us in other ways during the day.

The mind is not a mirror of reality. It is more like a holographic studio, creating images and projecting them through consciousness to become what we take to be reality. The mind does more than watch life go by; it does more than spin mental computations. The mind is a living, active, *creative* force in our lives. Who is at the helm of this powerful force? You can be. Let's begin by lifting the curtain on the surface of the mind and seeing what lies below.

PART 1

The Secrets of the Mind

THE MIND, as invisible as it seems, is quite powerful. It is clearly something other than what we usually think of it. How can it be that the window through which we look out onto life, the human mind, is actually a light shining a mysterious image onto the stage we call life? How can it be that life is but a dream? How can the mind possess the amazing qualities suggested by Cayce's psychic trance state? To answer these questions, we need to explore the secrets of the mind.

To do so, we'll begin by looking at some of the common mysteries of the mind. We'll make some of these mysteries seem less strange. We'll learn about our silent partner, the subconscious mind. This hidden genie, just outside our awareness, has some amazing abilities.

If you have ever wondered about ESP, you'll be interested to learn about how the subconscious mind picks up telepathic impressions. Cayce has a surprise in store for us as we explore the meaning of telepathy. One of the secrets of the mind is that it doesn't actually exist where you might expect it to be. As Cayce explains the nature of telepathy, we learn that the mind exists not in your brain, but in a fourth-dimensional world of its own. What you consider to be "your mind" is but a small representative of the whole mind, which is infinite in scope.

You have access to the infinite mind through ideas. Ideas are simultaneously everywhere and always, not just when and where you think them. As we explore the meaning of this unusual perspective, we find that Cayce turns reality on its head. As he does so, he puts the mind within a cosmic and spiritual perspective. You will learn that one of the most important secrets of the mind is that it is a dimension of soul. Cayce explains how the soul projects its reality through the use of the mind and he gives us a formula for creation of reality. We'll learn just exactly how it can be that what we experience in life is a dream of the soul.

Understanding Cayce's metaphysical perspective on the mind will prepare you for a new experiment in living. What you learn here will help you to appreciate the dynamic power behind the practical advice Cayce presents on using the mind's hidden powers to create for yourself an ideal life. That the mind is the way to achieve a better and more meaningful life is truly its greatest secret.

CHAPTER 2

THE SUBCONSCIOUS: HIDDEN GENIE OF THE MIND

> The study from the human standpoint, of subconscious, subliminal, psychic, soul forces, is and should be the great study for the human family, for through self man will understand its Maker when it understands its relation to its Maker, and it will only understand that through itself, and that understanding is the knowledge as is given here in this state.
>
> *Edgar Cayce 3744-4*

ISN'T THE MIND what we experience it to be? It's only natural to assume so. The mind is simply there, a living mirror of who we are and of the world around us. Sometimes, however, we may suspect that some part of the mind must be outside of our awareness. Who drove the car while we were daydreaming? Where do our hunches come from?

Terms like "subconscious" or "unconscious" are quite familiar today. We have all heard of Freud and psychoanalysis. But the subconscious that Freud made famous has a reputation as some dark and dismal region, better left alone.

"Who knows what dark and evil secrets lurk in the hearts of men? The Shadow knows!" We'd rather not know what the Shadow knows. That seems to be the general attitude toward the subconscious mind.

Let's shine a new light beneath the surface of the mind. The unconscious has received some bad press. Let's take a different look. Stories of the monsters of the deep won't frighten us away if we can learn to explore the depths of the mind and discover the wonderful resources waiting there.

Dipping Into the Stream of Consciousness

Is your mind out of your control? The idea is offensive. No one likes to think that they have lost control of their mind. A mind out of control means a person has gone crazy. You probably assume that you have control over your mind.

When we say we are "of two minds," it usually means that we think about something in more than one way. We have mixed feelings. That may be our attitude about the unconscious. It may have some tremendous riches for us, but it also implies that we are not always in control of our mind. There are parts of our mind that may control us. Yet we need to get past this barrier.

Let's dip into the subconscious a bit and see what it is like. I have an experiment for you to try. Afterward, you will recognize that I am showing you a familiar, but not always understood, side of your mind.

Let's assume you are in control of your mind. You should be able to decide what it thinks about. So pick something, anything, to think about. Why not make it easy—pick a single word, or a mental picture. Pick something simple to focus on.

Now begin concentrating on that one thing. Close your eyes and say to yourself that one word over and over, again and again. Hold in your mind that mental picture and focus on it. Don't think any other thoughts or imagine any other pictures. Just keep your concentration on that one thing. OK, stop reading for a moment and try it. Try it for maybe thirty seconds . . . So what happened? Were you able to maintain your concentration without interruptions? Or did other thoughts and images appear? Did your mind wander? If you are like most people, you found that your mind has a life of its own. There is a stream of thought. You find yourself thinking many other thoughts besides the one you wanted to focus on. If you think that you just got bored, that you could do the experiment if you really wanted to, prove it! Try it again. Otherwise, you'll have to admit, your mind is less under your control than you suspected.

Have you ever had moments when you wanted to control your mind but couldn't? Sometimes it's hard to go to sleep at night because the mind is racing with thoughts. At other times, we think thoughts we'd rather not think. Sometimes we can't locate our thoughts, or can't recall something we want to remember.

You may have also had moments when your mind was working quite well and without any help from you. Thoughts and ideas flowed freely. Perhaps you were having a good talk with a friend about some important topic. You found yourself saying all sorts of wise or thoughtful things that you didn't realize you knew. You didn't have to work to think up what to say, because the thoughts just came to you. It was like being inspired.

The better acquainted you become with your mind, the more you realize that it isn't something that you control in the usual manner. The mind may be a tool to use, but that doesn't mean it sits idle when you are not using it. Although you can learn to direct it, the mind has a "mind of its own." It certainly isn't just a passive mirror, waiting to reflect what comes in front of it. It has its own, active, full life. It has more of a life than you realize.

This stream of thought that you experienced is coming from your subconscious. Although you didn't consciously *decide* to think them, you probably recognized many of these thoughts. They didn't seem strange. As you became aware of them, they felt like they were your own thoughts. They were you thinking of other things. These were the thoughts that were "on your mind," so to speak. You see, there is more depth to you than simply the surface of your mind. Behind that surface are background thoughts, images, and feelings. If all these thoughts came to the surface at the same time, they would confuse you. That's where the subconscious helps out.

The very top surface of the subconscious mind is like a valet or assistant. It prepares your thoughts, holds them at the ready, and lets you choose among them. When you confront a situation, your subconscious immediately gathers many thoughts and has them ready for you. It allows you to think only a couple of thoughts at a time, at your choosing. Probably you are already familiar with this part of the subconscious mind, although you may not have called it by name. It is not at all unfriendly, and actually quite helpful.

Consciousness, or thinking, is like a stream. The water flows at many depths. With our attention, we dip into this stream, and bring to the surface what we need at the moment. We don't control this stream in the sense of being able to turn it off or on. Nor do we directly control what flows through it. Yet we have some say in what we attend to and what we bring to the surface. There is much beneath the surface that we could use, if we knew how to dip that deeply.

The conscious mind is narrow and fragile compared to the depths and power of the subconscious. The subconscious is an ally. It is like having a superman or wonderwoman at our side ready to assist us. Although hidden, it is truly a genie. Let's examine some of its spectacular abilities.

The Subliminal Power of the Subconscious

The conscious mind is like a focused light. It shines very brightly, but only upon a limited spot. What it gains by being able to concentrate intently, it looses in other capacities. While the direction of your attention focuses your conscious mind, your subconscious mind has a diffuse awareness in all directions. It is as supersensitive as the latest radar equipment.

Nothing escapes the notice of the subconscious mind. While you are paying attention to a task, it is quietly absorbing much information around you. It is much like a dog or cat that sits by your side, guarding you. It allows you to go about your business without your having to monitor events around you. It knows the difference between normally occurring events and unexpected ones. While you read this book, for example, you are almost deaf to the various noises happening in your environment. Should a strange noise occur, your subconscious immediately alerts you and cocks your ears.

You can tell that your subconscious mind pays more attention than you do when someone unexpectedly speaks to you. You may instinctively respond by saying, "Huh?" You weren't paying attention when the person started to speak, so you assumed you didn't hear them. Almost before they can repeat themselves, however, your subconscious mind repeats the statement for you. You can hear in your mind a tape-recorded playback of their words. It's like a tape recording because you can even hear the tone of the person's voice. Your subconscious mind registered perfectly the event even though you weren't paying attention.

The subconscious mind is so sensitive it can perceive things your conscious mind would consider impossible to notice. It has almost unlimited powers of perception. You could say it had "bionic senses," a sensory system technologically advanced beyond normal human abilities.

You may have heard about subliminal advertising. You may have seen ads for subliminal tapes that deliver suggestions to your subconscious mind. We'll look at the suggestion angle later in this book. For the moment, however, let's focus on the power of your subconscious mind to simply perceive subliminal stimulation that escapes your awareness. Just how sensitive the subconscious can be will surprise you.

Subliminal stimulation can happen in a variety of ways. It can flash before your eyes. It can be a whisper of sound. It can come as a touch, a smell, or a taste. In fact, it can come through intuitions, too. We receive a lot of telepathic information in a subliminal fashion. All that "subliminal" means is that the information does not register in the conscious mind.

Using sensitive microelectrodes to record brain activity, scientists can determine when the brain registers sensations. Researchers have found that the brain detects touches to the body that are so slight that the person notices nothing. The same is true for visual stimulation. The brain sees more than the person notices. Furthermore, such brain-recording experiments have shown that the brain not only detects the stimulation, but also analyzes its meaning. The subconscious mind perceives things and understands their significance while the conscious mind remains totally oblivious.

Consider this situation: You are listening to some instrumental music. You hear nothing unusual. However, there is actually a verbal message recorded in with the music. The message is so soft that you cannot hear it. A person's voice says, "You are walking up an endless flight of stairs." Although you are unaware of any message, your subconscious mind hears the message. How do we know? Experiments have shown that the message affects how you respond to the music.

If you daydream to the music, or simply list words the music suggests to you, your thoughts will show hints of the message. Compared to people listening to the same music without any subliminal message, your associations will contain more references to topics related to walking up stairs. Your daydream will contain more ideas about making an effort, exertion, being tired, walking, exploring, climbing, achieving, and related topics. Your subconscious mind perceived the contents of the subliminal message as if it were a part of the music.

The subliminal effect also works even if you can consciously detect the presence of the subliminal stimulus. Re-recording the verbal message at a higher speed again and again reduces it to squeak. When that little squeak is added into the recording of the music, you can hear it. It almost sounds like another note, although out of place. Afterward, your daydream about the music will again show the effect of the subliminal message. It was just a pip of a squeak to your conscious mind, but was a fully decipherable message to your subconscious mind.

Think about it for a moment. Think what these experiments show about the perceptive power of the subconscious mind.

The subliminal power of your subconscious mind extends to the sense of smell, too. You react to odors that your conscious mind doesn't even notice. Cayce noted, in fact, that odors have a more powerful effect upon us than any other sensory stimuli. Most of these effects are subliminal. Scientists have just begun to measure the effects of such invisible odors.

Women's menstrual cycles, for example, are sensitive to the odors of other women. When women are together for a long time, their periods become synchronized. Researchers have collected armpit odors from women with regular periods and applied them to women with irregular periods. As these women wear these odors, their periods become regular.

Scientists in England have placed male armpit odors, without noticeable scent, on the doors to public toilets. Men, but not women, avoided those toilets. The experimenters speculated that men apparently preferred toilets that give no indication that another man was recently there. A subconscious reaction to a subliminal odor revealed the men's territorial behavior. Animal instincts die hard.

We think we have only five senses. The subconscious has at least a sixth sense. It responds to electromagnetism. The ability to dowse for water comes from the response to subliminal electromagnetic stimulation. It also helps us in our sense of direction. One researcher drove blindfolded schoolchildren far from home, and then asked them to point to the way back. They were able to do so. In another experiment, however, the blindfolds contained magnets. The magnets confused the children's sense of orientation and they were unable to point to the way home. The subconscious probably contains other senses that await discovery.

The sensitivity of the subconscious mind seems to have no bounds. It is so sensitive, in fact, that it registers when someone is just *thinking* about us. There's truth to the saying that if your ears are burning, someone is talking about you. The subliminal powers of the subconscious mind extend to ESP. We'll learn more about that later.

Try to create an image for yourself of your subconscious mind. Visualize it as an ultrasensitive receiver of information. How would you picture it? You might see it as a network of antennae that surround your body. Or you might see it as a set of invisible eyes, ears, nose, etc., but much larger than your physical sensory tools. Develop a positive image of the subconscious mind so that you may feel more friendly toward it.

The Perfect Memory of the Subconscious

Not only is the subconscious extremely perceptive, it has the memory of an elephant. You've probably heard about the use of hypnosis to retrieve long-lost memories. Recent court decisions have recognized the legitimacy of hypnosis as a means of enhancing the memory of witnesses to crimes. People see a lot more than they notice or can remember, but the subconscious notices and remembers. Using hypnosis, a person can mentally replay the past with such accurate vividness that one can describe previously disregarded details.

Under hypnosis people have gone back to early-childhood experiences and relived them in surprising detail. In one study, for example, hypnotized adults regressed back to their tenth, seventh, and fourth birthdays. They described the events of each of these days. They also answered a test question about the day of the week of that birthday. Calendar checks proved the accuracy of their recall. The accuracy rate was 93 percent for the day of their tenth birthday. It was 82 percent for their seventh birthday and 69 percent for their fourth birthday. A four-year-old child might only be subliminally aware of the day of the week. Years later, however, the subconscious mind still has an accurate memory for the day.

Dreams are a common place to discover the perfect memory of the subconscious. That's how I first experienced it for myself. I dreamed of a young girl celebrating her tenth birthday. She was running with her friends while carrying a bottle of champagne. She dropped the bottle and the champagne came pouring out. She was upset, and I rushed to her aid. I bent down to rescue the bottle from emptying itself. I hesitated, however, and watched the last bit of sparkling yellow fluid drain from the bottle.

At the time of the dream, I was a newly recovering alcoholic. I saw my action in the dream reflecting my decision to let alcoholic beverages vacate completely from my life. Someone asked me what ten-year anniversary I was celebrating. I wasn't aware that I was experiencing any such anniversary. I checked the calendar, went back ten years, and searched through what records I had kept. It amazed me to discover that it was the ten-year anniversary of my first drink! The dream was marking the anniversary of that event. My subconscious had remembered the date. It indirectly referred to it in my dream to make a comment on my decision to stop drinking.

Dreams are a frequent source of subconscious memories. By contemplating the feelings in a dream, you will quite likely recall a surprising early-childhood memory. The memory will also contain the feelings of that early experience. Research has shown the effectiveness of this technique. It is something you can experiment with yourself. How much your subconscious remembers will surprise you.

The subconscious even remembers subliminal experiences. It registers and retains childhood events, for example, that the child does not consciously perceive. These subliminal experiences affect the child's behavior into adulthood.

Such invisible memories appear sometimes in dreams. It is almost impossible, however, for us to detect them there. We are not even aware of originally having the experience in the first place. We cannot recognize the experience as a memory. It is primarily from the work of psychotherapists that we know dreams can bring up subliminal memories from childhood.

I once read the case study of a woman who was seeking treatment for bulimia, the gorge-purge eating disorder. She had a dream that suggested to her therapist that she had subconsciously perceived a dangerous secret when she was an infant. It was that her father was having an affair with another woman. The patient said that she knew that the therapist was wrong. She spoke with her mother, who assured her that there had been no affair.

At the therapist's urging, the woman contacted her father. She asked him about it. He reluctantly confided that there had been an affair, but that no one, including her mother, had ever known about. He asked her to please keep it a secret. The revelation came as a terrible shock to the woman.

With the therapist's help, she realized she had an unconscious tendency to protect her mother from having bad feelings. She would try to absorb these feelings herself. This habit had begun in infancy, when she had unconsciously sensed the father's secret and its implications for her mother. When the father asked her, as an adult, not to reveal the secret, the pattern became obvious. The revelation proved to mark the turning point in the therapy. The woman was able to unburden herself of feelings that were not truly her own, but which really belonged to her parents. When she stopped absorbing their feelings, she no longer needed to purge herself.

Her dream had dredged up a crucial secret. It concerned something that as an infant she could have sensed only subliminally.

This story shows that the subconscious is able to search for an important buried memory that only it knows exists. Not only is its memory perfect, but it shows intelligent use of its memory. It recognizes critical moments in our lives when certain memories would be useful. It finds them and brings them to light.

The Creativity of the Subconscious

The subconscious does more than simply register and retain information. It is also able to operate on this information. It can think creatively. It can analyze information to detect patterns the conscious mind fails to notice.

One of the places that reveals the creativity of the subconscious is our dreams. Consider, for example, this puzzle: Here are five letters, O,T,T,F,F. What two letters do you think would come next? If you can't figure out the answer, you are not alone. Stanford University students were unable to solve it. Then they tried to "sleep on it" to see if their dreams might solve the puzzle.

Some of the students were indeed able to solve the puzzle in their sleep. The researcher, Dr. William Dement, reported one of the dreams. A student dreamed of being in an art gallery looking at a row of paintings on the wall. He began to count them. He counted one, two, three, four, five pictures, then saw that the next two frames were empty. He then realized that the numbers six and seven were the answers to the puzzle.

The subconscious noticed the subliminal message in the letters. They were the first letters of the numbers, one through five.

In another experiment, a professor of mathematics tested his ability to solve calculus problems. The experimenter then hypnotized the professor. He gave him a posthypnotic suggestion that he could solve calculus problems rapidly in his head. The professor then did so. Rather than using a pencil to work out the answers, he worked them out mentally. His speed and accuracy improved significantly over the first testing. He claimed that he could skip steps and the answers just came to him.

The subconscious mind can also stop the clock to gain more time to solve problems. In one demonstration, a hypnotized dress designer followed suggestions to slow time to a standstill. The hypnotists suggested to her that the next ten seconds would seem like an hour. During that hypnotic hour, she was to design a new dress. Ten seconds later, she awakened and drew her new design. She was very happy with the results. She said that to create such a new design she would have needed at least an hour! Her subconscious had provided it in ten seconds.

Relative to the conscious mind, the subconscious mind may appear like a genius. The subconscious has the reputation of being something that is a disturbance to the conscious mind. But it is really the reverse: the conscious mind tramples on the subconscious and holds it back. When the conscious mind can get out of the way, the subconscious can show its talent.

There is a mental abnormality called the "idiot savant" syndrome. The conscious mind is severely retarded, but there are signs of a creative genius. A person with this malady has some remarkable ability. Someone who doesn't know how to read or write can nevertheless perform amazing feats of mental arithmetic. Mentally multiplying 8,356,356 by 356,453 requires only seconds. Someone with no musical training is nevertheless able to listen to a complex classical piano solo and then replay it perfectly. Some are able to compose new music or create beautiful drawings. Idiot savants reveal that hidden in the subconscious mind is a genius waiting to awaken.

The Subconscious Mind in Daily Life

One of the main jobs of the subconscious, to which Cayce pointed our attention, is the monitoring of actions that have become habitual. When we first learn a skill, such as tying our shoes, riding a bicycle, typing, or driving a car, it requires all of our attention. Once we have mastered it, we pay it little attention. The subconscious takes over and carries out the task for us. Only when some unexpected, nonroutine event occurs does the subconscious call our attention to the task at hand. Perhaps you have noticed that sort of thing while driving. You didn't realize you were daydreaming until you were suddenly pressing on the brakes. The subconscious had alerted you to come back.

The subconscious mind is also a faithful, behind-the-scene servant in most of our mental operations. When we talk with someone, we are able to speak in an unending flow of words. We don't have to pause after each phrase in order to think up the next phrase. Our subconscious mind gathers thoughts for us in large groups, then presents them to us as we need to speak them.

When we listen to someone else speak, we can only hold about seven words in mind at one time. Yet we don't have to ask the person to pause every few words. Our subconscious remembers all the words and helps us understand what the person is saying.

While we are listening to the other person, our subconscious mind is also gathering replies for us. It has them at the ready when it is our turn to speak. Sometimes you notice this process in action. When you do, however, it is harder for you to listen to what the other person is saying. At such times, it is better to let the subconscious do its work unnoticed. Otherwise, we defeat its purpose.

The subconscious mind also controls the operations of our body. Cayce noted how the subconscious monitors our bodily functions and keeps them running smoothly. You didn't think, did you, that the body ran without an intelligence directing it? Who keeps your heart beating, regulates its speed so it goes faster when necessary, or slows it down when you are resting? Your subconscious mind. It also regulates the digestive process. It slows it down, for example, when you decide you're going to work immediately after a meal rather than rest. The various bodily functions work together, changing as needed to differing circumstances. The subconscious mind is the conductor of this harmonic symphony.

Neurophysiology has come to understand how the bloodstream and the nervous system network the body's various organs. The final master of this network of organization is deep in the brain, according to standard textbook physiology. Cayce noted, however, that it is the subconscious mind that is using the brain as a tool in its efforts.

The brain is *not* the mind! Instead, the mind uses the brain as a tool. In fact, the subconscious mind uses every atom in the body in its expression. Every atom in the body has its portion of mind. Being "of one mind," as in single-purposed, means having every atom in the body acting in harmony.

Cayce anticipated psychically what modern neurophysiology would later learn through laboratory research. By learning to make contact with the subconscious mind, we can ourselves direct the functioning of the body. Experiments have shown that this control extends to single nerve cells and to individual blood cells. In the future, science will have the means to observe this control extending to the atomic level of the body.

The Nature of the Subconscious Mind

When giving readings on the nature of the subconscious mind, Cayce often recommended that we read Thomson Jay Hudson's book *The Law of Psychic Phenomena* for more information. Although written in 1892, it continues to be a valuable textbook on the nature of the subconscious mind. Here we will mention but a few of the attributes of this hidden genie, suggesting that you, too, read Hudson's book for more information.

The subconscious mind is subjective, while the conscious mind is objective. Our conscious mind focuses on external appearances. Its world is the "objective reality" of the senses. The subconscious mind accepts internal appearances. What seems true for us from a subjective viewpoint is reality to the subconscious. While objective reality seems to be the master of the conscious mind, the subconscious is the servant of our subjective reality.

While the conscious mind relies on the senses and reasons logically, the subconscious operates on the principle of suggestion. When we talk to ourselves, the subconscious listens and accepts what we say to ourselves as true. When untended, this power of suggestion can work against us. Our subconscious registers the negative things we think about ourselves and accepts them as reality. The reverse is also true. It accepts our wishes and hopes as facts and can help bring them about. That's why it is worthwhile for us to harness the power of suggestion and use it to our benefit.

The use of pictures, or imagery, is another example of the subjectivity of the subconscious mind. It uses a picture language to do its thinking. In one experiment, for example, a hypnotized subject listened to a series of numbers and made up a dream about them. The experimenter read them aloud at a normal speed: 6, 5, 3, 9, 8, 8, 0, 1. Immediately afterward, the person reported the dream. It was of a curved pipe (shaped like the number 6), with a five-pointed star in the bowl. The man breaks the pipe in half, because half of six is three. He then turns it upside down to make a golf club (a nine iron). He sees two symbols for infinity (figure eights), and announces that all is nothing (0): it's all the same one thing (1). The subject was able to repeat back the numbers perfectly. The experiment shows how quickly the subconscious can turn facts into images.

The subconscious mind also thinks symbolically. The conscious mind thinks in a literal fashion, responding to the factual meaning of words. The subconscious responds to the emotional meanings of words, and gives free rein to its imagination. Symbols are not true to literal facts. Instead, they express feelings and subjective appearances. The symbolic logic of the subconscious is what gives rise to dreams, myths, and fairy tales. These stories, although not factually accurate, speak of truths of the soul.

For example, while the conscious mind sees no immediate relationship between a turtle and the planet earth, to the subconscious mind they are very similar. The curves on the turtle's shell are like the surface of the planet, with its bumps and valleys. The planet is a home that travels, just like the turtle carries its home on its back. There is an American Indian legend that reflects these symbolic parallels. According to this legend, the origin of the earth was the back of a giant turtle. The legend wisely speaks of the importance of a certain quality, both shy and modest yet strong and patient, that is necessary to sustain life on earth.

Because of the free play it gives to the imagination, the subconscious sees multifaceted, quaint connections that go beyond strict logic. It can also show as much insight as an ancient sage. Although it doesn't seem realistic or objective, it is nevertheless intelligent. Although innocent and gullible in its unquestioning acceptance of suggestions, it can be very wise.

Speaking symbolically, the conscious mind is like the sun while the subconscious is like the moon. The sun's bright light reveals details to our eyes. The diffuse light of the moon arouses our feelings. When the sun shines brightly during the day, lighting up the sky, the moon is barely visible. At night, when the sun has left the sky dark, the moon shines brightly. The workings of the subconscious also appear more readily when the conscious mind relaxes or sleeps. The sun's role in the life of the planet is obvious. Yet the moon also has powerful effects. It is smaller than the sun, but closer to the earth. Its gravitational force affects the tides, the growth of plants, and the fluids in our own bodies. The moon may not give off its own light, but its energies nevertheless affect us. In the bright light of day, our conscious mind operates through the senses and the intellect, two sharply focused powers. The moonlight gives the subconscious mind the quiet stealth of intuition. It uses the subtle play of feelings to help it reveal an equally important reality.

The conscious mind is also symbolized by a man. The male often thinks itself the ruler and the wisest of all. The subconscious is symbolized as a woman. She has a quiet wisdom of her own that often confounds the man's more focused, linear intelligence. As we appreciate the special wisdom and intelligence of the feminine perspective, we realize the special value of the subconscious mind.

This hidden genie, the subconscious mind, a servant and guardian with bionic sensitivity and creative vision, deserves our respect. As we attend to its subtle promptings, it can lead us toward still more mysteries of the mind.

CHAPTER 3

ESP AND THE TRANSPERSONAL MIND

Mind, then, may function without a form or body.

Edgar Cayce 262-78

EACH OF US is a separate person. We each have our own mind. That seems pretty obvious.

Our skin defines the boundaries of who we are. Our separate brains operate separate minds. Your mind stays inside your head, while my mind keeps its place inside my head.

Each of us is obviously separate from the environment, from the world. We're not glued to it. We're free to walk about freely while the world holds still. The world doesn't move with every step we take. The rest of life passes by while we watch. We don't move with it. We each lead our own lives, separate from the world.

It's also clear that what's inside our minds is something different from the stuff that's "out there" in the world. You can touch things, but how do you touch your mind? It's "stuff" that makes the world matter. It's the concrete reality of chemistry and physics. The body and the brain is part of this physical world, but what about the mind? The mind is somehow different. It's made of something else—thoughts and images.

All this is obvious. So what? It seems so obvious, but it's just not true. It's only a working convenience the conscious mind uses. The separation, between ourselves and others and between inside and outside, is the creation of the conscious mind. It is its most significant achievement and its major curse.

To avoid this curse, we'll need to see beyond the illusion of the conscious mind. To use the mind to its fullest creativity, we must introduce the conscious mind to its source—the transpersonal mind. It is not an easy task.

Subliminal ESP Powers of the Subconscious Mind

Our conscious mind may accept the idea of an unconscious. When it does, however, it typically puts a limit on it. Our normal conception of the unconscious is like a pocket, a hidden drawer, or the cellar of our house. It is a container, a place to put memories.

We have already seen that part of the unconscious, the subconscious, is more than just a pocket. It is an active power and extremely perceptive. It is not a container at all, nor is it bounded or contained. In fact, it may have no walls. Besides being our secret servant, it also has invisible connections with other subconscious minds.

When we are with others, for example, our conscious mind can create for us the lonely feeling of "self-consciousness." We peer out from behind our eyes across the crowded room and sense other people peering out from their eyes at us. We become the objects of their seeing as they are the objects of ours. The conscious mind creates impressions of separateness.

The subconscious mind experiences the situation in a different way. It is very sensitive to the emotional atmosphere in the room. These vibrations are the reality for the subconscious. It is something the subconscious intuitively feels even if there are no sensory cues that the conscious mind can perceive. We can feel one another's feelings almost as if there were a connection between us.

Our conscious mind rejects such thoughts. That is, unless it has studied the evidence for telepathy. Nevertheless, our conscious mind sometimes feels uncomfortable focusing on such feelings. The subconscious, however, cannot ignore them.

I'm sure that you have had such an experience yourself in a room of people. Perhaps you wanted to ignore the impression you were picking up. You didn't know if you could trust it, and you didn't know what to do with it. Nevertheless, it probably affected how you approached the situation in the room.

The subliminal ESP powers of the subconscious mind influence your thoughts, feelings, and actions. Your conscious mind is not aware of this influence, but it exists. Research has repeatedly demonstrated that the subconscious mind detects other people's thoughts.

Douglas Dean of the Newark College of Engineering devised this test of subliminal ESP. The subject provides the researcher with ten names of people who are emotionally important in the person's life. The researcher adds ten additional names randomly chosen from the phone book and copies all twenty onto individual cards. The researcher goes into another room and hands all the cards to another person. This person silently reads each name while the researcher records the subject's reaction on a plethysomgraph. This machine records blood flow in a fingertip and detects minute changes in the person's emotional state.

When the sender reads a name known to the subject, the subject's blood flow shows a response. Somehow the subject knows when the sender is thinking about someone of significance. Consciously, however, the subject doesn't experience anything in particular. Just sitting there quietly, the subject isn't even aware of the nature of the experiment. The subconscious, however, and the body it controls, show uncanny sensitivity.

Other experiments have demonstrated that other people's experiences affect the contents of our thoughts through subliminal ESP. Dr. Thelma Moss from UCLA's medical school, for example, showed that what one person concentrates on can leak into the daydreams of another person in a nearby room. Dr. Montague Ullman and his colleagues at the Maimonides Hospital in Brooklyn found that a sleeping person can pick up on the thoughts of other people and weave them into dreams.

We are not usually aware that telepathy is influencing our mind. Evidence of a subliminal ESP effect is quite clear to the observing researcher, however. In the experiment just mentioned, people contemplated colorful pictures. Images from these pictures made obvious appearances in the dreams and daydreams of the experimental subjects. The subjects assumed that their thoughts were their own. The researchers knew otherwise.

These scientific findings are but a few examples of what Cayce meant by the connection between subconscious minds. Your subconscious mind is in contact with all other subconscious minds. It is not only Santa Claus who knows what we have been thinking! Everyone has access to everyone else's thoughts. Even if we are not consciously aware of what others are thinking, their thoughts nevertheless affect us.

The Unconscious Connection

What are we to make of the subconscious mind if we are to accept that it has no boundaries? Isn't our mind our own? I know I experience my own mind as something that floats inside my head. I don't normally experience it as extending outside of me to be in direct contact with other minds. Although I can appreciate the evidence for subliminal ESP, it's still hard for me to visualize the connection between minds.

Edgar Cayce gave a pictorial model of the link between minds. What his model shows is stranger than fiction. It shows there is one mind and people share it. The drawing in Figure 1 is Cayce's image of the mind.

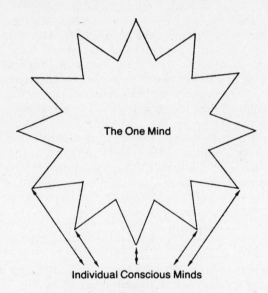

Figure 1

The Relation between Individual
Conscious Minds and the One Mind

The drawing is of a multipointed star. The star itself represents the entire mind. Each arm of the star represents a portion of the mind for a different person. To be more accurate, we would need a star with billions of points, but what we have will do. The very tip of each point represents the conscious mind of an individual.

The mind you usually think of as "your mind" is but one of the points on the star. It is your conscious mind. Our conscious minds are only a very, very small portion of the entire mind. If you value your conscious mind, and I trust that you do, then look how much more mind there is to value! Our conscious minds are quite wondrous themselves. So imagine the wonder of the whole mind!

The appearance of conscious minds is the result of the growth of the star. Beginning as a round shape, it developed arms that grew to very sharp points. A conscious mind is capable of very exact, penetrating focus. Yet it also becomes isolated from the rest of the mind by this very narrow focus. As one point on the star appears distinct from the others, one conscious mind seems separate and distant from other conscious minds.

Looking out upon the world with the eyes of our conscious mind, we see through our own point on the star. The conscious mind operates through its sensitivity to physical sensations. When we look out upon the world through our hearts, we use the intuitive ability of the subconscious. Through the unconscious we make connections through the inner part of the star.

In Figure 2, we see how the unconscious mind is a continuous connective

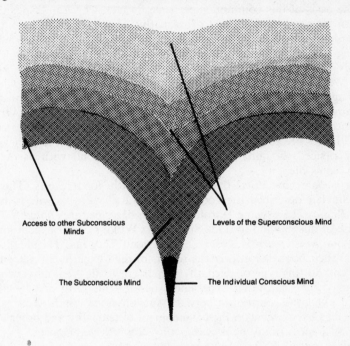

Access to other Subconscious Minds

Levels of the Superconscious Mind

The Subconscious Mind

The Individual Conscious Mind

Figure 2

Regions of the Mind

layer of the inner parts of the mind's arms. The star tips only seem separate from one another. The arms of the stars are clearly like fingers on the same hand. The arms represent our subconscious minds. All subconscious minds are connected. The core of the mind is available to us all, via what Cayce termed the superconscious mind.

An Experiment in Telepathy

With our conscious mind, we cannot make contact with any other point on the star except by way of sensory contact. You can't talk to anyone who is not present with you, except by aid of a telephone to bridge the gap. To "reach out and touch someone" with the conscious mind, you need a special tool. All of our senses are special tools for detecting physical energy. The communication devices that we have developed are tools to extend the range of the senses.

Only the conscious mind needs such tools. With the subconscious mind, we can directly reach out to someone with our feelings. How else to explain that phone call from a friend you were just thinking about?

On the basis of this common experience, in fact, Cayce indicates that you can learn for yourself the secret of telepathy. He suggests that you conduct this simple experiment. Make an agreement with a friend to stop what you are doing at the same time every day and tune in to each other.

Simply focus on that feeling of your subconscious connection with that person. What does it feel like to be in the presence of that person? That is the "wavelength," as it were, to attune to. Then let your thoughts, images, and daydreams have a free run. Note what passes through your mind. Arrange to speak with your friend, over the phone perhaps, every few days to compare notes. Chances are very good that you and your friend will find that each of you experienced thoughts and images that correspond with events in the other person's life.

Other people have tried this experiment with good results. The author Upton Sinclair described the good results he had with his wife in his book *Mental Radio*. The psychic Harold Sherman described in *Thoughts Through Space* use of this method to track Sir Hubert Wilkins on his expedition to the South Pole. Most recently, researchers Russell Targ and Harold Putoff reported in their book *Mind Race* the results of their experiments showing that anyone can do this type of telepathy, which they call "remote viewing."

You may have had other experiences besides this form of telepathy that suggest to you the connection between subconscious minds. You can learn more about Cayce's view on the development of telepathy and other forms of psychic awareness in my book *Awakening Your Psychic Powers*.

Certainly, not all ESP is subliminal. Furthermore, as the center of Cayce's star model suggests, our connection with one another goes deeper than the subconscious.

Archetypes:
Pictures From the Universal Unconscious

While making his rounds of the psychiatric hospital, Dr. Carl Jung was approached by an excited patient. He asked the good doctor to please come to the window. He wanted Jung to look up in the sky at the sun. "See, the sun is wagging its tail!" exclaimed the man. "It is making the wind!"

Some time later, Dr. Jung had reason to marvel at the patient's hallucination. It wasn't that the person could see something that was not there. Hallucinations were commonplace in the hospital.

It was something that Jung later discovered, when reading a translation, for the first time in German, of an obscure Greek text over two thousand years old. The text concerned an initiation ceremony into a religious cult. During the ceremony, the initiate experiences a secret revelation of the sun's tail and learns that it is what makes the wind. The details of this long-obscure religious ceremony were remarkably similar to the patient's hallucination.

How could the imagination of this poor, uneducated peasant parallel so exactly an obscure myth from an ancient culture? How could he have heard of it? That was the marvel. There seemed to be no way that it was possible.

This incident led Jung, a Swiss psychiatrist and a contemporary of Sigmund Freud, to research the deepest depths of the mind. He found himself in search of the source of universal symbolism. He found evidence of such symbolism not only in the hallucinations of the mentally ill but also in the dreams of ordinary people. He found it in the religions of the world, as well as in myths and fairy tales of all ages.

Cultural heritage or learning cannot explain the appearance of these common symbols. They are innate, arising directly from a universal level of the mind.

It was this discovery that forced Jung to develop a branch of psychoanalysis distinct from that created by Freud. When Freud discovered the unconscious, he thought he had found a pocket of repressed memories and urges. It was his theory of the unconscious that influenced our envisioning it like a cellar. Jung, however, found that the unconscious is more like a spring from a vast underground reservoir.

Jung noted, for example, that patients who had recovered all their repressed memories through years of psychoanalysis nevertheless continued to bring up fresh material from the unconscious. The unconscious doesn't run dry, but flows from an infinite source.

Jung proposed a psychoanalytic theory based on what he called the archetypes of a universal unconscious. These archetypes are a set of universal patterns from which all symbols evolve. They point to a region of the mind that exists as a common link between all people, living and dead.

Each person's mind, regardless of what it has, or has not, taken in through learning, shows evidence of having deep roots into a universal mind. From these roots, ancient symbols spontaneously arise into the minds of unsuspecting individuals. These symbols represent ideas that the person has never consciously experienced. They do not result from learning or experience. They reflect instead an archetypal thought pattern that is innate to the mind itself.

Let's look at one example, from the case records of psychiatrist Dr. Edward Whitmont, as he presented it in his book *The Symbolic Quest.*

There was a young child with asthma who had a recurrent dream. It was about trying to climb out of the water onto the dry land of an island. A great "goat man" was always pushing her back into the water. From the dream we might suppose that her growth was being somehow suppressed. Her asthma was the result of some type of drowning. But by what force?

When Dr. Whitmont interviewed the mother, he learned that she, too, had a recurrent dream. It was that an Eastern potentate was trying to break into her house. He threatened that if she did not let him in, he would kill the child.

Dr. Whitmont recognized that both dreams were referring to the Eastern goat god, Ammon, worshipped by Egyptians two thousand years before Christ. This deity relates to the earthy instincts of natural life. It is the same energy that the Christian church later rejected as the horned "devil."

The devil that was drowning the child, however, was not the Christian devil. It was the devil of the mother's rigid attitude. She denied the instinctual, spontaneous, joyous, and sensual side of life in favor of rigid opinions. Even though the mother verbally expressed a liberal attitude, her emotional stance toward her child was quite controlling. She always knew best where her daughter was concerned.

The daughter didn't even have room to breathe. Her mother's anxiety concerning the basic life energies made it impossible for the child to gain a handle on them for herself. When the mother was able to "loosen up," the child could literally "breathe easier."

The two dreams go together hand in glove. Their similarity shows the subconscious connection between mother and child.

The child's dream also shows that she had an unconscious understanding of what was happening to her. The symbol of the goat man, however, was not part of the child's own language or experience. It reflected the recognition by the archetypal unconscious of the source of the girl's difficulty. It expressed this understanding using an image four thousand years old. The archetypal mind produced an image from an ancient vocabulary and used it appropriately to diagnose the situation. An ancient and universal awareness spoke through the child's dream.

The archetypal unconscious is not simply a source of universal symbols. It also seems to be alert and aware of the current situation. It speaks in an ancient tongue, but makes an important point.

Carl Jung, as well as those who have further explored this area of research, found that this archetypal mind is very wise. It is as if it were a sage who had lived for thousands and thousands of years. Yet it keeps up to date on current events in the lives of people. The main concern of this ancient sage seems to be a spiritual question: How can the fullness of God be expressed in the particular life of this individual?

Can it be that in the depths of your mind, of my mind, and the mind of every person, there exists the mind of God? Cayce's source indicated so, and called it the superconscious mind. It is the infinite mind that exists within all life and knows no boundaries.

Whereas it is the subconscious mind that handles telepathy, it is through the superconscious mind that clairvoyance and intuition operate. Edgar Cayce demonstrated a clairvoyant ability in his psychic trance. It is the ability to gather information at a distance without the intermediary of another mind. Whereas Cayce indicated that he could diagnose a distant person's illness by telepathically reading the person's own subconscious knowledge of the body's condition, it was through the superconscious mind that Cayce operated clairvoyantly. One of these impressive feats was to specify the location of a needed medicine. It was no longer manufactured, but Cayce's clairvoyance impressed upon him the vision of a dusty bottle of this remedy on the back shelf of a particular pharmacy in a distant town. When the pharmacist was called and convinced to look where Cayce had suggested, he indeed found the bottle, hidden behind the current stock.

Our clairvoyance most frequently operates through intuition. Cayce indicated that intuition was the highest form of psychic functioning. Intuitions arise as they are needed, and are meant to guide us. They alert us to opportunities, warn us of dangers, and suggest particular actions. Intuition is a prompter. It is the nudge of the superconscious mind.

It is because of the superconscious mind that Cayce reminded us constantly that all knowledge is within. Although we look outside of ourselves to learn, to gain advice, to obtain assistance, everything that we experience and learn is the result of our inner response. We must learn to look within.

We will learn later about meditation and dreams, two of the places that it is the easiest to begin the process of turning within. We will see how the superconscious mind is the most active when we are asleep and our conscious mind merges with a universal level of awareness. Our dreams are the footprints of intuitive impressions.

The Transpersonal Mind

Jung's discovery of a universal level of the unconscious shared by all people fits with Cayce's model of the mind. There is only one star in that model because there is only one mind. Although the mind may have many points of conscious awareness, as in individual human beings, there is only one mind. In religions and spiritual traditions this mind has gone by several names; the universal mind, the mind at large, or the mind of God.

In the language of today's leading-edge psychology, we would say that the mind is transpersonal. The word *transpersonal* is a recent term invented to express in a new way the same ancient idea whose time has come once again. People from many different branches of science and philosophy have been embracing it, for as many different reasons, since the consciousness revolution of the sixties.

Transpersonal means that the mind has a life beyond what appears in individual persons. The mind is not just what happens inside a person. It is a reality in itself.

The mind is like the air we breathe. Does air exist just when it is in our lungs? Of course not. Does mind exist only when it is active within a brain? It does not, although we usually think of the mind that way.

We could say that you have your air and I have mine. Like the mind, however, air is transpersonal. Air is everywhere. There is one large body of air, but it occupies many different places. Some of it is flowing through my lungs, some of it is flowing through yours. Air threads together all the plants, animals, and people, as well as all the boxes, bottles, homes, and other hollow containers.

Air exists independently of what houses it. The mind exists independently of those who use it. There is only one air. There is only one mind. It is a *single,* living reality.

While it's hard to think of mind as being a single reality, we can think of nature that way. We can picture nature as an impersonal whole and as a law unto itself. We can see nature as a primary reality of its own, even though it has many and various appearances. The reality of nature transcends the specifics of any single piece of nature.

Try thinking of mind in the same way. Imagine the mind as an impersonal whole. Picture it as a world of its own, with its own life, and laws of its own. The life of the mind goes beyond any one individual's experience with it. It exists independently of any living body and continues after the death of that body. The mind is transpersonal.

Ideas: The Fourth Dimension

What is the mind made of that it can exist independently of a living body? Actually, the mind exists independently of more than just a body, but of time and space as well. The mind is of another dimension. According to Cayce, the mind exists in a fourth dimension. It is the world of patterns we usually call ideas.

Where do you go to find ideas? Into your mind, of course. Another name for the mind might be "idealand," or the "ideaosphere." Idealand is a world of its own.

An idea doesn't live in time and space—how long is an idea? How much does it weight? It's an obvious fact, but often overlooked, that ideas do not have physical properties.

Consider the idea of danger. We know what the idea means, but what physical measurements can you make on it? As an idea, it does not exist in just one place, nor at just one time. Danger is a meaning that is universally experienced by both animals and humans (and perhaps plants, too) throughout history. It is an example of what Jung meant by archetype, because it is a universal pattern of experience. It is an idea rather than any one specific thing or event.

The things that ideas refer to are of this world, but the ideas themselves are not. We can't really measure ideas by a ruler, a bathroom scale, or a clock. We sometimes talk about them as if we could: we "toss ideas around," we "stomp on ideas," we "look for ideas," we "weigh ideas against one another," finding some ideas "more forceful" than others, and we say "an idea's time has come." As someone once said, however, "You can't shoot an idea!" You can burn a book, but not the ideas it contains. An idea is not of this world.

Specific manifestations of an idea may appear at a certain time, or at a certain place, but the ideas themselves live in different kind of reality. The real world of ideas is the world of the mind.

In the time/space world, we understand how one event causes another, as a matter of the law of chemistry and physics. In the reality of the mind, one idea may also invariably lead to another. Yet the way one idea causes another is through the laws of the mind.

At the level of the conscious mind, the force of logic rules. Logic is not a physical force, but it still operates as a lawful power in the mind.

Ideas are also linked to one another by patterns of meaning. Through similarity of meaning, one idea attracts another. There is a type of gravity in the ideaosphere. It is not based on the weight of the matter but on the similarity of meaning ("like attracts like"). At the subconscious level of the mind, the gravity of affinity follows symbolic, rather than logical, patterns.

Although people may be separated by time and space, they can still be close to one another through the ideas they share. Ideas define the geography of a culture or a religion. A nation is a state of mind.

The communication of ideas may not require sending signals through physical space. Telepathy, for example, is an ability that goes beyond time and space. If ideas live in their own fourth dimension, then they don't have to travel in order to reach telepathically from one person to the next.

When an idea falls out of the ideaosphere and lands in one person's mind, it is very likely it will appear in the mind of another person, too. The same inventions often appear simultaneously in several laboratories. Einstein is said to have remarked that if he hadn't developed his theory of relativity, someone else would have, because the idea was "in the air." When an idea is in season, it blossoms everywhere.

A British biologist, Rupert Sheldrake, has developed a theory he calls "morphic resonance" to explain such simultaneous inventions. In his book *A New Science of Life,* he presents a vision of the transpersonal reality of mind quite similar to Cayce's perspective. His term for the fourth-dimensional status of ideas is the "morphogenic field." He suggests that mental events in individual brains are patterned by this fourth-dimensional field. When a new pattern, or idea, successfully resonates within the receptive field of one brain, it becomes increasingly easy for that idea to resonate within other brains. The more people that are able to conceive the idea, the easier it becomes for other people to have the idea. It is the way that the time for an idea actually comes. To prove his point, he staged a demonstration with the help of the BBC television system.

In Sheldrake's experiment, he sent field researchers to remote parts of the world and showed people two visual puzzles. They were both the type you have seen in the Sunday comics: "Find the figure hidden in this picture." His researchers measured the percent of the population that could detect these hidden figures. Sheldrake then showed one of these pictures on television, broadcast to millions of British viewers. Using a special close-up shot, he pointed out the location of the hidden figure. Sheldrake now sent his field researchers back out to these same remote locations, where the television show could not have been seen. Again the researchers presented the same two pictures to hundreds of people. This time, however, about twice as many people as before were able to locate the figure in the picture that had been shown on television. People were no better at finding the figure hidden in the other picture. Sheldrake suggested that, according to the terms of his theory, when the millions of television viewers discovered the hidden figure on television, it made that perception easier for other people to see.

It's natural to think of your mind as something that floats in your head. It's easy to imagine your ideas as little things hanging around inside your brain. Try a different image.

Imagine your brain to be a television set. Imagine the broadcast airwaves to be the mind itself. Ideas are vibrational patterns in those waves. Airwaves permeate everything. The airwaves don't sit inside the television set, and neither does the mind sit in the brain. Instead, the brain is sensitive to the energy of the airwaves and is able to tune in to them.

Cayce indicated that the individual brain resonates to the vibrations of patterns that exist within the mind. The brain tunes in to ideas that are in the air.

Remove all the television sets from the planet, and the airwaves remain. The mind is a reality itself, independent of physical bodies. The connection between the mind and the body is the reverse of what we usually think.

Mind and Matter: Patterns of Oneness

A television set does not create the airwaves. The situation is the reverse. The airwaves drive the television set. The pattern of vibrations in the airwaves determine the pattern of activity on the television screen. Similarly, the mind is the active force behind what we see around us.

The mind is a primary reality of its own. It is a universal reality. It feeds us all with some very similar mental patterns. That same mind gives the world the patterns in nature. As Herman Melville wrote in *Moby Dick,* "Oh nature, and O soul of man! how far beyond all utterance are your linked analogies! Not the smallest atom stirs or lives on matter, but has its cunning duplicate in mind."

There is an intimate relationship between mind and nature, or between mind and matter. Cayce refers to this link as the "image." God created the world, mind, and nature from images. The same images that are found in the mind are found in the forms of nature. Another term he used was "pattern." Both terms are in use today to describe the link between mind and matter. Cayce would have us understand the mind and nature are as one—they share the same patterns.

Artificially stimulating the brain, for example, can create some strange visual patterns. Similar patterns will appear as a result of head injuries or taking LSD. These purely imaginary patterns, however, resemble patterns found in nature.

Recall Jung's discovery that the hallucinations of a patient mirrored the revelations in an ancient religious ceremony. Years after his discovery, the *Mariner 2* spacecraft made a related discovery. It revealed that there is a wind on the surface of the sun! Astrophysicists later discovered a comet wagging a tail of charged particles. They supposed that it was connected with the movements of the solar wind. A few years later, *Mariner 10* discovered that the planet Mercury also has a tail that always points away from the sun.

This story reveals a universal pattern at work. The pattern found its way into a religious ceremony and the hallucinations of a patient. It also expressed itself in the workings of the sun and its neighbors. As above, so below. Mind and nature have the same patterns.

Perhaps the most significant example of this relationship comes from mathematics, the queen of the sciences. Mathematicians give free rein to their imagination. They invent totally imaginary mathematical systems. Like science-fiction writers who make up fantastic worlds and then follow the implications to see where they might lead, mathematicians conduct research on their inventions.

Such is the life of the pure mathematician. Yet they get paid for it. They earn their money because their imaginary worlds usually pay off down the road by helping scientists. Mathematical inventions often prove to match a newly discovered pattern in nature.

A recent example is the "fractal," invented by IBM mathematician Benoit Mandelbrot. We are familiar with the first, second, and third dimension. We have heard of a fourth dimension. What would the half dimension be? A fractional dimension is basically unimaginable except to a mathematician. Yet with this concept, Mandelbrot created a mathematics that made sense of aspects of nature never before understood. Fractal geometry is now useful for explaining the patterning of squiggly coastlines, of rolling hills and valleys, and of many other apparently random irregularities in nature. What began in the imagination of the mathematician became a tool for the scientist to explore and understand physical reality.

The Creation of the Conscious Mind

We can use images, analogies, and examples to point to the existence of the one mind as a reality of its own. Yet we still experience mind, and our identity, through our conscious mind. The conscious mind is the mind of separation. It separates our consciousness from an awareness of the one mind. Knowing that there is but one mind, what are we to make of the conscious mind?

Imagine that once, long ago, there was only the one mind. There was only being-in-existence, but no one to behold it. Then the conscious mind appeared in humans. People instantaneously appeared to themselves.

It was like waking up from a sleepy daydream. All of a sudden, people realized they were persons walking in a world. "Here we are," they said to themselves at the moment of their birth into self-consciousness, "alive in a world." Immediately, there was the question, "Where did we come from? Where were we before now? How did we get here?"

Ancient myths of creation, from all over the world, tell similar stories of this event. All involve an act of separation. In the Bible, for example, God separates the light from the darkness, the waters from Heaven, and the dry land from the waters. Before this act of creation through separation, all was a dark, formless void.

An act of separation was required to create conscious life. Why was this so? Acting as free agents in the sensory world of physical reality requires being able to perceive ourselves as separate from that world.

If you have had a child, or have watched a child grow from infancy, think about the difference between before and after the "terrible twos." That is the point where the kid learns how to say "No!" and perfects it to a perplexing art. Prior to learning how to say "No!" the child is simply a reflexive part of the family environment. Not that the child is always agreeable, for it may fuss, resist, and go its own way. Yet compared to standing right in front of you, looking you right in the eye, and saying "No!" the earlier resistances seem minor.

When it learns to say "No," the child's days of innocent, instinctive resistance to your wishes are over. The child now seems to know what it is doing when it says "No." The child is intentionally opposing your will with its own will. The child has become a separate being—and it knows it! Becoming a separate being, learning to say "No," opposing the parents' wishes, and becoming self-conscious are all part of an important stage in the growing-up process. Without this development, the child could never become a real person, nor have a life of its own.

The act of saying "No" is both a negation and an affirmation. With the power of the sword to cut and divide in two, saying "No" both states "You are not me!" and affirms "I am me!"

The child's development of the self-consciousness of a separate being is much the same as the development of the conscious mind in the origin of human beings.

The conscious mind is capable of focusing on something in particular by ignoring what surrounds it. When we focus our attention, we are performing an act of separation, saying "Yes" to what we want to attend to and "No" to everything else. If you didn't have the power to focus your attention, you couldn't read this book very well. How this book smells could capture your attention as easily as the words printed on the pages. The conscious mind is the mind of sense discrimination.

What distinguishes the conscious mind from the unconscious, as we learned in the last chapter, is this power of attention. While you are able to focus your conscious mind, your unconscious is picking up all sorts of other messages. If you were conscious of what the unconscious was sensing, you would be helplessly distracted. There needs to be a separation between the conscious and the unconscious mind, or else there would be no conscious mind as we know it.

The young child needs to be able to forget that he or she is contained within a parental world and be free to play and become involved in make-believe games to develop skills. At the same time, there is a need to also recognize one's roots and source of sustenance. There is a reason for separation, yet the separation is only in the mind, it is not real.

The ancient wisdom of the East recognized this important aspect of the conscious mind. It is expressed in their image of the relationship of yin and yang, shown in Figure 3.

The yin-yang symbol shows two objects. Can you see them? One is a black comet swirling around a white sky. The other is a white comet swirling in a black sky. That's right, there are two comets, but you tend to see only one at a time. Depending on how you look at the picture determines which color you see as the object and which you see as the background.

Figure 3

Yin and Yang

Looking at a pattern and making some part of it object and the rest background is the conscious mind at work. That's the way it wants to see. It's hard to see both at the same time. Yet the purpose of the yin-yang symbol is to remind us that the seen and the unseen are part of the same reality. It shows us the power of the conscious mind as well as what it forgets in order to exist.

Yet that same power to focus our attention and to perceive separateness has also made us appear to ourselves as separate from each other, from our environment, separate from earth, separate from creation, separate from God. It has cut us off from our spiritual heritage, the invisible bond that unites all life. To our conscious, sensation-based mind, there is no invisible unity to life. There are just a bunch of things, including atoms, rocks, plants, animals, people, buildings, and automobiles, that somehow interact with one another.

All religious traditions, in the East and in the West, have developed forms of discipline for the conscious mind to help it to wake up from its illusion of separateness and recognize its roots in nonseparated wholeness. It takes the conscious mind a great deal of effort to realize that the perception of separateness is but a useful tool, not the ultimate reality.

If we are to ask the conscious mind to surrender its grip on its own cutting edge of sensory consciousness, it will help to offer it something in return. We can introduce it to the *soul* of the mind.

CHAPTER 4

THE SOUL OF THE MIND

An entity body-mind was first a soul before it entered into material consciousness.

Edgar Cayce 4083-1

WE'VE DUG DOWN into the depths of the mind, exploring some of the fascinating splendors of the unconscious regions. At first, it seemed that we were digging down into a dark cave. Then, upon digging deeper, this dark region of the underworld of the mind opened up onto a vast vista.

Looking deep within ourselves, deeper than the subconscious mind, we see the enormous sky of the superconscious. The infinite world within and the heavens above are as one. What are we to make of this surprise? How can it be that we have such a connection with the infinite?

The psychiatrist Carl Jung found that deep within each individual, at the central core of their being, was a religious entity. He called it their real Self, or soul. It was from this level of consciousness that Edgar Cayce gave his psychic readings. He called the soul's awareness the superconscious mind.

While Carl Jung was struggling through his research efforts in Switzerland to understand his discovery of the universal level of the mind, Edgar Cayce was devoting his life in America to giving the universal mind a voice. Whereas Jung was finding indirect evidence of the superconscious soul and examining its footprints, Cayce allowed the superconscious to speak directly. By going into his trance state, Cayce was like an ambassador of good will, helping the superconscious mind to speak to us and tell us about itself.

From this source, we learn something important about the nature of the human being: We are spiritual beings, we are souls. Our physical existence is a reflection and a byproduct of our spirituality, manifested into physical reality through the creative power of the mind.

The Creation of Souls

As a child did you ever wonder about the origin of things and your place in the universe? I can remember looking up at the sky and trying to count the stars. The enormity of the universe was overwhelming. What or where was the earth in all this? And what of little me?

From science class I knew my body was composed of millions of atoms. Were all the stars in the sky like atoms, too? If the stars were atoms, whose body did they make? Was that God? If so, then was I a particle in God's body? Where in that giant body was my atom—nearer God's nose or the toes? Could God feel me, I wondered, jumping up and down?

Compared to the universe, I felt so tiny. Yet my mind, something invisible but still something I could feel inside me, seemed large somehow. It could reach into the heavens. Although my body could be zillions and zillions of miles away from one of God's eyes, my mind somehow felt close to God's mind, as if our minds might almost touch.

I can remember discussing such ideas with my childhood friends. Outdoor slumber parties under the starry sky were favorite occasions for such speculations. For us kids, these fantasies were very real. It was all so wonderous and believable. We were natural mystics. Sometimes kids can be wiser than grown-ups. The image of each of us being an atom in God's body is exactly how Cayce, in his superconscious state, described the origin and nature of the soul.

Out of a black hole that hid the original, dark and lonely mystery, God burst forth in a flash of creative impulse. Like an only child who creates imaginary playmates, so God burst out into souls. The creation of souls was an act of God's creative generosity. It was also an expression of a desire for companionship.

How would you imagine it? How would you envision a soul as being a piece of God? My childhood friends and I imagined it pretty much as in Cayce's description, "an atom in the body of God." Just as the shape of atoms resembles the shape of solar systems, as an atom of God, we may in some sense resemble God. As the Bible puts it, we are created in the image of God. What does that suggest to you? One meaning is that we were created through God's imagination. It's an important concept that will become more meaningful to you as we go along. Another meaning is that we are somehow a reflection of God, that we correspond to God in some way.

Cayce indicates that the Bible is giving a true and accurate description of the relationship of the individual soul to that of God. The soul is both a piece of God, right out of God's mind, and at the same time an image of God. Cayce used words such as "model" and "replica" when describing how the soul is a carbon copy, in a smaller version, of the creator. In modern terms, we might say our souls are clones of God.

In simple terms, we are children of God. If God had kids, wouldn't they be Godlike themselves? But God's kids are souls, not people as we normally experience them. We've become hardened by our concrete, physical existence, and forget that we are souls. So to say that we are children of God seems only like a wistful, poetic image, certainly not a literal truth. It is true, however, and it is coming time to get back to that truth. It will set us free. It should also enhance our self-esteem and give us the will toward assuming a creative responsibility toward life.

In Shirley MacLaine's TV miniseries *Out On a Limb,* her guide asks her to try saying, "I am God." She hesitates, understandably, then tries saying it. I can imagine that to most viewers, watching Shirley declare herself to be God seems insane, at the least sacrilegious. In fact, many people locked away in mental institutions declare the very same thing.

Cayce would have us understand, however, that what Shirley is saying is essentially true, *provided,* and it is a big proviso, that we know who we mean when we say "I." It is not the ordinary "I" who is God. It is not the little self, the ego Cayce called the "personality." Rather, it is the larger self, the soul, who can claim some identity with God.

To most people's ears, to hear "I am God" is an egotistical statement. Yet what Cayce wants us to focus on is the spiritual identity of a person, the fact that we are souls and as such, a part of God. Moreover, as souls, we have all of the attributes of God. Not that individual souls are all of God, but that each soul possesses the qualities of God. Each soul is God in miniature.

It is somewhat like the waves on the ocean. Each wave appears like a separate thing, yet each is a part of the ocean. And each wave is water, like the whole ocean, and contains the molecular components of the ocean. The soul is made up of the same stuff as God and has the same characteristics of God.

The most important quality of God is as the creator. Perhaps that is why "the Creator" is one of the most common names for God. And as souls, we have the same creative powers as God. Hearing this, our little "I," our ego would love to have such power, and drools at the prospect. Yet once we begin to appreciate the nature of this creative power, and how it derives from the soul, we realize that it is a responsibility as well as a glorious opportunity. It is the role the mind plays in this creative power that is the essential theme of this book.

Dimensions of Soul: Spirit, Mind, and Will

How do you speak about the soul? The word has a long and mixed history. Usually, the soul is talked about as something that we "have": we are not to lose it, let it be destroyed or tarnished, but we are to have it saved. It's something we are to look after, as if it were a thing in our care. Where do you keep your soul? Do you know where your soul is tonight?

Edgar Cayce turns our ordinary reality on its head. He explains that, in fact, we *are* souls. It's not that we *have* them. In truth, souls have us, *souls are us!*

The soul has created the body it uses in the material world, the body we think of as us. The soul has the creative power of mind, originating in the heart of the superconscious and extending to the fingertips of the conscious mind—that small piece of mind we identify as being who we are. But our bodies and our conscious minds, as we normally think of ourselves, are but the tip of the nose of the soul. Our true being is on a much grander scale.

As lofty and mysterious as soul may seem, we do have some instinct for it. We talk about a "loss of soul" when we sense that something important is missing in life. It may be love that is missing. It may be sadness at the loss of the human element in the modern mechanical age. It may be the spark of spontaneity. Soul refers to something especially human.

When we say that something has killed a person's "spirit," we are referring to an important and vital element of life. When the spirit of an activity disappears, or the spirit with which we do something is gone, we feel sad. We miss the energy and spark that the spirit brings.

We each have a "mind of our own." A person who can no longer think for himself is no longer a full human being. Followers of dogmatic indoctrination, no longer with minds of their own, don't seem completely human, but appear more like robots or trained animals. We say that "a mind is a terrible thing to waste," recognizing its importance to living a full human life of self-respect and self-directedness. When we criticize an activity as mindless, or mind-deadening, we are recognizing that anything that kills the mind is dehumanizing.

Having our own free will is also something we recognize as essential to being human. When we meet someone who has lost his will, we are quite concerned that something important to life is missing. We find offensive leaders who steal the will of their followers. We disapprove of torture and brainwashing that is directed toward the breaking of the will. To be forced to do something against our will feels dehumanizing, and we naturally rebel against such pressure. The freedom of our will is something we cherish as particularly essential to a human being.

Spirit, mind, and will are the soul dimensions to human life. They are mourned when they are missing. Each of these has soul connotations for us. Soul as spirit, mind, and will is something that makes humans people rather than machines or animals, free rather than slaves.

These are the aspects of soul that Cayce identified. We have always known these qualities were important. We just didn't necessarily connect them with the soul. Cayce would have us recognize and appreciate these three qualities as the dimensions of soul.

He was specific in his reference to the "dimensionality" of the soul. He wanted us to understand how the finite, conscious world of material life necessarily interprets the infinite. The conscious mind of the senses lives in a three-dimensional world. We have height, breadth, and width. There are also the three dimensions of space, time, and mass. From this three-dimensional viewpoint, the soul is also understood in terms of three dimensions.

Spirit, mind, and will are each a basic dimension of soul, each a distinct quality. When any dimension gets shrunk to a minimum, we feel sad. There is a deadening in us, a flattening of our lives, as if we lived in a two-dimensional world, not really human. To be truly alive as human beings, all three need to be present for us.

Spirit: The One Life Force

Spirit is the life force. It is energy, the one and only energy in the universe. God is energy. When God created souls, this same energy, or spirit, became a part of each soul. Each soul consists of the same life force as God and the rest of creation.

Science recognizes today four forms of energy: gravity, electromagnetism, and the strong and the weak atomic forces. Theorists believe, and are attempting to prove, that all four forms of energy are variations on the same one basic energy.

Cayce taught that all energy is of the same source. Atomic energy, solar energy, love, hatred, etc., are different aspects of the same one energy. The first law of creation is that everything proceeds from the same one source, the same energy. That is the spirit.

As physics defines it, energy is the ability to do work. Energy is the ability to apply force through a distance or over a period of time. There is power in energy, the ability to affect change, to do work, to make a difference. Energy is the dynamo, the spark, the life. Energy is vibration, it is pure excitement.

We never encounter pure vibration. We always encounter it patterned in a certain way. This same one energy can assume different forms, different guises, depending on the circumstances. If life is approached in one manner, atomic energy is experienced. Through a different set of circumstances, electrical energy can be realized. Humans experience energy in terms of stamina, motivation, drives, and feelings. These are but different faces of energy. What gives spirit, or energy, its face is the mind. The mind patterns energy.

Mind: The Pattern Generator

The spirit in which we do something is the quality of energy we put into it. The quality of the energy has to do with how it is patterned. It means the ideals or purposes we have in mind.

The spirit in which we do something is often more important than what we actually do, for it reflects our intentions. As William Blake said, "A truth that's told with bad intent / Beats all the lies you can invent."

Love is the ultimate spiritual force. We know that something done in the spirit of love is done in the best possible way. In the Gospel of John we read, "God is love." That is the ideal form of creative energy. It is energy patterned as a caring, empathic embrace of respect and good will.

It is the mind that patterns energy. There is only one energy, or spirit. When we speak of the spirit in which something is done, we are referring to the mental pattern that is shaping that one energy. How we experience energy is a reflection of how it is being patterned by the mind. The mind is the second attribute of the soul.

The Mind of God that created the whole universe was given to souls at the time of their creation. All the wonderful patterns in nature are the creations of that Mind. The mind of God gave shape to the spirit by means of those patterns. That same mind is active within each soul.

Mind organizes and creates patterns. A good mind is one that is particularly perceptive of patterns. A creative mind can see unusual patterns that others ignore. An alert mind is aware, awake and present in a situation, ready to recognize old patterns and create new ones.

By working with patterns, mind is the builder. It shapes energy into particular patterns and thus has an affect on how the energy is expressed.

The desire for a new job, a new house, or a new relationship is a source of energy. It is the mind that begins to create patterns that will satisfy that desire, that will give shape to an opportunity. In the imagination new patterns of working are conceived, blueprints for better living are constructed, scenarios of satisfying relationships are envisioned.

The mind operates at several levels. We are most familiar with the conscious mind. But now we know that behind the conscious mind there is the subconscious, and behind that, the superconscious mind. Each has its own realm of specialty.

The conscious mind is good at focused detail, discriminating the finer facts of one pattern from another.

The subconscious mind is less focused, but it is better at perceiving subtle or broader patterns that the conscious mind misses. When we can't see the forest for the trees, it is because our conscious mind is totally in charge. Lay aside the conscious mind, as in sleep, and the subconscious will reveal patterns in our lives that we hadn't noticed. It was through a dream, if you recall, that the student recognized that O,T,T,F,F were numbers.

The superconscious mind is aware not only of the patterns in our lives, but of the patterns from all our lives and the patterns of their interrelationships. Its access to universal awareness gives it a perspective on the eternal patterns of truth and law that govern all aspects of existence.

Recall our example from the last chapter concerning the girl with asthma. It was the subconscious of the mother and child that recognized the pattern that linked the mother's attitude with the child's physical disturbance. It was the superconscious that recognized the relationship between that pattern in the family and centuries-old patterns of energy that people had once regarded religiously.

Will: The Chooser

The mind can create endless patterns to direct and shape energy. To the mind, one pattern is not necessarily better than another. The choice of pattern is not the job of the mind. It is the job of the will. We have choices to make about which mental patterns will shape the flow of energy in our lives. We have that choice because we have free will. It is the third dimension of the soul.

One of the most significant choices made by God when creating souls was to give each soul free will. God gave souls free will because of the purpose God had for souls. According to Cayce, it is God's intention that souls be companions to God, not slaves or robots. Although that is God's intention, it is our free will to choose this companionship, to ignore it or reject it. It is important to God that we *do* have the free will to make that choice.

Think about it for a moment. When you spend time with a friend, isn't it important to you that the friend *wants* to be with you? If you thought the person didn't really want to be with you, but was doing it for other reasons, wouldn't that affect your feelings? When you ask your friend, or spouse, "What would you like to do?" and the answer is, "I don't know, whatever you would like," don't you find that frustrating?

A woman may feel ill at ease when her male partner seems always to act in a way that is designed to please her but that reveals nothing about the man's own feelings. Likewise, men are not attracted to women who seem to do whatever is asked of them, for they get the feeling that such women would act that way with any man. A man wants to know that the woman is responding to *him*.

We want the acts of love we receive from our friends to be the result of free choice. We want our friends to *choose* to love us, not to feel obligated to do so.

In the same way, God wants each soul to be a conscious companion by choice. It is God's intention that each of us realize that we are souls, children of God, and assume our rightful place as cooperative co-creators. In order to fulfill that intention, God gave souls free will and permits its wide use. The soul is free because it has the will to make choices.

With the mind, you can think of many different ways of spending your time. Obviously, you can't do them all. Will is the ability to make choices. It is the choosing function.

We can see our will at work in what captures our attention. This is our unconscious will, not consciously applied. To a great extent, we have lost our free will. When we are not conscious of our beliefs, our perceptions, and our values, we make our choices subconsciously, without conscious deliberation. Habits free the conscious mind of having to reinvent the wheel at every turn. Yet habits based on old choices can prove later to be dictators that steal our will.

To regain the freedom of our will, we must become consciously aware of what we have been subconsciously choosing. Then we can choose anew.

Cayce wants us to realize that there is no power in the world that can resist the power of our will. Astrology, drug addiction, karma, ironclad circumstances, bureaucracy, even the laws of nature—none of these is stronger than our will.

Even the laws of nature are not as strong as our will. In this startling statement, Cayce anticipated modern thinking about natural law. Truth itself is a growing thing, he said. He indicated that the laws of nature are but habits of the universe and subject to change through learning and will. It is something to ponder as you begin to discover the creative power of the mind.

Creation: Soul Projection

Suppose you are feeling fidgety. Your mind wanders from topic to topic, your arms and legs are restless. You are experiencing energy that wants to be expressed. But what shall you do? You think of various chores that need to be done, but you don't know if you feel like doing them. You think of that painting or knitting project that is unfinished, of some friends you have been wanting to visit, or of a book that you have been reading. None of these things does the trick, and you fuss about as your mind continues to flip through its files of ideas, memories, and other images of how you might express your energy.

Somewhere in that process you find yourself cleaning up the house or straightening out the garage. It may have been a conscious decision, or you may have only stumbled onto it. In either case, among the various possibilities your mind considered, you chose that one. Your will selected one of the patterns provided by the mind for the expression of your energy. Now that fidgety energy has been transformed into a physical reality: your house is clean, the garage is reorganized. And you feel different.

This example is something that is familiar to most all of us. It also illustrates a very important secret about the process of creation. What began as energy, and was experienced as a bodily feeling, evolved into a variety of mental patterns, or images. Through an act of choice, the exercise of either conscious or unconscious willing, a particular mental pattern was used to channel the energy into a specific activity. The result was a physical, concrete reality. Energy was patterned by the mind to achieve a resulting manifestation in the physical world.

The sequence, from pure energy, through a mental pattern, and into an observable manifestation, is the process of creation. Cayce expresses this process as a formula: "The spirit is the life, the mind the builder, and the physical is the result." The formula works in all areas of life. It is true for the condition of our own bodies, as well as the creation of all life forms. It is also true for the experiences we have in life, as well as the course of history. What we see around us and what we experience in life began as energy that was patterned in the mind.

Look around you, at your living conditions, your job, your family and the other elements of your life. What you are seeing is a bit of history. The circumstances of your life are living relics of thoughts you chose to entertain in the past. Some you recognize. The job you hold now, for example, you may recognize to be the result of earlier desires, fantasies, and hard work. Other aspects you may not recognize. There are probably circumstances in your life that do not please you, that you did not choose. These are the circumstances that you will be able to address as you become more fully aware of how the mind creates reality.

Life as we experience it is a projection of the soul. The word *projection* provides a useful way to imagine the process of creation. There is an analogy I find especially appealing that was developed by Herbert Puryear and Mark Thurston, two psychologists who are experienced students of the Cayce readings. It involves the workings of a film projection camera in a movie theater.

Within the camera is a powerful light bulb. It only does one thing—it shines a bright, white light. The light bulb represents the spirit, the one energy of all creation. The projector accepts the insertion of film, transparent sheets filled with colored patterns. Whereas the camera bulb remains a constant, the film can contain almost anything. It is the creative pattern-making ability of the mind that invents what will be on the film. The film represents the mind's mental pattern. The pattern on the film shapes the light coming from the bulb. As the light passes through colored portions of the film, the light appears colored, even though the bulb is itself emitting only white light. The patterns on the film blocks light here and lets it pass there, creating the impression of shapes. When this filtered light is projected upon a screen, images appear.

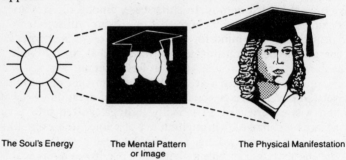

| The Soul's Energy | The Mental Pattern or Image | The Physical Manifestation |

Figure 4

The Creation Formula

The screen makes it possible for the images to be seen. Cayce refers to this screen as the "skein of time and space." The three-dimensional world is like a screen, or device that allows mind-patterned spirit to be visible. Without the screen, the projected images would travel along the light beam out into infinity. The screen "captures" the projected image, allowing it to become visible. So it is with life in our material existence. The existence of the time/space continuum allows physicality to exist for our consciousness.

What we take to be our bodies, the flesh, blood and bones that feel so concretely real to us, are really projections of consciousness, like images on a screen. Originating in the energy of the spirit, and patterned by our minds, our soul creates a body in its own image, just as souls were created in the image of God. Your soul "grew" your body from its mind. Your body is the soul's physical symbol for itself. Your soul also creates, by projection, the experiences that you have in the movie you call life. The body that seems so fixed and slow to change, as well as the circumstances of your life, are as easy to change as it is to place a different film in the projector. That makes the mind quite a magical instrument.

The "magical lantern," as a movie projector was first called, is magical indeed. You know what it's like to go to the movies and get caught up in the picture. The movie is hypnotic. We forget our own reality and enter the reality of the movie. A light bulb is being filtered by a series of colored patterns and projected onto a screen. Meanwhile, we are transported to faraway places and taken on an emotional journey. We become part of another life, another reality.

The invention of the film projector has had a tremendous impact on our culture. No doubt its power is based on the fact that its mechanics and effects mimic something about the nature of reality. The source of the invention was also possibly the result of an unconscious knowing on the inventor's part of this secret of reality, that it is a projection of consciousness.

Life, like a movie, is a dream. We first imagine it, and then what we imagine we project. We are hypnotized by the projection, and the dream becomes real. That life is like a dream is part of the magic. That it becomes our reality is, however, somewhat of a problem.

Souls at Play Lose Their Way Home

Little Johnny was hard at play when it happened. Armed with his two six-shooters, one in each hand, he was courageously holding off a band of outlaws. He had mortally wounded all but two of the bad men and was about to face off his last opponents. He stepped out of his hiding spot and was marching toward his destiny, issuing the final challenge to surrender or else, when the scene was shattered by a piercing voice announcing, "John-ny! Come ho-ome! Dinnertime!" In an instant, the world of this little hero, who was about to be crowned and badged as the Shining Sheriff, shrunk to that of a little boy called home by his mother. As much as he liked to eat, he wished he could have taken his chow back at the saloon, where he could have enjoyed his reward with his admiring fans. What a letdown!

Johnny's situation is like Cayce's story of souls, except that, unlike Johnny, few souls have heard the call to come home. The movies that souls have projected, their dreams, have become so real that they have forgotten that their creations are but playthings. They have forgotten about home. All they have, it seems, are their dreams.

Using the spiritual energy granted from God, and with the patterns in their minds, souls co-created with God the three-dimensional world we call earth life. It began as a legitimate foray into what a sensory existence would feel like. It was a creative extension of the Kingdom of God. But the sensory world, like the movie on the screen, had a hypnotic power. Souls began to get caught up in the world of the senses.

Souls fell in consciousness from their natural, superconscious birthright, to identifying solely with the conscious mind and its life of sensations. Like the two-year-old, souls had to say "No!" to their connection with the creator, perhaps to fully explore the implications of using their own will.

Relying on their own will, choosing the sensory world of the conscious mind, souls have pursued the hypnotic dream of their projections. In their enchantment, seeing nature not as part of their very being but as a playground for exploitation, they have enmeshed themselves in a mechanical nightmare. It is somewhat like the situation of the "Sorcerer's Apprentice" as seen in Walt Disney's *Fantasia*. Things have gotten out of hand.

What will be the outcome? There needs to be an awakening from the nightmare. This awakening is occurring. It is part of what has been called the "New Age."

Science, as a refinement of the conscious mind, not only has created some of the technological threats to our existence, but has also begun to realize the interconnectedness of life as well as its nonmaterial essence. A different perspective on life is gaining acceptance.

Yet the awakening is also part of an ageless process. God has never ceased calling us home. There have always been those individuals who have responded to the call and have awakened from their sleep. They, in turn, have tried to help God wake up others. The pressures of modern existence have been a recent incentive to hearken to the call of the spirit.

Edgar Cayce predicted these troubling times, and advised that we view the pressures in our lives as an opportunity to develop a new mind-set.

There are those who believe that nothing that mankind can do will make a difference in the outcome of the world, for it is totally up to God. And there are those who believe that it is totally up to human beings to try to fix up what is wrong with the world.

Cayce's view agrees with both sides of this debate. It is the God part of mankind that is the ultimate power, yet God acts through the mind and actions of human beings. When human beings become aware of the spiritual basis of the mind, they become even more creative in their ability to help themselves, each other, and God to help make life on earth as it is in Heaven.

The Creative Use of the Mind

The bursting of Johnny's bubble, from the imagined invulnerable, conquering hero to the reality of being a little boy son of a mother calling him home, is something like the disappointment of the conscious mind in discovering the truth of its status in the scheme of things. As Johnny marches home, he feels that his he-man world has been forever stolen from him, that he will never get to play again.

Of course, that is not true. As his mother would be the first to admit, Johnny's play is vitally important to his maturation. While chasing the outlaws, he develops initiative, courage, persistence, and other skills and self-confidence that will help him in the world. At the same time, he does have a family life, and needs to eat.

Likewise, the conscious mind, when it learns that its reality is of its own construction and is contained within a larger, unconscious reality, is afraid it won't be allowed to play its games anymore. On the contrary, the creative games the conscious mind plays are very important. It needs to learn to play them well. Yet it does need to realize it has a home, one not of its own making, but one that supports and feeds it. Then it can be free to do its job, which is to play its games in the most creative of ways.

The mind is the creator of consciousness. With our consciousness, we become aware of aspects of existence that might otherwise go unnoticed. Consciousness helps the world come alive. What would happen to the world if no one was aware of its threatened existence? Becoming consciously aware of more and more details of existence, as in science for example, helps more and more of the world become alive and real for us. This creative part of consciousness seems to also be important to God.

In one of his prayers, Cayce affirmed that to God "we [are] as lights in thee." As a soul, each of us is one of God's ways of experiencing the world. We each shine our light onto the world in our own way. We each reveal the world to God in our particular way. Carl Jung, in his later life, imagined God as a giant being who was peering out from the minds of individual people relying on their consciousness to get new glimpses of the world. God's creation continues through our own, individual responses to life.

The way we see the world affects the way we respond to it. The way we respond to it affects the world itself. God wants us to become more conscious and aware of this fact so that we can assume more responsibility in our role as co-creators with God. We are given the freedom and responsibility to create our lives as we choose.

You can have it your way. What way will you choose? If you get the big picture, if you realize that life is a dream, then how do you choose what kind of dream you want for your life? The implications of such a question must now be examined.

PART 2

What Do You Have in Mind? Have It Your Way: Creating An Ideal Life

THOUSANDS OF PEOPLE suffering from physical disease, financial misfortune, problems at home or at work, and every other human predicament imaginable wrote to Edgar Cayce for a psychic reading. In the diagnosis of the problem, Cayce often revealed the existence of some unsuspected hidden factor. It might have been a condition in the body, a past life memory, the activity of a disincarnate spirit, or the negative thoughts of someone in the person's environment. Regardless of what surprising revelation Cayce offered, he also repeated what was a constant theme throughout his career of helping people overcome the obstacles in their lives. He insisted that the people drop the notion that they were a victim of their circumstances. In gentle ways, in ways that were forceful and direct, or in an indirect manner, Cayce indicated that we are the creators of our own troublesome circumstances. If we will assume the responsibility for our misfortunes, we can then create our own fortunes.

Cayce did not share this revelation to blame us for our problems, to accuse us, or to make us feel bad. He was offering a gift, a road to freedom and to the inheritance of our divine birthright as creative souls.

His message was actually a restatement of the ancient and timeless revelation of all mystical experience. The "Perennial Philosophy," the universal core of all religions, states, "That art thou!" You, God, and reality are one. What you meet in life, as Cayce would say, is your self, the reflection of a soul projecting into the three-dimensional world. Cayce explained in great detail the meaning of this perennial wisdom. His explanation ranged from the most general of religious truths to the most specific facts of psychological functioning and the workings of the body.

Today this precept has become the motto of the New Age: "You are a God! You create your own reality." *The Course in Miracles,* EST training, Shirley MacLaine's workshops, and many others are based on this precept. Recognizing the power of the mind to shape our lives is indeed an important part of the new way of thinking that characterizes the New Age. If you suspect that those slogans, however, are a bit inflated, then you have detected, in fact, their fatal flaw. To assume that you are a god and that you create your own reality gives you a burden that can be too heavy to carry. The value of the Cayce readings on this topic is that it presents the notion of creating your own reality in a manner that avoids the pitfall of increased self-aggrandizement and self-blame. In this section of the book, therefore, we will discover how Cayce approached the question of creating an ideal life.

First we will explore the proposition that there is no objective reality independent of a subjective point of view. Such an idea is the modern scientific and philosophical equivalent of the Perennial Philosophy. The principle of universal subjectivity forces you to decide upon what subjective viewpoint you wish to adopt.

At this crucial point, Cayce indicates the importance of establishing your values, especially spiritual values. He considered the choice of a spiritual ideal the most important task we have in life. In the exploration of this topic, we will learn about the role of ideals in shaping reality. Here is where Cayce will help us avoid the pitfall usually encountered by the naive application of the slogan "You create your own reality."

We will then follow Cayce's prescription for using an ideal to deal with life circumstances and to mold them to match our values. The way ideals shape the creative powers of the mind is through our attitudes. Attitudes can be used creatively to reshape circumstances. How we respond to a situation, and whether the situation claims us as its victim or we claim it to be our opportunity for growth, is a matter of attitude.

Mind is the builder and the physical is the result. Attitudes become reflected in physical reality, in the health of our body and in the physical circumstances of our lives. Cayce also knew the secret of using a reverse strategy, and we will learn how to use the physical level of existence to gain leverage to change destructive attitudes and emotional states. Even when we feel caught in the trap of a negative mental framework, there is something we can do to free ourselves from its grip.

Finally, we will learn about the use of the will in creating an ideal life. Cayce appreciated the proper use of willpower but wanted us to learn how to take advantage of a higher level of will. The use of willpower can be a tiring exercise and is limited in its effectiveness. Ideals have a will of their own, and we can learn how to harness their power. Finding the harmonious marriage between conscious willpower and divine will transforms the challenge of creating one's own reality to the opportunity for spiritual self-realization.

You are not a passive target of the arrows of misfortune, but the active creator of your life. Your life, and everything you experience in it, is a creation and a reflection of the ideas and values you accept. You can choose to take this fact and blame yourself for your misfortunes, or you can use it to take charge and create an ideal life. Begin by trying to look at your problem as an opportunity to learn something about yourself and as an opportunity to develop new skills and new levels of awareness. By patient practice, you can develop the ability to master everything.

CHAPTER 5

REALITY IS A SUBJECTIVE EXPERIENCE

> That ye think, that ye put your mind to work upon, to live upon, to feed upon, to live with, to abide with, to associate with in the mind, that your soul-body becomes! That is the law. That is the destiny. That is as from the beginning, that each thought of the Creator bore within itself its own fruit as from the beginning.
>
> *Edgar Cayce 262-78*

TWO PEOPLE LOOKING up at the clouds will see different patterns in the sky. One may see a giant riding in a carriage while the other sees a giraffe. We recognize in this situation that what each person sees is something subjective, something based on the person's own needs and interests. On the other hand, we realize that the cloud is actually a floating mass of water vapor. That's what we call *objective* reality.

From an early age we learn the difference between subjective and objective. Subjective is what we feel, what we wish for or fear. Subjective is our personal point of view. Objective is what is really there, the plain truth. Knowing the difference between objective reality and subjective belief is the basis of sound mental health.

This obvious truth is fundamental to our upbringing and to our worldview. To contradict it will cause objections, create confusions, and even elicit fears. Nevertheless, let it be said: there is no objective reality, only subjective experience.

We have examined Cayce's metaphysical model that explains the source of this subjectivity. Physical reality is the by-product of the mind's mental patterns giving form to the one single energy of creation.

Cayce also expressed this point of view in more practical terms. He often remarked that the thoughts a person entertains shape the experiences the person encounters. He was fond of quoting from Proverbs: "As he thinketh in his heart, so is he." (27:3) Were he alive today, he might well quote the

Beatles: "What's within you is without you." Our life circumstances reflect the history of our thought patterns.

Our expectations, our beliefs, and even the thoughts we use to understand our world determine what we experience. We see what we understand. Perhaps that is why, in our language, "I see" and "I understand" mean essentially the same thing. Each person's experience is subjective, a personal point of view. There is no other reality.

We may regard science as the ultimate in human objectivity. It is a questionable assumption. Science is governed by the same expectancy principle, because science is an activity of human beings. When confronted by scientists wishing to test his ideas, Cayce questioned the purposes of the scientists. He knew that behind their instruments and their methodologies there was the same subjectivity as in any other area of human experience. This subjectivity expresses itself in expectations, in purposes and attitudes. Science creates a reality to match its vision.

The purpose of this chapter is to explore the assumption that there is such a thing as objectivity. We'll look at what we typically assume to be examples of objective processes. We'll see that there is good reason to suspect the presence of subjectivity in any experience of reality.

Expectations Create Reality: The "Rosenthal Effect"

We spend much of our lives interacting with people. People play a role in many of our endeavors. How we get along with others has a lot to do with our successes and failures. How do people respond to you? Do you find them to be kind and helpful, or do they stand in your way? Do they please you or annoy you?

The truth of the matter is that people will tend to mirror back to you your own expectations. The way they treat you reveals the thoughts you carry, your assumptions and beliefs. What you expect from people tends to become a self-fulfilling prophecy.

Consider the case of psychologists. They study people in the laboratory using scientific methods. They are highly trained in the careful observation of people's behaviors in strictly controlled situations. Psychologists have found, however, that their experiments also tend to create the very reality their research is supposed to objectively observe and measure. Self-fulfilling prophecies occur in laboratory research as well as in daily life.

This disturbing fact is sometimes called the "Rosenthal effect," named after the Harvard psychologist Robert Rosenthal, who first discovered it. I'm going to go into some detail, because it shows, in a way that is rarely considered, that our expectations are indeed self-fulfilling. It will make you think twice about how you interact with other people.

The experimental subjects in Rosenthal's original research weren't the usual ones. He studied research psychologists while they performed their own experiments. He would recruit ten researchers to each perform a certain experiment that he had designed. He would ask them. "Find out if it is really true that . . ." and then he would tell them his hypothesis. However, he didn't tell them all the same thing. He told half the researchers that his theory was one way, while he told the others that his idea was the reverse. Then he sent them to work in the laboratory and awaited their results. For the most part, the researchers returned with results that *confirmed what they thought to be the hypothesis.*

Rosenthal and others have confirmed this phenomenon in hundreds of experiments. Some have involved the researchers' testing human subjects on various tasks: studies of perception and learning, personality and intelligence testing, and studies of physical reactions within the body. Others have involved researchers working with animals. The results have all been the same. Somehow the researchers unintentionally affected the people or the animals they were studying to produce the results they were expecting.

You can imagine how upsetting the Rosenthal effect has been to the science of psychology. Many experiments have been conducted to find out the source of this problem. The first suspect was observational error. For hundreds of years we have known that scientists make mistakes, either in what they observe or how they record their observations. More often than not, the errors are in favor of the experimenter's bias. Errors of this sort, however, are rarely large enough to account for the Rosenthal effect. In fact, even when the experimenter is only conducting the experiment and not recording the data, Rosenthal's expectancy effect still occurs!

Then researchers began to observe experimenters through one-way mirrors, to see if they could find out if experimenters behaved in some manner that could explain their ability to produce the results that they were expecting. In this way it was discovered that it was indeed because experimenters interacted differently with their subjects in small, but apparently significant, ways that they led their subjects to confirm their expectations. How this happens is still not totally clear.

In one research project, for example, involving an experiment comparing "smart" with "dull" mice, the observer saw the experimenters handle more often the mice they believed to be smarter, giving them, literally, "more strokes." On the other hand, the experimenters talked more to the mice they believed to be duller. Is it possible that handling mice makes them do better at their tasks, while talking to them makes them do less well? When you try to think of an answer to this question, keep in mind that the Rosenthal effect has also occurred when experimenters were studying microscopic worms!

Because of the tremendous implications, researchers have conducted hundreds of experiments studying experimenters' interaction with human subjects. Examining movies and videotapes of an experimenter's behavior has revealed many disturbing facts. In another example, experimenters, both male and female, tended to smile more at female subjects than at male subjects. Many so-called "scientific facts" about the differences between the sexes may be the unintentional effect of sex stereotypes on the behavior of experimenters. This unfortunate effect occurs because experimental subjects behave differently when they receive a smile!

Smiles aren't the only thing that affect the experimental subject. The experimenter's sex and personality, need for power or approval, personal warmth, degree of anxiousness, and talkativeness affect the way a subject responds in an experiment. Whether the experimenter has had a good day or a bad day affects the outcome of the experiment. It has even been demonstrated that whether the experimenter is sweating or not, or how fast the experimenter is breathing, also affects the subject's behavior!

What isn't clear, but is now an active area of current research, is how the experimenter communicates his or her scientific expectations to the subjects through such acts as sweating or bodily movements. From what we've learned about subliminal perception, it shouldn't be a surprise that a subject would subconsciously notice such details about the experimenter's behavior. Perhaps the communication occurs through the subconscious—through that invisible link between minds.

Experiments attempting to control the Rosenthal effect have discovered how pervasive it can be. It seems almost impossible to prevent. It is able to seep through so many boundaries, however, that it almost does seem psychic.

Even when the experimenters conduct their experiments through remote control, the effect is evident. In one case, researchers had the experimenters give their instructions to the subjects on a tape recorder. There was no personal contact with the subjects. Nevertheless, the experimenter's expectancy was somehow relayed to the subjects and affected the results. In another case, experimenters used proxies to conduct the experiment. These assistants didn't know the experimenters' expectancies, yet they still affected the subjects in such a way to confirm those expectations.

If well-trained psychologists tend to confirm their expectations in their scientifically controlled experiments with people, you may suspect that it is quite likely that in your own interactions with people, you also tend to confirm your expectations. The Rosenthal effect shows us all that our expectations about how people are going to behave around us are indeed self-fulfilling.

Sensation Is Subjective

Social relations are certainly a subjective matter. So let's bring our examination of subjectivity down a notch to a more concrete level. Let's look at the senses, our eyes and our ears, and how they perceive the facts of reality. Aren't our senses themselves objective? Don't our eyes, ears, nose, tongue, fingers, and other physical organs of perception within our body tell us about the world of reality?

We don't experience the chemical interactions that occur on our tongue or in our nose. What we actually experience are tastes and smells. The chemical compounds that excite these events don't themselves contain the emotional reactions we experience. The joy in the smell of freshly baked bread is in the mind.

We don't experience the pulsing of physical energy in the air that vibrates in our ears. What we do experience is sound. Sound is a mental event, not a physical one. There is nothing in the physical characteristics of the pulsating air in the opera house that would explain why so many people are crying.

We don't directly experience the electromagnetic energy that hits our eyes; we experience light. Light is a subjective experience, a creation of the mind. We don't experience the wavelength of this energy; we experience color. Color isn't an aspect of the objective world, it is an attribute of the mind.

Our physical senses respond to physical processes in the external, objective world, but what we experience are subjective phenomena created by the mind. A cluster of photons passes through the eye's pupil and reaches the retina. There they stimulate nerve endings on the surface of the retina. These nerves send electrochemical impulses to the brain. Then nerve cells within the brain fire. A chemical chain reaction occurs, moving from the surface of the retina to the inner part of the brain. We experience none of this. We experience the sensation of light.

Our senses don't speak objectively, but in a subjective language of their own. They don't inform us of the actual physical events that are stimulating them. Instead, they provide us with subjective sensations that are the stuff of the mind. Sensations are a subjective translation of physical events into psychological experiences.

Translating physical processes into mental events isn't the only subjectivity of sensation.

The Senses Are Biased

Another dimension of subjectivity exists because the relationship between the physical events that stimulate the senses and the sense impression that it creates isn't a simple one. Twice the light isn't always twice as bright. It depends upon the situation. A candle in the dark appears brighter than at midday. Plain rice is very tasty when you are very hungry. Red glows when placed against green, but is dull next to orange.

The mind uses the brain in complex ways to form its experiences. When forming a sense impression, it takes into account contrast, changes in levels of stimulation, movement, relative sizes, timing, and a host of other physical relationships among the available stimuli. The world of perceptual illusions is an entertaining place to discover how sensations fool the mind. Illusions have revealed to psychologists just how innocently and creatively the mind interprets its sensations.

The mind designs its perceptual system to optimize its functioning for the most common circumstances. In order to achieve this optimal performance, it sacrifices accuracy under certain conditions. For example, our senses pay attention primarily to changes in stimulation. There is no information in the status quo; only change is news.

Our nervous system expresses this bias for change by tiring of sensing the same old thing. Most nerve cells can't fire time after time in quick succession. It's called fatigue. Nerve networks will stop passing a message if it continues to be the same one. This process is called inhibition. You hear the air conditioner when it first comes on, but soon its sound fades away. It has been inhibited. When the air conditioner turns off again, the silence is very loud.

You can experience some intriguing effects of this aspect of your perceptual system by discovering the visual afterimage phenomenon. Look at a solid black square against a white background. Now take away the black square and look at the white background alone. You will see a white square glowing brighter on the paper. That is the afterimage. Staring at the black square has tired your eyes of the message. It begins to block the "black square" message from its neuronal firing. When you take away the black square and look at the white paper underneath, your brain interprets the retina's inhibition of "black square" information as meaning "white square." That area of the paper is so "un-black" that it appears whiter than white.

Afterimages appear in all the senses. There are afterimages of color. Try looking at a red square and the afterimage will be green. There are afterimages in bodily sensations. Taking off your roller skates after an afternoon's ride makes your feet feel so light you can almost fly. Tastes leave images. After eating a sweet roll, orange juice is too sour to drink.

Afterimages are one class of contrast effects. They are produced by your senses inhibiting the impression from a stimulus that remains constant, only to be caught overcompensating when a stimulus of opposite characteristics is presented.

Contrast effects are but one example of an unexpected consequence of what is, in most circumstances, a useful bias within the nervous system. It can lead to some powerful subjective experiences that go beyond simple perceptual illusions. A person who has suffered unkindness from others for many years will perceive someone who extends even the most basic consideration as a wondrous saint.

Science Is Subjective

Sensory information, the most mechanical foundation of our experience of the world, is highly subjective. It is a creative interpretation of physical data, data that is largely invisible to the conscious mind. We are utterly vulnerable to this level of basic subjectivity. Knowing about it doesn't help. Most perceptual illusions persist in spite of their being explained. This level of subjectivity is inherent in the way the mind designs the wiring of the brain.

While the senses aren't accurate and have built-in biases, we might expect that science, with its high-powered measuring instruments, can perceive reality objectively. Whether or not we value science and technology, we all respect its power. We hold it up as representing the ideal of objectivity.

Our faith in the pure objectivity of science, however, is misplaced. All science is a subjective enterprise. It is an important point to consider. As we consider some of the ways that subjectivity affects science, we must conclude that all human experience must also be subjective. You may well come to the conclusion, as have several other philosophers, that objective reality, if it exists at all, remains unknown, and perhaps unknowable, to human beings.

Science Is a Value System

Science is really the statement of a value system. What it calls its "objective" stance toward reality—detachment, analysis, prediction and control—is actually a statement of values. It is a bias in favor of a certain attitude toward knowledge.

Suppose someone proposed to get to know you. What if that person said to you, "The best way of getting to know you is for me to remain aloof from you. I will break you up into pieces and analyze your parts. I want to examine all the little facts of your life with a computer. I am going to learn how to predict your every move. Furthermore, to prove that I have obtained this real power of knowledge of you, I will gain total control over you, and make you behave as I choose." Would you rush to reveal yourself to a person making such a proposal? You'd probably be amused or horrified.

Yet that is exactly the stance that science takes toward nature. It calls it "objective," and values detachment over intimacy, analysis over experience, prediction over involvement, and control over dialogue. Women have sometimes recognized this set of values in their male friends. In fact, some modern philosophers have proposed that the supposed objectivity of science is no more than a rationalization of masculine values.

In reaction to some of the negative consequences of this approach to science, some scientists have begun experimenting with an alternative approach, one that values respect for the integrity of nature. Perhaps we can learn as much valuable truth about nature by communing with it as we can by poking at it or tearing it apart.

Science Invents Stories About Reality

Science doesn't touch reality bare-handed, but through the gloves of its theories. It doesn't stare with the naked eye at nature, but views it through the glasses of concepts.

We usually assume that science deals only with facts. The facts of science, however, are really determined by concepts and theories. Gravity, magnetism, energy, electricity, atoms, and other such terms aren't actual facts. They are ideas. There is no such *thing* as electricity or gravity. They are shorthand terms for describing how certain aspects of the world behave. They are concepts developed to explain the sensations and experiences of scientists. These are the stories science invents about nature.

The sensations, or facts, that scientists seek are based on the theories they hold. Without a theory to make it meaningful in the first place, a fact isn't even noted. The history of science is full of new discoveries coming from facts that had always been ignored as irrelevant. Scientists are like other people: they see what they are looking for, and ignore everything else.

I'm sure you've had the experience of being with someone who professed to understand you but who was dealing with you on their own terms. No matter what you revealed about yourself, the person didn't really understand your point of view. Instead, the person assumed an air of understanding and analyzed everything you said in terms of their own pet theories and ideas. They would only notice those things about you that were relevant to the theory. Wasn't it infuriating? You wouldn't say the person was being objective. No, quite the contrary. The person, however, might profess profound objectivity, but they would be seeing only in terms of their own understanding.

We all use models and concepts to perceive and understand the world. Here's a demonstration that shows the difference between the raw facts and experience. It shows how automatically we use concepts to form our experiences.

The example concerns a visual demonstration that was developed by a psychologist, Fritze Heider. He designed an abstract, animated cartoon. It was a moving diagram involving a circle and a square. He used a mathematical formula to define the movement. Imagine this: The circle starts in one spot, and then begins to move in a particular direction at a certain speed for a certain period of time. At that point, the circle changes direction and speed, and later it changes again. Using a similar formula, he programmed the motion of the square. He changed the numerical values, however, for the square. It started at a different location than the circle. It began its first movement slightly after the circle began to move, and all the other changes in motion were slightly delayed relative to the circle. After developing this complicated program, he ran the cartoon and showed it to people.

When people saw the circle and the square move according to the formulas he designed, what do you think they thought they saw? You can bet they didn't say something like, "Oh, I see, you've created a pair of equations to define the motion of a circle and a square. The motions of the two are correlated. Very clever." No, of course not—no one said that. Instead, the invariable and immediate reaction was, "Oh, my goodness, the square is chasing the circle and the circle is trying to escape!"

The observers, being human, immediately used their imagination and perceived the events on the screen in terms of the concepts of running, chasing, and escaping. They created a meaning for what they saw and attributed purposes to the two "actors." Their reaction was natural. Their perception has a certain poetic truth to it. Yet it is a subjective creation.

Heider's purpose in creating this demonstration was to show that human beings respond to what they experience by organizing that experience into meanings they can recognize, and into stories that make sense on the basis of their previous experience.

The language of science, and the way it organizes its perceptions, is the same. The only difference is that the stories scientists create are more abstract and use more complicated terms. Humans, whether scientists or not, experience the events in the world in terms of meaning, not raw facts. There is little choice, except to choose which concepts to use when forming our perceptions.

Suppose you see an automobile for the first time in your life. If you "saw" it as a sculpture, the facts you would look at would be its shapes and lines. If you saw it as a container, the facts you would look at would be the spaces inside. You might measure how much water the trunk held or how many books you could store in the passenger compartment. If you saw it as some type of calculator or computer, the facts you would look at would be the readings on the dials. You might push buttons and pull levers to see how these dials responded. If you saw it as a conveyer, you might see how much weight it could carry and how fast it would go when loaded. In any event, the facts you would observe would depend upon your conception of what the car is.

The problem of how to understand a car shows that objectivity isn't simply a matter of being accurate in your measurements. Seeing what is really there —being objective, in other words—requires that you know *what* to look at and how to organize in your mind what you see. Knowing what to look for assumes that you have in mind some concept, or model, that applies to what you are looking at.

If you have no idea what you are looking at, but want to learn about it, you will have to ask some questions, take some measurements, or poke at it in some manner. What you learn about something depends upon the kinds of questions you ask. To formulate these questions, you will have to try out some concepts. There is no way around it.

Meaning involves concepts. Yet concepts are concepts, not direct reality. Concepts impose a subjective point of view. In a real sense, perception is idolatrous. We worship the concepts that form our perceptions and mistake them for the real thing.

Scientists are no different from poets, who invent connections between experiences. The poet understands love and writes that the rosebud opens as an expression of love for the sun. The scientist understands photosynthesis and writes that the rose opens in response to the sunlight's action upon the plant cells.

Science only has its models, its symbols, its metaphors, and theories. Science is science fiction, it is the product of the imagination. Science lives in a dream world of its own making. Scientists would agree with this statement, but you may already be rushing to their defense by pointing out that science tests its theories to see where they are wrong. The assumption is that science is objective because it considers the implications of its dreams, and invents tests to detect errors in the models. Science pinches itself to see if it is dreaming. Scientists do take measurements of the world, but sometimes their yardsticks dent what they measure and alter the nature of the reality that is being observed.

Science Affects Reality

We would like to be able to assume that there is a reality independent of our own subjectivity. Science develops theories about this reality and tests their adequacy. Testing theories requires performing experiments and taking measurements. The idea is to find out what is happening.

We have seen, however, that in the science of psychology, the experimenter's expectations tended to make things happen on their own. We have seen that science generally, as well as our own senses, tend to have certain biases in the perception of reality. Our observations seem to mirror our assumptions. This problem just won't go away, and seems to get worse the closer we get to looking at the bottom line of physical reality, the atom.

The deeper science stuck its nose into the reality of the atom, the more the atom ran away from the scientist's intrusion. Atomic physicists found that their measurements disturbed what they were trying to measure. They discovered an enormous catch-22 about the task of observing reality: observing something changes it.

The principle of indeterminacy, as science calls it, states that it isn't possible to make an exact determination, or measurement, about the condition of something without simultaneously changing at least some aspect of its condition.

The principle is really no news to you. You already know how differently you act when someone is watching you. If you have ever been the subject of an interview, you know that the kind of information the interviewer gets from you depends on how the person approaches you. The interviewer has an effect on you, and that alters the kind of information you have to give. If you have ever wanted to watch animals in the wild, you know how frustrating it can be, for as soon as they see you, the animals change what they're doing or run away.

The observer affects the observed. This effect extends down to the most basic layer of reality. Atomic physics discovered that it is just not possible to look at an atom without the atom's feeling an impact of the scientist's observation. To see something, you have to shine light on it. The light bounces off the object and strikes the eyes. At the atomic level, in order for the measuring instrument to detect the presence of an atomic particle, it has to have some form of contact with that particle. That contact, however, affects the particle, changing its position or its direction of movement. Seeing affects the seen.

What is seen is also determined by the observer. What is an atom? We think of it as a thing. We call it a particle. Sometimes, however, it acts as if it's not a thing, but an event, an energy reaction in the form of a wave. Whether or not an atomic physicist finds a particle or a wave of energy when observing these minuscule aspects of reality depends upon the type of observation made. In the subatomic world, reality is quite sensitive. It has a way of shifting back and forth, from matter to energy, in a manner quite perplexing to the scientist who wants to get a firm handle on what is actually there. What is there seems to depend upon how the scientist wishes to grasp it.

Many of us consider that the foundation of reality, the very basic reality, is atomic. If that is reality, then physicists have discovered that you just can't observe reality without affecting it. Reality changes the moment it is seen. It is quite sensitive to the observer. Experiencing reality affects it. Some physicists believe that there can be no description of reality without also describing the observer of that reality. Consciousness itself must be part of the equation, because it is part of the process of creating reality.

The Science of Subjectivity

When we experience the world, we engage it in an interaction. Reality doesn't just stand still, but responds to our glance, moves to our touch and reflects our assumptions. The world tends to mirror our beliefs, understanding, and expectations, and this is true even for scientists looking at the world carefully through technological devices.

There is a subjectivity both in our sense organs as well as in the scientist's microscope. There is a self-fulfilling aspect to our interactions with other people, whether we are socializing, engaged in business, or observing subjects in a psychological experiment.

The science of subjectivity understands that we are only objective when we recognize that truth is an interactive event. Observer and observed together create what we have called objective reality.

Facts, circumstances, and the other ingredients that would constitute the atoms of our lives are subject to our own creative perceptions. The first step in learning to have life on our own terms, to "have it your way," is to realize that there is actually no other way. We cannot avoid our own role in creating the reality we experience.

CHAPTER 6

YOUR IDEAL LIFE

The most important experience of this or any individual entity is to first know what is the ideal—spiritually. Who and what is thy pattern?

Edgar Cayce 357-13

WHAT WOULD YOU do if you were lost in outer space? Everywhere you look, above you, below, on all sides, all you see is the enormity of space—full of stars. Which way is up? Which way is home?

There is something equally disorienting about the idea that all our experience is subjective. If all we experience is a reflection of ourselves, then what do we have to hold on to? If expectations are self-fulfilling, if reality is our own creation, then are we not caught in a vicious circle of our own selves? Doesn't the science of subjectivity abandon us in a hall of mirrors?

Janet's Predicament

I remember a woman, Janet, who came to seek counseling from me. She was depressed and felt lost. She felt her life was a mess and she blamed herself.

She had a good job once and led a creative life, full of excitement and self-expression. She had decided to go to college and get an education that would advance her career. Before she acted on that decision, she got married. Her husband didn't like her working. She gave up her job for him. They moved to another town, and while he went to work, she stayed home and cared for their child.

Janet was satisfied with this life for a while. Then her husband developed a drinking problem. He lost his job. He began to beat her, not just with his fists, but also verbally with words of criticism and blame. Finally, he left her. What he left behind was not only a broken marriage, but a pile of debts, deep wounds, confusion, and guilt.

When Janet came to see me, she was staying with her mother. She had no money, no job, not even a driver's license. All she had was her child, bills, and lots of guilt. Her depression was twofold. First, she had lost her life as she knew it, and second, she blamed it all on herself.

She didn't know how she could ever recapture the good life she had lived before her marriage. Her self-confidence was lost, and she didn't think she could ever get it back.

She was angry with herself for creating such a mess of things. She echoed her husband's opinion that it was all her fault. She felt guilty for driving him to drink. She felt as if she must have deserved his beatings. She didn't blame him for leaving her. She was guilty, but she didn't know where she had gone wrong. That's why she had come to see me.

She expressed a passing acquaintance with the New Age slogan "You create your own reality." I watched her use it as another club to beat herself over the head. Her predicament proved to her that deep down, she was a mean, bad, and ugly person.

The Trap of Self-Blame

It's a normal reaction to blame ourselves when we suffer a loss. It's an unfortunate response, however, because the self-punishment adds to our misery and further depletes our resources for recovery. In Janet's case, and I have seen too many like hers, the suffering was even further intensified by her elevating self-blame to a spiritual principle. If we create our own reality, she reasoned with me, then she created this mess herself, on purpose! Her reaction is an example of what I meant when I said that the idea of creating one's own reality can trap a person in the vicious circle of oneself.

How can you avoid that trap, or get out of it if you happen to get caught? The trap does seem almost unavoidable. If there is no reality beyond what we create ourselves, then how can we avoid blaming ourselves when things go wrong? If the world is a mirror of our own selves, then what else do we have but ourselves? There seems no other place to stand, no place to get a foothold to get out of the maze of mirrors.

Sometimes puzzles appear unsolvable only because we have limited our options by our assumptions. Consider this example:

Below are nine dots arranged in a square. Connect all nine dots with a series of four straight lines, but without lifting your pencil from the paper.

Did you figure it out? The task is impossible if you limit your options by the assumption that your lines must remain within the square suggested by the dots. The statement of the puzzle doesn't require you to limit yourself in that way. The arrangement of the dots, however, does subtly suggest the limitation to your imagination. If you can break out of that box, you can solve the puzzle.

[Note: The solution is to draw a horizontal line through the second and third dots in the first row, but to continue the line to where a fourth dot would be. From there, continue with a diagonal line that cuts through the third dot in the second row, the second dot in the third row, and down to where the first dot would be in a fourth row. From there, continue by drawing a line straight up through the first dot in each row. The fourth and final line section will then be obvious.]

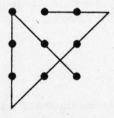

In the phrase "You create your own reality," there is also the suggestion of a box. Do you know what that box is? It is suggested by the word *you.* How did you interpret the word? Did you assume it meant your conscious self? Perhaps it could include your subconscious as well. Perhaps the metaphysical statement is actually addressed to your higher self, your soul. What if *you* meant God?

In an earlier part of the book, we examined Cayce's perspective on our spiritual identity. That entity is clearly a much larger reality than what we identify as our conscious personality. Creating your own reality is quite a large proposition, spiritual in scope. We have to interpret each word in the statement from a spiritual perspective. If we take the word *you* in its everyday sense and then try to work with the statement, we get into trouble. We fall into the trap of self-blame.

Let's approach the problem the way Edgar Cayce did and see if things don't work out better.

If You Are Lost, Where Do You Want to Go?

Janet's situation was not hopeless. It only seemed that way. There was another way of looking at it. I shared with her my impression that her unhappiness showed just how well she knew what her life was supposed to be like. "You wouldn't be unhappy," I told her, "unless you knew a better life was possible." I asked her, "What kind of a life is it that you know you're supposed to have?"

At first, Janet was somewhat puzzled that I saw her unhappiness as such a good sign. She was focused on her misery, while I was concentrating on the deeper feeling that her misery implied. She was depressed because she felt she had ruined her dream. I was happy for her because she knew she *had* a dream. I wasn't just trying to cheer her up, or get her to look at the bright side. I wanted her to focus on what was real and enduring rather than on what was a temporary condition. After all, her unhappiness was a reaction. It was really pointing to her dream of an ideal life.

Look at it this way. If all experience is subjective, if our experience of the world mirrors who we are, if we create our own reality, then what do you have? You can say, "All I have is me!" and look at that. You can also say, "All I have is choices," and look at them. If life is but a dream, then what dream will you have? The choice is up to you. Upon what foundation will you base your choices?

Begin by Knowing Your Ideals

For most of us, it is through having problems that we learn what we want to fight for. It is through becoming unhappy that we begin to question what we want out of life. Most of the people who sought advice from Cayce contacted him because of a problem. The problem initiated the person into a broader perspective on life.

When Cayce provided his commentaries on how the mind builds reality, he was not trying to tell people that their problems were illusory. When he indicated that what people meet in life is their own selves, he was not suggesting that they were to blame for their problems. He was trying to remind people that circumstances in life don't just happen, they are created, and for a purpose. He was not suggesting that people feel bad, but that they remember their purpose.

We create circumstances, from a deep level within our being, in order to learn from them. What we're all trying to learn is what works for us and what doesn't. We're learning what choices are good for us. We're testing our ideals and learning how to implement them.

Cayce would ask the person to consider what ideal was being tested.

Problems initiate us on the path of conscious spiritual development. Learning that our life experiences reflect who we are informs us that there is a path. The first step on that path is to become aware of the ideal that is governing our journey. The ideal is the guiding star that we use for navigation.

We begin with an ideal. That is the first, most important step, in our conscious use of the mind.

How to Choose an Ideal

What would make Janet happy, I asked. She wanted to get a job and she wanted the best for her daughter. She also wanted to have a man to love and who would love her. I asked her to reflect upon happy times and to see if there were other things that she wanted. She thought she had some talent, especially with people, and she enjoyed being able to help people. She wanted to develop that talent. She wanted to be good at something and to get pleasure from doing it.

She had mentioned things having to do with family and with career. What was it about those things that would make her happy? Why would it make her happy for her daughter to have the best in life? Why would it make her happy to be able to express her talent in a skillful way? I asked her to think about it. What did she sense in those things that made her believe they would make her happy? She said that it was something good, but she wasn't sure exactly what it was.

I asked her to close her eyes and focus on what it felt like. I suggested that she imagine the feeling and savor it. Did any pictures come to mind? Perhaps it reminded her of some incidents in her life when she felt that certain "something good."

"It's a rosy feeling," she said, "all around me. It seeps into me and I feel very warm inside."

"What else?" I asked her. "What else do you notice?"

She was smiling to herself, then remarked, "It sounds silly, but there is a good feeling in my heart and it is pouring out of me. It's warm, pink and very clear. It's alive and it . . . it knows it!"

"It doesn't sound silly at all," I replied. "What does this sensation of a good feeling pouring out of your heart remind you of?"

Janet was quiet for a while and then told me, "I don't know what it means, but I am remembering a time when I was working as a sales clerk in a department store. There was a woman customer who couldn't find any bed sheets that she liked. She described to me the colors and patterns in her bedroom. I could see it in my mind and it reminded me of some sheets I had seen somewhere in our stock. I spent some time looking, but I found them. When I showed them to her, her eyes lit up. She was really pleased. I felt really good, almost glowing. I had been able to think of those sheets and then find them. The customer thanked me, saying that she appreciated my taking so much time for her, and especially for being able to imagine just the kind of sheets she would like. It seems like a silly memory, but that's what came to mind."

I pointed out to her that earlier she had expressed a desire to develop the talent she had for helping other people. The incident that she remembered seemed like a good example of just that. We discussed the glowing feeling she had during that event. What did it say about why she was so happy at that moment?

We talked about how good it is to feel loved and appreciated. She described instances of feeling special, of being the only person just like her. She had felt grateful for that incident with the customer. Her love of fabrics, her knack for color and design, being able to help someone in a special way, being appreciated—all these things came together in that moment. She said, "That's the way it's supposed to be for me!"

Janet realized that her experience contained two qualities that were important to her happiness. First there was love. She noted, "Of course, it's a good feeling to give or receive love, but more than that, it brings out the best in a person!" Her eyes lit up and she said, "There's more to me than love—I'm smart, too!" She described the second quality as something like knowledge, or intelligence. She called it "a knowing."

"If there's a God," she explained, "then God wouldn't just be love, like some people say, but a *knowing love,* a love that was *intelligent!* It's like, I want what's best for my daughter and just loving her is not enough—I have to really know her to love her as best as I can. It's the two together that makes the magic. By itself, love can just be a warm feeling, while knowing, by itself, can be critical, like an eye staring at you and seeing through you. What I'm talking about is like a heart and an eye combined . . . seeing with the heart, knowing with love. It's what I've been feeling in our counseling sessions. When I first came here I was knowing myself in only a critical way and that just doesn't work. It's intelligence and love combined that makes life work."

Janet was in the process of formulating her ideal. Janet's statement of her ideal was "intelligent love." Her image of it was a heart with an eye. That was Janet's personal statement of *her* ultimate value, her vision of the Absolute Good. Another person would come up with a different ideal. A person might formulate an ideal based upon a religious tradition, such as using the word *Christ,* or *Buddha,* to express the composite of qualities that came together in that religious figure. Another person might value an abstract expression, such as Truth, Beauty, Quality, Harmony, Oneness, Bliss, Peace, Joy, Equality, or Freedom.

In each case, the word chosen only approximates the ideal it is trying to express. A symbol or an image is also useful as an alternative expression.

An ideal is something for the individual who formulates it. It is something the individual *does* believe in, not something an individual thinks everyone *should* believe in. On the other hand, one way to see if the ideal you've chosen is really what you want is to ask yourself what kind of world it would be if everyone followed that ideal. Would it be a kind of world you would want to live in?

It is often difficult to express our feelings or intuitions about an ideal. We can recognize an example of it when we encounter it, as in an experience we had, but sometimes it can be difficult to define directly.

What Is an Ideal?

One definition of an ideal might be a person's highest value. Janet came up with an interesting definition when she used the phrase "If there were a God, then God would be . . ." and described a certain quality. It was her way of saying that an ideal is an ultimate value, a vision of an Absolute Good.

To explain the meaning of an ideal, Cayce often used the phrase "perfect standard." An ideal is a standard by which we measure the value of something. Since it is a perfect standard, we never encounter anything but approximations to it in real life. It is like a guiding star, something we can steer by and aim toward, but which is never reached.

Mathematics is the easiest place to understand the perfection of ideals, because there ideals can be precisely defined. Mathematics works with ideals that easily exist in theory but are not found in actuality. A circle is defined as a set of dots that are equally distant from a center. That definition gives the perfect expression of the ideal of a circle. The value of a circle is that it is perfectly round. In real life, however, there are no perfect circles, only approximations.

A straight line, a square, and a right angle are but a few ideals in mathematics that are defined quite precisely. They exist, but only as ideals. Although we use these concepts all the time as standards, in actuality we work only with approximations. We all know what a straight line is, but no one has ever seen one. No line is perfectly straight. Yet we use the ideal of a straight line as a standard all the time.

An ideal is a valued pattern of perfection that is used as a standard of excellence, quality, or spirituality. Ideals having to do with spiritual values cannot be defined exactly. An ideal is contained in the spirit of the law, not its letter. The "Spirit of '76" was the expression of an ideal for the founding of America. The Declaration of Independence and the Constitution were attempts to put that spirit into writing. These documents are imperfect attempts to define the ideals of a nation. America itself is an imperfect expression of its own ideal, yet the spirit of the ideal is there, alive and functioning as a guide.

Ideals and Ideas

Earlier we learned that ideas exist in a fourth dimension, what we called "idealand." Ideals are similar, in that they live in an eternal dimension of their own. Ideas and ideals both exist as patterns of energy in the mind. They both operate through the mind to give shape to physical things and to events in the world. Yet ideals and ideas are not the same.

There is an idea called a "mousetrap." The idea itself is in another dimension. You could destroy all the mousetraps in the world, but you would not destroy the idea of a mousetrap. Like an ideal, the experience of an idea does not depend upon there being any actual examples in the physical world.

Unlike an ideal, however, the idea of a mousetrap does have perfectly satisfactory manifestations in the world. A device that catches a mouse satisfies the idea of a mousetrap. The idea of a mousetrap does not imply a standard of perfection that can only be approximated but never reached. While an ideal cannot find fulfillment in any concrete example, an idea can.

One mousetrap can be better than another. It is possible to build a better mousetrap. If one mousetrap is better than another, it is not because it is a closer approximation to the idea of a mousetrap. Both mousetraps fulfill the definition, but one may have an additional feature. A mousetrap that doesn't snap on little children's fingers is better because it's safer.

Evaluating a mousetrap for its safety is evaluating it according to an *ideal,* not according to the *idea* of a mousetrap. We can think about an ideal mousetrap, but it means going beyond simply the mousetrap idea. It means thinking about some absolute standard of perfection, in terms of an ideal like safety, humaneness, or efficiency, that would be used to distinguish a better mousetrap from an ordinary one. Yet a mousetrap can still be a mousetrap without being even close to an ideal one.

Because an ideal can never be satisfied, it acts as a perpetual motivator. An idea can be a motivator, but since it can be satisfied, it doesn't motivate for long. A teenager may have an ideal of freedom and daydream endlessly about owning a car. A car is an idea, and it can be satisfied. One day, the teenager will have a car and he or she will be satisfied, temporarily. Soon, however, the person will discover that although a car provides a certain freedom, in the sense of independence of movement, it brings with it certain requirements and responsibilities. Owning a car is not a free ride, nor does it allow total freedom of movement.

The *ideal* of total freedom of movement, its source deep within the intuition of humanity, has motivated many *ideas.* There was the shoe, the horse, the car, the airplane, and the rocket ship. The car came from the idea of a horseless carriage. The idea of a plane came from watching birds. Each of these ideas has been since improved upon, motivated by various ideals. Yet the ideal of total freedom of movement continues to motivate us to search for new ideas for transportation. Today we may consider its ultimate expression to be travel by thought, as in astral travel, remote viewing, traveling clairvoyance, or out-of-body experiences. In future years, the fulfillment of those ideas will probably reveal that the ideal is somehow still over the horizon. Unlike being motivated by an idea, to be motivated by an ideal means that we are forever reaching beyond our grasp.

Ideas and Ideals Create a Life

Although ideals never find perfect fulfillment, they are like ideas in that both operate through the patterning power of the mind to govern the shape of the material world. Mind and nature are one because of the patterns they share. Earlier we learned how image patterns in the mind give rise to the forms we encounter in life. This process is true both for the connection between the infinite mind and nature as a whole and for the connection between images in an individual's mind and that person's life experiences.

A person's conceptions, expectations, and beliefs govern what is experienced—even for scientists! It is the patterns in a person's mind that create the person's reality. It will make a difference whether or not ideals, and not just ideas, are among those patterns. A life centered on ideals will continue to grow fruitfully. A life centered on ideas alone, however, will run dry, because ideas can easily be satisfied.

As Janet and I reviewed her life history, for example, we encountered many ideas that had captured her attention: getting good grades in school, getting a good job, finding a suitable husband, and owning a home. Most of these ideas were goals and were capable of being achieved. She had, in fact, persisted with these ideas and achieved them, although some of them were later lost.

We also encountered some ideals: doing her best in life and being a good mother. With regard to ideals, since successful fulfillment is not possible, sincere trying is what counts. She had tried to live up to these ideals. Her conscience was clear on that score.

Janet and I were able to view much of her life history as a reflection of the ideas and ideals to which she devoted her attention. I pointed out to her that it was those mental patterns that created her life, not the "mean, bad, and ugly Janet" she had been blaming. If she did not like the way her life was developing, we should examine more closely her ideas and ideals, and especially the relationship between them.

We started with what happened in her marriage, because she felt that it was while being married that she lost the self-confidence that she had earlier. In particular, she realized that she regretted obeying her husband's request that she quit her job. Doing so left her totally dependent upon him. Why did she go along with his request? We uncovered several reasons.

Janet's ideal of doing her best extended to pleasing her husband. Janet's idea of being a good wife meant obeying his wishes. Needless to say, her husband probably agreed with that definition.

On a more general level, we learned that one of the ways that Janet measured whether she was doing her best was by the reaction of other people.

When people were pleased with her, she was happy and satisfied. If they were not pleased, then she tried harder.

She gave lip service to the notion that you can't always please everyone. In her secret emotions, however, she hoped she could always be pleasing. Janet harbored the idea that it is necessary to please people in order for them to love you. Like most of us, she wanted people to love her. Her idea of people loving her was that they would approve of her, care for her, and be sensitive to her needs. Most especially, if a person loved her, they would not abandon her and leave her alone. Since her husband left her, it must have meant that she had not tried hard enough to please him.

Most of us can readily identify with Janet's system of thought. It is somewhat like an economic philosophy of relationships: I'll rub your back and you'll rub mine. The relationship is based on a system of exchange. I try to please you and you try to love me. If you have trouble loving me, I try harder to please you.

It is a common approach to relationships, one that certainly does not distinguish Janet as a unique individual. If it doesn't work, it is not because Janet is a failure, but because the system of thought is faulty. Ideas have consequences. If you harbor an idea, you'll receive its consequences. Janet experienced the consequences of the thoughts she held about love. The disappointment Janet experienced wasn't the result of Janet's failure as a person, it was the result of the limitations inherent in the ideas she believed in.

Given enough time, most ideas reveal their limitations. Cayce warned us to make sure that we held genuine ideals, and did not try to guide our lives by ideas. Ideas are tools to use, but must be under the influence and direction of ideals. There were many ideas governing Janet's life, but very few of them, if any, were under the supervision of an ideal.

Wasn't Janet guiding her life by the ideal of trying her best? It was a question I had Janet examine herself. I asked her to compare that ideal with the one she had recently formulated concerning seeing with the heart, "intelligent love." After some thought, her first response was that the ideal of trying her best left out some important things, like what her best really meant.

Did her best mean being satisfied with what pleased others, or did it mean what is best for others and herself as well? She realized that she never used it to mean pleasing to the best that was inside herself. In fact, she often had to ignore her own sense of best in order to please others. From the standpoint of her newer ideal, she was somewhat angry that she hadn't loved herself enough to develop confidence in her own standards of excellence.

I suggested that her anger was perhaps misplaced. We all need love. If we believe the idea that we must please others in order to have them love us, wouldn't it be natural to try to please others? I explained that I saw her as being very conscientious in fulfilling her duty to that idea.

As we continued our discussion of her older ideal of doing her best, Janet confided that she now felt that it really wasn't much of an ideal, if it was an ideal at all. She realized that the feeling behind it—in other words, the spirit of it—wasn't an expression of any vision of an ultimate good. Instead, it was based on a feeling that she was not inherently lovable. It was a formula, or a strategy, for obtaining the love that might not otherwise come her way.

Janet's life experiences confirmed the ideas she held about herself. No matter how hard she tried, she was not able to please her husband sufficiently, and her husband left her. The ideas we hold, even the erroneous ones, do tend to be self-fulfilling. In Janet's case, unfortunately, she didn't have a true ideal to live by, one that could have guided her in her evaluation of the ideas she used in making her way through life.

In the earlier part of her life, before she got married, her idea about doing her best seemed quite adequate. In general, she was dealing with people who were basically loving toward her, or who were expecting no more than a day's work for a day's pay. The inherent flaw in trying to please others to win their love had not yet been revealed.

Janet's approach to life was severely tested, however, when she got married. There she became involved with someone who was extremely self-involved and insecure. Her husband took advantage of Janet's formula for having a relationship, took it to its limit, and exhausted it. Janet's lack of an ideal left her vulnerable to her husband's insatiable requests that she live up to his expectations and meet all his needs. Her own ideas were of no help to her. Instead, they acted as if in conspiracy with her husband. As might be expected from their implications, her ideas about love led to Janet's burnout. Her husband then abandoned her.

Janet was not happy to have her ideas confirmed. Even when they are good ones, however, how many of us are truly happy when our ideas come to pass? How many times has it happened that you wanted something, a certain car, a type of job, only to find that after you had it for a while, it wasn't as satisfying anymore?

Perhaps you have sometimes suspected that things appear in their best light only while we are wanting them. When we finally get them, we see their faults or we lose interest. Cayce described ideas as "dead," because when they materialize, they lose their power. By themselves, ideas are unsatisfactory guides to living. They are fickle motivators. Ideals, on the other hand, reach toward the infinite, toward the unreachable standard of absolute perfection. Ideals shape our lives in the same way ideas do, through patterning, except that ideals don't lose their power, their magic, or fascination as they bear their fruit. They carry us forward to ever more tasty fruits.

Ideas focus our lives on results, the realization of the ideas, the end of a journey. Ideals have us focus on the process, on the journey itself. Working toward a goal is often more pleasurable than its accomplishment. Focusing on the process of doing a job, on how we obtain a goal, on the quality of the journey through life, ensures satisfaction.

In a study of creative writing, for example, two groups of students wrote poetry, but under different conditions. One group was asked first to imagine how well people would like their work. They were asked to imagine applause and congratulations. The other group was asked to imagine the fun it is to play with words. Then the two groups were asked to compose poems. The students who focused on the joy of writing wrote poetry that impressed the judges far more than did the students who were focused on the rewards of their efforts. Enjoyment of the process produced better results than did the anticipation of success.

Ideas and ideals both create the reality of a life, but only ideals will create a life that is satisfying. The true measure of a person is the ideal the person steers by. Rather than saying "You create your own reality," it would be more accurate to say, "You choose the ideas and ideals that create your reality."

Developing an Ideal Life

Defining an ideal is the first step in an adventure into higher consciousness. It is the beginning of learning to work with the mysteries of the mind for a more creative and fulfilling life. Developing an ideal life begins with the definition of an ideal.

Defining an ideal is not a once-and-for-all proposition. If you decide upon an ideal today, you can still change to a different ideal later. You may very well change your ideal as time goes on. Don't let the notion that you will be stuck with the ideal you state today stop you from formulating one now. In fact, reevaluating and reformulating your ideal is a normal and natural part of the journey to an ideal life. The important thing is to start developing your awareness of an ideal.

To begin this journey, Cayce recommended that you write down your best guess concerning your ideal and start keeping a journal. He suggested that you make notes about daily experiences in various areas of your life. Some of these general areas might be yourself, your family, your job, and your community. These will be areas that you will observe for the next few months to see where they reflect your ideal and where you would like to see an improvement. This journal process is a way for you to make an honest evaluation of your life in terms of an ideal.

Each night, make some notes about your experiences in each of these areas. Include your thoughts, actions, events, as well as emotional reactions and inner experiences.

For example, you may have had thoughts such as trying to figure out a solution to a problem at work. You may have had some positive thoughts about a particular success and some negative thoughts about some paperwork you had to do. Among your actions, you may have observed that you worked hard on certain tasks, while you procrastinated on others. You may have experienced some frustrations as well as had some moments of satisfaction.

Cayce suggested that you *not* read over these daily journal notes for at least thirty days. Simply allow them to accumulate.

After a month or so, set aside some time to review the notes in your journal. Take a candid look at the quality of your experiences in each of the areas of your life.

What were the best moments? What were the worst? You will be able to pinpoint aspects of your life that most closely approximate what you would consider ideal. You will also be able to find aspects that are far from ideal.

You can analyze the positive aspects to find out what it is about them that you particularly like. Your best moments are celebrations and expressions of positive values. Look at those values. There you will find clues about something that you actually held as an ideal, at least at that moment. How does it compare with the ideal you formulated?

It's also important to analyze the negative aspects to find out what it is about them that you particularly dislike. Again, you will find clues about a standard of excellence that you used at that moment.

When you were frustrated, for example, what values were being frustrated? Recall that when Janet came to counseling, she was aware of being despondent and angry with herself. But it took some reflection to realize that her frustration was a response to the loss of something she valued. When we get angry or frustrated, or become sad or anxious, it is usually in response to a sense of loss, or the threat of loss, of something we value. Look behind the surface of your negative moments to discover the values you are guarding. Compare these values with your statement of your ideal. Does you ideal express these values? Does your ideal need to be modified to include these values, or do your values need to be brought more into harmony with your ideal?

Cayce's approach to working with ideals is to apply them to concrete situations in life. He followed the sequence of creation we discussed in an earlier chapter: The spirit is the life, mind is the builder, and the physical is the result. Thus, for any given situation, Cayce suggested that you allow your spiritual ideal to suggest a corresponding mental attitude, and let that attitude suggest a specific action or approach.

The remaining chapters in this section will explain the details of this process. They will show you how ideals can be used to both chart the course of your ideal life and to arrive at your goal. You will then have built a solid foundation at the spiritual, mental and behavioral level upon which to learn how to use the powers of even deeper regions of the mind to bring your ideal life into reality.

CHAPTER 7

A MATTER OF ATTITUDE

There is much more to be obtained from the right mental attitude respecting circumstances of either physical, mental or spiritual than by the use of properties, things or conditions outside of self. . . .

Edgar Cayce 5211-1

ATTITUDE CAN BE a dirty word. So it seems when you are being accused of having one. Like bad breath, an attitude can be a condition you don't know you have until someone informs you, "You've got an attitude problem."

Your attitude is something other people are more aware of than you. If they mention it, you often don't know what they're talking about. If someone says, "I don't like your attitude," about all you can guess is that you're not being the way they want you to be. If someone says, "You've got a good attitude," you suppose it means you are doing what they want.

An attitude can be a social thing. Generally, if you have a good attitude, people will like you. If you have a bad attitude, you'll get into trouble and have a tough life.

I don't think that any of us got too much of an education in school about attitude beyond learning that it could be good or bad. Education's approach to attitude traditionally has been that it is the key to socialization rather than the secret of self-realization. I don't remember a teacher ever explaining that we could choose a specific attitude, from a wide range of options, that expressed our values and use it as a tool to shape our lives. No one ever discussed how to go about selecting an attitude and cultivating it as a creative personal tool. It was just a dirty word.

Edgar Cayce, on the other hand, was quite emphatic and specific about the importance of attitude. Second to working with ideals, he considered the choice of attitude and its cultivation a crucial aspect of a person's learning to use the powers of the mind. For Cayce, choosing an attitude and learning to cultivate it was a specific strategy to focus the creativity of the mind. Until a person has learned, from personal experience, the practical power of mental attitudes, none of the other powers of the mind can be mastered.

An Attitude Is Creative

The ideas in the mind fashion the life energy to create our experiences. Ideas complete themselves in physical reality and our expectations become self-fulfilling. To create an ideal life, therefore, we have to first establish what our ideal pattern is to be. These are the fundamental Cayce teachings we have been learning so far.

The next step is to focus on those thought patterns that are consistent with our ideal. It is a matter of attitude. An attitude is creative. Attitudes pattern thoughts and determine the ideas we use to create our experience.

Is the glass half empty or half full? The optimistic attitude draws our attention to what remains in the glass, while the pessimistic attitude focuses on what is missing. In actual fact, the glass is both half empty and half full. Both ideas are correct.

Which idea will grip your mind is a function of attitude. Each attitude leads the mind and its perceptions in a different direction. The two resultant thoughts have different implications for action, for your reactions to the glass, and for your future reality.

In terms of practical experience, then, we have a choice. How do you want to look at the glass of water? This choice is what Cayce called deciding upon an attitude.

An attitude is a way of looking at something, a point of view, a perspective, an outlook, a frame of mind. An attitude is like a window in a house. A window can be small or large, placed high or low and facing attractive scenery or a dismal view. How we face something is an attitude. Our attitude shows in the expression on our face.

An attitude is an orientation. Our posture expresses our attitude toward the world. The style of our physical gestures toward what is in front of us communicates our attitude. It is a style of interaction.

When riding your bike around a corner, you adopt an attitude of leaning into the curve, going with the turn. If you adopted an upright attitude, you would fall off the bike.

When you approach an angry person with a bossy attitude, you receive the full brunt of the person's anger. If you approach with a humble attitude, you find the person calmer.

An attitude is creative because it structures reality through its influence on the patterns of our thoughts. Like the concepts we use in perceiving things, an attitude influences which ideas will govern what we notice and how we understand it. Like the scientist's theories used in research, our attitude shapes how we experiment with situations. How we approach a situation influences how the situation itself responds. Life mirrors our attitudes. An attitude becomes an active ingredient in the creation of reality.

The Attitude of Self-Reliance

Of all the attitudes Cayce discussed, the one he considered to be the most fundamental is the one Ralph Waldo Emerson called self-reliance. It is a frame of mind that assumes "I can make a difference." It is an active style of interacting with events.

When people received a psychic reading from Cayce, his first suggestion, no matter what the problem, was invariably to discard their attitude of helplessness. The success of the specific help and remedies he might give depended upon the person's letting go of the attitude of victimization by circumstances. Cayce emphasized the necessity of an attitude of self-reliance, or, in his terminology, the realization that everything comes from within oneself.

No matter what cards life deals us, a self-reliant attitude insists that how the cards are played will determine the game.

The attitude of self-reliance rejects being the passive pawn of outside forces. As Emerson put it, "No man can come near me but through my act." It also declares, "No matter how oppressive a situation, nothing can take away the fact that I can choose how I will respond."

Where we direct our attention expresses and defines our attitude. An attitude of victimization focuses on the pressure of circumstances: "My bills are so big I am hopelessly in debt." The fixed focus is hypnotic and the circumstance is compelling. The effect is numbing and depressing. A self-reliant attitude, however, focuses on the available choices: "How shall I manage what money I have?" Attention meanders among the possibilities, and there is a sense of freedom in the opportunity to make choices. The effect is motivating and creative.

No matter what happens to you, there is always the choice of attitude in how to respond. Realize this fact and you have a creative edge of freedom in dealing with circumstances. Ignore this fact, Cayce warns, and you will never discover the true purpose of your life. Even if your only choice is to turn a situation of defeat into an opportunity to learn something, that attitude can make the difference between ultimate defeat and survival.

Survivors of Solitary Ordeals

Survivors of catastrophes, where one's choices can be extremely limited, have found that the exercise of at least some choice was crucial to survival. The loss of freedom, whether caused by the constraints of the environment or by the limitations of the body in sickness, can be a source of depression and loss of the will to survive.

Those survivors who have endured this state have found that by limiting their attention to just a few things or areas of awareness, they can gain a sense of freedom. Simply deciding how to tie one's shoes can be a place to start. If the shoes are lost, or taken away, the survivor still has toes to count, to name, to dedicate the day to. Nothing matters except to find some place, even if only in the imagination, to play the game of attention, to make choices in that game, and to remain in charge of the game. So long as there is choice, there is life.

Richard Logan, a psychologist at the University of Wisconsin, studied survivors of such solitary ordeals as capture and imprisonment, long solo voyages, or being lost on a trek, and examined how they turned their situation around to help them survive. He found that they learned that their own attitude, and nothing else, determined how their predicaments affected them. Some experienced moments of transcendence while absorbed in their activities, even while enduring great suffering. For example, they would have experiences of merging with the environment. In such moments, the ego is lost or forgotten and the person and the environment become one. Even though that environment would seem distasteful by normal standards, when merger occurred the distastefulness would disappear. It was an extreme example of the dictum "If you can't beat them, join them." Not being able to beat the environment, these survivors found a way to merge with it that helped them keep their spirits up.

A judgmental attitude confines a person to an awareness of how things are not OK and of how helpless the person feels. By the suspension of judgment, the person is instead able to become more centered in the moment, and is rewarded with experiences of peace, harmony, and flow. Thus Cayce advocated that we adopt an attitude of acceptance toward everything we experience. A judgmental attitude cuts us off from the flow of life, while an attitude of acceptance carries us to the next unfolding moment and to the possibility of change.

A Sense of Personal Control

Stanford University psychologist Albert Bandura uses the concept of "self-efficacy" to explain the vital sense of personal control people can claim over their experiences. The term is another way of expressing the attitude "I can make a difference." It is an attitudinal, not necessarily a factual, control. Yet it can be the single most active ingredient in determining the outcome of events.

Research has demonstrated that people who believe they can exert some control over a situation will make more of an effort, will persist longer, won't stop when confronted by obstacles, and are less stressed by negative events.

People with a sense of self-efficacy have been found to be less fearful, get sick less often, and recover from illness faster. People who feel that they have some control over events find those events much less stressful. A sense of personal control makes a big difference in how we experience things.

If a person has no sense of personal control, the person is a hostage to circumstance. Bandura had found, however, if he can teach a person to control even a minor aspect of the situation, self-confidence improves and the person will gradually become in control of more aspects of the situation.

Cayce often recommended that we not underestimate the value of taking one such small step at a time. Many a time he patiently explained to a person who seem buried under unsolvable problems to simply make a beginning somewhere, anywhere. A ball of string is rarely in such a knotted mess that there isn't some place to begin unraveling it. We can pull ourselves up by our bootstraps if we'll first bend over and reach for the straps. It's a start.

I've experienced this effect myself many times and watched it with others I've counseled. Problems can seem so overwhelming that anxiety and depression further deplete a person's ability to cope. A free-fall of doom and gloom can be very frightening and intensify feelings of helplessness to the point of panic. At such moments, the suggestion to relax seems ridiculous.

"How can I relax at a moment like this? Besides, relaxation won't take away the bills, the disease, the lawsuit, or any of the other problems that are killing me!"

It's hard to argue with that kind of logic. It's an attitude of hopelessness that makes any action short of a miracle seem pointless. It's also a self-defeating attitude, rejecting any possibility of recovery from the misfortune.

With some persistent instructions to relax, taking advantage of the growing fatigue, the person can begin to calm down. With further instructions, the person can totally relax the body and begin to imagine peaceful scenes. In this tranquil space, the person begins the process of recovery. The mind clears and energy returns. Self-confidence begins to grow. In most cases, a person emerges from a few minutes of relaxation by announcing some strategy for dealing with the problems at hand.

By discovering that they could relax in spite of their problems, these people found that there was at least one thing they could control. They were able to stop the free-fall into devastation. The relaxation, beyond its sedative qualities, brought another gift. It provided a foundation of personal control that these people could build upon.

Thus research has shown that having a person learn to relax helps the person cope with a crisis. People taught relaxation prior to surgery experience less postoperative pain and recover faster. The relaxation itself is not necessarily the active ingredient. The increased sense of personal control is what makes the difference.

Turning Stumbling Blocks Into Stepping-Stones

An attitude of self-reliance says, "I'm the bottom line in this experience." A situation may seem out of control. There may be no choices for actions. But the self-reliant individual will find, or even invent, some choice to make. Choosing to remain calm, if that is all that can be done, can be the first step. By choosing one's own mental response, the whirlwind of chaos slows down. The person has found something to hold on to to begin a process of becoming responsible for how the experience unfolds.

One of Cayce's favorite expressions was that we learn how "to turn stumbling blocks into stepping stones." Perhaps you are familiar with the saying "If life gives you a lemon, make lemonade." If something bad happens, turn it to your advantage. It's not talking about whitewashing or overlooking the negative, but finding something useful in everything.

Cayce's expression was somewhat more explicit. It means using the negative event as a means of making some progress toward a personally defined goal. If nothing else, you can learn something from a bad situation, something that you can use to help you later.

Thomas Edison tried hundreds of ways to make a light bulb before he was able to finally make it work. When asked how he felt about all his failures, he denied that he had any failures. He indicated that he had learned hundreds of ways *not* to make a light bulb. He learned something from each experiment.

Deciding to learn something from a situation was Cayce's favorite strategy for coping with adversity. No situation can be so bad that you can't examine it to see if you can learn something from it.

Cayce is not suggesting that you ask yourself, "What lesson am I learning?" in the sense of being punished. Sometimes our parents said to us, "I'm going to teach you a lesson" as they began to spank or otherwise punish us. But instead, ask yourself what you can learn simply for the purpose of asking the question. It quickens your curiosity, helps you search for novelty in the situation, and helps you become absorbed and to go with the flow.

Simply by asking what you can learn from a bad situation, you have changed your attitude. You are no longer focusing on being the victim. Instead, you are taking control by choosing to make the situation your servant of your education. It will serve your needs to grow in self-awareness. It will serve your needs to assume creative mastery over events. It will serve your development as you strengthen your commitment to your ideals. The stumbling block becomes the stepping stone to furthering your evolution into greater consciousness.

Cayce reminds us that the purpose of life is not simply to go on living. Although we need to eat in order to live, we do not live to eat. We live to grow in awareness and understanding of the creative endowment we have within us. By accepting every situation as an opportunity for growth, we invite the discovery of our purpose for living.

Cultivating Attitudes Consistent With Ideals

Maintaining a positive attitude in adversity is the key to survival. As someone once said, "Any problem that doesn't kill me will make me stronger." Growing from adversity is one way to claim victory from disaster.

For some people, discovering this secret in the midst of their misfortunes is what initiates them upon the spiritual path. Adversity forces them to explore the magically creative role of attitude, and they discover the existence of higher levels of consciousness. Ask many people how they were introduced to spiritual concepts, those of Edgar Cayce or another tradition, and many will tell you that it was through adversity.

But why wait for problems to begin the spiritual journey? We can embark on that quest right now, by looking at our attitudes from the perspective of our ideal.

The road to higher consciousness is guided by a spiritual ideal. The choice of ideal is up to you. It is your vision of the Ultimate Good. It is the spirit in which you wish to live. To do so, the attitude you bring to situations will have to gradually become consistent with your ideal.

Cayce described the use of a practical strategy to bring about the desired relationship between your ideal and the life of your mind. You can use your ideal to guide you in your choice of attitudes.

In the last chapter, we described the initial stages of the process of working with ideals suggested by Cayce. It began with keeping a journal, and examining your experiences in light of your ideals. You can quickly determine those areas in life that challenge your ideals. These are situations that threaten your sense of peace and security, evoke reactions you don't like, or arouse feelings that are not in keeping with the spirit of your ideal. These are circumstances that hamper your freedom, depress you, hold you back, or divert your energies away from where you would put them.

Pick one of these situations to work with. Remind yourself that even though you don't always get to choose what you have to face, you can choose how you face it. Sometimes, that's the only choice you have.

Even if you have no other choices, remind yourself that you can choose your attitude. By deciding to make that choice, you can assert your own creative input on the situation. You can also invite the spiritual energy of your ideal to help you.

Cayce suggests that you next take a moment to reflect upon your ideal. Recall how you went about choosing it. If you used a past experience where you felt at your best, then recall that past experience. Get yourself in the mood of the spirit of your ideal.

Suppose your ideal is joy. Perhaps you made this choice based upon a memory of a sunny day when you took delight in everything you experienced. Your image of joy is the radiance of the sun with its smiling face. These are the various elements of your spiritual ideal. Contemplate all these elements to create in yourself a joyous atmosphere. Recall that wonderful memory of the sunny day and begin to feel the way you felt that day. Imagine being the sun smiling upon the earth. Imagine being a bird enjoying flapping its wings in flight. Imagine the soil of the earth warming itself in the sun. Think about the truth of your intuition, that all of creation is actually joyful. Be joyful in your realization.

Once you are filled with the spirit of your ideal, when you are in that mood, then look upon that unfavorable situation. From the perspective of your ideal, how do you view that situation? How does it appear to you? Imagine how you would react to that situation when you are in the mood of the spirit of your ideal. Note the attitude that you naturally adopt as you interact with the situation. What is that attitude? Can you sense it? Give it a name, as best you can.

In such a way, you can determine what your ideal attitude would be toward that situation. It is the attitude that defines the mental pattern that is most consistent with your spiritual ideal. It is the attitude that will channel the spiritual energy of your ideal into your approach to the situation. If you can cultivate that attitude, you will have your ideal to help you reshape that situation through constructive action.

An Attitude in Action

Suppose you are facing a bad situation at work. Your boss asks you, for example, to perform an impossible task. Maybe it's to develop and maintain a set of statistics concerning productivity. You just don't have the necessary resources to keep these statistics and also get your job done. What are you to do?

This sort of thing happens a lot. If you attempt the impossible, you will be overstressed and there will be consequences. If you tell your boss you can't do the job, there will be consequences. Can your spiritual ideal help you?

Suppose your ideal is love. Meditate on the feeling of this ideal and then ask yourself, "If I were approaching this situation in the spirit of love, what attitude would I take toward it?"

The first thoughts that come to mind might be to love yourself, love your boss, and love your work. What would be a loving attitude toward these three? Loving yourself, you would respect your limitations, care about your health, and would also have faith in your abilities, including your abilities to grow to new levels of competence in the face of new challenges. Loving your boss, you would respect the boss's perceptions of what needed to be done, care about your boss's needs and aspirations, and have faith in your boss's good intentions. Loving your work, you would respect its requirements, care about the quality with which it was done. You would have faith that it is possible to find an optimal solution to such a work crunch. Three attitudinal words are implied: respect, caring, and faith or optimism.

These attitudes certainly stand in contrast to what might be typical reactions to this predicament. You could easily resent the boss's new assignment. Your attitude could be defensive. You could look for reasons why you couldn't do this new job. But as you did so, your feeling that the boss didn't care about you and your already heavy workload would make you feel more desperate, resentful, and trapped. You might think of ways to get even, but as you did so, you would fear more and more the boss's ability to retaliate. Your defensive and fearful attitude could easily send you into a spiral of anxiety and rage.

If for no other reason than to protect your own sanity and to have some hope for coping with the problem, you would be better off to choose the positive attitude than the negative. Approaching this difficult situation with respect, caring, and optimism will be more beneficial to your state of mind than approaching it with disdain, resentment, and pessimism. It might also lead to a better outcome at the office.

Attitudes suggest the actions. They shape not only the way we respond inside, but also how we behave outwardly toward circumstances. Optimistic, for example, that a solution could be achieved and respectful of your boss's needs, you might get to work on the assignment while you also make a list of the consequences of attempting the job with inadequate resources. Caring about your boss's aspirations and optimistic that he will want to do his best, you might anticipate some of the negative consequences to him of your pursuing the job as assigned. Optimistic about your own creative abilities, you might try to come up with a proposal for a solution to the dilemma that minimized the negative consequences of the work crunch and resource shortage.

Then you might approach your boss and first tell him that you had begun the assignment. You would then inform him of the negative consequences you had discovered that would follow from your working on the assignment in the way he had originally envisioned, including those that would have a negative effect upon the boss's aspirations. You might present a proposal for how to restructure the assignment in the context of the other work requirements in order to minimize the negative consequences. You would leave the final decision to the boss.

In this hypothetical but all too common situation, you would be approaching your boss in a loving spirit of support, not confrontation. You would not be resisting the boss, but rather looking out for the boss's best interests, while you respected your own needs. You would be willing to put in an extra effort, yet you are not defensive about having limitations. By accepting realistic limitations, you are protecting both yourself and your boss from disappointment and other negative consequences.

This approach, although expressive of your ideal, cannot be perfect. You cannot control your boss's reaction. You can only control your own response. Don't expect to manipulate the boss into doing what you see as right, but maintain an optimistic view of your boss.

The example I've given of using an ideal to develop an approach to a difficult situation may seem too "idealistic" and not "realistic." Admittedly, working with ideals will lead to idealistic approaches—that is the purpose of ideals. On the other hand, such approaches need not be unrealistic. An idealistic approach requires more patience and effort, but may also, in the long run, be more realistic.

The *Challenger* space shuttle disaster brought to the public's awareness the tragic consequences of knuckling under to pressure from one's boss without fully communicating the consequences of pursuing an unsafe course of action. I know, from years spent training workers in the use of communication skills, as a stress-reduction and work-innovation tool, that most people respond with a knee-jerk reaction to receiving impossible job assignments. The instinctive reaction is a defensive attitude. It can be dangerous to all concerned. The idealistic approach is worth the time it takes to make it work.

Reactions at work are more often governed by ideas, not ideals. Ideas such as "the other guy doesn't care about my needs" and "I've got to look good or I'll be fired" are common culprits, and they are intensified by stress. One of two stereotyped, black-or-white responses to impossible assignments are usually evident. Full of resentment, the worker attempts the job, while developing excuses and ulcers in anticipation of the negative effects of attempting the impossible. Alternatively, the worker speaks up to the boss, but in a confrontational manner, communicating nonverbally if not also verbally, a lack of interest in cooperating with the boss's perceived need to get the job done. The reaction of the boss is equally stereotyped. It needn't be that way.

As the stresses of modern life intensify, as the demands upon available resources multiply, the need for innovation in approaching situations demands better communication and enhanced creative functioning among all concerned. Working with ideals, in the manner Cayce suggested, becomes a powerful way of guiding such an adventure into creating an alternative future.

Healing Negative Attitudes

When you begin keeping a journal, you will probably discover certain negative attitudes that you tend to adopt. Once you begin working with your current ideal to develop positive alternatives, you will no doubt find, to your dismay, that some of these negative attitudes are clearly your favorites. You might have a hard time giving them up.

Thousands of people asked Cayce for advice on problems. No matter what the nature of the problem, whether it was physical, financial, or marital, Cayce often pointed to the role of a negative attitude.

Attitudinal problems were so commonly addressed that there are three volumes of published Cayce readings on this topic, covering over 160 different attitudes, from animosity to zealousness. Some of the most common negative attitudes were self-doubt and fearfulness, judgment, fault-finding or condemnation, and hopelessness.

Cayce traced the mental source of negative attitudes to a common root—an erroneous self-image or faulty understanding of the true nature of the self. He often used the word *selfishness* to express this faulty self-image. He was not referring to being stingy, or to being self-preoccupied. Rather, he was referring to being attached or fixated on a narrow conception of self. By selfishness he meant being hypnotized by the little self, or the ego of the conscious mind.

It is like the situation portrayed in the common dream of being naked or scantily dressed in a public place. It is a situation of extreme self-consciousness. All eyes are upon you, and you are hypnotized by your self's existence. Most negative attitudes grow out of the preoccupation with that level of our being.

Consider the problem of self-doubt. Cayce described it as a "shadow of selfishness." It is the result of a misplaced focus on one's own ego. Given the focus on self, the question naturally arises, "Can I really do this or that? Will other people really approve?"

A person asked Cayce, for example, why he always assumed that he would not be able to "put over" to an audience what was really in his heart. Cayce's answer was that self-doubt was the culprit. Having stage fright, or being shy, are instructive examples of self-doubt, because the self-preoccupation is easy to see. Self-doubt arises from a focus on the self and can be overcome by a change of focus.

I have found from personal experience that Cayce's analysis is correct. When I am shy, or have stage fright, or difficulty communicating to an audience, in public speaking or in writing, it is invariably because I am focused on myself and my performance. There is always a performance anxiety in self-doubt. If I shift my focus away from myself, and pay more attention to the audience and to ideas that wish to be expressed, my doubt vanishes. I become more concerned with introducing the audience to the ideas. I am out of the picture. I become the servant to the ideas and the audience. No one notices the servant. The audience responds to the ideas, not to me.

In this situation, I have traded in the attitude of self-doubt for one of love of the ideas and caring about the audience. I have become a channel for the ideas. Not only have I lost the unpleasant burden of self-doubt, but I have also experienced the pleasure of being able to ride the wave of the energy of the ideas. The ideas themselves carried the day, while I simply served as a conduit of something I cared about. By getting out of my way, I have become a channel of the ideal of communication. It was a good trade-off.

Healing negative attitudes usually involves making such a trade. One gives up one's negative attitude by surrendering one's grip on the little self and allowing something greater to take its place. It is Cayce's simple secret, but one with profound implications for healing.

Love Conquers Fear

Cayce's general approach for dealing with something negative was to not fight it, but to replace it with a positive alternative. Quoting from the Bible (Matthew 5:39), he would advise, "Resist not evil!" It is sound psychology.

Imagine stopping a runaway horse that is galloping toward you. Would you try to fight it? Would you stand there in its path with your arms outstretched signaling for it to stop? No, because you know you would get run over. It would be better to turn and start running in the same direction as the horse's path so by the time the horse passed by, you'd have enough speed to jump on it. Then you could ride with it for a while and gradually calm it and slow it down.

It does little good to try to subdue a negative attitude by trying to knock it out, fight it back, or suppress it. Would you stop a baby from crying by covering its mouth? Negative attitudes arise from a false sense of self. They can be healed by education, by gentle leading toward a positive alternative.

Charles Thomas Cayce, Edgar Cayce's grandson, provided a good image for this process. Imagine a glass of water that is contaminated with oil. How can you get the oil out? By gentling pouring in more water, the oil is forced to the top and over the side of the glass. The water displaces the oil. It is the same way that positive attitudes can displace negative ones.

With regard to fearfulness, for example, Cayce indicated that love displaces fear. Fear is created by the illusion of separateness. It is based upon an illusion. Love is based upon the truth. The truth will dispel the illusory.

Find a way to be loving toward some aspect of a situation you fear and the fear will gradually subside. That was the principle behind Cayce's strategy for dealing with stage fright. It was also the basic strategy of those survivors of ordeals. They were in fearful situations. The natural tendency would be to try to get as far removed as possible from the situation. Instead, they found some aspect of the situation to embrace and had an experience of flow.

In my own experience, I had difficulty learning to ice-skate because I was afraid of falling on the ice. I moved rigidly and tried to stand straight up to avoid falling. I could not lean to the side to enable the edges of my skates to cut a secure path through the ice. I fought the experience every stumbling step of the way.

What was my fear? It was a concern for the safety of my body. I assumed that to fall on the ice would be the end of me. I was clinging to a limited concept of myself. I saw myself as Humpty Dumpty. My fear was convincing me that if I fell off the wall, I would not be able to get back together again.

My skating instructor kept encouraging me, "Love your edges." She demonstrated stroking the ice with the edge of her skate as she pushed off on a graceful glide. She made it look so appealing that I had to experience it myself. I leaned on the edge of my skate and pushed off into a glide. I could feel the skate's edge cutting a smooth path through the ice, making the ice almost feel as soft as ice cream. I loved the sensation.

I started making two or three strokes in a row, large steps for me, before pulling myself back upright, rigid on the ice. I needed to reassure myself that I could stand right there, in one piece. Then I pushed off again, into the wonderful sensation of a glide along the ice. Suddenly I fell. I hit the ice with a thud and slid. Momentarily I was in shock. But I was OK! I got up laughing and skated away in tears of joy! I had survived a fall. My love of gliding along the ice had freed me from my fear.

Love transports us beyond the boundaries of our separate selves and projects our attention, our caring, and our energies outward toward the focus of our love. It helps build a bridge between us and the rest of life. It delivers us from the illusion of separateness and introduces us to the truth. The truth is that we are one with life. The truth is that there is nothing to fear.

The Healing Power of Forgiveness

I have seen many people apply the formula "Love is letting go of fear" in a manner that is being cruel to themselves. They chastise themselves for being afraid. They sentence themselves to love as if they were issuing a condemnation of punishment. They struggle to love and they push away their fear, only to have their fear return the stronger. They feel defeated and guilty.

Using that formula in that way is not loving. It is instead an act of self-condemnation. Cayce warned against the evils of a judgmental attitude, whether toward another person or toward oneself. The solution is an attitude of forgiveness. It means not to blame ourselves for our limitations, but to assume that we had been doing as best we could.

When Janet, for example, came to me and told me that she blamed herself because she created her own reality, we had to get beneath the surface of that philosophy to reveal that she had not directly created that reality she called a failure. The patterns she held in her mind, her ideas, had created it.

She realized her life had been based on the feeling of being unloved and unlovable. Her father had left the family when she was a youngster. She had always wondered if it had been her fault. Perhaps she had not pleased him. She noted that her mother always seemed most loving toward her when she was pleasing her mother. From such experiences, she had formed the idea that it is important to please others if you wish to receive love.

Realistically, Janet could assume only partial responsibility for choosing to entertain such ideas about love. She needed to forgive herself, because forming such ideas were natural for a child who is totally dependent upon the love of others.

The experience of forgiveness releases our grip on anger and fear. It can heal us from negativity and make it possible to make a fresh start.

Guidance by Ideals

Adopt an attitude that is consistent with your ideal and you will invite the spiritual energy of that ideal to influence your life. The ideal will guide your actions, develop your character, and expand your awareness of spiritual states of mind.

Take good sportsmanship, for example. It is an ideal that has a long and honorable tradition. It is expressed in the attitude "It doesn't matter whether you win or lose, but how you play the game." In recent years, professional sports, and to some extent school athletics, have made a mockery of this ideal. The slogan has become "The bottom line is that winning is everything!"

The attitude expressing good sportsmanship contains an apparent contradiction that is sometimes too hard for the pressures of modern life to endure. Good sportsmanship can put you between a rock and a hard place. It's hard to be a good sport when so much is riding on winning. Not everyone can bear the strain.

Nailing yourself to the cross of contradictions, to playing your very best while not being concerned about the game's outcome, initiates you to the transcendent value of sportsmanship. You discover an extra dimension of genius in true creative play. Focusing on the process of the game rather than the outcome, you are free to focus only on the immediate moment rather than cluttering your mind with the anticipated consequences of winning or losing. By not cheating, or by not taking medicinal stimulants, you risk losing to an opponent who may not be a good sport, but you gain in other ways.

When we choose an ideal and then design optimal attitudes toward situations based on that ideal, we soon become more aware of our choices. Life becomes more intense. Your ideal will begin to guide and shape your life, but it will test you in the process.

Making a commitment to an ideal is like getting onto a roller coaster. Once you're strapped in, you're in for the duration of the ride. Negative attitudes protect us from taking risks, from getting on the roller coaster. Positive attitudes open us up to the thrill of the ride. If you can surrender to it, the ride will transport you outside yourself to an experience of exhilarating thrill!

CHAPTER 8

LET'S GET PHYSICAL

To be sure the attitudes oft influence the physical condition of the body. No one can hate his neighbor and not have stomach or liver trouble. One cannot be jealous and allow anger of same and not have upset digestion or heart disorder.

Edgar Cayce 4021-1

MARGARET WAS A very pleasant person. She had an engaging smile and reached out with her eyes to greet her visitor. She showed an interest and concern for the other person, wanting to put the person at ease. The other person was the doctor who was examining her. Margaret had shown signs of epileptic seizure, and the doctor was going to check her brain waves for signs of abnormalities. It was characteristic of Margaret that although she was the person who was in distress and who needed reassurance during this testing procedure, she was nevertheless reassuring the doctor that he needn't worry that the electrodes he was placing on her scalp might be bothering her.

The EEG record of Margaret's brain waves showed signs of irregularities. There were the telltale squiggles that indicated the presence of an epileptic condition. From this test, the doctor confirmed that Margaret indeed suffered from some form of epilepsy. The evidence was clear.

Jack was a different case entirely. He was irritable and angry as the doctor entered the examination room. He complained about having to take the brain-wave test and complained about the electrodes. He challenged the doctor's competence and was sarcastic about the value of the test. Jack talked constantly, often making off-color wisecracks. He made the doctor feel ill at ease and defensive. It was like Jack to express his nervousness in the form of aggressive teasing and snide remarks. The EEG record of Jack's brain waves showed no signs of irregularities. All the brain-wave patterns were perfectly normal. The results were as they should be, as Jack had no history of seizures. The doctor's examination confirmed that this man, although somewhat obnoxious, had a perfectly healthy brain.

Margaret was pleasant but suffered from seizures. Jack was rude and argumentative but had no signs of brain malfunction. What was perplexing was that Jack and Margaret inhabited the same body. Jack and Margaret were two different personalities of the same person. It was a case of multiple personality.

The case illustrates one of the fascinating mind-body phenomena associated with the multiple-personality disorder. The problem of multiple personality first came to public attention with the story *The Three Faces of Eve*. In recent years, therapists have discovered many similar cases and have examined them thoroughly. Multiple personalities raise a number of fascinating questions about our view of personhood. One of the most interesting are the physical aspects associated with each different personality.

Each personality inhabits the body in a different way, creating quite noticeable differences. Each personality has a distinct tone of voice, a different set of social expressions, gestures, and postures, as well as different ways of moving about. Each is clearly a different personality, and it shows! What is surprising is the extent to which the body changes in response to the personality that is currently active.

Many details of the body's functioning are affected. In the case of Margaret and Jack, each had different brain-wave patterns. One suffered from epileptic seizures while the other did not. In other cases it's been found that different personalities show different reactions to medication. One personality is allergic to sulfa drugs, another is not. One personality suffers from asthma, while a different personality has normal breathing. One personality smokes addictively, while another is a nonsmoker. One personality is right-handed, while another is left-handed. One is so nearsighted that very strong glasses are needed to read, while another personality sees quite well with no glasses at all. Even bodily functions that would seem to be rigidly fixed by physical constraints give way to the influence of the personality.

What these cases of multiple personality show so clearly is that the body and its neurochemical functioning is under the control of the mind. The mind directs and shapes the body. Given a dramatic change in mind, there is a corresponding shift in the appearance and functioning of the body. As Cayce indicated, different attitudes create different chemical climates in the body. Our attitudes become drugs in the body. The results can be startling. The implications are immense.

We've learned how to approach the design of an ideal life. We've seen how attitude can make a difference in our experience. It's now time to get physical, to see how our attitudes affect our body, and how we can use the mind-body connection to our advantage.

Stress and Disease

Hans Selye, the originator of research on stress, coined the term, "fight-or-flight reflex." It is based on animal instinct. When something or someone threatens us, our choice is to stand and fight or to run away. Our body prepares itself for action.

Faced with a charging bear, we flush with fear. Our adrenal glands kick into gear, quickly bringing about many physical reactions. Our heart pounds harder to activate our lungs and muscles for what may ensue. The blood vessels in our fingertips and toes shrink to prevent blood loss in case of a wound. We are charged up, ready to face the grizzly opponent or run for dear life.

Whether we run away or stay and fight, our body is energized for action.

When we take action, either running or fighting, we use up the adrenaline our body has produced. We get charged up with energy and we expend it. The cycle is completed. We are back to normal.

In the forest, the fight-or-flight reflex serves us well. In modern life, however, we encounter few actual bears. In today's forest, it is grizzly worries that confront us. We are never free of them.

Imagine that you are alone and helpless in a hostile world. How would you feel? Karen Horney, an eminent psychiatrist, defined *anxiety* by referring to just that very attitude. It produces its own mild fight-or-flight reflex. There are chemical consequences of anxiety within the body.

The stresses of modern life keep us in a mild state of anxiety. Anxiety keeps our adrenaline level above normal. Yet we don't actually throw spears and chase after our worries or run away on foot. We sit on our worries. We get charged up emotionally, but we do not take the vigorous action required to expend the juices and flush our system. The anxiety juices build up in our system and wear down our body. Chronic stress is bad for our health.

It was through just such an explanation that, in 1936, Hans Selye initiated the study of how stress affects the body. By the 1980s, a tremendous research explosion into the body's immune system verified much of what Cayce had described about the health consequences of attitudes. It has now become clear that mental attitude is one of the most crucial determinants of physical health.

The Mind Cures

In Charlie Chaplin's memorable movie *Modern Times,* the stresses and strains of technological life were clearly cast as the meat grinders of the human spirit. This movie made it easy to see how pressures of modern life could crush the body's ability to stay free of illness. Selye's research confirmed Chaplin's impression and helped ulcers become accepted as a physical result of psychological stress.

In later years, rumors began spreading that another form of stress played a role in disease. Lurking behind the development of cancer was the subtle culprit called grief. Hidden, unexpressed, chronic depression over a past loss was suspected as a predisposing factor in the initiation of this dread disease. As the years went by, the evidence mounted.

As it became clearer that emotional factors were involved in disease, it was also becoming clear that the mind and emotions could be involved in healing. The first "mind cures" occurred on the fringes of society. Hypnosis played a role in this early history, before the turn of the century.

Mary Baker Eddy was cured of a nervous disorder through hypnotic treatments. She later disavowed hypnosis herself and founded Christian Science. Eddy's development was but one of the several "new thought" groups formed during the turn of the century. These traditions mixed religion, positive thinking, and sometimes hypnosis into an approach to health—physical, mental, and spiritual. It wasn't until the consciousness revolution of the

1960s that their ideas began to enter into the mainstream of scientific thinking.

One of the hallmarks of the medical profession's otherwise reluctant acceptance of the role of the mind in disease and healing was the publication in 1986 of *Love, Medicine and Miracles,* by Dr. Bernie S. Siegel. Written by a Yale University surgeon, this book is a personal and professional affirmation of how the mind creates disease and how it heals it. What was most significant about this doctor's work was that he was actively practicing it himself with his patients. Using psychotherapy and other means, he helps his patients rid themselves of depression and build positive attitudes. He has taken seriously the evidence showing that attitudes such as hope, optimism, humor, and love have a curative effect upon the body's immune system. Building first upon attitudinal change, he then encourages his patients to learn the use of imagery techniques to help their bodies recover. His book is an excellent resource for seeing both the spirit and the methods of the Cayce readings on healing put into action.

After decades of research into how the mind plays a role in the creation of disease, the reverse is now as clearly established. The mind also heals.

The Physiology of the Mind

Cayce explained the relationship between attitudes and the health of the body by reference to the nervous system and the endocrine glands. He was the first psychoneuroimmunologist, presenting a holistic and integrated view of how the mind, the nervous system, and the endocrine system operate to produce health and illness. At the time of his psychic readings, his statements about the endocrine system seemed invalid. Time proved Cayce right, however, as revelations of the body's immune system became regular news items.

According to Cayce's model, we have three nervous systems. They are each associated with a different level of mind. Through a proper understanding of their functioning, however, Cayce indicated that we can gain some control over their activity.

There is the cerebral-spinal or voluntary nervous system. It controls the body's muscles and is under the voluntary control of the conscious mind. This is the nervous system that relaxes and sleeps at night. It is also the system that we can use to gain indirect control over the other systems.

There is the autonomic nervous system, controlling the functioning of the body's organs, such as the heart and digestive processes. It used to be called the involuntary system, because it seemed to function outside conscious control. Cayce, however, anticipated modern research by explaining that the autonomic nervous system, controlled by the subconscious mind, can be indirectly controlled by our attitudes and through visualization.

The autonomic nervous system contains two subsystems. One is called the sympathetic nervous system and the other is called the parasympathetic nervous system. Both respond to emotional arousal. They are like the accelerator and brake pedals of the body. The sympathetic system is the activating system. Its job is to excite the body. The parasympathetic system's job is the opposite, to calm the body. The fight-or-flight reflex is the job of the sympathetic system. Falling asleep requires the action of the parasympathetic system. The functioning of body systems is closely integrated with the functioning of the endocrine system.

Cayce identified the endocrine system as a third nervous system of its own. The endocrine system consists of the body's various glands: the pituitary, pineal, thyroid, thymus, adrenals, leydig, and gonads. Cayce indicated that this system corresponded to a series of psychic centers, known in the East as chakras. For example, the chakra name for the pineal center is the "third eye."

The superconscious mind makes its contract with the body through these psychic centers and the endocrine system. The soul's awareness, as in past-life memories and ideals, affects the physical body through this system.

Through the network of the bloodstream the endocrine glands communicate with each other and the brain through the chemicals they secrete. They also have a network of nerve fibers for communication. Taken together, the endocrine system is almost a brain unto itself. Cayce sometimes referred to it as a brain, and modern science is learning just how intelligent it is.

Research on the body's immunity response has increased our knowledge of the functioning of the endocrine system and its interaction with the autonomic nervous system. The thymus gland controls the production of the "killer cells" that fight disease. The functioning of the thymus is affected by the activities in the pineal and the adrenal glands. The activity in the adrenals is also affected by the nervous system. There are thus many different pathways by which the activity in the thymus gland can be influenced.

As neurophysiologists trace these complex paths of influence, others have discovered the truth of Cayce's major proposition about the power of the mind over the body. The essential way to influence the health and harmony within the endocrine system is through mental attitude.

The Emotional and Physical Effects of Attitude

Looking at the world through rose-colored glasses will give you a rosy disposition and a rosy complexion, too. It's about that simple, and it's true.

The attitude we assume determines the emotions we feel. Emotions have physical consequences and determine how our body functions. The creative power of attitude thus extends beyond our state of mind. Attitudes become physical.

An attitude is a frame of mind. As a perspective, it governs both what we look for and how we arrange what we see. Is your glass half empty or half full? A person with a pessimistic attitude looks at the upper part of the glass to see the empty portion. An optimist looks at the bottom part of the glass to see the full portion.

Seeing the empty portion of the glass, the pessimist feels sad. The optimist feels gratitude for what the glass still contains. Each emotional reaction is appropriate to the reality perceived. Attitude determines the nature of the reality experienced, which determines the quality of the emotional reaction.

The sadness of the pessimist is translated into physical terms. The nervous system provides a slight depressive effect. The person "loses heart" and the thymus gland responds accordingly. The immune response is weakened. Research has confirmed that loneliness, sadness, and depression weaken the immune response. Even though the glass may indeed be half empty, the pessimistic attitude is a hazard to health.

The gratitude of the optimist translates into an upbeat physical expression. Even though optimism may be unrealistic, from an objective point of view, it creates such a positive physical effect that it gives a person an edge in overcoming difficulties. Optimism is not only healthy, but also is a good strategy for coping.

Depression and Pain

Pain is a part of life. No one escapes having at least some encounter with it. We all know what pain feels like. None of us likes it.

Accidents and illness are occasions of actual physical pain. Damage to the body stimulates nerve endings to send warning signals to the brain, and we experience pain. It's a very real, physical experience.

As physical and real as it may be, pain is also a matter of psychology. Attitude plays a role in the creation of pain. Research has shown that optimism and pessimism have different effects upon the experience of pain.

Suppose you had to place your hands in a bucket of ice water. It would hurt. How much would it hurt? It depends upon your attitude.

People who believe that they have little or no control over what happens to them in life find the ice water more painful than people who believe that their own actions can make a difference. People who are optimistic in that way experience less pain than people who are pessimistic. Research has proven that true, even though the optimism may have little practical relevance to dealing with the source of the pain.

If someone gives you a painkiller before you stick your hand in the ice water, you will feel less pain. That would be true even if the pill was a placebo, a phony. Expectations and beliefs affect pain. If real pain pills are used, optimistic people require smaller dosages to eliminate pain than do pessimistic people.

If you are taught how to relax before sticking your hand in the water, you will feel less pain. Relaxation can reduce pain, but it is not the essential ingredient. As research has shown, it is the attitude and not the actual facts that determine the subjective experience.

Using false feedback, people can be fooled to believe that they have learned the relaxation trick when, in fact, they have not. Similarly, people who have indeed learned to relax can be fooled to believe that they have not learned the trick. People who believe they have learned some control feel less pain than people who are actually relaxed but believe they have no control. Note the implications of this study: the belief of having some control has more effect on the experience of pain than does actual control.

Depression and feelings of helplessness add to the experience of pain. It is a factor in many cases of chronic pain. If the depression can be alleviated, the physical pain will also be alleviated. Alternatively, when a patient with chronic pain learns relaxation, or some other form of self-control, pain diminishes. The reduction in pain does not necessarily result from a new ability to control the source of the pain. It results as much from the release from feelings of helplessness.

The body's response to an actual, physical threat, such as something causing pain, depends upon the person's perception of the situation. Recall Cayce's advice to turn stumbling blocks into stepping-stones. His advice is based on sound physiological evidence. When the body is threatened and the person feels helpless, there are different chemical secretions in the body than if the person responds to the situation as a challenge.

Whatever the source of stress, if we can find a way to regard it as a challenge, our body will help us out. The body's ability to fight off disease, and our ability to invent creative solutions to problems, is dependent upon our taking a constructive attitude. The body is sensitive to such feelings of helplessness and such sentiments as, "I give up." Finding some way, even trivial, to believe that you can make a difference in the situation initiates a positive response within the body.

Even contemplating an upbeat approach has positive physical effects. Movies are a good way to stimulate a particular frame of mind. They can help us look on the bright side and inspire us to think positively. On the other hand, they can agitate us, incite fear, or make us feel depressed. Movies affect our body as much as our mind.

In one experiment, conducted by Harvard psychologist David McClelland, subjects viewed either a depressing movie about Nazi concentration camps or an inspiring and hopeful movie about the work of Sister Teresa. You would not be surprised to learn that afterward people who saw the first movie felt depressed while the people who saw the second movie were feeling pretty good. What might surprise you is that the chemistry in the blood of these two audiences was quite different. Blood tests revealed that the people who watched the Nazi movie left with depressed immune systems, while the people who saw the Sister Teresa movie left with their immune system strengthened.

Finding something positive to think about, reading inspirational literature, seeing a movie full of optimism, or even engaging in daydreaming about a pleasant topic can tip the scale toward a more optimistic frame of mind.

Evidence suggests that optimism actually affects the brain's preparation for pain, stimulating an increase in the secretion of natural painkillers within the bloodstream. These painkillers, called "endorphins," seem to be the body's own form of morphine. A person's state of mind has a lot to do with their production.

Pessimists are not just complainers. Their brains do not produce as much painkiller. These people have something to complain about. They can also learn how to use optimism, and other more specific skills, to make their lives more pleasant.

Modern research on pain is a good case study in appreciating the principles Cayce taught concerning how attitudes affect our body. There is a very intimate relationship between mind and body. A change in attitude has physical consequences. If a change in attitude doesn't come easily, we'll see how a minor change in behavior, applied consistently, can lead to the desired change in attitude.

Humor Medicine

We know from *Reader's Digest* that laughter is the best medicine. Cayce was also an advocate of humor. He considered it to be healthy, a sound preventative to the effects of life stress, as well as an attitude that reflected just the right approach to spiritual realities. Being able to laugh at ourselves reflects both self-acceptance and humility. It keeps the little self, the ego, in proper perspective.

The value of humor in physical healing made headlines when Norman Cousins, formerly editor of *Saturday Review,* came out with his book *Anatomy of an Illness.* There he told the story of how he cured himself of what the doctors called an incurable, terminal illness by daily doses of laughter. He watched countless hours of videotapes of old comedy shows, like Groucho Marks and the Three Stooges. He described how, after a good laugh, he felt less pain in his body. He challenged medicine to understand the mechanics of what he had accomplished. Medical research was ready to respond to the challenge.

The role of humor in the body has been suspected for a long time. Ancient Greeks viewed the functioning of the body in terms of the activities of what they called the four "humors." These were four basic bodily fluids that created corresponding temperaments—blood, phlegm, choler, and melancholy. Although the specifics of this ancient theory have been displaced by better anatomical science, the basic understanding has remained in our vocabulary. We still say that someone is in a good or ill humor, referring to their temperament. Medical science is learning just how attitudes are translated into chemical reactions within the body.

With regard to good humor, research is uncovering some of the positive effects of laughter. By showing people cartoons or comedy films, experimenters are learning about the physical side effects of laughter. They have discovered, for example, that laughter is a painkiller, as Norman Cousins observed. After viewing comedy films, subjects are much less sensitive to pain. Blood tests indicate that the immune system is stronger after a period of laughter.

Strong and hearty belly laughter is almost like exercise. It increases the rate of deep breathing and exercises the abdominal muscles. Afterward, there is a decrease in physical tension and a sense of peaceful relaxation.

Laughter can be cleansing. If you have ever experienced laughing until your side hurt and your eyes were watering, you know for yourself the sensation of having had tension washed out of your system. Laughter is clearly a tonic for stress, a purgative for the body's ills. It's what makes laughter the best medicine.

Using Physical Techniques to Improve Attitude

Being able to laugh at a time when things are not funny isn't a skill that most of us have. It would be a cruel joke if Cayce were simply to suggest that people adopt a humorous attitude at a time of crisis. He had enough compassion and understanding to know that such a suggestion would cause more harm than good. Fortunately, there is a way around this problem.

Body, mind, and spirit operate as a unit. Recall Cayce's creation principle: Spirit is the life, mind is the builder, and physical is the result. In this formula, the physical expression is at the bottom of the hierarchy. It is at the result end of the equation, not at the cause end. Thus we have explored how our ideals lead to our attitudes, which in turn affect our concrete experiences of circumstances and the operation of the body. This equation can also be reversed.

We can have our bodies perform actions that are consistent with certain attitudes. The corresponding attitude becomes easier to manifest. We can build an attitude by our bodily actions. The attitude can then take over and direct the body to produce the chemical changes consistent with that attitude.

A good case in point is the bodily reaction to panic. When a person is overcome by fear, one of the body's reactions is quickened breathing. Sometimes the fast breathing takes over to the point that the person suffers from hyperventilation. The overcharging of the system with oxygen, without the corresponding physical discharge through actual fighting or running, intensifies the panic reaction. The person becomes frozen in their steps.

One way to pull out of this nosedive into despair is to grab on to the throttle of the breath. Hold the breath momentarily and then forcefully make the breathing go slowly and deeply. Forced slow and deep breathing stops the panic reaction. It calms the person down and gives them back control over what was an out-of-control situation. Not only is the body calmed, but the panic sensation goes away. Operating on the body can affect the emotions.

When we are afraid, we can act bravely. Taking small physical steps into the face of danger, mimicking the actions of the courageous, results in small emotional changes. By acting bravely, we can come to feel more courageous. The change in attitude will translate into a chemical change in the body, giving us the energy of an uplifted and courageous heart, more stamina, and greater tolerance for pain. We can literally lift ourselves up by our bootstraps.

Actors employ this method to get into the mood of the part they are to play. They start by pretending to feel something. They act *as if* they feel it. They make faces that correspond to the mood and feeling they are supposed to enact. Researchers studying the physiological effects of actors' methods have found that the playacting does indeed bring about the physiological and chemical changes that would naturally occur if the feelings were real. These results show that actors know the secret of a "priming effect," using physical actions to create moods.

Did your parents or teachers ever suggest to you that you keep your head held high? We know moods are expressed in posture. But the reverse is also true. Postures effect mood. Walking in an upbeat, proud posture will elevate your spirits and give you a feeling of courage. Walking with your eyes to the ground, shoulders slumped, will make you feel blue.

In one study, researchers trained subjects to walk in one of two ways. In the happy gait, subjects held their head erect, swung their arms, and looked out at the horizon while they walked at a brisk pace. In the sad shuffle, subjects lowered their heads, looked at the ground, and walked in small, slow steps. At the end of the hike, those who had adopted the happy gait were feeling up and energetic. Those who had practiced the sad shuffle felt tired and blue.

It's interesting that popular speech expresses this wisdom. We'll say that life is just "getting the person down." We know what it is like to be so tired and discouraged by events that we become literally slumped over. The physical posture not only expresses but also adds to the chemical effects of our discouragement. We can give ourselves an energy boost, begin to change the chemistry in our bodies, and prepare ourselves to master the situation by simply standing tall. Walk as though you are on top of the world and you'll soon feel that way.

It's not just a way to trick yourself out of feeling bad. Walking, and exercise in general, has been found to have positive effects on elevating mood. It has been shown to be a good antidote to depression. It changes the chemistry of the body and strengthens the immune system. Besides, getting out in the fresh air and taking an enjoyable walk simply feels good.

Cayce also often recommended smiling as a way of elevating one's mood. He gave it as a formula for producing happiness when one didn't feel happy. Laboratory research has demonstrated the effectiveness of his recommendation.

In one rather unusual study, researchers manipulated by hand people's facial expression. By pushing on eyebrows and lips, they created the facial equivalents of frowns and smiles. They found that these forced masks had emotional consequences. Frowning makes people feel sad, while smiling makes them feel happy.

What if you just don't feel like smiling? What if you don't have someone who can put a smile on your face? The results of one study suggest that you can stick a pencil between your teeth and enjoy the effects of smiling. In this experiment, people looked at cartoons and rated them for humor. Some people held a pencil in their teeth, as instructed, or held a pen in their lips. Holding the pen in the lips creates a pucker that makes smile impossible, while holding the pen in the teeth forces a smile. The people with puckered mouths didn't find the cartoons very funny, while those with forces smiled were amused. Regardless of the people's intentions, the smile muscles in their face opened their hearts to humor.

If you were feeling depressed, would you be willing to stick a pencil between your teeth to force a smile? Research has proved the effectiveness of Cayce's ideas about using physical techniques to improve mood. Are you willing to have your mood lifted? It is an important question. It brings it back to you and your choices. How do you choose to feel? If you want to feel better, if you want to adopt a more constructive attitude, if you would like to feel that you can create an effect on your circumstances, there are things that you can do for yourself to prepare the way.

Cayce thus paints a picture that runs the full circle, with a place for everyone, no matter what their condition, to enter the creative process of life. You can begin by setting a spiritual ideal. Then adopt a corresponding mental attitude. Let that attitude suggest appropriate actions. The spirit thus is channeled into the physical. If things are so bad that you can't quite summon up a motivating image of your ideal, if you can't bring yourself to adopt a positive attitude, you can start with something very simple. You can find some way to act as if you felt better, you can act as if you held that constructive attitude. You can go for a walk, you can smile at someone, even though you are feeling blue. That very action will have an effect on the body to make it easier to consider adopting a more upbeat attitude; it will make it easier to envision your ideal. You can gain an edge on your situation, rekindle your belief that you can make a difference, and then take another step forward. Step by step, inch by inch, you can turn a situation around. You can survive a crisis, you can create circumstances that will help you toward having it your way.

It does require some effort. On the other hand, you are not alone. The ideal you believe in has its own power to help you. It is not a matter of your own willpower. It is more a question of whether or not you are willing to do what you can do—nothing more is asked—to allow your ideal to manifest itself in your life.

CHAPTER 9

WHAT IS YOUR WILL?

The ability to choose is *will*; as well as the ability to allow self to be used by influences.

Edgar Cayce, 1608-1

WHEN JANET'S HUSBAND reappeared at her doorstep, her commitment to her newly formulated ideal was tested. What was her will?

Perhaps it was because his life had not improved by ridding himself of what he considered to be an inadequate wife. Perhaps he now missed having someone else to blame for his difficulties. Whatever the reason, Janet's estranged husband returned suggesting a reconciliation.

He approached her full of apologies. The problems were all his fault, he said, and he would now be a changed man. He said he needed her to believe in him. He needed his family to inspire him toward a good life.

Janet was tempted to please him and rejoin their old marriage. Old habits do die hard. He clearly needed her. She could regain her esteem by winning his approval and praise. It was a familiar pattern. It was close at hand and easily available. He wanted her back, and she liked to be appreciated.

Although she could feel the pressure to make an immediate decision, Janet hesitated and asked for some time to think about it. She evaluated the options from the point of view of her ideal of intelligent love. She knew she needed time to regain her bearings on a new foundation in life. She accepted her desires and respected her needs.

She confessed to him that she did not have what it seemed to take to satisfy his cravings. She suggested that he enroll in an alcoholism rehabilitation program while she worked on trying to get back on her own feet. When he had achieved sobriety and was employed, and she had regained some confidence as a self-supporting woman and a working mother, then she would be willing to look at the prospects for a life together. She said she hoped it could be so. Time would tell.

Janet expressed to me her amazement at what had happened. She was surprised that she found his offer so tempting. She still loved him, and was more than willing to consider the possibility of an eventual reconciliation. She was also surprised that she had the will to counter her husband's plan with an alternative. She said that when she meditated on the feeling of intelligent love, she discovered that, more than anything else, she trusted the wisdom of respecting her need for self-confidence. She was willing to do what was necessary to get it back.

It didn't feel right to Janet to go back with her husband at this point. Janet's response to her husband's invitation, however, made her quite nervous. Wouldn't a good mother want her child to have father and mother united under one roof? What if he didn't come back a second time? Wasn't she being selfish to consider her needs over his? She suffered many anxieties as a result of her idealistic decision, but she was also excited at the prospects of a new life. She had no guarantees that it would work out. All she had to hold on to was that her decision felt right when viewed from the spirit of her ideal. She was willing to be guided by that feeling.

An Alternative to Willpower

You can choose your ideal; you can have it your way. But, like Janet, you may have to face the question of whether you are willing to have things as you choose. Cayce paints a pretty optimistic picture about the possibilities that are available to you when you build upon an ideal with the powers of the mind. It may sound good but feel unrealistic. It depends on what you are *willing*.

It's easy to say: pick an ideal, design your attitudes to keep them positive, and take a walk when you are feeling blue. It's easy to say, but not easy to do. It seems like we are talking about a heroic amount of willpower. It seems like a lot of work. When we are depressed, feeling blue, or even tired, or when we are sick, frightened, or overwhelmed, who needs help in the form of making greater effort? What if you can't bring yourself to smile when you're depressed? Anyone who says you can always do as you choose just hasn't been in any tough situations.

To believe that you can do anything you choose also sounds somewhat grandiose. It doesn't seem right somehow that by sheer strength of will you can expect to always have things your way. It seems selfish and manipulative. It also sounds a bit deluded. It's one thing to accept that faith can move mountains, but it would seem that greed could only destroy a mountain.

The Cayce readings offer a perspective on will that helps us get around both the willpower trap and the evil of self-centered willfulness.

Studying the problem of healing negative attitudes, we saw that it did little good to try to beat down the negative. It required, instead, supplanting the negative with a positive alternative. Similarly, relying on raw willpower is often counterproductive. Tapping into a higher form of will will prove to be a better strategy. Relating to a higher will, first expressed in the form of an ideal, also helps guide our behavior according to spiritual values and leads us to the use of higher powers of the mind.

Qualities of the Will

Hidden in the shadows, behind the superhero willpower, the true will is the dynamic, propelling force of every soul. Cayce viewed the will as one of the three dimensions of the soul, along with spirit and mind. In *Paradox of Power: Balancing Personal and Higher Will*, Mark Thurston provides an in-depth discussion of Cayce's perspective on the will. Examining the many times Cayce referred to the activity of the will, Thurston found that it had nine essential qualities.

The will is the *chooser*. Souls have the same free will as their Creator. It is a freedom of choice. Among the various patterns the mind generates, the will can choose the one upon which to focus attention. The path of attention, in fact, is a good place to watch the footprints of the will. Our attention follows our will. When the will is inactive, our attention and our behavior follow the path of habits. When the will is active, we become more aware of our choices and more in touch with our reality as creative souls.

The will is the *active principle* within the soul. The spirit dimension of the soul is pure energy, without pattern or direction. The mind patterns the energy while the will directs it. It is the will that provides the soul with its impetus for growth and evolution. Without the will, the mind's past patterns completely determine the manifestation of spirit. When this active principle is dormant, or hidden, our actions appear to be the passive follower of habit or mood.

The will is the *motivator*. That is the quality of the will that helps us take initiative. It gets us moving in a particular direction. It channels our energy into action. When the will is dormant, it becomes hard to take action on our wants. We are stuck in the daydreaming, wishing stage of living. We are full of good intentions, but can't seem to start anything.

The will is the *changer*. It is the will that stops us in a chain of thought and says, "Hold on here! I don't have to think this way!" Mental patterns have a life of their own, following the rules of the mind. It is the will that can give the mind a turn and steer it in a new direction. It is the ability of the will to release us from the grip of a particular mental pattern. When the will is active, it can change our habits. Cayce indicates that it is the will that frees us from our past.

The will is the *developer*. While the patterns of the mind are governed by the past, the will is directed toward the future. The mind knows patterns; the will knows objectives. While the mind may shift from one pattern to the next, the will holds to a particular pattern and perseveres to the completion of the goal. Whereas the mind is easily bored with repetitious stimulation, the will has the patience to remain focused until it meets its objective.

The will is the *individualizer*. It is what distinguishes our individuality, our true self, from our personality. Much of our personality is learned, and represents only a certain surface part of our being. During the course of a lifetime, we are presented with thousands upon thousands of choices. Each choice takes us down a different road. The sum total of our choices is our individual path.

The will is our *guide*. How can we choose among the patterns in the mind without some basis of selection? The will guides the choices. The will can also direct the creative function of the mind. Once it is awakened, the will is a source of guidance that we can turn to for help and direction.

The will is also the *agent of obedience*. It is that part of us that is *willing* to be subject to influence. The will is what makes it possible for us to be guided by influences beyond the individual self. It can open us to the influence of the spiritual forces contained in ideals.

Finally, the will exists in *opposition to the mind*. Many of the qualities of the will that we have discussed involve some kind of opposition to the mind. The will can oppose the habits of the mind, it can oppose the momentum of the mind, and it can reactivate the inertia of the mind. Most of the time that we speak of willpower, in fact, we are talking about the struggle of the conscious mind to oppose or control the activity of the will. Willpower is the domain of the conscious mind. It is a counterfeit will. Willpower is the creation of the conscious mind to make up for the loss of contact with the true will. To learn to awaken the authentic will, we will need to go deeper than the workings of conscious mind.

The Physical Will

Will is an active principle. It is dynamic. It is physical. Getting our body to move as we wish is the first place we experience the will in action. Our eyes and head move with our attention. Our arms reach out to what attracts our interest. We crawl and then we walk. As body coordination develops, we are able to express more of our will through physical action.

As adults, our bodies express our will without our thinking about it. Bodily movement becomes so automatic that we take it for granted. Only when trying to develop a new skill, or when confronted by injury or infirmity, do we realize that our will and our bodily motions are not automatically one and the same thing. Learning to dance ballet, to play golf or tennis, or to finger a guitar, we have to become more intimately aware of how the body moves to be able to express our will in action. Under ordinary circumstances, however, our bodies are controlled through an unconscious will rather than through conscious willpower.

Operating outside of conscious awareness, the will directs the life force of the human being. Cayce indicates that the spiritual level of the will acts through the throat chakra, corresponding to the thyroid gland. One of the main purposes of the thyroid is to regulate metabolism, the energy-combustion process of the body. As we learned in the last chapter, the glands of the endocrine system communicate with one another and with the nervous system. Thus, the activity in the thyroid affects and is affected by activity in other regions of the body.

The autonomic nervous system, under the control of the subconscious mind, regulates the body's machinery. Here is another aspect of the functioning of the will. It is the body's will to have the heart beat and the lungs breathe, to digest food and metabolize it as energy for the body's use. The very will to live plays an important role in health and in the recovery from illness.

The will to live is expressed in instincts, reflexes, and appetites. The survival of the body is dependent upon the functioning of the will at this basic physical level. Jerking our hand away from a hot stove and blinking our eyes when objects approach them are both critical to survival. As the body is depleted of water or food, we automatically develop feelings of thirst or hunger. The regulation of eating and drinking is an automatic process governed by the healthy functioning of the will.

Appetites are one place that we can see how distortions to the body's chemistry play havoc with the healthy will. As an extreme case, mice given a choice between food, water, and cocaine will very soon opt only for cocaine. Forsaking food and water for this drug, they will consume cocaine to the point of a very premature death. People who have developed drug addictions will demonstrate similarly self-destructive behaviors. Addictions are an obvious example of how a chemical effect within the body can kidnap a person's will, holding the person hostage to a craving.

As in any hostage situation, addictions gain their power by applying leverage to the body's will toward survival. Addictive cravings actually express, in a distorted manner, the body's inner wisdom. When we ingest a drug, or overeat, the body attempts to compensate in order to regulate an internal balance. With continued ingestion of that substance, the body habituates to the chemical additives and calculates it into its balance sheet. The result is that when the ingestion doesn't occur, the body misses it. The body would gradually return to a normal balance, but the craving experienced in the meantime stimulates the person to ingest more. Thus an addiction is formed.

Edgar Cayce took this compensatory physical process into account when giving suggestions for how to overcome addictions. He interpreted the cravings as a chemical process expressive of the body's now distorted will. He didn't suggest fighting that will, but reshaping it. He gave prescriptions for alternative substances to ingest, to help the body adjust to the withdrawal of the addictive substance. To people with overeating problems, he suggested taking a glass of water with four to six ounces of grape juice before meals to curb the appetite. For alcoholics, depending upon the individual, he recommended gold chloride mixed in water with bromide of soda. For some smokers, he suggested the vegetable salsify. Other suggestions can be found in Reba Ann Karp's *Edgar Cayce: Encyclopedia of Healing.*

We express through a body and we are dependent upon a healthy body to be able to have our will function in harmony with our purposes. Sufficient exercise, a well-balanced diet, and a minimal intake of addictively reacting substances (sugar, coffee, alcohol, salt, tobacco) help ensure that the body's will is not diverted away from its mission. Abuse of the body in these areas sidetracks the will into the task of counterbalancing our self-destructive actions. This same principle can be seen in other disturbances of the will, where Cayce's approach to healing—supplanting the negative with a positive—remains the formula for regaining harmony with oneself. Healthy habits and appetites can be cultivated in the same way as positive attitudes.

Will in Conflict

Joe was always late. He was late for work, for his appointments, for dates. He joked that he was even late for his own birth, as it was a delayed delivery. Although he joked about it, Joe seemed quite upset about his habitual tardiness, for it brought him a lot of grief.

His co-workers were annoyed with him. He had lost credibility with his friends. He tried many different strategies to learn to be on time. He even got himself a watch. He maintained a written schedule of activities and wrote himself notes. No matter what he seemed to try, it didn't work. His work supervisor was understandably concerned about the problem. After repeated attempts to work with Joe on a solution, he suggested that Joe get some counseling.

Joe presented himself to me as an abject failure. He had developed a shamedog manner because he was always apologizing. He was obviously hurt by the frowns he received. He wanted to please other people. He had many commitments, he made many promises, but kept only a few. He was ashamed of how he so frequently disappointed other people. He appeared to be a person who was totally out of control. Joe was hoping that I could help him make his willpower more effective so he could straighten up his life.

Joe was a typical workaholic, attempting to do more than he was capable, working on several tasks at once, and always in a hurry. Not only was he tardy, but he was constantly behind schedule. Besides his regular job, he had a part-time job and ran a business on the side. He had little time for himself and seemed to derive little satisfaction from his life.

The more I learned about Joe, however, the more I suspected that his life was more under control than he cared to admit. Joe's predictable tardiness appeared to be a compensation for his apparent lack of control. He didn't know how to say no, to turn down an assignment, but he did know how to be late. Being late was his way of saying no. It was his way of protesting the hurriedness of his life. It was his inner nature in rebellion. Without the tardiness factor, what would keep Joe from spinning wildly into oblivion? Being behind on his work was Joe's way of controlling his schedule.

Joe didn't have the will to control his life, because it would mean he would have to assume responsibility for his choices. He couldn't please everyone, and someone would be angry at him for not choosing in their direction. Joe's hectic schedule took the blame rather than Joe himself. His tardiness was something that people tried to help him with, and people learned to make allowances for it. He was afraid he wouldn't get that kind of understanding and support if he were to stand up and declare, "I don't want to do this or that, and I'm not going to do it." Instead, he paid lip service to wanting to accomplish so much and to being a team player. He was *trying* to be on time; he was *trying* to get his jobs done on schedule.

Joe wasn't aware of his secret feelings of resentment. He wasn't aware that he was being late on purpose as a form of protest. He sincerely believed that he was trying to exert his willpower to getting himself places on time and his work done on schedule. During our counseling sessions, he became aware of his feelings of resentment and rebellion. It was a secret part of himself that he didn't want revealed. He felt more comfortable resisting it, fighting it, and condemning it. His willpower was on the side of his public self—the diligent, overscheduled worker. His will, however, was on the side of the tired, neglected, rejected self.

I had Joe practice claiming his will. I asked him to affirm his "bad" behaviors, saying to himself, but not necessarily to others, that he was late on purpose. He was then to ask himself what his purpose was. In that way, he learned to thank that rebel part of himself, for it was the only part that actually stood up for his feelings. He wouldn't do that for himself. He learned that this secret part had a more intuitive reaction to events, whereas Joe's conscious reaction to things was always to think about them endlessly. What he called his lazy self was actually more gifted in ways than Joe. It had a lot to offer. His rebel part taught him how he felt inside. It was also the seat of his will, and its strength was more powerful than Joe's conscious willpower.

Our counseling work involved his learning to respect his secret self and to listen to its advice. He had to learn to make allowances for his needs for time out, for a more balanced approach to living. He found it hard to go public with his desire to work less, but gradually he found ways to do so. Finally, he was able to quit his part-time job and let his business go. He had less money, but he had more time for himself. He refound his enthusiasm for arts and crafts and returned to his pastime of going to the movies. He was much happier. At his regular job, he was now on time and caught up in his work. He soon received a substantial promotion, with a salary increase that more than made up for the lost income from his part-time job.

Joe now felt much more in control of his life. He also felt more in touch with himself. Learning to listen to that secret part of himself became listening to that still-small voice within. He was now in touch with an inspiring source of guidance from within his being. At times, he had to assert his independence from its advice. He found that it took a lot of willpower, however, to fight his inner will. He began to discover that it wasn't worth the effort. When he was willing to follow the inner voice, his life went so much more smoothly. He had discovered the power and the peace that comes from being in harmony with his true will.

Joe's story has something to teach us all. Very often the very symptoms or habits that we are trying to change by strength of willpower are in fact expressive of our will. It is a will that is unconscious because we are unconscious of our true feelings. Willpower is often what the conscious mind substitutes for actual will when it is only the conscious mind that wants something.

It usually pays to look at the symptom, to ask it what will it is expressing. It is the principle of *resisting not evil*, looking instead for the purpose behind the symptom, the need it is serving. When the need is known, a more constructive manner of meeting that need can be found. This procedure also puts the conscious mind more in harmony with the truer will, where they can cooperate to bring about better results.

As Joe found, being in touch with the inner will also brings the advantage of an intuitive guidance. Will is not only a motivator but also a source of guidance. If the conscious mind is overly dominant with its willpower, this source of guidance from the will is usually hidden. It can be hidden behind a symptom, a certain laziness or resistance to doing things demanded by the willpower. If the conscious mind is willing to surrender its control and listen, the voice of the will can speak.

The Experience of Willingness

Very little of our will originates from within our conscious mind. It can be made conscious, but to do so requires honest self-evaluation and learning the freedom that comes from surrendering to one's true nature as a spiritual being. The conscious mind has to let go of willpower as its model of the will and adopt a model based more on willingness.

The experience of willingness is the closest approximation the conscious mind can get, at first, to the experience of will. Willingness would seem like the opposite of will, especially if willpower is held as the standard. Willpower seems like strength, while willingness seems like weakness. There is strength in true will, a strength similar to that we associate with conscious willpower, but its best representation in the conscious mind is the experience of willingness.

When we say, "I am willing to do whatever is necessary to . . ." we are expressing true will. When we make such a statement, we are confessing that our choice of direction or goal is coming from a place of deep decision. Our resultant actions almost feel involuntary, for we have no choice but to act as we do. That compelling quality is the action of the will. It is a different feeling than willpower.

The exercise of willpower brings with it the feeling of effort in the overcoming of resistance, while the expression of will has more the feeling of determination. Using willpower requires us to continue to decide in its favor. Each moment is a temptation to give in to impulse and let go of willpower. The expression of authentic will, however, doesn't ask us to keep making a decision in its favor. The decision feels locked in place.

Most of us can distinguish between those times where we have to continue to invoke willpower and those situations where our authentic will is active and we are its willing servant. The first situation becomes quickly tiring. The second situation feels like we are "in for the ride." The decision carries us along. From the standpoint of the conscious mind, an act of will is somewhat like a voluntary surrender to a choice so that what follows is more like an involuntary going along. Willingness is a voluntary act that leads to involuntary compliance with the will. One does what must be done.

The Willingness to Surrender to a Higher Power

People who have come to moments of decision in their lives and have had experiences of will find that same sense of freedom. It requires no effort to carry out the decision. It is not a struggle. Willpower is not involved. One is simply willing to do what is necessary.

It is not surprising that religious conversions often involve such acts of will. When alcoholics experience turning their drinking problem over to their higher power, they discover a relief from not having to struggle with the issue. It is over. A higher will was invoked and took the issue out of their hands.

I can testify to this effect. The first step in my recovery from alcoholism was the experience of realizing I was not willing to stop drinking. Most of us alcoholics maintain that we are in control. It took a particularly bad experience for me to recognize that I loved drinking so much that I would never voluntarily stop. I know I was sincere in what I said, because I was terrified at the admission. It was like having my fate sealed. I was truly despairing. There I became in touch with my true will.

Later, I became aware of why I was willing to do anything necessary to have my drinks. Alcoholism is truly a questing after spirit. Feeling relaxed, feeling in the flow, through drinking I was able to give way to the river of life. Yet it was not a true surrender to the flow of life. I maintained control. I kept the genie in the bottle. I would uncork it when I wanted the experience of flow. Afterward, I would return to my normal state of consciousness. I wanted access to the experience of flow on my own terms. I wanted the power to control the flow.

Alcohol, however, was controlling my life. I attended meetings of Alcoholics Anonymous. I accepted the fact that I was an alcoholic. My personal story was not unique to me; my story was the story of alcohol—all such stories are essentially the same. I was possessed by a spirit that took advantage of my need for power. As long as I insisted on my being in control, I would continue to be possessed by the alcoholic spirit. It was a sobering realization.

It was also freeing to realize that if I was willing to surrender my need for personal control, I could invite a higher power to pattern my life. It could displace the power that alcohol had over me. I didn't know how to act on that realization. All I could do was to imagine what it might be like and wait.

One day I found that I could no longer drink. When I went to the liquor store that afternoon and reached for a bottle, I found I was hesitating. I didn't understand what I felt, but I felt it clearly: drinking was no longer an option.

As I left the store empty-handed, I wondered what was going on. Had my higher power taken the decision out of my hands? I hadn't made a decision to stop drinking. I felt some sadness at the loss. Even though it seemed that I had no choice in the matter, I accepted it. I was willing not to drink. Never did I experience, since that moment, having to use any willpower not to drink. That is the freedom granted by the willingness to be guided by a higher power of will.

Later I learned a clue about my participation in the action of my higher power. Browsing through my dream journal, I found a dream that preceded by a few days the cessation of drinking. In this dream I found a bottle of whiskey in a cabinet and threw it away. That dream may have reflected the soul's decision to quit.

Although the drinking stopped, the quest after spirit did not. My own case is but another of those examples of a spiritual journey initiated by a personal crisis. My will toward spirit was redirected from a destructive approach to a more constructive search for inner freedom and peace through dream study, therapy, meditation, and the application of the gifts of the spirit in my family and social and work relationships. I will always be thankful that my experience with alcoholism directed me to the secret of surrender to a higher power.

Imagination and the Will

Invoking our higher will is the surrender to guidance from our ideals. It is important that we are able to visualize our ideal so vividly that the ideal is compelling. When the ideal is compelling, we can surrender to it. We accept it and are willing to do what is necessary to stay in harmony with that ideal.

An ideal then becomes like an ark. It is something that you can hang on to; its power becomes your power. It is a lot better than gritting your teeth trying to do right.

If you make a tight fist and hold it until your arm gets tired and sore, and then try to hold the fist a bit longer, where is the will? The decision to keep your fist clenched is an act of conscious willpower. The aching along the back of your hand is the expression of the will, asking that the tension be released. Holding the fist clenched is a voluntary act, while the aching is involuntary. The willpower to keep the fist closed requires your continuing to decide to keep exerting that effort.

Now imagine that you are holding something very precious in your hand, but someone wants to rob you of it, to pluck it out of your hand. Try to imagine this situation as vividly as you can. The robber pries at your fingers to force you to let go of your fist. The prospect of having your valuable belonging stolen horrifies you, and you hold fast. Your fist clamps shut like an iron lock. The clenching of the fist is now almost involuntary. You can't help but hold back from the efforts of the thief. The aching along the back of your fist doesn't feel quite the same as it did before. Instead of a pleading ache, it feels more like the strength of your determination. You are willing to keep your fist clenched as long as necessary until the thief gives up. The power to keep your fist closed comes from the compelling value of what you are holding on to, not from your conscious willpower.

This example illustrates an important secret about the will, the imagination, and the hidden powers of the mind. We will be discussing these powers in the next section of the book, where it will be helpful to you to be familiar with how to access your higher will through the willingness to imagine.

In our example, by the use of the imagination, you were able to invoke your will. By imagining that you were holding something valuable in your hand and that someone was trying to steal it, your will automatically determined to keep your hand closed. Your imagination created a reality and your will responded accordingly in an automatic fashion. You did not have to decide, or use willpower, to keep your hand closed.

Finally, note that as you imagined your hand holding something valuable, it was your will that was active in clenching your fist, while your role was the more passive one of being *willing* to hold your fist as long as necessary. We mentioned earlier that willingness is the conscious equivalent of the expression of the true will. The use of the imagination plus willingness will be the key to learning to invoke your will to accomplish things that you could not do through conscious willpower. In the next chapter, for example, you will learn how to create an effect in your body by imagining the effect and then being willing for the effect to occur. Imagining something, and then being willing to allow what you imagine to be true, is the secret of invoking your will.

Besides through the functioning of our body and through our actions, our will expresses itself through the imagination. Every day we spontaneously have daydreams. We do not plan to have them. They occur involuntarily. What comes to your imagination involuntarily is an expression of your inner will. One way to come to know the direction of your will is to listen to your imagination. It can be a form of meditation, or a mode of self-exploration.

There is a subtle interplay between our conscious willpower, the inner will, and the imagination. The imagination is a place where your conscious willpower and your inner will can dialogue. You can use conscious willpower, for example, to initiate a sequence in the imagination.

Think of two different animals, for example. What animals came to your mind? You consciously commanded yourself to think of animals, and your imagination complied. Yet the particular animals that came to mind were a spontaneous expression of your inner will.

Conscious willpower can initiate a sequence in the imagination, nation, but it is of limited value in directing the sequence. Your will also gives direction to your imagination. Two forces collide: what you consciously decide to imagine and what your will imagines. As you explore this phenomenon, you will learn that an attitude of willingness is the way to coax your will to imagine what your conscious mind directs.

Think of your two animals again and have them interact. Make them do things together that you decide for them to do. Have them get along the way you want them to. See how much control you have over their actions.

How were you as an animal trainer? If you are like most people, you found that you could get them to do most of what you thought to command them to do. How did you decide what commands to give? Was it a conscious, deliberate decision, or did certain thoughts just come to you? It's a hard question to answer. You probably also found that not everything you commanded was performed with the same vividness in your imagination. Some things you could easily see, and others were more vague and more like thoughts.

Whatever it is that your inner will wants to imagine, the more vividly you will see it and the more spontaneity it will have. The vividness of your imagination is also a function of the degree to which your willingness matches your will, because you can otherwise try to distract your attention away from your imagination. The more willing you are to imagine what is in your heart, the more vividly you will see it in your mind's eye.

Shaping the Will With an Ideal

In our example of the clenched fist, it was the power of values, or ideals, that guided the functioning of the will's power. The action of your will to keep your hand closed was determined by the fact that you were valuing what you held in your hand. When you imagine an ideal so vividly that it is real for you, your will automatically guides your actions to be in accord with the values expressed in that ideal.

By imagining your ideal, you can shape your will. At first, your will may not be in accord with your ideal. As you examine your actions, you may find they express a contrary will. You can try to imagine an ideal alternative, but you may find your imagination spontaneously presenting some contrary images, expressive of your contrary will. It isn't effective to try to force your imagination, through willpower, to comply with your ideal.

When willpower and the imagination are pitted against one another, the imagination wins because it expresses the inner will. The conscious mind does have some input, and can coax the imagination of the inner will. With your conscious will you can decide what to imagine, but then you have to switch over to the seemingly passive willingness. As you are then willing to surrender to the imagination, your will may assent to your expectation, or it may modify it with something of its own.

When Janet's husband asked to return, Janet tried to visualize her ideal of intelligent love. For a while, however, her imagination came up with images of being alone and afraid. We did not try to force the issue, but instead examined the meaning of her frightening images, for they were the authentic expression of her will at that moment. We realized that her will was responding to the eruption of her habitual idea that one needs to please others in order to be loved and secure.

Janet began to feel angry about being kept hostage to that false notion. Her anger was the expression of her will to be free, to be herself. I asked her if she was willing to love herself no matter what, for that would be necessary to break free. She said she was willing, but didn't know if she could. I suggested that she forget about the situation with her husband for a moment and get into the mood of her ideal of intelligent love. As she did so, I asked her to experience herself from that perspective. I asked her to imagine what she might do with the habitual notion that she needed to please others in order to be loved. She saw herself taking herself by the hand, turning away from that notion, and embracing herself. She started to cry. She could indeed love herself, and it freed her from her fears.

Discussing this experience, Janet expressed some relief to discover that it simply felt better to love herself than to be afraid about pleasing others. That discovery made it easier for her, because she was certainly willing to feel better. Now when she tried to visualize her ideal of intelligent love and view the situation with her husband, her will spontaneously expressed in imagination her confessing to her husband that she just couldn't get back together with him at that time.

Janet's experience shows how the inner will cannot be forced but can be developed and shaped. It required that she know her ideal and that she engage in some honest self-evaluation of her feelings. She was then able to forgive herself for harboring the false notions that created her fearful attitude. When she ceased condemning herself, she was able to redirect her will toward her ideal, and her imagination now expressed her single-mindedness of intention.

Authentic will, approached not through willpower but through willingness to be influenced by an ideal, stands at the threshold between the use of the conscious mind in the ways we have explored in this section of the book (setting an ideal, working with attitudes, and taking physical actions) and the use of the hidden powers of the mind, as in creative visualization, self-hypnosis, and autosuggestion. It is through these hidden reserves that we can develop and apply the will to create an ideal life.

PART 3

Hidden Powers of the Mind

MEDITATION, HYPNOSIS, TRANCE, deep relaxation, reverie, visualization, and suggestion—these are some of the more dramatic phenomena associated with the mysteries of the mind. Perhaps it was an interest in one of these altered states of consciousness that originally attracted you to this book. We are going to deal with these things now and we are going to learn how to use them.

In Part One, we learned about Cayce's metaphysical perspective on the mind. We learned that the mind is a reality that transcends individual persons. We also learned that the mind exists in levels of reality that are normally outside our awareness, in the subconscious and universal unconscious regions. We are about to learn how to contact those levels of the mind.

We have learned how God exists in this world as spirit, mind, and will. As creations of God, as souls, we too share in having these three dimensions of being. We learned Cayce's formula for creation: The spirit is the life force. It is pure energy. Mind, called "the builder," is what gives energy its patterns. The will chooses the mental pattern that the energy then shines through, creating the visible forms of matter. That is the process of creation. As souls, we are co-creators with God of reality.

In Part Two, we applied Cayce's metaphysical formula of creation to the matter of daily life. First we faced the fact that experience is subjective, that our expectations do get fulfilled. We learned that it is more true to say that we see what we believe than to say that we believe what we see. That realization posed a problem. If life is a dream, then how do you decide what dream to have? Cayce's answer to that question is that it is important that you begin the process of conscious creation by deciding upon your spiritual ideal. What is your highest value, what is your vision of the Ultimate Good, that you would use to guide your life? We modified the slogan of the New Age, "You create your own reality," to a more accurate statement: the ideas you adhere to create your reality. Following the formula for creation, spirit-mind-physical, in daily life led to the sequence: ideal, attitude, action. Choose an attitude that is consistent with your ideal, then act as dictated by that attitude. We learned that the development of the will was important in being able to discipline the spontaneity and freewheeling aspect of the mind so that we keep our attention on the desired mental patterns.

In Part Three, we will continue with the theme that has been presented and now bring an extra dimension of power to the formula for creation. Knowing the metaphysics of creation and the important role of the mind, knowing the vital importance of ideals and attitudes in domesticating these metaphysical truths, we are now ready to begin to use the deeper powers of the mind that are hidden within altered states of consciousness.

We have more than the conscious mind to use in our efforts to apply the spirit (ideal), mind (attitude), physical (action) formula to creating our life. We have the hidden powers of the subconscious and the universal unconscious mind. We will begin by learning about the nature of altered states of consciousness, how to meditate, what happens when we fall asleep, and the value of dreams. Then we will learn about deep relaxation and how to open ourselves to the creative powers of the subconscious.

Knowing how to drop down to these deeper regions, we will learn about the importance of mental imagery, expressed both as the visionary capabilities of the imagination and the creative power of visualization. We will then learn how to combine the power of visualization and the power of suggestion to train the subconscious mind to help us in our quest to manifest our ideals.

By learning to explore the unconscious in a manner that is designed to help us and bring good into the world, we can feel more comfortable about our explorations of these deeper mysteries of the mind. In learning how to create our own ideal life, we can also learn how to channel the spiritual wisdom of our higher self. In so doing, we become co-creators with God, thus fulfilling the spiritual purpose of our being.

CHAPTER 10

ALTERED STATES OF CONSCIOUSNESS

In deep meditation there descends the influences to open the channels
. . . to the inmost recesses of the Creative Forces in body.

Edgar Cayce 275-39

YOU SEE LYING before you a woman reading a book. Suddenly, as she gets up, the space between you and her is disrupted and distorted. As she swims away, you realize that all this time you have been looking through water at a woman under water.

This description is of a visually stunning television commercial advertising a pool cleaner. The idea is that it cleans the water so perfectly clear, you don't even know the water is there. The water is invisible until it begins to move.

This scene is an instructive analogy to the mind and consciousness. When the mind is steady and clear, we don't notice its presence. We see the world directly, our vision passing right through an invisible, transparent mind. But when our consciousness is altered, when the mind is no longer steady and clear, the ripples awaken us to the mind's existence. Thus, the psychedelic drug movement of the 1960s earned its name. Psychedelic means "mind-manifesting." By dramatically altering consciousness, these drugs revealed the creative presence of the mind in all we experience. It was part of the beginnings of the consciousness revolution.

Altered states of consciousness do not have to imply such risky and dubious activities as drug use. Every day we alter our consciousness as we go to sleep. We can begin with this normal psychedelic trip to learn to explore other altered states that we can use to our advantage.

Sleep: The Daily Psychedelic Trip

What happens when we fall asleep at night? Have you ever stayed up to watch? Cayce indicated that doing so would be very instructive. There is a lot to learn from staying awake while you fall asleep.

That we say "falling asleep" or "drift off to sleep" is revealing of what we understand about the process. The first step, Cayce notes, is that we withdraw our attention from the external world. As our eyes and ears shut down, we ignore the external world. The inner world of our own thoughts becomes our reality.

The story *Alice in Wonderland* begins with Alice falling asleep as her sister reads to her. As she goes to sleep, she no longer hears what her sister is reading. Instead, she falls into a hole in pursuit of a rabbit.

I'm sure you've had a similar experience. Perhaps while watching TV you have drifted off to sleep momentarily. Awakening, you realize you must have been asleep because you have lost track of the TV show. Only moments ago you were experiencing something else, you were somewhere else, but you didn't suspect you were asleep.

As we relax the body and the physical senses, Cayce explained, the conscious mind begins to shut down. The conscious mind is dependent upon the activity of our senses. As the conscious mind shuts down, the subconscious mind emerges as our consciousness. Here we have a normal, everyday, but very significant altered state of consciousness. The altered consciousness of the presleep state is subconsciousness.

Falling or drifting, as we go to sleep, the conscious mind surrenders its existence by letting its senses shut down. Our attention drifts with the stream of thought into the upper regions of the subconscious mind. One of the things that happens is that our thoughts become more visual. If the conscious mind thinks with words, the subconscious mind thinks with pictures. As the sun sets, words disappear and the pictures within us become more visible.

We begin to imagine scenes. If we were awake, we would realize we were daydreaming. We would know where we were, and that the pictures in the mind were just that—pictures in the mind. But as we fall into the subconscious, we take these mental pictures to be our reality. It is jarring to wake up suddenly and realize that although we thought we were awake and visiting with a friend, we were actually falling asleep into a daydream.

Falling into a daydream is an important part of the process of falling asleep. It gives our fading consciousness something to hold on to, like a security blanket. The images that come to us as we fall asleep distract our attention from the process of falling asleep. The conscious mind needs to be lulled asleep.

As we continue to fall asleep, our consciousness alters further. Very few of us are able to stay awake this far into the journey toward deep sleep and dreaming. Through his psychic trance, Cayce was able to describe what happens.

The conscious mind and its sensory system collapses down to a single sense. Cayce calls it a "sixth sense" and describes it as most closely resembling hearing. We fall into a state of listening. It is not an ordinary listening, but a cosmic resonance to universal vibrations. It is as if our individual being dissolves back into its source. All that remains is listening. It is a state of psychic union with all of life. It is a state of pure intuition.

Deep sleep is such a dark and remote state of unconsciousness that it's hard to believe any awareness could exist there. But there is evidence that we do listen while we sleep. I'm not referring to the fact that our baby's cry will wake us up while we will sleep through the sounds of traffic. This everyday phenomenon suggests that we are always listening, ignoring innocent sounds, but are ready to get up at the sound of trouble. Instead, what I'm referring to is the recent revelation that patients under heavy anesthesia are often able to hear the conversations of the operating staff during surgery. Doctors were resistant to the evidence for a long time, because it violated both common sense and traditional medical thought. But now, a newsletter devoted to educating surgeons about the implications of this surprising revelation, "Human Aspects of Anaesthesia," suggests that every operating room contain a sign reading, "Be careful, the patient is listening."

The conscious mind considers deep sleep a void of utter darkness, but the unconscious mind finds it full of life. Cayce described sleep as a "shadow of, that intermission in earth's experiences of, that state called death." Falling asleep is like dying. We give up the world and our control over it to surrender to a dark unknown. From the perspective of the conscious mind, we cease to be. But like death, sleep is not a termination of existence, but a transformation of existence into the realm of the unconscious. We fall asleep, but awaken into a dream.

What Is a Dream?

Going to sleep is a night sea journey. On this trip, we encounter an island of light. As the subconscious mind takes the helm normally held by the conscious mind, the soul awakens. The soul is actively conscious, Cayce indicates, only when the conscious mind is laid aside and the subconscious mind becomes the consciousness.

We are sleeping on our portion of universal awareness. It lies dormant within us until we are asleep. The soul brings its own light to our darkness and peers about in our dreams.

A dream is an experience the soul has while we are asleep. With its universal awareness its reach for information knows no bounds. It remembers all its past lives, the lessons learned, as well as the purpose for incarnating this lifetime. It looks upon our daily activities and our experiences and views them in the context of its ageless wisdom. Knowing that a dream is an experience of the soul makes it easy to understand the source of the extraordinary phenomena that happen in dreams.

Dreams have been the most frequent source of psychic experiences. On the one hand, surveys have shown that people who have had psychic experiences (telepathy, contact with the dead, seeing the future) indicate that dreams were the most frequent source of these experiences. On the other hand, laboratory investigations attempting to demonstrate the reality of ESP have found dreams to be the most reliable state of consciousness for producing verifiable telepathic events. Psychic dreams can be understood as resulting from the soul's reach beyond time and space.

Most religions can trace their origins to dreams. Besides the dreams heralding the birth of Jesus, dreams also figured in the birth of Buddhism and Mohammedism. The autobiographies of religious leaders and mystics often contain stories of special dreams of spiritual significance. It is common for people who meditate on spiritual matters or lead an active prayer life to have dreams concerning religious themes. Religious dreams can be understood as resulting from the soul's concern that our daily activities fulfill the soul's mission on earth.

The ideals of the soul, truths it has garnered from countless experiences, are the standard the soul uses in evaluating the experiences of the physical personality. The impressions the soul receives, comparing our daily activities to its storehouse of wisdom in the superconscious mind, are the basis of the dreams we have at night. The soul has an "ah-ha" experience of revelation, but what we remember of that experience is a dream.

We remember few of our dreams and only incomplete portions of those we do recall. The symbolic stories we call dreams are the translations made by the subconscious for the conscious of the soul's experience while we slept.

They are an indirect record of what happened. Yet our dreams are perhaps the primary source of clues that we live more than the material life of time and space. For many primitive cultures, dreams were the primary evidence for the reality of the soul.

Dreams are an instructive altered state of consciousness. In our dreams, reality is rubbery. People change identities easily, scenes change instantly. We do impossible things, ridiculous things. We perform miracles and commit horrors. Yet we take this make-believe world to be reality. Dreams prove to us that we ourselves create the sense of reality. The dream is real while we are dreaming it. Only after we awaken do we conclude that we were "only dreaming."

We call some of our dreams "realer than real." We may meet someone special in a dream, perhaps a loved one or someone deceased, and we experience such closeness with that person that upon awakening, we can't believe that it was just a dream. This strange quality of ultrareality makes it easy to accept the evidence for telepathy. Furthermore, dreams that later come true suggest that our dreams are one step ahead of reality.

Cayce emphasized that dreams are real experiences. They are real experiences of the soul. The evaluations the soul makes serve as subconscious guides to our future activities. While we dream, the soul scans ahead to forecast the likely outcome of various attitudes and actions that are competing for our attention. It sorts through various mental patterns and selects new ones to place within the projector to be cast out upon the screen of life. Dreams thus are like seeds of our future experiences. What we call real life is but the consequence of our dreams.

Voluntary Control of Altered States of Consciousness

Sleep and dreams are everyday occurrences of altered states of consciousness. Hidden within them are the secrets of the mind and its creative link with reality. For the most part, we are their passive subjects. We *fall* asleep; we do not drive ourselves to sleep. Dreams *happen* to us; we do not consciously choose to dream, nor what to dream. At least that is the way we experience these two states of mind.

It does not have to be that way. These two activities do not have to remain as involuntary instincts. We can learn to have some conscious control over these and other altered states of consciousness. Being able to enter a desired state of consciousness for a specific purpose is an important part of using the powers of the mind.

We can learn to fall asleep at will. We can approach sleep with a purpose, such as to change our mood, to heal ourselves, or to merge prayerfully with universal awareness. We can learn to cultivate the power of dreams. Dreams are also a means of healing, as well as a source of guidance. We can learn to prepare ourselves to have dreams that provide help with specific problems.

How can we learn to voluntarily enter a special state of consciousness?

Learning to go into an altered state of consciousness requires a special approach. It is learning to initiate processes that would ordinarily happen involuntarily. It involves invoking the will through an indirect means. Cayce gave a general principle for learning this type of skill. He called it "setting self aside."

Setting Self Aside

Squeeze your right hand into a fist. As you do so, notice that it requires that you make an effort. Feel the tension along the back of your hand and along your forearm. Squeezing your fist is something that *you do*. It is an active, direct action on your part. The tension you feel in your arm and hand is the experience of what *you are doing*.

Now allow your fist to open, allow your arm to relax. Can you *make* your arm relax? You can try shaking it or rubbing it. Such actions may help your arm relax, but it doesn't *make* it relax. Your arm can only relax itself, as you *allow it,* if you are *willing* to have it relax. Try it again. Make a fist momentarily until you can feel the tension, then release your fist and allow your arm to relax. See if you can set yourself aside, get out of the way, and simply allow your arm to relax itself. It relaxes when you *do nothing*. Relaxing is something your body will do itself when you allow it. It requires nothing from you other than that you allow it to happen and do nothing to interfere with the natural, unfolding process of relaxation.

Learning to voluntarily enter an altered state of consciousness requires learning to set self aside and allow the altered state to happen by itself. Yet it requires that you intend for it to happen, to be willing for it to happen, and then to allow it to happen.

It is learning the secret of a paradox, of a seemingly contradictory maneuver. How do you get out of your own way? How do you pick yourself up and set yourself aside? Who picks up whom and who sets whom aside? Setting self aside in order to enter an altered state of consciousness isn't something you can do in the same active way that you can make a fist. You have to intend it, yet you have to allow it to happen by itself.

The paradox of setting self aside will prove important not only in learning to enter altered states of consciousness but also in learning to use visualization. It is also the key principle in learning how to allow your ideals to guide the development of your life. It is a key to spiritual unfoldment. The secret to this seemingly mysterious yet quite simple principle is discovered within our will. It is the special, active receptivity we have called *willingness.* You set yourself aside, you allow your body to relax, you enter altered states of consciousness and use visualization techniques by your focused willingness to have it happen.

To learn this quality of willingness, we need to turn to another altered state of consciousness. It is the one Cayce would have us become skilled in first. It will help in all the others.

Meditation

Meditation may evoke images of shaven heads, colorful robes, strange postures, exotic chants, and religious cults. Yet meditation is actually something more ordinary than its publicity would suggest, while more profound and important than any publicity statement could ever convey. Cayce stressed it above any other activity, except for the setting of ideals, and it has the support of a substantial body of scientific evidence. We will approach meditation from a starting point that is quite familiar to you.

In the second chapter of this book, I suggested an experiment for you to try. I asked you to see if you were in control of your mind by trying to hold your thoughts to a single focus. Perhaps you might repeat that experiment for a moment to refresh your memory for how it feels to try it and what happens. The result is a convincing demonstration that you can't control your mind. No matter how hard you try to pin your thoughts to a single focus, the spontaneous flow of your mind is stronger than your efforts.

You can't bring enough willpower to bear to keep your mind from wandering. We discussed the problem of will in Chapter Nine. We use our will to make choices. It expresses our individuality. The wanderings of our attention reflect the activity of our will. Our will, however, is not the same as willpower. Willpower alone cannot make our mind stay focused. Until we can learn how to have our mind settle on a single focus, we cannot say that we have gained any mastery of our will.

Meditation is the practice of the will. It is an altered state of consciousness that happens when we intentionally are willing to allow the mind to rest on a single focus. It is the practice of becoming mentally attuned to our ideal. It is the training ground for learning to set self aside. Let's learn to meditate.

How to Meditate

Here is a simple way to begin to meditate. It is as simple as releasing your fist, if you are willing to allow it to be that simple.

Get into a comfortable, upright position in your chair. Assume a posture that will allow your body to balance itself so that you will not have to make any effort at all to remain in that position. Close your eyes and sense your body. Make any necessary adjustments to your posture to make yourself comfortable.

Keeping your eyes closed, take a deep breath and hold it. When it becomes stressful to hold it any longer, let it go. Notice how good it feels to let your breath go. Meditation can feel that good.

Gently focus on your breathing. It comes and it goes. Notice the feel of your breathing. When it comes, your abdomen expands as your lungs fill with air. There is a slight tension. When the air goes, your body relaxes. The cycle of breathing is irregular. Some breaths are long and some are short. But breathing always happens!

Follow your breathing closely while allowing the breathing to happen by itself. For days, months, and years your breathing has functioned without any assistance from you. Now that you are paying attention to it, that doesn't mean you need to interfere with it. In fact, one of the easiest ways to learn the secret of setting yourself aside is to learn to be able to watch your breath without interfering with it. You may have noticed that as you watched your breathing, you automatically stepped in and began regulating it in some manner. Now step aside and simply observe your breathing without interfering with it. Allow yourself to trust the breathing process. It can be quite comforting.

It's natural for your mind to generate thoughts about your breathing as you observe it. That's OK. Your mind will also naturally wander and think about other things. Your breathing's not *that* interesting. That's OK. When you notice that you are thinking thoughts, think to yourself the thought, "That's OK." Then let your attention return to your breathing, resting in the comforting rhythm of the waves of breath. Your mind will soon wander again, off into its own thoughts. That's OK. Gently return your attention to rest on your breath. Simply practice the willingness to have your attention remain peacefully focused on your breathing. That's meditation.

You may well fall asleep. It's that comforting. Many people reported to Cayce that they fell asleep when they tried to meditate. He indicated that it was perfectly OK to do so. It was a sign that the body needed the rest. It is also a way for the conscious mind, when it is first introduced to meditation, to use sleep to seek reminders from the soul's universal awareness concerning the meaning and purpose of meditation. If you fall asleep when you first practice this meditation, assume you did so to receive reassurance from your soul about the safety and value of meditation.

Add Meaning to Meditation

Meditation is not a meaningless activity. Focusing on the breath is a natural way to place the mind in harmony with the flow of the spirit. It is the breath of life. Another word for inhalation is *inspiration.* Being infused with the spirit, and receiving spiritual or creative insight, share a common word because they share a common process. Allowing yourself to be inspired while you meditate begins with setting self aside and allowing your breath to come to you on its own.

You may wish to explicitly add a mental component to your meditation to reflect your greater awareness of the meaning of meditation. To do so, think the phrase "I am" as the breath comes in. Think the word *One* as the breath goes out. As you let go, letting your breath go out, as you set self aside, preparing for the moment of receiving inspiration, your thoughts follow a parallel track: "I am . . . One . . . I am . . . One." Physical sensations and mental meaning now coincide. Still, your mind will wander. That's OK.

When you find your mind thinking other thoughts, simply return your attention to your breathing and allow your mind to reflect, "I am . . . One . . . I am . . . One." That is meditation.

Echoes in Your Mind

Let's pause for a moment and try another experiment. Take a single word, like *apple,* and say it silently to yourself. As you do so, listen to what it sounds like in your mind as you say it. After you say it once, listen carefully. You can hear the word echo in your mind. See how many repeating echoes you can hear of the word *apple* before it fades away.

What happened? I trust that you could hear the echo. Maybe just a few times, perhaps many times. Perhaps you also noticed the intriguing fact that it became hard to tell if you were hearing an echo or were listening to yourself repeat the word. Listening to the echo has both the qualities of listening to something and thinking something. It is like listening because you have to be receptive. It is like thinking because it is concentrating on a process happening in your mind.

Listening to a word echo in your mind is a way to allow your mind to think the same thought over and over. It's a much easier way than to directly try to force your mind to stay focused on a single thought. Rather than tightening your jaw and forcing your mind to stay focused, you relax and allow yourself to listen to a thought that automatically repeats itself. It repeats itself as long as you are willing to listen to it. When your will takes your attention to other thoughts, all you have to do is think the original word again, and be willing to listen to it repeat itself. Listening to the repeated echo of your own thought is practice in the paradox of setting self aside. It is an indirect approach to a goal that can't be reached directly. It is meditation.

The Ideal of Meditation

Clearly, meditation is not emptying the mind. It is not making the mind go blank. Cayce emphasized that the goal of meditation is *not* a blank mind. The goal is to attune the mind to a single focus. Cayce's approach to meditation is to attune the mind to our chosen ideal. That ideal could be the breath and the idea of oneness with the spirit, if that is your ideal. If love is your ideal, then make love the focus of meditation. Meditation is the willingness to listen to the reverberations of your ideal. It is the discipline, not of making the mind empty of all thoughts, but of choosing to bring the mind back to the ideal every time it strays to other thoughts.

Here is where meditation is a training ground for the will. Here is where we can learn to be willing to choose to entertain only a specific mental pattern and ignore others. During meditation, we practice returning to our ideal, even though other mental patterns compete for our attention. It is where we learn that, rather than using will power, we must be willing to surrender to an ideal. We set self, and all the ideas its will is bringing to our attention, aside, in favor of attuning to our ideal.

An ideal is an image of perfection or ultimate good that cannot be achieved in actual practice. It guides the way, but is never a goal that can be reached. Similarly, in meditation, the goal of having nothing in mind except the thought of the ideal, to have every cell in one's body, all our feelings and thoughts in total harmony with the ideal, is itself only an ideal. It guides the process of meditation, but shouldn't be used as an expectation of what we will always experience. It is something that we can aim for, but it cannot be forced. Yet the process can happen by itself, if you'll simply set self aside.

Fear of Meditation

Since you become more aware of the presence of your subconscious mind during meditation, you may judge that it has become more active. You are aware of a lot of thinking. You may experience thoughts or emotions that disturb you.

Some people believe that meditation is like taking the lid off the subconscious. They feel that it is almost like inviting disturbing thoughts that would normally be held in check to now flood the mind. They experience anxiety during meditation. They find meditation fearful.

It is that mental picture of meditation as opening Pandora's box, and the resulting expectation, that is partly responsible for this effect. Meditation, however, is the practice of allowing yourself to maintain a focus on a positive affirmation while ignoring other thoughts. It is not an invitation to the subconscious to speak up, nor is it required that negative thoughts be stopped.

An interesting laboratory experiment in "thought stopping" may be instructive. Researchers at Trinity University asked subjects to observe their stream of thought for five minutes, but to *not think* of a white bear. Subjects were only fairly successful. Thoughts of white bears managed to creep into the stream of thought. Afterward, they were allowed to think whatever they liked. During that rest period, they found that thoughts of white bears were even more frequent! In other words, not only was it difficult to try *not* to think a particular thought; but also, after stopping this effort, the thought persisted with a vengeance!

The researchers then tried a different tactic with a new group of subjects. These subjects were also told to not think of a white bear. In case they did, however, they were told to then think of a red Volkswagen instead. These subjects were better able to avoid thinking of a white bear than the first group of subjects who had no alternative focus. Moreover, during their subsequent free-thought period, hardly any thoughts of white bears came to mind.

There is a lesson here. Fighting a thought is next to impossible. If you do fight it, then once you rest your defenses, the thought attacks more ferociously. Don't fight your thoughts. Don't say, "I won't think about that!"

Rather, say, "I will choose to think about this instead!" Meditation is not the attempt to stop thinking. It is the practice of choosing to return one's attention back to the ideal when other thoughts come into mind.

What Happens in Meditation

Although you do very little during meditation, a lot happens.

Your body slows down. Breathing becomes more regular, heart rate and blood pressure decrease, and there is a general relaxing effect.

The subconscious mind is also relaxing. It becomes less active and less responsive. Because your body is relaxed, there is less emotional response to the thoughts that arise from within the subconscious. Whereas one thought might normally trigger ten more thoughts, during meditation a thought finds comparatively little response. The subconscious is settling down, even though it may not seem that way to you.

Cayce's description of what happens in meditation emphasizes the activity of the spiritual ideal upon the thoughts, the emotions and the body of the meditator. We can think about an ideal, but when we meditate upon it, it has relatively more power to shape our being. As the body and the subconscious mind relax, the effect of the ideal increases as our imagination is filled with its meaning.

Imagine watching a movie when all the theater lights are on. The picture on the screen is not very bright, and it is easy to be distracted by the sights and sounds within the theater. When the lights go out, the picture on the screen becomes the reality. Similarly, during meditation, the thoughts and bodily reactions that would normally reduce the influence of the ideal are turned down. The patterning power of the ideal then has maximum effect.

Every atom in the body begins to resonate with the ideal during meditation. The activity of the endocrine system begins to reflect the influence of our ideal. The body's immune system, governed by the thymus gland, becomes stronger. This documented and measured effect is evidence of Cayce's statement that meditation on a spiritual ideal improves the harmonious functioning of the psychic centers and their corresponding endocrine glands.

While your ideal is transforming your mental, emotional, and physical being during meditation, you are learning to turn to the will of your higher self. You are learning to substitute a spiritual willingness for personal willpower. You are also learning to enter an altered state of consciousness where you allow a particular pattern of mind to become your reality. You are also, as research has verified, increasing your sensitivity to psychic awareness. The practice of meditation, grounded in absorption in your ideal, will help you learn to master other states of consciousness. It is the gateway to the hidden powers of your mind.

CHAPTER 11

SELF-HYPNOSIS AND THE POWER OF SUGGESTION

> Begin with the study of self, which may be best done by suggestive
> forces to the body through hypnosis.
>
> *Edgar Cayce 3483-1*

NO DOUBT YOU have heard stories of the dramatic power of hypnosis. Hypnosis has been used to remove warts, stop bleeding, and eliminate pain.

After undergoing a period of scorn, hypnosis was accepted in 1959 by the American Medical Association as a useful adjunct to medical analgesia. Hypnosis can be so effective as a painkiller that it has been used in place of surgical anesthesia in both cesarian section deliveries and amputations.

These miracles of hypnosis reveal the powers of the mind. Yet such amazing stories make hypnosis look like some deeply mysterious and magical potion. It makes hypnosis seem far removed from our ordinary life. One moment we glimpse the powers of the mind, then they disappear behind the veil of a secret process.

The truth of the matter is that hypnosis is quite ordinary. We enter states of hypnosis every day. Each night as we fall asleep, we pass through a hypnotic state. We become lost in thought, hypnotized by our daydreams. Our favorite television show absorbs our attention. The story is real to us, and we laugh and cry. We are hypnotized by the electronic reality in front of us. We are subject to the suggestions implicit in television commercials. Our days are filled with the events of hypnosis. Three very ordinary processes are involved in hypnosis: relaxation, suggestion, and imagery. Under the right circumstances, any one of these processes may create a hypnotic effect.

Hypnotic effects occur through the action of the subconscious mind. The subconscious operates through suggestion and imagery. When the conscious mind is relaxed, the subconscious mind can be reached directly. It is thus easiest to work with hypnosis in a special state of relaxation. Hypnosis is simply a way to communicate with the subconscious.

The Presleep State: Self-Hypnosis Every Night

The time of falling asleep at night, Cayce noted, is the most natural hypnotic state. You've experienced hypnosis every night of your life!

As we fall asleep, you may recall, the body relaxes and the senses shut down. The conscious mind dims. As external reality fades away, our own thoughts become reality. The subconscious mind emerges as the dominating consciousness. The subconscious accepts its imaginings as reality.

The time of falling asleep is a perfect time to make suggestions to the subconscious mind. Cayce often recommended the presleep state as a golden opportunity to plant thought seeds of a new life. We will learn how to use the presleep state ourselves, to give our subconscious mind positive programming. It can become a major tool in using deeper mind power to achieve our goals.

Cayce also advised parents to use the presleep state to the child's advantage. It is a natural extension of the bedtime story and bedtime prayers. It is a time to help the child establish a positive outlook on life. It is also a time to plant positive alternatives to problem behaviors.

Cayce prescribed to parents the use of presleep suggestion for children's psychological, psychosomatic, and physical problems as well: nightmares, bedwetting, bad habits, as well as conditions such as hyperactivity. The subconscious mind controls the operation of the body. It stands in between our thoughts and their physical consequences. Thus, Cayce recommended the use of presleep suggestion to shape the influence of the subconscious in bringing healing to the body.

The Miracle of Jennifer

One of the most dramatic cases of the use of suggestion in restoring a child to health is told by a mother, Cynthia Pike Ouellette, in her book *The Miracle of Suggestion: The Story of Jennifer.* Because of her mother's own sudden, severe infection, Jennifer was born eleven weeks prematurely. She weighed only two pounds and was infected herself. The doctors said she had no hope of survival, as she was severely jaundiced, suffered from seizures and hydrocephalus, and was experiencing occasional cardiac arrest and difficulty in breathing. Jennifer's mother, however, had reasons to believe that her baby daughter would survive. The next day Jennifer almost died and was saved through a blood transfusion. The doctors were now predicting that *if* Jennifer survived, she would be severely handicapped, with damage to her eyes, brain, and lungs, and would very likely be mentally retarded.

Almost every day in the Newborn Intensive Care Unit, Jennifer suffered some type of setback. Almost every day the doctors discovered another malady in Jennifer's tiny body. Cynthia's faith in her daughter's recovery was unshakable, and she found herself constantly talking to her. She couldn't touch her, as Jennifer's body found touch painful, so mother's only way to be in contact with Jennifer was through talking. She reassured Jennifer that everything would be fine. Then she began to describe for Jennifer how her body was healing itself. Without knowing it at the time, she was giving her daughter suggestions of healing.

By one month, Jennifer weighed three pounds. She was able to leave the intensive-care unit and move into an observational unit. By nine weeks, weighing about six pounds, Jennifer left the hospital to go home with her mother. The problems were not left behind, however, and there were further discouragements. By the seventh month, the doctors' prediction that Jennifer would develop cerebral palsy was confirmed. In a moment of despair, when Jennifer's mother was wondering how her daughter was managing to survive all these problems, it occurred to her that it was because of all their talks. She was convinced of it, and began to research the power of suggestion. It was at that point that she discovered the work of Edgar Cayce and his advice concerning presleep suggestion with children.

What had begun as an instinctive expression of positive suggestions to Jennifer now became a consciously planned and intentionally programmed set of regular suggestion sessions with Jennifer. "You are a perfectly normal creation," she said to Jennifer in a natural tone of voice.

"You are perfect, whole and healthy. Your spine is perfect, whole and healthy. . . . You have perfect control of both hands. . . . You are capable of doing anything you want to do. . . . You wake up feeling very good every day." These statements are a small sampling of the positive thoughts Jennifer's mother repeated to her over and again. She also made tape recordings of these suggestions to play for Jennifer on a regular basis.

It may seem strange to expect such verbal suggestions, delivered to a tiny infant, to have any effect on the body. Can the small baby understand such words? Does the baby's subconscious mind understand? Cayce indicated that the subconscious does understand, that mother and infant are bonded at the subconscious level and that these communications would be acted upon.

Jennifer's mother also had to train herself to consistently think in a positive manner. If a visitor asked, "What is wrong with Jennifer?" mother learned to say that nothing was wrong, that Jennifer was perfectly healthy, and to believe it.

Against terrible odds, having only the will to live, the atmosphere of positive suggestions, along with the massages and other forms of tender loving care, Jennifer gradually evolved into a healthy young girl.

Subliminal Suggestion and Self-Help Tapes

Positive thinking and autosuggestion has been a popular self-help strategy since the early 1900s. Today it has taken on more sophistication. Prerecorded audiocassettes containing self-help suggestions have become a mass-market item. Especially appealing are the tapes that offer subliminal suggestions hidden within pleasant background music.

Stick a portable cassette player in your pocket. Place a tiny earphone discreetly in your ear. As you go about your business, at work and at home, you hear soothing music. All the while, you realize, subliminal messages are silently nudging your subconscious. You are free from smoke, you are thin, you are healthy, wealthy, and wise. As you pursue your normal routine, your subconscious mind is imprinting a new program for living. It requires no effort on your part. You simply reap the benefits of the principles of dynamic psychology applied with the latest in modern technology.

It sounds too good to be true. Although based on sound and established principles, subliminal tapes promise more than they deliver. Cayce would suggest, on the other hand, that they deliver something that they don't mention. The issue of commercial tapes, offering suggestions and subliminal suggestions, deserves some detailed discussion.

It is true that the subconscious mind is capable of detecting information that is invisible to the conscious mind. It is quite sensitive to subliminal stimulation. We have already examined some of the research that indicates the incredible extent of this sensitivity. Subliminal stimulation definitely is a way to bypass the conscious mind and communicate directly with the subconscious. That much is true.

One problem, however, is that subliminal stimulation is a fickle process. For example, to place a voice script into some music so that the voice functions as a subliminal message requires experimental testing to get it right. If the voice is too loud, anyone can hear the message. It's no longer subliminal. If the voice is too soft, only the most discriminating subconscious mind detects it. Many others miss it. The conditions under which the recording is then listened to will also influence whether or not the subliminal message will get through.

Laboratory research on subliminal stimulation requires extensive pretesting to find the exact intensity needed to create the subliminal effect for the average listener. Because any melody will vary in loudness from moment to moment, the laboratory must calibrate each insertion to fit with the loudness of that part of the music. These seemingly minor technical considerations are very important. They are also time-consuming and can be expensive.

Assuming that a commercial producer of subliminal tapes performs the necessary experimentation to properly calibrate the subliminal message, another question then arises. What is the effect on the listener of the subliminal message? As of this writing (spring, 1988), no commercial producer of self-help subliminal-suggestion cassettes has published any studies to indicate that their product does indeed produce changes in people's behavior.

Laboratory research has established that subliminal stimulation affects how a person experiences the foreground stimulation. If I show you a picture of a person's face, for example, I can use subliminal stimulation to affect how you will interpret the expression on that face. If I subliminally flash the word *angry,* superimposing it over the face, you will interpret the person's expression as being more angry than if I flash the word *happy.* Earlier we saw how subliminal messages hidden in a piece of music affected the listener's daydream and associations to the music. In other words, what researchers have learned most about subliminal stimulation is how it influences conscious experience. It tends to bend our conscious perceptions in a direction suggested by the subliminal message. That fact is quite well established.

Contrary to popular opinion, however, most of the research on subliminal stimulation has *not* focused on motivational suggestion. It is commonly assumed that research on subliminal stimulation has studied the effect of messages like "Buy popcorn!" on people's popcorn-buying habits. There have been very few published studies, actually, of that sort, and they have yielded contradictory results.

The popular imagination may assume that Big Brother has been working hard in secret laboratories learning how to influence people through subliminal suggestion. Big Brother, however, has not published the results of this research.

Mommy and I Are One

However, there has been a substantial body of published research investigating the positive effects on behavior of one particular subliminal suggestion. To be effective, it requires a situation where a person is *already motivated* toward a particular goal and is *already making active efforts* to reach that goal. In such cases, exposure to this subliminal message has proven to substantially improve a person's success. Mathematics students scored higher on their math quizzes. People in therapy for depression experienced an elevation of their mood. People in treatment for drug addiction, alcoholism, or smoking were able to abstain for much longer periods of time. These are just the sorts of subliminal-suggestion effects we would desire.

What was the suggestion? It will surprise you. It's not the sort of suggestion you would think to give to yourself. In fact, Lloyd H. Silverman, Ph.D., the psychologist who invented the suggestion, has indicated that the suggestion works only because the conscious mind is *not* aware of its contents. The suggestion is, "Mommy and I are one."

Arguing from a psychoanalytic point of view, Dr. Silverman explains that the suggestion activates an unconscious fantasy of returning to the womb. It is a fantasy that most of us would not consciously find appealing. Planted as a seed thought in the subconscious mind, however, it inspires visions of blissful union with Mom. The visible result is an overall positive one. There is evidence of increased relaxation, improved mood, decreased dependency upon drugs, and improved competitive performance. You couldn't ask for more.

A commercial firm advertising a "Mommy and I are one" subliminal tape could promise, with some validity, that listening to its product will produce profound effects. No such tape is available commercially. It's uncertain whether or not such a theme would have public appeal. It doesn't have the ring of success.

In his book *The Search for Oneness,* Dr. Silverman states, "Unconscious oneness fantasies can enhance adaptation if, simultaneously, a sense of self can be preserved." It is interesting that, even though coming from a different point of view, Edgar Cayce made a similar proposal. On many occasions his psychic source said that the purpose of each human life is to realize oneness with God *while simultaneously* developing one's true individuality. The conscious mind, as we have explained, has difficulty understanding and accepting this seemingly paradoxical statement. Presented as a subliminal suggestion, however, it bypasses the conscious mind to find an exuberant reception in the subconscious.

I find an important lesson in Silverman's research. By using subliminal stimulation, motivational suggestions can be given to the subconscious mind in a way that totally bypasses the desires of the conscious mind. These suggestions, however, must appeal to the mentality of the subconscious mind. When they do, the subconscious has a strong response. The response cannot always be predicted. Psychoanalytic reasoning, based upon the peculiar logic of the subconscious, is necessary to adequately steer the suggestion process. Thus, when we use subliminal tapes we are dependent upon the insights and wisdom of the manufacturer in their choice of suggestions. Even then, we are not certain of the outcome.

Side Effects of Subliminal Suggestion Tapes

Cayce's readings on the possibilities of influence through the subconscious mind suggest another reason to avoid subliminal tapes until such time as they might be made in a different fashion. When we listen to a subliminal tape, we are giving permission to our subconscious mind to be influenced by outside stimulation. Cayce indicates that the influence is not limited to the actual verbal message that might be subliminally embedded on the tape. The influence goes much further than that. The thoughts, feelings, and subconscious motivations of everyone involved in the manufacture of the tape is a potential source of subliminal influence upon the listener!

A similar situation may exist in the reaction the postal-delivery person receives from many dogs. Dog bites are the most serious and frequent occupational hazard of the postal delivery system. Our dog barks and threatens to attack most every person who approaches our house, but he saves his most menacing welcome for the postal worker, regardless of who that might be. No salesperson or UPS delivery person receives the kind of treatment that the postal worker has to endure. I've asked around for some explanation to this phenomenon. The most convincing explanation that I uncovered was that the problem was the bag of mail. A couple of hundred letters, each one handled by several different people, created a very confusing sachet. The postal worker arrives with an ambiguous and mixed message bombarding the dog's nose.

Our subconscious mind can be as sensitive to the emotional vibrations of others as a dog is to scents. When we open ourselves to influence by listening to a tape containing suggestions, subliminal or otherwise, we can pick up the emotions and thoughts not only of the person who voiced the suggestions, but also from the people who handled your particular copy of the tape when it was manufactured.

Those experienced in hypnosis will verify that a hypnotic subject often picks up on the thoughts of the hypnotist. I once experienced a dramatic example of this phenomenon. I was attending a hypnosis workshop and was entering a hypnotic trance following the suggestions of the hypnotist. As I became more relaxed and his voice became my only thought, I suddenly had a brief dream. I was in a room that was totally empty. I noticed that one wall was developing a hole in it close to the floor. It was as if the wall were a curtain and someone was lifting the curtain at one spot. Then a person came through that hole and entered the room. I found that curious, but then returned to listening to the hypnotist's voice. As I listened, however, I was startled to discover that there was now a difference in how I was experiencing the voice. I was having my own thoughts, and I was thinking the suggestions myself before the voice spoke them. It was hard to believe, but as I allowed it to continue, I was able to verify that I was indeed thinking the suggestions, word for word, before I heard them.

Afterward, I discussed this experience with the hypnotist. He explained that what I had experienced was telepathy, that we had entered into a mind lock together. I reflected on my dream. A room can represent a state of mind. Under the relaxed, hypnotic state, my mind was empty. The wall, or mental barrier, was flexible, like a curtain. The hypnotist had penetrated that wall and had entered my mind. He told me that I should remember that experience when I used hypnosis when working with others. The subject will be influenced not only by the suggestions that you verbalize, but also by your silent thoughts.

In giving instructions on the preparation of healing materials and devices, Cayce indicated that it was necessary for those involved to first purify themselves with meditation and prayers prior to starting each work session. Those handling the physical materials as well, such as the blank tapes, the copying machine, and the packaging of the tapes, should also be involved in these purification practices. Until such time as manufacturers produce tapes in such a manner, it would be better if we made our own suggestion tapes, or with the help of a like-minded person.

Cayce's instructions about the manufacture of healing aids are no different from what was traditionally practiced by spiritual healers among so-called primitive groups. Native Americans, for example, would dip their healing objects in sacred smoke to purify their vibrations. Such practices seem strange to someone who doesn't appreciate the power of the subconscious mind to be influenced by the thoughts of others. Evidence for psychometry, the ability to read someone's thoughts by holding an object that person has touched, further supports the wisdom of Cayce's advice.

To appreciate how open you are when you avail yourself of a subliminal-suggestion tape, you might try observing your responses to listening to such a tape. My first exposure to such a tape was with one offering suggestions to quit smoking. Playing in the foreground was the sound of the ocean. It was quite a pleasant listening experience. I couldn't hear, of course, what subliminal suggestions I was receiving. But I found that I was constantly thinking about what they might be, wondering what my subconscious was hearing. Not knowing what the facts were, I found that my imagination went wild, supposing all sorts of suggestions. I also found that any resistances I had to the idea of quitting to smoke was being drained away from me involuntarily, and I was not necessarily willing to have that happen. I would smoke during the tape and would also feel guilty about doing so. Was I defeating the purpose of the suggestions, or was their subliminal power so strong that they would overtake my willful continuation of smoking? I realized that even if there were no suggestions on the tape at all, I was submitting myself to a potent placebo treatment. The very idea that you are listening to a tape containing subliminal suggestions is a very suggestive experience in itself! I found that one clear value of listening to a subliminal-suggestion tape was discovering, by monitoring my thoughts, whether or not I was actually willing to have the suggestions take effect.

Suggestion and Pretending

In the second chapter, we noted that Cayce emphasized that we respect the subconscious mind. He noted its special qualities. In particular, he noted that, in contrast to the conscious mind, the subconscious responds to suggestion. Let's examine what that statement means.

Let me suggest to you, for example, that this book is as light as a feather. What happened?

You probably checked the weight of the book, feeling it in your hands and noting its weight. In other words, you automatically attempted to evaluate my suggestion. The response of the conscious mind to a statement is to immediately evaluate it. It attempts a verification. The conscious mind tests the statement for truth or accuracy.

Unless it chooses to ignore a statement, or doesn't understand it, the conscious mind automatically tends to agree or disagree with it. It checks it for logic, for consistency with past experience, or with information from its senses, and then either denies or affirms the statement. The conscious mind cannot accept suggestion. As Cayce pointed out, the conscious mind can only respond to a statement as a proposition. It must evaluate the statement, and either validate or deny it.

Let me now instead ask that you *pretend* that your book is as light as a feather. Pretend that the book is so light that you can relax your hands and arms and the book will simply rest in your hands, suspended by itself. Try that and see what happens.

If you pretended, could you experience the book as light? If you did, then try it again, and notice how you go about pretending that the book is light.

How did you do it? You probably focused on certain things and purposefully ignored others. To pretend that the book is as light as a feather, you might focus on how relaxed your hands and arms feel. You might notice the book sitting in your hands, but ignore any sensation of pressure from the book sitting upon your hands. You could then imagine the book sitting weightlessly in your hands.

While pretending, your conscious mind doesn't respond to the statement as a proposition. Instead, it agrees to accept the statement as true and acts accordingly. It focuses its attention on aspects of its experience that would be consistent with that assumption. It ignores contrary data.

Pretending is the best way to explain to the conscious mind what is meant by a suggestion. Otherwise, the conscious mind has no way to respond to a suggestion other than taking it as a proposition.

Recall, from our earlier discussion about attitude change, that we presented Cayce's idea that behaving *as if* you were experiencing a certain attitude, that attitude would come about. We are seeing this principle once again, this time as we see how pretending is a way for the conscious mind to cooperate with the power of suggestion. We can see now how Cayce's advice that we take actions consistent with an attitude we would like to adopt is actually based on an understanding of how suggestion operates.

All Suggestions Are Affirmations

There is nothing about a statement itself that qualifies it as a suggestion. A statement becomes a suggestion when it is accepted, when it is acted upon, when a person is willing to pretend that it is so, or believe that it is so.

The subconscious mind automatically accepts statements as affirmations of what is true. This characteristic of the subconscious, however, comes with a particular proviso. The subconscious mind does not understand the meaning of the negative *no,* or *not.* If you are given the suggestion, "You will *not* think about the eye of a camel," the subconscious mind drops the word *not* from what it hears. The phrase "eye of the camel" is implanted in the subconscious, and you can't help but think about it. Recalling the experiment in thought stopping we described in the last chapter, we realize it would be more effective to suggest instead, "If you think of the eye of a camel, you will immediately begin thinking about a red Volkswagen."

Understanding of the logic of the negative *not* is the sole province of the conscious mind. In Chapter Three, I described how the creation of the conscious mind arose from an act of negation, separating itself from the subconscious by saying "No." It was likened to a child going through the terrible twos who separates from the parents and establishes its own will by defying the parental will with a constant "No." It is another reason why statements made to the subconscious mind become suggestions, whereas the same statements made to the conscious mind are taken as propositions. The conscious mind always has a "No" ready, and will be quick to use it if the statement doesn't ring true.

The subconscious mind cannot be directed away from an undesirable focus by asking it *not* to do this or that. Instead it must be *re*directed, by asking it to do, or to look at, something else. Here again we have the general Cayce principle of supplanting negatives with positives. Suggestions must be phrased in an affirmative manner. What is it you want the subconscious to believe, to do, to experience?

I have witnessed the use of suggestion to redirect the smoking habit, for example, into other avenues of expression. In one case, this suggestion was gradually established: "When you have the urge to smoke a cigarette, you will experience the taste and smell of vomit and you will reach for your polished stone and feel peaceful while holding it." In another case, the suggestion was based on a spiritual ideal: "When you feel the need to smoke, you will take a deep breath and feel grateful and at peace as the Spirit of God enters you, filling you with love and warmth. You will sigh a deep sigh of relief that the Comforter is so close at hand."

In both cases, there was real motivation to stop smoking, reinforced by their doctors' warnings concerning imminent health dangers. There was also a sincere willingness to quit. Both people had quit smoking except for two or three times a day during moments of stress. At those moments, they couldn't get the mind off having a cigarette. The use of these suggestions planted a different thought habit for those moments. The suggestions didn't have to create a willingness in these people, only a new route through which to express that willingness. In each case, the suggestion was phrased in terms of creating an alternative habit.

A good place to begin learning about how the power of suggestion works through affirmation is with your statement of an ideal. Try wording your statement so that it reads as an affirmation of a fact—not a wish, or a desire, but a fact. Rather than "I want to be a loving person," affirm "I am a person created by love and expressing love." An alternative might be, "Only love is real."

Working with suggestion does not mean pounding the thought into your mind in an attempt to drive out other thoughts. A suggestion, as an affirmation of truth, is expressed in a casual, matter-of-fact manner, in a normal tone of voice, as if to imply, "Of course, no doubt about it." If you announce your affirmation to yourself, shouting it in your mind, as it were, you challenge your conscious mind to take it as a proposition to evaluate. You invite negative reactions.

Repeat your ideal to yourself gently from time to time, willing to pretend it *is* true, willing to believe it as fact. Let yourself *feel* it in your body, let your imagination play with the implications of the affirmation. Let it grow on you. In this way, you will discover for yourself how suggestions operate through affirmation.

Pretending Your Way Into Hypnosis

One of the major difficulties in learning self-hypnosis is not fear of the unknown, but the habit of the conscious mind to evaluate. It's hard not to ask yourself, "Am I really hypnotized now?" You can learn to hypnotize yourself more easily if you are willing to pretend that you are hypnotized.

Choosing to pretend that a proposition is true is not the same as evaluating it and deciding it is true. It means to accept the statement as true and direct attention in such a way as to help make the proposition appear true. The conscious mind pretends by focusing on what is consistent with the proposition and ignoring any contradictory information.

Pretending is a good equivalent of suggestion. When the conscious mind becomes so active in its pretending that it forgets that it is pretending, when it begins to now believe what it was pretending to be true, it has come the closest it can to accepting a suggestion.

Entering hypnosis is simply the process of accepting one suggestion after another. Hypnosis is the state of mind of accepting suggestions. As in other suggestions, the conscious mind can help the process of entering hypnosis by the use of pretending.

Researchers have found that instructing people to pretend that they are hypnotized can produce as good hypnotic results as does actual hypnosis. Some argue that this fact shows that there is no such thing as hypnosis. Don't be fooled by this argument. When the conscious mind pretends, it is performing the conscious equivalent of what the subconscious mind does when it accepts a suggestion.

The conscious mind can cooperate with what the subconscious mind is doing. If the conscious mind is still active under hypnosis, it will experience its response to suggestions as pretending. That doesn't invalidate the experience. It only helps.

Traditional hypnosis theory maintains that people vary in their ability to be hypnotized. Cayce maintained that anyone could learn how to enter a hypnotic state simply because it is a natural state of consciousness. Modern thinking about hypnosis is changing in favor of Cayce's point of view. Research has now demonstrated that the conscious mind can cooperate with the induction of hypnotic suggestions by agreeing to pretend. By being willing to imagine the suggestions, the conscious mind can pave the way for the subconscious to accept suggestions.

The ability to pretend, to imagine or act, initiated by the willingness of the conscious mind, is good for hypnosis. Learning how to become absorbed in an imaginative activity, in fact, is a close equivalent to hypnosis. As we will now discover, a willingness to pretend or imagine can be used as a method of entry to the more traditional hypnotic state of deep relaxation.

Deep Relaxation

Learning to relax is the first step in learning self-hypnosis. The vitality of the conscious mind depends upon the activity of the body and the alertness of the senses. If the body relaxes and we ignore information from our senses, the conscious mind loses the stimulation it depends upon and it begins to evaporate. This is what happens as we begin to fall asleep and it is what happens when entering hypnosis.

There are a number of ways to begin to learn deep relaxation. None requires *doing* anything. Relaxing is the opposite of doing. It is a process of letting go. Relaxation is another example of "setting self aside."

To relax, it is best to either lie down or sit in an easy chair that leans back. Having a pillow under your knees and ankles, as well as under your neck, helps support those areas of the body and adds to your comfort.

An excellent way to begin is with the eyelid method described by Henry Bolduc in *Self-hypnosis*. Cast your gaze upon a spot across the room and close your eyelids slowly, as slowly as you can. Then slowly open them and close them once again, very slowly. Repeat this process ten times. By the tenth time, the area around your eyes will feel very tired and relaxed. The sensation of relaxation can then spread to the rest of your body.

You can focus on the breath and imagine the whole body breathing. Relaxation naturally occurs in the chest and abdomen during every exhalation. Begin by focusing in that region of the body and then moving out to other areas. With each exhalation, for example, pretend that your knees are also exhaling breath. Imagine your knees relaxing as they exhale tension along with the air. Continue this process as you move along to every part of your body.

Some people enjoy saying to themselves "Re-" as they inhale, and "-lax" as they exhale. It provides a mental focus. It also helps to prevent falling asleep until such time as sleep may be the goal.

Another approach to relaxation is to focus on one limb at a time and imagine it as feeling heavy. The sensation of heaviness is what happens when a limb relaxes. It doesn't feel like a lead weight is bearing down on it with pressure. Instead, it feels heavy, as if it were made of lead itself and were melting. It feels very good to let it go and allow it to relax. Here is a way to relax that is based on suggestion and that automatically introduces you to a self-hypnotic state.

Begin by experiencing your right arm as heavy. Say to yourself, "My right arm is heavy." Don't do anything to make it heavy. Simply imagine it as heavy, and be willing to experience it that way. Why don't you try that right now?

Put down this book. Rest your arm on your lap or on the arm of the chair. Close your eyes and let yourself imagine that your arm feels heavy. Pretend that it is heavy by noticing any sensations in your arm that feel like heaviness. Let those sensations spread through your entire arm. After you've enjoyed the experience for a moment, wiggle your fingers and the heaviness will go away.

Wasn't that easy? It's a very natural experience. It's also one of the most common suggestions a hypnotist gives when first beginning a hypnotic induction. You can easily do it yourself.

To go further with this procedure, don't stop at the right arm. After a minute or so, move your attention to your other arm, thinking "My left arm is heavy." Then move along to each of your legs. You can go back and summarize your experience with suggestions such as, "My arms are heavy," "My legs are heavy," or "My arms and legs are heavy."

By imagining your body as relaxed, then experiencing relaxation, you've successfully responded to suggestion. You are on your way to even deeper levels of hypnosis. By imagining your arm as feeling heavy, you have begun, without realizing it, to use imagery in your autosuggestions. As we now turn to the topic of imagery, remember this experience. You do have imagery, and you can use it to control your state of consciousness and your body.

CHAPTER 12

THE MIND'S EYE:
IMAGINATION AND VISUALIZATION

Physical conditions—whether pertaining to social, to money, to station in life, to likes and dislikes—are the application of those mental images builded within the body, seated, guided, directed, by the spiritual. . . .

Edgar Cayce 349-4

As THE EYES are the window to the soul, so is the mind's eye the window to the soul of the mind. The mind's eye sees with images and it conceives with images. Nowhere is the creative magic of the mind more evident than in imagery.

We value people with "vision." It is not their eyesight we applaud, but their imagination, their ability to see what is not yet before their eyes. Such people trust those images in their minds and steer by them, creating actual realities from what was first only imagined.

Beethoven composed his best symphonies after he had gone deaf. All he had was his imagination to invent and polish his music. He never heard it played. Einstein developed his theory of relativity by first imagining what it would be like to ride upon a ray of light. Much of his theorizing was based upon imaginary experiments. It wasn't until after his death that scientists were even capable of making the actual observations he imagined. Out of his imagination, Walt Disney created a cast of characters and the means to bring them to life. He not only invented an entire reality, but the means to create it in actual physical terms.

Such pioneers, and there have been many, provide proof positive of the saying "What the mind can conceive and believe, the person can achieve."

Cayce would have us know that each of us is a similar pioneer. Each of us is using the powers of what he called the "imaginative forces" of the mind to create our life experiences. Whether or not we are conscious of the process, or are actively engaged in making intentional choices about its use, each of us is drawing upon the creative forces through the imagination to conceive possibilities, to believe in certain eventualities, and to manifest circumstances in the body of our lives. Cayce would have us become more conscious of this process, choose our ideal, and work with the imagination in a more deliberate and constructive fashion.

To do so, we must first recognize that our bias is to think of the imagination as relating to the imaginary, as distinct from the real. We often use the word *imaginary* to mean something that is not real. Instead, if we would lean toward the implications we grant to the term *visionary,* we will be off to a better start in appreciating what Cayce meant by the imaginative forces.

The Intuitive Radar of the Imagination

Your visionary mind is like a television set. It is capable of tuning in to vibrational patterns from around the world and translating them into pictures upon its screen. In fact, it is through the image-making capabilities of the mind that intuitive, psychic, and creative experiences are manifested. The imagination is a mode of experience, of sensing, of picking up information.

Dreams are the place where most of us become aware of the sensitivity of the imagination. While dreaming, our imagination faithfully captures any intuitions or psychic impressions sensed through the soul's infinite reach of perception. We may dream prophetically about an event that later comes true. We may dream telepathically about the troubles of a distant friend. We may reach out clairvoyantly to locate the existence of something that we need. We may dream intuitively the solution to a problem. In our dreams, we may peer into our body with microscopic precision to diagnose the source of a pain. In each case, the dream state uses the imagination to translate impressions into informative, if not also symbolically expressed, visual imagery.

Sometimes it is through feelings that the imagination receives its first intuitive signal. Contemplating these feelings will lead to their translation into images that can then be more easily read for informative meaning. It is like turning the television to a channel that gives some indication of sound, suggesting the presence of a station broadcast, then fine-tuning the television to bring in the picture as well as possible.

For example, consider what happened to a friend of mine, Jane, who confided to her husband, Edward, that she had an uneasy feeling about his boss, Mr. Jones. She was referring to the dinner they had shared with Mr. and Mrs. Jones, where there had been much discussion about the business and Edward's role in developing the company. Edward, enamored with the prospects for the future he was envisioning as a result of that dinner conversation, was reluctant to pay much attention to his wife's vague feelings.

Partly because her husband didn't encourage her to vent these feelings, and partly because his reaction showed her that he wasn't taking seriously her implied warning, Jane found herself reviewing the feeling over and over in her mind. She knew she had to find a way to express herself in a manner that would make her husband sit up and take notice to the threat she just *knew* existed. Focusing on the gut feeling, she experienced various images appearing in her mind. In her imagination, she saw Mr. Jones pulling a rug out from under Edward, and she saw the surprised look on Edward's face as he began to fall. Edward's look of being betrayed, though, didn't quite match her own gut feeling, and she looked again at her image of Mr. Jones. She didn't sense Mr. Jones as intending to harm Edward, but saw him juggling several balls in the air. One ball started to get away from him, and as he chased after it, he inadvertently pulled the rug with him, causing her husband to fall over. Had the rug been nailed down, or not attached to Mr. Jones, his response to this runaway ball wouldn't have affected her husband in the same way. This imaginary scene gave Jane the information she needed.

Jane now approached her husband in a different manner, directing his attention in a more specific direction. She asked him if it was possible that, if Mr. Jones followed up on certain growth directions that might prove promising, company resources would be drained away from the growth projects Edward was going to direct. Edward had to agree that it was a possibility. Jane suggested that Mr. Jones, without intending to, might thus undermine Edward's efforts. He did have a tendency to suddenly grab on to something that was hot, forgetting about previous commitments. Wouldn't it be a good idea, she wondered, for Edward to get some kind of specific contract from Mr. Jones concerning the resources to be committed to Edward's projects? It hadn't occurred to Edward to doubt Mr. Jones's planning, but the more he thought about Jane's insight, the more he suspected she was right.

A few days later, Edward revealed to Jane that he had had some further discussions with Mr. Jones. They had clarified their plans, and in so doing, Edward realized that without Jane's insight, he might have inadvertently accepted an untenable assignment. Edward expressed his gratitude to Jane, who felt relief that her husband's position was now more secure. She herself was grateful that she had spent the time with her feelings, coaching them to reveal what they had to say in such informative imagery.

Jane's story is a good example of how the imagination can tune in to an impression and clarify it by way of mental imagery. Jane trusted her intuition, although she did not understand the meaning of her initial feeling of unease, and allowed her imagination to speak to her more clearly. She was not "imagining things," in the cliché meaning of the phrase, but was instead using her imagination as a channel of ever-clearer intuition.

In our exploration of the subconscious mind in Chapter Two, we saw how its powers of subliminal ESP and creativity operated through the intuitive mode of imagery. We can learn how to intentionally tune in to this level of consciousness and use the intuitive, creative, and psychic skills of the imagination. Our preliminary work, in the previous chapter, learning how to relax ourselves and enter a self-hypnotic state, prepares us for this capability. We are already well on our way.

The Formula for Inspiration: Hypnosis Plus Daydream

John was a free-lance writer. He had been researching an article on a local cooperatively run store. He had gathered all the necessary facts and had written a few paragraphs, but he hadn't been able to come up with an approach to the story that had quite the emotional punch he wanted. John tried hypnosis.

John relaxed in an easy chair. He listened to music, while at the same time listening to instructions designed to take him into a hypnotic state of consciousness. Fifteen minutes later, when the music was over, John listened to further instructions, suggesting he visualize his problem. "Picture in your mind's eye," it was suggested, "all the elements of your magazine article."

John saw three piles of papers. One pile was neatly stacked and was full of writing. It was the completed article. The second pile was quite large, but loosely stacked, papers lying every which way. It was full of little bits and pieces of writing. He saw that all these bits and pieces were the elements of his research, quotations from people in the store, descriptions of the premises, some trial sentences and paragraphs. The third pile was much smaller and was in the dark. There wasn't much in those papers yet, and they troubled John.

John then received a second set of instructions. "Let the images disappear from your mind," it was suggested, "and forget about your problem." John sighed, for he was happy to relax and relieve himself of the burden of thinking about his article. He then heard this suggestion:

"Even though you cannot see these elements any longer, they are still very alive in the back of your mind, out of sight. In fact, they have a life of their own where you can't see them, and in a moment they will cause a dream or dreamlike experience to come into your mind's eye."

Moments later, John was daydreaming about floating in the air down Main Street. He floated right into the second-story window of the store he had been writing about. Once inside the store he continued floating about, viewing the premises from the air. He saw the various departments, the sales personnel, and the customers. He felt the store's atmosphere, and everything within the store took on a special quality. The merchandise vibrated on the shelves, sparkling with light, inviting the customers, "Take me home, I'm good!" He experienced the special feeling that existed between the sales personnel and the customers, who both had a cooperative interest in the store and its success. John found himself feeling very good being in such an atmosphere.

When John woke up from this dream, he was very enthusiastic about writing his magazine article. Within a few minutes he was busy at work, writing the story of a visit to the store. Within an hour, he had completed a rough draft of the entire article. He liked the tone of the article. It had never occurred to him to simply describe the store from the point of view of someone who comes in to visit and browse. He had been bogged down by the technicalities and had missed the spirit of the place. Within a week of leisurely work, he revised his draft, submitted his article, and it was published.

John's story is taken from one of the cases reported by Robert Davé, a psychologist at Michigan State University who studied the usefulness of hypnotic daydreams in creative problem-solving. In his experiment, he invited people who were stuck on a problem to try one of two approaches. The first approach was the hypnotic daydream method John experienced. The second method was to try a rational approach, thinking about the problem without allowing any irrational feelings to interfere with the problem-solving efforts.

People who experienced the rational method received coaching on how to stay focused while they logically thought through each element of their problem. They explained aloud their problem in detail and went over every possible element of a solution. Spending up to an hour with their coach, they examined every relevant idea for its rationality and appropriateness. At the end of this session, the person felt quite enthusiastic and expressed the opinion that the process had been quite helpful.

One week after this experiment, all participants reported on the status of their problem. The results were dramatic. Six out of the eight people who had experienced the hypnotic-daydream method had since worked out a successful solution to their problem. Of the eight people who had engaged in rational problem-solving, however, only one person had so far arrived at a satisfactory solution. Even though all the people who had the rational treatment had thought it beneficial, while only a few of the people experiencing hypnosis felt that way, the hypnotic daydream had certainly proven to be the more effective formula for inspiration!

You can learn from John's experience in this research project. You can use this method to obtain inspirations of your own. Using the method of self-hypnosis described in the last chapter, you can enter a relaxed state of mind. You can then allow your imagination to bring you inspirations on whatever you suggest.

The philosophy in the Cayce readings would recommend that you begin work with hypnotic daydreams by focusing on your ideal. Learn how to have daydreams that portray the spirit of your ideal in pictures and scenes you can feel. Once you are relaxed and ready for suggestions, mentally repeat to yourself your ideal and allow it to create in you the feelings that it suggests. Then allow those feelings to develop into images. Let yourself have a daydream based on your ideal.

The next step would be to use the hypnotic daydream experience to help you imagine how an ideal attitude might help you respond differently to a particular situation. In your hypnotic state, allow yourself to get into the feeling of your ideal and then view your current situation. Have a daydream about this situation as you approach it in the mood of your ideal. Very likely, you will find that in your daydream you find a novel way of approaching the situation.

Cayce indicates that the imaginative forces operate within patterns set by an ideal. If you wish to ensure that your use of the inspiration formula yields constructive results, it is important to first develop familiarity with having daydreams centered about the theme of your ideal. As you practice these daydreams, you will likely evolve one or two imaginary scenes that immediately place you in the mood and frame of mind of your ideal. It may be an image of yourself surrounded by light, or sitting in the sun at the beach, or looking out at the world from a mountaintop, or cuddled in the arms of a loving giant. Whatever it may be, you will have developed an image of inspiration. It is just this sort of image that hypnotists often suggest when guiding a hypnotic induction on creative problem-solving. You will have evolved your own imaginary scene and you will find it a very powerful tool for further work with the use of imagination for inspiration and problem-solving.

Presleep Imagery for Seeding Dreams

Using the inspiration formula as you fall asleep at night is a wonderful way to increase the creative power of this technique. It will plant a suggestive seed within your subconscious that will very likely sprout into a full-fledged dream for you to ponder in the morning. The use of dreams for creative inspiration is a powerful approach that invites the participation of the full scope of the superconscious mind to help you in your endeavors.

There is no question, no problem, Cayce indicated, that can't be solved or answered by asking our dreams for help. He indicated that for personal problems, scientific and religious questions, whatever the topic, the superconscious mind was available in the dream state for guidance and wisdom.

History bears proof of Cayce's claim. In *Our Dreaming Mind: History and Psychology,* Bob Van de Castle, Professor of Psychiatry at the University of Virginia Medical School, describes the great dreams from the past that have led to political innovation, scientific invention, philosophic and artistic inspiration, as well as religious illumination. Such great dreams do not have to be relics of the past. They also happen today. You can have them.

The essential method is to begin to relax in bed and use your image of your ideal to get into an inspirational frame of mind. While in that mood, let the elements of your problem dance in your mind's eye, just as John did in his hypnotic session. Then let them go, and allow yourself to have a daydream about your problem and its solution. Finally, let that daydream go, and allow yourself to drift to sleep. In the morning, write down whatever you remember of your dreaming, no matter how irrelevant or trivial it may seem. As you ponder this dream, you may be surprised to discover that it speaks more to your problem than you initially suspected.

I have researched several methods for obtaining inspirational dreams and how to work with them. I have described these approaches in *Getting Help From Your Dreams* and *The Dream Quest Workbook.* Of all the methods for seeding a dream, research has shown that using presleep suggestion and imagery is the most critical ingredient. In the previous chapter, we noted that the presleep state was an ideal condition for responding to suggestions. The use of imagery, as in the inspiration formula, is a natural extension of this fact and has been found, in countless experiments, to have a profound impact on a person's ability to have dreams about a desired topic.

If you have trouble remembering dreams, you can use the imagery method to help you recall them. As you lie in bed, imagine yourself waking up in the morning and writing down a dream. When you do wake up, immediately write down whatever is on your mind, regardless of whether or not you consider it to be a dream. If you will make a commitment to write one full page of thoughts and feelings immediately upon awakening, and follow through with this commitment for seven days in a row, I can almost guarantee that before the week is up, you will find that one morning you are writing down a dream.

The Power of Visualization

Dana and his father had just purchased an antique bicycle. It was one of those from the turn of the century, with a large front wheel almost five feet in diameter. It was a rusty bike, and many of its parts were in need of replacement. It took them six months of leisurely work to restore the bicycle to mint condition and to make it operable.

All during the period of restoration, Dana wondered if he would be able to ride that bike. It was quite tall and unwieldy. He had tried riding a bicycle like his, belonging to members of the High Wheelers Club, but he had found it almost impossible, and somewhat frightening. It wasn't going to be easy, but Dana was determined.

Dana began to dream about the bicycle. In his dreams, he struggled to climb up on the bike and ride it. He dreamed time and again of riding the bicycle, experiencing its balance, experiencing its height, experiencing the thrill.

When the day came that the bicycle was completed, Dana and his father wheeled it out of the garage and onto the street. He remembered his dream experiences of climbing up onto the bike and pushing off down the street. This would be the moment of truth. He gave the bike a push as he climbed on from the rear, and he was off and riding! On the very first try, Dana was riding comfortably atop the high-wheeler.

Dana told me about this experience as he was teaching me to ride his bicycle. I can verify what a nerve-racking experience it is to climb aboard that very tall wheel. Dana was convinced that it was his practice sessions in his dreams that enabled him to ride his bike from the very first day.

Dana had discovered the power of visualization from his experience with dreams. Practicing something in the imagination pays off when the real test comes. In one study, student basketball players attempted to improve their free-throw shooting. One group practiced the free-throw shots for an hour every day. Another group practiced the same amount of time, but only in their imagination. In their mind's eye, they would see themselves standing at the line holding the ball. They would see the basket and feel the body movements of making a perfect throw. At the end of a week, when the students were retested, the students who had practiced in their imagination had improved significantly more than the students who had practiced with the real ball.

You can give yourself an immediate demonstration of this effect. Turn your head slowly to the right as far as you can. Make sure that you can turn it no farther. Relax your neck muscles and see if you can't turn your head a bit farther, but without forcing it or causing pain. Notice how far you can turn it by sighting a spot on a distant wall. Return your head to normal and close your eyes. In your imagination only, very slowly turn your head to the right. Imagine the feeling in your neck allowing you to continue turning your head much farther than you did before. Then bring your head back to normal. Do this imaginary head turn three times. Then open your eyes and actually turn your head slowly to the right as far as you can. Sight with your eyes across the room and you will see that you have now turned your head farther than you were able to before. Through your imagination you have been able to actually increase the flexibility in your neck!

Using imagery can extend the body's capacity and improve physical performance. Charles Garfield, Ph.D., describes in his book *Peak Performance* a personal experience that convinced him of the power of visualization. He found himself in the company of Olympic sports trainers from the Soviet Bloc countries and asked for a demonstration of their latest training techniques. Garfield had been a serious weight lifter in college years before, but he hadn't even been to a gym for several months. When he did work out, he could manage to lift 280 pounds. The trainers asked him if he thought he could lift 300 pounds. Garfield was reluctant, but gave it a try. It required all his effort, but he managed to do so. He was pleased with himself, but was utterly exhausted from the effort.

The trainers asked him how long it would take to get himself back in shape to be able to lift 365 pounds. He had once lifted that much weight and estimated that it would take about nine months of rigorous training to work back to that level of strength. They announced that he would do it within the hour! He said that was impossible. He had barely managed to lift 300 pounds and could do no more. Weight lifters know that it is necessary to increase weights in small increments, and what these trainers were suggesting represented more than a twenty percent increase in weight. They nevertheless proceeded with the demonstration.

They asked Garfield to lie down and relax. They guided him through imagining that his arms and legs were heavy and warm. They took him into a deeply relaxed state. Then they coached him in the visualization of every step of the weight-lifting feat he was about to attempt. He saw the additional weights added to the barbells. He saw himself lie down beneath them. He visualized the feeling of his breathing, the feel of his weights, the feeling of exertion in his arms as he made the press and the sound of the weights landing back on their stand. He visualized the successful completion of this experiment in every detail.

Garfield then got up and walked over to the bench. He was quite apprehensive. Doing it in the imagination is one thing, but to attempt it in reality was another. When he started his lift, he balked. He just couldn't do it. The trainers patiently talked him through a brief review of his relaxation and visualization experience. They reviewed it a second time.

During that second review, Garfield noted that suddenly there was a switch in his frame of mind. It was no longer an effort to perform the visualizations. An effortless and clear image of his success translated into a sense of confidence. He knew he could do it. He opened his eyes and lifted the weight!

The Secret of Visualization

What is it about imagery that gives it such impressive power? How is it possible to use visualization to imagine something and have it come about?

Recall Cayce's description, discussed in Chapter Four, of the soul's projective activity, how spiritual energy is patterned by the mind to shape physical manifestation. Cayce insisted that these attributes—spirit, mind and the physical—were really all one and the same aspects of a singular reality.

His term "the imaginative forces" was a special one he used when the emphasis was upon the creative aspect of the soul. The imaginative forces refers to that process whereby energy is creatively transformed into pattern. It also refers to that process whereby mental patterns are transformed into physical manifestation. Thus, the imagination is both a means of receiving new information, or the creativity of conceiving, and of manifesting, or giving birth. In other words, it has both receptive and active aspects.

The subconscious mind holds the key to working with the imaginative forces. The conscious mind can set the intention, but it must relinquish control to the subconscious mind to get the job done. The subconscious mind speaks the language of imagery, the pictorial patterns that shape the creative energies.

To see for yourself how you can expand upon the power of suggestion by use of imagery, try this experiment. Sit back and relax for a minute, then begin suggesting to yourself that you will salivate. "My mouth is becoming moist, my mouth is watering, it is becoming juicy." Let yourself feel your mouth becoming moist. See how much of a mouth-watering effect you can experience through suggestion alone.

Now try it a different way. Relax again and begin imagining a lemon. In your mind's eye, see its yellow skin. Imagine cutting it in half with a knife. Pick up one of the lemon halves and squeeze it to make beads of juice form on the surface. Now bring the lemon up to your mouth and suck on the juice. Notice just how sharp the tangy lemon juice can be. It makes you pucker. Notice how much your mouth is watering.

Imagining sucking on a lemon made your mouth water a lot more than simply giving yourself the suggestion to salivate. Verbal suggestion is somewhat effective, but when imagery is added, the suggestive power is irresistible. The response is involuntary and automatic. There is visualization's secret.

In the last chapter, when you were learning how to relax, you imagined that your arm was heavy. That image automatically produced a relaxation effect. When you imagined sucking on a lemon, that image automatically produced salivation. If you want your body to respond in a particular way, you can imagine a situation in which such a response would be natural, and your subconscious mind will direct your body to match the image!

Learning how to make your hands warmer, for example, is easy if you imagine wearing gloves on a hot day. You can feel how sweaty your hands are inside those gloves. It has been demonstrated that learning how to increase the blood flow to the hands is an effective treatment for migraine headaches.

It is also used as a training device for more advanced work in the use of imagery in healing. Garrett Porter, the boy described in Chapter One who healed himself of a brain tumor through visualization, began his self-healing work by learning how to make his hands warm.

Controlling Body Cells Through Imagery

That it is possible to control the activity of cells in your body through visualization may come as a surprise to you. Cayce indicated that every cell in your body has its portion of mind. That was a radical notion until the discovery that people could control the functioning of their body through the proper use of their mind. Learning to control the "alpha state," that particular brain-wave pattern associated with relaxation, was one of the early discoveries of the power of the mind over the body. More recent research has established even finer levels of control, down to single nerve cells!

In one experiment, described by Dr. Jeanne Acherberg, associate professor and Director of Research in Rehabilitation Science at the University of Texas Health Science Center, in her book *Imagery in Healing,* medical students were shown colored slides of a particular class of white blood cells called neutrophils. The students saw how these cells removed waste from the bloodstream. They learned that these cells could change their "adherence factor," meaning whether the cells clung to the walls of the blood vessels or whether they released themselves from the walls and floated freely. These students then practiced visualizing these cells. After training in visualization, the students demonstrated the ability, as verified by blood tests, to command these cells either to increase or decrease their adherence factor. Their control was quite specific, because their visualizations did not affect the activity of any of the other classes of white blood cells.

Imagining Your Ideal Day

My own first experiment with a concept presented in the Cayce readings concerned visualizing my ideal day. I was visiting with Charles Thomas Cayce, Edgar's grandson and a psychologist like myself, at his farm in southern Virginia Beach. At the time, I was teaching psychology at Princeton University. Academic life was not appealing to me as much as I thought it would, and Charles Thomas Cayce used my expression of discontent as an opportunity to talk about his experiences visualizing an ideal life.

Edgar Cayce indicated that ideals were like the rudder of a ship. Without an ideal, one would drift randomly upon the sea of life. A clear ideal is needed to begin the process of creating a life more to your liking. Charles Thomas likes to think about ideals in a concrete and specific fashion, and he challenged me to try to visualize a sample day from my ideal life. He suggested that I imagine how I would spend my time, what I would *do,* not just what I might *have.* He said that when I was ready, I should write down all the events of that ideal day on a piece of paper and then put the paper away. He promised me that one day in the future I would discover that I was living that day. His promise was fulfilled.

Here are some of the things that I wrote on that piece of paper. I was living in a home of my own close to the beach. I got up in the morning and worked on my current book. I was at leisure in the afternoon, riding my bicycle, walking along the beach, or working in the garden. People came to visit me at my house in the late afternoon and early evening for counseling sessions. One night a week I taught a psychology class at a local college. Most evenings I engaged in social activities with my wife.

That is exactly the life that I am living today as I write this book. It feels like a dream come true. It is like walking about in my own visionary reality. It's a good feeling.

My ideal life did not come about overnight. It took a few years to manifest, and it came one step at a time. One of these steps makes another good story about the visionary power of the imagination.

In 1978, my wife and I were living in seasonal rental housing in Virginia Beach. We were tired of moving every season, so we decided we wanted to buy a house. We visualized this hypothetical, ideal house and wrote down on a piece of paper all its characteristics. We put the paper away.

Some months later, a crisis situation entered our lives and we decided that, ready or not, we had to find a house. We called a real estate agent and made an appointment. The next morning, my wife told me that she had dreamed of a house. She described it as full of light, and through a back window she could see water. We liked her dream image, because being on the waterfront was one of the items on our descriptive list of our ideal house.

When we met with the real estate agent, we explained our situation. We had almost no money for a down payment, or full-time jobs to qualify for a mortgage. We had great faith, however, that if we could find a house that would inspire us, we could work out those problems. The woman was amused, but having known us as rental customers for some years, she agreed to give it a try. She cautioned us that, realistically, we would have to come up with $500 to even make an offer and then we would need to get jobs fast to even have a chance at getting a mortgage. She suggested that we take a look at a house she knew would be coming on the market soon. It would give us a chance to face what we were up against.

She drove us to an unfamiliar neighborhood four blocks from the oceanfront and stopped at a house that wasn't very inspiring. We were disappointed but went inside. As we started to look around, my wife commented on how bright it was inside, how full of light. It reminded her of her dream, so we went into the rear of the house and saw outside the window that the property was indeed a waterfront place, sitting on the bank of an inland lake. This house was the one my wife had dreamed we would inhabit.

We told the agent that we wanted it and we would get right to work. We could use our MasterCard to come up with the earnest money. We would see if we could turn our part-time jobs into full-time. She was cautious and said that she would call us that night. When she called, it was with the news that she had spoken to the owner. She had negotiated a lower price for us and had arranged for the owner to provide a second mortgage. All we had to do was to come up with a twelve-thousand-dollar down payment and qualify to assume the existent mortgage.

Every night for a week we drove over to the house and sat outside in our car and meditated on the prospects of moving into this house. We began to call on friends and relatives, and with a few hundred dollars from some and a thousand dollars from others, we raised the down payment. My wife was able to increase her hours at her part-time job to approximate a full-time position. I was a substitute crisis-intervention counselor for the City of Virginia Beach, and within a couple of days a full-time position came open, which I took. We submitted the offer on the house the agent had arranged. By the time the mortgage company managed to evaluate our mortgage application, we looked quite acceptable.

There is an interesting side note that shows the fourth-dimensional quality of an idea. The neighbor across the street greeted me one day after we had moved in. She seemed to know me. She said that the year before I had been over to her house on an emergency call. Then I remembered. It was to deal with a runaway teenager. His name was Henry, my name. I remember because another social worker was also there on the case and her last name was Henry. We joked, because the name isn't that common, and there were three of us in one room. The name Henry means "ruler of the home." The house across the street from where the three Henrys met, the house my wife dreamed about, has been our happy home for the past ten years.

Can You Imagine It?

Claims about the power of imagery invariably bring up the question about a person's ability to imagine, to see mental images. Not everyone believes they can visualize.

When asked about what it means if a person doesn't remember dreams, Cayce answered that the person was being negligent. The same can be said about mental images. If you don't think you have mental imagery, you're just not paying attention.

The truth is that everyone does visualize. People do vary in the extent to which they accept the suggestions of their visualizations sufficiently to experience them as clear visual images.

Let me describe a situation that may demonstrate what I mean. Suppose you have an ordinary shoe box and a shipping crate ten feet tall and ten feet wide—in other words, a fairly small box and a pretty large box. Suppose you had two rubber bands, and you stretched one around the shoe box and the other around the shipping crate. Inspect each box to verify that when you stretch a rubber band around a box, the band contacts only four sides of the box, leaving two other sides untouched. Does the rubber band touch only four sides of the shoe box? Does the rubber band touch only four sides of the shipping crate? Would it be the same for a box that was one *mile* wide?

How long did it take you to make this mental confirmation? Did it take longer to inspect the shipping crate than the shoe box? What about the mile-wide box? With each box, the logic of the problem is the same. If the problem were approached simply in terms of the abstract logical principle, the size of the box would be irrelevant to the question being posed. To the extent that imagery is used, no matter how subtly, it takes longer to trace the path of a band around a shoe box than it does to trace that same path around a shipping crate. You may not be aware of your use of imagery, but if you can notice the difference in time it takes you to *think* about the different-size boxes, you may be able to infer that your thoughts are being governed by images. We all have imagery and use visualization. To have them appear to our mind's eye as pictures involves the same principle that we learned about suggestion. It is a matter of being willing to engage in an "as if" frame of mind. To visualize a box, simply pretend that you are looking at one. Ignore all your thoughts that are telling you that you are just *thinking* about a box, that you don't really see it. Pay attention only to what the pretending *feels like.* The more you pay attention to what the pretending feels like, and less to your thoughts, the more you will allow yourself to experience the picture image that is actually there. It *is* there. It can become more vivid as you close your eyes and relax.

The more willing you are to accept what you *do* experience as being a mental image, the more you become absorbed in that experience of your imagination, and the more vivid the imagery becomes.

Are you *willing* to experience the imagery? The question is important and to the point. You can choose whether you will focus on how what you experience is like an image, or whether you will focus on how it is *not* like an image, but more like a thought. To allow yourself to accept it as an image, to let yourself go into your pretending, you are taken into the images of the imagination.

We have come full circle, back to the issue that initiated us into this section on altered states of consciousness and the hidden powers of the mind. It is the matter of the inner will, the deeper source of will than willpower. With our conscious mind, we can direct our imagination only to a limited extent. Whether or not the images we conjure will come to life and grab our awareness depends upon a deeper will. It is more a question of our true willingness.

Confirm Your Visualizations in Action

It is hard to consistently visualize something, even something very desirable, if we are not willing to accept it as true and act accordingly. Cayce indicated that we shouldn't expect to rest upon the power of visualization alone, but need to express our intentions in action. If the key to visualization is a mental process of *acting as if* you are seeing something, then the key to manifesting visualizations is to *act as if* they will manifest.

We can demonstrate this willingness, and reinforce its suggestive power within the subconscious mind, by our conscious actions. By working with our attitudes, and taking appropriate steps in behavior, we indicate the sincerity of our desire to manifest what we imagine. My wife and I visualized our ideal house for some time, but it did not manifest until we took a step in faith and acted as if it was there and we were prepared to buy it. We made a commitment in action, and the means to follow through materialized.

Cayce would remind us of the saying "Pray hard, as if everything depended upon God, and work hard, as if everything depended upon you." It applies as well to using the hidden powers of the mind in conjunction with conscious efforts in the world. Both are required. Even to be in the right place at the right time, which some would call luck, requires getting up from the meditation chair. It is with the love of our ideal in our heart, with a vision in our mind, and with very busy hands, that we become inspired creators.

CHAPTER 13

THE SPIRITUAL MYSTERY OF THE MIND

> The earth then is a three-dimensional, a three-phase or three-manner expression. Just as the Father, the Son, the Holy Spirit are one. So are our body, mind and soul one—in Him.
>
> *Edgar Cayce 1567-2*

IS THERE ANY greater mystery than life itself? It is a wondrous, self-perpetuating carnival. There is the magical symphony of vibrating atoms, the gallery of masterful and stunning landscapes, the exciting circus of animals and the infinitely complex and varied stories of the human creatures.

The forces of nature may be blind. Life may play out its patterns in an unknowing and automatic reflex chain of electromagnetic and atomic actions and reactions. Yet the human being is aware. We behold the bounty of life. We are conscious of our existence. The players in the cause and effect sequence of the life of chemistry and physics may not question why they act the way they do, but we humans notice, we question, and we are filled with wonder.

If there is a mystery to life, it is because there is human consciousness to pose the question. What is the purpose of life? What is the story? What is going on? And who are we? What does it mean that we are aware of ourselves, that we know we are conscious?

A Key To the Universe

What if out of the swirl of creation there appeared a clue to the puzzle of life? What if in the midst of all the elements and their varied formations there appeared in nature a magical sculpture that revealed the secret of the universe? Its features and the patterns in its construction expressed the Creator's signature. Its movements revealed the Creator's thoughts and feelings. When properly addressed, it shone forth with pictures upon a magical screen that was a veritable encyclopedia of the secrets of the universe. What a prize this sculpture would be!

There is such a sculpture. It's the human being—it's you and me. Cayce revealed that the human being is a mirror of creation. Within our very being, sometimes right before our eyes and sometimes buried deeply within the unconscious, lie all the secrets of the universe.

It may surprise you, but of all these secrets there is none greater than that God exists! It is the cornerstone to understanding creation and our role in it. We are like time capsules created by God, ready at any moment to break out of our shell of material egocentricity and give expression to God's intention in creating us.

Cayce tells us that it is God's intention that we be companions with the Creator. In full realization of our true essence, with full awareness of our oneness with God, the purpose of our coming into being is to share in the responsibility of continuing the process of creation, to add to the glory of life by the way we channel God's creative energy that flows through us.

Each human being is one of God's experiments in conscious living, each having a portion of the divine energy, or spirit, a mind and a free will by which to make choices and accept influences. Each of us represents God's attempt to become aware, in a finite material body, of the nature of the infinite creative forces. Each of our experiences is therefore very important to God, and within our being we can sense the Creator's reaction to our responses to those experiences.

God awaits our recognition. The meeting comes within. The honoring of God is to be expressed outwardly, in our thoughts and actions toward the rest of creation.

The Prime Directive

Deep down we are more alike than different. We share with the animals various survival instincts. Among one another, we share the need for love and companionship; we all face the task of leaving our parents and making our own way in the world. We all face death. Most of our personal experiences, though they seem personal to us, have a universal, archetypal heritage. If you have ever shared deeply with another person your experiences in life, especially your feelings about these experiences, you most likely have discovered that your confidant had similar feelings. The human story is universal, even though no two are identical.

One of the common dimensions of human experience is the attempt to reconcile the need for security with the desire for freedom. We all long for the freedom to be ourselves, to express our individual creativity. On the other hand, we realize that we need to make a place for ourselves in the world if we are to survive. The need for security compels us to fit in with society, to do what is expected. Complying with the needs of the whole sometimes requires our sacrificing what would be good for us as individuals.

This universal human experience has an important spiritual dimension. God expresses in multiple individualities. God is millions upon millions of souls, and then some. Each soul is an expression of God, an individual and unique expression. The life of an individual human being is a symbolic manifestation of its soul. Each human being has the potential to reveal its spiritual origin in a unique way. That, in fact, is the task God sets before each of us.

As Cayce explains it, we are all One in God, yet each of us, as souls, is a unique creation. Our task in life is to develop and express this individuality while at the same time expressing that Oneness of God, who is our essential identity. The primary commandment is to love God and to love our neighbors as ourselves. Each of us is to do this in our own individual way. Yet there is only one way to comply with this commandment. It is to be yourself.

It is a paradoxical and contradictory assignment, at least to the conscious mind. On the one hand, it is such an easy and natural task that a baby does it quite instinctively. We grown-ups, on the other hand, find it an almost impossible job. Perhaps that is why we have to become again as children in order to know how to do it.

To be yourself, with no holding back, requires self-acceptance and a lack of anxious self-consciousness. Giving no thought to your separate self, life itself becomes your self, and you accept being one with that experience. In that way, you bridge the opposites of the paradox, living life like no one but you can, while embracing in a spirit of love all of life. That life is God. It is you.

Experiencing and loving life as yourself, you naturally reach out with whatever unique perceptions and talents you have and serve that life. You do this in your own unique way, expressing your individuality. Your link to life is your security; your expression of your uniqueness is your freedom. You can have it all. All you have to do is become aware that the You we're talking about is not the little separate you constructed by your conscious mind. It is the bigger You, the divine You.

Your soul grew that separate, little you in order to better experience itself in fuller awareness. Let that separate you be a tool of your soul, not a runaway caricature of your true essence, a tragic illusion, the Sorcerer's Apprentice up to its ears in its own mess. The conscious mind is an able servant and apprentice of the soul. The Prime Directive is to act accordingly. To follow it willingly is to awaken to awareness of the blessings of co-creatorship.

The Holographic Soul of Reality

Cayce's primary teaching on the soul is that it is both a piece of God as well as a miniature replica of its Creator, and thus a model of the whole of creation. But how can something be broken into pieces so that it also still reflects the whole thing? How can it be that we are each separate and unique, yet all essentially one and the same being? Edgar Cayce's teachings on the soul and the projection of reality through consciousness has recently gained a new source of support. We can now think about his teachings on this subject with a new conceptual tool, thanks to modern technology.

Cayce predicted that the crystal would someday be the source of an important invention. The use of a ruby crystal to create a laser beam has indeed led to many important inventions. In particular, laser holography, the exciting three-dimensional image-projection system, has provided an even more magical image of the creative power of consciousness. This advance in technology has also led to new theories on the nature of consciousness itself and its role in creating what we perceive as reality. Holographic theory parallels Cayce's teachings in many important respects.

The hologram has proven to be an even more astounding example of how the part can reflect the whole. Here is how it works.

When a normal camera takes a picture, it uses a lens to focus the light reflected off an object before it is allowed to expose the light-sensitive film. The result is a two-dimensional picture, reflecting only what can be seen of the object from the camera's momentary perspective.

In laser-beam holography, no camera lens is used. The laser beam itself is already highly focused. To take a picture of an object, the laser beam is shot at the object and a photographic plate picks up the light as it bounces off the object. To show the picture, a laser beam is aimed at the developed photographic plate. The markings on the plate cause the laser light to bounce off it in a way that casts an image of the original object out in space. No screen is used. The object appears as a lifelike, three-dimensional form. You can walk around the image and see it from all sides. It literally appears to exist as a real object, an illusion of the real thing!

In a normal, two-dimensional picture, there is an exact correspondence between a spot on the picture and the portion of the object shown. The top of the object appears on the top of the picture. If you cut the top off the picture, you lose the top of the object. In a holographic picture, there is no such correspondence. The laser light reflected from the original object is allowed to scatter all over the photographic plate. As a result, and here is the surprise, every piece of the plate contains the whole picture.

You can cut up the plate in hundreds of pieces. Each piece contains a unique set of patterns as a function of its position on the plate when the exposure was made. No two pieces are alike. On the other hand, if you shine the laser light on just one of those pieces, you will still get a three-dimensional projection of the *whole object* out in space. All that is affected by using smaller and smaller pieces of the original whole plate is that the sharpness of the image begins to get a bit fuzzy, but it still remains the whole image. Here is a modern, technological equivalent of Cayce's concept of a soul as being both a piece of the Creator and an image of the whole!

Many theorists have pointed to the holographic phenomenon as a suggestive image to explain the universal mystical experience of oneness. The hologram has become a metaphor for the transpersonal mind and has shed new light on ESP. It suggests a new way to understand the nature of consciousness.

According to Cayce's model, consciousness is a projection of the soul and the reality we experience is like a dream upon an invisible movie screen. The discovery of the hologram has led to the development of a scientific theory of consciousness much like Cayce's perspective. Karl Pribram, a brain scientist at Stanford University, has concluded that the brain must operate like a hologram. For one thing, we are learning that memories are not stored in any one particular place in the brain. You can cut out large chunks of the brain and still find the memories intact. The memories are stored all over the brain, just as a holographic image is repeated countless times all over the holographic plate.

Cayce indicated that the brain resonates to vibrations. Dr. Pribram has come to the same conclusion. He theorizes that the brain interprets vibrations both from the world of stimuli through the senses as well as from the world of ideas that exist in another dimension. Consciousness operates through the brain like the laser light striking the holographic plate. The result in both cases is similar: a three-dimensional image projected out into the appearance of space. Pribram is saying that we do literally experience holographic movies, living dreams created by our brains.

Spiritual Use of the Creation Formula

The stunning, illusory reality of the holographic image gives added meaning to Cayce's formula of creation. The spirit of the laser beam, cast through the holographic mind, projects the reality of manifestation in the three-dimensional realm.

We have learned how to apply this formula in both the conscious and subconscious mind. Through the setting of an ideal and the cultivation of a corresponding attitude, we can shape our behaviors to construct a life of our choosing. Through suggestion and visualization, we can tap into the hidden powers of the mind to create manifestations of our choosing. We can create an ideal life for ourselves.

The Prime Directive would ask us to be mindful of our spiritual mission. It can be achieved through the choosing of an ideal that includes a vision of the interrelatedness of life, that reflects the spirit of love. No matter how much power we can attain through the use of the mind, no matter how much understanding or psychic ability, how would it benefit us if we didn't learn the secret of love? Only in learning to love will we gain entry to the paradise that life offers. Otherwise, we will find ourselves imprisoned in a world of our own making, a lonely world of self-absorption and self-defense. It is to our benefit, as well as a benefit to life, for us to use the creative formula of the mind in a manner based upon an ideal of love.

If we are willing to submit voluntarily to the Prime Directive, if we are willing to do what is necessary to act in acceptant patience, love, and cooperation with the whole of life, with all circumstances that we meet, we will find that such an ideal will carry us through any of the circumstances that we might confront. It will save us the aggravation of doubt and fear. It will leave us free to enjoy life.

The Christ Consciousness

Cayce indicates that if we were to adopt such an ideal to guide the use of our creative energies, we would receive more than enough help from that ideal to transform our lives. When we work with an ideal, the ideal works with us.

Cayce gave many psychic readings on the life of Jesus and its meaning for the development of humanity's consciousness. In distinction to the historical person, Cayce also refers to the Christ Consciousness, an exalted state of mind that Jesus developed within himself.

God incarnates in each and every one of us. What was special about Jesus was that he was directly aware of his oneness with the Creator. This awareness was not just an assumption or a concept, but as a living reality. In developing the Christ Consciousness, Jesus fulfilled God's intention that a human being could simultaneously manifest in a material, three-dimensional ego consciousness while simultaneously living in oneness with God. Jesus willingly carried the cross of the Prime Directive and discovered the integration of the two levels of experience, the earthly and the heavenly.

Jesus died on that cross, but he also had a rebirth experience. In his teachings, Jesus made many references to the theme of death and rebirth. The seed must surrender its self-contained shell and crack open if the plant is to sprout. As the ego yields its fearful defensiveness of its self-contained reality to the love of life itself, a wider consciousness is expressed. The kingdom of Heaven lies within, waiting patiently for us to die to it. Cayce indicates that we practice that process every night, as we fall asleep and awaken into the soul's consciousness, the dream.

Less common, but receiving more attention in recent years, are the experiences of near-death. Perhaps as a result of an accident, a heart attack, or during surgery, a person dies, but is revived within a few minutes. Many people who have been brought back from death have reported incredible visions of beings of light and environments of infinite love, peace, and tranquility. As astounding as such experiences may be, what is more important is the impact that such experiences have had on these reborn individuals. They report they have lost any fear of death. They now *know* that consciousness survives; they have *experienced* their oneness with life. Their personal values change. They become less concerned with material things, less interested in competition or in winning recognition and approval. They feel at peace with themselves and are more interested in the quality of their daily experience. They spend more time enjoying loving interactions with others; they find they are more naturally concerned with the welfare of others. Many also discover their psychic ability, especially that of healing.

The movie *It's a Wonderful Life* provides a touching, and instructive, portrayal of the effects of a near-death experience. The character played by Jimmy Stewart was about to commit suicide because of financial difficulties when an angel gave him an unusual review of his life. He was able to see what life would have been like for all his friends and loved ones had he never been born. Although the man thought his life had been a failure, he saw that, in fact, his very presence had been an important influence on the lives of others in ways he had never considered. He had to surrender his narrow focus on financial matters and accept a larger perspective on the meaning of a life.

The development of the Christ Consciousness doesn't necessarily involve a dramatic flash of light. The surrender of the little self doesn't always mean a total renunciation of our personal concerns. It can mean getting out of our own way, getting past self-*preoccupation* and making allowances for the fact that we have more to offer to life than just our accomplishments.

The Mind Is the Way

Near-death experiences confirm the fact that the Christ Consciousness is a potential hidden within the mind of all of us, regardless of our particular religious faith. To develop the Christ Consciousness, we do not have to have a near-death experience. Nor do we have to suffer the trials of crucifixion. If we can accept pain and suffering as the inescapable chafing of the truth against the shell of our defended egos, we can ask of any experience that it teach us something, that it help release us into the fuller light of the truth of our ideal. It is a matter of attitude. Our frame of mind is the key to the Christ Consciousness.

In his readings on the mysteries of the mind, Cayce often made reference to a certain analogy between God and the human being. He explained that in our three-dimensional world, we experience God as Father, Son, and Holy Spirit. Likewise, he explained, we humans are as a body, a mind, and a soul. The Father dimension of God is like our body, our soul is like the Holy Spirit, and our mind is like the Son. In other words, Cayce identified the mind as being like the Son of God.

Such an analogy makes the mind extremely important and reveals its spiritual significance. Jesus insisted that no one could get to God except through Him. Cayce explained this statement in a way that is similar to other modern theologians and psychologists of religious experience. Even though every human being is a part of God, a child of God, we experience God directly only through the intermediary of our higher self as it develops the Christ Consciousness. This development requires, Cayce indicated, that every atom in the body resonate harmoniously with the ideal.

The conscious mind plays a vital role in this development. It is the conscious mind that decides to work with an ideal. It is the conscious mind that focuses the effort to develop constructive attitudes and habits. It is the conscious mind that can invite into awareness the deeper levels of consciousness.

The conscious mind can direct the development of the will to come into accord with the ideal. In the Bible, Paul laments that although he chooses to do right, he often does otherwise. He concludes that he must "die daily" in order that Christ may live within him. In other words, he chooses to surrender to his higher power to develop his will. He imagines and believes that this higher power will come to direct his actions, and he is willing to have it so.

Cayce indicates that our part is to make the conscious decision concerning what ideal we will serve. The ideal will then help us in our efforts. The life of Jesus, Cayce indicates, established the Christ Consciousness as a pattern in the universal mind. That Jesus "died for our sins" means that he found a way for a material body consciousness to submit to God's will. The way he found is now available as a pattern in the fourth-dimensional domain of ideas and ideals. It is a pattern within the superconscious mind capable of influencing and guiding our own consciousness, should we choose to invite it.

Becoming Channels of the Higher Self

One recent afternoon I accompanied my friend Jim to pick up his five-year-old daughter, Jessica, at school. Loaded with papers, she climbed into the back seat of the car. As we drove away, Jessica reached forward between the two front seats, announcing, "Here, Daddy, this is for you!" She presented him with a cutout drawing of a person in the form of a flower that she had made. The colorful flower person was smiling happily. So was the artist, as well as the artist's father, who commented, "She's the master of all she surveys, and she shares it willingly."

I marveled at the innocent beauty and joy of Jessica's creation. She created out of the joy of her own experience, and her sharing her work brought joy to us all. Her handing her unique creation to her father as a gift of love seemed such an exquisite image conveying the spirit of Cayce's revelation about the human being. We are like flowers, drawing upon the life energy of the sun and patterning it, each in our own way, to create love offerings of beauty to those we meet.

The incredible powers of the mind are for us to use as we choose. Each of us perceives the world with a uniquely creative subjectivity. How we see things, and react to them, not only determines our own experience, but is also our gift to the events of the world. With our imagination, we can reach out to an infinite realm of possibilities and cast a wish upon whatever star suits our fancy. If we are willing to make the effort, we can channel the creative potential of that vision into a living reality.

When we focus on the highest values and stretch ourselves to share our best efforts with others, we complete a circuit that allows the life energy to adventure forth into new patterns of being. Our own awareness is expanded as we become channels of our higher self, servants of our souls' quest toward the long-lost paradise on earth. If such would be your ideal, if you can imagine it, if you are willing, then act as if it were so, knowing that the thoughts of your heart will come to pass. That is the way of the mysteries of the mind.

SUGGESTED READING

Cayce, Hugh Lynn. *Venture Inward*. New York: Harper & Row, 1964.

Cayce, Hugh Lynn. *Faces of Fear*. San Francisco: Harper & Row, 1980.

Hudson, Thomson Jay. *The Law of Psychic Phenomena*. New York: Samuel Weiser, 1969.

Jampolsky, Gerald G. *Love Is Letting Go of Fear*. Millbrae, CA: Celestial Arts, 1979.

Pike, Cynthia. *The Miracle of Suggestion: The Story of Jennifer*. Virginia Beach: Inner Vision Publishing, 1988.

Puryear, Herbert. *The Edgar Cayce Primer: Discovering the Path to Self-Transformation*. New York: Bantam Books, 1982.

Puryear, Herbert, and Thurston, Mark. *Meditation and the Mind of Man*. Virginia Beach: A.R.E. Press, 1978.

Reed, Henry. *Getting Help From Your Dreams*. New York: Ballantine Books, 1988.

Reed, Henry. *Awakening Your Psychic Powers: Edgar Cayce's Wisdom for the New Age*. San Francisco: Harper & Row, 1988.

Reed, Henry. *Channeling Your Higher Self*. New York: Warner Books, 1989.

Rossi, Ernest Lawrence. *The Psychobiology of Mind-Body Healing: New Concepts of Therapeutic Hypnosis*. New York: Norton, 1986.

Siegel, Bernie. *Love, Medicine and Miracles*. New York: Harper & Row, 1986.

Thurston, Mark. *Paradox of Power: Balancing Personal and Higher Will*. Virginia Beach: A.R.E. Press, 1987.

EDGAR CAYCE

On Reincarnation

By Noel Langley
Under the Editorship of
Hugh Lynn Cayce

CONTENTS

FOREWORD

Who Was Edgar Cayce?

THE SIX BOOKS which have been written about Edgar Cayce have totaled more than a million in sales. More than ten other books have devoted sections to his life and talents. He has been featured in dozens of magazines and hundreds of newspaper articles dating from 1900 to the present. What was so unique about him?

It depends on through whose eyes you look at him. A goodly number of his contemporaries knew the "waking" Edgar Cayce as a gifted professional photographer. Another group (predominantly children) admired him as a warm and friendly Sunday School teacher. His own family knew him as a wonderful husband and father.

The "sleeping" Edgar Cayce was an entirely different figure—a psychic known to thousands of people, in all walks of life, who had cause to be grateful for his help. Indeed, many of them believed that he alone had either "saved" or "changed" their lives when all seemed lost. The "sleeping" Edgar Cayce was a medical diagnostician, a prophet, and a devoted proponent of Bible lore.

In June, 1954, the University of Chicago held him in sufficient respect to accept a Ph.D. thesis based on a study of his life and work. In this thesis the writer referred to him as a "religious seer." In that same year, the children's comic book *House of Mystery* bestowed on him the impressive title of "America's Most Mysterious Man"!

Even as a child, on a farm near Hopkinsville, Kentucky, where he was born on March 18, 1877, Edgar Cayce displayed powers of perception which seemed to extend beyond the normal range of the five senses. At the age of six or seven he told his parents that he was able to see and talk to "visions," sometimes of relatives who had recently died. His parents attributed this to the overactive imagination of a lonely child who had been influenced by the dramatic language of the revival meetings which were popular in that section of the country. Later, by sleeping with his head on his schoolbooks, he developed some form of photographic memory which helped him advance rapidly in the country school. This gift faded, however, and Edgar was only able to complete his seventh grade before he had to seek his own place in the world.

By the age of twenty-one he had become the salesman for a wholesale stationery company. At this time he developed a gradual paralysis of the throat muscles which threatened the loss of his voice. When doctors were unable to find a physical cause for this condition, hypnosis was tried, but failed to have any permanent effect. As a last resort, Edgar asked a friend to help him re-enter the same kind of hypnotic sleep that had enabled him to memorize his schoolbooks as a child. His friend gave him the necessary suggestion, and once he was in a self-induced trance, Edgar came to grips with his own problem. He recommended medication and manipulative therapy which successfully restored his voice and repaired his system.

A group of physicians from Hopkinsville and Bowling Green, Kentucky, took advantage of his unique talent to diagnose their own patients. They soon discovered that Cayce only needed to be given the name and address of a patient, wherever he was, to be able to "tune in" telepathically on that individual's mind and body as easily as if they were both in the same room. He needed, and was given, no other information regarding any patient.

One of the young M.D.'s, Dr. Wesley Ketchum, submitted a report on this unorthodox procedure to a clinical research society in Boston. On the ninth of October, 1910, *The New York Times* carried two pages of headlines and pictures. From that day on, troubled people from all over the country sought the "wonder man's" help.

When Edgar Cayce died on January 3, 1945, in Virginia Beach, Virginia, he left well over 14,000 documented stenographic records of the telepathic-clairvoyant statements he had given for more than six thousand different people over a period of forty-three years. These documents are referred to as "Readings."

The Readings constitute one of the largest and most impressive records of psychic perception ever to emanate from a single individual. Together with their relevant records, correspondence and reports, they have been cross-indexed under thousands of subject headings and placed at the disposal of psychologists, students, writers and investigators who still come, in increasing numbers, to examine them.

A foundation known as the A.R.E. (Association for Research and Enlightenment, Inc., P.O. Box 595, Virginia Beach, Virginia, 23451) was founded in 1932 to preserve these Readings. As an open-membership research society, it continues to index and catalogue the information, initiate investigation and experiments, and promote conferences, seminars and lectures. Until now, its published findings have been made available to its members through its own publishing facilities.

This is the first volume in a series of popular books dealing with those subjects from the Edgar Cayce Readings.

This volume presents data from 2500 Readings given by Edgar Cayce from 1925 through 1944, and deals with psychological problems rather than physical ailments. Such subjects as deep-seated fears, mental blocks, vocational talents, marriage difficulties, child training, etc., are examined in the light of what Edgar Cayce called the "karmic patterns" arising out of previous lives spent by an individual soul on this earth.

Karma, as he saw it, was a universal law of cause and effect which provides the soul with opportunities for physical, mental and spiritual growth. Each soul (called an "Entity" by Cayce), as it re-enters the earthplane as a human being, has subconscious access to the characteristics, mental capacities and skills it has accumulated in previous lives. However, the "Entity" must also combat the influence of lives in which such negative emotions as hate, fear, cruelty and greed delayed its progress.

Thus the "Entity's" task on earth is to make use of its successive rebirths to balance its positive and negative karmic patterns by subduing its selfish impulses and encouraging its creative urges. One of the most provocative concepts deals with the logical why and wherefore of apparently "needless" suffering.

The purpose of this volume is to present in simple, straightforward language some of the strange and exciting stories from the Edgar Cayce records which can help one to achieve a practical philosophy for every-day living.

—*Hugh Lynn Cayce*

CHAPTER 1

"HAVE I LIVED BEFORE?"

ON THE WARM afternoon of August 10, 1923, in a hotel room in Dayton, Ohio, the famous American seer Edgar Cayce woke from a self-imposed hypnotic sleep to receive one of the greatest shocks of his life.

As he listened to the stenographer read back a transcript of his words, Cayce, the most devout and orthodox of Protestants, a man who had read the Bible once for each of his forty-six years, learned with increasing bewilderment that he had stated flatly and emphatically that, far from being a half-baked myth, the law of reincarnation was a cold, hard fact.

His first fear was that his subconscious faculties had suddenly been commandeered by the forces of evil, making him their unwitting tool; and he had always vowed that if ever his clairvoyant powers were to play him false, he would permit no further use of them.

Now, with his confusion mounting, he sat and listened to Arthur Lammers's excited account of what he had said. Lammers had requested these sessions. He had paid Edgar's expenses all the way from Selma, Alabama. And, though Edgar had been diagnosing and helping to cure the ailments of the sick with his "Physical Readings" for over twenty years, he had never been asked to expound on the forbidden territory of the occult before. Lammers, on the other hand, had made a thorough study of psychic phenomena and Eastern religions at a time when such pursuits were frequently confined to elderly ladies at phony seances trying to trace their pet pugs in a canine hereafter.

Lammers was as jubilant as Edgar was dismayed. The questions with which he had bombarded the sleeping psychic had all been categorically answered. The last of Lammers's doubts had been swept away.

And Edgar was at another—and perhaps the most critical—milestone of his uphill path through life. His first impulse was to turn and run. Merely to entertain the possibilities that a man lived more than one life as a human being on this planet seemed to him sacrilegious and contrary to all the teachings of Christ.

It was even a repulsive concept—illogical, defeatist, and macabre. The best of good Christians found it hard enough to keep firm their faith in Christ's promise to His believers that He went to prepare a place for them in His Father's house. But, sacrilege apart, the unfamiliar words that had emanated from his own mouth were almost gibberish to him.

Unlike Lammers, his education was confined to a literal acceptance of the Bible. He accepted it verbatim, had taught it verbatim in his Sunday Schools, and had drawn total spiritual comfort from it. Thus he was the least equipped clairvoyant Lammers could have chosen to voyage into such strange, uncharted waters.

What would have happened if Edgar had begged to be excused and taken the next train back to Alabama? Perhaps a great deal more than we can rightly measure. Certainly greater issues would have gone by the board than the minor one that this book would not be in your hands. Certainly the psychiatrists would not have locked horns in controversy over *The Search for Bridey Murphy* in the mid-fifties—and inconclusive as that case may or may not be, it served as another milestone in Edgar's pilgrimage toward the eternal verities. Though he had been dead for eleven years, the attention attracted by Bridey publicized his philosophy in areas where it had never penetrated before, enabling his words to bring that much more aid and comfort to the sorely tried, the lonely, and the disenfranchised who had drifted from their own denominations, yet found no solace in the arid wastes of agnosticism.

It was only when Edgar conquered his doubts that day in Dayton and permitted Lammers to continue with his questions, that a new concept of reincarnation saw the light of day. This concept neither challenged nor impugned the teachings of Christ, but laid the foundations for a spiritual philosophy powerful enough to withstand the secular cynicism of this most turbulent of centuries.

Edgar Cayce made it a rule never to convert or convince by tub-thumping or "blinding with science." He left all judgment to the discretion of his hearer, and this book's only purpose is to give as clear a picture as possible of his theory of rebirth.

Over twenty-five hundred people went to him to learn of their previous life histories on this planet. The first logical question must be: "Did it do any of them any good?"

The answer is yes, in the cases where the "Readings" were seriously studied and their counsel applied.

It was to be expected that a fair percentage of lazy people, while prepared to recognize the home truths and timely warnings, still left their Readings to yellow on the shelf while they continued on their unrepentant ways. But the great majority were the gainers, to one degree or another. Some even transformed their lives from moral drudgery to purposeful use. Edgar taught that all human natures have one thing in common: they are only operating at full potential when their concerns are directed away from self-preoccupation and towards the assistance of their less fortunate brothers.

The most straightforward place to begin, then must surely be with the study of two of these Life Readings in detail.

Once we have followed the practical application of previous experience to a man's present endeavor, we can more comfortably move to the broader implications of reincarnation. These will logically include the inflexible laws to which reincarnation conforms, its implied presence in orthodox religion, and the reasons why it has suffered such rejection at the hands of Western civilization.

On August 29, 1927, Alice Greenwood asked for a Life Reading for her younger brother David, who had turned fourteen three days earlier. Though Alice had already received her own Life Reading, her brother was personally unknown to Edgar Cayce. Edgar's wife, Gertrude, usually conducted these sessions, but on this occasion the only people present were Edgar's father, Leslie, substituting for Gertrude, Gladys Davis, the stenographer, and Beth Graves, a visitor.

Gladys Davis was Edgar's permanent secretary, a woman whose impeccable record of staunch and faithful service continues to this day.

All that was known of David Greenwood was that he was a good student, bought his own clothes and schoolbooks by working as a newsboy, and liked to collect stamps. Beyond this, the sister possessed no special insight into his character.

It should also be made clear at this point that Edgar never undertook a reading except at the request of the subject or someone responsible for him. Once in self-induced hypnosis, he would answer to no other voice save that of the conductor of the questions. Any deviation from this procedure would result in silence, or his curt statement: "We are through for the present," whereupon he was given the suggestion to return to consciousness.

When this procedure was in any way violated, Edgar was in grave personal danger. On one occasion he remained in a catatonic state for three days, and twice had been given up for dead by the attendant doctors.

In response to Alice Greenwood's request, Edgar pursued his usual routine of reclining on a couch, hands folded across his chest, and breathing deeply. Then his eyelids fluttered—the signal for the conductor to close them and make contact with Edgar's subconscious by giving the suggestion for the Life Reading. In this case, Alice's written request for help for her brother was read. Unless this procedure was timed to synchronize with the fluttering of his eyelids, Edgar would proceed past his trance to a deep normal sleep from which there was no rousing him until he himself chose to awake.

CONDUCTOR: "You will have before you the Entity, David Roy Greenwood, born August 26, 1913, between Perry and Hale Counties, eight miles north of Greensboro, Alabama. You will give the relation of this Entity and the universal forces, giving the conditions which are as personalities, latent and exhibited, in the present life; also the former appearances in the earth's plane, giving the time, the place, and the name, and that which in each life built or retarded the development for the Entity, giving the abilities of the present Entity and that to which it may attain, and how."

A pause followed, during which Edgar's subconscious made contact with the subconscious of David Greenwood. (Had this reading been only concerned with the physical health of the subject, it would have been imperative that Edgar be told the exact geographical location of the boy at that moment, just as a tracking station must know the precise location of a satellite before it can make radar contact.) Then he began to speak in a quiet, unemotional undertone.

His first comment was that most of the boy's present characteristics consisted of latent instincts rather than recognizable traits responding to an effort of will. "We find indications, then, of one who is strong of body, yet with inclinations and tendencies towards physical defects which afflict the body by manifesting themselves in the digestion, or physical body. Hence the Entity should be warned against indulgences which may bring about strain and stress on the digestive system."

At this time there was no indication of any kind that the boy would eventually suffer from digestive trouble. It was an excellent example of Edgar's power of precognition. He then proceeded to laud the boy's friendly nature, but suggested he learn to curb his quick temper before it became a problem.

He warned that without responsible application of will power and a stable religious faith to guide him, the boy's impulses might continue to hamper his course of action throughout his life.

According to the unconscious memory the boy retained of his previous lives, his best chance for success was to associate with businessmen whose trade pertained "to materials, clothing, and of such nature. These will be the natural trend and bent of the Entity . . . for with the ability to make friends, the turn is seen towards nobleness of purpose . . . hence the training which the Entity needs under such conditions should begin, as soon as it may, to supply the correct groundwork for such a development."

He then proceeded to describe the boy's life immediately before this one.

It spanned the last years of Louis XIII and the early years of Louis XIV in France. Edgar referred to an approaching rebellion that could well have been the public uprisings against the Queen Mother and Cardinal Mazarin which lasted intermittently from August, 1648, until their final subjugation by the Prince of Conde in July, 1652. David's name then was Neil, and he occupied a substantial place at the King's Court, a kind of Master of the Robes and arbiter of fashion, personally responsible for the King's wardrobe.

Neil served his royal master faithfully, and Edgar made the point that he would stand to reap the benefits of his devotion to duty in this present life—a kind of good conduct medal, as it were, handed down from one self to the other.

What other characteristics did he inherit?

"There is seen, in the present, the urge to be particular with himself as to dress, and the ability to describe well the dress of a whole roomful of people, if he sets his mind to it."

It should be noted that the Reading occasionally employed cautious, sometimes pedantic phraseology, and for a very good reason. The subconscious mind of Edgar Cayce seemed to be dealing with the colloquial French of the seventeenth century, which it must then have transposed into the modern English idiom of his conscious mind.

The subconscious does not consist of tangible matter; only thought exists. Therefore, all languages are one. The danger of misinterpretation could only begin when Edgar spoke aloud. Thus his perpetual concern, once he had successfully transferred the "mental pictures" from his subconscious to the "teletype" of his conscious mind, was to retain the true original sense.

This care and caution became more and more evident as Edgar receded further and further back in time, and was confronted not only by obsolete idiom, but languages which made muscular demands on the throat and lip-muscles which his own would have been totally incapable of reproducing. Here his task was not so much to translate from one language to another, as to paraphrase unintelligible symbols into their nearest modern equivalent.

In short, he had to "crack the code," much as archeologists have had to reduce ancient sign languages to their approximate grammatical equivalents.

Edgar then proceeded to the life before the boy's French incarnation as Neil. This was on the isthmus of Thessaloniki on the Aegean coast of Greece. There, in a town called Solonika, he lived as a tradesman called Colval.

No exact date was given, but the times were referred to as unsettled, leaving one to assume that one form of government was being overthrown and replaced by another, enabling Colval to attain to a position of power which he subsequently misused. Therefore he forfeited some of the benefits he might otherwise have passed on to himself in the present. Nevertheless, "the influences in this life in the present are seen in his ability to fit himself into any place or position among whatever people he finds himself associated." He was also told, with truth: "Especially is the love of family, and of those closely associated with same, seen from that experience."

The next serial life might well have coincided with Alexander's invasion and conquest of Persia.

Whatever invading power it was, it suceeded in dividing the country against itself. The boy's name was then Abiel and he took advantage of the times to rise to the status of court physician. Here the intrigue and corruption had its effect on him, but even though he again misused his authority, he was still commended for standing his ground when he faced the threat of persecution by his conquerors.

The influence on his present life was also seen in his innate desire "to study chemical compounds . . . the urge toward a desire to be a physician." This was perfectly correct; but instead of being told to encourage it, he was advised to put more store by the later experience as a tradesman in Greece.

In other words, the boy was warned away from his daydreams of becoming a great surgeon, the obvious implication being that he was not only economically and temperamentally unequipped for it, but also that his penchant for intrigue at the Persian court would restimulate facets of his nature that were better left dormant.

From here Edgar proceeded back to times so ancient as to border on prehistory—Egypt during one of its invasions by an alien race. It now became possible to identify the recurring factors in the path of this soul's progress. Both in France and Persia he enjoyed the privileges of royal favor. His familiarity with court procedure in Persia clearly enabled him to adapt his instinct, or flair, to his environment in France. Living twice in countries which had been overrun by invading cultures, the tumult and unrest had given him a clear insight into the psychology of crowds.

In Egypt his name was Isois, and once again he was able to make himself invaluable to his conquerors. From a humble beginning he rose to authority as a type of lay preacher who enjoyed the trust of the common people. As a result, the priests of the new dynasty used him as a go-between and "general interpreter" of the new form of worship.

"Hence he was among the first in the land to take on a special class of raiment, or garment, to distinguish self from other peoples."

The boy was told that his life had gained such luster from his concern for the welfare of the man in the street that relics still remain among the ruins of Egypt which commemorate his sanctity. After his death he was worshipped as a saint or minor god. "The Entity gained in that experience, and the gain manifests in the present, in his ability to apply himself to the masses as well as to the individual."

Egypt was invaded many times in its long history, but the presence of priests among the conquerors suggests that this period predated the Babylonian and Ethiopian invasions, and belongs as far back as the early Aryan invasions from the North.

This would place the time at about 10,000 B.C., which would seem far enough back for any soul. But next Edgar came up against the controversial subject of Atlantis, which science flatly dismisses as legend, and which Edgar Cayce defined as three huge bodies of land spanning what is now the Atlantic Ocean, possessing in common a civilization far in advance of our own and a practical command of nuclear energy which contributed to its own destruction and inundation. Large groups of survivors reached South and Central America and North Africa, and one group, not so easily assimilated because of its isolation, survived as the Basque race in the Pyrenees between France and Spain.

The material on Atlantis in the Cayce files is imposing enough to warrant a book of its own, and reference to it will of necessity occur in subsequent chapters of this one, but it is only necessary at the moment to establish the fact that its civilization spanned a period of two hundred thousand years, the last of its islands finally subsiding in 10,000 B.C.

"Before that, the Entity was in the Atlantean land when the floods came and destruction ruled the land, (and) was among those so destroyed. The name then was Amiaie-Oulieb."

Most significantly, he was heir to the throne; so from his very beginnings, the blood of royalty was familiar to him. Despite his death by drowning, he had lived long enough to indicate that he lacked the discipline and dedication necessary to his station, but "the present (evidence of that incarnation) is seen in the ability to know materials, especially those that apply to wearing apparel."

Thus we find that in only one of his lives was he lacking an affinity for fine cloth and ceremonial vestments, even though the lives delineated by Edgar Cayce were not necessarily the only appearances the boy made on earth. (Indeed, his cycles suggest that he may well have been one of the members of a tenacious soul-group who pride themselves on the number of times they are reincarnated—almost as if some sort of Olympic Championship were involved! But these were the only lives that had a constructive bearing on his problems in the life on which he was now embarking. This became apparent in the final summing-up of David Greenwood's potential talents at the close of the Reading:

"As to the present abilities of the Entity, then, it is seen that many conditions arise which are to be met by the Entity in the application of himself to the environs of the present experience.

"First beware of those conditions which might bring detrimental forces to the physical well-being through the digestive system. Then, in this channel, follow specific diets and the correct application of food values for the physical well-being.

"In the mental and the body building, the Entity needs to apply himself first to that which will give the more perfect knowledge of his relation to Creative Energy, *i.e.* to the spiritual lessons which may be gained from a study of the Master's experience in the earth's plane as the son of man.

"In the material sense, apply self toward salesmanship and to the abilities of meeting the needs of man as pertaining to business relations.

"Keep self physically, mentally and spiritually fit, for in service the greatest blessings are given. Choose thou whom thou will serve; for no man can serve two masters.

"Keep the law, as is befitting to man's relation to God. Keep self unspotted from the world. Not as eyeservice, but as service of the heart to the Maker.

"We are through for the present."

The Reading was duly typed and forwarded to the boy's parents. It made so little sense to them that the boy was never given it to read. Fortunately, his sister was not so easily discouraged. She put the Reading in a safe place, and the case does not appear in the files again until seven years later, August 22, 1934.

At this point the twenty-one-year-old David Greenwood was the main support of his mother and other sister. He was earning a modest salary as the circulation manager of a small-town newspaper, and had little or no promise of substantial advancement. His mood was both frustrated and restless when Alice finally presented him with his Reading and suggested he apply its counsel to his problems. His response was not much warmer than his parents' had been. There was nothing wrong with his digestion; he had no interest or aptitude for the clothing market; the idea of rebirth left him cold; and the possibility that he was some kind of repressed couturier was utterly ridiculous. However, he did admit that almost anything was preferable to spending the rest of his days in the obscure penury of the newspaper office.

Even so, it was not until the spring of 1940 that David's sister persuaded him to make use of an introduction she had obtained for him to the two partners of a third-generation clothing factory which confined itself exclusively to manufacturing uniforms. Alice had been aware that the partners were familiar with the work of Edgar Cayce and held it in high regard. Thus David's Life Reading left no doubt in their minds that he possessed a natural bent for their particular trade, and without further ado they offered him an opening as a traveling salesman. His main line was high school band uniforms, but he also catered to civic groups.

In the following year, David developed such a gift for anticipating his customers' needs that he added several southern states to his territory, outstripping every other salesman in the company, even though he was the youngest and least experienced.

In February, 1943, he was classified 4F by the Army. The reason: food allergies, the origins of which predated the Reading's warning that he could look for trouble with his digestive system!

Then gas rationing, crowded hotels and overburdened railroads wrote *finis* to his flourishing career as a salesman. So David volunteered to work in one of the largest Army induction centers, where an average of fifteen hundred officers a week were outfitted for combat.

By July of the same year he had been promoted to O.C.S. Clothing Shop. When the war ended, he returned to his old firm to be placed in sole charge of the retail section, while the two former owners concentrated on reorganizing the wholesale department as a separate corporation.

It is not surprising that the grateful Greenwood continued to work closely with Edgar Cayce, and a revealing fact emerged from the subsequent Readings: the weak digestion he inherited was a direct consequence of his love of rich food at the French court, where the gourmet Neil literally destroyed his body by his excesses in gluttony. (Gout was probably the least of the agonies that attended his death in that life.) The fact that Greenwood was confined to the most Spartan of diets in this life was not only restitution for the harm he did himself at the King's table; his own subconscious was also warning him never to inflict such needless and unattractive punishment on his physical self in any of the serial lives that still awaited him!

This is by no means a unique example of the 2,500 Life Readings made by Edgar Cayce, but it conveys in a clear-cut line of progression how the latent abilities of a fourteen-year-old boy, which would otherwise have remained fallow and unsuspected throughout his lifetime, were apparent to Edgar Cayce, correctly identified by him, traced to their source, and presented to the boy in terms of practical application.

Edgar lived long enough to see David Greenwood inherit his rightful destiny.

No less singular was Cayce's power of prophecy in a Reading he gave, six years before he died, for Grover Jansen.

The Call of the Wild

When he applied for his Reading in 1939, Grover Jansen was in a more fortunate position than David Greenwood. He was a nineteen-year-old student who had doubts about his future. After two years in college, he could find no occupation to which he responded.

Edgar left him in no doubt as to his natural bent. In his previous life, during the War for Independence, he had worked as an agriculturist whose duty it was to estimate the amount of produce the Army could expect to obtain from a given terrain. Thus, there was little he did not know about the fertility or barrenness of any given area in which major battles were to be fought.

"The Entity, in the name of Elder Mosse, was associated with Andre as well as with Arnold, Lee and Washington, in those lands about the upper portion of what is now New York State . . . hence we will find in the present that mountains and streams, the outdoors, all those activities which relate to physical prowess, have an innate, subtle influence upon the Entity in its choice of its dealings with others."

In the life before that, the youth had lived in the Roman Empire during its period of great expansion.

"There we find the Entity was among those who were the choice of at least three emperors—the early Caesars, but not the first—for activities in England, Ireland, portions of France, portions of Spain and Portugal, as well as the northern coasts of Africa and Grecian lands and the Palestine land. All of those were a part of the Entity's activity.

"For the Entity was among those (and there was only one other) who had the ability to judge as to what could be best produced in the varied lands with the least effort to supply the greater benefit to the empire in its various spheres of activity.

"Hence we find that every activity of nature comes under the Entity's judgment—whether to furnish adornment, food, a means of exchange, including the feathered tribes of those that were the fur bearing, or the production of seeds or woods of various kinds.

"In the present, then, as indicated, the Entity has the ability—from that very sojourn—to become a judge of those influences for conservation . . . the name then was Agrilda.

"Before that we find that the Entity was in the land now known as the Egyptian, during those periods of reconstruction following the inundation of the Atlantean land, of which the Entity had been a part.

"For the Entity, though younger than some of those who were in authority, soon grew in favor in that Egyptian land, not only for instructing and edifying the various groups, but aiding the bond of union and strength that comes from united efforts for the better conservation . . . the name then was Ex-en.

"As to the choice of how the Entity will act in the present then: as to whether it will fulfill that purpose for which it entered, or glorify self or a cause, or an individual, that must be decided by the Entity alone.

"In those fields of conservation—whether it be of fishes in waters, birds of certain caliber, needs for food, or protection of certain portions of the land or timbers, or the better conservation of soil for certain seeds or crops—all these are the channels in which the Entity may find contentment and harmony.

"Of course, the land continues to grow—for it is God's footstool—but man's abuse of same can cause it to become no longer productive. But if there is the conservation of its strength—the lands, the timbers, and God's creatures that manifest through same—it is a continuous thing. For 'Ye grow in grace and in knowledge and in understanding' is applicable to man's secular life just as much as to his mental or spiritual."

Q: "Should I continue at Penn State College next year?

Cayce: "If there is a course in which this particular study is stressed, yes. If it is found that there can be a greater study through the Government's activity in those fields, choose that! And it will be opened if ye look for it!"

The youth followed the advice in his Reading promptly and to the letter. And just as Edgar had told him, he developed a natural affinity for wild life and conservation.

It was a thoroughly contented and fulfilled man in the National Park Service of the Department of the Interior who wrote to Hugh Lynn Cayce seven years later:

"Dear Folks: We are finally located for the summer at the south gate of this beautiful and biggest of our National Parks. It is a big thrill to me to have the title of 'Ranger,' since I have always looked upon these guardians of our natural resources as 'real men' ever since I was a little shaver. I'm starting in as 'Ranger-Naturalist' July first, which is an even bigger event in the climb up the ladder.

"Well, the bragging is over now, but I just had to let you all know that the Readings have made me and my little family very, very happy since we at least know that we are on the right road.

"This Ranger-Naturalist job is a perfect opportunity to show the people a little of God's work untouched. Every stream is pure and good to drink, chock full of trout ready for fly. All of the old mountain men, as well as the Crow, Sioux and other Indian tribes, once roamed this very country so rich in history. The antelope, buffalo and elk and moose are as common as they were when the pioneers first cut a trail through this great wilderness. The grizzlies and black bear make one aware that some danger lurks behind each tree. . . . I find a spice here that I have never experienced before.

"Intend to return to the Agricultural College in September to finish up a few credits for a sheepskin, and then into the National Park Service for good maybe.

"Come on out—I'll give you all a complimentary pass!"

Then in 1951, he wrote from the Fish and Wildlife Service to a friend who was sufficiently concerned for her son's future to ask his advice: "If only Edgar Cayce were living now I am sure that a Reading would be the answer to many of those knotty problems that you are now dealing with. I was very fortunate in contacting the Association at an early age, and as the result of a Life Reading and several Check Readings, I have found the kind of work for which I am best suited.

"As you can see from the letterhead, I am no longer with the U.S. National Park Service. Last August we moved to North—— where I have assumed the title of U.S. Game Management Agent and enforce the Federal fish and game regulations in this State. The Life Reading advised Government work in the conservation of natural resources, and I can assure you that I enjoy the position immensely!"

The Boy Who Remembered

It would hardly be logical if the soul-history Edgar Cayce traced for himself were not both imposing and unique. But by the same token it is so complex and recondite that only a volume wholly devoted to its evolution could make it comprehensible to the orthodox layman.

Without trying to inflate him to a Grand Panjandrum, his spiritual antecedents place him in a high echelon of human souls. His various lives took him from sublime heights to plateaus in which he was neither particularly exalted, nor gifted with more than the normal five senses.

For example, in the life he spent on the American continent immediately prior to his return as Edgar Cayce, he had not been a minor saint. He had been a mercenary in the British Army prior to the War for Independence—a jovial rolling stone with an eye for the ladies and the bottle.

He was born in 1742 of swashbuckling Cornish stock—a Celtic race which in those days felt little if any love for England and gloried in smuggling and ship wrecking. He was christened John Bainbridge. Originally, he landed in America in Chesapeake Bay (significantly near to Virginia Beach which, like a Lorelei, had called him back to its shore in this life). His involvement in the intermittent skirmishes with hostile Indian tribes took him as far north as Canada, and finally confined his theater of war to Fort Dearborn, the site of present-day Chicago. The frontier life there was rough and rowdy, a foretaste of the shenanigans that were to paint the California boom towns scarlet in the following century, and he was a man of his own times in every sense of the word.

When the beleaguered Fort Dearborn finally fell to the Indians, he aided a large group of men, women and children to escape down the Ohio River on a clumsily assembled raft. They had insufficient supplies to sustain them and were unable to go ashore to forage, the Indians having pursued them along both banks of the Ohio. One by one the unfortunates died of exposure and starvation, but Bainbridge's own life ended in an act of heroism; he died enabling a young woman to escape to safety.

Apart from this, his soul had made no great spiritual progress in that life, and it would merit no further comment, save for two singular links with his present life. The woman whose life he saved sought his help again in this life, and through her he was able to aid many of the souls he had known in Fort Dearborn, for as a group, they had remained intact, bringing their unfinished problems with them to be resolved in the environs of the Chesapeake peninsula. (See Chapter 16.)

A minor but much more disarming fragment of evidence was forthcoming when the Cayce family first moved to Virginia Beach in September 1925. Edgar had accompanied his son Hugh Lynn to a barber's shop where the barber's son, a sleepy five-year-old, was fretfully awaiting his mother's return to put him to bed. His father had given him a box of animal crackers to keep him pacified, and when his drowsy gaze suddenly focused on Edgar, he trotted over to him and handed him the box. "Here," he said impulsively. "You can have the rest. You must still be awfully hungry!"

"Leave the gentleman alone! You know better than to pester folks you don't know!" his father chided him.

"But I do know him!" protested the child, gazing up at Edgar with complete confidence. "He was on the raft, too! And you were real hungry then, weren't you, mister?"

"Thank you, young man," said Edgar gratefully. "I'll take just the one cookie," and then added in a confidential whisper, "and you're right! I was real hungry on that raft!"

CHAPTER 2

IF WE HAVE LIVED BEFORE, WHY DON'T WE REMEMBER?

THE SUBCONSCIOUS MIND does remember its past experiences, but there is every good reason why the conscious mind is spared that rather dubious privilege.

Imagine yourself to be a soul before it returns to earth. Imagine yourself a diver seated on the deck of a salvage ship in the Caribbean. It is a calm, bright day. The water is smooth and transparent, the skies unclouded; only a slight breeze stirs.

Somewhere below you is the wreck of an old galleon, reputed to have been laden with golden bullion when it sank. You can even detect the shadowy skeleton of its few remaining timbers, though most of it is buried in silt. What you cannot see from the deck of the ship are the intricate crosscurrents flowing at that depth; they are too far down to disturb the surface calm of the sea.

Because of the length of time you must spend submerged, you now don an old-fashioned canvas diving suit with lead-weighted boots, and a copper helmet is screwed into place over your head. Its small oval windows confine your vision. As you climb overboard, your body feels as if it weighs a ton. The sweet drowsy ozone you were breathing undergoes a deglamorization as it is pumped into your helmet through the airhose. As soon as you disappear below the surface, however, you adjust to weightlessness and sink down comfortably to the sea bed. It is all clear-cut and straightforward: your success is a foregone conclusion. You will merely have to reach the ocean floor to walk straight to the wreck, locate the treasure, dig it up, and then signal to be drawn back to the surface.

The only thing you have failed to take into account is the fickleness of the sea itself. As your feet touch the seabed, you find yourself fighting against a strong current. You pitch your full weight against it and start approaching the wreck. But the force of the current, pushing you first this way and then that, doubles the dead-weight of the cumbersome suit and helmet you are wearing.

Let us call this suit the physical body which the soul inhabits while it is on earth. All goes well with it while the currents are just right, and the light is just right, and you are in full control of it. But the filtering light may suddenly be obscured by clouds over the sun, and the ocean floor suddenly becomes grey and murky. The perpetual resistance of the crosscurrents begins to weary you; your muscles begin to ache. What had promised to be such a simple and rewarding task from the safety of the deck of the ship now becomes complex, confusing and frustrating. Nothing is made any easier by the appearance of a couple of hungry-looking twelve-foot sharks, who skulk menacingly nearby. As you reach the wreck, your lifeline and airhose tangle with the upturned beams of the wreck. You struggle afresh to disentangle them. The air coming down the hose is impeded. You begin to feel short of breath. You also begin to wonder what on earth you are doing down there, and whether any amount of treasure will be worth the discomfort. You try to remember the chart you had studied so carefully on deck, which clearly indicated which part of the wreck would contain the treasure. Now you are no longer sure which is the stern of the wreck. You begin to experience what Thoreau describes as "quiet desperation." Time tends to stand still. You feel you had been on the sea bed in your unwieldy diver's suit since the beginning of time, and that you will remain there for all eternity. The normal life on shipboard becomes more and more an unreal dream—something that you yourself had never experienced personally. The voices filtering down to you through the speaking-tube become equally inhuman and unreal. The *only* reality is the battle you are waging not to be pushed this way and that by the currents. You are keeping such an alert eye on the slowly circling sharks, who seem to be imperceptibly moving closer and closer, that you have little time to search for your bearings and concentrate on your original mission.

At last such weariness, claustrophobia and defeat overwhelm you that you can barely signal to the men above to haul you back aboard. On your way up you develop a case of the bends, and when you are finally dragged aboard and rescued from your stifling suit, you are more dead than alive.

In the period it takes you to recover, while you lie on your back gulping in the fresh air, the memory of those interminable hours down below, in their turn, became the vague dream. The unreality now is the period you spent on the ocean floor; the reality is now the deck of the ship and the security you feel in the companions around you.

The whole memory-process has been reversed.

In like manner does the human soul re-enter the world of the living too often too over confident, and likewise it returns after death to its original state with too little confidence, having forgotten that the two separate worlds coexist, and that one is just as real as the other.

"One Man in His Time Plays Many Parts"

If you prefer a more tangible frame of reference to account for your apparent lack of karmic memory, think of yourself as a professional actor.

Put yourself in the shoes of the great Shakespearean actor, Sir Laurence Olivier, whose theatrical genius has given us definitive portrayals of Henry V, Hamlet, Richard III and Othello. Each one of these roles is a perfect and fully resolved creation in its own right; none of them derivative of the others. Olivier actually had to live these roles to imbue them with such intensity and conviction.

Between each of these achievements, Olivier, the professional actor, has had time to rest and take stock of his progress toward the position he now enjoys. He may be the greatest living classical actor in America and Europe, but away from his profession, his problems are no different from yours. He makes appointments with his dentist, has income-tax headaches, colds in the head and an occasional hole in his sock. But the difference becomes instantly apparent when he stands in the wings of the Old Vic Theater, about to make his first entrance as Othello.

Is he worrying about Laurence Olivier's tax problems? Most certainly not. Laurence Olivier is fast becoming a vague dreamy blur in his memory. His sole identification is with Othello. He concentrates only on the emotions he must soon evoke. The canvas scenery disappears, and a real street in Venice takes its place. The voices of the other actors continue, but are now emanating from the throats of flesh-and-blood sixteenth-century Venetians.

To a very real extent, Olivier is in self-induced hypnosis as he makes his entrance onto the stage.

Now—imagine him passionately declaiming, drawing on the last reserves of his emotional energy, yet maintaining split-second discipline as he times each syllable—and tell me if he would have time to dwell proudly on his press notices for his Hamlet, or glow with nostalgia at the memory of the ovations he received for his Richard III, or suddenly wish he had used a different accent and makeup in his film of Henry V.

Let me assure you he would be incapable of remembering anything beyond Othello's immediate infatuation for Desdemona. Even during the intermissions and offstage waits, he would still be Othello—an Othello relaxing, perhaps; as the body does in sleep; but still Othello. Not until the final curtain has fallen and the audience left the theater, not until his costume and makeup are removed, can he be in any sort of condition to discuss the critical pros and cons of his previous triumphs as Henry V, Hamlet and Richard III.

And, if you take the parallel further, not all Olivier's theatrical portraits were successful. But it would be needless sabotage of his own confidence, if he never permitted himself to forget that he once allowed himself to be hoaxed into making an abysmally dilettantish film version of *The Beggar's Opera.* What kind of performance could his "Othello" audience expect of him, if his mind were so obsessed by that one failure that it impelled him to stop short in the middle of his performance as Othello to whisper to Desdemona: "Ye Gods, old dear, what an absolute jackass I made of myself as MacHeath! I've no right to be out here taking their money!"

What would happen to the rapport he had so carefully built up between his Othello and the audience?

Apply this to yourself. Suppose you were allowed voluntary access to all your previous lives, and one day, by chance, you stumbled across the memory of having been the greatest monster in history!

How would you deal with the horror, the belated remorse? How would you deal with the fear that your soul might be in such arrears that you would have to put in another million lives of bitter compensation to atone for the harm you did your fellow-souls in that one incarnation? What hope would be left you?

Actually this situation can never arise, for the simple reason that it would throw the whole karmic law of cause and effect out of balance, and the workings of that law are fixed and unalterable. No soul will ever be permitted such calamitous knowledge of its own past blunders. Whatever the debt a soul owes to its fellow-souls, it will never be called upon to settle it until the soul has progressed to a sufficiently mature level to make such compensation possible and practical. Meanwhile, from this point on, let us jettison the idiotic concept that "karma" is brutal and senseless punishment unleashing itself on us unworthy sinners.

"For the Lord does not tempt any soul beyond that which it is able to bear," said Edgar Cayce. But many times he had to exorcise the dark tenets of Predestination and Original Sin from the hopelessness and confusion in the minds of the people who came to him for help.

"Most individuals in the present misinterpret karmic conditions," he said. "Each soul or Entity should gain the proper concept of destiny. Destiny is within; it is of faith; it is as the gift of the Creative Forces. Karmic influence, in this case, is rebellious influence against destiny."

"The Entity puts a stress upon karma," he reproached one of his questioners. "If ye live by law, you must judge by law; but if ye live by faith, ye judge by faith.

"This is not intended as criticism, nor as sarcasm," he told another, "but that ye may know that it is the law of the Lord that is perfect—not men's conception of it. The law will be fulfilled. Will ye do it, or let someone else do it? . . . He who seeks will find. He who knocks, to him it will be opened. These are irrefutable, these are unchangeable laws."

And here he analyzes it in greater detail:

"Karma is a reaction which may be compared to the reaction within the body when a piece of food is taken into the system. The food is translated into a part of the body itself, penetrating to every cell, and influencing the health of the body and mind.

"Thus it is with a soul, when it enters the body for an experience in the earth. The person's thoughts, along with the actions which result from these thoughts, are the food upon which the soul feeds.

"These thoughts and actions, in turn, have been generated by thoughts and actions behind them; and so on back to the birth of the soul.

"When a soul enters a new body, a door is opened, leading to an opportunity for building the soul's destiny. Everything which has been previously built, both good and bad, is contained in that opportunity. There is always a way of redemption, but there is no way to dodge responsibilities which the soul has itself undertaken.

"Thus a life is a way of developing, a preparation for the cleansing of the soul, though it may be a hard path, at times, for the physical consciousness and the physical body.

"Changes come, and some people say luck has intervened. But it is not luck. It is the result of what the soul has done about its opportunity for redemption."

And here, in the simplest of terms, he presents the Law of Grace which supersedes atonement: "Karma is rather the lack of living up to that which ye know ye should do. As ye would be forgiven, so forgive in others. That is the manner to meet karma."

Throughout the Readings one comes across cases of individuals whose karmic sin was their determination to clutch onto their obsolete guilt and shame, rather than make a positive effort to balance them by the "forgiveness of others."

Obviously no one can be forced, either by his God or his fellow man, to forgive himself, or anyone else, until he himself decides to. He is at liberty to remain in his chosen purgatory for as long as he prefers it to any other state.

But until he has evolved himself to a sufficiently enlightened outlook to pull himself up by his own bootstraps, what will he gain by asking: "Why don't I remember?" Isn't it more circumspect to say: "I'm glad I don't remember!"— even if this means he is denied the gratification of reviewing those lives in which he was a ministering angel to his fellow souls and died loved, honored and respected?

All the good achieved in any life remains permanently with the soul. A soul can never undo the good it has done, and later in this book we can examine how this can be set against the law of cause and effect by the application of the Law of Grace.

CHAPTER 3

MAN'S SUBCONSCIOUS IS IMMORTAL

IN THE EARLY days, the difference between the "waking" and the "sleeping" Edgar Cayce was as fundamental as the difference between East and West Berlin. There was, of course, no antagonism between the two minds, either, even though one was vulnerable and human, and the other was spiritually insulated against the "sea of sorrows" to which man falls heir.

Perhaps the simplest frame of reference is the ship-to-shore radio—you cannot talk on it and listen at the same time. It is simply a mechanical device which enables the man at sea to make contact with the man ashore. As for itself, it records no impressions and retains no memory of the words that enter and emanate from it.

Toward the end of Edgar Cayce's life, there was definite evidence of a merging of the two levels of consciousness, but in his early years, he was as startled as the next man to learn he had given medical counsel to an Italian, in fluent and flawless Italian. Nor was the complicated medical terminology that rolled off his tongue any more intelligible to him in his waking state than was the fluent Italian.

Perhaps the most popular misconception foisted on him was that he was a kind of secular Moses crying in a metaphysical wilderness. What *did* give his mind uniqueness was its apparent ability to recall its own beginning in Creation.

His purpose—perhaps his whole purpose, for all we know as yet—was to serve as a "paver of the way" to those who believe their heritage began in God. "What I can do today, every man will be able to do tomorrow," is a recurring theme in his philosophy.

That every soul possesses the same potential is implicit in the words he uses to describe the soul's first appearance on this earth.

"In the beginning, when the first of the elements were set in motion that brought about the sphere called 'earth plane,' when the morning stars sang together and the whispering winds brought the news of the coming of man from his indwelling in the spirit of the Creator to manifest as a living soul, this Entity came into being with this multitude."

If we bear in mind that at this time the orthodox "waking" Cayce's interpretation of the Bible was diametrically opposed to his "sleeping" interpretation, it is interesting to compare the above statement with this passage from Job 38: "Then the Lord answered Job out of the whirlwind, and said. . . . 'Where wast thou when I laid the foundations of the earth . . . when the morning stars sang together, and all the sons of God shouted for joy?'"

Even as they were awaiting creation, according to Edgar Cayce, some souls were already predestined to use their new-found free will to serve God's purpose on the earth, while others were equally designated to use their free will to do as they chose. . . . The newly-born earth offered them an opportunity to usurp God's role as Creator and become petty Creators in their own right. In short, the souls brought sin with them. It was not here awaiting them "in the flesh" on a planet where even animal evolution had not yet begun. Indeed, the density of "solid" matter, as we know it now, lay millions of years ahead. Thought was the original motivating force. Dense matter was a subsequent mutation of thought after it "bogged down." To simplify— thought can be compared to molten lava—malleable, perpetually moving, changing, capable of resuming any form. Solid matter is its inanimate aftermath, responsive only to the chisel and the hammer.

Hence you will find throughout the Readings the perpetual reiteration that "Thought is the Builder"—the wet clay responsive to the potter's hands— and that the survival of the soul depends utterly on its power to mold its destiny at the subconscious level, where the clay is moist enough to respond.

Just as a series of chain reactions alters the atom from a harmless particle of solid matter to the mushroom cloud that obliterated Hiroshima, the chain reactions of positive thought can eventually release the soul from solid matter and return it to the freedom of its fluid state at the astral level.

It is because we lack the equivalents of such convenient scientific terms as "atomic fissure," that we are reduced to referring to the process which releases the soul as "the tragedy of death."

This is akin to throwing away the potato and glorifying the potato peel.

It is far simpler to think of the soul in terms of Telstar. It takes two booster-rockets to free it of gravity and set it in astral orbit. As soon as the rockets fulfill their function, they burn out and fall away, just as the flesh body—the earthly shell of the soul—burns out and falls away in death, to be followed by the expended "ego," the discarded conscious mind of the earth shell.

The soul is no longer entrapped in matter. It is free. All that it retains from its sojourn in its earth shell is the total recall of its worldly experiences, now safely stored in its "memory bank." But only the "conscious" mind has been discarded.

The subconscious mind has survived because it neither consists of, nor depends on, matter. It now becomes the conscious mind of the soul, and will continue to function as such until the soul returns into the earth's dense matter to begin its next life.

Meanwhile the superconscious mind assumes the functions relinquished by the subconscious mind, and the soul is now articulate as it could never be on earth. The "ecstasy" that certain Saints achieve is probably akin to a momentary recapturing of the exhilaration the soul enjoys at this level of existence.

When the time comes for the soul to return to earth and assume its next body, the process is quite simply reversed. The conscious mind returns to the subconscious level, and the subconscious mind returns to the superconscious level, where it subsides back into a womb-like sanctuary in the flesh body. It neither seeks nor desires emotional association with the pursuits of the subconscious mind and the new-born conscious mind, as they accustom themselves to their new ego.

Only very rarely, in a very few cases, can the superconscious mind be contacted—and then only by expert deep hypnosis. (While Edgar Cayce was able to contact his superconscious by means of his own quite unique form of self-hypnosis, it must be born in mind by the reader that he is the exception, not the rule, at this present level of our universal development. He is a glimpse of ourselves as we will be tomorrow.)

The "new-born" conscious mind, then, can never be older in age than the new body which is temporarily housing it. The new-born's accumulated store of wisdom, its caution and its intuitive appraisal of both itself and its fellow men all lie at the subconscious level. Thus the only friend and counsellor to which it can turn is its own subconscious mind. Moreover, it can only make this contact while asleep in the "dream state," or by the enlightened process of meditation. Here, by dint of self-discipline, it trains itself to sit and listen for the "still small voice of conscience."

In its waking hours, at the conscious level, the newborn must meet again all the novel distractions of material existence, picking its way as best it can across the stepping stones that span the treacherous crosscurrents of life, avoiding—if it heeds its "still small voice"—the excesses of self-indulgence that have so often tripped it and sent it headlong into the waters churning round it.

Has it any means of anticipating in advance the problems it will have to face?

Yes, indeed, if we liken the lives of the soul to the installments of a serialized novel in a magazine. As your soul dies at the end of a life, "to be continued in our next issue," is parenthetically added in small print to that installment. When you appear again in a new body, you do not start from scratch; you pick up exactly where you left off.

If you had failed to curb a passion for pitching rocks through greenhouse windows in the life before, you can resign yourself to being born into the equivalent of a greenhouse, where you will have to learn to enjoy the discomfort of being at the "receiving end" of the rocks. If you grin and bear it while the panes are bashed out one by one until the score is evened, you will not be doing so badly. But if you collapse in self-pity, insisting that you have done nothing to deserve your fate, you are obviously in a sad way, and your overall gains are doomed to be minimal.

Edgar Cayce himself had no false pride about admitting, that some of his lives could have been better spent—that he had often given in to anger and impatience—that the fleshpots of prehistoric Egypt, for example, had offered sufficient temptation to distract him from the thorny path of total advancement.

It was as much to put his own spiritual house in order as to help his fellow creatures that he shouldered the onerous responsibility of his clairvoyance in this life.

Where did he obtain his information, when he set out to give a Life Reading?

In a talk he gave at the Cayce Hospital in 1931 he explained it in these words: "Let me tell you now of an experience of my own. I feel that it was a very real experience, and as near an illustration of what happens at death as it would be possible to put into words. On going into the unconscious state, on one occasion, to obtain information for an individual, I recognized that I was leaving my body.

"There was just a direct, straight, and narrow line in front of me, like a shaft of white light. On either side was fog and smoke, and many shadowy figures who seemed to be crying to me for help, and begging me to come aside to the plane they occupied.

"As I followed along the shaft of light, the way began to clear. The figures on either side grew more distinct; they took on clearer form. But there was a continual beckoning back, or the attempt to sidetrack me and bring me aside from my purpose. Yet with the narrow way in front of me, I kept going straight ahead. After a while I passed to where the figures were merely shadows attempting to urge me on, rather than to stop me. As they took on more form, they seemed to be occupied with their own activities.

"Finally I came to a hill, where there was a mount and a temple. I entered this temple and found in it a very large room, very much like a library. Here were the books of people's lives, for each person's activities were a matter of actual record, it seemed. And I merely had to pull down the record of the individual for whom I was seeking information. I have to say as Paul did, 'Whether I was in the spirit or out of the spirit, I cannot tell'; but that was an actual experience."

Free Will Is Stronger than Destiny

When he touched on the previous lives of the people who came to him for help, Edgar Cayce constantly insisted that karma was memory, thus the laws of cause and effect were elastic. The soul, like a "trusty" in a penitentiary, can always get its sentence "reduced for good behavior" by cooperating with authority. One lifetime of genuine sacrifice to the welfare of others, such as Schweitzer's or Father Damien's, might well equalize five or six sterile existences where progress stood still and the soul fell behind in the parade.

Free will, in short, is always stronger than pre-ordained destiny. No soul is ever so encumbered with old debts that it must drearily resign itself to pay and pay and pay.

But we must also allow for the fact that the soul can sometimes advance itself by methods that need not be immediately apparent to our powers of conscious reason. The blind man healed by Christ, for example, was not blind because he had sinned, but because his soul was gaining stature from the experience of blindness.

It is absolutely essential to understand and accept this simple concept before proceeding to deal with the more complex issues which will arise, as we treat individual cases in more detail.

However sore the straits may be in which you find yourself, you put yourself there by your own previous indifference to the laws. Whatever laws you broke, you broke of your own free will, the free will given you in the beginning by your Maker. You alone chose to be where you are at this moment. This, at least, allows you the dignity and self-respect of knowing that you made your own mistakes—even if it destroys the convenient sugar-coated alibi that you are the victim of an angry, vengeful and palpably half-witted Jehovah, who controls you with invisible strings from the flies of a most naively ill-conceived marionette-master's Hereafter.

To conceive of a fretful God of Vengeance at the controls of this immaculately operating Solar System is to credit a tin lizzie full of Mack Sennett cops with the ability to break up traffic jams on a crowded eight-lane freeway.

That is why the hell-fire doctrines of original sin and the enlightened tenets of true religion have never been able to coincide.

The only God the sleeping Edgar Cayce knew was a loving God of infinite mercy, who has already forgiven us all.

As the reader begins to take more heed of the processes involved in the theory of reincarnation, let him bear in mind that every one of its laws stem from such a concept, and could not function otherwise.

CHAPTER 4

PHYSICAL AND EMOTIONAL KARMA

The Wages of Virtue, and the Wages of Sin

WHEN PAUL DURBIN was thirty-four years of age, with a wife and a child to support, he was stricken with multiple sclerosis, or creeping paralysis, and his right leg and arm began to wither.

Though Paul's family was all but destitute, good friends rallied to his aid. They paid for his hospitalization, obtained his Physical Reading, and even administered the massages which the Reading advised. His condition soon began to improve.

But significantly, the Reading also made reference to a past incarnation in which he had indulged his negative passions to excess.

"The Entity is at war with itself. All hate, all malice, all that will make men afraid, must be eliminated from the mind. For, as given of old, each soul shall give an account of every idle word spoken. It shall pay every whit. Yet the Entity knows, or should know, that there is an advocate with the Father.

"For, as given, 'Though ye wander far, if ye call I will answer speedily!' Then, right about face! Know that the Lord liveth and would do thee good, if ye but trust wholly in Him!"

In short, a soul had but to acknowledge by its penitence that it had gone astray, and help would be forthcoming in exact proportion to his sincerity.

The warning fell on deaf ears. Durbin, saturated with bitterness and self-pity, dismissed such an idea as rubbish and demanded to know why Cayce had failed to cure him miraculously and instantaneously. He even vented his frustration on the people trying to help him, playing them off against each other until they regretted their involvement.

Nevertheless his condition improved for a while. When the improvement failed to stabilize, he complained even more bitterly than before.

His next Reading was phrased in blunter language: "This is a karmic condition, and there must be measures taken for the body to change the attitudes towards conditions, things, and its fellow man.

"First there should be a change of heart, a change of mind, of purpose, a change of intent. If this is done, then keep up the massages and the use of the appliances suggested. But all the mechanical appliances that ye muster will not aid complete recovery, unless thy soul has been baptized with the Holy Spirit! In Him, then, is thy hope. Will ye reject it? The body is indeed the temple of the living God, but what does it appear to be in the present?

"Broken in purpose, broken in ability to reproduce itself.

"What is lacking? That which is life itself, that influence or force ye call God. Will ye accept, will ye reject? It is up to thee!

"As long as there are hate, malice, injustice—those things which are at variance to patience, long suffering, brotherly love—there cannot be a healing of this body. What would the body be healed for? That it might gratify its own physical desires and appetites? That it might add to its own selfishness?

"Then, if so, it had better remain as it is!

"We are through—unless ye make amends."

This Reading was deliberately selected for its uncharacteristic austerity. The correspondence in the A.R.E. files is mute testimony to the recalcitrance of this patient, determined not to stir a finger in his own behalf, demanding the restoration of his health as his due.

Why did Paul Durbin suffer? Why do any of us suffer, if it comes to that?

"All illness is sin," said Cayce, and he does not necessarily mean sin committed consciously in the present life, but sin expressing itself as illness because it has not yet been expiated by the soul.

Karma, the abacus on which the gains and losses of the soul are scored from life to life, is often wrongly and unjustly confused with retribution. It is too meticulous and dispassionate for that; its ultimate purpose too benign. But while it is acting as a painful cure for an even more painful relapse, it can be bitter gall indeed.

Apparently a certain type of mortal suffering can be a salutary astringent to the torpors of the subconscious mind, when all subtler warnings have failed to persuade the ego to exert itself in its own best interests. "Whom the lord loveth, he chastizeth," has more kindness than irony in it, when viewed in this light.

The Readings divide karma into two rough categories—emotional karma and physical karma. Each of these has, of necessity, its positive and negative aspects—its good and bad.

Under the negative emotional heading, we find such symptoms as incompatible marriage, alcoholism, impotence, neuroses such as manic depression and paranoia, mental perversions, and even possession in its medieval sense.

On the physical side, it manifests itself in such defects as deafness, blindness, speech impediments, and the killer diseases such as leukemia and multiple sclerosis.

Through his entire life as a seer, Edgar Cayce devoted the bulk of his efforts to the successful diagnosis of bodily ailments. On many occasions, however, he traced them not to physical causes, but to an inevitable moment of truth at the subconscious level, when self must answer to self. The murderer who shed innocent blood in one life will balance the scale in another by symbolically shedding his own. More than one case of leukemia was directly attributed to this reckoning.

But the remedy need not always be so drastic as it was in the case of Paul Durbin. The Law of Grace is a perpetually available alternative to the soul— the working off of accumulated debts, by unselfish dedication to the welfare of others even less fortunate than itself—in Edgar's own words, "what you sow you reap, unless you have passed from the carnal, or karmic, law to the Law of Grace." Most souls seem to hover between the two extremes.

The next case of physical karma deals with a woman who successfully overcame the challenge which faced her.

Stella Kirby, a quiet, retiring woman, divorced and with a child to support, was advised by a friend to take up nursing. She had no sooner completed her training than she was sent to apply for a private post at nearly twice the normal fee. She was interviewed by the housekeeper of an imposing mansion, a pleasant woman who took an instinctive liking to her and hired her on the spot. The house was well staffed and elegantly run, the food was excellent and her quarters almost luxurious. All this, coupled with the generous salary, was more than Stella had dared hope for. But when she was taken to her patient's bedroom, she was confronted by a man of fifty-seven in a state of imbecility. His bed was encased by an iron cage, and in it he sat systematically shredding every article of his clothing, blank-eyed and incapable of all normal functions. He could neither speak nor respond to speech. He had to be fed like an infant, sometimes forcibly, and he resisted all and every effort to keep him clean.

Dismayed, but determined to do her best despite the revulsion she felt, Stella entered the cage to give him his bath, and the moment she touched him she was overcome by such nausea that she had to retire to the bathroom and vomit.

When the revulsion showed no signs of abating, she realized she had to give up the job and the security she badly needed. Fortunately, she was able to journey to Virginia Beach and appeal personally to Edgar Cayce for help— and thus, one of the most bizarre of his case histories unfolded.

Twice before, the paths of Stella and her patient had crossed. In Egypt he had been her son. The revulsion she felt for him stemmed from a life in the Middle East when he had been a wealthy philanthropist of high standing, greatly honored for his generosity. Privately, however, he retained a kind of seraglio of young women who were obliged to participate in his abnormal sexual practices, and she had been one of the unfortunate women involved.

The memory of the degradation and disgust had returned the moment she had touched his flesh, while he, poor devil, again surrounded by every material luxury and comfort, had met his karma—with a vengeance. It is hard to conceive of a soul more destitute and debased.

Yet Cayce insisted (as he did in every similar case) that the crippled mind was capable of responding to love—that Stella must, in short, learn to love him if she ever hoped to surmount her own karmic barriers. To leave the house would be no solution: the bond between them would simply continue, unresolved, into their future lives.

Years later, Stella described her first reactions to her Reading. The idea of reincarnation was completely new to her, yet she instinctively responded to it. God had never been clear or real to her before; now she found herself able to comprehend Him. All her life she had felt such a compassion for cripples that before the birth of her daughter, her one fear had been that the child would be born with deformed legs. This stemmed from a life she had spent in Palestine, where she had nursed and healed the weak and maimed—an experience which could now reward her a hundredfold. Even the housekeeper who had employed her had been with her in Palestine, and this had accounted for the mutual liking they felt for one another as soon as they met.

Stella remained, but the idea of conveying love to the pitiful creature she was nursing all but defeated her. Several times she felt she must admit defeat, but the Readings always urged her to keep trying, and eventually her patient began to show signs of responding. He obeyed her utterly, ate his food instead of rejecting it, began to keep himself clean, and no longer tore his clothes to shreds. And as she moved about the room, his eyes followed her with dog-like devotion.

Her love had conveyed itself to his paralyzed brain, as Cayce had insisted it would; and with the realization that he was once more loved, he was released from his own immediate hell. He might well have lingered on for an interminable span of years, yet he was able to die peacefully within two years, and Stella was able to go forward into a balanced and rewarding life of her own.

The Readings were too compassionate to refer to the relationship between the two when she had been his mother in Egypt, but since there is no effect without cause, she would hardly have been subject to his obscene fetishes in the Near East unless she already owed him a debt. One can assume that she had failed her son in Egypt, either by neglect or rejection, at a point in their mutual destiny where her help could have prevented him from plunging off onto the self-annihilating path which brought them together again in the Middle East. Here again, where her love might have wakened a response in his profligate soul, she withheld it, thus stretching out the misery to span yet another life.

The Case of the Mongoloid Child

Physical and emotional karma combine again in the following case history of a man and his wife who had been closely associated in at least two of their previous lives. Both could be called highly developed souls, but they were nevertheless meeting a challenge, a test, which they might well have failed without the help of their Life Reading.

The six-year-old child of Myra and David Cobler was a Mongoloid. The Coblers asked if their conduct in their past lives was to blame, and the answer was phrased with great delicacy.

Not all the lives "were pretty," and though the present life had been so far disappointing, Myra's sublimated longing to be a novelist could yet express itself if it would use for material the very lessons she was learning from the sorrow in her own home. Her passionate nature, her longing for affection and her deep spiritual loneliness could all be turned to positive account. In regard to the love and patient care the child needed, as she gave of it with more and more freedom, so could she build a life of beauty for the next child she would bear.

"Do not blame self," Edgar told her, "do not blame thy companion. Do not blame God." She and her husband had reached that plateau where "self must meet self" and jointly put their records to rights. If they succeeded in this, they would so aid the soul of their child to free itself from its own karma that it would never again need to incarnate in a deformed shape.

The child's soul, said Edgar, "is thy problem with God, not to be put aside until He, who is the Giver of Life, sees fit to call it home to prepare for the better life that ye have made possible in thy kindness to thy follow man."

What had Myra done to reach such a fate? Her previous life had been wretchedly spent in a frontier post in the early middle west under the name of Jane Richter; yet for all its squalor it had laid the foundation for her intense longing to make her home secure and congenial in this life.

Her Reading then traced her back to Palestine "when the Master walked in the earth." The name of Dorcas established her as a woman of Greek or Roman origin, as did her sophisticated skepticism of the miraculous powers attributed to the Messiah. Not having bothered to seek Him out and judge for herself, "the Entity made fun of, yea rebuked those" who believed he was indeed the Son of God. It was not until the day of Pentecost that His path crossed hers. When she saw the outpouring of the Holy Spirit, she was converted, but felt it was too late to atone for her apostasy. "But it is never too late to mend thy ways," Edgar exhorted her. "For life is eternal, and ye are what ye are today because of what you have been. For ye are the co-creator with thy Maker, that ye may one day be present with all of those who love His coming."

In this Palestinian life, her husband's fate-line converged with hers. He was one of the Seventy chosen to spread the gospel throughout the land. He failed because he took certain of the Teachings literally instead of symbolically.

Particularly had he been offended by the purely spiritual content of "Except ye eat of My body, ye have no part of Me."

His name was Elias and he was a friend of two of the disciples, though he "leaned more towards the staid Andrew than the boisterous Peter," for he could reason with Andrew whereas he could only argue with Peter.

The Reading then suggested that if both David and Myra reattuned their memories to the arguments they had once heard from these two disciples, it would awaken positive attitudes in their own thinking in the present.

"For the law of the Lord is perfect. It converteth the soul if it is used, not abused, in the application," The Reading continued. "As the Entity learned in his experience as Elias, healing of the physical without the change in the mental and spiritual aspects, brings little real help to the individual in the end."

One last sojourn is suggested—and only very lightly—in the Egypt of 10,000 B.C. where David, under the name of Atel El, had served as an aide to the surgeons in a Temple of Healing, and Myra had been educated in the cultural arts in a similar type of Temple.

This period saw the development of a sub-race of primitive souls from a retarded evolution, only slightly above the animal level, to the full stature of bodies "fashioned in God's image." These humanoids or mutants feature extensively in the Atlantean records as a primitive form of antediluvian life, the last faint echoes of which linger in Shakespeare's Caliban and in the fauns, centaurs and minotaurs of Greek mythology. They were for the most part defenseless and pitiful beasts of burden which had been used for slave labor by the Atlanteans, and the purpose of the Temple was to hasten their evolution by corrective surgery. This involved the use of the laser, followed by ritual purification in the name of the One God. In these far distant beginnings, then, we may infer that these two souls were first taught to care for the maimed and helpless; and that the troubled soul who came to them in the present as a mongoloid child did so because it remembered their aid and compassion when it was first struggling to acquire human status.

This would account for the compassion and deep concern the Reading conveys to all three of them throughout. If they have strayed off their appointed path, one feels they have strayed very slightly. The bonds forged in Palestine were too strong to fail them entirely.

Which one of them had gone most recently astray? David, perhaps.

His last life before his present incarnation had been as William Cowper, "a keeper of the records" at the time of the American Revolution when Washington was rallying his demoralized forces at Trenton, prior to turning the tide of battle towards eventual victory. Here William Cowper, in charge of the victualing of that section of the Army, was involved in some kind of disaster which resulted in loss of limb to some of the volunteer patriots.

"Here a word of warning would be given," says the Reading cryptically. "Beware of a body that is malformed, or where some portion of a limb or activity is amiss; it may bring thee great distress."

Cowper had apparently been one of a group that stumbled into a British ambush. In his anger at the carnage, Cowper held his own officers responsible, even though it was not the fault of "those in authority, but was by accident." The shock of seeing his companions killed and mutilated had burned deep into his memory, however. Unable to forgive his officers in that life, the inability to forgive had manifested itself in his present life as a major hindrance to his peace of mind. The sight of a cripple would automatically rekindle his old bitterness and sense of injustice, thus inflaming and clouding his judgment—even when it affected his helpless child.

His urgent need was to practice forgiveness, tolerance and understanding in all his dealings with others. Only thus could he approach his emotional problems constructively.

The almost paternal kindness in which these two Readings were couched leave little doubt that Myra and David Cobler cared for their Mongoloid child until "He who is the Giver of Life saw fit to call it home."

This might be an example, then, of the Law of Grace superceding the law of karma, thus sponging the slate clean of accumulated debts.

What of the child itself? An indication is reflected in another Reading for a chronically retarded child. This soul held a position of authority in the court during an English incarnation, much akin to the voluptuary Lord Buckingham, whose rapacious exploitation of his privileges and influence contributed to the beheading of Charles I and even had repercussions in the French court, where his liaison with the Queen all but destroyed her.

"The Entity turned away from those who were without hope, who were disturbed in body and mind, preferring to indulge the appetites in self. Here we find the Entity is overtaken, and what he has sown, he is reaping."

To the parents who faithfully nursed the child with protective affection, the Reading was particularly approving. "For through your love and service, the soul-consciousness of this Entity may become aware of the power of true, abiding love to inspire individuals to protect those who are dependent on their care, for the soul of this Entity is entering an awakening in the present. Sow the seeds of truth, hope and mercy, of kindness and patience, that this soul shall learn at last that 'I am my brother's keeper!' "

Irene McGinley first came to Edgar Cayce's attention when she applied for a Physical Reading at the age of seventeen. An attractive, intelligent and talented young girl, she was already bedridden with an erosion of the femur, and her doctors had recommended amputation of the leg at the hip to prevent further spread of the cancer. She was a member of a large well-to-do family, and the wife of an elder brother also lived in the house. Though she had children of her own, Kit, the sister-in-law, was very ably filling the role of Irene's companion and part-time nurse. The treatment suggested by Irene's Physical Reading obviated the need for the amputation and placed her on the road to recovery. But we are concerned here with the Life Reading she subsequently requested.

Yet again we find physical and emotional karma meeting at a predestined crossroad. All the people involved were aware of mutual ties, but on the surface there were none of the character conflicts that appear so often in situations of this kind. All that manifested itself was the apparent injustice of Irene's affliction.

"One refined of taste," the first Life Reading described Irene. "The mental abilities are keen; love's influence bringing the greater experiences . . . as in the seeking for something in a constant manner in the developing of mental and physical abilities in self."

Straightaway the tone is optimistic. It presupposes a normal and productive life. Cayce calls her a dreamer, a builder of castles in the air, and suggests that writing is the form of creative expression best suited to her, but that it should always be anchored to reality. In the life before, she had been an early settler in America. Pretty speeches meant little to her, for she judged people by their actions, not their good intentions. She was honest and forthright in her religious convictions, and skilled in sewing, knitting and spinning.

But the life before that found her in the Rome of the Emperor Nero during the persecution of the Christians, the daughter of a wealthy and influential government official. Among the women of the household she observed with discreet caution the impact of Christianity on their lives. Here we find the first clue to her misfortune—"laughing at another's sincerity has brought physical defects . . . as does the holding of grudges, as does selfish interests."

Cayce began the second Life Reading with a deft analysis of the soul's memory bank. This, as it registers its experiences in the Akashic Record, "is to the mental world as the cinema is to the physical world."

Now we find that Kit, her present sister-in-law, had been the daughter of one of the guards assigned to the Roman household. There was presumably a close bond between the two girls, for they shared a deep love of music, and Kit was treated as an equal. Kit was also a secret convert to Christianity, and Irene found herself being drawn more and more to the teachings of the Master, although she took care to conceal her sympathies when she attended the persecutions in the Coliseum. This was perfectly logical and understandable conduct when one took Nero's insanity into account. Any high-born Roman lady expressing leanings towards Christianity stood a good chance of joining the martyrs in the arena.

Cayce's allusions to unhappy love affairs are always tactfully phrased, but we are led to assume that Kit attracted the affection of a man Irene herself favored. In Irene's angry desire to punish the man she betrayed her friend to the authorities so that her lover could witness his loved-one's death in the arena. Seated beside him in the audience, she laughed at his horror as the girl he loved was mauled to death by a wild beast before his eyes. Irene's laughter had obviously stemmed from a hysteria of jealousy, and not from callous glee, but the karmic bond was forged. Retribution followed swiftly. The man, broken-hearted, never recovered from the horror of the spectacle, and she was forced to watch him waste away before her eyes. Her conscience was further tormented whenever she heard the music Kit and she had sung and played together, "especially of the lyre, harp, or of the zither." Then her remorse caused her interminable suffering.

"Hence in meeting same in the present, the Entity passes under the rod, as it were. She is now being pitied, laughed at, scorned for the inability to take part in any activity that requires the full use of the physical body.

"The Entity may now overcome those things that have beset, knowing how life is to be met: no scorn, no sneer, but with patience and fortitude, with praise, with the giving of pleasure in music, in kindnesses, in gentle words, in bespeaking of that which may build for a perfect mind, a perfect soul, a perfect body . . . for the weaknesses of the flesh are the scars of the soul, and these can be healed only by making the will one with His, being washed, as it were, in the blood of the Lamb."

The punishment here seems to be not for the laughter itself, but for the *crime passionel*—the cold betrayal of a rival whose religious faith she secretly shared.

What of Kit's own karma?

In prehistoric Egypt and again in Arabia, she had gained and lost. In Egypt she developed the talent for nursing which enabled her to care for Irene in the present; but she had been vain and jealous of her social position in Arabia, and resentful when age caused her to relinquish it.

In the Roman period she had made a great spiritual advance; the sermons of Paul himself, delivered at the secret meetings in the catacombs, had converted her so thoroughly that she died bearing Irene no grudge.

In the next life, however, as a child of twelve in a French inn, she witnessed the recognition and arrest of Louis XVI and Marie Antoinette just as they were about to escape to safety on the eve of the Terror. The fever-heat of the times stimulated an ambition in her to be part of the Revolution, and as soon as she was old enough she sped to Paris, where the turbulence of the times soon lifted her to a position of influence in political circles, and where her self-aggrandizement eventually brought about her own downfall.

In her present life, she had restrained this ambition in herself and pursued the wise course of marrying and concerning herself with her family's well-being. The help and care generously given her younger sister-in-law did much to balance the karmic debts she had acquired elsewhere. She even overcame her inborn fear of animals, derived from her death in the arena.

Irene, in her own turn, restored to health by her Physical Reading, followed Edgar's advice to take up the harp, and discovered she possessed an inborn talent for it to a professional degree. Retired from the concert stage, she still uses the harp even today, in the kindergarten she conducts, to create and mold a love of music in her charges.

Thus Irene and Kit represent an example of the positive application of both emotional and physical karma. Indeed, it is seldom one comes across the manifestations of one without the other operating somewhere in accord nearby.

A notable exception is the following case, where emotional karma came into its own with none of the overtones of physical disability—only a soul inheriting the rewards awaiting it for "good conduct."

Two years before Edgar Cayce died, Norah Connor, a widow of thirty-one, applied to him for vocational guidance. "Yes," began the Reading, "we have the records here. What a muddle-puddle; and yet what a talented soul!

"Here we find an Entity who may be said to combine all that is beautiful, gracious and lovely; and all the mischief-making that one might imagine.

"Suffering has cleansed the mind much. It has set it towards helping others. This is marvelous, for it is well for most individuals even to be in the presence of this Entity.

"What a wonderful companion this Entity would make for a school that would teach spirituality as well as graciousness in the home, in motherhood, in things having to do with the making of a home! These should be the activities of the Entity.

"True, through the periods of the present conditions (World War II), give thyself to the activities in Red Cross Service. For ye can encourage many in such a way that they will never again grumble at their hardships.

"But when these conditions have passed, begin and work with groups in music or art, in social science, even in political economy, any undertaking that deals with the emotions, with all forms of character-building for teen-aged girls. Do apply yourself in these directions, for abilities here are far, far beyond the ordinary.

"Do not allow the ravings of others to deter thee from what ye know to be thy spiritual and mental duty. Do keep that beauty of love, of hope, of gentleness, of graciousness, that is the innate characteristic of the Entity."

The Reading then proceeds to delineate her previous life as the wife of a frontiersman in the early settling of America. There she learned to tend to the women and children, hold the settlement together, provide against the harassment of the Indians by setting up storehouses for food, and dressing the wounds of the men after the raids. "Then in the name Anna Corphon, the Entity created the environs of home life in surroundings that would have put many a strong-hearted man to shame. For, despite the hardships and those conditions that existed among the natives, the Entity builded friendships, having learned that the self should not offend and not be offended by others. With such an attitude one will, indeed, eventually find peace in self. There must be harmony in self before ye can bring it to others.

"The Entity has found it, loses it at times; but keeping thy trust in Him, will never weary in well-doing.

"Before that, the Entity was in the Palestine land when the Master walked in the earth. The Entity was among the children at Bethsaida who were blessed by Him. Thus the desire, ever active and latent since that experience, to emulate His laughter, His thoughtfulness, His care for others. For as the Entity applied herself through that period when there were trials, then in the name Samantha, she encouraged those who became weary and weak from the temptations of the flesh which arise at times in every human in materiality. Hence the Entity is a most gracious hostess, a most loving individual with those close and those apart."

One of the written questions she put to Edgar Cayce was: "Is there any indication of what church I should join and associate myself with?"

"Remember, rather, the church is within self," he answered. "As to the denomination, choose one, whatever its name, not as a convenience for thee but where ye may serve the better. Let it be thy life proclaiming Jesus, the Christ."

"Any other advice?" was the final question.

"Why tell beauty to be beautiful? Just keep sweet," she was told with unwonted gallantry.

A fairly clear portrait emerges from her letter of gratitude to Edgar Cayce: "The Reading certainly expresses my most inmost desires and aspirations. My dominant desire and interest has always been in homemaking, and I love serving people. I find that at the present time I am very much interested in social studies—geography, history—and English as related to present day community and world affairs.

"As to the music and art referred to, my interest has been more in its use in connection with worship services. I think that the course in college that I liked best of all, and in which I received an A, was Fine Arts in Religion.

"I know I must have 'peace and harmony' in myself if I am to give it to others. And when I lose that peace and harmony I'm like a lost soul struggling to get back on the right path again.

"I have changed jobs so many times that it seems as if I should stick to one over a year. I realize that I can only decide on opportunities as they come along, but I do get in such a stew. (As you say 'What a muddle-puddle!')"

For the rest of the war years Norah devoted herself to the Red Cross and discovered she had a natural propensity for organization. She rose to a position of executive responsibility equaled by very few. Emergencies brought out the best in her, and at the end of the war she was decorated for her services. She continued to serve with the Red Cross, specializing in rescue work in disaster areas.

As Hugh Lynn Cayce notes in his check report, made in 1957, "Mrs. Connor continued to work for the Red Cross, as was suggested in the Reading. We wondered whether the rescue work along the Delaware River and Louisiana took her into the areas associated in her Reading with the 'pioneer days when she overcame insurmountable difficulties and did a good job.'

"She also described her problems with a superior official in the disaster work, when the word 'ravings,' indicated in her Life Reading, might well apply to the supervisor's criticism of her over-zealousness in giving help and comfort to the flood survivors.

"She is now employed in Boston University in charge of a dormitory of 150 girls. She intends to take courses that will prepare her for work in a smaller establishment where she can devote herself to the education of younger girls, as suggested by her Reading. She also indicated that she enjoyed Girl Scout work, especially the outdoor life, camping, etc.

"As a matter of interest, the interview with her was most pleasant throughout, and in my observation, confirmed the Reading's assessment of her character in full measure."

Fear of Childbirth

"I'm almost on the eve of insanity and suicide, the most miserable woman on earth and almost a dope fiend," reads an excerpt from one of the more extensively documented cases. Flora Lingstrand, born 1879, was forty-six years of age when she wrote for help. Her troubles began with a neurotic mother whose terror of death in childbirth increased with each successful birth of her six children. Flora's childhood was warped by her mother's lugubrious harping on her one fixation. And when Flora eventually embarked on her own marriage, she found her reason paralyzed by the inherited phobia. Her husband was a decent and sympathetic man who did all he could to understand and help, but birth control was apparently out of the question, and she was so obsessively terrified of pregnancy that eventually she separated from him. He still helped her with what money he could afford, and in an ill-advised moment she decided to have her ovaries removed.

In her incoherent letters to Edgar Cayce, Flora implied that radium was used, and that the "bromides" they subsequently administered, created in her an addiction to narcotics. This was compounded by chronic over-eating and haphazard consultations with various psychiatrists.

"I cannot go to another sanitarium for the analysts do not talk anything but sex life . . . they say my suppressions have caused my nerves and dread of children, and after they told me the trouble, it stuck in my mind until I cannot bear my husband near me. I am afraid all the time, and fear is horrible," Flora wrote.

Flora was a tragic figure. Her self absorbtion blinded her to the needs of others, and in that area lay her only chance of salvation. To this day, her voluminous letters make pathetic reading, yet one cannot quite reject the impression that her occasional bursts of remorse for the suffering she is causing her husband are "words for the sake of words."

Her Life Reading patiently assures her that her case is not as hopeless as she is determined to make it, but states quite clearly on its first page that the source of the trouble lies in the need for the soul to correct and overcome its old preoccupations with self-aggrandizement, "desires of the flesh," and lack of consideration for the human rights of others.

"One lovable in many ways, one with high aspirations, many never attained! The goal is always whisked away just as she is about to attain it. In the purpose, good. In the actions from within, and of the use of will towards self, not good. Its relations with others, in the greater portion excellent . . . with itself, negligible."

Her previous life was as Sara Golden, one of the steelers who came to Roanoke in Carolina—the "Lost Colony" which disappeared without trace in 1590.

Here she was forced to witness all her children "taken and scourged in the fire, and the Entity lived in dread throughout her remaining days." As her reason failed her, she began to curse God in fury for allowing her children to be destroyed. "This, in the present, brings the dread of the Entity for the bearing of children . . . and has brought destructive forces into the Entity's (present) sojourn."

She had, in brief, returned without hope of forgiveness from the God she had reviled. But this is a manifestation of her own guilt, not the retaliation of a secular deity; therefore her sin is only against self.

The life before that was squandered at the French court of one of the Charleses, which means prior to 1515 . . . "a somber age of traitors and cut-throats." As one of the King's clerks given to excesses of debauchery, the forfeiting of subsequent domestic happiness had its beginnings. We have to search all the way back to ancient Greece to find the soul as yet uncorrupted. And in prehistoric Egypt she had "stood immaculate and tall" as a priestess in one of the Temples of Initiation.

The Reading ends with no promise of quick panaceas: "The Entity may gain only through service to others, for in serving self without respect for the good that may come into the lives of others, self blocks the way. When we build a barrier between ourselves and our associates, our friends, or our families, this we must, of our own volition, tear down, would we fill that place that is necessary for each and every individual to fill, that has its existence in the physical plane.

". . . . Those spirit forces which are innate may become so subjugated by the desires of the flesh that they become as nil. Yet these are ever ready to be awakened and to exercise their prerogative in the life of each and every individual. But self must be subjugated before such may come about."

Following this is a suggestion that Flora develop a latent talent for writing, and that she choose for her subject matter a positive philosophy that would have an uplifting influence on its readers.

Flora Lingstrand seized the help Edgar offered, with the frenzy of someone drowning, but one cannot but feel that despite the protestations of gratitude that poured from her, she had been expecting some kind of miraculous intercession which would exempt her from having to make any personal effort in her own behalf.

One will often come across this tendency to expect of Edgar, contrary to his explicit warning, that he be not a counsellor but an extension of the Angel Who Troubled the Waters at the Pool of Bethesda. The act of immersion alone was expected to constitute a complete cure. Whereas Edgar never deviated from his one principle: only faith in a benevolent God enables the soul to reassess itself and put itself to rights.

By the same token, Cayce was never a man to mince words if he was confronted by lassitude or self-pity trying to pass itself off as a hapless casualty of karma.

"Is there some karmic debt to be worked off with either or both of my parents?" a young woman asked him. "And should I stay with them until I have made them feel more kindly towards me?"

"What is karmic debt?" he answered crisply. "You have made this a bugaboo! It is not a karmic debt between you and your parents; it is a karmic debt to self which may be worked out between you and your associates in the present! And this is true for every soul!"

"Would it be best to remain in the same apartment with my family for the present, or try to borrow money enough to get a place of my own?"

"It would be better to remain," he advised. "If the antagonism between self and family continues, then change. Separation at the moment would leave not only animosity and a feeling of spitefulness on the part of self, but also on the part of the family, which would build that which you have learned, or been taught, to call karma."

Her next question was suitably chastened:

"What is there wrong about my personality which is holding me back, physically and mentally?"

"Nothing," he said amiably, "save improper evaluation of self in the present experience!"

Arrogance and Self-righteousness

We now concern ourselves with the emotional karma of a beautiful girl in her early thirties, a compulsive drinker, who was involving herself in one promiscuous affair after another. When she was sober she bitterly condemned herself, but remained incorrigible. Her Reading informed her that her avid nymphomania originated in a French incarnation when she was a king's daughter. It was a period of immorality and materialism, and she had not hesitated to sit in judgment over weaker women than herself, leaving little room for tolerance or pity in her self-righteous condemnations. She ultimately retired to a convent to avoid further "contamination" by her fellow-creatures, obviously leaving a trail of persecution behind her.

"Ye condemned those whose activities were in direct disobedience to the law," her Reading informed her. "But he who is weak in the flesh, is his error the greater? For one should know that the condemning of others is already a condemning of self. Which is the greater sin?"

Hate and self-centered arrogance had also dogged a woman who took her own life in a Persian incarnation. She had been the proud daughter of a wealthy tribal chief who was captured by Bedouins and given in marriage to a young captain who had fallen desperately and sincerely in love with her. This could have been an opportunity for soul growth, but to a woman of her ferocious pride it was intolerable degradation. When she bore him a daughter, she found no consolation in motherhood. Unable to overcome her hatred and contempt for her abductors, she committed suicide, abandoning her baby to its own fate.

Today, lonely and unmarried, she longs for a baby girl with such intensity that she is even prepared to adopt one. She is thwarted in this because she has been embroiled in an obsessive love affair which has dragged on interminably and frittered her life away. Of her incompatible lover, she asked: "Why have I only received unfairness from him, when I have tried so hard to be fair?"

"As he is treating you in the present, so you treated him in that Persian experience," Cayce told her. "As ye mete it unto others, it shall be meted unto you!"

The same boomerang struck a young man who had been a caricaturist in the French court of Louis XVI. He had lampooned those unfortunate members of the court who were unable to conceal their homosexuality. In this life he is mortified to find himself struggling against the same compulsion, and though his Reading was able to help him, it again pointed out that "Whatsoever we mete unto others, we mete unto ourselves."

A Definitive Credo

The philosophy of the Life Readings takes on such a universality in the following excerpt that one is tempted to call it a definitive credo for every living soul, regardless of sex or age.

"From Saturn we find the sudden changes that have been and are a characteristic of the Entity—in this, Mars plays a part. When these two planets are together, there is an adverse influence, a wrath or madness, bringing great disturbance to the mental being of the Entity.

"Hence it behooves the Entity to keep before itself an ideal, not merely for the sake of being idealistic, but as a standard by which it can judge its own deeds. For the ideal of what is right can never apply only to self.

"For if ye would have life, ye must give it! As the laws apply in the spiritual, so do they apply in practice. For Mind is the Builder.

"If ye would have love, ye must show thyself lovable. If ye would have friends, ye must show thyself friendly. If ye would have peace and harmony, forget self and make for harmony and peace in thy associations.

"For each soul is in the process of developing itself to become fully aware of its Maker. And as thy Lord hath given: 'In the manner ye do it unto the least of these ye meet, day by day, so ye do it unto thy God.'

"Be not deceived and do not misunderstand. God is not mocked. For what man soweth, man reapeth, and he constantly meets himself!

"If ye attempt to meet it alone, by thyself, then it becomes karma. But do good, as He gave, to those that spitefully use thee, and then ye overcome in thyself whatever ye may have done to thy fellow man!"

"Suffer Little Children to Come Unto Me"

Perhaps the most moving case of emotional karma in its most positive sense belongs to Edgar and Gertrude Cayce themselves.

Their second son, Milton Porter Cayce, had been born on March 28, 1910, at 8:30 p.m. and had died two months later, May 17, at 11:15. Edgar, who had been able to save the lives of so many children, had been unable to save his own child, and though he never discussed the subject, the tragedy had haunted him until he dreamed, during the First World War, that he met and talked with a group of his Sunday School pupils who had been killed in the battlefields of Flanders. Still dreaming, he reasoned that if he had been allowed to see these young soldiers still alive and happy, there should be some way of being able to see his own son. At once he found himself in the presence of tiers of babies, and in one of the higher tiers he saw his own baby smiling down at him in recognition. He awoke consoled and never again grieved for the welfare and security of the child's soul.

Then, nearly twenty years later, on May 25, 1936, he began to give a routine reading on a thirteen-year-old boy, the son of a doctor, born in Peking, China, on March 31st, 1923. He began as usual by counting back over the years from the present to the date of the boy's birth, noting the vast change in his outlook in 1932 when his family returned with him to the States.

Then unexpectedly he announced that "those associated in this undertaking" were in a position to study the case at firsthand. "For this Entity, now called David Hoffman, entered the earth's plane in the previous experience for only a few weeks—on March 28, 1910, 8:30 in the evening, departing on May 17 at 11:15.

"The mother would know, in the present," he added, referring to Gertrude, and implying that she would respond in instinctive recognition once she saw him again. He explained that the boy had died because "there was too great a disturbance in the mind and experience, during that period of gestation, for the soul to remain." By the same token, there was little or no opportunity for the soul to develop. But now that David was established as having once been their son, "the knowledge and association of same will bring helpful experiences in the development of the soul of the Entity."

He then dealt in great detail with the potential physical weaknesses the boy faced. The digestive system was delicate, might adversely affect the colon and appendix . . . "be warned of these, that there be not a cutting short of the opportunities for the Entity; for . . . those weaknesses exist as a material overlap from other experiences in the earth."

In the life before his brief sojourn as Milton Porter Cayce, he had served as a secretary to Adams and Hamilton in Boston, during the framing of the Constitution; hence in the present he would find himself able to serve men in high authority without awe or confusion, "for the ideals of the Entity naturally are high."

In the life before that "the Entity was among the children of one Bartellius, in Palestine, and was blessed by the Master, Jesus. The boy was among those who later suffered material hardships for the causes held, not only by his people and his parents but for those tenets held by himself."

It was from this experience that he had developed his high ideals, for in every Reading where a child had once received the touch of Christ's hand in blessing, the memory remained indelibly in the soul-memory as a benediction.

His earliest life had been in prehistoric Egypt, one of the refugees from the subsiding continent of Atlantis. "The name then was Aart Elth. This, to be sure, was the Egyptian name for a consecrated teacher in the service of the Temple.

"Though young in years when journeying into Egypt, the Entity aided in the development of mechanical appliances for the cutting of stone in the temples of service, as well as the temples of sacrifice.

"Hence, in the present, these things (though of a much higher order) make for peculiar experiences at times, as does music, upon the whole of the bodily forces.

"These should aid the Entity in first learning to know itself, its own weaknesses physically, its own abilities mentally . . . and thus, in a coordinated, consecrated effort may great experiences come to the Entity in this sojourn . . . for, as the body-mind develops, each of these branches should be offered as an opportunity or outlet: those of a mechanical nature, those of a musical, or those of a biological nature, which would include insect life and its influence on man's environ."

When Edgar returned to consciousness, his wife told him with tears of joy that he had been aiding his lost son to prepare for his new life.

A year later, Dr. Hoffman brought the boy to New York to meet Gertrude and Edgar. David, of course, was never told of the link between them; but just as Edgar had warned her, Gertrude was so magnetically drawn to the boy that she had difficulty in concealing her true feelings.

It is hard to conceive of a more unique situation in the history of Edgar Cayce's tireless service of his fellow men. It served the double purpose of consoling the parents of a child they had lost, and aiding the parents of a thirteen-year-old boy to preserve him against the illnesses most likely to beset him in his formative years.

CHAPTER 5

THE ELEMENT OF FEAR IN EMOTIONAL KARMA

The Root Cellar

PATRICIA FARRIER, a spinster of forty-five, was told in her Reading that in her previous life she had lived and died near Fredericksburg, Virginia, under the name of Geraldine Fairfax, while America was still a British Colony. She was told that records, "even in stone," still existed. So she and her sister Emily journeyed to Fredericksburg in the hope of tracing them.

During their search, the sisters had occasion to put up at a small rural hotel one night. Having retired to bed healthy but tired, they soon fell asleep —a sleep from which Emily was awakened by a choking noise from her sister's bed. She turned on the light and found Patricia literally suffocating to death. Her face was red, and she was fighting desperately for breath, yet Emily was unable to wake her from the deep coma in to which she had fallen.

In panic, Emily sought help from the proprietor, but nothing would rouse Patricia from her coma, and she seemed to be on the verge of death. On the arrival of the doctor, she was brought back to consciousness with difficulty and normal breathing was finally restored. The two sisters fled the hotel that morning and hastened back to Edgar Cayce. In her subsequent Reading, Patricia asked: "Why have I so much fear in the present?"

She was told that she had been subject to many fears, in the physical sense, in her previous lives, and these had come through with her into the present as subconscious memories.

As a thirteen-year-old girl in Fredericksburg, she had been playing at "gardening" in the root cellar, where all the seedlings, cuttings, potatoes and herbs were stored on shelves during the winter. It was presumably a place where the child was forbidden to go unattended, and on that day a minor earth tremor shook the countryside, causing the floor of the farmhouse to cave in. The shelves collapsed and buried her under an avalanche of roots, bulbs and damp soil. She had smothered to death in such an hysteria of panic that it manifested itself in this life as claustrophobia, a terror of crowds, a fear of smothering. Its direct association did not manifest itself, however, until she and her sister had stayed the night at the hotel. This hotel must either have been built over the site of the old frontier homestead, or was sufficiently near to it for her memory to reenact the actual death throes of the child in the previous life.

Her Reading advised her to harness the energy she was expending in fear to a positive ideal of some kind, whereby she could profit rather than lose from its influence. Her karma offered her full reason to develop her capacity for deep religious faith. In Palestine at the time of Christ she had been a member of the household which witnessed the resurrection of Lazarus by the Master, and the New Testament was accordingly familiar to her at a high subconscious level of personal identification.

She took this advice and achieved success in full measure, developing a prayer group which devoted certain hours of its day to prayers for Edgar Cayce when his own energies were occupied helping others.

The immense dignity of Edgar Cayce's simplicity is movingly illustrated in the letter of gratitude he sent her:

"My dear Miss Farrier: It would be very hard indeed for me to express to you my appreciation of yours of the fifteenth. I realize a great deal more than I'll ever be able to tell you, how much your prayer group—as a group, and as individuals—have helped me. I have come to depend upon them a great deal. I feel very much as Moses must have felt when it was necessary that Joshua and Aaron hold up his hands! I am willing, but the flesh is weak—and it's very necessary that we have those upon whom we can rely when our own strength fails. I assure you I have found a great deal of strength in the efforts and the cooperation of every member of the group.

Thanking you, and with all sincerity, I am,
Ever the same,
Edgar Cayce   Dec. 18, 1931."

Patricia Farrier died of cancer in January 1939, and he corresponded with her to the end, advising her sister by Physical Readings how best to nurse her. When she asked how much longer she would have to "remain in this suffering condition," he consoled her with the assurance that it was in no way a punishment, merely the soul's completion of its lesson in patience, "even as Jesus in the Garden learned obedience through suffering."

Equally moving is the understanding Cayce showed for Jane Clephan, a college girl of twenty-one with an almost disabling inferiority complex.

He commented at once on her inborn musical ability and urged its development. He also assured her that she had a latent talent as a concert pianist and teacher, once she developed sufficient confidence in herself. But he advised against marriage unless it was late in life "else it will bring later discouragements and discontent, even of a greater nature than exist at present."

This he traced directly to her former life in France, where she was the wife of a disgruntled physical bully who so resented the "beauty and affability of the Entity that he sought to keep her submerged, even at times using force." The weals on her body from his floggings were still vivid in her memory. "Hence the fear of punishment in the present, of being misunderstood or misinterpreted.

"The Entity then was a musician, but was cut short in same because of the association. Thus, in the present, the Entity will be required to determine what type of friendships with others she would like, then set about to plan them. . . . For they that make themselves friendly, have friends."

The Reading then described her life at the time of the Christian persecutions.

"The Entity accepted the teachings of the followers of Jesus; yet the torments of the persecutions became so abhorrent that the Entity became submerged in mere drudgery in order to keep away from the words, the hurts, the slights and slurs. . . .

"But know, as ye live in thy conscience in such good faith with thy Maker that ye can look every person in the face and know that ye have done naught but good in thought or deed, ye stand exalted before thy Maker. And if the Lord be on thy side, who can be against thee? . . .

"Before that, the Entity was in the Egyptian land, during those periods when there was the purifying of the body for active service in the Temples. The Entity then entered into a life of service, being what today would be called a nurse, one who cared for those physically or mentally ill.

"These phases can be a portion of the Entity's present experience or desire, unless timidity prevents the putting of same into practical application.

"As to the abilities of the Entity in the present: first find thyself and thy ideal, mentally, spiritually, physically, then apply same to thy relationships to others.

"Study music and apply same, either as the instructor or as the one giving the concert, or the like. For in that field ye will find harmony of life, harmony of expression, harmony of relationship to the Creative Forces. Ready for questions."

Jane: "Will I ever make close friends?"

E.C.: "If practiced in those things indicated, yes."

Jane: "What causes my absentmindedness?"

E.C.: "Self-condemnation! Do not condemn. Rather know, and live in self, that which we have indicated."

Jane: "What musical instruments should I take up?"

E.C.: "The piano as the basis, to be sure, but any stringed instruments."

Jane: "Is my mental ability and physical condition suitable to continue my college education?"

E.C.: "By all means! Continue such!"

Jane: "Why didn't I get in a sorority last February?"

E.C.: "Because of fear! As indicated, practice those things you would like others to do for you, by doing the same for others!"

Jane: "What is my I.Q.?"

E.C.: "This would depend on the standard by which it would be judged. It is sufficient for all your requirements, if ye will but apply self—first from the spiritual and mental, then from the material angle."

Jane: "How can I overcome my intense fear—fear of meeting and conversing with other people?"

E.C.: "As has been indicated!"

How much more simply and lucidly could constructive counsel be given to an inhibited girl, who, until the time of her Reading, had no practical means of resolving her own confusions!

Obviously no one in Jane's position could be expected to identify her fears with those of an ill-treated wife whose spirit had been broken by the sadism of a boorish lout. Yet, once she understood the source of her social timidity, it had the effect of exonerating the innocent people she had needlessly been fearing, and enabling her to see them in an objective, congenial light. Her confidence was being taught to emerge like a baby being taught to walk. How very clearly this illustrates Cayce's answer to: "Why don't we remember past lives?"

"We do not have to remember," he said in effect. "We are the sum total of all our memories." We manifest them in our habits, our idiosyncracies, our likes and dislikes, or talents and blind-spots, our physical and emotional strengths and vulnerabilities.

Because of his life as Bainbridge, for example, Edgar Cayce never had the slightest desire to gamble or drink. The memory of the cost, the waste of endeavor, was still too recent. This is why he insisted that anyone with sufficient honesty to examine his own nature, would find in it a complete lexicon of do's and don't's . . . the still small voice of conscience never lies. It is simply that we conveniently choose not to hear it occasionally, and then wonder why we walk slam-bang into a glass door that all but flattens our nose.

There is something infectious in Cayce's exuberance when he chaffs a soul for having relinquished self-confidence in the face of life's buffeting.

"You have belittled yourself and cramped your own abilities!" he exhorted a woman of forty-six. "Turn yourself loose! You may go anywhere so long as you keep your faith in the one God, and just apply self to being kind, patient, showing brotherly love.

"Too long have you been under a cloud, as it were, and rather timid and lacking in self-expression. You need to get out in the wilds and yell, and hear your own echo back again!

"Do not be subdued by others who try, or have tried, to impress you with their importance, for God is not a respecter of persons! And anyone can act the fool by appearing to be important!

"The greatest among those of the earth are those who serve the most; but this doesn't mean keeping so quiet, being so uncommunicative.

"There is a lack of flash and show. If you would dress up in a red dress, you could cut a nice caper, and this is not meant as a pun, either! Such urges have been so subdued, the love and deep emotion kept hid so long, that little of your real beauty has emerged.

"You need to change your environment, to be where you will meet lots of people and have to do a lot of talking, and a lot of explaining to people that you realize don't know nearly as much as you do.

"Give to those who think they know a lot! If you will only realize it, you know a lot more than they do, on any subject! These conditions, once changed, will make a great deal of difference to you. . . . So don't be afraid of having troubles; know that whatever you want, you can have. For the Lord loveth those who love Him, and He will not withhold any good thing from such!"

And in the same vein, he rallied a nervous young man of twenty: "Overcome timidity by having something particular to say! Many individuals talk without saying anything—that is, anything constructive or anything which even has meaning—but you take their opinions of you literally!

"We are given only two eyes, two ears, but we should hear and see twice—nay, four times—as much as we speak! Never be boastful, but never attempt to be 'just as the other boys, and do what people say lest you many be thought different.'

"Dare to be different! And if ye will begin with Deuteronomy, thirtieth chapter, and Exodus 19:5, you will know the reasons deep within self!"

CHAPTER 6

VOCATIONAL KARMA

The Frescoes of the Pantheon

THE FOLLOWING IS an outstanding example of Cayce's encouragement earning him the undying friendship of the youth he helped.

John Schofield, aged twenty-three, suffered much early frustration in a dead-end mechanical job in a commercial engraving firm. This suffering was aggravated by a possessive family which allowed him no mind of his own. He was a fair-to-middling amateur artist in his own right, but lacked any confidence in his own creative worth. He had painted himself into a corner of the room, as it were, and the paint showed every sign of taking a long time to dry.

As many did, Schofield applied to Edgar Cayce as a last resort, all other sources of help having failed. He was briskly advised to put a healthy distance between himself and his parasitic family. In his past lives in Egypt, Greece and Rome he had many times been involved with the designing of frescoes for the temples, law courts and seats of government. This is a highly specialized vocation, not confined to purely architectural skill, yet not as informal as mural painting. Nevertheless he was directed to go to New York and seek his place among the major architectural firms, once he had completed his vocational training at an art school.

Cayce explained that architectural styles in different lands were the sum total of the inspiration of the men who labored to create them over the centuries, even though their immediate rewards had been little more than their own dedication to their artistic ideals. He cited Leonardo da Vinci as an example of a genius whose soul was expressing itself, now in the present, as it had never been allowed to do in his own lifetime. The genius of da Vinci could only be expressed when the world had progressed sufficiently to recognize it and put his creations into practice. Thus his true immortality manifested itself in his universal influence, not in his personal fame.

The same argument applied to John Schofield's inborn talents.

"Why should this be?"

"Because this soul, having gained so much in the decorative influence in the temples, in the public buildings, in the tombs, is now beginning its true career in America. And there may be seen in the decorative style of the frescoing, or second panels, in the Pantheon and its casements, influences which derived from the same school in which the Entity once studied."

"Just how should I prepare myself to contribute to this?" asked Schofield.

"By learning to combine the modernistic with the Phoenician and Egyptian, for they combine beautifully, their simplicity, their decorativeness."

Schofield proceeded as instructed, and five years later he was able to report on his progress.

"I received a sudden message to appear at the Barnes' Foundation, where I am a student, to be awarded a traveling scholarship for four months study in Europe with a group of his students this summer . . . from May 18 to September 18. It includes travel and instruction in seven countries.

"This year terminates my fifth and final year at the Academy of Fine Arts, and my second at the Barnes' Foundation. I am seeking new values and new inspiration for that ultimate course which I am to pursue.

"I feel very lucky and very grateful for the opportunities that have come to me. My sincere and humble wish is that I may prove deserving of them and develop an expression that is meaningful to those who seek an experience in art."

"My trip this summer was a wonderful series of experiences and I must have lived a lifetime in that period," he subsequently wrote to Hugh Lynn Cayce after Edgar's death. "Since my return I have been true to the Reading, and with much experimenting, have completed my first fresco, and am well along on planning my second. My first was rather successful, and my second one is hopeful. I have had a very good year, probably the best yet in the way of actual accomplishment."

Nine years later, Hugh Lynn Cayce was able to make the following appraisal:

"It is natural that we have watched with interest this young man's years of work and study in art school and his rise to remarkable heights in his field. Anyone who could compare the suppressed young man of a few years ago and the young scholar and artist whose work is being recognized today would see why we feel that the Life Readings are so worth studying."

The Intelligence Officer

It is a far cry from Schofield to the complex soul who is involved in the next case history—too complex a soul to make full use of his Life Reading, even though it correctly foretold the how and the where of the role he would play in World War II.

Calvin Mortimer, Ph.D., was a psychologist, whose Reading defined him as "an extremist in some of his ideas," a soul who had returned for a very definite purpose, who possessed a well-developed talent for dealing with "very large groups of people in many varied spheres of activity."

"Before this, the Entity was in the land of the present nativity, during the period just following the American Revolution . . . among the soldiery of the British, acting in the American land in what would be termed the Intelligence Service. Not as a spy, but rather one of those who mapped and laid out the plans for the campaigns by Howe and Clinton.

"However, the Entity remained in the American soil after hostilities ended. Not as one dead, but as one making for the cooperation between the peoples of the Entity's native land and those of the land of adoption.

"Then in the name Warren, the Entity gained by successfully establishing these relationships.

"Hence, in the present, we will find diplomatic relationships, the exchange of ideas and plans of the various nations, becoming of interest to the Entity."

Before that, he had been an English Crusader who was taken prisoner by the Saracens in the Holy Lands, and was profoundly impressed by the civilized handling he received from the "heathen infidel."

He lost in that life by uncritically defending a false cause rather than serving an ideal he genuinely believed in. This lent him a skepticism in the present towards religious or philosophic principles, though he retained his fascination for dogmas that can sway whole masses of people.

In a Persian incarnation before that, he lost again by indulging the carnal to excess, though he came under the influence of Esdras, of whom it was said:

"According to tradition, all the writings of the Bible were destroyed, but they were restored by Esdras who 'remembered in his heart' and rewrote them."

He had also mastered the science of astronomy; "thus a knowledge of the movements of the earth are still a portion of the Entity's record."

In prehistoric Egypt "the Entity made for the greater progress in his development of the mental, or soul experiences. With the gathering of various races and creeds, the Entity made a study of same, classifying and interpreting them for the many, not only in the Egyptian land, but in the Indian, the Mongolian or Gobi, the Carpathian, and the Og, and those lands across the seas."

It is now possible to follow his destiny from the account supplied by his third ex-wife.

At the time of the bombing of Pearl Harbor "he was too old for active duty, and being a specialist in Public Opinion, he dashed off to Washington to see if he could be of use in this field.

"After a number of barren interviews, he came home discouraged, but it was not long before he had a new idea. Living on navigable water and having the means with which to indulge himself, he had considerable experience with sailboats, and so he applied to the Coast Guard.

"He passed the Navy I.Q. test with the score of 175, was slated to be a Lieutenant Commander, and came home to polish up on his navigation. Then he was urgently called back to Washington.

"Within a few months he was switched to the O.W.I. Domestic Intelligence Service as an Opinion Expert, where he worked closely with the O.S.S., and then with O.W.I. Overseas. He finished the war in charge of a technical school, training men to drop behind enemy lines, on the selfsame spot in Long Island where he had once mapped and laid out the plans for the campaigns of Howe and Clinton in the War of Independence."

In 1957 Dr. Mortimer married again for the fourth time. His third wife reported that her own marriage had lasted ten years, longer than any of the rest, presumably because they had been together before, harmoniously in Persia, and incompatibly as man and wife in the War of Independence.

In the latter years of their marriage he had insisted on too much drinking, and that she drink with him, "so that even now it is still quite a problem for me." She mentioned the terrific sex drive which had dominated their marriage.

She wrote again in 1963 to announce his death, during his sleep, after he had suffered two strokes and lost his sight.

She herself died very suddenly in the following year, having spoken of the "terrific pull" which she felt from him, "as if he were hypnotizing me to join him."

It is possible that, had Mortimer heeded Cayce's warnings against self-indulgence and excesses, he might have stuck to the very definite purpose for which he returned. This presumably was a continuation of the advance he had begun to make in Egypt at a high responsible level of international diplomacy. But Mortimer's nostalgic appetite for the erotic fleshpots of Persia proved an insurmountable obstacle.

It is not out of keeping here to consider the Oriental belief that the soul is allowed one "comfortable" reincarnation for every six lives of arduous development, the theory being that the lives grow correspondingly tougher as the soul sheds the ties that bind it to earth. Without this "sabbatical," the soul might well weary of the constant upward struggle and allow itself to become unduly discouraged.

By this same token, it could be possible that the Mortimers had reached the sixth life of such a cycle, and that Dr. Mortimer and his wife will return next time to a more tranquil existence, where they can put their house in order and assess their spiritual progress more clearly.

CHAPTER 7

LIFE READINGS FOR CHILDREN

WHENEVER EDGAR CAYCE was dealing with children, his loving concern was detectable even in the flat pages of the transcripts.

In ordinary life, children were drawn to him instinctively. In his time, he had been a most successful children's photographer, due to the magical rapport he was able to establish between his young sitters and himself.

From as far back as the turn of the century, he had taught Sunday School, and his pupils kept in affectionate touch with him long after they went out into the world.

The Doctor in Spite of Himself

Roddy was born at 4:43 a.m. January 9, 1943, and his parents requested his Reading the following June.

"As will be seen, in the not too distant future," the Reading begins, "all those souls who enter the earth plane in the years '43, '44 and '45 will apparently be destined to fulfill interesting roles in their service to their fellow man, and find a very unusual approach to same.

"This Entity, if given the opportunity in its early environs, is destined to be a professional man in this experience, preferably in the fields of medicine, or dentistry, or as a pharmacist. Any of these will be channels through which the Entity may attain the fulfillment of his purpose.

"As the Entity develops, it will be seen that he will have a great imagination. Do not rebuke the Entity for telling 'tall tales,' for, to the Entity, they will be true. Just impress on him how these may be used more constructively in the application of self towards spiritual, mental and material unfoldments.

"He will be inclined to be extravagant in his words, in his attitudes. This, too, will need to be—not curbed by 'you can't do this,' or 'you can't do that,' but by encouraging him in other interests that will create in him a constant appreciation of being consistent, in that he 'does as well as he speaks.'

"Astrologically we find Venus, Mercury, Mars and Jupiter as influences. In Venus we find the love of the beautiful.

"This will make for the determination that everything he attempts, if he is directed well, will be well done. And it will require patience on the part of those responsible for the Entity!

"We find in Mercury the high mental abilities. In Mars with Mercury we find quite a busybody, not inclined to interfere with others, but wanting to have his own way, and knowing how to do things just a little bit better than anyone else!

"We will find in Jupiter, as the unfoldments come, the greater universal consciousness, giving the abilities which were expressed by the same Entity in a previous experience as Harvey—Dr. Harvey, discoverer of the circulation of the blood.

"Though proven to be in error in many things, he still insisted, even then, that he knew best! His activities are well known, and, if studied, will give those responsible for the Entity an idea of the problems to be met.

"But do give the Entity the opportunity to study, either as a pharmacist, or as a dentist, and he will do the rest himself as he goes along."

Here indeed is a very big fish in a very small five-month-old pond!

In France, at the time of Cardinal Richelieu, the Entity had been "Count Dubourse, and had made great contributions to the advance of cleanliness in relationship to disease. Though the Entity made no pretenses, yet he indicated to others he knew better than they did. (And in that instance he did!) Especially in relation to diseases commonly called the "catching" diseases, for he insisted that these came not only from microbes but could be carried by individuals.

"Thus, in the present experience, it will be found that the Entity will be inclined to be clean about its person, though 'messy' about a house. These were the natural extremes indicated in the characteristics in that former experience, and will find expression in the present.

"And the Entity will be one of those who keeps his friends quite separate!

"Then, in the guidance you give him, do keep the spiritual life balanced with the purposeful life. And, as a normal balance is kept, we will find those abilities manifesting themselves in a way and measure as to bring blessings to many people."

When Edgar declared himself ready to answer questions, the mother asked when and where she had been associated with her boy in the past. The answer: "In many places—especially in Egypt as a directing influence. Thus care should be taken that not too great a disagreement ever arises between the two!"

The father had been with the boy in the French experience, "as well as in the Egyptian—where we find them in opposition to one another. So, expect a good many spats between 'em!"

Though this was of sad necessity the only Reading the child was ever to obtain, his mother made the following report to the A.R.E. ten years later.

"Roddy has shown particular interest in the physical body since a tiny child, and especially anything having to do with the heart and the circulation of the blood. He also definitely has the trait of insisting he is always right! He never wants to admit that another's explanation of anything is better than his. Has been an A-1 student; boasts of having had better grades than anyone else in school! Has a mind that researches into knowledge along whatever line he gets started. Has a phobia about germs—washes his hands all the time— definitely 'hipped' on the subject. Doesn't want to live in a big city because of 'all those people breathing germs on you'!

"Although we have never discussed his Reading with him, he insists he's going to be a doctor. At ten years old, he has his own paper route and is saving money towards medical college.

"We have four other children, all entirely different. These traits are definitely peculiar to this one child, just as Mr. Cayce stated when he was five months old. . . ."

All the eccentricities Edgar had foreseen in the baby had fully developed in less than ten years. Edgar indicated but never insisted on the course a child should follow. The responsibility lay directly with the parents as to whether they would encourage the child's medical ambitions or direct them into other channels. But at least they knew where his own instinctive proclivities lay, and why they were there.

The Purity of a Child's Soul

In the files of children's case histories many are simple, unassuming human documents. The children often face uneventful destinies in quiet obscurity, the problems are not major or dramatic. But every so often one emerges with such unique overtones that it deserves inclusion for its human interest alone.

One young "original," aged three, received this Life Reading in 1936:

"Much crowds in to be said!" Edgar began, "for the Entity is very sensitive, very high-strung, inclined to be very stubborn, and very expressive of feeling. . . . For the Entity is an old soul, and an Atlantean who, properly guided and directed, may not only make for his own development but make his surroundings, his environs, his world, a much better place for others.

"It will be found that few people will appear as strangers to the Entity, yet some will remain strangers ever, no matter how often or in what manner they are thrown together! The Entity will ever be tending towards an idealistic nature. Hence, unless it be made clear to the Entity as to why there will be faults and failures in the promises made by individuals and associates, he will tend to lose confidence, not only in others, but in self.

"And the loneliest person, the loneliest individual, yea the loneliest Entity, is the one who has lost hold upon his own self!"

In his previous life this Entity had been a gold miner in California who had become disgusted by the lawlessness and violence which had robbed him of his just rewards and brought him a violent death. Thus the child had inherited a terror of firearms, and they were never to be allowed in his presence. "Such explosions are fearful experiences to the Entity.

"But the Entity never lost hold upon self . . . and if asked in the present: 'Can you do this or that?' he will always answer that he can 'if you show him how!'

"He will ever seek new fields of activity, for everything about the Entity must be new. Hence a word of counsel to those who aid the Entity in the formative years: do not be overawed or surprised when he informs those about him that they are 'out of date'!"

The Entity had been an imposing figure in Roman times, a wealthy and influential supervisor of the collection of tithes and taxes, and during the final inundations of Atlantis, he had been a key official in the directing of refugees to resettlements in Egypt, the Pyrenees and Central and South America. In the present, "law should be the vocation," preferably international law.

His father was an old friend who had been with him through the disillusion of the gold fields, and again in Egypt at the time of the Exodus. And in that same incarnation his mother had been his daughter . . . "hence there will arise periods in the present when the son will doubt his own parents' authority!"

There were obviously stormy days ahead, but Cayce was confident that as long as the parents always explained why they expected a high standard of conduct from him, he would understand and obey.

This Reading is absolutely unique in the following respect. Cayce, having consulted the boy's Akashic Record, made this aside during the session: "The cleanest record I've ever experienced. The book is the cleanest. And yet I had never thought of any of them not being perfectly clean before."

The Accident-prone Child

Frederick Leighton was five months old when Edgar Cayce gave him a Life Reading in 1931. He commented on an as yet unformed character (which is unusual in itself), thus placing the responsibility for the child's development squarely on the shoulders of the parents. Not until the second half of his life would the inner characteristics from his previous lives begin to manifest. He would have a natural affinity for music, having been an itinerant entertainer or "barnstormer" in the south and southwest just after the cessation of the War Between the States, and he had brought with him a predilection for folk songs.

He would develop a talent for business and law "but not confining same in a closed space such as a store, office or the like. Rather will he tend to express himself in the open, in the crowd, on the stage, or as the political leader or speaker." A strong religious influence was traced back to a life in Jerusalem as a harpist in the temple. In ancient Egypt he had again dedicated his life to music, as well as becoming rich "by service to many in the distributing of food from the royal granaries. (Thus) we will find in the latter portion of the present, the Entity will accumulate much of the word's goods from the world's storehouse."

Then came a warning to the parents: "As to whether the Entity becomes one broken in will, broken in its ability to think, to recall much from the spiritual side of its life, depends on what is trained in or trained out by those in authority in the formative years." Otherwise the child was assured of a fully rounded and successful life, either in politics or music.

The implied warnings were not without foundation. When Frederick was four, he suffered a major accident to his head. Allowed to play with a pair of scissors, he stabbed them into his right eye, narrowly avoiding permanent damage to his frontal brain. An immediate operation was performed, but he developed a cataract, and his sight was endangered.

As a result of the seven Physical Readings obtained for him in the next two years, he regained his sight. His grateful response to this is conveyed in this excerpt from a report: "And in walking down the road with little Frederick, I found that he loves Mr. Cayce as far as the stars. . . ."

A Triple Debt

Sarah Crothers was thirteen when her parents belatedly requested a Life Reading for her. For some time Edgar Cayce had been supplying Physical Readings to counter the particularly stubborn case of epilepsy which had plagued her since birth. Under the Physical Readings she would make progress and then slip back. Possibly the Readings were incorrectly applied, or the parents had to deal with doctors hostile to the unorthodox diagnoses. No other explanation offered itself until Edgar got right to the heart of the matter in the opening paragraphs of the Life Reading.

He stated flatly that if the karmic records were to be of any use, the parents would have to shoulder their own share of the responsibility.

"Those responsible for this Entity, who oft are inclined to pass off the epileptic attacks as chance, or as conditions that are unavoidable, should parallel their obligations to her. For, with such a paralleling (through their own Life Readings, you see), there would be a much greater comprehension of the . . . self-aggrandizements or indulgences that now find expression in the physical condition of the Entity, who also is reaping her own whirlwind."

As a very young girl during the American Revolution, she had been used by her parents as a spy against her own countrymen, for the parents were afraid that the defeat of England would bring them financial ruin.

The girl was then called Marjorie Desmond, and possessed a certain amount of latent psychic ability that neither she nor her parents properly comprehended. Her father encouraged her to channel this energy into alluring susceptible young officers into sexual indiscretions, and "she excited the fires of the physical in many." The karmic crime was not so much the treachery to the young colony as the dangerous harnessing of psychic energy to sexual practices for sordid gain, and Edgar made no bones about placing equal blame on the parents. The child herself, however, had blundered twice before—in both lives she had been a Levite—and resentment and rebellion had left their imprint on her character.

"Before that, the Entity was in the Egyptian land, among the offspring of the Atlanteans, though born and reared in Egypt for the (purpose of serving in) what is now known as the hospitalization of individuals ill of body or mind."

Here one may suspect that her neglect or indifference caused the first fissures in the fabric of the soul, though Edgar Cayce, with his usual discretion, made no direct implication.

When he answered the parents' questions at the close of the session, he pointed to no easy solution.

Q.: "Has the condition of the body for the past ten years had any effect upon it physically and mentally?"

E.C.: "Necessarily, these have not been—nor are they yet—coordinated."

Q.: "What type of education should she have to prepare her for life?"

E.C.: "The musical education, as well as the encouragement towards nursing."

Q.: "What effect has destiny on the present appearance?"

E.C.: "This depends, as indicated, upon the application of those who have brought the Entity into its present environ. The gain will be according to how well the obligations due the Entity are met."

Q.: "What will aid her to overcome her physical and mental ailments?"

E.C.: "As indicated—physical exertion, exercises and activities for the body."

It is difficult to ignore the subconscious reluctance implicit in the father's subsequent correspondence, and at the end of the voluminous file on this case, one is left with the regretful impression that the child's progress was minimal, and the karmic debt by no means expunged.

The Bubble Reputation

This seems an opportune moment to point out that the "celebrities" of history represent a very small minority in the Life Readings. Cayce suggested that most souls made their greatest spiritual advances while living obscure and uneventful lives, usually under fairly straitened circumstances. The serf and the peasant had few pleasures and many burdens until the middle of this century. Nevertheless, the average initiate to reincarnation toys rather wistfully with the possibility that he has, at least once, caused the earth to bow down before him.

Unfortunately, it matters very little how important you once were, and very much that you are conforming to decent standards in the immediate present.

Alexander Hamilton (1775–1804), soldier-hero and a founding father of the American Constitution, whose life was cut short by the famous duel, would seem to have been a highly-evolved soul at a mature level of unselfish dedication. Yet this did not prevent him returning as a rather harassed young man of the Jewish faith whose parents obtained his first Reading from Edgar Cayce when he was five weeks old.

Edgar Cayce at once warned against an erratic temper that could cause trouble in later years, and emphasized that the boy should be protected from tampering with firearms. The Entity had brought with him no preconceived pattern of soul development; this he would have to develop as he grew. He was advised to study "in law and in the financial forces and principles of the land."

Before the boy was five, his father fell in love with another woman; the parents were divorced, and the mother retained custody of the child. (Broken homes were always somber hazards to Edgar Cayce. He put intense emphasis on the need of every soul to have a secure background during its formative years, and maintained that the preservation of a congenial home was the highest achievement that a soul could aim for in terms of its own progression.)

At the age of twenty-five, the young man was displaying "a very dogmatic attitude about life in general," which a year and a half in the Navy had failed to cut down to size.

The following year found him under psychiatric care and in hospital for shock treatments. His innate tendency to violence had caught up with him. Having met every conflict head-on, he had added to his problems by an impulsive marriage to a divorcee with a child. The repercussions of the broken home revealed themselves here, in that the girl who had broken up his father's marriage and the girl he himself married were of the same ethnic origin, had the same red hair and were both wives of men laboring in the same mechanical field.

When the marriage only served to compound his miseries, he began to suffer belated remorse that he had not kept on friendlier terms with his father during his lifetime. Towards the end of the following year he seemed to feel his only hope of salvaging himself lay in becoming a rabbi, but a further attempt to contact him by the A.R.E. resulted in the return of the letter marked "Address Unknown."

From his Life Reading, one tends to assume that the bad debts accrued in an earlier Greek life had taken precedence over the gains he had made as Hamilton. Elsewhere in the Readings, the Trojan War gives evidence of having roused sufficient violence in many of its protagonists to deter and confuse their subsequent soul-development. Being in essence a civil war, the passions generated by this war bit deep enough for their scars to reach down the centuries. Using the average patterns of the Readings as a yardstick, this unhappy young man will need yet another life to expunge from his own karmic records the ugly warp left by the Trojan War.

What is most illuminating in the study of this case history is the fact that, as Alexander Hamilton, he had been able to rise to the occasion when his aid was urgently needed by this young nation in crisis. He had been able to come to his task stripped for creative action. All his negatives had been left in abeyance against a future day, when he could apply himself to them in a more settled and resolved period of his country's history. This alone denotes a basic selflessness struggling to express itself in the soul. In which case, he has justly earned and justly deserves the altruistic prayers of his fellow men for his ultimate welfare—as long as they are couched in terms of "prayer for the living" and not "prayer for the departed."

The Memory of the Master

The Readings leave one in no doubt that the most permanent benediction that a soul can bring with it to its lives on earth is the memory of a blessing bestowed on it by Jesus himself.

In one instance a little girl of five would never say her prayers unless her mother stood beside her with her hand on her head, symbolizing in the present the reassuring touch of the Master's hand when he blessed her as a child in the Holy Land.

And when Edgar gave a Reading for another one-year-old child in 1935, he laid special emphasis on the fact that "during the period when the Master walked in the earth, the Entity was among those children who were blessed by Him on the way from Bethany.

"The Entity then beheld and knew Him as one who drew children to Him, and heard that spoken by Him: 'Lest ye become as little children, ye will in no wise enter in.'

"For if one would be forgiven as a child, one must forgive those who would err against self.

"Then the Entity was of the household of Cleopas, in the name Clementina," and in her early teens, having followed the training of the disciples to follow in His steps, attached herself in service to Mark and Luke during their journeying across the land, becoming so closely associated with Mark as to aid in the preservation of "those lessons as we find in the gospel recorded by Mark."

Thus her parents were urged to encourage the child's memories as Clementina, for her present life would be best expressed in unselfish service to others.

Child Care

The A.R.E. files contain an abundance of grateful correspondence from people Cayce helped physically and spiritually. But none are more affecting than the letters from parents of children too young to understand the source of their help.

His views on upbringing consistently emphasized the need for absolute honesty with the child. He condemned pampering as firmly as he condemned indifference. Without a secure and solid background, a child's insecurity and lack of self-esteem left it susceptible to the negative habit-patterns of the faults and woes of its previous lives. Cayce urged the parent always to explain the reason for proper discipline, never to apply it autocratically "because *I* say so." By always appealing to the child's faculty for reasoning, a stable foundation could be laid for its character. When Cayce came across indifference or lack of affection in a parent, he had no hesitation in saying so bluntly. Nothing disturbed him more than the parent who tried to force his own fears and prejudices down the throat of the young soul entrusted to his keeping. The source of most neuroses in later life was this "force-feeding" in childhood of illogical do's and don'ts, as if the child were merely a puppet-extension of its parents' repressions and frustrations.

Cayce constantly urged that the encouragement of the best in a child was a twenty-four-hour job, and must be done gladly, never as a chore. The child must be reasoned away from its own weaker characteristics, not bribed away, or made to feel unduly conscious of them. Religion should be presented in its most benign and spiritual aspects, free of any intolerance or coercion. The development of a good sense of humor was essential to the balance and perspective in adulthood. Any inclination towards music should be warmly stimulated because of its harmonious aid to the child's growing self-awareness. "Just as exercise for the hands and arms, music used for creative purposes is helpful. Through music, you may find the greatest expression of self."

In answer to a mother's question: "How can the mother best cope with this temperament for the best development?" Edgar Cayce replied: "It isn't so much 'cope with it' as just meet it! Be just as patient as you would like thy child to be. The child will then be more patient with you also."

"What course of studies should she pursue in secondary and higher education?"

"Music! History of, the activity of, all of its various forms. If you learn music, you'll learn history! If you learn music you'll learn mathematics! If you learn music, you'll learn all there is to learn—unless it's something bad!"

Children in Wartime

Towards the close of his life, as World War II loomed darker and darker, Edgar Cayce's concern for the children who would be innocently caught in its meshes became more and more evident and urgent. He was not alone in the fear that the souls of children, bewildered by violent deaths, would wander in equal bewilderment in the lower astral planes, unable to proceed "towards the Light," and that they would tend in their confusion to return to earth too swiftly, merely for the sake of the temporary sanctuary of a womb. Joan Grant, the English psychic, was equally concerned, and her psychiatrist husband, Denys Kelsey, using the regression technique in hypnosis, came across many cases of these "war children" reincarnating too soon, into uncongenial families, in search of makeshift shelter from the terrors of the bombing and extermination camps which had clung to them like malignant thought-forms after death.

Fletcher, the spirit-guide of the psychic Arthur Ford, had taken care never to reincarnate after his death on a Flanders battlefield in World War I. He was then a young French Canadian soldier of seventeen. He is an "original," in that he is perfectly happy on the plane he inhabits for the time being, a cheerful, gregarious sprite with more *joie de vivre* than many of the people who come to Arthur Ford to consult him.

The first poignant chord struck in the Readings occurred in August, 1943, when Edgar was asked by the distressed mother of a four-year-old girl to account for her nightmares and constant terror of city life.

Edgar discreetly refrained from overstressing the soul's previous lives; advising the mother to wait until the girl was in her eleventh year before requesting a second Life Reading. (This sometimes forewarned of a potential tragedy or even an early death.)

"For here we have a quick return to earth," he observed, "from fear, back to fear, through fear." He counsels that the child must be protected from all "loud noises, darkness, the scream of sirens.

"For (in her previous life) the Entity was only just coming to that awareness of the beauty of associations, of friendships, of the beautiful outdoors, flowers, birds, and of God's manifestations to man of the beauty, of the oneness of purpose in nature itself, when the tramping of feet, the shouts and rattle of arms, brought destructive forces."

The child had then been only a year or two years older than she is now, he explained, thus the past and present were inextricably interlocked in her mind, and she could not distinguish between the ordinary din of New York city and the Nazi hooliganism that had shattered her world and brought about her death.

"The Entity then, in the name Theresa Schwalendal, lived on the border of Lorraine and Germany. The Entity had no sooner passed on than she reentered the material world in less than nine months.

"Be patient. Do not scold. Do not speak harshly. Do not fret nor condemn the body-mind. But *do* tell her daily of the love that Jesus had for little children, of peace and harmony. Never tell her those stories of witches, never those of fearfulness, of any great punishment, only those of love, patience.

"Do this, and we will find a great, a wonderful soul, that has come again to bless many.

"We are through for the present."

The King's Jester

Edgar's hesitancy to detail the future prospects of a doomed child is again evident when he gives this Reading in 1944 for a seven-year-old boy living in London, England, during the Battle of Britain.

"Thus we would confine the direction to the training, the counseling. And then, when the Entity has reached that period of his own choice, or, at thirteen years of age, we would give further directions, if these are sought by the Entity himself.

"With all the horrors of destruction, with all the trials in the minds of men in this period through which this Entity and his associates in his early experiences are passing, *do* keep alive in him the ability to see not only the sublime things of life, but the humor, the wit—yes, the ridiculous also—that may be drawn from the cynic as well as the pessimist, as in cartoons and the like. For the Entity should be trained in the abilities as a writer, using historical facts as the background of such writings . . . for in the experience before this, the Entity was a jester in the Court of England, in the name of Hockersmith . . . and set many things in order, when there were those great stresses owing to the selfishness of men.

"Also the Entity was among those peoples of Israel who entered the Holy Land, who were married to the Canaanites. Yet the Entity was not among those who led the children of Israel astray. For he forsook Astheroth and served rather the God of Abraham, Isaac and Jacob, as did the one who led the children of Israel through the Red Sea, across the Jordan.

"But when the Entity is thirteen years, we would give further directions.

"Train him especially in English, and at Eton.

"We are through with this reading."

This letter from the mother, written to Hugh Lynn Cayce in February, 1947, confirms Edgar's concern.

"My son passed quickly into the other plane of consciousness at about 4:30 p.m. on February 6. I am in the hospital today, expecting my third child. Timmy was looking forward eagerly to 'his' arrival and was most anxious he should be a boy. He also said, a few weeks before he died: 'I'd like you to be my Mummy in my next life.' I told him he might not be able to arrange that, but he persisted; 'I'm going to ask God anyway.' I remember answering, 'Well, there is no harm in asking.' I feel he was well prepared for what we call 'death.' I had told him, in resumé, the story in *There Is a River,* and before that I had simplified for him Stewart Edward White's *The Unobstructed Universe.*

"My first thought was that he would come back to us in the body of this tiny baby, especially as I had felt and told my husband that I felt that this baby had no personality as yet, and I wondered what type of soul we would attract this time. . . . I do not, however, now feel that he necessarily will choose to return so soon, even though he 'would like me to be his Mummy in his next life.'

"It may be too soon; there may be things for him to learn on another plane of consciousness. It may also be too much the same situation, which was unsettling to him. He (this is hard to explain in a few words) was sensitive to the chaos in the world, and to the financial insecurity of the last two years which we have had due to his father's generosity and kindness to his mother, who died 1/23/47 after living with us as a helpless invalid . . . I had to neglect my children to nurse her at a time when I was pregnant. It was all too much for me, and Timmy suffered with me and for his father, who was at a loss what to do about it, and was consequently impatient and nervous, and not his usual loving, cheerful self; so that the loving, happy atmosphere of our home was completely destroyed from about August '46 until 3/26/47, when I feel Timmy succeeded in restoring it with our cooperation. He always was most solicitous that his Daddy and Mummy should be united and loving, as we were, except when our house became the home of either my family or his, even if only for a visit of a few months. . . ."

She enclosed a newspaper clipping which described how Timmy and a friend had "ventured onto a frozen pond; the ice broke and they disappeared together. Death was due in both cases to shock. . . ."

In his answering letter of sympathy, Hugh Lynn Cayce made the following comment: "I wonder if you realize that his Life Reading was unusually short, and that there was a reticence about giving any information until he could ask for himself. I think there is much that we must come to understand regarding the interrelation between this plane of consciousness and those on the other side of the state we call death. Perhaps Timmy can get his Reading now, and go on preparing for the work which the Reading indicated he could accomplish. . . ."

The Call of the Sea

At the age of seventeen, Fred Coe terminated an adolescence of restriction and incompatibility by running away from home. Two months later he was still missing, and Edgar Cayce was requested to trace him. The Reading, though brief, is as intriguing as any, telling its own story with lucid economy and vigor.

"Yes, we have the Entity here," Edgar began. "In entering the earth plane, we find he comes under the influence of Neptune and Uranus, with influences from Jupiter and Mars. Hence the condition exhibited in the present is a love of the sea. (See? The body has gone to sea).

"In the planetary influence then, we find one of many exceptional abilities.

"One who is considered eccentric and peculiar, having many changeable moods.

"One loving mystery tales of the sleuth or detective order, and every condition regarding a mystery of the sea.

"One who should have been guided close in the study of those things pertaining to the mystery and the occult.

"One who will find his greatest abilities in the present earth's plane in the study of the occult forces.

"One who loves the use of firearms, and likes the display of same.

"One that in the present year finds the greatest change coming in the life, when he will find many experiences in many lands, returning only to the present surroundings of birth in middle age.

"One who finds little need for that called a religious life.

"One who will bring much joy and much sorrow to many, especially to the weaker sex.

"One with the ability to give much counsel to many.

"In the previous appearances, we find many of the various urges influencing the present existence. In the existence before this, we find the Entity often referred to as Captain Kidd. The Entity gained in the first portion of the life, and in the latter portion gave much to others, though the cost to self was rather severe. In the urge is found the love of the sea, of those things which pertain to the mysterious, the ability to gain mystery in the eyes of others.

"In the life before that, we find the Entity known as Hawk, in the English navy. The Entity then was aide to the first of the navigators to the eastern portion of the world (John Cabot, 1497); and in the latter days came to the northern shore of this land.

"The urge, again, is the love of adventure and of mystery.

"In the life before that, we find him in that land of the Bedouins, when the war was made between the then Grecian forces and the peoples of the plain (circa 900 B.C.). The Entity then was in the name Xenia, and was the second-in-command of those plainsmen who brought consternation to the invading forces by turning hornets loose among them! That life, as we see, brought power to the Entity, and in the end proved his undoing. Here is seen the present love of outdoors and the mysteries of nature.

"In the life before that (circa 10,000 B.C.) in that period when there were divisions in the land now known as Egypt, the Entity wrought then in iron, in the service of the ruler. And in that service brought much counsel to many. The urge in the present—a desire to be of service to, and in direct communication with, those in power.

"Many, many, developments will be necessary before this Entity attains oneness with the higher forces. Study, then, those conditions; and let those who would assist, take warning.

"We are through for the present."

This is one case where his sympathies were clearly with the boy and not with the parents; and when they requested a second reading, the only information Edgar would vouchsafe was that the boy had shipped aboard a seagoing vessel in New York, eastward bound for Europe.

In the next case, however, one is suddenly pulled up short by the jolt of stark tragedy.

The Grapes of Wrath

The mother of a twelve-year-old boy, Lennie Talbot, asked for her son's Life Reading in the hope that it would aid her to understand his mercurial behavior-pattern.

Despite the great tact Edgar always employed, the Reading clearly reveals his serious concern for the boy's future welfare, and a note of sober warning is implicit in every line.

"In giving the records here of this Entity, it would be easy to interpret them either in a very optimistic or a very pessimistic vein. For there are great possibilities and great obstacles. Here is the opportunity for an Entity (while comparisons are odious, these would be good comparisons) to be either a Beethoven or a Whittier; or a Jesse James! For the Entity is inclined to think more highly of himself than he ought; and that is what these three individuals did. As to the application made of it, this depends upon the individual self.

"Here is an Entity who has abilities latent within self which may be turned into music, or poetry, or writing in prose which few would ever excel. Or there may be the desire to have his own way to such an extent that he will disregard others altogether, in every form, just so he has his own way.

"In giving the astrological aspects, these are latent and manifested: Mercury, Venus, Jupiter, Saturn and Mars. These are adverse in some respects, one to another, yet are ever present, and indicate that the body will go to excess in many ways, unless there is real training in the period of unfoldment. And the Entity is beginning to reach that period when—while the spirit must not be broken!—everyone should be very firm and positive, inducing him through reason to analyze himself, and to form a proper concept of his ideals and purposes, and in doing this, we will not only give to the world a real individual with genius, but make for proper soul development. Otherwise, we will give to the world one with a genius for making trouble for somebody!

"As to the previous appearances in the earth, these naturally—as indicated from those tendencies—have been quite varied:

"Before this, the Entity was in the present land during the French and Indian wars.

"The Entity was among the French in the activities about Fort Dearborn, determined to have his own way, irrespective of the trouble or the great distress he caused others.

"In the end, the Entity by sheer illness gained a great deal. For it may be said of this Entity, as of the Master, through suffering he learned the more.

"The name then was John Angel.

"Before that, the Entity was in what is now known as France.

"Then the Entity, with certain groups, made forays into the Hun land, and yet eventually escaped to the southern portion of Italy.

"The Entity was then of a disposition in which artistic or musical talents came into greater play, the ability to write verse and compose music to it.

"The ability to become an orchestra leader or a writer of song or verse may be a part of the Entity's experience in the present, provided he doesn't have the 'big head,' or think more highly of himself than he ought. Every other individual has as much right in the earth as you have yourself, even though he may not be in some respects as far advanced in his learning. God is not a respecter of persons because of their good looks or abilities. He respects the individual according to his purposes, his aims, his desires. Remember that.

"Before that, the Entity was in the City of Gold, during the early evolution of the various lands of Saad, the Gobi and Egypt (10,000 B.C.).

"The Entity was among those who acted as guards to the ladies in waiting, and was active in his ability to entertain in verse and in song, using these not only to entertain, but to aid the greater development and unfoldment of those people.

"Before that the Entity was in Atlantis, during those periods just before the second breaking up of the land (28,000 B.C.).

"The Entity was among the Sons of Belial who used the divine forces for the gratifying of selfish appetites, and the formation of this desire to gratify self became the stumbling block.

"As to the abilities of the Entity in the present, these are unlimited. How will they be directed by the Entity? How well may others aid the Entity to become aware of such activities? These questions should be put to self.

"Study first to know thy ideals, spiritual, mental and material. Then apply self towards these in such a manner that there will never be a question mark after thine own conscience nor in the eyes of others.

"Ready for questions."

Q: What should be his chief work?

E.C.: "This depends upon what he chooses—whether in directing of music, writing of music, or writing of verse—any of those are the realms through which the Entity may *exceed* as well as succeed."

Q: Should all of his talents be developed?

E.C.: "All his talents will either be developed, or run to seed and be drained off."

Q: Any other suggestions that may help his parents to guide him?

E.C.: "Let the parents study to show themselves approved unto God, workmen not ashamed, putting the stress where stress is due, keeping self unspotted from the world.

"We are through with this reading."

The Atlantean Sons of Belial will be dealt with in the following chapter. For the moment, the reader may assume that this was the worst blot on his record, and the long-delayed karma which demanded its reckoning from this boy in the present had its ill-omened beginning in this period.

Excerpt I from the correspondence of the mother, February, 1944:

"Your reading for Lennie was no surprise to my husband and me. We early saw that such tremendous energy should be set to work, and he is in his third year at a very strict, very religious boarding school. Idleness would destroy him. He must always be in the big world, where he will be just a 'drop in the bucket,' not the 'big frog in a small pond'. . . ."

Excerpt II, September, 1949:

"We are in great distress now over the condition of our only child, who has a distressing mental and nervous upset which as yet has not been diagnosed. . . ."

Excerpt III, July, 1951, to Hugh Lynn Cayce:

"The press has been cruel to us in our sorrow, and no doubt you have read of our tragedy. My son Lennie, who has been emotionally unbalanced for three years, last Wednesday shot his grandfather and grandmother.

"Hugh Lynn, your father was my friend, and I brought Lennie to see him and also he gave a Life Reading for him which had plenty of warnings in it. I am writing to ask you to please get one of your prayer circles to work for us. . . ."

Excerpt IV, August, 1951:

"Lennie is now in the State Hospital. The doctors there, and elsewhere in other sanitariums where he has been, have, of course, labeled his trouble dementia praecox, schizophrenia, etc., but you and I know it is bad karma. Thank God his intellect seems intact, he writes for books he has always liked, and he takes two newspapers. . . ."

Excerpt V, October, 1951:

"My husband and I have arranged to send him to a psychiatrist, Dr. Baker. He is very fine, one of the pioneers in insulin and electric shock treatment. I see no reason why Lennie should not receive osteopathic treatment while under Dr. Baker. He tells me that he will keep Lennie for a whole month for observation before he gives him any treatment, and I am going to urge that in this month he be given osteopathy. With our love and thanks again. . . ."

Excerpt VI, November, 1951:

"(This is Lennie's last letter. Please return to me)

"Dear Mother: I was indeed glad to hear about your trip through the Middle West, but have not yet heard about the results.

"I certainly feel better since Brother Lindsay prayed for me, and am less tense and worried about the future than before.

"Will you please take me to a healing revival? I could probably benefit from this more than from any other form of treatment. Do please find out where one is being held and let's go to it.

"Could you please send me my tweed suit and those new shoes which I wasn't allowed to wear at the other place. I could certainly use them here, as certain regulations are much more lenient.

"Also I would like my wrist watch, which I am also allowed. Please tell Father to buy me some canned goods and delicacies from the food market. All these items are very useful and they would come in very handy around here.

"You probably have not yet felt this year's tax increases, but your '52 income tax will be higher, leaving you less money to live on if you don't do any tax dodging. Business property, however, yields about the highest income after taxes for any investment.

"Love, Lennie."

Excerpt VII, June, 1956:

"Miss (Gladys) Davis recommended Hildreth Sanitarium as being one that Mr. Cayce approved of, and for two years Lennie has been there. This is the only place where he has been content, and we think it the very best, regardless of price. Lennie, with only one setback, has steadily improved there, and we have great hopes that he will ultimately recover . . ."

These cases, more than any other type, serve to emphasize that Edgar Cayce viewed the future in two quite separate ways. While the personal destiny awaiting a given soul may consist of the inevitable consequences of his own past actions (and thus lend itself to psychic predetermination) the future can never be entirely preordained. A given country, for example, has the power to alter and reshape its destiny in exact accord with the altering behavior patterns of that people of that country. A stronger, more determined effort on the part of the responsible German majority could easily have prevented Hitler's rise to power. Europe could have followed a saner, more serene evolution. The earthquakes which threaten in California and South America can likewise be averted by a swing away from materiality and social indifference on the part of their inhabitants.

Cayce never put it more clearly than he did in one of his lectures, given in his normal conscious state to an A.R.E. prayer group.

"A warning was once given to a man of God that a certain city would be destroyed," he said. "But the man talked with God face to face, and God promised that if there were fifty righteous men, he would save it . . . then, finally, if there were just ten righteous men, He would spare the city.

"I believe that the just people in the world keep it going. The just people are the ones who have been kind to the other fellow . . . in patience, long-suffering, brotherly love, preferring their neighbor before themselves.

"When there are possibly fifty—or a hundred, or a thousand, or a million —then the way may well have been prepared for His coming.

"But all these just men must be united in their desire and supplication that the Christ physically walk among men again."

CHAPTER 8

MAN—THE STRANGER IN THE EARTH

IT MIGHT BE good to call a halt here, while we recap Edgar Cayce's reasons for placing in God the only power to alleviate the soul's mortification when it reaches a despair beyond the succor of man.

While Edgar's subconscious mind in hypnosis was still orthodox enough to envision the soul as a creation of God which contains a minute particle of Him at its core, the reader will have clearly seen by now how adamantly he maintains that all mortal sorrow comes from the soul's own misuse of the free will given it by its Maker.

In short, God can neither denounce, sit in judgment condemn, mete out punishment, be cajoled by lip-service, nor award special dispensations to a favored few. He relinquished all these privileges when he gave every soul freedom of action, choice and decision. Now, He can only wait in patience and genuine compassion for the souls to decide how soon they will use their free will to return to Him, once they have conceded that He makes a better Creator than they do.

The reader may argue that as a theory it may all be very fine, and even acceptable to the subconscious, but it leaves conscious man in the uncomfortable position of having nowhere to pass the buck, and the ego depends for its self-preservation on the illusion that it is more sinned against than sinning.

If we return to that first session with Lammers in 1923 we should by now find it easier to trace the fundamental logic underlying Edgar's philosophy.

LAMMERS: "What is the soul of a body?"

CAYCE: "That which the Maker gave to every individual in the beginning, and which is now seeking the house—or place—of the Maker."

LAMMERS: "Does the soul ever die?"

CAYCE: "It may be banished from the Maker. That is not death."

LAMMERS: "How does the soul become banished from its Maker?"

CAYCE: "To work out its own salvation—as you would term the word—the individual banishes itself."

LAMMERS: "What is meant by the personality?"

CAYCE: "The personality is that which is known on this physical plane as the conscious. When the subconscious controls, (e.g. under hypnosis) the personality is removed from the individual and lies above the physical body. This may be seen here (in my own case).

"Hence the disturbing of these conditions would bring distress to the other portions of the individual."

This point was dramatically illustrated some years later when Hugh Lynn Cayce, Edgar's son, was conducting a public session. One of the men present scribbled a note and handed it to Hugh Lynn across the sleeping body of his father, who instantly broke off speaking and relapsed into a cataleptic silence, which thoroughly disconcerted his son. The situation was without precedent and he had no means of resolving it. Some hours later, Edgar suddenly jack-knifed from his recumbent position and catapulted himself to his feet at the base of the couch. This was done with unbelievable rapidity, more akin to the speeded-up action of a film than anything in reality, and while Hugh Lynn was still grappling with his own amazement, his father asked in a perfectly natural voice for something to eat. He had an intense hunger and thirst.

In a subsequent Reading he explained that his "personality"—evicted from his physical body by the self-hynotic process—had levitated about a foot and a half above his physical body. And when the gentleman had handed the note to Hugh Lynn, he had thrust his fist through the astral equivalent of Edgar's rib cage. The impact was the equivalent of a kick from a horse.

This ability of the body to separate itself into at least three separate levels of electric vibration—much as the atomic scientists have divided the atom into separate energies, all different but all coexistent—can only manifest itself in cases as unique as Edgar Cayce's. He could move from plane to plane of consciousness with the ease of a man switching from AM to FM and then to TV on the same console.

The basic logic is perfectly simple: the least effective part of any unit—spiritual, human or mechanical—is its most temporary component. In the human makeup, the physical body, the "temporary shelter" of the eternal soul, is the most expendable.

The lizard who can always grow another tail (should he happen to lose one through no fault of his own) is not likely to attach exaggerated importance to that particular section of his anatomy. He is secure in the knowledge that, while he can grow another tail, the tail cannot grow another him.

Unfortunately, the human ego is incapable of such lucid reasoning. To mix the metaphor and take it to its logical conclusion—in the human psyche, the tail stubbornly insists on wagging the dog. Therein lies the beginning and the end of all human misery. This is what led Sartre's existentialists to blind themselves with inexact science, and avante-garde clerics, seeking to escape still further from all spiritual responsibility, to create Instant Religion out of God-is-deadism.

The Same Law Governs All Planets

"The unbalancing of the truth brings normal results to both the physical and soul matter," Edgar Cayce told Lammers. "Each individual must lead his own life, whether in this sphere or in the other planes."

We might take this to mean that the eternal laws of cause and effect, to which every soul is personally answerable, work on all the other planets in our system exactly as they do on earth, even though this is the only planet where physical life as we know it exists.

The components of the other planets may be as diversified as the atoms in nuclear physics. Their *genera* may range from one-dimensional to the cube root of x-dimensional. But each makes its proper contribution to the eventual evolution of the soul.

"All insufficient matter is cast into Saturn," said Cayce at this time, implying that the planet in question may operate as a kind of oven, slow-baking the accumulated drosses out of those souls who have fallen so far behind the others that immediate return to the earth would cause hardship for all concerned—the bigots of history, possibly, from Herod down through the Roman and Byzantine tyrants to this century's dictators and their schizoid worshippers.

Thus, if Edgar Cayce is correct in suggesting that each planetary environment tempers the wind to the shorn lamb, the soul's reception here must always be dictated by the condition in which it arrives, whether from another planet in the solar system, or from the various astral confines of our own.

LAMMERS: "Where does the soul come from, and how does it enter the physical body?"

CAYCE: "It is already there. As the body of the human, when born, breathes the first breath of life, so it becomes a living soul, provided it has reached that development where the soul may rightly enter and find a lodging place."

LAMMERS: "Is it possible for this body, Edgar Cayce, in this state, to communicate with anyone who has passed into the spirit world?"

CAYCE: "The spirits of all that have passed from the physical plane remain about that plane until their development carries them onward, or until they are returned for their further development here. While they remain within the plane of communication of this sphere, any may be communicated with. There are thousands about us here at present. . . ."

The Planetary Influences

LAMMERS: "Give the names of the principal planets, and their influence on the lives of people."

CAYCE: "Mercury, Mars, Jupiter, Venus, Saturn, Neptune, Uranus, Septimus."

LAMMERS: "Are any of the planets, other than the earth, inhabited by human beings or animal life of any kind?"

CAYCE: "No."

LAMMERS: "Give the description of the planet nearest the earth at the present time, and its effect upon the people."

CAYCE: "That planet now fast approaching the earth, under whose influence the earth minds trend for the next few years, as time is known here, will be Mars, which will be only thirty-five million miles away from the earth in 1924.

"The influence will be felt as this recedes from the earth and those who have sojourned on Mars will express, in their lives upon the earth, the troublesome times that will arise. This will only be tempered by those who will be coming from Jupiter, Venus and Uranus, those strong ennobling forces tempered by love and strength."

The Astrological Influences

LAMMERS: "Please define astrology."

CAYCE: "The inclinations of man are ruled by the planet under which he is born, for the destiny of man lies within the sphere or scope of the planets.

"In the beginning, our own planet, the Earth, was set in motion. With the planning of other planets began the destiny of all created matter.

"The strongest force affecting the destiny of man is the Sun first, then the closer planets to the earth, or those that are coming to ascension at the time of the birth of the individual.

"Just as the tides are ruled by the Moon in its path about the earth, just so is the higher creation ruled by its actions in conjunction with the planets about the earth.

"BUT LET IT BE UNDERSTOOD HERE: NO ACTION OF ANY PLANET OR THE PHASES OF THE SUN, THE MOON, OR ANY OF THE HEAVENLY BODIES, SURPASSES THE RULE OF MAN'S OWN WILL POWER: the power given by the Creator to man in the beginning, when he became a living soul with the power of choosing for himself. . . .

"In the sphere of many of the planets within the same solar system, we find souls again and again and again return, from one to another, until they are prepared to meet the everlasting creator of our Universe, of which our system is only a very small part. (But) only upon the earth plane, at present, do we find men in flesh and blood. Upon others do we find those of His own making in the preparation of His own development."

The Soul's Immunity to Death

How does the world of the living appear to the soul who is temporarily free of an earth-body? The simplest frame of reference might be to compare the weight and density of an astronaut on the ground with his weight and density in orbit.

There is definite evidence that an astronaut, once he is beyond the pull of earth's gravity, attached to the capsule only by a thin nylon cord, experiences moments of exhilaration, euphoria, a disassociation with the earth below him, and a desire to remain suspended in space.

Suppose we argue, then, that the difference between the soul freed by death, and the same soul encased in a living body is only a difference of density and vibration, no more complex than the difference between the astronaut floating in space and the same astronaut securely strapped to his controls before takeoff. Before takeoff he has little or no freedom of action; in outer space he has more than he needs, but in essence he is still the same man.

Once you feel you can accept this comparison, it may be easier for you to go back to the Creation and imagine the souls as they first became aware of themselves.

The earth was still cooling from its fiery birth; the division of land and water had followed. Then came the emergence of animal life from its amoeboid origins. The only solid matter the souls had ever known was now manifesting itself on the earth proper. In other words, only the earth itself conformed to the laws of density and gravity as we know them now.

Hovering above the earth, the souls had been following this evolutionary progress with fascination, and now, with the division of animal life into male and female species, their curiosity tempted them to digress from their own evolutionary path and assume mortal shape instead. At this time, remember, their bodies were still of rarified spiritual texture. In terms of the astronaut, they were "weightless."

Cayce constantly employs the term "thought-forms" when dealing with their condition at this stage of their development. A thought-form is exactly what its name suggests: a form created by concentrated thought, yet lacking the solidity of mundane matter. On all mental levels other than the conscious mind, "thoughts are things," and thus a thought-form, once it is created, is as real and tangible as the mind which created it.

It can only manifest itself to the conscious mind as a vision or a hallucination. Injudicious doses of lysergic acid break down the protecting barrier and submit the user to direct contact with thought-forms, usually his own; though he is equally vulnerable to the thought-forms of others. When these outside contacts are evil, his encounters with them can have a disastrous after-effect on his own sanity.

When a competent hypnotist tells a susceptible subject in a trance that he is holding an orange in his empty hand, and the subject obediently begins to eat it, he is, to all intents and purposes, eating a real orange. He has created a thought-form of it at that level of his subconscious where thought *is* matter.

Cayce explained that the uncorrupted soul could enter and withdraw from denser matter at will, being able to "push out of itself" and adapt to the conditions which had already taken shape in its thought "much in the way and manner that the present-day amoeba sustains itself in the waters of a stagnant bay or lake."

Because it had never been God's intent that the souls should ever manifest themselves on this earth in human bodies, there was as yet no division of the souls into male and female. Therefore, the animals' means of reproduction was inaccessible to them. Their only alternative was to "occupy" the animal bodies, much as a hermit crab might occupy the empty shell of another species, except that in this case, the shells were already occupied!

Thus two entirely alien forms of life were attempting to share a common physical heritage. The hazards were obvious. Nevertheless, a few of the bolder souls employed their free will to intrude into this denser vibration of animal matter.

The wiser and more prudent souls hesitated, and it was well that they did.

Those souls which now found themselves entrapped in their flesh prisons were unable to extricate themselves. The alien matter of the material world acted like the cogs of an implacable machine. It engorged the souls and swept them along with it. They became hopelessly entangled in the procreative processes. And onto the earth came an anguished hybrid, neither human nor animal—a half-man, half-beast—unable to conform to or escape from the laws of animal evolution.

"We find these sons of the Creative Forces," says Cayce, "looking upon those changed forms, the Daughters of Men. And there crept in those pollutions; or rather, they polluted themselves with those mixtures. This brought contempt, hatred, bloodshed, and those impulses which build for self-desire, without respect for another's freedom."

The souls who had remained free were unable to come to the rescue. They could only look on, helpless and bewildered.

It was this that caused God to create a perfect physical mold, or flesh body, into which the "rescue-souls" could incarnate with safety. Symbolized in Genesis as the creation of Adam, man appeared in his present form at five different places on the earth, and each of the five newly created groups was ethnically distinct from the others.

The souls who now incarnated through these pure channels are referred to by Cayce as the *Sons of God* to distinguish them from the souls trapped in animal matter. These he called the Sons of Man.

The Bible's admonitions to "keep the race pure" have their origins in this first appearance of uncontaminated souls on the earth. To them, the hybrid souls with their animal deformities were in the Hindu sense "untouchable."

The Sons of God, in their five separate race categories of white, black, brown, red, and yellow pigmentation, built up their separate civilizations on continents now destroyed or altered beyond recognition by the subsequent earth-changes. The Atlantic ocean now covers the submerged continent of Atlantis (cradle of the red race), just as the Pacific covers the sunken continent of Lemuria (cradle of the black race).

Because so few questions were put to Edgar Cayce concerning it, the Readings record very little of Lemuria. But Atlantis (200,000 B.C. to 10,700 B.C.) is generously documented. Indeed, according to the Readings, it is fair to assume that it was the cradle of our present civilization.

This vast soul-group was both the most aggressive and the most resourceful the world was ever to know.

For the most part, the Atlantean influence is still as headstrong as ever it was. This influence applies particularly to those soul-groups who chose *not* to reincarnate at a steady rate of progress. At their zenith, the Atlanteans commanded the powers of ESP and telepathy, harnessed electricity, mastered the mechanical propulsion of air and sea vessels, established short wave communications, induced longevity and performed advanced surgery, using as their source of energy the Tuaoi Stone of "Terrible Crystal" their own forerunner of the maser or laser ray. It was the misuse of this same source of energy which destroyed them.

They were a peripatetic, restless expression of human life, perpetually striving to meddle with, alter and improve the laws of Nature. They attained to a fantastic height of power, and then proceeded to abuse it.

From their spiritual beginnings as a civilization that only recognized the One God, they eventually rejected Him for a totalitarian god of brute force, which is the same as saying that they worshipped their own vices instead.

They reduced the backward hybrid souls, or mutants, to slavery, subjecting them to every degradation and abuse.

They remained perfectly aware of the laws of karma, but made the error of assuming that their accumulating debts could easily be paid off at any given time in the future. Here they reckoned without one factor—that the path of evolution might suddenly veer in its course and return them to meet their debts in bodies shorn of all their Atlantean prescience and might.

This is exactly what befell them. When man's senses were reduced to the minimal five he possesses today, the Atlantean miscreant found himself as impotent as the hermit crab bereft of its shell.

The karmic debts that were to be so easily paid off in a life or two were suddenly magnified into infinity. Instead of two lives, some of their offenses against God now demanded thousands of lives of restitution.

Rather than shoulder such eternal burdens, they chose spiritual bankruptcy. The vast accumulation of debt remains, however, and still has to be paid.

Early in this century, Edgar Cayce began to prophesy the return of both types of Atlanteans in vast numbers. He warned that for every advance of science and material emancipation the Sons of the One God might bring with them, the Sons of Man could also bring corruption and chaos.

"Atlantean souls are extremists; they know no middle ground," Cayce stated uncompromisingly, adding that Atlanteans of every genre were to be found among the leaders of all the nations involved in the two World Wars. So, as a rough standard of comparison, we can set Roosevelt and Churchill at one end of the scale and Hitler and Stalin at the other. In like manner we can contrast Pope John XXIII with Mao.

The advances which civilization has made from barbarism to practicable democracy leave the impenitent type of Atlantean unmoved, except when his stupefaction that "his world is not as it was" reaches a psychotic level. Then he stuffs himself with LSD, or climbs into a college bell tower and shoots the "usurpers who have altered the earth." At a cannier level of self-preservation, he is the scofflaw whose cynicism undermines his society. You will find him behind the corrupt politician, the rabble rouser, the lunatic fringe dedicated to religious and racial discrimination, and the gougers of the sick, fat buck, who are reducing the popular cultures to semi-literate trash.

"As we have indicated, the Atlanteans were those who had reached an advancement and had been entrusted with divine activities in the earth, but forget the One God in Whom all live and have their being. Thus they brought about that which destroyed the body, though not the soul. There are numbers, great numbers, of Atlanteans in the earth in the present."

Against the extremist Atlanteans who still worship lust, violence and death, are aligned the sober forces of their tempered, experienced fellow-souls, who have gained a sane perspective from their many and varied reincarnations down through history—"those strong ennobling forces tempered by love and strength." With these marches the Christ. With these may lie our descendants' only means of averting another cataclysm akin to the annihilation of Atlantis.

This concept is thrown into sharp focus when the Life Reading for a very young child warns its parents that in its Atlantean life, it had worshipped the One God.

The usurpers of power at the time of the third and final inundation, however, were the Sons of Belial, whose god of evil was destined to survive the Deluge in the corrupted form of the Biblical idol Baal. The child had suffered persecution at the hands of these same Sons of Belial, "as it will again here in the present. Let the Entity be warned to guard against all those who seek for self."

"Granting that reincarnation is a fact," Edgar Cayce said elsewhere, "and that souls once occupied such an environ as Atlantis, and that these are now entering the earth's sphere—if they made such alterations in the earth's affairs in their day as to bring destruction on themselves—can there be any wonder that they might make such like changes in the affairs of peoples and individuals today?"

This same warning is reiterated in another Reading: "Beware lest material or vain things bring thee forgetfulness of Who is thy Redeemer, and whence cometh the Voice which is deep within! For what is needed most in the world today? That the Sons of Belial be warned that those who are, and have been, unfaithful to the One God must meet themselves in the things which come to pass."

In one of his Readings for a child, Edgar urged the parents to direct his interests towards the technical side of "radio, television and the like" because his experience in electrical communications stemmed from a life in Atlantis in which he had been an expert in the use of sound-waves "and the manner in which light was used as a means of communication. And Morse's dots and dashes were already 'old-hat' to the Entity in that experience."

Elsewhere he counsels a young man with an Atlantean "memory-bank" to choose electronics as a career because "none of the modern conveniences are a mystery to the Entity, even though he may not understand them as yet. For the Entity has always expected to see these again!"

The advanced technology which Atlantis's scientists brought back to this century with them has controlled disease, conquered the skies and split the atom, but it has also bequeathed us the H-Bomb—that selfsame exploitation of nuclear energy which destroyed its original creators and buried their arrogant ramparts deep in the mud of the ocean floor.

Why has this totalitarian cross section of a once mighty race learned nothing from its blunders? Because it refused to keep abreast of the world's spiritual progress by reincarnating in its proper soul-cycles. But surely its greatest lack is its ignorance of Christ. Its last memory of life on earth predates, by nearly two hundred centuries, the Redemption brought to the soul of man by the Master. It is hardly likely, then, that our articles of faith are imposing enough to command the comprehension or respect of such atavists. Remembering nothing of Christ, they have no cause to abandon their ancient belief in the brute survival of the fittest. They would be as eager today to enslave the more backward nations as they enslaved the backward humanoids of their own time . . . those selfsame "things" or "monstrosities" whom the Sons of the One God led out of Atlantean bondage into prehistoric Egypt, where the surgeon-priests in the temples of healing eradicated the physical evidence of their animal antecedents and "made them men.

"This is the purpose of the Entity in the earth," Cayce taught, "to be a living example of that which He gave: 'Come unto Me, all that are weak and heavy-laden; Take My cross upon you and learn of Me.' These are thy purposes in the earth. And these thou wilt manifest beautifully—or again bring to miserable failure, as thou didst in Atlantis, and as many another soul is doing in this particular era."

The final Armageddon, said Cayce, will not be fought on the earth. It will be fought between the souls leaving the earth and the souls endeavoring to return to it—the souls returning to the God they once deserted, and the lost souls who hope to reject Him into eternity, by holding fast, at all costs, to this failing planet.

In terms of orthodox dogma it will be a war fought between the dead, not between the living.

But Edgar Cayce makes no more differentiation between the dead and the living than he does between the caterpillar, the cocoon and the butterfly. Thus the souls involved in the final Armageddon will be the same souls they always were from the Beginning. Nothing will have changed except the plane of consciousness they occupy. They will only have moved from the confines of matter to the eternal plane of their origin.

CHAPTER 9

EDGAR CAYCE'S OWN CREDO

IN 1941 EDGAR CAYCE had occasion to give a Reading to two members of the Association for Research and Enlightenment, in which he commended them for resolving their own karmic differences in their dedication to the work of the Association. They had successfully buried the hatchet and worked side by side to such a harmonious extent that the writer Thomas Sugrue was able to assemble his biography of Edgar, *There is a River,* from the material they had patiently indexed from the Readings.

There had been mutual forgiveness by both members, the Reading explained, "for each has met himself well. Remember the injunction given by Him: 'When thou art converted, strengthen thy brothers.' Do not depart from the awareness that He, the Master, Jesus, will walk with thee—if ye desire to walk with Him."

In the distant past, these two members had been enemies in more than one life—not so much because their ideals conflicted, but because they were serving the same ideals at cross-purposes. Rather than hating one another, they had been jealous of each other's glory; the war between their egos had taken precedence over their service to their fellow men and delayed their spiritual progress down the centuries.

It is in this same Reading that Edgar gave voice to his own intense concern for the unenlightened soul in the period immediately following physical death. If the soul has lived in ignorance of the unbroken flow of life from one plane of consciousness to the next, he may "pass over without understanding until the opportunity for understanding is seemingly past."

He voiced a hope that the A.R.E. would succeed in building the truth "in each phase of an individual's experience while he is on earth—in books, in pamphlets, in lectures, by conversation—in such a manner that knowledge, and the wisdom to apply it, be made available to all who choose to seek it."

His total reliance on the power of Christ to preserve and enlighten the human soul underlies his every thought. In 1932, when he was asked to give the strongest reason against reincarnation, he answered: "That a law of cause and effect should exist here in material things. Yet the strongest argument against reincarnation is also the strongest argument for it, as in any principle reduced to its essence. For the law is set, and it happens—even though a soul might will itself never to reincarnate, but would prefer to suffer and suffer and suffer—for both Heaven and Hell are built by the soul.

"But does a soul have to crucify the flesh, even as He, when it discovers that it must work out its own salvation in the material world by entering and reentering until it achieves that soul-consciousness which would make it a companion with the Creator? . . .

552

"Rather is the law of forgiveness made available in thine experience through the Son who would stand in thy stead."

Cayce never professed to be a man of letters in his waking state, but what he did write is impressively lucid and never obscured by pretension. The proof is evident in this talk he gave to the A.R.E. in 1933, where he explained his own attitude to his psychic power in words that would be hard for another pen to better.

"As to the validity of the information which comes through me when I sleep—this is the question, naturally, that occurs to everyone. Personally, I feel that its validity depends largely upon how much faith and confidence lie within the one who seeks this source of information.

"In regard to this same source of information, even though I have been doing this work for thirty-one years, I know very little about it. Whatever I might say would be largely a matter of conjecture. I can make no claims whatsoever to great knowledge, for I also am only groping.

"But then, we all learn by experience, do we not? We come to have faith and understanding only by taking one step at a time. Most of us don't have the experience of getting religion all at once, like the man who got it halfway between the bottom of the well and the top, when he was blown out by an explosion of dynamite! Most of us need to arrive at our conclusions by weighing the evidence along with something that answers from deep within our inner selves.

"As a matter of fact, there would seem to be not just one, but several sources of information tapped when I am in this sleeping state.

"One source, apparently, is the record made by an individual in all of its experiences through what we call time. The sum total of the experiences of that soul is written, so to speak, in the subconscious of that individual as well as in what is known as the Akashic Records. Anyone may read these records, if he can attune himself rightly. Apparently, I am one of the few people who may lay aside the personality sufficiently to allow the soul to make this attunement to the universal source of knowledge. I say this, however, not in a boastful way; in fact, I don't claim to possess any power that any other person doesn't possess. I sincerely believe that there isn't any person, anywhere, who doesn't have the same ability I have. I'm certain that all human beings have much greater powers than they are ever aware of—provided they are willing to pay the price of detachment from self-interest which is required to develop those powers or abilities. Would you be willing, even once a year, to put aside your own personality—to pass entirely away from it?

"Many people ask me how I prevent undesirable influences from entering into the work I do. In order to answer that question, let me tell an experience I had when I was a child. When I was between eleven and twelve years of age, I had read the Bible three times. Now I have read it fifty-six times. No doubt some people have read it more times than that. But I have tried to read it once for each year of my life.

"Well, as a child, I prayed that I might be able to do something for other people—to aid them in understanding themselves, and especially to aid children in their ills. One day I had a vision which convinced me that my prayer had been heard and would be answered.

"So I believe that my prayer is still being answered. And as I go into the unconscious condition, I do so with that faith. I also believe that the source of information will be from the Universal, if the connection is not made to waver by the desires of the person seeking the Reading.

"Now, some people think that the information coming through me is given by some departed personality who wishes to communicate—some benevolent spirit or guide from the other side. This may sometimes be true, but in general I am not a 'medium' in that sense of the term. If the person who seeks a Reading, however, comes seeking that kind of contact and information, I believe he receives that kind.

"For instance, if that person's desire is very intense to have a communication from Grandpa, Uncle, or some great soul, then the contact is directed that way, and such becomes the source.

"Do not think I am discrediting those who seek in such a way. If you're willing to receive what Uncle Joe has to say, that is what you get. If you're willing to depend upon a more Universal Source, then that is what you get.

" 'What ye ask, ye shall receive' is like a two-edged sword. It cuts both ways."

Two years earlier, he had told the A.R.E. audience he was addressing: "Now who is to be the judge as to what is the proper way and manner in which to conduct research into the mysteries of life? We are able to judge only by their fruits, only by the results people obtain, when they delve into these phenomena of life.

"I am constantly asked by people who have just come to know me: 'Are you a spiritualist? How did you ever become interested in psychic phenomena? Are you a medium? Are you this, that, or the other?'

"It has always been my desire to be able to answer for the faith that lies within. It seems to me that if one cannot answer for that faith that one professes to live by, then such a one is not at his best. For we live by faith, day by day. If we don't know what we believe or why we believe it, we are indeed getting far afield from that which the Source of Life would have us be.

"What is Life? What is this phenomenon of life? Where and how do the various phenomena manifest themselves?

"We have a physical body; we have a mental body; we have a spiritual body, or soul. Now each of these has its own attributes. Just as the physical body has its divisions—all dependent one upon the other, and some more dependent than the rest—so the mind has its own source of activity that manifests in various ways through the individual body.

"The soul also has its attributes, and its various ways of gaining, maintaining or manifesting itself among men. The psychic force is a manifestation of the soul mind.

"Let us go back into sacred history. Do you know where the first lines were drawn concerning psychic phenomena? Where the first line was drawn as to what a psychic phenomenon is—the division as to what is real, and what is not?

"It was when Moses was sent down into Egypt to deliver the Chosen People, and he was told to take the rod he had in his hand and—with Aaron, his brother—to go before Pharaoh. God, through him, would show mighty wonders to the people. Then Moses went before Pharaoh and cast his rod down, and it turned into a serpent. The magicians cast their rods down, and they turned to serpents, too. But Aaron's rod or serpent ate up all the rest of them!

"Then there began what were called the plagues in Egypt. In one, Aaron stretched out his rod over the waters and they turned to blood. The magicians stretched out their rods, too, and the water turned to blood for them. Next came the plague of frogs, and the magicians could do this also, with their enchantments. Then came the plague of lice, when the rod smote the dust of the earth; and this plague was the first instance of blood being drawn from the body. The magicians attempted to do the same thing but nothing happened. They turned to Pharaoh and said: 'The finger of God is in this thing!' (Ex. 8:18, 19.)

"At this point, we can draw a dividing line between enchantments and the things of God. When we know, when we are convinced, when we see by the results, that the finger of God is indeed in what is taking place, then we can know whether the phenomenon we are seeing and experiencing is of divine origin or otherwise!

"How may it be otherwise? Well, we say all force, all power, comes from one source. With that I agree; but when there is a misapplication of this Force of Life itself, the phenomenon does not fail to occur—even though misdirected. Just as we see people born among us who are mentally deficient, physically disabled. Apparently such afflictions have nothing whatever to do with the individuals. (I say apparently.) Yet the phenomenon of life moves on, just the same. At some point there has been a misdirection or a guiding-away from the purposes of the All-Powerful. Yet it moves on just the same.

"Possibly there wasn't a greater parable than the one about the wheat and the tares growing up together. The tares were not to be rooted up at once, else the wheat would be destroyed also. But the time would come when the wheat would be gathered and put into the granary, and the tares gathered to be burned.

"If the soul is in a proper accord with the Source of life, may not the phenomena be directed by the same One that directed Aaron, rather than that which directed the magicians in their activity? In the plagues, there was a point at which the magicians failed. So if psychic phenomena come from some source other than the one Divine Source, they, too, must reach a point where they fail.

"The Master was in accord with the One Source of all Good. I think many others also were, at various times, when they presented themselves as a living sacrifice, holy and acceptable unto Him. Therefore, it must be possible for any of us to be in accord with the One Divine Source of all information, if we will but pay the price.

"Often I have fallen far short in presenting myself as a living sacrifice for whatever source might manifest through me. In that sense, I suppose I may be called a medium. But I hope I may be, rather, a channel through which blessings may come to many, rather than a medium through which any force might manifest. For if it is of God, it must be good. Or, if it is good, it must come from the All-Good, or God. This good, I trust, is the type of psychic phenomena manifesting through me."

This is a serene manifesto of perfect faith, couched in a simplicity that lends it beauty. And Cayce's personal love and trust in the Christ is, if possible, even more intimate in its total dedication when he spoke to the same group in 1934.

"In John 14:1-3, Jesus said: 'Let not your heart be troubled; ye believe in God, believe also in Me . . . And if I go and prepare a place for you, I will come again, and receive you unto myself; that where I am, there ye may be also.'

"When we look into the history of the world as we know it today, how often has a great religious leader or prophet arisen? Plato said that our cycle of entering is about every thousand years. Judging from history itself, the period of time between each religious teacher who has come into the earth varies from six hundred and twenty-five years to twelve hundred.

"Do you ask: 'Is that how often you say Christ has come?'

"No, I don't say that. I don't know how many times He has come. However, if we will consider the following passages of Scripture for a few moments, an interesting idea may be formulated: 'In the beginning was the Word, and the Word was with God, and the Word was God. The same was in the beginning with God. All things were made by Him; and without Him was not anything made that was made . . . And the Word was made flesh, and dwelt among us. . . . He was in the world, and the world was made by Him, and the world knew Him not.' (John 1:1-14.)

"Many people tell us that this is speaking of spiritual things. You must answer this for yourself. But if the Word was made flesh and dwelt among men, how can we be sure that this is not speaking materially, too?

"In talking with those who should have been and were the judges of Israel at the time, the Master said: 'Your father Abraham rejoiced to see my day, and he saw it, and was glad.' Then said the Jews unto Him, 'Thou art not yet fifty years old, and hast thou seen Abraham?' Jesus said unto them, 'Verily, verily, I say unto you, before Abraham was, I am.' (John 8:37-44.)

"Did Jesus mean that in a spiritual sense or a literal sense—or both? What do you think? I don't know. But what we have been told psychically is this— take it for what it is worth and apply it in your own experience.

"Now turn to the fourteenth Chapter of Genesis and read where Abraham is paid tribute by a certain royal priest, Melchizedek, who brought forth bread and wine. 'For this Melchizedek, King of Salem, priest of the most high God, who met Abraham returning from the slaughter of the Kings, and blessed him. . . . Without father, without mother, without descent, having neither beginning of days, nor end of life, but made like unto the Son of God; abideth a priest continually.' (Hebrews 7.)

"Was this the Master; this Melchizedek? I don't know. Read it yourself.

Maybe I'm wrong in thinking it was the Master; the man we know later as Jesus.

"Consider now the book of Joshua. Who directed Joshua when he became the leader of Israel? Who walked out to lead Joshua, after he crossed the Jordan? The Bible says that the Son of Man came out to lead the armies of the Lord. And after Joshua's experience in meeting this man of God, all the children of Israel were afraid of him. (Joshua 5:13-15.)

"From the above references, let us draw a few conclusions, and supplement them with psychic information. The Spirit of the Christ manifested in the earth many times before the coming of Jesus; at times it manifested through one like Melchizedek, and at other times it manifested as a spiritual influence through some teacher upholding the worship of the One God.

"What has this conclusion to do with the second coming? Well, in the light of the above, there ceases to be a second coming! Also, by considering the conditions that made His appearance possible at various times—or, if you prefer, the one time as Jesus—we can deduce certain facts about the return of the Master.

"How did He happen to come as Jesus of Nazareth? There had not been a revelation to man, of which we have any record, for over four hundred years. Then did darkness and dissipation on the part of man bring Christ into the World? If so, it's a reversal of the natural law Like begets Like. The laws of God are not reversed at any time, and never will we find them so. They are immutable and hold true throughout any kingdom we may find in the earth.

"Then what brought about the coming of Jesus? A people who were sincere seekers—a little group founded to make themselves channels whereby this great thing could come to pass. Who were these people? They were the most hated of all those mentioned in profane history, and are scarcely mentioned in the Bible, the Essenes, the hated ones, the lowest of the Jews. . . .

"These Essenes, then, were consecrating their lives to make possible a meeting place for God and man, that Jesus the Christ might come into the world. Thus there was a *preparation;* and if we will prepare a meeting place—in our heart, our home, our group, our church—then we too can have the Christ come to us again, and He will come as He is. His spirit is here always. It will abide with us always. . . .

"We all believe that He descended into Hell and taught those there. We read it in the Bible and we say it is true. But we don't really believe it. If we did, we would never find fault with any soul in the world—never! For if we believe that He went into Hell and taught the people there, how could we find fault with our next-door neighbor because his chickens got into our garden, or because he doesn't believe exactly as we do?

"He, for our sakes, became flesh. How many times? Answer for yourself. How soon will He come again? When we live the life He has laid out for us, we are making it possible for Him, the Lord and Master of this world, to return.

" 'I will not leave you comfortless, but I will come again, and receive you unto myself; that where I am, there ye may be also.' "

Thus in his waking hours Cayce the man reveals himself as a tolerant and sincere churchgoer of orthodox antecedents, with no desire whatever to push his personal beliefs down other people's throats . . . or for them to push their beliefs down his throat. Nevertheless, it would be difficult to proceed beyond this point to a fully-balanced explanation of reincarnation as he saw it, unless we understood his insistence that Christ was a Divinity manifesting himself through a highly-developed human soul named Jesus. Furthermore, that same Divinity had had to manifest Itself several times on earth before It was able to prepare a human body of sufficiently advanced spirituality to sustain It in Its ultimate task of salvation.

The reader may be assured that no Reading exists in which Edgar Cayce infers that sections of the Bible had been re-edited with malice aforethought. When he was asked if such might be so, he replied that the spirit of the Bible was still whole, and that its power lay in its spiritual strength, and was not dependent on its literal context. In short, it was still God's assurance to the human race that He would never abandon it.

On the other hand Cayce did not, in permissive sleep, deny that many sections had lost their original clarity in the course of their translations from Hebrew to Byzantine Greek, to classic Latin, and then to Jacobean English. A thorough study of the Readings centering round the Palestinian period at the time of Christ reveals that they gave the Essenes far greater credit for preserving the true wisdom of the ancient scriptures than the established Hebrew Church, which was, in effect, passing through the type of period which Pope Pius XII has defined as "heresy of action."

When Christ preached in the synagogues, he introduced nothing new or unfamiliar into his sermons, but, more devastatingly, he revived those sections of the old teachings which had either fallen into convenient disrepute, or been reinterpreted to suit the political exigencies of the Sanhedrin.

It is pertinent to inject here that the Dead Sea Scrolls, even in these cautious early stages of their deciphering, have established that much of Christ's teaching is present in the same form, indeed often in the same words, in the Essene scriptures which were in existence at least a hundred years before His birth.

This proves that He was in basic accord with the tenets of the Essenes, although in His own lifetime they were in such militant conflict with orthodox Judaism that no reference to them was permitted in the Hebrew Scriptures.

Unfortunately the sect possessed its fair share of firebrands and hotheads who believed that the ends justified the means, even to the extent of guerilla attacks on the caravans of the Sadducees and the Pharisees. This group obviously found itself in conflict with Christ's exhortation to resist all forms of violence, and even the two or three Essenes among His disciples forgot themselves often enough to provoke incidents which achieved no better purpose than to heighten the antagonism of His enemies.

At this time, Jerusalem was occupied by the Romans very much as France in our century was occupied by the Nazis—but the Essenes were a sect which had for so long been underground that they were virtually unaffected by the superimposition of Roman persecution over the existing persecution of the

Sanhedrin. Nevertheless, the sect met eventual annihilation at the hands of the Roman army, at the instigation of the Sanhedrin, the same governing body which had instigated the crucifixion of Christ.

To some, what the Dead Sea Scrolls are slowly establishing is that the Essene beliefs were rooted firmly in the laws of reincarnation.

Furthermore, they were the only sect which correctly prophesied the coming of Christ. Just as the books of the Apocrypha and Revelation were obscured in symbolism to preserve the truth they contained, the Essene prophecy is worded in the past instead of the future tense, and in it Christ is called by variations of the Good Man, the Messiah, and the Son of Light, never by His real name; and the Sanhedrin is referred to as the Wicked Priest. In every other respect it is an exact foretelling of the events which came to pass a century later.

Cayce states categorically that the Essenes, being the only sect that was prepared for Christ's appearance on earth, not only aided in the birth in the manger and the flight to Egypt, but taught Jesus in his childhood. Many of these teachers were recognized by Cayce in the present:

"Then, the Entity was brought up in the tenets or school of thought that attempted to be a reconstruction of the former sect established by Elijah in Mount Carmel. . . .

"Because of the divisions that had arisen among the peoples into sects such as the Pharisees, the Sadducees, and their kind, there had arisen the Essenes, who cherished not merely the traditions which had come down by word of mouth, but had kept records of all supernatural experiences—whether in dreams, visions, or voices—that had been felt throughout the experiences of this peculiar people. . . .

"These pertained, then, to what you would call today astrological forecasts, as well as all those records pertaining to the coming of the Messiah. These had been part of the records in Carmel given by Elijah, who was the forerunner, who was the cousin, who was (John) the Baptist. . . .

"Hence the group we refer to here as the Essenes was the outgrowth of the teachings by Melchizedek, as propagated by Elijah and Elisha and Samuel. The movement was not an Egyptian one, though it was adopted by the Egyptians in an earlier period and made a part of the whole movement. They took Jews and Gentiles alike as members . . . preserving themselves in direct line of choice as channels through which might come He of the new or the divine origin. . . .

"The Essenes were to aid in the early teaching of the life of the child Jesus, as well as of John. For John was more the Essene than Jesus. For Jesus held rather to the spirit of the law, and John to the letter of same."

Throughout the detailed and exhaustive references to Jesus in the Readings, one is constantly struck by the urgent reality of the prose. Edgar Cayce always refers to Him as an immediate, living Force, never further from man than his own elbow.

Christ the Messenger; Jesus the Man

If, as Edgar Cayce reasons, Christ manifesting Himself through the body of Jesus was completing His own soul development in the earth, it brings conviction to His assurance to His disciples that they were capable of doing all the things that He had done. This was obviously impossible if they were to remain as spiritually imperfect as they were at that time. It presupposed that they would return many times before they could attain to His enlightenment.

Otherwise, we would have to believe that Christ was demanding of His followers an almost superhuman exercise in blind faith. He was offering a hit-or-miss, one-chance-only hope of survival . . . only if we sin no more, may we enter heaven. Is it so easy to conceive of Him as such an impractical perfectionist? All His other teachings are, in every sense, practical and realistic.

Cayce found it much more consistent that He defined the eventual redemption of the soul as a slow, patient retracing of the footsteps, rather than "instantaneous apotheosis." In this context, reincarnation appeals to the self-doubter not to despair as he watches his nimbler brothers apparently outstrip him. It teaches him that his free will can work for his best interests just as easily as it can work against them. He is shown the way—after that, it is up to him. He must take up his own bed and walk, not be transported bodily to an ersatz Heaven by an all-too-mortal Redeemer.

He is taught that if an innocent man, having suffered injustice at the hands of a powerful enemy, grimly takes a "just" revenge, he will gratuitously handcuff himself to that same enemy, and both of them will be compelled to return together and reenact the whole dreary, negative conflict until they develop enough common sense to bury their hatchets and call it quits. The more advanced soul of the two is bound to delay his own spiritual progress, for he has forced himself to proceed at the speed of the less developed soul he has harmed.

If, on the other hand, he is smart enough to "turn the other cheek" rather than attempt a futile retaliation, he frees himself of all further involvement with his enemy. The onus is then on his enemy, who must return alone, in his own time to repair whatever damage he left in his own wake.

Who Is Without Sin

Why did Christ make no social distinction between Pharisees and whores, publicans and weighty scholars? Surely because their outer trappings were temporary and transient, and He was concerned solely with the ultimate welfare of the soul within, as it struggled onward through its slow and painful self-exile.

What else is Christ saying, when He bids us love our neighbor, except: "Don't be such a fool as to hate him, and involve yourself with the dead weight of another gratuitous enemy!"

Christ was never more tolerant and merciful than in His treatment of the woman taken in adultery. Indeed, He was putting the law of love into practice in a way that very few of the churches bearing His name seem anxious to emulate. And yet all He was saying, in effect, was: "As ye judge, so shall ye be likewise judged." He was warning the woman's tormentors that in their subsequent lives they ran the danger of being caught in *flagrante delicto,* if only to teach them to shun persecution and hypocrisy, the two drabbest cancers of the soul.

His parable of the Prodigal Son restores God to the perspective that had been distorted in the Old Testament, when the scattered nomad tribes used the avenging Jehovah as a big stick to keep their spear-happy warriors from exterminating first their fellow tribesmen and eventually themselves.

Thus the parable of the Prodigal Son only takes on its true universality when God becomes the forgiving Father, and the Son becomes the lost and wandering soul on earth, afraid to return to its Father in metaphorical rags.

The Chalcedonian Decree of 451 A.D., which split Christ into two separate natures, human and divine, is confirmed by Edgar Cayce's answer to the same question:

"Christ is not a man! Jesus was the man! Christ was the Messenger! . . . Christ in all ages! Jesus only in one!"

Unless He was preparing himself to return to His disciples in a body akin to the purified shape they themselves would one day assume when they, too, eventually returned to their Father, why did Christ, on the cross, withdraw from his mortal form long enough for Jesus to call to Him in bewilderment: "Eli, Eli, why hast thou forsaken me?" It is utterly contrary to all His own teachings that Christ should have given way to inexplicable misgivings at the eleventh hour, and called those words to God. It would have served no better purpose than to harrow and demoralize those of his followers whose faith in Him, till then, had been absolute.

Surely Christ's logical purpose in submitting to the crucifixion was to show His followers not only the ease with which the earthly ties of flesh can be discarded, but the total unimportance of the body after it ceases to house the soul.

It is in this regard that Edgar Cayce puts forward a theory which occurs nowhere in dogmatic controversies, yet seems the most lucid of them all.

(Here it must be borne in mind that he refers to the living body as the body material, and the body after death as the body physical.)

"Just as an Entity, finding itself in one of those various realms abounding in the solar system, takes on, not an earthly form, but a pattern conforming to the elements of that particular planet or space, the Prince of Peace came into the earth in human form for the completing of His own development. He overcame the flesh and all temptation. So He became the first to overcome death in the body, enabling Him to so illuminate and revivify that body as to take it up again, even when those fluids of the body had been drained away by the nail holes in His hands and by the spear piercing His side. . . ."

Cayce insisted that Christ had already begun to assume His own immortal form when Mary Magdalene saw Him in the company of the two angels:

"As indicated in the spoken word to Mary in the Garden: 'Touch me not, for I have not yet ascended to my Father' . . . the body as seen by the normal, or material, eye of Mary was such that it could not be handled until there had been the conscious union with the Source of all Power. . . .'"

Cayce then proceeded to analyze verses nineteen through twenty-nine, from the twentieth chapter of St. John:

"Just as indicated in the manner in which the body-physical (the spirit body) entered the upper room with the doors closed, not by being part of the wood through which the body passed, but by forming itself from the ether waves that were already within the room, because of a meeting prepared by faith . . . 'Children, have ye anything here to eat?' indicated to the disciples present that this was not transmutation but a regeneration of the atoms and cells of the body. . . .'"

It may at first glance seem curious to place such vital emphasis on this concept of Christ, which on the face of it would have little bearing on the attitude of the western churches to reincarnation. But it is over this very issue that the grimmest controversies in the church's early history raged, and one of its many consequences was the rejection of reincarnation from western faith.

Before we proceed to trace this from its source to its effect on present-day orthodoxy—which in its turn served to increase the burdens under which Edgar Cayce labored—we submit the parallel views on the same Biblical passages as they are put forward by the famous English cleric, Leslie D. Weatherhead, M.A., Ph.D., Hon. D.D., Minister of the City Temple, London, and Honorary Chaplain to Her Majesty's Forces:

"Students of the resurrection never seem to me to have paid enough attention to the meticulous details about the grave-clothes which the fourth Gospel gives. This narrative—unlike some parts of the Gospel—seems to me to be based on the account of an eyewitness.

"It is made clear that the grave-clothes, covering the body up to the armpits, had collapsed as if the body had evaporated. We are told that the turban wound round his head stood on its edge, as if the head also had evaporated. If the student will turn to the twentieth chapter of the fourth Gospel and read the first twenty verses, he will realize that it was the way the grave-clothes were lying that convinced Peter and John that Christ had disposed of his physical body in a way which we do not understand, but which suggest words like 'evaporation,' or 'evanescence.'"

It would seem a far cry from the testimony of a lone clairvoyant to an established pillar of orthodox English Methodism, but almost nowhere else does so much corroboration exist for Edgar Cayce's religious philosophy than in the clear and forthright prose of Dr. Weatherhead.

The Christianity of Constantine

In his *Psychology, Religion and Healing,* Abingdon Press, Dr. Weatherhead states: "The conversion of the Roman Emperor Constantine to Christianity in 325 A.D. was a very doubtful gain to the cause of Christ. He may have seen a cross in the sky surrounded by the words In Hoc Signo Vinces, but he produced a Christianity that dispensed with the Cross, and might as well have used a cushion as its symbol.

"The Name above every name had once been written on the pale foreheads of the young knights of Christ who had either died for Him in the hundreds, or ridden forth to declare to a sneering and indifferent world the good news of the Gospel. That was over now. But it was a disaster that Constantine was 'converted.' . . .

"Christianity became, in fact, a polite veneer without power or beauty. All the Court darlings were Christians now. The spineless sycophants who giggled out their fatuous days in the luxury of the Roman court, and the sleek, shrewd parasites who battened on its energy and power, were 'converted' overnight. . . .

"Paganism remained, but now it was labelled Christianity as it is today. The religion of Christ has never recovered either, except for brief periods of revival, and without a nucleus of real saints it could not have survived."

Voltaire

If we now turn to the genius of Voltaire (1694–1778), one of history's greatest scholars as well as a founding father of democracy, we find that these excerpts from his *Philosophical Dictionary* anticipated Dr. Weatherhead's arguments with admirable acerbity.

"By the end of the first century there were some thirty gospels, each belonging to a different society, and thirty sects of Christians had sprung up in Asia Minor, Syria, Alexandria and even in Rome," says Voltaire. "Two or three antiquaries, either mercenaries or fanatics, enshrined the barbarous and effeminate Constantine, and treated the just and wise Emperor Julian as a miscreant. Subsequent chroniclers, copying from them, repeated both their flattery and their calumny. Finally, the age of sound criticism arrived, and after fourteen hundred years, enlightened men reviewed the judgment of the ignorant.

"Constantine was revealed as an opportunist who scoffed at God and men. Here is how he reasoned: 'Baptism purifies everything. I can therefore kill my wife, my son, and all my relatives. After that I can be baptized, and I shall go to Heaven.' And he acted accordingly. But he was a Christian, and he was canonized. . . ."

The Council of Nicaea, 325 A.D.

One school of dogma claims that reincarnation was condemned at the Council of Nicaea, in which case Voltaire's own analysis of its purpose deserves inclusion here:

"Alexandras, Bishop of Alexander, saw fit to preach that God was necessarily individual and indivisible—that He was a monad (a single unit) in the strictest sense of the word, and that this monad was triune (three in one). Alexandras's monad outraged the priest Arius, who published a denunciation of the theory. Alexandras quickly summoned a small council of his adherents and excommunicated his priest. . . .

"The Emperor Constantine was villain enough to send the venerable bishop Osius with conciliatory letters to both warring factions, and when Osius met with justified rejection, the Council of Nicaea was convened.

"The question to be considered was: Is Jesus the Word? If He is the Word, did He emanate from God in time, or before time? If He emanated from God, is He co-eternal and consubstantial with Him: or is He of a similar substance? Is He made or begotten? And how is it that, if He has exactly the same nature and essence as the Father and the Son, He cannot do the same things as these two people who are himself?

"This I cannot understand. No one has ever understood it. And that is why so many people have been butchered.

"The final decision of the Council of Nicaea was that the Son was as old as the Father and consubstantial with the Father . . . and war raged throughout the Roman Empire. This civil war gave rise to others, and down through the centuries to this day, internecine persecution has continued. . . .

"(Yet) Jesus taught no metaphysical dogmas. He wrote no theological treatises. He did not say: 'I am consubstantial; I have two wills and two natures with only one person.' To the Cordeliers and the Jacobins, who were to appear twelve hundred years after Him, He left the delicate and difficult task of deciding whether His mother was conceived in original sin.

"The Socinians, or Unitarians, call the acceptance of this doctrine of original sin the 'original sin' of Christianity. It is an outrage against God, they say. . . .

"The Socinians place much emphasis on the faith of the first 'heretics' who died for the apocryphal gospels, (and) refuse therefore to consider our four divine Gospels as anything other than clandestine works.

"To dare to say that He created all the successive generations of mankind only to subject them to external punishment, under the pretext that their earliest ancestor ate of a particular fruit, is to accuse Him of the most absurd barbarity.

"This sacrilegious imputation is even more inexcusable among Christians, since there is no mention of original sin, either in the Pentateuch or in the Gospels, whether apocryphal, or canonical, or in any of the writers called the First Fathers of the Church.

"Souls were either created from all eternity (with the result that they are infinitely older than Adam's sin, and have no connection with it), or they are formed at the time of conception. In which case God must create, in each instance, a new spirit which He must then render eternally miserable, or God is Himself the soul of mankind, with the result that He is damned along with His system. . . ."

And finally Voltaire gets to the heart of the matter thus: "None of the early Fathers of the Church cited a single passage from the four gospels as we accept them today.

"(They) not only failed to quote from the gospels, but they even adhered to several passages now found only in the apocryphal gospels rejected by the canon.

"Since many false gospels were at first thought to be true, those which today constitute the foundation of our own faith may also have been forged."

Origen

This brings us logically to the teachings of Origen (185 A.D.–254 A.D.), around which all the controversy was now to center.

Origen's teachings were vital to the preservation of the original gospels. His pen had been as prolific as Voltaire's, but according to the *Encyclopedia Britannica* the ten books of "Stromata," his most provocative work, have disappeared leaving almost no trace. This is of paramount significance, in that Origen occupied himself here in correlating the established Christian teachings with the "Christian" dogmas of Plato, Aristotle, Numenius and Corrutus. He devoted his life to the preservation of the original gospels.

"It was not so much the relation between faith and knowledge that gave offense, but rather isolated propositions such as his doctrine of the preexistence of souls. . . . Origen was able to explain the actual sinfulness of all men by the theological hypothesis of preexistence and the premundane fall of each soul."

Origen states in his own *Contra Celsum:* "Is it not more in conformity with reason that every soul, for certain mysterious reasons, (I speak now according to the opinion of Pythagoras and Plato, and Empedocles, whom Celsus frequently names), is introduced into a body according to its desserts and former actions? Is it not rational that souls who have used their bodies to do the utmost possible good should have a right to bodies endowed with qualities superior to the bodies of others?

"The soul, which is immaterial and invisible in its nature, exists in no material place without having a body suited to the nature of that place. Accordingly, it at one time puts off one body—which was necessary before, but which is no longer adequate in its changed state—and it exchanges it for a second."

And in his *De Principiis:* "Every soul . . . comes into this world strengthened by the victories or weakened by the defeats of its previous life. Its place in this world as a vessel appointed to honor or dishonor, is determined by its previous merits or demerits. Its work in this world determines its place in the world which is to follow this."

Pythagoras and Plato

Exactly how did the "pagan" philosophies of Pythagoras and Plato (who both subscribed to reincarnation) complement the beliefs of the Early Christian Fathers?

The views of Pythagoras (582–507 B.C.) exist only in his biographies by Diogenes Laertius and Iamblichus, but the former quotes him as asserting that "he had received the memory of all his soul's transmigrations as a gift from Mercury, along with the gift of recollecting what his own soul, and the souls of others, had experienced between death and rebirth."

From Plato (427–347 B.C.), we can obtain direct context: "Soul is older than body. Souls are continuously born over again into this life.

"The soul of the true philosopher abstains as much as possible from pleasures and desires, griefs and fears . . . for in consequence of its forming the same opinions as the body, and delighting in the same things, it can never pass into Hades in a pure state, but must ever depart polluted by the body, and so quickly falls into another body, and consequently is deprived of all association with that which is divine and pure and uniform.

"Know that if you become worse, you will go to the worse souls, and if better, to the better souls; and in every succession of life and death, you will do and suffer what like must fitly suffer at the hands of like."

It should also be established here that St. Jerome (340–400 A.D.) once impulsively hailed Origen as "the greatest teacher of the Church since the Apostles." This is hardly plausible if the New Testament was then as ambiguous in its references to reincarnation as it is now. Surely for Origen to have held pride of place among the Early Church Fathers for nearly four centuries, his tenets must have been based solidly on what at that time were accepted as the true gospels.

St. Clement of Alexandria (150–220), in his *Exhortation to the Pagans* is also clearly influenced by Plato: "We were in being long before the foundation of the world; we existed in the eye of God, for it is our destiny to live in Him. We are the reasonable creatures of the Divine Word. Therefore, we have existed from the beginning, for in the beginning was the Word. . . . Not for the first time does He show pity on us in our wanderings. He pitied us from the very beginning."

To St. Jerome's and St. Augustine's views on Plato must be added those of St. Gregory (257–332), who affirmed that "it is absolutely necessary that the soul should be healed and purified, and if this does not take place during its life on earth, it must be accomplished in future lives."

St. Augustine (354–430) held Plato in such veneration that he writes in his *Contra Academicos:* "The message of Plato, the purest and the most luminous of all philosophy, has at last scattered the darkness of error, and now shines forth mainly in Plotinus, a Platonist so like his master that one would think they lived together, or rather—since so long a period of time separates them —that Plato was born again in Plotinus."

To come full circle, Plotinus (205–270) was a fellow-disciple with Origen under Ammonius, who founded the famous Alexandrian School of Neoplatonism in Egypt in 193 A.D.

Plotinus, in *The Descent of the Soul,* is perhaps the most articulate and expressive: "Thus the soul, though of divine origin, having proceeded from the regions on high, becomes merged in the dark receptacle of the body, and being naturally a postdiluvial god, it descends hither through a certain voluntary inclination, for the sake of power and of adorning inferior concerns. . . .

"Yet our souls are able alternately to rise from hence, carrying back with them an experience of what they have known and suffered in their fallen state, from whence they will learn how blessed it is to abide in the intelligible world, and by a comparison of contraries, will more plainly perceive the excellence of a superior state.

"For the experience of evil produces a clearer knowledge of good . . . the whole of our soul does not enter in the body, but something belonging to it always abides in the intelligible world, which is something different from this sensible world, and that which abides in this world of sense does not permit us to perceive that which the supreme part of the soul contemplates."

Here we have the testimony of four Saints of the early Church. They cannot *all* have had bats in the belfry, nor would they have embraced beliefs that were hostile to the contemporary tenets of their own church. The fact that they repeatedly adhere to the "Christian" dogmas of Plato indicates their conviction that Christ had included those same dogmas in His own philosophy.

Exactly when did these original versions of the Gospels undergo such drastic reinterpretation? In all the research material that is reasonably available, there is not one source which can supply a clear-cut, substantiated answer, and only the *Catholic Encyclopedia* even hints at one.

CHAPTER 10

DOES THE BIBLE CONDEMN REINCARNATION?

"I CAN READ reincarnation into the Bible—and you can read it right out again!" Edgar Cayce once said with his usual dry humor. Though he had read the Bible once for every year of his life, his first reaction in Dayton was to read it straight through again to find where it actively condemned the theory of reincarnation. Nowhere did it do so. Nowhere did it endorse reincarnation per se, either; but in Proverbs 8:22-31 he found this strangely moving reference to Creation: "The Lord possessed me in beginning of His way, before His works of old.

"I was set up from everlasting, from the beginning, or ever the earth was.

"When there were no depths, I was brought forth . . . when He prepared the Heavens, I was there. When he appointed the foundations of the earth, then was I by Him, as one brought up with Him. And I was daily His delight, rejoicing always before him, rejoicing in the habitable part of His earth. And my delights were with the Sons of Man."

Are we beholden to take this as the abstract imagery of an obscure poet? Or can we ask who "I" was? Obviously not a mortal creature with a life-span of three score years and ten; no matter how obscurely he was expressing his poetry. If we credit "I" with being a human soul, speaking of its own origin from its subconscious memory; every line makes logical sense. Its nostalgic yearning for the uncorrupted joy of its beginnings, its longing for its rejected God, these epitomize perfectly the weary soul's disenchantment with the arid cycle of its materialistic lives on earth, having cut itself off from its loving Father as the Prodigal Son had done.

This is not the dour "predestination and original sin" of Calvin's luckless humanoid, damned before he draws his first breath, potential fuel for the eternal fires even before he quits the womb. It is not the despair of the damned; it is only the cry of the lost sheep.

With this as our model, how should we interpret this line from the Wisdom of Solomon 8:19-20: "Now I was a good child by nature, and a good soul fell to my lot. Nay, rather, being good, I came into a body undefiled."

The King James Version, with curious circumlocution, takes this liberty: "For I was a witty child, and had a good spirit. Yea, rather, being good, I came into a body undefiled," making a non sequitur of the whole passage. But in both versions, who is the arbiter of what is good and what is bad? Clearly the soul itself, using its own standard of previous conduct as its gauge, in that it makes no claim to having been designated 'good' by standards other than its own. And surely it could have no means of knowing what 'good' was, unless it was equally familiar with its opposite?

That souls had been both good and bad at various stages of their manifestation on earth is again implied in Romans 9:11-14: "For the children being not yet born; neither having done any good nor evil. . . . it was said unto (Rebecca), 'The elder shall serve the younger. As it is written: Jacob have I loved, but Esau have I hated.' What shall we say, then? Is there unrighteousness with God? God forbid."

If there is "no unrighteousness" with God, why is God showing a most ungodly bias by loving Jacob for no reason, and hating Esau for no reason? What opportunity would either of them have found, before their creation, to choose such divergent natures? If they had come directly from their Maker to Rebecca's womb, where else could Esau have committed his crimes, except in Heaven? If he did, why wasn't he cast out with the rest of the fallen angels and deposited directly into hell? It would seem far more likely that he learned to sin on earth, in a mortal body, and his return as the servant of his younger brother was an act of restitution.

"Even from everlasting to everlasting, Thou art God," says the Ninetieth Psalm. "Thou turnest Man to destruction, and sayest 'Return, ye Children of

Men.' . . . Thou carriest them away as with a flood; they are asleep; in the morning they are like grass that groweth up." Here we have the ambiguity of the word "turnest" to contend with; the lyrist having combined the tribal Jehovah with the Creator. A fairer reading would surely be, "Thou failest to turn man from his destruction." Even so, the concept of Heaven in those days was an eternal state of static perfection. "If 'Return, ye Children of Men' meant 'return to Heaven' (the only alternative being the Fiery Pit), then the three transpositions from flood to sleep to growing grass are not only bad imagery but disjunct. Even if we accept the 'flood' literally to mean death by drowning (the Flood, after all, was fairly recent history), and the 'sleep' to symbolize an interim period between death and resurrection in Heaven, 'the grass that groweth up in the morning' is still a peculiar symbol for a Heavenly life where all is perfect and nothing alters. The earthly seasons, on the other hand, do alter. The grass grows up with every spring to die again with every winter; and the reincarnating soul follows an identical cycle."

The theme suggests itself again in Job 1:20-21: "Then Job arose and rent his mantle, and shaved his head, and fell down upon the ground and worshipped. And said: 'Naked came I out of my mother's womb, and naked shall I return thither!' "

Obviously if Job is referring literally to the same mother, the old gentleman has lost his marbles. But if we accept the fact that Job was not an historical character but a symbol for the soul, the parable is exhorting man never to despair when all seems lost, and the symbolism of the womb at once becomes self-evident. The soul cannot possibly embark on its next life on earth without first "returning naked to the womb."

And what is the reward of the soul, once it completes its earth cycles and can return like the Prodigal Son to the Father it rejected when it chose to glorify itself instead? "Him that overcometh," Revelation 3:12, "will I make a pillar in the Temple of the Lord, and he shall go no more out."

In Malachi 4:5, we come to perhaps the most persuasive example of all, for Elijah and Elias are only variations in spelling; both refer to the same prophet. "Behold," says Malachi in the fifth century B.C., "I will send you Elijah the prophet before the coming of the great and dreadful day of the Lord."

Five hundred years later, according to Matthew 16:13, "When Jesus came into the coasts of Caesarea Philippi, he asked His disciples, saying, 'Whom do men say that I, the Son of Man, am?'

"And they said, 'Some say that Thou art John the Baptist, some Elias; and others, Jeremias, or one of the Prophets.' " This is continued in Chapter 17, Verse 10. "And His disciples asked Him, saying, 'Why then say the scribes that Elias must first come?'

"And Jesus answered and said unto them, 'Elias truly shall first come and restore all things. But I say unto you that Elias is come already, and they knew him not, but have done unto him whatsoever they listed. Likewise shall also the Son of Man suffer of them.' Then the disciples understood that He spake unto them of John the Baptist."

What logical thought-process induced the disciples to draw such a conclusion so promptly, unless Jesus had made them thoroughly familiar with the laws of reincarnation? John the Baptist had been beheaded by Herod in their own lifetime, and Elias was five hundred years dead.

The idea that the soul could reincarnate must have been equally familiar to Herod, for in Luke 9:7-8: "Herod the tetrarch heard of all that was done by (Jesus); and he was perplexed, because it was said of some that John was risen from the dead; and of some that Elias had appeared; and of others that one of the old prophets was risen again. And Herod said, 'John have I beheaded, but who is this of whom I hear such things?' And he desired to see Him."

The curiosity of an orthodox monarch would hardly have been aroused by irresponsible talk. He would have cleared his court of the superstitious idiots who entertained such fancies and attached no further importance to Jesus.

And in the light of the above, what are we to make of this passage from John 9:1-3? "And as Jesus passed by, he saw a man which was blind from birth. And his disciples asked him, saying, 'Master, who did sin, this man or his parents, that he was born blind?' Jesus answered, 'Neither has this man sinned nor his parents. He was born blind that the works of God should be made manifest in him.' "

If reincarnation was a totally rejected theory, surely Jesus's answer would have been a reproach for such an idiotic question. Obviously a newborn babe is incapable of any kind of sin: if sin had been the cause of the blindness, then the question would have been phrased quite differently: "Master, is this the sins of the father's visited on the child, or are the parents innocent of sin?" Jesus was in all things merciful. Even when he "cursed" the fig tree (in the nonmelodramatic sense of blighting it). He had obviously divined that it was rooted in subsoil sufficiently contaminated to poison its fruit. He would never have painted such a forbidding picture of his Father as to suggest He inflicted a defenseless child with blindness merely to "manifest His works in him." But if the soul inhabiting the man had voluntarily elected to be blind, to advance itself more swiftly in patience and understanding, then the works of God would most assuredly be made manifest in him.

Interpreted from the point of view of karma, Jesus's restraining doctrine of "as ye sow, so shall ye reap" makes perfect good sense. Shorn of its basic link to reincarnation, it dwindles to fatuous banality. Very few people are fortunate enough to reap what they sow in the same lifetime.

The disciples were simple fishermen and men of the soil, and Jesus's tone changes when he debates with an educated man of the world like Nicodemus.

The following passages from John 3:3-14 are usually interpreted as applying only to the pros and cons of baptism; but the text does not imply it, and it is hard to conceive of Jesus descending to a straw-splitting quibble over the niceties of proper church usage with a mature scholar of Sanhedrin law. The passages make a great deal more sense if we assume that Jesus is chiding a man who should know better than to give His symbolic words a purely literal interpretation.

He hardly seems to be prescribing secular baptism as the solution for Nicodemus's confusion, when He makes the unequivocal statement: " 'Verily, verily, I say unto thee; except a man be born again he cannot see the kingdom of God.' Nicodemus said unto Him: 'How can a man be born when he is old? Can he enter a second time into his mother's womb and be born?' Jesus answered: 'Verily, verily, I say unto thee, except a man be born of water and of the Spirit, he cannot enter into the kingdom of God. That which is born of flesh is flesh, and that which is born of the Spirit is spirit. Marvel not that I say unto thee, "Ye must be born again." The wind bloweth where it listeth, and thou hearest the sound thereof but canst not tell whence it cometh or whither it goeth. So (it is with) everyone that is born of the Spirit.'

"Nicodemus answered and said unto Him, 'How can these things be?' Jesus answered and said unto him, 'Art thou a master of Israel and knowest not these things? . . . . If I have told thee of earthly things and ye believe not, how shall you believe if I tell you of heavenly things? And no man has ascended up to Heaven, but that he came down from Heaven; even the Son of Man which is in Heaven.' "

If we proceed to Chapter 8, Verse 34 of the same gospel; Jesus, arguing with the orthodox Jews in the temple, speaks with such slight concern for their prejudices that he is stoned for his pains. If we are still to assume that the argument centers only around the right way and the wrong way to conduct a baptism, it is hard to understand why He wasted His patience and energy over such a trivial issue. If the issue is their rejection of reincarnation, however, His following words and the resultant fury they arouse fall into a very logical perspective. " 'Verily, verily, I say unto you, whosoever committeth sin is the servant of sin. And the servant abideth not in the house (the flesh) for ever; but the Son abideth ever. If the Son, therefore, shall make you free, ye shall be free indeed. . . . I speak that which I have seen with my Father; (but) ye do that which you have seen with your father.'

"They answered and said unto Him, 'Abraham is our father!' Jesus said unto them, 'If ye were Abraham's children, ye would do the works of Abraham. But now ye seek to kill me . . . this did not Abraham. . . . Your father Abraham rejoiced to see my day; and he saw it and was glad.'

"Then the Jews said to him, 'Thou are not yet fifty years old, and hast thou seen Abraham?'

"Jesus said unto them, 'Verily, verily, I say unto you; before Abraham was, I am.' "

Why are these allusions to reincarnation in the Bible so isolated and fragmentary? Is it possible that the few that do exist were accidentally overlooked during a systematic expurgation of the original Greek and Hebrew texts?

For the moment it is sufficient to establish that Edgar Cayce satisfied himself that an acceptance of reincarnation in no way went against Holy Writ: it did, in fact, add teeth to many of its arguments.

Without question, it supplies force and logic to the warning: "He that killeth with the sword must be killed with the sword, and he that leadeth into captivity, must be led into captivity." (Revelation 13:10.)

"As thou has done, it shall be done unto thee; thy reward shall return unto thine own head." (Obadiah 1:15.)

But perhaps the most impressive warning of all, directed, it would seem, to those who might be tempted to tamper with the true meaning of the Gospels to further their own aggrandizement, is given by Jesus in Luke 11:52: "Woe unto you, lawyers! for ye have taken away the key of knowledge; ye entered not in yourselves, and them that were entering in, ye hindered."

In the newly discovered Coptic Gospel according to St. Thomas* this is directed squarely at the church: "The Pharisees and the Scribes have received the keys of Knowledge, and have hidden them. They did not enter, and they did not let those who wished."

CHAPTER 11

WHY ISN'T REINCARNATION IN THE BIBLE? THE HIDDEN HISTORY OF REINCARNATION

OUR ORTHODOX VERSIONS of the Old and New Testaments date no further back than the sixth century, when the Byzantine Emperor Justinian summoned the Fifth Ecumenical Congress of Constantinople in 553 A.D. to condemn the Platonically inspired writings of Origen.**

Contrary to the belief of our contemporary Churches, this was not an unsecular Congress. The Pope was forbidden to attend, and his denunciation of it was flouted. It was instigated by the same substratum of moronic barbarians who had "converted" to Christianity under Constantine.

If the reader should find it singular that this Congress is given so much attention in the following pages, it is because the events which led up to the Fifth Congress represent practically the only surviving evidence as to why reincarnation disappeared from the Bible.

The Byzantine Emperor Justinian (483–565), as a fatherless youth, was brought up in austere obscurity by his mother and his uncle, the "peasant" Emperor Justin, while they rigidly groomed him to inherit the throne of Constantinople. The severity of his upbringing was responsible for an arid, erratic streak in him. He early developed an intellectual passion for law that is hardly commensurate with normal adolescence, and though he considered himself essentially a "good" man, he was easily swayed by flattery and his judgment of his fellow men remained superficial and immature.

Only in his intuitive grasp of military strategy was he consistent. His youthful General, Belisarius, successfully subdued the Ostrogoths in Italy and the Vandals in Africa, thus restoring the foundering Roman Empire to a modicum of its former power.

Byzantine architecture flowered under Justinian, and he revised Roman law to the extent that it subsequently became the basis for all western civil law.

On the face of it, he should have risen to the heights of a Charlemagne.

* Harper and Row (N.Y. 1959), p. 25.
** See appendix A.

That he did not was due in part to his temperament—an incompatible mixture of dedicated zealotry and infirmity of purpose—and in part to his deterioration to the rank of pawn in a ruthless woman's bid for self-deification.

Theodora (508–547), the commoner who became Justinian's Empress, wielded sufficient authority over contemporary records to suppress most of the evidence of her dubious background, and her only contemporary biographer, Procopius, so bitterly detested her that his *Secret History* is rejected in as many academic quarters as it is accepted in others.

It is generally agreed that Theodora was the daughter of a bear-feeder in the amphitheatre in Constantinople, and made her debut as a child actress at a time when that profession ranked with the world's oldest. Of this, too, she rapidly became an accomplished member, and her insatiable ambition made capital of the obstacles that confronted her.

Theodora's strategy was always to create a condition of organized confusion in which every man eventually found himself in conflict with his neighbor, enabling her to divide and conquer at her leisure. Once she had become Justinian's mistress, she set her stakes even higher. She determined to become his Empress, and though Justinian's mother opposed her with all the power at her command, Justinian proved to be too emotionally unstable to resist such a blitzkrieg.

Where his knowledge of his fellow men was faulty and erratic, Theodora's was expert and innately predatory. Where he vacillated, she was as inflexible as iron. Although the law forbade men above senatorial rank to marry actresses, the law was conveniently abolished by Justinian on the death of his mother, and Theodora took her place beside him on the throne.

There is nothing historically unique about an unworldly monarch reduced to thralldom by a ruthless courtesan, but few courtesans in history possessed Theodora's diabolism.

Witness the *Encyclopedia Britannica:* Officials took an oath of allegiance to her as well as to the Emperor. The city was full of her spies, who reported to her everything said against herself or the administration. She surrounded herself with ceremonious pomp, and required all who approached to abase themselves in a manner new even to that half-Oriental court.

"According to Procopius, she had before her marriage become the mother of a son, who when grown up, returned from Arabia, revealed himself to her, and forthwith disappeared for ever."

In every short order she became a tyrant in the grand manner of the more psychotic Caesars.

Her favorites catapulted to power and her enemies died in such numbers that eventually the public rose up against the royal couple. Confronted by the Nika insurrections of 532, Justinian, terrified and demoralized, would have fled before it, but the indomitable Theodora preferred death to obscurity. She made him sweat it out, and the riots were finally subdued.

After that, Justinian was no more impressive than a glove-puppet on her strong right hand, and she was free to concentrate her energies on the most formidable of her foes, the Church of Rome.

Theodora saw the Christian Church as her equivalent of the Great Pyramid—an eternal monument to her ego—and to ensure its permanency she set about the total reconstitution of its credenda, which were far too sublime for her purposes. That she actually succeeded was due to the fact that the Vatican had barely had time to recover from its subjugation by Theodoric the Ostrogoth before it found itself under the over-solicitous "police protection" of Belisarius's army of occupation.

Her first and most influential teacher, Eutyches, a devotee of the Eastern Church, first emerged when Theodora was the mistress of Hecebolus, the governor of Pentapolis in North Africa. When Hecebolus eventually threw her out of the city, Theodora and Eutyches gravitated first to Alexandria and then to Constantinople, she as an ascending power in the lists of profane love, and he as the doyen of a series of Monophysite religious schools.

The Monophysite Doctrine

The Monophysite doctrine is, as it were, the villain of the piece.

It was this sect that was later to discredit all allusion to reincarnation in the early gospels, and split the church into two warring factions.

It must be remembered that not only had an unending series of conflicting schisms plagued the solidarity of the Christian Church from about 300 A.D. onward, but it also faced active resistance and sturdy competition from the pagan religions it had not yet superseded, many of which were not only gayer and more escapist, they even threw in the odd saturnalia.

Now the Monophysites added to the confusion by contending that Jesus's physical body was wholly divine, and had never at any time combined divine and human attributes. (It seemed to cause them no embarrassment that Jesus himself had declared that there was a spark of the divine in every human soul. They adhered militantly to their conviction that the mere act of donning the outer trappings of a mortal body would have defiled Jesus's true origin.)

Unfortunately, under the influence of Eutyches, Theodora became a convert to this controversial Monophysite dogma. Its principal claim to her affections was its total rejection of those teachings of Origen which had so profoundly influenced the early Church Fathers. Origen not only believed in metempsychosis, but argued that Christ the Logos, or Word, inhabited the human body of Jesus, thus sanctifying it.

It is fair to assume that Theodora conscripted two of her most devoted deacons, Virgilius and Anthimus, on the suggestion if not the insistence of Eutyches, to this viewpoint.

It is difficult, today, when one wades through these laborious arguments between the Eastern and Western branches of the Church over the divinity of Christ, to realize the manic antagonism they aroused in both camps. The Monophysites continued to provoke strife and discord until the year 451, when a specially summoned Church Council, loyal to Origen's teachings, split Christ into two separate natures, human and divine.

The Chalcedonian Decree, 451 A.D.

The well-intentioned decision known as the Chalcedonian Decree, while protecting the teachings of Origen, became, in effect, the launching pad for all the black mischief that followed.

Indeed the split between the Monophysites and the Vatican eventually reached such violent proportions that "one of Justinian's first public acts was to make the Patriarch of Constantinople declare his full adhesion to the creed of Chalcedon."*(Encyclopedia Britannica)*

This constitutes solid evidence that, prior to Theodora's arrival on the scene, Justinian was in complete sympathy with the Origenist leanings of the Church of Rome; yet in 543, at Theodora's urging, he permitted a local synod to discredit and condemn the writings of Origen.

Very much as the hero of Orwell's *1984* "purified" the public files of the newspapers by rewriting political history and eliminating all reference to previous "Big Brothers," Theodora now pursued a campaign designed to obliterate all and any passages in the Bible which might reduce to absurdity her hopes of instant apotheosis upon departing this life.

Anthimus

Theodora's first move in her grand strategy was to subdue and unify the various feuding factions of the Eastern Church until it was utterly under her domination. In open defiance of Vatican protocol, she appointed her lackey Anthimus as Patriarch of Constantinople.

Now Anthimus is a minor figure in the overall picture, but he was equipped for great mischief at this moment. Theodora had appointed him for the express purpose of revoking the Chalcedonian Decree. Justinian's role, as usual, was to plead ignorance of the whole affair and play Pilate.

At once she ran afoul of Pope Agapetus.

Pope Agapetus

This dignified old worthy traveled from Rome to Constantinople in bleak February weather, and when he discovered the full enormity of Theodora's intent, he became the only prelate ever to denounce her in Constantine's presence.

"With eager longing," he informed the outraged Justinian, "have I come to gaze on the most Christian Emperor Justinian. In his place I find a Diocletian,* whose threats, however, terrify me not!"

This unexpected rap on the royal nose pulled Justinian up short, and "being fully convinced that Anthimus was unsound in faith, he made no excep-

* One of the tyrant Caesars.

tion to the Pope's exercising the plenitude of his powers in deposing and suspending the intruder Anthimus and, for the first time in the history of the Church, personally consecrating his legally elected successor, Mennas." *(Catholic Encyclopedia,* p. 203)

Unfortunately for the spiritual destiny of Europe, the saintly and incorruptible Agapetus died in the same year of 536; but he leaves a nobler and more honorable record behind him than any of the other participants in this sorry charade.

His expedient demise followed his triumph so swiftly that one can only assume that Theodora was instrumental in speeding him to a happier world.

With Agapetus dead, Mennas was easily brought to heel, and accommodatingly condemned the entire Diocese of Origenism in the Emperor's name.

From this point on, Justinian obediently sanctioned all Theodora's further purges of Origenism.

Pope Silverius

It seems relevant at this point to illustrate from a completely independent source, the *Vita Silveri* (Gesta Pont. Rom. I. 146), just how malevolent Theodora's self-deification had become:

"Because the Empress was grieving for the Patriarch Anthimus, the most holy Pope Agapetus having deposed him on the grounds of heresy and replaced him with Virgilius, she sent this letter to (Agapetus's successor) Pope Silverius at Rome: 'Make no delay in coming to us, or without fail recall Anthimus to his own place!'

"And when blessed Silverius had read this, he groaned and said: 'I know very well that this affair has brought an end to my life,' but replied by letter to the Empress: 'Mistress Augusta, I shall never consent to do such a thing as to reinstate a man who is a heretic and who has been condemned in his own wickedness.'

"Then the Empress, in a fury, sent orders to the patrician (General) Belisarius by the deacon Virgilius: 'Seek out some grounds of complaint against the Pope Silverius that will remove him from the office of Bishop, or at least send him quickly to us. You have there the Archdeacon Virgilius, our most beloved deputy, who has promised us to recall the patriarch Anthimus.'

"The patrician Belisarius undertook the commission, and under urgent orders, certain false witnesses issued forth and actually made the statement that they had discovered the Pope Silverius sending messages to the King of the Goths. Upon hearing this, Belisarius refused belief, knowing that these reports were motivated by envy. But when many more persisted in this same accusation, he became afraid.

"Therefore he caused the blessed Pope Silverius to come to him in the Pincian Palace, and he stationed all the clergy at the first and second entrances, and when Silverius and Virgilius had come alone into the salon, the patrician Antonina was reclining on a couch, and her husband Belisarius was seated at her feet. Antonina said at once: 'Tell me, Master Silverius, Pope;

what have we done to you and the Romans, that you wish to betray us into the hands of the Goths?'

"And even while she was speaking these words, there entered John, the regional sub-deacon of the first ward, who lifted the blessed Pope Silverius' collar from his neck and led him into a chamber. There he unfrocked him, put on him monk's garb, and spirited him away.

"And Virgilius took him under his personal protection, as it were, and sent him into exile in Pontus, where he sustained him with the bread of tribulation and water of necessity. And he weakened and died and became a confessor."

Theodora now stood revealed in her true colors, and her next move was her most ferocious so far. She became the only Empress in history to succeed in enthroning her own Pope, Virgilius, in Rome in 538.

She had, in effect, ascended the papal throne in person, and it is more than likely that this is the source of the legend of the mythical Pope Joan.

Before we turn our attention to the eyewitness accounts supplied by Procopius, it is fitting to preface them with one last excerpt from an independent source.

Among the accredited historians of Byzantine history of this era are three of importance—Agathius (530–582), John Lydus (490–565), and Evagrius (536–594). Evagrius in his *Ecclesiastical History* (iv. 32), makes this comment:

"There was also another quality latent in the character of Justinian—a depravity which exceeded any bestiality which can be imagined. And whether this was a defect of his natural character, or whether it was the outgrowth of cowardice and fear, I am unable to say, but in any case it manifested itself as a result of the popular Nika insurrection."

Here is a side of the Emperor which Procopius documents in detail, yet it is discreetly ignored in the standard references, most of which content themselves with discrediting Procopius outright and whisking a whitewash brush lightly across Theodora's diabolism.

The Secret History by Procopius

The version of the *Anecdota,* or *Secret History,* from which we now quote is one of seven volumes which include the *History of the Wars* and *History of the Buildings* (Harvard University Press), translated by H. B. Dewing, Ph.D., L.H.D., in 1935.

According to Dewing, the personable and well-educated Procopius arrived in Constantinople from Caesarea in Palestine while still a young man. Almost at once he was appointed legal adviser and private secretary to the patrician Belisarius, Justinian's youngest and most illustrious General. This is hardly a privilege accorded an anonymous scribbler of salacious gossip.

Indeed, we are immediately confronted by an unexpectedly articulate and imposing figure, the official historian of Justinian's three wars against the Persians, the Vandals, and the Goths respectively, in which capacity he traveled in the personal entourage of Belisarius and observed the wars firsthand.

"Besides his intimacy with Belisarius," says Dewing, "it should be added that his position gave him the further advantage of a certain standing at the imperial Court of Constantinople, and brought him the acquaintance of many of the leading men of his day. Thus we have the testimony of one intimately associated with the administration.

"One must admit that . . . the imperial favor was not won by plain speaking; nevertheless we have before us a man who could not obliterate himself enough to play the abject flatterer always; and he gives us the reverse, too, of this brilliant picture (in) the *Anecdota,* or *Secret History.* Here he freed himself of all the restraints of respect or fear, and set down without scruple everything which he had been led to suppress or gloss over in the *History of the Wars,* through motives of policy.

"It is a record of wanton crime and shameless debauchery of intrigue and scandal, both in public and private life . . . we seem to hear one speak out of the bitterness of his heart. It should be said, at the same time, that there are very few contradictions of fact.

"It was the intention of Procopius to write a book on the doctrines of Christianity (and the long and often bitter debates, in the course of which these were formulated), as he definitely states in Chapter XI 33 of the *Secret History*—a promise which he repeated in the eighth book of the Histories XXV. 13.

"It is most unfortunate that he was prevented from fulfilling this promise, for his point of view was that of a liberal who was puzzled by the earnestness with which his contemporaries entered into the discussion of these matters."

Even a cursory study of the War Histories reveals Procopius not only as a diligent and meticulous chronicler, but conscientious to such a degree that he was prepared to risk the ire of Justinian by rightfully crediting Belisarius with the success of the three campaigns.

If he promised to write a treatise on the religious confusion of the time, it is more than possible that he did write it. The fact that it is missing does not necessarily point to foul play by his enemies, when one recalls the widowed Lady Burton burning her husband's exotic translations from the Arabic "to keep his memory pure." Even so, we cannot ignore the fact that Procopius's *History of the Church* could have been so explosive in content that a timid bibliophile, discovering it on some forgotten shelf, would be impelled to deliver it into the hands of the authorities rather than offer it for sale to a private collector.

It was, after all, a private collector who discovered the *Anecdota* manuscript in Rome in the mid-nineteenth century. Written in Greek, and intact, it had obviously been lovingly protected for more than fourteen hundred years. But as far as we may ever know, the *History of the Church* vanished as utterly as the Imperial Court archives in Constantinople, which did not even survive the remorse-ridden senility of Justinian.

Those gifted with the patience to endure the archaism of Procopius's style will find that a series of very real, convincing portraits will emerge from the *Secret History* as distinct from the expedient effigies which adorn the standard references. It will even become apparent that the accounts of Justinian's insomnia and schizoid outbursts have a disturbingly familiar ring. They follow the same behavior-pattern as Hitler's—a fact which would have been inaccessible to Dewing in 1935, the year he completed his translation.

A Portrait of Theodora

Procopius supplies such a vivid firsthand account of Theodora's sexual promiscuity that most of it is too disgusting for inclusion here, although, when it is measured against the excesses of the more degenerate Caesars, it is credible enough. He then continues with a description of her after she became Empress:

"Now Theodora was fair of face and in general attractive in appearance, but short of stature and lacking in color; being, however, not altogether pale but rather sallow, and her glance was always intense and made with contracted brows. She lavished more care on her body than was necessary, but never as much as she considered adequate. For instance, she used to enter the bath very early and quit it very late, and go thence to her breakfast. After partaking of breakfast, she would rest. At luncheon and dinner, however, she partook incontinently of food and drink, so that sleep would constantly lay hold of her for long stretches of time, not only in the daytime up to nightfall, but at night up to sunrise, and although she indulged herself in every excess for so major a portion of that day, she still claimed the right to administer the whole Roman Empire.

"And if the Emperor should impose any favor upon a man without her consent, that man's affairs would suffer such a turn of fortune that not long thereafter he would be dismissed from his office with the greatest indignities, and would die a most shameful death."

All of which has the ring of firsthand reporting of a highly responsible order.

A Portrait of Justinian

Procopius then presents in detail his theory that both Theodora and Justinian were "possessed by demons." And here the same manic disorders that distinguished Hitler come into sharp focus, even if the language of that time lacked the advantage of modern psychiatric idiom:

"And I think it not inappropriate here to describe the appearance of this man. He was neither tall in stature nor particularly short, but of medium height, yet not thin but slightly fleshy, and his face was round and not uncomely, for his complexion remained ruddy even after two days of fasting. But his character I could not accurately describe, for this man was both an evildoer and easily led into evil, a perfect artist in acting out an opinion which he pretended to hold, and even able to produce tears . . . not from joy or sorrow, but contriving them for the occasion, according to the need of the moment . . . always playing false, yet not carelessly, but adding both his signature and the most terrible oaths to bind his agreements, and that, too, in dealing with his own subjects. . . .

"And they say that a certain monk who was very dear to God . . . set out for Byzantium in order to plead the cause of the people living near the monastery who were being wronged in unbearable fashion, and immediately upon his arrival he was granted admittance to the Emperor. But just as he was about to enter his presence, having already placed one foot across the threshold, he suddenly recoiled and stepped back.

"Now the eunuch who was his conductor, as well as others nearby, besought him earnestly to go forward, but he, acting like a man who had suffered a stroke, made no answer but departed thence and went to the place where he was lodged.

"And when his attendants enquired why he had acted thus, he declared outright that he had seen the Lord of the Demons sitting on the throne, and had declined to suffer his presence long enough to ask anything from him.

"And how could this man fail to be some wicked demon, who never had a sufficiency of food, or drink, or sleep, but, taking a haphazard taste of whatever was set before him, walked about the Palace at unseasonable hours of the night, though he was passionately devoted to the joys of Aphrodite? He was not given to sleep as a general thing, and he never filled himself to repletion with either food or drink, but he usually just touched the food with the tips of his fingers and went his way."

Justinian's split personality is shrewdly and articulately observed in the following: "However, he did not, on that account, blush before any of those destined to be ruined by him. Indeed, he never allowed himself to show anger or exasperation, thus to reveal his feelings to those who had given offence, but with gentle mien and lowered brow, and in a restrained voice, he would give orders for the death of thousands of innocent men, for the dismantling of cities, and for the confiscation of all monies to the Treasury. And one would infer from this characteristic that he had the spirit of the lamb. Yet if anyone sought to intercede through prayers and supplications for those who had given offence, thus to gain for them forgiveness, then, 'enraged and shewing his teeth,' he would seem to be ready to burst, so that none of those who were supposed to be intimate with him had any further hope of obtaining the desired pardon.

"And while he seemed to have a firm belief as regards Christ, yet even this was for the ruin of his subjects. For in his eagerness to gather all men into one belief as to Christ, he kept destroying the rest of mankind in senseless fashion, and that, too, while acting with a pretence of piety. For it did not seem to him murder, if the victims chanced to be not of his own creed.

"And I shall show further, how . . . many other calamities chanced to befall, which some insisted came about through the afore-mentioned presence of this evil demon and through his contriving, while others said that the Deity, detesting his works, turned away from the Roman Empire and gave place to the abominable demons for the bringing of these things to pass in this fashion.

"Thus the Scirtus River, by overflowing Edessa, became the author of countless calamities to the people of that region, as will be written by me in a following book.

"And earthquakes destroyed Antioch, the first city of the East, and Seleucia which is close to it, as well as the most notable city in Cilicia, Anazarbus. And the number of persons who perished along with these cities, who would be able to compute?

"And one might add to the list Ibora and also Amasia, which chanced to be the first city in Pontus, also Polybotus in Phrygia, and the city which the Pisidians call Philomede, and Lychnidus in Epirus, and Corinth. And afterwards came the plague as well, mentioned by me before, which carried off about one half of the surviving population."

Substitute the Allied bombing raids of Germany in World War II for the natural disasters, and Hitler's "voices" for the demons which "possessed" Justinian, and the parallel is neither fortuitous nor farfetched.

Procopius has drawn two very real portraits, and it seems unconvincing to reduce his observations to malicious chatter.

The Fifth Ecumenical Church Council

Theodora, having contrived the murder of two Popes, expected to instill their successor Virgilius with her own mania for exterminating all traces of the Chalcedonian Decree and its division of Christ into two separate entities, human and divine. She failed.

What caused her death no one seems to know for certain. The *Encyclopedia Britannica,* finally giving Procopius the benefit of the doubt, set the date as 547.

One thing is certain: Justinian continued to conduct his affairs exactly as if she still stood at his elbow. He was determined to deify her and himself by totally obliterating any facet of the Christian religion that might in any way disqualify such a grotesque conceit. What religious doctrine could possibly have deranged him more than reincarnation's dispassionate law of cause and effect? What other law could obliterate both his and his consort's imperial status at the moment of death, reduce them both to the common denominator of backward souls, and then bundle them back into lives of abject atonement to balance the scales?

The Three Chapters Edict

Justinian's opening gambit was to disinter a toothless and forgotten civil law, passed in 531, called the Three Chapters Edict. This had lashed out indiscriminately at three long defunct heretical author-bishops, Theodore, Theodret and Ibar. This unimposing edict had apparently alarmed no one except Virgilius at the time; and now, in 553, his fears were fully confirmed when Justinian found it necessary to convene the lumbering weight of the

Fifth Ecumenical Church Council to incorporate this very minor tempest in a teapot into canon law.

When he went so far as to exclude all but six Western bishops from the Council, while permitting the attendance of one hundred and fifty-nine Eastern bishops (all of them, presumably, faithful Monophysites), Justinian provoked Virgilius to belated but courageous action.

Pope Virgilius demanded that the Eastern and Western bishops be given equal representation, a demand that was promptly and predictably quashed by Justinian.

Robbed, thus, of his last shreds of superficial authority, Pope Virgilius refused to attend the Council, though his motive might have been less loyalty to the Vatican than self-preservation. Justinian was not above hastening his end with the same dispatch that had been meted out to Agapetus and Silverius.

If the Church of Rome had not been powerless to oppose the military supremacy of Byzantium, Virgilius could have forbidden Justinian to convene the Fifth Council on pain of excommunication. Again, if there had been a bit more of the stuff of martyrs in Virgilius, he might have aroused sufficient protest in the West to make Justinian think twice, for the Emperor would have been in no haste to provoke a public uprising on the scale of the Nika insurrection of 523, which was still raw in his mind. Unfortunately, like Becket, his past was against him. He found himself at odds both with the ill-omened pyrotechnics of his master and his own conscience.

There is something stupefying in the haphazard lack of concern for the keeping of the Council's records. None were kept. When the Council ended in an atmosphere suitably obscured by organized confusion and high-sounding bombast, Justinian officially announced that the Council's sole purpose in convening was to legalize the well-worn Three Chapters Edict, and that this was now accomplished.

Pope Virgilius was served official notice that the Three Chapters Edict was now law. And so, to all intents and purposes, the Council had fulfilled its declared function, and the Bishops departed.

Now the Three Chapters Edict, in itself, was very small political beer. If that had been Justinian's only concern, he could easily have had it incorporated into canon law without recourse to the elaborate machinery of a full-scale Ecumenical Council. This was like chopping down a whole orchard to pick one apple.

If, on the other hand, the Emperor's purpose was to delete all reference to metempsychosis from the original Gospels, he most certainly would have needed the imposing might of the Fifth Council to cloak his mischief.

What exactly was the real purpose of the Congress?

It was to condemn the writings of Origen, the immediate effect of which would, of course, be the obliteration of the Chalcedonian Decree of 451. It is therefore imperative that we never confuse the Chalcedonian Decree of 451 with the ridiculous Three Chapters Edict of 531; for the sleight-of-hand of the Fifth Council was designed to deceive the eye in exactly this fashion.

Who really instigated the Council?

The unquiet wraith of Theodora. It was her posthumous coup d'etat to the autonomy of the Western Church in Rome. The Monophysites were henceforth to realign the church from their Eastern stronghold.

In brief, concealed beneath all the pomp and circumstance of the Fifth Council there was a witchhunt in full cry, and its victim was reincarnation in all its Platonist, Origenist, secular, and unsecular forms.

Yet, Emperor or no Emperor, Justinian was a layman tampering with ecclesiastical law. The titular head of the Roman Church had been refused admittance to the Council and only six Western bishops had been permitted to vote.

The findings of the Council did, of course, annihilate Origenism in the Christian church, even if a few stubborn sects, notably the Troubadours of Southern France, went underground for a few more centuries.

Moreover, the attack on Origen now stood revealed as an attack on all the Early Church Fathers whose writings reflected their veneration of him. Copies of their works were not numerous and could easily be tracked down and expurgated. The early gospels were either in Latin or Greek, and were never allowed to fall into the hands of laymen.

Few, if any, monasteries would have had the courage to defy their Emperor and hide their original versions. The imperial spy system was as efficient and thorough as any conceived by Stalin or Hitler; it would have possessed detailed records of all the religious libraries. Justinian's deletions and alterations of the Gospels would have been completed in very short order, and so would the elimination of all and any evidence of the vandalism.

Even so, certain questions remain stubbornly unanswerable. Surely, if Pope Virgilius had not felt assured that the Western church was solidly behind him, he would never have taken on Justinian. Yet he did oppose the Council.

If we are expected to believe that the full sympathy of the Western bishops was solidly behind the Monophysite dogma, why should Justinian have gone to such lengths to bar them from the Fifth Council? Surely he would have welcomed them in?

By what process did the Vatican eventually arrive at the conclusion that their Pope had voluntarily approved the anathemas and officially accepted them as canon law?

The absence of all but six Western bishops at the Council was hardly calculated to instill into the heart of the Mother Church a sudden trust in its bitterest foes, Theodora and Justinian. Was the Vatican prepared to submit to their intimidation for all eternity? Fear of Theodora's avenging arm is understandable during her lifetime. . . . but in his old age Justinian distintegrated into a demoralized dotard, repenting his ways and desperately seeking absolution. Why was the issue never reexamined by a properly authorized Ecumenical Council?

The *Catholic Encyclopedia* informs us that Virgilius and the four Popes who followed him give recognition only to the Three Chapters Edict when referring to the Council, and speak of Origenism as if they knew nothing of its condemnation.

Five hundred years later, in 1054, the Roman and Greek churches excommunicated each other. Surely no division of ideologies could be more total? But yet another puzzling aspect of the suppression is the ambivalence shown by the Greek church at the Council of Florence during the Renaissance. George Gemistus, attending as the Greek Church's deputy, urged Cosimo de Medici, then at the height of his power, to form a Platonic Academy in Florence. This served to introduce metempsychosis into European philosophy, even though the Church remained firmly uninvolved. Voltaire's caustic comment that "today Roman Catholics believe only in the councils approved in the Vatican, and Greek Orthodox Catholics believe only in those approved in Constantinople" implies an ironic reversal of loyalties to Platonism. Rome had to condemn it before the Greeks would condone it, even if they, too, still excluded it from their creed.

This is tantamount to saying that the real findings of the Council, never having been submitted to the Church of Rome, were therefore never ratified by it.

The Council had been no more than an elaborate thimblerig to conceal a much more intimate conclave which had been held in secret a few days earlier. In this secret cabala, according to the *Catholic Encyclopedia,* "the bishops already assembled at Constantinople had to consider, by order of the Emperor, a form of Origenism that had practically nothing in common with Origen, but which was held, we know, by one of the Origenist parties in Palestine."

The *Encyclopedia* concludes with the statement that the bishops obediently subscribed to the fifteen anathemas proposed by the Emperor against Origen*, and that Theodore of Scythopolin, an admitted Origenist, was forced to retract. But (and we may attach the most vital significance to the following) "there is no proof that the approbation of the Pope, who was at that time protesting against the convocation of the Council, was asked. It is easy to understand how this extraconciliatory sentence was mistaken, at a later period, for a decree of the actual ecumenical council."

For whom is it so easy to understand?

During the nearly fourteen hundred years which have elapsed since the Council, no ecclesiastical authority has subjected the problem to examination, or even evinced the slightest desire to do so.

Head and Cranston in their *Reincarnation, An East-West Anthology* supply this cogent summing-up: "It seems clear that. . . . Catholic scholars are beginning to disclaim that the Roman Church took any part in the anathemas against Origen; suggesting that during the many centuries when the Church believed it had condemned Origen, it was mistaken.

"However, one disastrous result of the mistake still persists; namely, the exclusion from the Christian creed of the teaching of the preexistence of the soul, and, by implication, reincarnation."

---

* (See Appendix A)

CHAPTER 12

THE SALEM WITCH TRIALS: THE "PURITAN ETHIC" IN THE AMERICAN PSYCHE

IT IS UNDERSTANDABLE that references to the Salem Witch Trials of 1692 are given special emphasis in the Life Readings, in that they were the first examples of religious persecution to leave their indelible stains both on the New World and the human souls who were involved.

Fourteen men and five women were hanged, and one man was pressed to death for refusing to plead innocent or guilty. Fifty-five others only escaped by turning informer on the innocent, and when the authorities finally regained their sanity, a hundred and fifty people were still languishing in jail.

Here again the "scars stretch down the centuries." The overall impression conveyed by the Readings is that among the innocent men, women and children who were persecuted was a core of devout visionaries and genuine clairvoyants.

Most significantly, the cases which appear in the Cayce files are nearly all linked in some way with psychic problems in the present. In this first example we find physical and emotional karma converging again.

The Witch-ducking Case

Some thirty years ago an A.R.E. member requested urgent help for her sister, Moira Schaeffer. A struggling artist of thirty-three with a shy, introspective and somewhat self-pitying nature, Moira had been invited to a Greenwich Village party where she was to meet "artists and dealers who would help her forward her career." She eventually returned home in a state of traumatic shock which deteriorated so rapidly into self-inflicted violence that it was necessary to confine her to an institution for the insane.

In her delirium she constantly cried out in terror that someone was trying to hurt her, and was in abject fear that she would be visited again by "the man with the black umbrella."

Her Life Reading regressed her to New England at the time of the witchhunts. Here Cayce found her as Mana Smyrth, possessing to a minor degree a talent for clairvoyance which swiftly brought her to the prisoner's dock. Her sentence was comparatively light. She was condemned to a series of public witch-duckings. But such duckings were often brutal enough in themselves to cause accidental drowning, and Mana Smyrth emerged from her ordeal embittered and vengeful.

"The Entity suffered under those persecutions, and often was brought under submission by the experiences of ducking.

"Thus the Entity inherits both good and bad influences from same in the present. Here we will find the needs for definite stands to be taken. While the Entity is afraid of water in a sense, we find that water—or color and water—must be a manner or a means or a channel for the greater expression."

The intensity of her hatred and anger canceled out whatever gains she might otherwise have made by forgiving her enemies. By thus abusing the Law of Grace, she found herself enmeshed once again in the karmic laws of cause and effect, where a deal of unfinished business awaited her from a life as an artisan in a distant Arabian incarnation. "Much disturbance physically and mentally arose through that period," Cayce told her, "and yet—as the Entity found, even then—a greater outlet for her abilities to depict the beautiful in art. So may she find the same in the present."

Despite this note of hope, the case remained a stubborn one in all its aspects. Moira's Physical Reading indicated that damage incurred in her spine was causing the insanity, but it was difficult to persuade the hospital authorities either to remove her from the "violent and incurable" ward or authorize osteopathic adjustments. Her weight was down to eighty pounds. In her total derangement she recognized nobody. However, Edgar was so vehement that she must be helped at all costs that David Kahn, a senior A.R.E. member in New York, used all the authority he could bring to bear. And after a long and laborious succession of appeals and minor miracles the girl was eventually restored to sanity and health by the aid of osteopathic treatments.

Her career as an artist took on full stature when her Reading told her that she had once been an apprentice in the atelier of the famous artist Peter Paul Rubens (1577-1640), and that if she hewed closely to his school of painting, her own style would evolve successfully. Her letter of gratitude to Edgar Cayce contains this touching excerpt: "I feel so much happier in spirit since I received the Reading. It seems incredible that any human being could see and feel things the way you do! The Rubens influence has been noticed in my work before, which makes this very convincing; I shall study up on Rubens's work and period, which I have already done, to some extent, in Boston. . . . Rubens was a master of the oil. As for the water color, it is peculiar the way things arrange themselves. I have always been somewhat afraid of a lot of water, and yet, as you said in the Reading, that's where water-color painting comes in."

No evidence was ever forthcoming of the exact nature of the outrage to which she was subjected, but her sister's impression, having listened to her delirium, was that a malign form of hypnotism had been used prior to the most brutal molestation.

If this was indeed so, could there be a boomeranging here of a revengeful Salem "witch" cursing her tormentors with more potence than she herself knew she possessed? And did she thus catch herself in her own trap? For to curse another "is to be cursed by self."

Two worthies appear in the Readings whose existence can be confirmed, though it should be born in mind that spelling in those days was often arbitrary and phonetic—John Dane, who took part in the general persecution, and the Rev. James Allen, a pastor who attempted to defend the persecuted.

John Dane (or Dain), was "among those who first landed in that country now known as Massachusetts, and among those called the Puritans. The Entity gained through service rendered to others, and through the application of self to the (spiritual) building in body and mind; for the Entity endured much suffering during that period."

An interesting sidelight to this incarnation is the Reading's reference to Dane's previous life as an English monk who had allowed "the weaknesses of the flesh" to cause him to break his vows. He was obviously atoning for it in his life as Dane.

At least two books contain historical reference to him as a member of the jury which tried the so-called witches: *More Wonders of the Invisible World,* published by Robert Calef in 1700; and *Witchcraft* by Charles Williams, published by Faber and Faber, London, in which is an account of how a group of jurors "signed a statement wherein forgiveness was asked for having had a hand in the persecutions." Among these names was that of John Dane.

The Reverend James Allen was a minister both in Salem and in Providence Town, "and there may be found yet, in the outer-portion of Salem, the monument, or the little slab, here of Allen, the minister of this church."

The Reading states that Allen was persecuted for his attempt to defend those of his parishioners who "had come to a free land that they might worship their God according to the dictates of their own conscience.

"Yet the Entity within itself gained throughout the experience. Though banished, he was loved by all those whom he served in body and in mind during that sojourn, bringing to self in his latter days the commendation of all that had known of the persecutions he had undergone.

"And to this Entity, this is the test of the fidelity of the soul even in the present."

Allen's existence is confirmed in *Records of Salem Witchcraft,* Vol. 2, by Elliot Woodward, but the graveyard where he was buried has been allowed to go to ruin. Even so, according to the Reading, his own headstone is still intact and decipherable, even if it is now part of a wall or a vestry floor.

Both these men fared well in their present lives, having retained the compassion and tolerance they exercised during the persecutions. Even Dane, though he had sat on the hanging jury, had dared to be as just as he could, and more than one poor creature must have owed her life to the vote Dane cast in her favor.

The Crows Come Home to Roost

Next we come to the complex case which might have derived from the pen of Poe or Hawthorne. In the early thirties, the Reading of Ezra Brandon, aged thirty-five, married with a young family, overlapped that of Marion Kramer, spinster, a few years older than himself.

Brandon was suffering from psoriasis, brought on by a back injury, but his Physical Reading had done much to alleviate it.

Marion was dabbling actively in the arcane. Possessing a slender gift for genuine clairvoyance, she was "spreading it around" by a dramatic use of automatic writing and impressive sessions with the ouija board. Her nature was restless, mischievous; her regard for the feelings of others, nil. When she met Ezra Brandon she developed a sexual obsession for him to which he responded. Directing her concentration to his weaknesses, she soon befuddled him with her dominating personality: the ouija board assured him that they were "soul mates" who belonged together, and urged him to free himself of his marriage ties. The merest modicum of truth underlay her theatrical sleight of hand, but it was enough to hook and gaff the credulous Brandon.

Both of them disregarded the warnings implicit in their Readings. Brandon divorced his wife and deserted his family. The moment he and Marion became man and wife, misfortune, which had till then remained in abeyance, descended on him. Not only did his livelihood crumble under a series of disasters, his ill-health returned, never to leave him again and eventually to bring his life to an end.

On the face of it, this was the kind of dreary tragedy that occurs every day at all levels of society. But in this case it was the playing-out of an unsavory relationship which had begun in Salem nearly three hundred years before.

There the couple were again man and wife, but the man, as Jacob Bennet, persecuted the women accused of witchcraft with unwholesome zeal, making no exception of his wife when she was discovered to be one of the victims "and oft was dipped—and once put in the stocks—for her activities."

Both Marion Kramer and Ezra Brandon had returned with positive potentialities. Marion was told that her ability could have been constructively channeled into some form of lay-therapy, working in conjunction with psychoanalysis or psychiatry, and Ezra was told that his remorse for his intolerance in Salem might be easily directed towards social and religious work in this life.

What reshackled them to each other, and wrecked their present lives, then? Clearly the incapacity to forgive, on Marion's part—the desire to be revenged for the cruelties in which her husband had played so large a part as Jacob Bennet. By reverting to a life in Greece which she had wasted gratifying the flesh when she had possessed unusual physical beauty, she had used a purely sexual coercion to entrap him.

And why had he passively allowed her to tear his life to pieces? He had been on the mend physically; he had not been unhappily married. It was almost a passive submission to destruction. No free will was used; indeed, it was abused. In this atmosphere of arid nihilism, the Law of Grace could not exist: therefore both of them were left to the tender mercies of the law of cause and effect.

The Good Friends

Yet good could come out of Salem, and never more surely than it did in the following relationship. It concerns a married woman and her brother-in-law, both by the name of Alden. He was the assistant to a stool-dipper, but found his task so thoroughly repugnant that he finally declared his sympathy for the oppressed. In the woman's case, "she suffered in body for the persecutions brought to her household. Hardships came upon the Entity, and she held grudges against those who had brought suffering to her loved ones.

"In the present there has ever been an innate awe of those who are teachers, ministers, or any who profess association with unseen sources," and a dread that they might come to harm for expressing their true opinions.

Had she been accused of witchcraft by association? The innocent invariably suffer twice as cruelly as the guilty in times of public persecution, and seldom if ever receive redress. Whatever the case, she was running a boarding house in Norfolk when she was made welcome by Edgar Cayce because of the intense sincerity of her power to pray. As a member of the A.R.E. prayer group, she developed the rare ability to "heal with her hands."

In this life, her brother-in-law was born a German national, and as a teenager he served as an infantryman in World War I. During the final defeat of Germany he was badly wounded and left to bleed to death on a deserted battlefield. Throughout the night, however, his wounds were staunched and he was kept alive by a luminous supernatural being. This he took to be his Guardian Angel—(and his is by no means a rare example of this type of phenomenon in the 1914-18 war)—for he was one of the first of the wounded to be discovered by the stretcher-bearers in the early dawn of the following day.

Subsequently he emigrated to America, and fate took him surefootedly to the boarding house in Norfolk where he was warmly welcomed by the sister-in-law of the old Salem days, now a widow of fifty-eight. Through her, he obtained a Reading from Edgar Cayce and even studied at the ill-fated Atlantic University which was organized in conjunction with the Edgar Cayce Hospital, and which likewise foundered with the '29 crash.

Cayce was able to clarify that the young man's Guardian Angel was not an angel in the scriptural sense but one of the Watchers, or Helpers, who have made sufficient spiritual progress to be able to come to mortal aid while they themselves are in the next dimension, awaiting rebirth.

This advanced soul had been able to repay, in full, the pity and kindness that Alden had shown to the victims of persecution in Salem. This is as good an example as any of the Law of Grace in action, superseding all the lesser laws of karmic cause and effect.

Another positive note is struck in the case of the woman who had escaped from Salem to Virginia as "the Witch, Jane Dundee," and though harassment and rejection of one sort or another followed her even there, she steadily continued to do what good she could until her death. Her Reading informed her that she had been one of the sick children healed by Christ during His lifetime, and that the desire to heal had persisted throughout the balance of her lives, defying the hangman's noose in Salem and manifesting now in a power to "heal with her hands."

The overall impression given by the references to Salem in the Readings is that the soul-group which incarnated there had shared a cycle of reincarnation which included France (from the Crusades to the Revolution) and Palestine in the time of the Master; then Greece, prehistoric Egypt and the cryptic and forbidding continent of Atlantis. Those souls who had responded instinctively to the preaching of Jesus tended to display strong spiritual fiber and courage during the Salem trials. Where and when they could, they strove to bring back sanity and tolerance.

Those who came to grief in Salem often had a record of intolerance, beginning in Atlantis, that led directly to their misfortunes in Salem. But it is cheering to observe how many profited by their mistakes and returned to the twentieth century prepared not only to live and let live, but to make themselves useful to their fellow men.

One captures vivid flashes of Salem's effect on a particular soul by such haphazard references as these:

. . . "The Entity was then one Sally Dale, who lost her life through the cold caught by dipping" . . . accounting in the present for her fear "ever to allow herself to express fully that which she feels within, when dealing with such subjects as witchcraft."

. . . "In the name of Marie Smith . . . heard and saw visions that were the imaginings of a mind far from home (this refers to the tall tales of a West Indian slave woman) who had heard in the groaning of the forests a sign that the souls of people live on.

"In the present, this may bring a curiosity, a wanting to know—yea, the listening to snatches of conversation not too nice—for oft ye will hear that which, if left unheard, would have made thee much happier!"

. . . "In the name Elsie Pepper . . . being among those who defied those who, as termed by Him, were wolves in sheep's clothing. Thus the interest in the present in all things of that nature (witchcraft)—and no wonder have there been the dreams and visions!"

. . . "The Entity was one Bill Edmundson, who made light of, yet experienced those close associations with earthbound spirits, or Entities, who had not found the Way. Yet the Entity put same aside, without analyzing or doing much about same. The Entity was then a storekeeper closely associated with some of the Ministers and councilmen . . . thus we find that commercial interests, the ability to speak in public, and those things pertaining to occult or psychic forces, are a part of the present experience. And all these things have their place, but the Entity must not become too rabid, or censor without due consideration of others. For freedom of speech does not entitle any individual to speak ill of his neighbor. Rather, it gives one the privilege of being a constructive influence through one's speech, thought and actions. And thus is freedom free indeed, as truth makes it so!"

. . . "During the persecutions of those who had familiar spirits, or those who saw, heard and understood much that is closed from material-minded men; the Entity was considered too lenient with those of the opposite sex as shared such experience, and suffered both in body and mind. In the present (the memory of) such experiences causes shudders in the region of the pineal and its center, as of shivers, quivers, or quakes; and sorrow enters in the mental being. These, if applied in the service of an ideal, may become worthwhile."

. . . "The Entity persecuted those who had visions or dreams, or those who were considered to have familiar spirits. Yet when those of his own household were counted among those who had seen visions and heard voices, the Entity found confusion even in self. Hence in the present there may be seen the interest in things of a psychic, occult or scientific nature. However, these but confuse. Beware of mysteries that may not be practical in the material experience, but beware as much of those who would make their soul—or psychic—experiences so practical as to impede the spiritual development of the soul itself!"

"A Sort of Sadducee"

A certain mystery arose over a Salem life attributed to an A.R.E. member, "then in the name of Robert Calvert. The Entity made for many questionings, and acted in the capacity as a judge in the tenets of the very orthodox relations of church, of state, of people."

The recipient of the Reading obligingly wrote the following to Gladys Davis Turner:

"For a matter of months, I searched the records for a Robert Calvert who fitted the description. The only representatives of that name in the New World were associated with Maryland, not Massachusetts. There was no Robert among them, and the line did not extend beyond the originals themselves, they being unmarried and having no heirs.

"The index of *The Devil in Massachusetts* revealed no Robert Calvert, but it did list a Robert Calef, whose character and activity fitted exactly with the details presented in the Reading.

"He was a Boston merchant, rather deprecatingly referred to as a weaver, who most assuredly made for many questionings and acted in the capacity of judge.

"The discrepancy of the name is easily accounted for as an error in transcription, since the shorthand symbols are quite similar, and substituting a familiar name for one unfamiliar would seem natural enough. I believe no one would hesitate to say that Robert Calef was the man whose record was referred to.

"He was born in England in 1648 and came to Boston sometime before 1688 with his family. Two of his eight children were born after his coming to

Boston, his eldest son being in 1693 a physician in Ipswich. In addition to his business and his justifiable meddling in the witchcraft matter, Calef was from 1692 to 1710 a constable, hayward and fence viewer, a surveyor of highways, a clerk of the market, an overseer of the poor, an assessor, and a tithing man! He retired to his own property in Roxbury, Massachusetts, where he died and was buried in the old burial ground opposite his home, April 13, 1719, aged seventy-one.

"He seems to have been one of the few sane heads in the place, and weaver or cloth-merchant though he was, he did not hesitate to make his own observations and draw his own conclusions. Nor did he hesitate to question repeatedly the decisions, theology, and reasoning of the two Mathers, Cotton and Increase. And, when they failed to give him satisfaction, he appealed to the clergy at large. He followed Cotton Mather's *Wonders of the Invisible World* with a book of his own, *More Wonders,* which was five times reprinted and is today recognized as the work of a mature and fair-intentioned individual possessed of an orderly mind.

"I shall forgo inordinate self-praise (although I am inclined to it) that father Increase, as President of Harvard, burned this man's book in Harvard Yard, and son Cotton called him 'a sort of Sadducee in this town.' And to have called the true infantile and fanatic character of these two divines to the fore is in itself a mead of praise and a modicum of comfort!

"Maybe I'm presumptuous and overhasty, but I'm proud of Robert Calef —he's just the kind of man, not only that I should have liked to be, but the kind I still want to go on being for some time to come!

"It might be harder, however, for another to see the connection between what Cayce says of the virtues and vices appertaining to Calef which still show in the present personality. But I feel they are there.

" 'Hence those influences in the present in which the Entity finds that he almost attains, and yet there is an influence or a force apparently outside or beyond his control . . . for as the Entity measured to others, so the Entity meets self in the present.'

"The exact explanation of anything is as important to me as ever. Although today not even as successful as a cloth merchant; and being wholly inexperienced as a surveyor, hayward, constable, or overseer of the poor; I still will take issue with anyone, so far as keeping the record straight. And I want to get it down on paper too, in just the way I see it—step by step—even at the expense of seeming tedious and pettish!

"Furthermore, I'm still unregenerate and a trifle stiff-necked: I'm a libertine in Puritan garb—and the 'Mathers' of this world and I are still at odds! Maybe they were right, and I am a sort of Sadducee!"

CHAPTER 13

THE REPERCUSSIONS FROM
THE SEARCH FOR BRIDEY MURPHY

THE THREE MEN who have done most to popularize Edgar Cayce's approach to reincarnation are the late Thomas Sugrue, who knew and loved him like a son; Morey Bernstein, who came to Virginia Beach after Edgar Cayce's death with the express intention of exposing him as a fraud; and, most recently, Jess Stearn.

Sugrue obviously needs no introduction here, and Stearn's book, *The Sleeping Prophet,* speaks for itself.

Bernstein was an intense, dedicated young man of independent means, whose medical study of hypnosis eventually led him to *There Is A River.* In Pueblo, Colorado, he discovered a young housewife, Ruth Simmons, who was so susceptible to hypnotic suggestion that he was able to regress her to the life of an Irish peasant woman who had lived in Belfast in the first half of the nineteenth century.

Bridey Murphy was thus destined to relive an obscure and uneventful existence in full view of the American public, and for a few years she reigned as queen of the newspaper headlines.

In 1956 Bernstein published *The Search for Bridey Murphy,* an account of the hypnotic sessions. In his favor it should be said that Bernstein was utterly unprepared (as were the rest of the people involved) for the best-selling overnight sensation the book became. He was likewise unprepared for the pained reaction such a vulgar success aroused in the more conservative echelons of the various Establishments; and retribution was swift to descend on his head.

For a while, the furore aroused by the book threatened to bring disrepute to everybody concerned, even those remotely involved in the proceedings. And because Edgar Cayce was featured in the first third of the book, the aims of the A.R.E. could have suffered a public setback if the drive against reincarnation in all its forms had succeeded in its aims.

For this reason the Bridey Murphy incident warrants more than a passing nod in the present volume.

In his zeal to get the full story, he presented his questions with the impartiality of a district attorney determined on getting the truth out of a recalcitrant witness, quite forgetting that the I.Q. of an uneducated servant-type of the early 1800's had less than nothing in common with the I.Q. of Ruth Simmons.

Bridey, on first being allowed to express herself, was more than delighted. She gossiped happily, flattered to be the center of an attention she had never enjoyed in the flesh. She was anxious to be liked and to make a good impression, and she was naturally reluctant to expose herself as an illiterate peasant.

She promoted her husband and her family to the lower-middle class she had obviously always held in wistful awe and envy. (Actually, she must have been as low down the scale as the wife of a coachman or the messenger for a Belfast solicitor.) Her boasting, alas, while only human and certainly forgivable, crumbled under the lie-detector methods of Bernstein.

As one listens to the tapes, one becomes aware of her gradual bewilderment, and then her active fear, as she finds herself being grilled by "hostile members of the upper class." The little white lies she had told were thrown back at her, implying that nothing she had said was being believed. With her reluctance to be exposed and made a fool of, a sympathetic reluctance began to evidence itself in Ruth Simmons on a subtler scale. She began to chafe at the imposition made by the sessions on her own life, and Bernstein was reduced to having to beg her to continue.

It is significant that on all the minor details that an uneducated servant could be expected to know, Bridey was checking out well. She correctly named shops in the town, the popular reading matter, (which she personally could never have read), the type of meals she served, the colloquialisms for domestic articles, and distinctly expressed her awe of Father Gorman, the parish priest, apparently a rather distant young cleric with waning hopes of better things than an impoverished parish. The stark, arid loneliness of existence of the poor in that century comes through the tapes in sober measure. Bridey had almost no pleasures to speak of, and a great deal of unrewarding slavery. She died of sheer exhaustion, prematurely old, cowed in death as she had been in life, unable to make her presence known to her senile husband and equally unable to progress beyond the primitive astral world that clutters the outer perimeter of life. In this "purgatory of the under-privileged," life-after-death took on the thought-form drabness of a workhouse or almshouse in permanent twilight. And in one of his less diplomatic moments, Bernstein included in the book Bridey's reference to a meeting at this level with Father Gorman, as dazed and disorientated as herself. (This, of course, offended the sensibilities of our present-day clerics who were later to denounce the book from their various pulpits.)

Two most affecting phenomena must be given mention here. As Bridey's uneasiness and bewilderment with Berntein's cross-examination increased, she resorted more and more to pitiful attempts to mollify him. She would develop a convenient cold which caused her to cough when his questions became too aggressive, or she would complain that her foot was hurting from a sprain incurred in dancing an Irish Jig.

Then, towards the close of the sessions, as the questions centered more on Bridey Murphy's last years, a voice emerged from Ruth Simmons that not even the most accomplished actress could have simulated. It was the slack-throated, utterly weary half-whine of a sixty-year-old woman, resigned to speaking with a toothless palate and now completely reconciled to abject poverty and physical misery. The accent was confined to the flat, inimitable vowels of the Belfast slum—an accent that has never crossed the Atlantic, in that it is never used by American actors. (All this was preserved on tape.)

If Ruth Simmons had been a vocal genius, she would still have had no means of re-creating these accents consciously. And Ruth Simmons was not a passably adequate amateur actress.

The behavior-pattern of Bridey on these last tapes is more convincing than fifty technical proofs that such-and-such a street existed in Belfast at that time, or whether Bridey as a child referred to her bed as an "iron bed" or a "foine bed."

If Bernstein had been the sly fox the press called him, he would never have been so naive as to publish his book before he had accumulated a solid backlog of evidence. And to obtain that evidence, he would first have had to permit a trained and tactful psychologist to do the questioning of Bridey, and he would have had to bury himself for at least six months or a year in Belfast, up to his ears in the records of the nineteenth century.

Even if he had done all this in overwhelming measure, it is still anybody's guess whether the book's reception would have been any more open-hearted.

The facts have been objectively analyzed and presented by C. J. Ducasse, Professor of Philosophy Emeritus, of Brown University, Rhode Island in his book, *A Critical Examination of the Belief in a Life after Death,* published by Charles Thomas, Springfield, Illinois, 1961.

In it Professor Ducasse devoted thirteen objective and impartial pages to the Bridey Murphy controversy which are required reading for anyone even mildly interested in the Hallowe'en hubbub after all these years.

Professor Ducasse quietly and sanely put the matter into perspective as no one else has been able to do. He defended Bernstein and came to the support of Ruth Simmons, whose real name was Mrs. Virginia Tighe of Pueblo, Colorado, exonerating her from all suspicion of fraudulent practice.

Mrs. Tighe was born April 27th, 1923. At the age of three she was adopted by an aunt, Mrs. Myrtle Grung, and grew up in Chicago. At the age of twenty she married a U.S. Air Force flyer who died in action a year later.

Virginia's second marriage was to Hugh Bryan Tighe, a Denver businessman, with whom she had three children. As both her husband and her own relatives were "very much opposed to the whole Bridey phenomenon on religious grounds," Virginia was unprepared and unequipped both for the sensationalism the Bernstein book aroused and the backlash that curled around her family's defenseless heads.

Life magazine began to zero in on Bernstein as early as March 1956, but it was the *Chicago American* which fired on Fort Sumter. In June it began a series of skeptical articles, using as its authority a Rev. Wally White of the Chicago Gospel Tabernacle, who had vowed to "debunk reincarnation because of its assault upon established religious doctrines."

White claimed to have known Mrs. Tighe from her childhood, but she herself stated that she had never met him until he appeared uninvited at her door in 1956 and informed her that it was his duty to pray for her soul.

The *Denver Post* came valiantly to the defense of Virginia and Bernstein, but its guns were silenced when *Life* dealt the coup de grace on June 25 with a summary of the *Chicago American*'s exposé, and a photograph of a certain Mrs. Bridie Murphy Corkell and her family, of whom more later.

As fascinating a piece of Freudian curiosa as any that emerged at this time was a book jointly written by three New York psychiatrists, which had as its purpose the total annihilation of the theory of reincarnation forever. This book, *A Scientific Report on "The Search for Bridey Murphy"* came to a singularly unscientific end as a discount bookstore remaindered it at forty-nine cents a copy.

Of the Rev. Wally White, Professor Ducasse has this to say: "It would seem, then, that the featuring of this clergyman's name at the head of several of the *American*'s articles was just psychological window-dressing for the benefit of pious but naive readers. Such readers, seeing articles under the by-line of a clergyman, and having been told that he is the pastor of the church Virginia attended in Chicago, would naturally assume that he has firsthand knowledge of her childhood and youth; that his articles are based on that special knowledge; and therefore that, since clergymen are truthful, the articles bearing the Rev. White's by-line must be authoritative. But although the reader is likely to infer all this from the articles, they carefully refrain from actually asserting any of it.

"The climax, however, of the *Chicago American* series of articles was the discovery of a Mrs. Bridie Murphy Corkell in Chicago, who lived across the street from one of the places where Virginia and her foster parents had resided, whom Virginia knew . . . but although the articles state that she 'was in the Corkell home many times,' Virginia never spoke with Mrs. Corkell— nor does the article assert that she ever did.

"Further, Virginia never knew that Mrs. Corkell's first name was Bridie, and still less that her maiden name was Murphy, if indeed it was. For when the *Denver Post* tried to verify this, Mrs. Corkell was not taking telephone calls. And when its reporter Bob Byers inquired from her parish priest in Chicago, he confirmed her first name was Bridie, but was unable to verify her maiden name as Murphy; nor could the Rev. Wally White do so.

"But the reader will hardly guess who this Mrs. Corkell, whom the *American* 'discovered,' turned out to be. By one more of the strange coincidences of the case, Mrs. Bridie (Murphy) Corkell happens to be the mother of the editor of the Sunday edition of the *Chicago American* at the time the articles were published!"

The farcical aspect of the whole story only emerges in full relief, however, when we examine the fate of the film version, which was already in production at Paramount Studios with Pat Duggan as the producer, when the storm signals were run up the mast.

The screenwriter-director of the film reports as follows: "In the screenplay, I was limited to the material Bernstein had published in his book, though there was far more dramatic and convincing material elsewhere on the original tapes. The climax of the picture was carefully constructed to scare the public off the irresponsible use of hypnosis as a party-trick, and I even wrote in a gratuitous scene where a Protestant minister and a Catholic priest gave their definitive opinions on the theory of reincarnation (subversive paganism), and hypnosis (for the birds).

"The salaries budgeted for the two principal actors were modest to say the least, but I managed to blarney Teresa Wright into such enthusiasm for the role that she agreed to work for the allotted pittance. So did Louis Hayward, who, because of his earlier costume pictures, had become inexcusably underestimated as an all-around character actor. The studio heads, instead of evincing pleasure at the casting, went out of their way to show the back of their hands to both stars, and only the fact that I am six-foot-five preserved me from having to carry a loaded fly-swat to defend myself in lonely corridors. Nevertheless, I soon began to call our unit the 'Contamination Ward.' My production manager had been privately informed by higher sources that the picture would never be finished, but that Duggan and I already were. My cutter, a gregarious type, spent happy hours on the stage disparaging the filming, but none, as far as I could gather, in the cutting room . . . nothing I was shooting would 'cut together.'

"We were able to defend the picture from open sabotage on the studio floor, but when it became necessary for us to use the special-effects laboratory—we had 'ghost' sequences and intricate mechanical dissolves from modern Colorado to Ireland in the 1860's—we were informed that Mr. De Mille had commandeered the effects lab in toto for 'The Ten Commandments.' We then requested that the rushes be sent to an independent effects lab outside the studio. We were told this was quite impossible. Finally my cameraman, Jack Warren, put the clock back fifty years and did all the double-exposures right on the set, using nothing more complicated than a prism, a mirror, and a two-foot strip of plain glass, lamp-blacked at one end, greased with Vaseline in the center and clear at the other end. This, when drawn slowly across the lens of the camera, was twice as effective as a modern lab dissolve.

"The worst, however, was yet to come. *Life* magazine had been paying close attention to the Bridey Murphy craze for some time, tracing its pernicious influence to teenage parties where irresponsible young 'beats' regressed equally irresponsible young girls into presumable seductability by the gross. Halfway through the picture, *Life* broke the story that the whole thing was a hoax.

"Our budget was low and we were bringing in between four to ten minutes of screen time a day (this with adequate covering shots), but from the Contamination Ward we were relegated to the Leper Colony. There was a move afoot to suspend production entirely, and I found myself not only directing but holding the bridge like Horatio, which at least kept the foe at bay during working hours. We brought the film in on time, but less than five minutes of it had been cut. I managed to get the cutter replaced at the eleventh hour, and in the short cutting time left to us, we had to protect Teresa's performance first—once that was in balance, we would have been able to bring Hayward's performance up to match it. He had worked with unselfish intensity, and Teresa's performance reflected his team-work; but it would have taken another week to cut him into the picture in his proper stature, and we were denied that extra week.

"Even in its maimed and limping state, the film got a round of applause at its sneak preview in a particularly rough and unresponsive neighborhood theater in Glenwood. This should have heartened the executives sufficiently to let us finish the job, if only to protect the shareholders' investment, but I never saw the film again.

"When it was released, the general press gave it the silent treatment and it obediently wilted on the vine.

"No one in Hollywood ever saw it, in case their presence in the audience could be interpreted as subversive malfeasance, yet Duggan and I were treated as renegades who had gratuitously smirched the proud heritage of the Four Freedoms."

It is a far cry from the uneasy fifties to the success of Alan J. Lerner's Broadway musical in 1966, "On A Clear Day You Can See Forever." The intervening years had seen the theory of reincarnation advanced in the public mind from a scaremongering bogey to a sedate muse, perfectly at home on the Broadway stage and responding happily to the warmth and charm of Lerner's genius.

The majority of the critics found it a little too defiant of orthodoxy to be treated cordially, but the audiences established their own standards, much as they will during a newspaper strike. In fact, the house was sold out for six months in advance when the show opened at the Mark Hellinger Theater.

Briefly, the plot deals with a modern Trilby, Brooklyn model, who is a natural hypnotic subject for a personable young psychiatrist. He regresses her to an earlier life in eighteenth-century England, and it is implied (though never flatly stated) that he was her inconstant lover in that period.

The psychiatrist proceeds to fall in love with the English belle, Melinda, while her contemporary edition, Daisy, falls in love with him, to their mutual frustration.

In her life as Melinda, the heroine had perished while escaping to America on the sailing ship Trelawney. Fleeing from her psychiatrist, Daisy almost meets the same fate by booking a flight on a transatlantic jet—also called (why not?)—Trelawney.

Representing the popular misconception of reincarnation is the Greek shipping magnate, Kriakos, who offers the psychiatrist a fortune to tell him who he will be in his next life, so that he can will his millions to himself in advance.

Daisy's ESP and the course of true love save the day. Ultimately she permits her previous personality to move in and "take over the management" of her present self. But before the happy ending, the audience has been treated to a painless but thorough grounding in the advances ESP has made in the last decade. Lerner contents himself with saying in effect: all this will soon be acceptable to society; this is the psychiatric logic of tomorrow.

In the November, 1965, issue of *Atlantic Monthly* is an interview with Mr. Lerner, in which the dramatist states: "Somebody asked me if I thought (the play) was a fantasy, because it touched on the possibility of reincarnation, and I said, 'Well, no, not to five hundred million Indians it isn't!' . . . .

"The only surprising thing about (the play) is that I haven't written it before. Extrasensory perception has been my hobby all my life. . . . I know, of course, that only twenty-two percent of our brain is in practical use. The rest of it must be doing something up there besides filling out the hat. I've never had any extrasensory experiences myself, except for one minor one when I was writing 'Brigadoon.'

"The first act of 'Brigadoon' ended with a wedding, which had to take place outside the church. I tried to figure out why in seventeenth and eighteenth century Scotland anyone would be married outside a church, and if they were, what the ceremony should be. So I figured something out and wrote it down.

"Several years later I was in London . . . and I stumbled upon a book called *Everyday Life in Old Scotland*—and there was my wedding ceremony, word for word! . . .

"When I began to think seriously about why I wanted to write a musical about (reincarnation), I realized that in recent months I had become increasingly outraged at all the pat explanations psychoanalysis was throwing up to explain human behavior. I was becoming more and more disgusted by the morality of psychoanalysis—that we are living in a world where there is no more character and where everything is behavior; that there is no more good, it is all adjustment; that there is no more evil, it is all maladjustment. Psychoanalysis has turned into a totally unsatisfactory religion which gives no life hereafter, and no divine morality to live by. And so I began to think, 'Well, yes, this might be a good thing to write about.' I would find a way of saying I don't think that we are all that explainable; that much of us is still unknown; that there are vast worlds within us, and that it's a thrilling possibility to contemplate."

1966 also saw the publication of Dr. Ian Stevenson's *Twenty Cases Suggestive of Reincarnation,* which we will examine next. Here we find reincarnation afforded the full dignity of acceptance by a distinguished professor in the Department of Neurology and Psychiatry of the School of Medicine at the University of Virginia.

CHAPTER 14

THE WORK OF DR. IAN STEVENSON

DR. STEVENSON, heading the vanguard of responsible investigators seeking firsthand evidence of reincarnation, has journeyed as far afield as India, Ceylon, Lebanon and Alaska. In 1966 he published his findings under the title of *Twenty Cases Suggestive of Reincarnation.**

The singular characteristic of the Eastern cases is the brief interval between the souls' death and the rebirth. While the Cayce Readings roughly measure rebirths in terms of centuries and half centuries, in Dr. Stevenson's cases the average is nearer ten years or less . . . sometimes instantaneous, as in the case of a Hindu youth of twenty-two, poisoned to death by a debtor, who

* Published by the American Society for Psychical Research; New York, 1966.

reincarnated into the body of a three-and-a-half-year old boy, presumably dead of smallpox. The boy revived, but from then on identified only with the characteristics and history of the twenty-two-year old, even to the extent of correctly describing his former family, and recognizing each one individually when taken to see them.

The most compelling example, in that Dr. Stevenson was able to observe it while it was still occurring in Lebanon in 1964, concerned a five-year-old Arab boy named Imad Elawar, living in the village of Kornayel. Before he was two he had begun to refer to his past life. His first words referred affectionately to his mistress of his previous life. Imad was fortunate to possess parents who did not subdue his chatter with the severity such children usually receive. Born December 21, 1958, he claimed to have lived, in his former life, in the village of Khriby, some twenty-five miles away, as Ibrahim Bouhanzy, who had died of tuberculosis on Sept. 18, 1949. Imad correctly supplied the dying words of Ibrahim, correctly identified the surviving members of Ibrahim's family, and never ceased to refer affectionately to Jarmile, Ibrahim's mistress. Ibrahim's village and house were likewise familiar to Imad. Dr. Stevenson traveled with Imad and his family to Ibrahim's village, and tabulates the fifty-seven items recalled from memory by the child as follows: "Of the fifty-seven items, Imad made ten of the statements in the car on the way to Khriby . . . of these ten, three were incorrect. Of the remaining forty-seven items, Imad was wrong on only three items. It seems quite possible that under the excitement of the journey . . . he mixed up memories of the 'previous life' and memories of the present life."

As much as it was possible to verify the evidence of the two families, Dr. Stevenson did so meticulously. Most of the proof was immediately self-evident. Neither family stood to gain, and both stood to lose by lying, in that it could not be denied that the child's memory had been correct fifty-one times out of fifty-seven.

Dr. Stevenson points out that if there had been collusion between the two families (who were unknown to each other until they met to satisfy the child), the motive would have been hard to establish. No family would assiduously accumulate evidence so reluctantly over so long a period for the mere sensationalism of getting their name in the papers. Indeed, Dr. Stevenson's reception by most of the Hindu families he interviewed was hostile, at first.

In the case of the "possession" of the three-and-a-half-year-old "corpse" of Jasbir by the twenty-two-year-old discarnate Hindu youth Sobha Ram, the embarrassment to the family of the child Jasbir was further aggravated by the child's refusal to eat anything except Brahmin food, which had to be prepared and cooked for him by a sympathetic Brahmin neighbor. Anyone familiar with the implacable ferocity of the Hindu caste laws will comprehend that a Jat child would normally sooner starve than eat Brahmin food, no matter how unbalanced his mental faculties might otherwise have become. It is also hard to conceive of a child of Jasbir's tender years suddenly behaving with the articulate authority of a youth eighteen years his senior.

"During my stay," writes Dr. Stevenson, "I easily noticed that he did not play with other children, but stayed aloof and isolated. Yet he talked willingly with my interpreter, although wearing always a sad expression on his quiet, pock-marked but handsome face."

The Brahmin family of the dead Sobha Ram were willing to treat Jasbir hospitably, but his own Jat family deeply resented his identification with a family of superior caste, and their opposition to the "previous" family of their son reached its zenith in their dogged refusal to let him meet his own "widow."

"Readers may wish to know, as I did," concludes Dr. Stevenson, "what account Jasbir gave of events between the death of the Sobha Ram personality and the revival of Jasbir (from his presumed death) with memories of Sobha Ram.

"To this question, Jasbir replied in 1961 that after death he (as Sobha Ram) met a Sadhu (a holy man or saint) who advised him to 'take cover' in the body of Jasbir.

"Although the apparent 'death' of Jasbir occurred in the period April-May 1954, close to the identified date of Sobha Ram's death, we do not know that the change in personality of Jasbir took place immediately on the night when his body seemed to die and then revived.

"In the following weeks Jasbir was still perilously ill with smallpox, barely able to take nourishment, and not able to express much of any personality. The change of personality may therefore have happened quickly or gradually, during the weeks beginning immediately after the apparent death of Jasbir."

In terms of documented evidence, this case is unique. In most instances of this nature, the soul is given time to depart from its adult body before its next body is conceived, even in cases of violent death.

The allusion to the "holy Sadhu" who directed the discarnate Sobha Ram to "take cover" in the dead or dying body of Jasbir suggests a state of emergency, a breakdown in the normal "laws of creation." Edgar Cayce has admitted that "sometimes there are mistakes, even in the firmament"; even though they are too rare to be placed in the category of hazards. He has also suggested that the first astral plane is primitive, in that it distortedly resembles the earth plane, and can be inhabited by the thought-forms of backward or undeveloped souls, able to assume all the menacing outward trappings of the nightmare.

If we assume that Sobha Ram's premature and unexpected death as a result of poisoning was not anticipated in the karmic laws to which he conformed, it might well have left him vulnerable to some hostile and vengeful soul who had been awaiting just such an opportunity to square accounts with him.

In his own state of disorganized confusion, unable to defend himself, one of the more benign Helpers or Watchers could have appeared to him in the reassuring form of a Sadhu and shown him the only sanctuary available—the uninhabited shell of the dead child. This could have been purely a temporary measure, until the immediate danger on the lower astral had been deflected and Sobha Ram could proceed safely to a more enlightened and protective level. (Here again we employ Cayce's argument that the forces of evil, no matter how stubborn or of what intensity, can always be dispersed by prayer from a pure and responsible source.)

It could be possible, however, that once Sobha Ram had reentered the material confines of human flesh (rather like a lobster crawling into a lobster-pot), he was unable to extricate himself again; and is now compelled to remain "earthbound" as Jasbir until he has lived out the requisite number of years still due him on his own karmic record. Mercifully his memory of his previous life will gradually fade.

Reincarnation in the Frozen North

The Eskimos of northwest Alaska, the Aleuts to the west, and the Tlingit Indians to the southeast, all base their religious beliefs on reincarnation. The Tlingits further personalize it by believing that souls return to their own immediate families.

Between 1961 and 1965 Dr. Stevenson made four visits to the Tlingits, obtaining thirty-six claimed cases of reincarnation. These cases were not difficult to collect, as most of the Indians spoke English and many of the claimants bore "sympathy" scars in the present life which identified the manner of death in the previous life.

In 1949, a Tlingit Indian fisherman of sixty, called William George, told his son and daughter-in-law he would return as their son. He promised them they would recognize him by his present birthmarks, and gave them his gold watch for safekeeping. A few weeks later, he disappeared from his seine boat without trace. Barely nine months later his daughter-in-law gave birth to a boy "who had pigmented naevi (moles) on the upper surface of his left shoulder and the volar surface of his left forearm at exactly the locations mentioned by the grandfather."

As he grew up, the boy displayed a behavior-pattern similar to his grandfather's, even extending to a physical limp which his grandfather had incurred in a basketball game. Before he was five, the boy identified his watch by picking it out of his mother's jewelry box unprompted, and stubbornly maintained his right of ownership. He referred to his uncles as "sons" and his great-aunt as "sister."

Dr. Stevenson wrote: "He shows a precocious knowledge of fishing and boats. He also shows greater than average fear of water for boys of his age. He is more grave and sensible than other children of his group."

Even more evidential is the case of another Tlingit, Victor Vincent (tribal name, Kahkody), who died in 1946.

In the previous year he had told his favorite niece and her husband Corliss Chotkin that he would return as their child, and promised that they would recognize him by the scars he bore—one on the side of his nose and another on his back, the remains of an operation that still revealed the marks of the stitches.

Eighteen months later Mrs. Chotkin gave birth to a son who possessed birthmarks which exactly duplicated Vincent's scars. At thirteen months he interrupted his mother's efforts to teach him his name, Corliss Chotkin Jr., by asking: "Don't you know me? I'm Kahkody!"

At the age of two he correctly identified his previous stepdaughter Susie, his son William, and his own widow. He continued to exhibit unusually detailed recall until the age of nine, from which age his memory began to fade, finally becoming inactive in his fifteenth year.

Dr. Stevenson tabulates each case meticulously and academically. He states his own views, doubts and rationalizations in great detail. Nevertheless, his book emerges as a responsible assembling of incontrovertible facts. In his conclusion, he makes no claim to having proved reincarnation, but the evidence for it has never been presented by a more responsible spokesman.

CHAPTER 15

THE LAW OF GRACE

OBVIOUSLY, THE SIMPLEST way to illustrate the Law of Grace is to show it in action.

Anthony Hollis had fallen in love with a girl while he was still in college in Connecticut. He lost her to his best friend without a struggle, and his subsequent Reading told him his subconscious memory had stood him in good stead: twice before in the past he had been married to her, and twice before she had been unfaithful to him. The Reading even specified a life in ancient Egypt in which she had run off with the same friend! It did not offer details of any other life with her, beyond the implication that violence and tragedy had always dogged them.

Hollis had taken full advantage of his opportunity to receive further Readings, and as he had put their morality into practice to the best of his ability, he could justifiably be called a "good Christian." He married well and the college infatuation was soon buried and forgotten. In 1944, he was called to active service and took his training as a transport officer at Fort Eustis, Va.

One day he happened to swallow a plum pit which lodged so firmly in his throat that he had to report to the hospital to have it removed. He thought no more of it at the time. But while he was based in England prior to the D-Day invasion of Europe, he choked again, this time on a piece of gristle. Once more the situation was serious enough to warrant medical aid. By this time it was too late to request a Reading from Edgar Cayce, and by the time Anthony Hollis experienced his third mishap in occupied Germany, Edgar Cayce was dead. Each mishap was more serious. In Germany he was all but strangled by a segment of bone from a stew.

Back in America after the war, he was dining with a friend in New York City, when a chicken bone lodged in his throat. He was rushed to hospital, where an inexpert doctor wasted valuable minutes trying to give him a barium test "to prove that the choking was psychosomatic."

When they finally rushed him to the operating table, Hollis was barely conscious, yet while they were working on him with oxygen masks and local anaesthetics, he found himself confronting a strange, vindictive face framed in straggling locks of dirty yellow hair. He was thrust deeper into this level of consciousness until he "merged" with the other personality and discovered it to be himself. The surroundings vaguely suggested a Nordic environment about nine or ten centuries back . . . and he was confronting a young woman. His grief and rage were homicidal; he knew she had been unfaithful to him. He knew she was his wife, but that was all.

At exactly the time this was happening, a friend of his in San Francisco received a vivid "photo-image" of this same demented face and associated it with Hollis. In this hallucination, however, no woman was present. Hollis was chained to a dungeon wall, one of a group of unkempt, ragged men. The impression was sufficiently vivid for his friend to phone Hollis the next day in some consternation. When Hollis and his friend compared notes, no shred of doubt remained that they had both seen the same face.

Hollis searched his Readings but could find no specific reference to the "fellow with the dirty yellow hair." The Readings had emphasized the karmic trait of a quick temper that Hollis at all times went to great pains to control. In Edgar Cayce's cautious, tactful notes, there were allusions to karmic debts still to be paid. The Readings made a great point of suggesting that instead of pursuing the "eye for an eye, tooth for a tooth" law of literal restitution, Hollis should attempt the more enlightened method of evening-up his reckoning by forgiveness and prayer.

This seemed a complicated task for a man in the twentieth century who had apparently hated a woman in Viking Norway in the eighth or ninth century. But the matter was taken out of Hollis's hands. Less than a week later he dreamed the same macabre dream. This time the unfamiliar features of the woman took on the "ghost" physiognomy of the girl who had jilted him in college, and he was strangling her in deadly earnest. On the split-level he now occupied between dream and karmic reenactment, Hollis began to pray with all the intensity and faith he could muster. He prayed for the spiritual strength to forgive the woman he was strangling; he prayed for her to be forgiven her adultery; he prayed for himself to be forgiven for having strangled her to death. Anyone who has literally prayed his way back from a deathbed will confirm that, once it attains to a certain intensity, genuine prayer manifests as energy that surmounts all other factors opposing it.

When Hollis woke the next morning, he was aware of a weight gone from his mind, a sense of newly found freedom he had never known before, and the feeling remained with him over the balance of the week. Yet he had no tangible means of assuring himself that his prayers had freed him permanently from the karmic yoke that had hung so heavily around his neck. Not, that is, until his phone rang on the Saturday, and he heard the voice of his victim in the dream.

She had long divorced his friend and married again. Her second marriage had also foundered; and now, a rich woman, she wandered the world on luxury cruises with her children, disconsolate and unfulfilled. For no reason at all, when her ship docked in New York, she found herself thinking of Hollis with remorse for the way she had jilted him, and her phone call a whim. "I do hope you've forgiven me by now? I did treat you so disgrace-fully!"

In a heartfelt burst of relief and gratitude, Hollis fervently assured her that he had forgiven her a thousand times over!

What would Hollis's karmic alternative have been? Surely an increase in the intensity of his choking fits, until one killed him. The debt he owed was to himself, for having once committed murder. The fact that in this life the girl, herself, spared him the misery of having to marry her again, and that he then suffered the same miserable ordeal of her betrayal, did not take him off the karmic hook. The murder had still been committed; the Law still demanded that it be accounted for. Thus, when the freedom of his throat was in any way obstructed, the symptoms of his physical response were of strangulation, not ordinary choking.

But his outward decency toward the girl in the present; plus the fact that once Cayce had explained the karmic cause, Hollis bore her no grudge and wished her no ill, worked in his favor. As soon as hurt pride and outraged vanity had been removed from the picture, the complications vanished also, and he was left to face a clear-cut test.

The source of the will-power and concentration Hollis was able to apply to his final prayer of forgiveness is defined very simply in the following words: "Yet it is a fact that a life experience is a manifestation of divinity. And the mind of an Entity is the builder. Then, as the Entity sets itself to accomplish that which is creative, it comes under the law which operates between karma and grace. No longer is the Entity under the law of cause and effect, or karma, but rather, in grace, he may go on to the higher calling set in HIM."

"To be sure, the law applies," said Cayce in a similar situation. "For in the beginning of man, in his becoming a living soul in the earth, laws were established, and these take hold. But do not lose sight of the law of grace, the law of mercy, the law of patience as well. For each has its place—especially when individuals desire to be channels through which God may manifest."

The Needless Despair of a Resolved Soul

The second case is that of Vera Aldrich, housewife, aged fifty-three. Here we see the error, made by an advanced soul whose path has been almost too physically hard to bear, in assuming that her karmic debts have demanded their reckoning, and that she is about to be visited by her old guilts.

"Why should I come into this life with such a broken physical body? It seems I have been through hell (but an interesting trip so far!) and I have often wondered what I have saved myself for. I have always wanted to be of service to humanity, but had no strength . . . angina, pernicious anemia, and so on, since I was young. Why did I bring such a broken body to live in? Have I committed a great crime in the past?"

Cayce's answers were couched entirely in warm reassurances.

"This Entity was associated with the one who persecuted the church so thoroughly, and who fiddled while Rome burned (Nero). That's the reason why this Entity has been disfigured by the structural conditions of the present body.

"Yet this Entity may be set apart! For through her experience in the earth, she had advanced from a low degree to the point where another reincarnation in the earth may not even be necessary.

"Not that she has reached perfection, but remember, the material, and material urges, exist in other consciousnesses, not in just the three-dimensional. . . . There are other realms for instruction, if the Entity will hold fast to the ideals of those at whom she once scoffed (the Christians in Rome).

"There is more that might be said, but we would minimize the faults and we would magnify the virtues. And little or nothing could be given that would deter the Entity in any way, for, as Joshua did of old, she has determined that 'others may do as they may, but as for me—I will serve the living God!'

"As to the abilities: Who would give glory to the morning sun? Who would tell the stars how to be beautiful? Keep that faith which has prompted thee! Many will gain much from thy patience, thy consistency, thy love!"

This woman, by her generous and unselfish way of life, had achieved Grace without even realizing it at the conscious level. Her long karmic wanderings were over.

"To be sure, individuals grow in grace, in knowledge, in understanding, and as they apply that which they know, the next step is shown to them. . . . For His promise is: 'I will be with thee always, even unto the end of the world.' He was with thee in the beginning. Ye wandered away. . . .'"

Gladys Turner Davis, Edgar Cayce's permanent secretary from 1923 to his death, transcribed nearly every Reading in the files, not once but five times over, and has remained as selflessly loyal to him as she was in his lifetime. No other member of the A.R.E. possesses her unique familiarity with the Readings, and perhaps no one else exemplifies so unobtrusively the application of the laws of Grace to everyday existence. She considers it was a rare occasion when he told someone their soul was so far advanced that they need not return to earth again.

On one of the rare occasions when she was persuaded to express herself on paper, she pays Edgar this tribute:

"During Mr. Cayce's lifetime, I can remember only three instances in which the individuals claimed their Life Readings were incorrect—only three out of nearly 2,500!

"Since Mr. Cayce's death, in gathering progress reports to index with the Readings, we have encountered only one unfavorable report—from a mother who complains that there was 'nothing personal' in the Reading for her six-year-old daughter.

"It has happened time and again that Life Readings for children were put away and forgotten by the parents, then, later, were found to be true in every detail. But let us think for a moment about these few instances in which the Readings were disclaimed. Even if one in twenty-four had been completely wrong—that is an unheard of percentage in the field of psychic research—perhaps in any line of research!

"Those of us who know from experience the value of these Readings are not only privileged, but in fact obligated, to press on toward perfection, carrying a torch not just for the theory of reincarnation, but for the whole Christian way of life as taught by Him 'Who, being in the form of God, thought it not robbery to be equal with God.'

"But what do the Readings mean to the millions who didn't even know or care that a man gave his life for them? What will it mean to the generations to come?

"It has been said that in the eyes of two or three witnesses, a fact is legally established. We have over two thousand living examples of correct analyses of capabilities and character based on akashic records of past lives.

"By a careful analysis and study of them, many of us are convinced that we can reach an understanding of the basic factors which govern man's thoughts and feelings. For these Life Readings represent interpretations of fundamental spiritual laws, applied, it is true, to personal problems. By studying a number of examples, we should be able to learn how to apply those same laws to our own personal problems."

CHAPTER 16

GROUP KARMA

The Survivors of Fort Dearborn

EDGAR CAYCE, in his former life as the frontier scout Bainbridge, had ranged the newly-emerged nation of America from the Canadian border to Florida, an amalgam of pioneer hero and the Gaylord Ravenal type of riverboat gambler-gallant.

The crossroads of his various sorties had been Fort Dearborn, a trading post on the site of present-day Chicago. And it was here that he made his strongest ties with his fellow men. Fort Dearborn was rough terrain, perpetually on guard against hostile Indians, and the inhabitants worked and played hard. The Puritan element was present, but cheerful lip-service paid to virtue (a legacy from Jacobean England) was still the norm, and the trading post had its full quota of taverns, gambling-dens and bawdy houses.

The memory of this life was still so vivid in his own day that Edgar still regretted Bainbridge's persuasive tongue and easy charm with the ladies, and the wasted opportunities he had left behind him. Cayce never gambled for any stakes or any reason, and seldom if ever took a drink.

Bainbridge forged a strong emotional bond with Fran Barlowe, the daughter of the petit-bourgeois storekeeper of a minor trading post nearby. She was one of a large, neglected and turbulent family, and at the age of seventeen she was more than grateful to elope with a young tavern keeper of dubious worth and settle in Fort Dearborn. The tavern was merely the front for gambling rooms which specialized in bilking the sucker. It was Bainbridge's favorite haunt during his periodic stop-overs.

Fran developed no mean talent as a singer and dancer in her husband's tavern. She forged a close bond with the good-hearted madam of the girls of easy virtue, a woman who concerned herself with the welfare and health of her charges "over and above the demands of duty." Fran also crossed swords with a conscientious priest who viewed her and her frivolous associates with a bleak eye, reserving his particular disapproval for a convivial sexton who prayed piously by day, cut a nimble caper in the dance halls by night, and also found time to court the priest's sister—a romance which that worthy very rightly nipped in the bud, to the chagrin of the lovers. Toward the end, Fran began to mend her ways and severed some of her more disreputable ties, but "the sounds of revelry by night" were only silenced for good when the Fort suffered a mass Indian attack that burned it to the ground.

Bainbridge—who had previously been as willing to fiddle while Rome burned as the best of them, despite the great good he had done as a scout in the surrounding countryside—rescued one of the larger groups of survivors and brought them safely to the Ohio river, where a large raft of logs was hastily assembled to ferry them to the eastern shore.

Hostile Indian tribes pursued them along the eastern shore, however, and Bainbridge had no choice but to head down river to seek a safe landing. Unable to go ashore to forage for food, even under cover of night, the exhausted occupants of the raft soon began dying of starvation and exposure, Bainbridge among them. But he had been able to keep Fran alive, and when the raft finally went aground she fell into the hands of friendly Indians and eventually made her way to Virginia. There she began life afresh.

By 1812, Fran was the proprietress of a modest boarding house where her warmth and kindness earned her the nickname of the Ministering Angel. She died at the age of forty-eight, honored and respected, the indiscretions of her youth apparently absolved and forgotten. But the life cycle in Fort Dearborn had not had time to complete itself. The scattering of the families by the Indian attack had left a deal of untidy and unfinished business.

Within seventy years, Fran returned to the self-same state of Virginia, where some of her competitors from Fort Dearborn had already begun to reassemble. As if by some tacit prearrangement, they had chosen the Chesapeake peninsula, within comfortable commuting distance of Virginia Beach, though Cayce himself was not to move there until 1925.

Fran soon found cause to feel she had been born under an unlucky star. She had made an early and disastrous first marriage and topped it with another, before the depression era of the early thirties found her on the run from herself in New York City, "slinging hash" in a workmen's cafe in a semi-slum district.

More benumbed than embittered, lacking confidence and direction, she had resigned herself to living from day to day with no real hope of finding her place in a world that seemed to consist of booby traps and built-in disillusions. It was here that David Kahn spotted her.

Kahn was the man who did more to bring Cayce to the attention of the people who needed him than any other single individual in the psychic's life. His business took him across the length and breadth of the eastern states and the middle-west, and wherever he went he extolled the powers of his best friend, Cayce, with eloquence and conviction. A garment-district hashhouse was not a usual port of call for him, but business having taken him there, he observed Fran shrewdly as she served him, and finally asked her the equivalent of "What's a nice girl like you doing in a dump like this?" When he learned that she lived near Norfolk, Virginia, he scribbled Edgar's address on a slip of paper and suggested that when she returned home, she apply for a Reading.

Fran figured she had better things to do with her money. Life had to apply a couple of more twists of the screw before she finally presented herself at Edgar's door a year or so later. He seemed to recognize her at once, and the atmosphere of peacefulness and calm radiated by the house and its occupants was the first real sense of sanctuary she had ever experienced in her twenty-five years.

There followed one of the most singularly compact series of Readings covering one soul-group. Nearly every member of Fran's large family was represented in it. Edgar felt he owed them reparation for the happy-go-lucky manner in which he had viewed their problems in Fort Dearborn.

Fran had been born back as a daughter to the madam who had befriended her in the Fort Dearborn days. Cayce cured her mother of a potential eczema, and she died at eighty-seven of nothing more toxic than "weariness of soul." Her father was likewise aided by Cayce to conquer a disgorged liver and an over-toxic blood count, and lived to be ninety. Her eldest brother Ned had also been her brother in Fort Dearborn. Joel, the second brother, had been the sexton who courted the priest's sister, and he had met and married that same sister in his present reincarnation. The marriage was a model of mutual happiness until the priest, true to character, incarnated as their first-born. As soon as he could express himself, his parents were never again to know an unharassed moment. Even as a very young child he played one against the other with such precocious zeal that he finally drove a permanent wedge between them. Singularly, he too, suffered from a third-degree skin disease that was finally cured by his Health Reading in his twenty-first year.

One of the most thoroughly documented of the Health Readings traces her sister Vera from advanced TB, diagnosed as incurable by her doctors, to total recovery with the aid of Cayce's "unorthodox remedies." Vera, secretive by nature, refused a Life Reading, perhaps fearing that her TB had been contracted in the dance halls of Fort Dearborn.

Fran's third brother, Hal, was fondest of her, protective, avuncular, and admiring. He loved to encourage her to sing and entertain, and would sit enraptured, applauding at the end and extolling her talents to the skies. Who was he? Her tavern keeper husband from Fort Dearborn. When he watched her conversion to the somewhat restraining standards of behavior laid down for her in her Readings, he developed an illogical antipathy for Cayce that he never overcame, refusing to meet him or even discuss him. His wife Sarah had no such mental block, having been one of the women whom Fran had nursed during the War of 1812. It was not until their first baby was three weeks old, and in such desperate need of expert medical help that was locally unavailable that her death seemed inevitable, that Hal, stonefaced, presented himself to Fran and asked her to get a Health Reading on the child from "that quack."

Fran explained that Cayce would only give a Reading if personally requested by the parent, but this far Hal would not go. At Fran's own request however, Cayce, aware that they had to fight the clock to save the child, broke his rule. The solution to the gastric problems of which the baby was dying was simply to dilute the formula and administer a dose of Castoria. Recovery was all but instantaneous, and three days later the baby was in perfect health, never again to suffer the same symptoms until colitis developed later in her childhood. This, too, was cured by a Reading.

Of the twenty or more Fort Dearbornites who had all reassembled in the Chesapeake peninsula, Hal and one of Fran's three husbands were the only who held out implacably against any aid, comfort or cheer that the Readings might have had to offer them. Actually Fran's second husband had not entered Fran's previous life until she was settled in Virginia, where he, too, had been nursed back to health in her boarding house.

During the War of 1812, Fran had made no distinction between friend and foe when she administered to the wounded. Thus, as Fran reestablished her own life on a more stable footing, the chips on her shoulders fell away and her whole family group began to improve in health and self-orientation. The feuds diminished and the tensions abated. The old "unfinished business" of Fort Dearborn was all but accounted for.

Then a Mary Barker arrived on the scene to open a small gift shop for the summer tourists. Mary, not much younger than Fran, suffered from a form of polio which had given her an obese and crippled body. She had been unable to walk unaided since the age of one. From the moment she met Fran she developed an almost neurotic obsession for her, haunting her in her leisure hours and overwhelming her with clumsy affection.

Fran overcame her resentful embarrassment and obtained a Health Reading in the hope that Mary was still not beyond medical aid. The Reading prescribed a series of massages that were far beyond Mary's means. By this time she was well-nigh incapable of earning an adequate living. From a deep-rooted sense of compassion, Fran's mother took Mary into her house and for three months Fran applied the daily massages and packs. The girl slowly rallied and was eventually able to walk. She then requested a Life Reading which informed her that she had been Fran's daughter in the life before, and had suffered malnutrition when the Indian servants had fled with her to save her life. In adulthood she had been an itinerant barnstormer and rolling stone, convinced that her mother had willfully deserted her. Her unforgiving bitterness and self-pity had manifested themselves in the form of the disfiguring polio. When she finally moved away to pursue her career elsewhere, she and Fran were able to part as good friends.

Today Fran is a dignified matron looking fifteen or twenty years younger than her real age because of her strict adherence to her Health Readings. She shows understandable discretion when she discusses the benefits derived from the Readings by her family and friends. They, like many solid citizens who owe their equanimity and longevity to Cayce, are timid about admitting his help in public, lest some newspaper reporter descend on their heads for being arrayed as "a host of witnesses, almost none of them named, who were snatched from certain decay by the diagnoses that Cayce delivered in his trances.

Group karma does not apply only to a select few who follow the same soul-cycle and reincarnate into the same families; it has more universal implications.

Edgar Cayce made it abundantly clear that all the souls involved in the Conquistador invasions of Mexico and South America by Cortez and Pizarro paid proportionately for their plunder and slaughter of the Aztecs. This annihilation of an entire civilization is sickening to read even now; but the gold-hungry adventurers, said Cayce, returned en masse to Spain during the period of the Spanish Civil War in this century. There, brother and mother and father and sister turned against one another until their civilization was a shambles. Does this throw a clearer light on the reason why certain groups of apparently innocent people are subject to undeserved horror and tragedy?

Whole races seem to move with their soul-cycles. It would seem that in contemporary America Negro leadership is guiding the race toward its inheritance of long-denied economic and social rights.

How then can we account for the unforgiving hatred of the small minority groups such as the Muslims; when we place it against the responsible and disciplined rationale of the majority of the Negro leaders?

It is possible that such implacability, far from reflecting the Negro group-cycles, stems rather from an intrusion into the Negro race of souls who hate Negro and white man with equal intensity. Such souls could well have belonged to the reversionist type of slave-owner in the ante-bellum South who subjected his slaves to brutal floggings and ill-treated their wives and children. Such souls would compulsively have condemned themselves to reincarnate as Negroes: but while the erstwhile slave-owner's dark skin in the present might inflame his conscious grievances, his subconscious mind could be equally inflamed by the guilt and shame he feels for the crimes he once committed against the Negro race to which he now belongs; making him hate them as much as he does the whites.

CHAPTER 17

THE PRESENT ATTITUDE TOWARD REINCARNATION

1. The Public

IF THE READER should question why reincarnation seems to thrive more in the Oriental and primitive societies, let him compare the permissive and tolerant upbringing of, say, a Tlingit Indian child with a child born into Colonial Salem possessing an equal aptitude for recalling its previous life. This would instantly be labeled as the work of the devil and zealously exorcized. Some of the women who were hanged were hardly more than children.

Such horrors are inevitably assimilated by what the great psychiatrist Jung calls the "collective unconscious" of an entire nation. And when a race contracts such infections of the psyche, taboos retard its intellectual reason for generations to come. In his grim play "The Crucible," Arthur Miller points the clear lineal descent from the mass hysteria of the Salem witch trials to the "monkey" trial of John T. Scopes for teaching evolution to his class in the twenties, and the un-American Activities Committee hearings of the early fifties.

If a brilliant scientist, educator or politician can be kept from assuming his rightful place in the affairs of his country by coercion, surely it is easy to see how children who believe the evidence of their own eyes and ears (and presume their parents do also) can be brainwashed into disowning their own psychic potential. A child who sees and talks to a very tangible replica of a dead grandparent, and is rash enough to say so, runs the danger of either being ridiculed, punished or sent to a child psychologist. It is inevitable that he will be reduced to repressing the evidence of his own spiritual senses until they atrophy.

2. The Churches

America, the youngest and strongest democracy ever to exist in the world's history, has proven capable of assimilating hostile ideologies and learning from them—provided a lunatic minority is restrained from harassing the level-headed majority. The brutality of Salem, for example, led directly to the inclusion of freedom of all worship in the Constitution.

If the Constitution is the rock on which democracy survives, then surely, when the Rev. Wally White vows to debunk Bridey Murphy "because reincarnation is an assault on established religious doctrines," he is just as misguided as his Salem forerunners.

What are the "established religious doctrines" that he and his ilk are always in such a fluster to protect? And how weak are they, that the protection of the Constitution is insufficient for their needs? Surely the faults in the established churches are more likely to resemble those criticized by Pope Pius XII in 1950: "We cannot abstain from expressing our preoccupation and our anxiety for those who . . . have become so engulfed in the vortex of external activity that they neglect the chief duty of the Christian: his own sanctification.

"We have already stated publicly in writing that those who presume that the world can be saved by what has rightly been called the 'heresy of action' must be made to exercise better judgment."

Fourteen years later, His Eminence Julius Cardinal Dopfner, the fifty-one-year-old governor of the See of Munich, defined the state of western religion today in terms so brilliantly lucid as to make it definitive.

Cardinal Dopfner's prestige is such that he was chosen by Pope Paul VI to be one of the four Moderators of the second session of the Vatican Council in 1964. In this capacity, he made pronouncements to an audience of twenty-eight hundred people in the Congressional Hall at Munich. Of this, *Time* magazine reported:

"Masses of the faithful have been lost, said Dopfner, because to many the Catholic Church appeared as 'an institution that enslaved freedom' and as a 'superannuated souvenir from the past age.' It spoke to man in an ancient tongue, through incomprehensible rituals, in preaching concepts that have no relation to current life. Instead of penetrating the world, the church seemed to sit 'in a self-imposed ghetto, trying to build its own small world adjoining the big world.'

"Tied to 'antiquated forms,' Catholicism often gave the appearance of resenting the inescapable presence of idealogical pluralism, political democracy and modern technology.

"These unpleasant truths persuaded Pope John XXIII that the council was needed, and gave new force to the traditional understanding of Catholicism as *ecclesia semper reformanda*—a church ever in need of reform.

"Christ himself was free of sin, but the continuation of His work, Dopfner pointed out, 'has been entrusted to frail, sinful humans.' Thus the church has sometimes been guilty of 'failing to achieve what God had desired. The presentation of the love of Christ can lag, if the church uses the means of power instead of humility—of force instead of service.'

"This means, according to Dopfner, that any reform can only be carried out by the church at the council in a spirit of penitence, or metanoia, in the knowledge that it is 'a community of sinners.' Reform also must be based on the teachings of Christ and Holy Scripture. It also must be in the nature of renovation rather than revolution, preserving what is good from the past tradition while remaining open to future possibilities of development.

" 'We are in danger of resisting ideas, forms and possibilities to which perhaps the future belongs; and we often consider as impossible that which will finally manifest itself as a legitimate form of Christianity,' said the Cardinal.

" 'Even in the area of church teaching, development is far from impossible,' said Dopfner, since 'a dogma as such is not finally synonymous with divine truth, but only incompletely expresses the wealth of divine truth, because it sees revelation in human terms.'

"This does not mean that the church can recant or change dogmatic definitions of the past, but it can discover new aspects of truth, and find new ways to express traditional teaching.

"Thus the ancient belief of Catholics that 'outside the church there is no salvation' can be amplified to make it less offensive to Protestants. It should also be modified to recognize 'that the word and grace of God is effective in many manifestations outside the church.'

"To recognize this in a statement by the highest teaching authority is undoubtedly an innovation which, in earlier times when the people of other faiths were merely considered in the light of formal heresy, would have been utterly inconceivable.

" 'But,' said the Cardinal in his peroration, 'the recognition of the Holy Spirit outside the limits of the Catholic church establishes a bridge to our 'separated brethren' and enlarges the order of the church as such. . . . This we view as the first step of the road along which God can ultimately lead us to each other.' "*(Time,* Feb. 4, 1964.)

These words resound with a somber magnificence because, in essence, they apply to all denominations where intolerance has made any kind of inroad.

You will also have observed that *Time*'s editors recognize Cardinal Dopfner as the "highest teaching authority." Yet I submit that in the eyes of an omniscient Rev. Wally White, the Cardinal's statements could just as easily be construed as "an assault on established religious doctrines" as any of the tenets contained in the "formal heresy" of reincarnation.

Religious intolerance undergoes an even more penetrating X-ray examination than the one administered by Cardinal Dopfner in this brief precept by the Jewish essayist Harry Golden.

"Perhaps, most important of all inspirations," submits Golden, "the anti-Semite often burns with a consuming hatred of Jesus, which he prudently expresses against the people who produced Him.

"Hating Jews also allows the anti-Semite to strike blows against the restraining ethics of Christianity without risking his standing in the community."

In short, the narcotic euphoria of false righteousness inevitably leads to persecution.

Persecution must invariably enforce retaliation, no matter how pathetic or ineffectual, even in the forsaken echelons of sexual inversion, where the homosexual is rated as a monster rather than a glandular cripple. Shorn of social rights and privileges, he has inherited the cloak of the outcast pariah which was worn, in the last century, by the immigrants fleeing the European despots and ghettos.

A hundred years ago, signs in office windows informed the unemployed that "Irishmen and Dogs Need Not Apply." The Jew found himself as isolated in his segregated quarter of New York as he had been in Warsaw or

Prague. The Negro was reduced to the bondage of the humanoids in Atlantis. This brave new race of free men, for all its unique birthright, still simmered in the melting pot; it was still polyglot; and even now the true indigenous American "conceived in liberty" has yet to emerge.

But *will* he; until all intolerance has vanished from the fifty states?

Cayce, in his self-imposed hypnosis, says no. This nation stuck its chin out as no nation had ever done, when it wrote its Constitution—as literal a covenant with God as any in the Bible. Other nations, not committed as this one is, do not have to achieve or sustain such idealistic standards, even though half Europe and most of Asia still adhere to cynical and obsolete manifestos that deny man's right to "equality, brotherhood and liberty."

Reincarnation reiterates in every tenet, theme and credo that a mock religion creates a mock people—that the root of all evil, the lethal poison man still feeds himself, is the sly and shameful hankering to persecute without being caught at it.

CHAPTER 18

REINCARNATION IN THE FUTURE

IN THE MATERIAL world, coming events always cast their shadow, even if these are discernible only to the hindsight of the historian.

Edgar Cayce was always reluctant to force his theories on others, but in the speeches he made to the people at the Cayce Hospital in the early thirties, he indicated his own beliefs of what lay ahead. He saw a development in man's faculties, a broadening of his five senses, and, by implication, a rational and logical acceptance of deeper truths.

If reincarnation lies inherent in these deeper truths, it will be automatically recognized and accepted by the human race as they attain to that plateau of deeper perception.

Cayce himself was already able to read minds and see auras, and described his reactions in these simple words: "Ever since I can remember, I have seen colors in connection with people. I do not remember a time when the human beings I encountered did not register on my retina with blues and greens and reds gently pouring from their heads and shoulders. It was a long time before I realized that other people did not see these colors; it was a long time before I heard the word 'aura,' and learned to apply it to a phenomenon which to me had always been commonplace.

"I never think of people except in connection with their auras; I see them change in my friends and loved ones as time goes by—by sickness, dejection, love, fulfillment. For me, the aura is the weathervane of the soul. It shows which way the winds of destiny are blowing.

"Many people have had experiences similar to mine, not knowing for many years that it was something unique.

"I have heard many people comment on the prevalence of eyeglasses among our civilized peoples. They seem to consider this a bad thing. Could it be that it is a result of constant straining on the part of our eyes to see more, and to bring us to the next step of evolution? I think this is true, and will be accepted in the future.

"What will it mean to us if we make this next evolutionary step? Well, it will mean that all of us will be able to see auras.

"An aura is an effect, not a cause. Every atom, every molecule, every group of atoms and molecules, however simple or complex, tells the story of itself—its pattern, its purpose—through the vibrations which emanate from it.

"As the soul of an individual travels through the realms of being, it shifts and changes its pattern as it uses or abuses the opportunities presented to it. The human eye perceives these vibrations as colors.

"Thus at any time, in any world, a soul will radiate its history through its vibrations. If another consciousness can apprehend those vibrations and understand them, it will know the state of its fellow-soul, the plight he is in, or the progress he has made.

"Imagine what that will mean! Everyone will be able to see when you plan to tell them a lie, even a little white one! We will all have to be frank, for there will no longer be such a thing as deceit!

"Danger, catastrophe, accidents, death, will not come unannounced. We will see them on their way, as did the prophets of old; and, as the prophets of old, we will recognize and welcome our own death, understanding its true significance.

"It is difficult to project ourselves into such a world—a world where people will see each other's faults and virtues, their weaknesses and strength, their sickness, their misfortunes, their coming success. We will see ourselves as others see us, and we will be an entirely different race of people. How many of our vices will persist, when all of them are known to everyone?"

In similar vein, he explained his attitude to the latent power of mental concentration, which is also due to increase in the human race.

"My experience has taught me that practically every phase of phenomena may be explained by the activities of the subconscious mind. First, let me tell you one of my own experiments along these lines—an experiment I have never repeated! In telling you why, I can give you my ideas as to how mental telepathy should and should not be used.

"Many years ago, when I was operating a photographic studio, a young lady who was really a musician was working in my studio. She had become interested in photography and in the phenomena which manifested through me.

"One day I told her that I could force an individual to come to me. I said this because I had been thinking about the subject and studying it. I believed that by deep concentration one should be able to hold a mental image within oneself, and by 'seeing' another person doing a thing, one could mentally induce that person to do it.

"The young lady said, 'Well, I believe most of the things you've told me, but this is one thing I do not believe! You'll certainly have to prove it to me!'

" 'All right,' I said. 'Who are two people you consider it would be impossible for me to influence?'

" 'You couldn't get my brother to come up here,' she said, 'and I know you couldn't get Mr. B to come here either, because he dislikes you.'

"I told her that before twelve o'clock the next day, her brother would not only come up to the studio, but he would ask me to do something for him. 'And the next day, before two o'clock,' I told her, 'Mr. B will come here.'

"She shook her head, and said that she couldn't believe anything of the kind.

"Now our studio was so arranged that from the second floor we could look into a mirror and see what was going on in the street below. At ten o'clock the next day, I sat in meditation for about thirty minutes, just thinking about her brother and wondering if perhaps I hadn't overstepped myself in saying he was going to ask me to do something for him, because his sister often told me that he had no patience with the work I did.

"After about half an hour of this concentrated thought, I saw the boy pass on the street below, then turn and come to the steps. He stood there a few seconds, looking up the steps—then walked away. In a few minutes he returned and came up the stairs to the second floor.

"His sister looked around and exclaimed, 'What are you doing here?'

"The boy sat on the edge of the table, turning his hat around in his hands. Then he said, 'Well, I hardly know—but I had some trouble last night at the shop, and you've been talking so much about Mr. Cayce, I just wondered if he couldn't help me out.'

"His sister almost fainted!

"The next day, at eleven o'clock, I took my seat in the same chair. The girl said, 'If you worked it on my brother, I guess you can work it on Mr. B!'

"I told her I preferred not to be there when Mr. B came, because he disliked me so much, and that he wouldn't know why he had come. She told me afterwards that he came in about twelve-thirty, after I had gone out. She asked him if she could do anything for him. He said, 'No. I don't know what I'm doing here!' and walked out!

"But as I studied these matters more and more, I decided never to do such a thing again. Anyone who wants to control another person, can do it—but beware! The very thing you wish to control in the other person will be the thing that will destroy you. It will become your Frankenstein!

"For, as the information of the Readings say, anyone who would force another to submit to his will is a tyrant. Even God does not force His will upon us. Either we make our will one with His, or we are opposed to Him. Each person has an individual choice.

"Then what part may mental telepathy play in our lives? For anything good can also be dangerous. I could mention nothing good that does not also have its misapplication, its misuse. How, then, may we use mind reading, or mental telepathy, constructively?

"The best rule I can give is this: don't ask another person to do anything you would not do yourself.

"When the Master went down into Judea, He was asked by one of the noblemen of the district, a Pharisee, to have dinner with him.

"So Jesus accepted this invitation, and His disciples went with Him. As they sat at the table, a woman of the streets came in and washed His feet with her tears and wiped them with the hair of her head. She also anointed His feet with precious ointment.

"The nobleman thought to himself—as many of us would today—'What kind of man is this? Doesn't he know the sort of person she is?' Jesus, knowing what was in his mind, said, 'Simon, I have somewhat to say unto thee. . . . There was a certain creditor which had two debtors; the one owed five hundred pence, and the other fifty. And when they had nothing to pay, he frankly forgave them both. Tell me, therefore, which of them will love him most?' Simon answered and said, 'I suppose that one to whom he forgave most.' And He said unto him, 'Thou hast rightly judged.' (Luke 7:36-50)

"Note that Jesus did not say to Simon, 'This is what you are thinking about,' nor accuse him of being discourteous in not having provided water for His feet, nor oil to anoint His head. Jesus simply spoke in such a way as to awaken in Simon the realization that he should not find fault with another.

"At times, we, too, are able to sense what people are thinking, and we may know the trend their thoughts are taking. At such times, our conversation and actions towards them can only be to show—even as the Master showed Simon—that the inmost thoughts can be known to those who are closely associated with the Divine.

"Those of you who have studied something of the history of Atlantis (in the Readings) know that such forces as mental telepathy were highly developed there. Numbers of people were able to think with such concentration that they could bring material things into existence by the very power of their will. To use such forces for selfish purposes, as they used them, can result only in destruction.

"That same force of mind still exists, just as it did in ancient Atlantis.

"The greatest sins in the world today are still selfishness and the domination of one individual will by another will.

"Few people allow other individuals to live their own lives. We want to tell them how; we want to force them to live our way and see things as we see them. Most wives want to tell their husbands what to do, and most husbands want to tell their wives what they can and cannot do!

"Have you ever stopped to think that no one else answers to God for you? Nor do you answer to God for others.

"If a person will seek first to know himself, then the ability to know another's mind will come. Most of those who will practice it for just a little while can develop along this line. But be sure you don't attempt to do God's work! Be content to do your own, and you'll have your hands full!

"We have a right to tell people our own personal experiences and let them decide for themselves, but not to force them, for God calls upon every man, everywhere, to look, to heed, to understand for himself.

"The answer comes to each one of us, as to whether these abilities are worth developing or not. If we have the proper conception of what 'psychic' means, then we know it is a faculty which exists—has always existed—and is ours by birthright, because we are the sons and daughters of God. We have the ability to make association with the Spirit. For 'God is Spirit and seeks such to worship Him.' (John 4:23)

"When we use the forces within to serve the Creative Forces and God, then we are using them correctly. If we use them for our own selfish interests, they are being abused. Then we become even as the Son of Perdition—call him whatever we will."

And once, when Edgar Cayce was in self-hypnosis, he was asked: "How should we present the work of the A.R.E. to one of orthodox faith?"

"Invite them to come and see," he answered. "Not by imposing, not by impelling. For only those who are in need of answers to 'something within' will heed.

"Do not disturb them, do not find fault. For if thy Father, God, had found fault with every idle word or every unkind act in thine experience, what opportunity would ye have had in this experience?

"If you would know mercy before Him, be merciful and kind to those of whatever faith or group ye may find."

CHAPTER 19

CONCLUSION

REINCARNATION, THEN, is not a theory; it is a practical code of ethics directly affecting human morality.

It was an essential part of the early Gospels, and its removal by two macabre pagans has never been satisfactorily accounted for. Scattered references to it still exist in the Bible, but the encyclopedias have been steadily diminishing their emphasis on it since as far back as 1911—the last edition of the *Encyclopedia Britannica* to deal frankly with it under the heading of Metempsychosis.

Edgar Cayce's Readings accept it unequivocally, and repeatedly insist that positive and negative conduct in earlier lives actively affect behavior patterns in the present. That which is negative can be resolved and overcome, once a man is prepared to accept his problems as being entirely of his own making, and therefore responsive to his un-making.

Nowhere does it seem to have been dangerous or harmful to man's spiritual or philosophic beliefs, save when it conflicts with an inflated vanity, or an ego which has become the tail that wags the dog.

Yet no belief has been so stubbornly denied the benefit of the doubt at the parochial level; never more loudly have its detractors clamored for "proof." But on whose shoulders should the onus of proof rightly lie?

There is no historic proof that Atlantis ever existed. But five hundred years ago there was no historic proof that America ever existed. For that matter there was no historic proof that the Dead Sea Scrolls ever existed until they were discovered by an Arab goatherd by a one-in-a-million chance.

On nearly every subject under the sun, most men will believe almost any lie —provided it is big enough, absurd enough and is repeated often enough— and never dream of demanding proof. Likewise he will believe what he reads in the papers, and what he sees on the newscasts, as implicitly as if Moses had brought them down Mount Sinai engraved on stone. He will totally accept the election promises of a demagogue. He is blindly convinced that his lawyer, his doctor and his dentist are infallible and incorruptible. If his doctor operates for appendicitis and inadvertently leaves a gauze pad behind when he sews him up, he will obligingly die before he demands to know why the operation had not been as successful as it was cracked up to be.

Apparently only reincarnation fills him with the superstitious dread, and only when he is plagued by dread as vague as that does he insist on proof so irrefutable that not even the Mother of All Living could supply it to his satisfaction.

Why is the karmic law of rebirth and restitution such a scapegoat for the orthodox mind? Is it the fact that every soul in creation will have to voluntarily return and experience the emotional equivalent, good and bad, of all that he has caused others to experience? The fact that whatever weakness we persecute in others we shall eventually inherit, with all its attendant persecution.

The fact that each soul is its own judge and its own jury, and passes sentence only on itself.

The fact that the hereafter shelters no bribable judge, no jury to be bamboozled.

The fact that in the last analysis, the only person anyone has ever kidded was himself—and unsuccessfully at that.

Our obsessive preoccupation with external superficialities, and our servile anxiety to conform to the modern not only rob us of individuality and stature, they corrode us until we become complacent and stultified. Is it only because we have rejected the law of reincarnation that we squander three quarters of our lives, impressing others, pretending to be what we are not? If so, there will have to come a time when we find it almost impossible to be honest with ourselves; and by then nothing will be more painfully and desperately necessary to our sanity.

Perhaps the unpalatable ingredient lies in the fact that, even when it is reduced to its humblest factors, reincarnation offers little if any consolation to the indolent neurotic who blames his blowsy mom and boozy dad for the fact that he has never taken the slightest trouble to make himself likable—let alone lovable—to others. It has no panacea to offer the drone who sullenly sits and waits to be loved for all his faults—for his shiftlessness, his goldbricking, his pharisaic buck-passing, and his furtive longing to play the bully-boy without being made to pay the piper for it.

"So oft is the ego so enrapt in self," Edgar Cayce said, "that it constantly fears it will lose its importance, its place, its freedom. Yet to have freedom in self, give it! To have peace in self, make it! These are immutable laws. . . .

For in patience possess ye your souls. In patience you become aware that the body is but a temple, an outward edifice. But the mind and the soul are the permanent furnishings thereof—the essentials in which you shall constantly abide."

This certainly clashes with the fine old materialistic maxim that the world hates a loser and admires a self-made big shot, no matter how many victims he leaves in his wake.

Have we, by discarding the law of reincarnation, discarded all concept of a just and loving Creator? Then we would seem to have created our own booby traps with a vengeance. For surely man's five senses are insufficient to enable him to deny the existence of God with any real conviction.

Isn't man on safer ground accepting rather than denying Him? For once he succeeds in reducing all belief to nothing, he himself, obviously, no longer exists.

This would seem to indicate that a professed atheist is only a man who cannot contemplate the firmament without getting vertigo, because it offers him nothing familiar to compare it against.

Perhaps this explains why he has equal difficulty trying to contemplate the idea of reincarnation. The idea that it is one of the logical cornerstones of a valid faith lacks a comforting solid, materialistic base. This fact alone is enough to make it suspect to any self-condemned penitent who believes that he was born in sin once and once only, and that the only way to his own conception of a bedraggled salvation is through senseless and interminable suffering.

To him, the abiding heresy of reincarnation is that man is a free agent and his God is a God of Love. This means that until he has learned to love his fellow men, no further knowledge of his Maker is available to him.

What confronts him next? The unpalatable fact that no man is capable of loving others until he has overcome the obstacles which prevent him from loving himself.

If he can never love or become lovable to others, it follows as logically as day follows night that others can never love or become lovable to him.

In which case, he is now in sore and mortal trouble, for if he can neither love nor be loved, he will be engulfed by the eternal night of implacable loneliness. Loneliness is man's most lethal adversary, for it is the only poison which can ultimately and inexorably exterminate the soul.

The reader who has realized by now that any serious study of reincarnation can not be approached through any other channel than the dependence on a benign Christ, will do well to de-dogmatize himself by resorting to the Rev. Weatherhead's beautifully conceived and simply written *The Christian Agnostic* (Abingdon Press, New York, 1965). No other cleric of such estimable authority has ever been more in harmony with Edgar Cayce's own interpretation of the Bible.

In the chapter *"Reincarnation and Renewed Chances,"* Dr. Weatherhead spearheads his own acceptance of metempsychosis in the following words: "I think of Betty Smith, born into a prosperous home, surrounded by every opportunity, given an ideal education, loving and marrying a man well able to keep her in the same kind of environment, giving life to half a dozen happy, healthy children, and passing into middle and later life with full health and every possible amenity.

"Then I think of Jane Jones, born blind, or deaf, or crippled, into a poverty-stricken home, where a drunken father makes life a hell for everyone. Jane cannot escape, can never marry and have her own home, can never be given the things Betty enjoys, and dies early, let us say, of malignant disease. . . .

"Some imagine that 'things will be squared up in heaven.'

"Is Betty, then, to suffer in another life because she was happy on earth? What would that do, in the matter of justice? Nothing. And certainly it would do Jane no good. Nor is she vindictive or mean enough to desire it. Is Jane to be 'rewarded' or 'compensated?'

"But what kind of compensation makes up for half a century of earthly misery? We cringe when we hear of a grant of money given to a man wrongfully imprisoned. How can that make up to him for the mental distress, the wasted years, the misery and pain to all his relatives? These things cannot be 'made-up' for.

"Is human distress just luck, then? If so, how unjust is life! Is it God's will? Then how unlike any human father he must be; for a human father who thus exerted his will would be clapped into jail, or into a lunatic asylum!"

These are strong words from the august Minister of London's City Temple, but Dr. Weatherhead hits as hard as Cayce ever did. Dr. Weatherhead believes passionately that Christianity is a way of life, not "a theological system with which one must be in intellectual agreement. . . ."

"If you love Christ and are seeking to follow him, take an attitude of Christian agnosticism to intellectual problems, at least for the present. . . .

"Frankly I often wonder why so many people do go to church. Christianity must have a marvellous inherent power, or the churches would have killed it long ago."

Even so, reincarnation will be allotted no logical place in our society until orthodox dogma ceases to cater to (and thus only attract) the guilt-ridden factor in its congregations. Reincarnation can never make sense to the man in the street as long as he secretly fears and rejects his obsolete concept of a vindictive and avenging God.

Dr. Weatherhead, as Cayce did before him, makes this the cornerstone of his whole argument, and he takes particular exception to an English cleric who, having used every specious bromide to discredit metempsychosis, ended with the defiant: "My alleged pre-existence can have no present moral meaning simply because I am debarred from remembering anything about it."

Here the well-intentioned worthy led with his chin, and Dr. Weatherhead was cheerfully in his rights to tap him on it.

"What a preposterous statement!" Dr. Weatherhead exclaims. "So if some drug were now given to Dr. Whale, blotting out the memory of his youth, any indiscretions of that youth could have 'no present moral meaning!' He forgets that they would just as effectively have made him and molded him to be what he is, as if he remembered them. A judge is not often ready to excuse a prisoner of all moral responsibility if he asserts that he can't remember anything about it now!

"None of us can now remember his earliest years. But any psychologist will stress their importance and the effect they had upon us.

"These childhood incidents happened, not to another, but to us, and, though now forgotten, determined many of our present reactions to life. The very pattern of adult life is a form of stored memory. We do not need to remember mental impressions to be influenced by them."

And in the same mood of amiable exuberance, Dr. Weatherhead presents this straightforward argument: "The intelligent Christian believes that God is working out a plan in the lives of all men and women, and that the consummation of this plan will mean that his will is 'done on earth as it is in heaven' . . .

"(But) how can a world progress in inner things—which are the most important—if the birth of every new generation fills the world with unregenerate souls full of untamed, animal tendencies? There can never be a perfect world unless, gradually, those born into it can take advantage of lessons learned in earlier lives instead of starting at scratch. True, the number of prodigies is small and so is the number of saints, but there may well be other planets more adequate than this is, to be their classroom. It may be that we must relinquish the idea of this earth being the venue of the perfect society.

"These thoughts make me agree with the late Dean Inge, no mean thinker, who said of the doctrine of reincarnation, 'I find it both credible and attractive.'

"One wonders why men have so readily accepted the idea of a life after death and so largely, in the West, discarded the idea of a life before birth. So many arguments for a one-way immortality seem to me cogent for a two-way life outside the present body."

But even if we confine the issue to life after death, we can do no better than conclude with one of Edgar Cayce's favorite parables from the Bible.

In Luke 17:19-31, Christ tells the Pharisees of the beggar Lazarus, "fed from the crumbs of the rich man's table," who died and was taken to Abraham's bosom. But when the rich man died, he found himself in hell, from which vantage point he could see Lazarus ensconced in Heaven.

"Then he said (to Abraham), 'I pray thee therefore, father, that thou would send him to my father's house; for I have five brethren; that he may testify unto them, lest they also come into this place of torment.'

"Abraham said to him, 'They have Moses and the prophets. Let them hear them.'

"And (the rich man) said, 'Nay, father Abraham: but if one went unto them from the dead, they will repent.'

"And Abraham said unto him, 'If they hear not Moses and the prophets, neither will they be persuaded, though one rose from the dead.' "

RECOMMENDED PARALLEL READING

BOOKS:

Twenty Cases Suggestive of Reincarnation by Ian Stevenson, M.D.
Many Mansions by Gina Cerminara, Ph.D.
The World Within by Gina Cerminara, Ph.D.
Reincarnation: An East-West Anthology by Joseph Head and S. L. Cranston

PAMPHLETS:

The Case for Reincarnation by Leslie D. Weatherhead
The Evidence for Survival from Claimed Memories of Former Incarnations by
     Ian Stevenson, M.D.

THE FIFTEEN ANATHEMAS AGAINST ORIGEN

HENRY PERCIVAL HAS printed in full the fifteen anathemas against Origen. They are easily available in Head and Cranston's admirable *Reincarnation: An East-West Anthology* (The Julian Press, New York, 1961) and seldom have such grandiose dictums carried such disproportionate substance. Indeed, they read more like illiterate bombast than responsibly conceived tenets, and literally nowhere do they quote Biblical authority for their condemnations.

"If anyone assert the fabulous pre-existence of souls," they begin grandiloquently, "and shall assert the monstrous restoration which follows it, let him be anathema (cursed)."

Clause 2: "If anyone shall say that the creation of all reasonable things includes only intelligences without bodies . . . and that there is unity between them all by identity of substance, force and energy, and by their union with and knowledge of God the Word; but that, no longer desiring the sight of God, they gave themselves over to worse things, each one following his own inclination; and that they have taken bodies more or less subtle, and have received names . . . let him be anathema."

(This would suggest an impeachment of the entire Bible, for even the Old Testament states that all living things were originally conceived in the mind of God, were given Entity by Him, and subsequently rejected their source and their Maker).

Clauses 3 and 5 submerge themselves in their own unintelligibility, but Clause 7 announces: "If anyone shall say that Christ . . . had pity upon the divers falls which had appeared in the spirits . . . and that to restore them He passed through divers classes, had different bodies and different names, became all to all, an Angel among Angels, a Power among Powers. . . . and finally has taken flesh and blood like ours and is become man for man. . . . if anyone says all this and does not profess that God the Word humbled himself and became man; let him be anathema."

(The unabbreviated text is even more labored in its effort to discredit Christ's incarnation in a human form; and yet it tries to imply at the same time that He might have done something vaguely similar, but too obscurely to be intelligible to mortal reason. This is typical of Theodora's constant anxiety-neurosis to have her cake and obliterate it too.)

Clause 8 is an even more complex non sequitur: "If anyone shall not acknowledge that God the Word . . . is Christ in every sense of the word, but shall affirm that He is so only in an inaccurate manner and because of the abasement of the intelligence, and *e converso* that the intelligence is only called God because of the Logos, let him be anathema."

(If any sense can be got out of this, it surely entirely discredits Christ's own affirmation that he was both the Son of God and the Son of Man.)

Clauses 9 and 10 and 11 entangle themselves in each other's verbiage to such an extent as to cancel out their combined rodomontade; but Clause 12 makes an effort to salvage the best of the preceding clauses: "If anyone shall say that the future judgment signifies the destruction of the body; and that . . . thereafter there will no longer be any matter, but only spirit, let him be anathema."

(This makes Christ's symbolic triumph over the flesh by His death and resurrection a pointless gesture, performed for absolutely no constructive purpose whatsoever.)

Clause 14 blunders even more unwittingly into passive atheism: "If anyone shall say that all reasonable beings will one day be united in one . . . and the bodies shall have disappeared, and that the knowledge of the world to come will carry with it the ruin of worlds . . . that in this pretended apocatastasis, spirits only will continue to exist, as it was in the feigned pre-existence; let him be anathema."

(In short, "all this shall not pass away.")

Clause 15: "If anyone shall say that the life of the Spirits shall be like to the life which was in the beginning, when as yet the spirits had not come down or fallen; so that the end . . . shall be the true measure of the beginning; let him be anathema."

Small wonder that even the intimidated Pope Virgilius moved heaven and earth to get such claptrap anathematized in its own turn; and that Justinian had to resort to a Byzantine filibuster to railroad it through.

But there was yet more idiocy to come.

In his auto-intoxication (for by now the whole process of creation must have seemed as clear as mud to the self-apotheosized Justinian), he personally contributed ten more gratuitous anathemas against Origen.

These are even more deranged in content than the first fifteen, except that two of the clauses are direct attacks on church concepts which even predate Origen. The first relates to the idea of Christ descending to purgatory and submitting to a form of crucifixion there, as the only means of redeeming the souls of the damned. (Reference to this appears often enough in the early church writings to establish that it must at one time have held an honored place in the Gospels.)

"If anyone says or thinks that Christ the Lord in a future time will be crucified for demons, as he was for man, let him be anathema," trumpets Justinian, gorgeously impervious to the possibility that he and his formidable spouse might one day languish among those selfsame demons, in abiding need of salvation from the Son of Man.

The next point lies even further back in antiquity—the poetic concept of the soul, once it is free of its material confines, as a luminous glow of pure light. It was one of Origen's pet images, and Justinian skewers it grimly: "If anyone says or thinks that at the resurrection, human bodies will rise spherical in form and unlike our present forms, let him be anathema."

(Here one senses the outraged Theodora refusing to conceive of herself on Judgment Day as anything less spherical than a heavily bejeweled Empress, diplomatic immunity intact.)

The last of the ten clauses is the most petulant:

"If anyone says or thinks that the punishment of demons and of impious men is only temporary, and will one day have to end, and that a restoration will take place of demons and impious men, let him be anathema."

(So you can forget the parable of the Prodigal Son.)

About Edgar Cayce

Edgar Cayce (1877-1945) was a man gifted with a unique clairvoyance. During periods of so-called "sleep," he was able to diagnose illness, often in people he had never met, and then to prescribe medical treatment. With no formal medical training, he healed thousands of people who had previously tried conventional medicine without success. The four separate works in this volume all explore Cayce's extraordinary abilities and their far-reaching implications for the psychic world. All were written under the editorship of the Director of the Association for Research and Enlightenment, the non-profit organization committed to making practical use of Edgar Cayce's psychic readings. Information on the A.R.E. may be found on the following page.

THE A.R.E. TODAY

The Association for Research and Enlightenment, Inc., is a non-profit, open membership organization committed to spiritual growth, holistic healing, psychical research and its spiritual dimensions; and more specifically, to making practical use of the psychic readings of the late Edgar Cayce. Through nationwide programs, publications and study groups, A.R.E. offers all those interested, practical information and approaches for individual study and application to better understand and relate to themselves, to other people and to the universe. A.R.E. membership and outreach is concentrated in the United States with growing involvement throughout the world.

The headquarters at Virginia Beach, Virginia, includes a library/conference center, administrative offices and publishing facilities, and are served by a beachfront motel. The library is one of the largest metaphysical, parapsychological libraries in the country. A.R.E. operates a bookstore, which also offers mail-order service and carries approximately 1,000 titles on nearly every subject related to spiritual growth, world religions, parapsychology and transpersonal psychology. A.R.E. serves its members through nationwide lecture programs, publications, a Braille library, a camp and an extensive Study Group Program.

The A.R.E. facilities, located at 67th Street and Atlantic Avenue, are open year-round. Visitors are always welcome and may write A.R.E., P.O. Box 595, Virginia Beach, VA 23451, for more information about the Association.